RUNNING BEHIND LAKSHMI

The Search for Wealth in India's Stock Market

Adil Rustomjee

JOHN MURRAY

First published in 2025 by Hachette India
(Registered name: Hachette Book Publishing India Pvt. Ltd)
An Hachette UK company
www.hachetteindia.com

1

The stock prices, market movements, and index values referenced in the book have been sourced from the official websites of the Bombay Stock Exchange (BSE) and the National Stock Exchange of India (NSE). The old names of some places such as Bombay or Calcutta have been used to maintain the historicity of the information.

Cover image courtesy Wikimedia commons. PD–US, Sridharbsbu.
Image on endpapers showing participants on the floor of the Bombay Stock Exchange, 1946.
Image by Margaret Bourke-White/The LIFE Picture Collection.

Print ISBN 978-93-5731-548-7
Ebook ISBN 978-93-5731-897-6

For sale only in the Indian subcontinent.

Hachette Book Publishing India Pvt. Ltd
4th & 5th Floors, Corporate Centre
Plot No. 94, Sector 44, Gurugram – 122003, India

Typeset in Adobe Caslon Pro 11.5/15.5
by InoSoft Systems, Noida

Printed and bound in India
by Manipal Technologies Limited

For

My Parents

and
Dorab Framji
who is always there

and
Pranay Gupte
who planted a tree

but mostly for
Nathan Krishnan
who made it all possible

CONTENTS

Preface ix
A Note on Numeraires xv

Prologue: The Road to Golconda 1

Part One: FROM THE BANYAN TO THE SIP

1. How It All Started: Under the Banyan Tree in 1875 17
2. A Century of Marking Time: Interregnum to 1991 60
3. New Beginnings: 1991 to 1999 132
4. Software Boftware: The 2000 Blowout 198
5. Rise and Fall in the Rate Cycle: 2003 to 2009 221
6. The SIP Bull and a Virus: From 2009 to the Present 259

Part Two: APPROACHES AND METHODS

7. The Temple of Brahma: The RBI in All This 305
8. Beating the Monkeys: Efficient Markets 327
9. And Finally, a Multi-Bagger: The Unitech Saga 349
10. Storming Lakshmi or Laying Siege: Speculation and Investment 372

11. Trade Selection: Technicals and Fundamentals 412
12. Searching for the Kohinoor: Stock Picking 439
13. Other Practical Approaches: Contrarianism, Growth, and Momentum 465

Part Three: PLAYERS

14. That Saviour of the Professional: The Public 483
15. *'Siddhu Borivali thi Churchgate'*: Why and How People Trade? 509
16. The Dervishes of Dalal Street: The Big Professional Traders 530
17. *Atithi Devo Bhava*: The Foreign Institutional Investor 547
18. The Buy Side: LIC and the Mutual Funds 568
19. Things Are Not What They Were: The Brokerage Industry and the Primary Side 599

Part Four: MISCELLANY

20. *'Did You Understand That?'*: Derivatives 635
21. The Howling: The Media and the Market 667
22. We're Only Going Higher: Highs and Lows 688
23. Evaluating Performance and the Financial Advisor 718
24. Why We're All Messed Up in Our Heads: Behavioural Finance 746

Conclusion: Catching Lakshmi 771
Glossary 796
Bibliography 815
Acknowledgements 846
Index 848

PREFACE

Much of the first draft of *Running behind Lakshmi* was written during the years I spent in Room 1014 of Phiroze Jeejeebhoy Towers, the Bombay Stock Exchange building. Casting around for material on India's stock market – both history and method – I found little. This is surprising, given the importance of the stock market and the various publics associated with it. During my research, I was struck by the stock market's long history and complex methods, together with the fragmented efforts that went into recording both. Stock market activity in India dates back to the early nineteenth century, and yet this is the first account on how it has all unfolded over the last two centuries. That the Indian stock market is at its bicentennial and that such an account had never been attempted before, speaks to the remarkable ahistoricity of India's culture. But it also speaks to the market's hold over its participants – everybody seems to have been too busy trying to make a living from the market to bother about sitting down to narrate its past or discuss its operations.

Veteran participants advise newcomers that a grip on the market comes only after living through a couple of its cycles. Yet vicarious experience, as lived through the documented experiences of previous participants is also one way of learning, and some would note that it is a relatively inexpensive way of learning as compared to, say, loading up at a market top. 'Fools learn from their own experience. I learn from other people's experience,' is attributed to Bismarck, a view that some might take as cynical but which others might see as the basic argument for vicarious experience in financial markets.

Of the stock market's importance, there can be little doubt, and it is a significance that increases by the day. Market capitalization was about $2.1 trillion in January 2020 – just before the distortions of the COVID-19 pandemic break and liquidity induced pullback – and in the modern era that value has moved typically between 60 to 90 per cent of the country's economy (its GDP). More broadly, the stock market raises capital, spreads risk, stores value, and provides an avenue for corporate control. Much of that importance is still of a local and domestic kind; as an emerging market, India accounts for between 2 and 3 per cent of world market capitalization. Usually featuring towards the end of a list of the world's 10 largest markets, the Indian stock market occasionally drops out of that list – because of volatility in market levels and the exchange rate – but then comes back in. So, the market is, locally at least, an important beast and coming into its own in a country that is finding its place in the world.

In fact, India is the world's oldest emerging market. By the 1820s, newspapers were carrying two-way quotes for stocks such as the Bank of Bengal and the Union Bank. Debt instruments of the Bengal government with coupons of 5 per cent date back even earlier, to the early 1800s. By the 1830s, shares of cotton presses and banks traded in Bombay. A 1993 study by the New York Federal Reserve Bank that attempted to measure market capitalization to GDP from 1810 onwards showed India as the only emerging market in a list of mid-nineteenth century markets that include the UK, the USA, and France. India's 1850 market capitalization to GDP ratio is a token 1 per cent in keeping with the nascent market of that time, but that it figures at all in the list is remarkable.[1]

Books about India's financial markets are rare. Economic and business history has been covered, but on financial history and method, there

[1] John Mullin, 'Emerging Equity Markets in the Global Economy,' *Quarterly Review*, Summer 1993, Federal Reserve Bank of New York, 72.

is little of note. Most people in India's stock market still make their money the old-fashioned way – by buying low and selling high – and as a consequence, books on the stock market tend to cluster around two poles, namely charting and stock picking, corresponding to the two dominant types of trade selection, i.e., technical and fundamental analysis. But, as the reader will find out, there is more to the stock market than just trade selection. This paucity of local material stands in contrast to the extensive literature on Wall Street, whether in the categories of investment methodology, academic research, market history, wisdom literature, or self-help material. As a result, market participants of an inquiring bent of mind who were also seeking to build competence, usually consult Western and more typically, American literature, but where are the local sources? It was this dearth of source material on India's stock market that got me started on the journey that resulted in this book. *Lakshmi* started out as spreadsheet comments entered next to the trades and investments I made, which were subsequently diarized. The search for context to these occasional observations then led to years of research and writing that developed into this book. Hopefully, participants from this generation and those yet to come will walk down the broad avenues this book cleaves through the market's story.

Various publics are associated with the stock market as market participants, and this book is written for them. Besides the stock exchanges themselves, commonly acknowledged participants include the trading and investing public, brokerages, the fund management industry, foreign institutional investors, the financial advisory business, and the myriad entities including depositories and clearing houses that make up the market's microstructure. But the term 'market participant' as used here suggests a wider taxonomy than those directly connected with the buying and selling of shares. The government, the regulator, the media, promoters, executives, banks, academics and their students, are all publics with a healthy stake in the markets. The *government*, more particularly the finance ministry, keeps a keen eye on markets and is happy to see an up move as an affirmation of its policies, though it is careful never to state it as such. The *regulator's* interest is more direct and mundane, and the Securities and Exchange Board of India (SEBI) enjoins the market's clean function besides acting as the locus of reform efforts in the modern era. The *media* covers it incessantly, and the stock market provides a framework that dominates the Indian business media's daily coverage much more than it does in other countries. *Promoters* find the biggest portion of their wealth, their holdings in the companies they control, being valued by the markets on a daily basis. *Company executives*, both at senior and lately also at middle levels, may wish to know how the mechanism that values their stock options really works. The *banks* that lend into markets through their loans against shares (LAS) departments and provide the all-important leverage have the simple concern of parties who want their money back. Finally, the *academics* find that markets provide the material for much research and their *students* will form the next generation of all these publics. So, they all participate in the markets, but less directly than the trading public or the brokerages.

A work of this sort has to deal with the problem of arrangement above all else, and both chronology and theme provide a basis for the book's structure. The first part traces the Indian stock market's evolution from the early decades of the nineteenth century and goes through a narrative arc culminating in the reform effort of the 1990s, followed by significant movements into the present – noteworthy among which are the Rate Bull between 2003 and 2007, and the bull move between 2009 and 2022 that is due in large part to the systematic investment plan, or SIP. It was the most difficult section of the book to write. For history to be meaningful and something more than a collection of facts, it must have form, but the market itself is largely a random beast and not amenable to having form driven into its story. Besides, my formal training is in finance and my experience in the market is as a participant. Yet, there was the realization that the market's history had to be told for the sake of completeness. Of necessity therefore, the perspective is of the historically literate participant rather than the financially literate historian, and yet I have tried to heed the Rankean dictum to tell it like it was, to simply find out 'what really happened'.

The second part of the book deals with the themes of buying and selling stocks in an inefficient market through the dominant approaches of speculation and investment, followed by a discussion of the methods of trade selection that flow from these approaches, among which are technical and fundamental analysis. The third part examines the participants in the market's drama; the third chapter of this section deals with the big professional traders, the dervishes of Dalal Street, and in a departure from the rest of the book, is written as a *roman à clef*. The final part deals with special topics such as derivatives and advisory services that are essential to completing the account.

Running behind Lakshmi is based on a fresh reading of primary and secondary sources. Archival material at the stock exchange was used extensively, together with extant academic research, both from India and abroad; as a result, sections dealing with academic insights and methodology are more technical than the rest of the book. In a society with a strong oral tradition, one would expect the oral history component to be important and yet that is not so. Most interviewed participants had hazy recollections of past events, perhaps because in the market, participants are so deeply conditioned towards looking into the future and discounting it, that the past is inconsequential and simply disappears into that haze. Rare also was the participant who wrote about past events, and so, the imprint into memory that comes from such writing was likewise missing. And yet, with the internet's arrival in the new millennium, access to the media's vibrant market coverage has become easier, and this aids the researcher immeasurably in accessing the first draft of history – for the first time in India's story, the written has begun to take precedence over the oral. Finally, sitting on Dalal Street allowed me to imbibe some of its lore, a portion of which is recounted.

Certain sources provided primary source material at regular intervals on the markets through much of the twentieth century. Eyewitness accounts from politician and participant Sir Dinshaw Eduljee Wacha (1910, 1913, and 1920) supplied much information on the founding episode of the stock market – the Cotton and Share Mania of the 1860s – together with market practice of that era. Successive commissions appointed to look into the Bombay exchange produced reports – usually after the first-hand examination of various participants – and those of Sir Wilfrid Atlay (1924) and Walter Morison (1937) provided extensive material on the market's workings. P.J. Thomas's report (1948) is a definitive account of the markets on the eve of Independence, and unlike the earlier works, is the first to give a national perspective, in keeping with Thomas's position as the first economic advisor at the Ministry of Finance. The 1951 report of a committee headed by A.D. Gorwala provided information on the first draft of the market's legislative framework, the Securities Contracts (Regulation) Act. The next account comes from K.R.P. Shroff (1962), the BSE's chairman and president for 43 years and the longest-serving exchange head in the history of the world's stock markets. A BSE report (1970) on the exchange then provides an update but reflects the uncertainty of that age. With the onset of the reform era, various committees looked into the stock market's affairs and produced reports. Noteworthy among these were committees headed by G.S. Patel (1985 and 1995), Abid Hussain (1989), M.J. Pherwani (1991), L.C. Gupta (1998), and J.R. Varma (1997, 1998, 2000, 2001, and 2002). With the creation of SEBI and the publication of its annual reports from 1992, formal and detailed coverage of the markets comes at regular intervals.

This is not a personal finance book that offers advice on using the myriad financial products out there. Neither is it a 'how to' book on stock investing or trading with some sort of central message or secret to successful operations in the market. In fact, there is no central message to *Running behind Lakshmi*, perhaps because my nature is uncomfortable with the preachiness of a central message, especially on so complex a subject in so complex a country. Just as there are various approaches to life, there will be various approaches to the markets. As a participant, you have to find an approach that works for you and for that to happen, you have to know who you are. If the reader wishes to get some message from this account, then let this be it.

As always, any errors and omissions remain my responsibility.

A NOTE ON NUMERAIRES

India has traditionally had its own numeraires that convert as follows.

INR conventions

1 lakh = 100,000

1 million = 1,000,000 = 10 lakhs

1 crore = 10,000,000 = 10 million = 100 lakhs

1 billion = 1,000,000,000 = 100 crores = 1000 million = 10,000 lakhs

USD to INR conventions (2021)

1 USD = ₹80

1 million USD = ₹8 crores = ₹80 million

1 billion USD = ₹80 billion = ₹8,000 crores = ₹80,000 million

Prologue

THE ROAD TO GOLCONDA

Every day they come to Golconda. You can see them troop in with their briefcases and *potla*s, some coming by 9 a.m. while others drop by during the day. Their arrival times are staggered, and the lowly arrive earlier than the lordly, to get things started but also because the lowly have more at stake on a daily basis. They are a motley crew, this lot who come to Golconda. At one time, their sartorial choices were as varied as India itself, though the Gujarati *angarkha* and the Marwari *dhoti* figured prominently. Many wore *topi*s, or caps, and some even had diamond-studded buttons on their tunics. Now, however, there is the overwhelming sameness of shirt and pant. Every day they stream into the rabbit warren of offices in Mumbai's Fountain area and into broker offices throughout the country. Even if they don't make the physical journey, there is that virtual Golconda of flickering prices just a button click away.

Once there was a real Golconda, and it is still around. A fort surrounded by a dusty plain in Telangana, it was an important centre of trade for the Kakatiya and Qutub Shahi dynasties during the fifteenth and sixteenth centuries. Today, Golconda[1] is almost deserted and just a tourist attraction, known especially for its unusual acoustics. Hyderabad's

[1] Spelt as Golkonda, it means 'the shepherd's hill'.

proximity makes Golconda convenient to visit, and that city's urban sprawl now laps away at the fort's magnificent stone ramparts.

There was a story in the stone. For at one time, Golconda guarded riches. Though not much grew in the barren hot lands of the Deccan, Golconda's diamond mines, notably Kollur, were at their most productive during the Middle Ages. These mines yielded big diamonds – really big ones – and for centuries, some of the most famous diamonds in the world came from Golconda. Several of their names still echo through the history of the *diamantaire*'s trade: Hope, Kohinoor, Regent, Wittelsbach, Princie, Daria-i-Noor.[2] India was the world's only known source of diamonds at that time, and Golconda, at the centre of the diamond trade, became a metaphor for wealth.[3] 'Hast thou from the caves of Golconda, a gem / Pure as the ice-drop that froze on the mountain?' goes the opening line from Keats's 'On Receiving a Curious Shell'.

Fables often arise over the accumulation of great wealth, and here it was the belief that whoever went through Golconda's gates would get rich.[4] In this case at least that story may have some basis in fact, as beyond those gates, Golconda's *toshkhana* (treasure house) had at one time guarded its diamonds. The tale – an outgrowth of Golconda's place in the diamond trade – persisted through the centuries, long after the mines of the Deccan ran dry of diamonds and places such as Brazil, South Africa, and Russia displaced them.

A similar fable arises in India's stock market. Whoever enters the stock market shall grow rich, and the diamonds of Golconda await the intrepid explorer. Except that they don't have evocative names such as Kohinoor or Hope or Princie but more prosaic ones such as Reliance, Infosys, HDFC Bank, Godrej Consumer, Hindalco, or ACC. And these diamonds are all lying around waiting to be picked.

[2] Well-known Golconda diamonds are discussed in Ian Balfour's *Famous Diamonds*, London: Antique Collectors Club, 2008.

[3] Edwin Streeter, *The Great Diamonds of the World: Their History and Romance*, London: George Bell and Sons, 1882, 27–33.

[4] John Brooks's *Once in Golconda: A True Drama of Wall Street, 1920–1938* also echoes this myth.

The stock market is modern India's Golconda.

The game that India's stock traders come to play at Golconda is not different from the game as played by their counterparts around the world. Simple in theory, it is difficult in practice. Promoters and entrepreneurs get together with people, materials, machines, and money to start a firm. Then they float pieces of paper that represent ownership stakes in these entities, and these papers, or stocks, subsequently trade on an exchange. Traders buy if they think the price quoted on the exchange is less than some calculated fair value for the firm; later they sell if the price of the stock has been driven up to its fair value. In many cases, they buy the stock expecting its price to get driven up at some future date because of a 'trigger' – a sort of displacement that will take the stock higher. The trader or investor brings capital, courage, and competence to the game.[5] Capital is needed to take part in the game and to drive the price up to fair value by buying. Courage is essential because the psychological environment for buying is hardly conducive when the opportunity arises. And competence, or judgment, on what constitutes value or momentum is vital. If the price of the stock differs considerably from some estimation of its future value, if the paper is heavily bought and that future value finally realized – well, then the traders have found their Kohinoor or their Princie.

So, this Golconda has its own diamonds, and there is a small army out to pick them. In this age without a name, they all come in search of Lakshmi – that elusive goddess of wealth and prosperity.

Associated as she is with grace, beauty, wealth, and prosperity, Lakshmi holds a special place in Hinduism's pantheon of gods. A large portrait of her adorns the lobby of the Bombay Stock Exchange (BSE), the fortress-like structure where – for over a century before the internet was invented – the traders came to enter Golconda. Before her portrait, marigolds are laid daily, and it is not unusual to see traders prostrate themselves before the likeness and then go to their offices.

[5] Philip Carret, *The Art of Speculation*, Wiley Investment Classics, Hoboken, NJ: John Wiley and Sons, Inc., 1997; first published 1930, Preface.

She is invoked especially on Diwali (celebrated among Gujaratis as the New Year), and for generations, the BSE closed and then reopened its financial books on that day, as though to say, '*Chalo, it's over for now, but a new year and a new dawn begin on her day.*' This end, this beginning, in a country that has no concept of either.

The association of Lakshmi with wealth and prosperity does not do her justice. After all, she stands for the final goal of life, fulfilment, and her name itself is derived from the word *lakshva*, or goal. In fact, *artha* (wealth or material prosperity) is symbolized only by one of her four arms – the other arms symbolize *dharma* (righteousness), *kama* (desire), and *mukti* (freedom from bondage). The lotus she sits on, representing peace and purity, is symbolic of the development of the full human being, and as the white lotus grows on muddy waters, so too the ability of those qualities to come through even in the most dismal circumstances. The four elephants that are often shown pouring water in the background symbolize her followers, who with wisdom, steadfastness, and faithfulness, worship her from all four corners of the compass. Her left hand – palm facing outward – signifies her watchfulness over her faithful devotees.[6]

But from her right hand pour out the gold coins that are often the main reasons for the devotees' worship. They signify unending material prosperity and abundance. Those coins are the real reason for her status as the patron deity of the Indian stock market, and those coins are also responsible for her worship by millions of its traders. In the minds of her devotees, her worship will somehow yield the mysteries of the stock market, and her watchfulness will protect them on their treacherous and dangerous journey through its vagaries. So, from all over India, they come to this modern-day Golconda to find Lakshmi.

Every day, many of the traders pouring into the BSE will genuflect and say a little prayer before the portrait of Lakshmi in the lobby. Perhaps, in the time-honoured manner of traders greeting one another

[6] Devdutt Pattanaik, *Lakshmi: The Goddess of Wealth and Fortune – An Introduction*, New Delhi: Vakils Feffer & Simons Ltd, 2009, 20–34.

anywhere in the world, they have already asked each other on Dalal Street, '*Kevo lagech market?*', or 'How goes the market?' in Gujarati, before stepping into the building.

Adjacent to the portrait of Lakshmi is another object of the traders' devotion. Here is placed a vast TV screen, perhaps 10 feet across, that dominates the BSE's lobby. The TV is usually tuned to one channel, CNBC's Indian avatar, CNBC-TV18. This is the media covering the market, and here earnest-sounding anchors ask movers and shakers the English equivalent of '*Kevo lagech market?*' Because of the penchant of business channels for studio interviews, the faces of the anchors and guests loom large on that massive screen. The faces dwarf the portrait of Lakshmi, almost as a sign of relative importance.

In a game in which luck and skill play an equal role, but in which if given a choice, it's better to be lucky than skilful, the invocation to Lakshmi is important. But this also makes deciding whether an investor was lucky or skilful always a hazardous task in any market, particularly difficult in India. Karma – a complex concept often seen as a cosmic law of cause and effect, but seen in this story as the local version of luck – and the inherent Indian tendency to attribute much of success to karma rather than to the odds, makes it so. The traders don't see it that way, but because of the position of Lakshmi's portrait and the screen, they're often genuflecting before both Lakshmi and that flickering TV coverage of the market itself. This is as it should be.

India finds a place in the origin of the world's first stock markets. It might come as consolation to those with an ethnocentric view of events that the real spur to the development of the first stock markets was Europe's search for the sea route to Asia and the riches of its spice trade, the sources of which stretched in a broad arc from South India to the Moluccas. After all, the world's first traded joint-stock company – and the trading in its shares that resulted in the world's first stock market – was called the Dutch East India Company for a reason.[7] Its counterparts from England and France had near-identical nomenclatures as the English and French East India Companies.

Drawing a series of curves southward from the western seaboard of Europe, and making those curves repeatedly touch the west African coastline till they arched around the African continent, and then extending the journey from a midpoint on Africa's eastern shores across the ocean to India and onwards to South-East Asia, graphically illustrates the concerted efforts of many voyagers in their discovery of one of history's fabled journeys – the Spice Route. Empires rose and fell, and fortunes were made and lost on that journey.

The quest for a sea route from Europe to the Orient and India obsessed navigators for centuries. The reason is spices, items that were desiccated and lightweight but very expensive, which made them valuable goods to trade in an age when wind was the dominant source of marine propulsion. Spices from the Orient were valuable in fifteenth-century Europe. Pepper, for example, was like black gold, functioning sometimes almost as a unit of currency with 'medium of exchange' and 'store of value' functions. And pepper was cheap on the Malabar Coast in Kerala, where it was grown and traded in abundance.

The actual catchment area for spices stretched in a broad arc from the Moluccas (or Spice Islands) which bordered New Guinea, all the way to Ceylon and the Malabar Coast in South India. But getting spices from Kerala's Malabar to Europe meant passing through the Middle East – then, as now, an area of some geopolitical instability. The spice trade's sea-land route through the Middle East had been dominated at the start of the Common Era by the Romans, followed by the Arabs, with Basra and Alexandria as the great entrepôts. Part of the trade passed through Basra and the Levant, before entering Europe through cities such as Aleppo or Constantinople. But Alexandria was always the larger locus, the end point of a maritime route up the Red Sea, followed by

[7] For early corporate forms – such as the Casa di San Giorgio, the Honor del Bazacle, the Muscovy Company, and the Company of Cathay – that predated the East India companies, see William N. Goetzmann, *Money Changes Everything: How Finance Made Civilization Possible*, Princeton, NJ: Princeton University Press, 2016, 289–315.

land haulage across the Nile Delta to the city. At Alexandria, the Italian republics then vied with one another for control of the route's final leg. One of them – Venice – would even develop a monopoly over the trade, given to it by Byzantium; fast-moving Venetian galleys crisscrossed the Mediterranean, picking up their fragrant cargoes from Alexandria and building a fortune for the Venetian Republic in the process. The Venetian monopoly presented an obvious hindrance, but traders also had to deal with customs and other levies that were put in place by waylaying potentates such as the Mamelukes, the Safavids, and the Ottomans.

A sea route to Asia would avoid these impediments and open up the Orient and its spices.[8] Finding a sea route to the Orient and India that bypassed the Venetian monopoly and other obstacles was commercially very valuable.[9]

The pioneer in all this was Portugal. Located at the western edge of the Iberian Peninsula and landlocked on three sides by Spain, the Portuguese were also shut out of the Mediterranean by Italian dominance of that inland sea. As a result, they turned to exploring the Atlantic and its coastal waters to their south. In this, they were led by that austere prince, Henry the Navigator.

From Sagres, his rocky redoubt at the southwestern tip of the Iberian Peninsula, where Europe ended and the Atlantic met the Mediterranean, Henry marshalled his captains and sent them down the African coastline to find where it led, probing and searching for a route around the African continent to Asia.

For a decade from 1424, Henry's ships repeatedly pushed along the western bulge of the African continent but never rounded it. The problem was a tiny blip on the map that later became Cape Bojador, presently in Western Sahara. Though not even the westernmost point of Africa's western bulge, that little promontory exercised the imagination of Henry's captains, and rounding it became the great navigation

[8] John Keay, *The Spice Route: A History*, Berkeley: University of California Press, 2006, 12–13, 46.
[9] Ibid., 62, 66–67.

challenge of the day.[10] Over time, as repeated attempts to get around it failed, myths grew around Bojador. It was the end of the world – *ne plus ultra*,[11] as the cartographers inscribed on their maps – something no one dared go beyond. Treacherous reefs and unmanageable currents were all that awaited those who dared its roiling waters. To Henry, a product of the Middle Ages and yet a nascent man of science, this smacked of nonsense. Impatiently, he kept sending his ships out, and fearfully, they kept coming back. Then in 1434, Gil Eanes, squire, and one of Henry's captains, headed west on approaching the Cape, risked the open ocean, and then tacked south. At the end of his manoeuvre, Eanes found himself on the southern side of the Cape. Bojador – that great barrier of the mind – had been surmounted.[12]

Once Bojador was rounded, what Europe called its Age of Discovery could begin. Portugal's fast-moving caravels, symbols of its maritime dominance, kept hugging the African coastline and pushing south, looking for a way around the continent. Cape Verde was touched around 1455 and the southern tip of the continent – the Cape of Good Hope – was reached and rounded in 1488. Finally, in 1498 came the breakthrough. Vasco da Gama, using the logs of the captains before him, rounded Cape Hope, picked up pilots at Malindi in present-day Kenya, followed favourable monsoon winds and made the open ocean run to India, landing at Kerala. The maritime Spice Route had been thrown open. But he was not the first. Da Gama would arrive only to discover that Arab trading along the Malabar had been ongoing for centuries before his arrival. Portuguese cannon then proceeded to blast Arab dhow, marking the start of over four centuries of European mastery of Asian waters.

The Portuguese discovered the maritime Spice Route to India and the Orient but could not dominate it.[13] The reasons for this are complex

[10] Daniel J. Boorstin, *The Discoverers: A History of Man's Search to Know His World and Himself*, New York: Random House, 1983, 165–66.

[11] 'No more beyond'.

[12] Daniel J. Boorstin, *The Discoverers*, 167.

[13] John Keay, *The Spice Route*, 246–47.

and varied – as they are for all major historical phenomena – but one reason they could not control the trade is because they did not know how to finance it. Many of their early voyages were financed by royal grants and subject to the whims of such a source. Significantly, the Portuguese simply did not know how to manage the Spice Route's dominant element – risk.

The spice trade was a risky and dangerous business. There were perils of the sea, spoilage, crew mutiny, piracy, and a host of other dangers that could take ship and spice. Even if the vessel survived those dangers, there was the peculiar problem of two or more ships arriving at their home ports at the same time. This would cause a supply glut and drive down prices, hurting profits for both merchants and investors. Supply, as modern parlance goes, was lumpy. Finally, the journey out and back could take over two years, and that was a long time to spend ruminating on whether the investment capital was safe.

Over time and because of various reasons – among which was its inability to manage and control risk – Portugal gave up its maritime dominance. A new power rose from the Low Countries of Europe, the Dutch.[14] In fact, it was early Dutch attempts to control risk on the outbound trip to India and the East Indies that resulted in the development of the world's first traded stocks and the world's first stock markets with recognizably modern features.[15]

Many of the building blocks of modern capitalism came from the Dutch. It is often claimed that those sober burghers of Amsterdam – as Hals the Elder and Rembrandt painted them – invented the world's first traded company, first multinational, first shares, first stock exchanges, and the first mutual fund.[16] After an initial attempt at Antwerp, Amsterdam derivatives trading exhibited features that found parallels

[14] Ibid., 235–49.

[15] Early stock trading is discussed in Lodewijk Petram, *The World's First Stock Exchange*, New York: Columbia University Press, 2014.

[16] See, for example, K. Geert Rouwenhourst, 'The Origins of Mutual Funds', *Yale International Centre for Finance*, Working Paper No. 04–48, December 2004.

in modern derivatives markets.[17] And they did much of this to finance the spice trade with Asia.

Behind all the battles for maritime supremacy and the shifting alliances and complex international relations that history books talk about, the Dutch glimpsed a simple and powerful truth – it would be better if the risks of such a perilous undertaking as sailing the Spice Route were shared by various persons instead of one. Dutch control of the Spice Route came for many reasons, but among them was that they discovered a unique way to finance the spice trade with the Orient.

Consider an entity with a single ship outfitted to undertake this hazardous journey. The risks outlined above meant it would be too much to finance for one person, but if some way could be found to divide up the ownership stake of the ship into shares, with each shareholder only responsible for his own investment, itself limited to the face value of the shares issued to him, then the ship could be financed.

The Dutch developed the idea of issuing pieces of paper (first called an *actie* but later called an *aandeel*) in return for which a person contributed a certain sum of money. The money so collected was used to buy and outfit the ship. Each piece of paper – or share – was a share in the share capital of the entity that owned the ship and represented the holder's ownership stake in the ship. If the ship went down, the person's risk of loss was limited to the face value of the *aandelen* in the entity that he held, which represented the money he had given up. The risk of the voyage suddenly became manageable. In return, the holder got cash payments as a share of the profits of the voyage, what in today's idiom we call dividends. By doing this, the Dutch discovered the two functions of a modern stock market – the capital-raising function and the risk-management function. A third function, that of a measure and store of value, would come later.

If on a paper sheet the balances of such an entity were drawn up, it would list on its asset side the item owned by the entity – a single

[17] Geoffrey Poitras, 'The Early History of Option Contracts', *Vinzenz Bronzin's Option Pricing Models: Exposition and Appraisal*, eds. Wolfgang Hafner and Heinz Zimmermann, Berlin, Heidelberg: Springer-Verlag, 2009, 493–95.

ship. On the other side, the paper sheet would list what the entity was liable to pay back its owners and capital providers. This liabilities side of the balance sheet would list the *aandelen*, the ownership shares of the various people who had got together to finance the ship. Besides the ownership stake and the right to receive voyage profits as dividends, each share also represented the right to receive what was left if the entity was liquidated.

But the third and vital innovation of the Dutch was still to come, and this was discovered incidentally in the coffee houses of Amsterdam. Usually, the company's shares, once issued, just stayed in owners' safehouses or desk drawers. But perhaps Pierre van der Spuy needed to buy a house, and Christiaan Weiland wanted to get a daughter married. They could not wait for those voyage profits to come in. Besides, the pieces of paper they held had value because they represented a share of future profits from the expeditions. So, van der Spuy and Weiland met in the coffee houses of Amsterdam or at a specific place – the Amsterdam Stock Exchange – and bought and sold their *aandelen*, among themselves and with others. Rather than just hold on to these pieces of paper and receive future voyage profits through dividends, they often sold them to one another at prices that were quoted in the coffee houses, prices that rose and fell depending on the news about the expeditions and their future profits. Trading had started in the world's first exchange with recognizably modern features.[18] The Dutch had discovered the traded joint-stock company with limited liability.

Trading meant price discovery, and price discovery meant value setting. By taking the number of *aandelen* outstanding and multiplying the figure by the price quoted in the coffee house, one arrived at the value of the ship, a value that rose and fell based on news about the expeditions or on different estimations of the future. Thus was discovered the third function of the stock market – the weighing machine function. The stock market is a guide to measuring and storing the value of companies, constantly weighing the future's effect on present price. Every day this

[18] The earliest trades were transactions in uncalled and unpaid subscriptions as recorded in a company register.

protean adjustment of current price to some perceived future value takes place in the world's stock markets. In fact, the stock markets represent nothing but the reasoned – and at times unreasoned – adjustment of current price to some definition of future value; at unreasoned times, the market would simply not perform its third function as a store of value, allowing van der Spuy and Weiland to buy that paper cheap (and sell it later when the market realized its error), buying that would itself act as the correcting mechanism that drove prices up to fair value.

This early maritime trade was funded through what is today called 'all equity' financing. Alternately, the ship could be part financed by a group of people who put up their own money as equity along the above lines, and then financed the rest by borrowing money and taking on debt. But this presented unique problems, besides the obvious issue of severe risk to the lenders. Not many of the bankers of Amsterdam would advance debt without collateral. In the case of the Spice Trade, the collateral – the ship – sailed across the horizon and went away for years on end. Not many bankers would advance money against collateral that disappeared in this fashion.

The above example was used for illustration, and reality modified the example, but only by so much. The entity that resulted from all this did not own a single ship, but many. Besides, some of its early stock issues were only for a specific sequence of voyages, and so, those issues lacked an important characteristic of modern equity contracts – perpetual existence. Further, the other basic financial instrument, debt, was also used as working capital to finance the individual voyages of ships. Finally, the shares themselves were not bearer scrips with nominal face values but more in the nature of receipts acknowledging subscriptions recorded in a register.[19] Yet the entity itself, founded in 1602 through the merger of various 'pre-companies', was a leviathan of its time. In English, the name translates to the Dutch East India Company, but the Vereenigde Oostindische Compagnie – the VOC – was not just a company. The VOC was almost a sovereign in its own right, and it

[19] Lodewijk Petram, *The World's First Stock Exchange*, 21–23.

was generally acknowledged that the entity also represented the nascent Dutch Republic.[20] Despite being a company, the VOC had powers that were virtually unprecedented in international relations, powers that were unparalleled in its own time and never replicated since. Like a sovereign, it could wage war, make peace, forge alliances, issue fiat money, and pronounce on life and death. Like a sovereign, it used those powers with impunity and immunity, and often to excess. Later day scholars, in their attempt to understand early corporate capitalism and stock exchanges, would make the Dutch East India Company the most studied corporation in business history. The VOC would dominate trade with Indonesia and South-East Asia; its north European cousin and counterpart, the English East India Company, founded in 1600, would do the same with the India trade, and in doing so create its own historical association with the country.

The first account of these Amsterdam markets – and the earliest work on a stock market – comes from a classic work by a Sephardi, Joseph Penso de la Vega. Appropriately titled *Confusion of Confusions*, it surveyed the chaos and madness in the coffee houses of Amsterdam as VOC and other company shares changed hands. De la Vega noted the deep-rooted speculative impulses in play among the two types of participants.[21] The first type was chronically happy and optimistic and cheerful about the future; the ship was just returning, the captain was true, and the hold was loaded with spices. Just as a bull uses its horns to toss a victim up in the air, these optimists with their feverish talk and buying attempted to drive up the price of the VOC's shares. The other group were chronically depressed and down, perennially fearful and timorous about the future; the ship had run into trouble, the crew had mutinied, and the spices were rotten. Just as a bear uses its paws to hammer its victim and drive it into the ground, these people, with their

[20] Ibid., 14–15.

[21] Charles Mackay, *Extraordinary Popular Delusions and the Madness of Crowds* and Joseph de la Vega, *Confusión de Confusiones*, ed. Martin S. Fridson, Wiley Investment Classics, Hoboken, NJ: John Wiley and Sons, Inc., 1995. De la Vega's descriptions of the early Amsterdam markets are structured as dialogues between a philosopher, a shareholder, and a merchant.

dampening talk and selling, were trying to drive down the price of the VOC's shares. And so, the behaviour of the basic types of participants – the bulls who buy for the rise and the bears who short sell and trade for the fall – was set right from the stock market's early days.[22]

Even today, despite the computers and sophistication and *dramabaazi* (histrionics), stock markets do the same three things they did at their founding: they raise capital, they share risk, and they measure and store value. A fourth function, evolved since their founding, is providing a market for corporate control; control of listed companies passes through traded ownership claims in the stock market. Yet to most people in India's markets, the above functions are all abstractions, ancillary, and perhaps downright irrelevant to what they believe is the market's main purpose – providing the backdrop, the Golconda where they can find that next Kohinoor. And so, they come to Golconda, sweating, heaving masses of them, down a road that has not changed much since the beginning.

[22] A related (but unlikely) explanation for the terms could be the juxtaposition of the two animals in the practice of bear and bull baiting. Another explanation for the idea of bears comes from the bear-skin middleman who presold pelts, hoping to profit by buying them back a little later – and lower – when trappers finally brought the pelts in and flooded the market, thereby reducing prices.

PART ONE

FROM THE BANYAN TO THE SIP

1

HOW IT ALL STARTED

Under the Banyan Tree in 1875

The search for a sea route to India and the Orient brought stock markets into existence, but over two centuries would pass before de la Vega's bulls and bears could make their appearance in the subcontinent. Despite that, the Indian stock market at Bombay – now Mumbai – is Asia's oldest, formally dating back to 1875 but with recorded trading from the 1830s. By contrast, the Tokyo Stock Exchange, the second-oldest trading centre in Asia, was founded in 1878.

But it all began with a bunch of banias under a banyan tree.[1]

Like cricket – and many other activities that India has absorbed and now calls its own – the stock market is a product of the colonial era. And like the game, the market does not come with much of the historical baggage sometimes associated with the colonial encounter. Calcutta newspapers such as the *Bengal Hurkaru and Chronicle* recorded trade in debt securities of the East India Company as far back as 1805 – which is not long after 1792, the year when a group of traders met under a

[1] The etymology of the banyan (or Indian fig) is variously derived from the Portuguese *baniano* and the Gujarati *vaniyo* (merchant or trader). Banias (*banyas* or *vanias* are alternate spellings) are members of trading communities, and they often gathered to trade under the extensive shade of the banyan tree. Many early accounts of India's commercial life refer to middlemen and guarantee brokers as *banians*.

buttonwood tree on Wall Street to trade among themselves.[2] The 1830s saw kerb trading in stocks of cotton presses and banks begin in Bombay.[3] Quotations for stocks started appearing in Bombay newspapers, with one of the earliest quotes – for Agra Bank at ₹250 – dating to 1835.[4] Trading also took place in derivatives, and the early traders bought or sold cotton using cotton futures.[5] Actual market participants never numbered more than a dozen during the 1840s. In 1850, the first law on joint-stock company registration was enacted, recognizing a company as a legal entity; subsequent legislation in 1857 granted the privilege of limited liability to all companies except those in banking and insurance, and within a decade, that privilege was extended.[6] As a result, the number of brokers increased to about two dozen in the mid-1850s and to about 60 by 1860.[7] As their operations expanded, they began meeting in South Bombay's Fort area, often under banyan trees.[8]

[2] See *Bengal Hurkaru*, Volume 11, No. 520, Tuesday, 1 January 1805. Early copies of the *Bengal Hurkaru* (it later merged to form the *Bengal Hurkaru and Chronicle*) are available at the Library of Congress's World Digital Library. See https://www.wdl.org/en/item/16067/ view /1/4/#q =bengal%20 hurkaru%201805.

[3] K.R.P. Shroff, *History and Present Position of the Stock Market in India*, Bombay: The Stock Exchange, Bombay, 1962, 2. Journalist Aditi Roy Ghatak, when documenting the early years of the Calcutta Stock Exchange Association from its yearbooks and jubilee publications, found that shares of the Calcutta Docking Company, the Bengal Bonded Warehouse, and the Calcutta Steam Tug Association traded in the 1830s. Aditi Roy Ghatak, *Down Lyons Range*, Kolkata: P.K. Ray for the Calcutta Stock Exchange Association, 2008, 40–41.

[4] *The Bombay Courier*, Saturday, 18 April 1835.

[5] Derivatives have pay-offs that derive from the value of an underlying instrument, such as a share, bond, commodity, or exchange rate; the underlying can also be intangible, like an interest rate or an index. Futures and options are the two basic types of tradable derivatives. Forwards and swaps are examples of non-traded derivatives.

[6] Banks and insurance companies acquired limited liability privileges in 1860 and 1866 respectively. Umakanth Varottil, 'Corporate Law in Colonial India: Rise and Demise of the Managing Agency System', Working Paper No. 2015/016, National University of Singapore, 2015.

[7] Dwijendra Tripathi, *The Oxford History of Indian Business*, New Delhi: Oxford University Press, 2004, 108.

[8] That the first cotton and stock traders met under banyan trees is an important part of the founding myth that is confirmed by eyewitnesses. Sir Dinshaw Eduljee Wacha, in his eyewitness account of the Cotton and Share Mania, mentions the *vad* (or banyan) tree – 'the trysting-place which offered a grateful shade in the mid-day sun to quite a swarm of brokers, panting and perspiring. It was under

Initially, the centre of their operations was the old Bombay Green, a large open area in front of the Town Hall building where cotton was stacked, and where it became convenient to trade in that commodity.[9]

Part of that old Bombay Green – the garden in front of Town Hall – still stands today, a serene oasis surrounded by the urban chaos of Mumbai. Under its banyan trees congregate lovers in need of privacy, drug addicts looking for a quiet place to shoot up, and the odd insurance agent taking a breather from his rounds. The nomenclature of this area has changed over the years – from Bombay Green to Elphinstone Circle and now Horniman Circle Garden.

The catalyst to transform this little scene into something resembling a stock market came not from India but the United States. The American Civil War had affected the cotton plantations of the South, with the North's blockade of the former's ports preventing Southern cotton from reaching outside markets. Cotton from India entered world markets as a substitute. As a result, prices in India soared, providing an opportunity to all those traders who bought and sold cotton futures. Some of the trading profits from cotton found their way into other stock schemes, and the mania that resulted led to the frenzied creation of India's stock market. Eyewitnesses to the Bombay events who were familiar with accounts of famous manias such as England's South Sea Bubble or Holland's Tulip Mania pointed out similarities of scale between the 1860s share mania and those episodes.[10] And yet, there is no detailed recounting of

---

that ancient trysting-tree that the minor spirits of speculation met.' Sir Dinshaw Eduljee Wacha, *A Financial Chapter in the History of Bombay City*, Bombay: A.J. Combridge and Co., 1910, 78. In her work on Premchand Roychand, one of the major players of the time, Sharada Dwivedi claims that the banyan tree near a freshwater well at the western end of Horniman Circle Park is the spot where Roychand reportedly stood. Sharada Dwivedi, *Premchand Roychand: His Life and Times*, Mumbai: Eminence Designs Pvt. Ltd, 2006, 19–21. Archives of the Calcutta exchange mention that early Calcutta traders gathered to trade under neem trees at Lyons Range. A.K. Sur, 'History of the Stock Exchange', *The Stock Exchange: A Symposium*, ed. A.K. Sur, Calcutta: Calcutta Stock Exchange Association, 1958, 2.

[9] Sir Dinshaw Eduljee Wacha, *Shells from the Sands of Bombay*, Bombay: Indian Newspaper Co., 1920, 326–29.

[10] Arthur Travers Crawford, 'Silver Times in Bombay', *Federal Observer*, Stock Exchange Special Number, Vol. 1, Nos. 42 and 43, 30 March 1941, 14.

the Bombay episode, and no name attaches to these events. Given the close connections and spillovers between the cotton and share markets, it is appropriate to call this the Cotton and Share Mania.

The phenomenon spanned the four years of the American Civil War, and saw cotton and share prices gyrate and fortunes rise and fall on the ebb and flow of the campaigns of American generals Ulysses S. Grant and Robert E. Lee. It was also the first recorded instance when international news impinged on Indian markets, offering a brief and dramatic break from a settled – almost timelessly domestic – cadence.[11] With the North's victory and the ending of the blockade came the re-entry of American cotton in world markets, resulting in the inevitable crash and dénouement.

The Cotton and Share Mania of the 1860s also produced the first noted Indian market participant. His name was Premchand Roychand, and he laid down many of the conventions and traditions that were to govern trading for the next century. Today, at the Bombay Samachar Marg entrance to the Bombay Stock Exchange stands a totemic sculpture – that of a massive, virile bull, muscles rippling in bronze. Opposite the sculpture is Bombay Paperie, a small paper-trading concern, and among the companies listed at its entrance is Premchand Roychand and Sons, still in existence. In the alcove within hangs a portrait of Roychand himself, complete in *dagli*, *fetah*, and white walrus moustache. India's first bull and his bronze avatar still stare at each other all day, almost in silent cosmic agreement on the need for rising stock prices.

India's first bull run followed a pattern that was to repeat itself in subsequent episodes. Initially, a displacement occurs, which changes people's belief in the future. This displacement is often based on sound economic logic and translates into larger profits for firms. The higher profits cause a major movement in paper assets such as stocks that are priced off firms' profits. Intuitively, people pay a multiple of these

[11] D.R. Gadgil, *The Industrial Evolution of India in Recent Times*, 3rd ed., London: Oxford University Press, 1933; first published 1924, 14.

profits – say 15 times – for such paper assets, and as profits surge, people keep paying 15 times for the increased profit, which moves prices higher; alternatively, the paper price stays the same and the profit surges, causing the multiple to fall, making the paper assets cheap, and this recognition causes further buying that takes prices higher.

The upward spiral in price is then followed by the search for capital by market participants. The capital is needed to keep the price rise going, and it is usually obtained by compromising elements of the banking system. Along the way, there is the search for newfangled instruments that can fully exploit the price rise. These usually involve leverage – buying in excess of the capital at hand, which is done by using the capital at hand as margin to fund a much larger position, or by borrowing to buy stock. As the price rise continues, it is often associated with a single personality, who is seen by the crowd as a person of dazzling virtuosity; following this demigod, this Pied Piper, will lead one to riches. There is also the spillover into related asset classes such as real estate. In turn, all this leads to *naya daur* or 'new era' thinking, and a tendency to view the new conditions as permanent.

At the peak, the last buyer has come in and news comes out about the transience of the displacement. A crash follows, resulting in prices falling so much that calls go out to participants operating on leverage to deposit more capital as margin to maintain their positions. These margin calls often cause financial distress among participants and lead to unsustainable pressures on them, which spreads to the banks that provided the earlier capital. Finally, all this ends with the public's outrage and search for a scapegoat – usually the Pied Piper who led the rise and who was most associated with the price expansion.

The American South and its cotton plantations were major sources of supply to the mills of Lancashire in England. When the American Civil War to end slavery broke out in 1861, one of Abraham Lincoln's first acts was the Northern blockade of the South's coastline and ports. Cotton exports to England, on which the South depended for hard currency, fell drastically.[12] Running the Union blockade was possible with faster ships carrying light, valuable items, but it was not a viable option for large-capacity ships carrying a bulk commodity such as cotton. By one estimate, cotton exports from the Confederacy fell as much as 95 per cent, from 10 million bales in the three years prior to the war to just 5,00,000 bales or less during the blockade period.[13] So crucial was the cotton textiles industry to England during the later Industrial Revolution that many Southerners even hoped that the crisis would force England to enter the Civil War on their side. But the mills of Lancashire, though starved of the South's cotton, exposed this as fantasy by quickly turning to alternate sources of supply from countries such as India and Egypt.

India became a preferred source for the commodity, despite the fact that it supplied short staple cotton as opposed to the long staple variety usually desired by England's mills. Cotton prices in India started rising as a result of this sudden displacement. Initially, moderate increases gained upward momentum as the Union blockade and Northern campaigns led by Generals Grant and Sherman into Southern cotton-growing areas further throttled the South's ability to sell its cotton in world markets.

Manchester's manufacturers encouraged cotton cultivation in other parts of the world, including India, Egypt, and Brazil, but were also happy to keep their options open when the American South came back into business after the war.[14] Consequently, these other areas were initially reluctant to commit to infrastructure investment in cotton – because of the obvious hazard from resumption of Southern shipments when the war ended – but as the Civil War progressed, many bet on its extended duration. So, cotton exports from Bombay increased considerably.

[12] US Department of State, 'The Blockade of Confederate Ports, 1861–1865', http://history.state.gov/milestones/1861-1865/blockade.

[13] Stanley Lebergott, 'Through the Blockade: The Profitability and Extent of Cotton Smuggling, 1861–1865', *Journal of Economic History*, Vol. 41, No. 4, December 1981, 881.

[14] Ricky-Dale Calhoun, 'Seeds of Destruction: The Globalization of Cotton as a Result of the American Civil War', Unpublished PhD dissertation, Manhattan, Kansas: Kansas State University, 2012, 326–29.

Volumes more than doubled – exports in bales to Europe (largely Lancashire) rose from about half a million in 1859 to 1.2 million in 1865.[15] By itself, this was not enough to qualify as a surge, but the price increases took the phenomenon into surge territory. Surats – the leading contract of that age – went from between 3 *d.* and 5 *d.* in 1862 to between 20 *d.* and 27 *d.* at the height of the mania in 1864[16] (quotes are pence per lb). It was this price effect rather than the volume increases that caused cotton export values to surge. Substantial fortunes accumulated for traders who had made it their business to deal in cotton futures. The situation also began to elicit a supply response as cultivators and farmers increasingly turned to cotton cultivation in response to the incentive of higher prices.[17] In this, they were aided by none other than the traders themselves. In fact, some of the speculative profits were ploughed back by farsighted businessmen into cotton cultivation, another instance in financial history when traders integrated backward into production.

Financiers hurried to help farmers raise output and buy better seeds, and here they were aided by Manchester's businesses. India's infrastructure – some things never change – was a major barrier to the trade, as transport infrastructure between cultivation centres such as Kathiawar, Dharwar, or Berar, and the western seaboard at Bombay was negligible.[18] Though the lack of infrastructure meant the market could not capture much of the surge (which explains the negligible growth in volumes), the impetus for future development of infrastructure was to come from the cotton boom.[19] The railway network's expansion in

[15] Sir Dinshaw Eduljee Wacha, *A Financial Chapter*, 17.

[16] Ibid., 12.

[17] Sven Beckert, 'Emancipation and Empire: Reconstructing the Worldwide Web of Cotton Production in the Age of the American Civil War,' *American Historical Review*, Vol. 109, No. 5, December 2004, 1411–13.

[18] Issues involved in transporting staple from the cultivation centres to Bombay are covered in Arthur W. Silver, *Manchester Men & Indian Cotton 1847–1872*, Manchester: Manchester University Press, 1966, 26–57.

[19] The 1854 inauguration of the first railway line between Bombay and Thane preceded the cotton boom, but directly attributable to the boom is a tenfold increase in track length, from 432 miles to 5,015 miles between 1859 and 1869. D.R. Gadgil, *The Industrial Evolution of India*, 18–20.

the early years, for instance, was dominated by efforts to connect the hinterland's cotton-growing areas with ports.

Despite the supply response, prices continued to rise during these years, and as the cotton market went into a frenzy, substantial surpluses were generated in 1862 and 1863. Some of the surplus made its way to cotton-growing areas, either to pay *ryot*s (farmers) or agency middlemen. So considerable was this wealth effect that some *ryot*s could briefly escape the eternal bondage they were held in by village moneylenders; it remains an enduring myth of the Cotton and Share Mania that *ryot*s even rimmed the wheels of their bullock carts with silver.[20]

But a substantial part of the wealth stayed in Bombay, where it searched for alternate avenues of deployment.[21] By some estimates, as much as ₹85 crores came in as specie or bullion payments against cotton exports, of which about two-thirds stayed on in Bombay.[22] The efforts of the surplus to go down the cotton chain and aid cultivation and production had been noteworthy, but now there took place the move into paper assets such as stocks. Much of the surplus was used to subscribe to shares of newly floated banks, financial associations, and reclamation companies. This led to the second phase of the bull move – mainly in the shares of these banks and reclamation companies – and was to have disastrous consequences.

The tendency of stock market profits to set off a boom in real estate prices in Bombay is peculiar and distinctive; it happened first in the Cotton and Share Mania and was to be a pattern in subsequent bull moves. Most old-timers will say that the real estate market in Mumbai does have a tendency to take off when the stock market does well, and it is not difficult to see why. Mumbai, the most land-starved city in the world, has property prices that are perennially out of reach. Little surprise that traders are inclined to book trading profits and buy that

[20] Sir Dinshaw Eduljee Wacha, *A Financial Chapter*, 19.

[21] Dwijendra Tripathi, *The Oxford History of Indian Business*, 102–04.

[22] Sir Dinshaw Eduljee Wacha, *Premchund Roychund: His Early Life and Career*, Bombay: The Times Press, 1913, 53–54.

sought-after roof over their heads, leading to a bump in real estate prices.

But in this case, the move into real estate was conceived on a larger scale. Bombay in the early nineteenth century was a patchwork of islands with little land available; population pressure on land was less relentless than it is today but was still felt. Besides, land was required to house the infrastructure for the cotton trade – almost half of India's cotton crop was marketed through the city. Reclaiming land became a laudable public policy objective, worthy in and of itself, and because it would improve the infrastructure for trade. In fact, land reclamation companies had a history that predated the Cotton and Share Mania, with land reclamation attempts ongoing since the early nineteenth century. So, the surplus's efforts to find an outlet also gravitated towards the formation of various land reclamation companies, among the largest of which was the Bombay Reclamation Company, more popularly known as the Backbay Reclamation Company.

Sir Bartle Frere, the governor of Bombay, encouraged the formation of the Backbay Reclamation Company, primarily to reclaim land so that the Bombay, Baroda and Central India (BB&CI) Railway could have a railhead in the city. The BB&CI line was to be extended from Grant Road, where it terminated, through to Colaba, where cotton was now stored for exports. The project called for reclaiming the foul-smelling and ugly foreshore that stretched in a wide arc from Malabar Hill to Fort's western gate, opposite St Thomas' Cathedral (an area that later became known as Churchgate). This foreshore – today, as Marine Drive, it houses some of the most expensive real estate in India – was considered worthless, as the sea's shallow draft did not allow vessels to dock there. With Frere's encouragement, the Backbay Company was formed in September 1863.[23] One of its promoters, flush with his cotton trading profits, was the Pied Piper of his day – Premchand Roychand.

[23] The original promoters of the Backbay Reclamation Company were Michael Scott, Cowasjee Jehangir, Premchand Roychand, Walter Cassels, and Gavin Steel. See Sir Dinshaw Eduljee Wacha, *A Financial Chapter*, 154–55.

Some of the surplus also found its way into the flotation of new banks like the Asiatic Banking Corporation. In particular, the launch of the Asiatic – here too Roychand featured, as he was appointed broker – led to the founding of a new animal, the 'financial association'. A financial association was a cross between a modern-day non-banking financial company (NBFC) and an investment bank, and committed itself to activities such as brokering, share issuance and financing, factoring, bill discounting, and market bulling and bearing. With the discovery of the financial association, there started a pattern of pyramiding using triad schemes that defined the next stage of the mania. A bank, in association with other parties, would promote a financial association and lend money against the shares of the company it had promoted. The other promoters of the financial association would, in turn, launch a reclamation company, against the shares of which both the bank and the financial association would advance funds. In this triad, the financial association was using the bank's funds to bull the reclamation company's stock. Banks were, in effect, advancing money to buy – and bull – shares of their own subsidiaries.

Capital to fund the run had suddenly become available.

Foremost among these triad schemes was the Asiatic Banking Corporation, which spawned the Financial Association of India and China which, in turn, formed the Backbay Reclamation Company.[24] The Backbay scheme was viewed as critical among the many reclamation projects, so to give the company some ballast, Sir Bartle Frere even promised to get the Bombay Presidency to subscribe to its share capital.[25] But Frere's proposal was rejected by his superiors in

[24] Sir Dinshaw Eduljee Wacha, *A Financial Chapter,* 33–35, 67–75. A competing triad consisted of Alliance Bank and Alliance Financial Corporation, with Mazagaon Land Reclamation as the reclamation company. Capital was raised to purchase government land at Mazagaon with the intention of reclaiming the bunder next to the land. The promoters – Dr Diver, Atmaram Madhavji, and George Taylor – were known as the 'gunpowder trio' as gunpowder had previously been stored on the Mazagaon land. When the triad's end came, Dr Diver absconded, leaving an umbrella as his only asset.

[25] Rekha Ranade, *Sir Bartle Frere and His Times: A Study of His Bombay Years, 1862–1867*, New Delhi: Mittal Publications, 1990, 68–71.

Calcutta as a violation of free trade principles, and so, in July 1864, the unsubscribed government allotment of shares was auctioned.[26] It was a smashing success, with each share of ₹5,000 listing at over ₹26,500 and subsequently getting bid up to ₹50,000. This sort of price move might seem negligible by contemporary 'multi-bagger' standards, but it was enough to be a sensation in that age.[27] The success of the Backbay issue spawned a host of imitators. Earlier, flotations were restricted to the triad of banks, financial associations, and reclamations, but now a large number of other companies were launched, some for essential schemes but many for dubious ones.[28] The Backbay auction also triggered a general advance in prices that defined the wild stage of India's Cotton and Share Mania.

As share prices lurched higher, banks and financial associations became convinced that the collateral – the shares they had lent against – was safe, and continued to lend into the advance, giving it momentum. By now, most banks and associations held shares in one another and counted these crossholdings as their largest assets; the price advances swelled their balance sheets, allowed them to lend more, and gave them a further stake in the continued price advance. Traders who borrowed at high rates from banks to purchase shares, gained, as the advances in share prices far outstripped the interest they were paying on their borrowings. This, in turn, prompted them to buy more and gave the bull more force. Borrowing to 'over apply' for limited allotments, and then flipping the few shares that were allotted also became a common practice among the public[29] (in later years, this practice would become widespread whenever primary markets flared up). Companies raised capital in the primary market and advanced that capital to the public

[26] Radhe Shyam Rungta, *The Rise of Business Corporations in India 1851–1900*, London: Cambridge University Press, 1970, 74.

[27] John Martineau, *Life and Correspondence of Sir Bartle Frere, Volume 2*, New York: Cambridge University Press, 2012; first published 1895, 5–6.

[28] Sir Dinshaw Eduljee Wacha, *Premchund Roychund*, 49, 55.

[29] Sir Dinshaw Eduljee Wacha, *A Financial Chapter*, 42–43.

on the condition that the public buy that company's shares; in the case of reclamation companies, the funds raised were anyway deposited into the banks that had promoted them, which gave the banks further funds that were promptly advanced out to buy more reclamation stocks.

Roychand himself was not just a trader in shares; in collaboration with others, he promoted a number of companies – Backbay among them – whose shares were sold at substantial premia. Even when not a promoter, he was often allotted shares to ensure the issue was a success. Financing purchases was not a constraint; prospective buyers often got advances from the Bank of Bombay on Roychand's recommendation and used those advances to buy shares in his ventures.

The Bank of Bombay had an Indian director who was usually consulted when loans and advances had to be made; his recommendation carried considerable weight because of his position and contacts in the wider business community. Roychand's standing in Bombay business improved so much that he was offered the directorship in the Bank of Bombay. His predecessor, Cowasjee Jehangir, had resigned in 1864, ostensibly on the grounds of ill health, though he was on record as being aware of the consequences of the unfolding folly and keen on avoiding them.[30]

The Bank of Bombay was at the centre of much market activity during the mania. Founded in 1840 as a note-issuing institution, it evolved into the de facto central bank for the Bombay Presidency, and the business, in keeping with that position, was initially conducted on sound principles. As a rule, it lent only against government securities, guaranteed railway shares, or bullion.[31] By 1860, the government had decided to issue its own currency and so deprived the bank of its note-issuing powers, but compensated by giving it the mandate to handle various government businesses like payroll and treasury. In 1861, modifications to the 1840 founding act removed many of that earlier act's restrictions, and crucial

[30] United Kingdom Parliament, *Report of the Commissioners Appointed to Look into the Failure of the Bank of Bombay*, Vol. 4, No. 4162, 1869, 22. Minutes of Evidence, 51, 113.

[31] Ibid., 1.

among these modifications was a provision that now allowed the bank to lend against securities of 'other public companies' in India.[32] This, in effect, allowed the Bank of Bombay to lend against the shares of many companies floated during the share mania, and was to prove its undoing. By August 1863, caught up in the tide of events, the bank also commenced lending against personal guarantees or promissory notes. The first such transaction was with Premchand Roychand's father.[33] Disguised – and oftentimes, undisguised – easing of lending norms by financial institutions to finance a bull run would also become a pattern in later years.

This easing of restrictions on acceptable collateral and the lending against personal guarantees gave Roychand an opening, and his directorship of the Bank of Bombay was promptly used to secure huge personal advances without collateral – both to him and his associates – which were then used to buy stocks in his own companies. 'My dear Mr. Blair, Kursondass wants a loan for four to five lacs [*sic*]. I think he is safe for any amount,' on a charming handwritten note from Roychand to the Bank of Bombay was all the worthy Kursondass Madhowdass needed to secure the capital to bull Roychand's companies.[34] In return for all this, the Bank of Bombay's management received allotments in shares of companies Roychand had an interest in, together with favourable business terms on share dealings.[35] So profitable were these arrangements that the Bank of Bombay raised further share capital to increase the scale of its engagement with this astounding and wonderful process – the bank's capital doubled in August 1863 and then doubled again by June 1864.[36] The augmented capital also found its way back

[32] Ibid., 5-6.

[33] Sir Dinshaw Eduljee Wacha, *A Financial Chapter*, 90.

[34] United Kingdom Parliament, *Report of the Commissioners*, 73.

[35] Sir Dinshaw Eduljee Wacha, *A Financial Chapter*, 93–94; United Kingdom Parliament, *Report of the Commissioners*, 14.

[36] The capital doubled from ₹52.25 lakhs to ₹1.04 crores, and then doubled again to over ₹2 crores. United Kingdom Parliament, *Report of the Commissioners*, 10–11.

into the market through further advances to participants, who promptly bought more stock, causing prices to roar higher. The bull move was now feeding on itself.

The rise in share prices and the search for sources of capital to keep the move going went together with the search for new instruments and the leverage they provided. Time bargains – a type of derivative forward contract that originated in the cotton market – were introduced.[37] They were a good fit for commodity markets like cotton, but less so for stock trading. Even so, they quickly became available in the nascent share market with tenors of up to six months.[38]

Trading in time bargains also did not require much currency to settle transactions, which was an advantage. Bombay was now facing a shortage of currency in circulation. On the surface this seemed a paradox, as the surge had caused an increase in specie and bullion pouring into Bombay, but some of it went into paying agency middlemen and farmers in the interior, while substantial amounts were absorbed by the increased velocity caused by the general rise in commercial activity; paper money was just coming into existence, so there was an overall shortage of specie and bullion as a medium of exchange. In such a situation, time bargains – where traders only paid or received the difference in prices – lessened the need for currency while settling transactions, and this was a convenient feature of the instrument.[39] The contracts did not call for physical settlement, so they were squared up without physical delivery. Without physical delivery requirements in a constantly rising market, time bargains were basically unmargined naked forward contracts that people closed out for a profit, and kept flipping at higher prices. Trader A contracted to buy from B (and have B deliver to him) a share at (say)

[37] Sir Dinshaw Eduljee Wacha, *A Financial Chapter*, 44–45.

[38] Sir Dinshaw Eduljee Wacha, *Premchund Roychund*, 137–38. Among the time bargains, reclamation companies such as Backbay, Mazagaon, and Colaba were trading favourites.

[39] 'Of the circulating medium there was not enough or to spare. But all the same colossal speculative business was daily transacted, involving crores of rupees – mostly at a fictitious price.' Wacha is referring to trading in the 'marked to market' price differences in unmargined naked forward contracts. Sir Dinshaw Eduljee Wacha, *A Financial Chapter*, 20, 17–23.

400 at the end of three to six months, the usual tenors of the contracts. As the price went up to say 450 at the end of three months – or even before that – A, forgoing delivery, simply sold at the higher price, 'squared up' as the parlance goes, and pocketed the difference.

This practice of trading in the 'marked to market' portion of unmargined naked forwards would become standard in later years, and in a modified version – badla – would continue well into the modern era.[40] In the coming years, currency for settlement would not be an issue, but later generations would discover that such contracts had another convenient and remarkable property – they did not require any capital to trade, and the effect of this unlimited leverage in a roaring bull market was similar to throwing fuel on a fire. The absence of a margin requirement – Trader A did not have to put up any capital even as margin to initiate the position – meant that the profits were astronomical (in fact, as the capital put up was zero, profits as a percentage of the capital put up were so large as to be undefined). The losses could be equally astronomical, but as prices continued their majestic march higher, there was little question of loss, and most people viewed the prevailing conditions as permanent.

In the final stages of the mania, companies – in one of the earliest cases of arbitrage – even bought their own shares in the cash markets and simultaneously sold them forward in the time bargain markets at high premia to lock in the differential. Despite considerable opposition from local trading interests, the Bombay Presidency tried to ban time bargains by treating them as wagers or bets – which would have made them unenforceable in a court of law. The Bombay bill had gone to Calcutta for final assent, but the Raj's summer capital between April and October would move to Shimla, and 1864 was the first time when this annual ritual would take place. In all this transit, the bill got misplaced and was finally passed only after substantial delay. It came into effect just after the crash.[41]

[40] The next chapter has a detailed treatment of the badla contract.

[41] John Martineau, *Life and Correspondence of Sir Bartle Frere*, 14–17.

In the mania's final stages, just as in England's South Sea Bubble of the early eighteenth century, companies were founded for all sorts of purposes. In predictable procession came 'banks and financial associations, land reclamation, trading, cotton cleaning, pressing and spinning companies, coffee companies, shipping and steamer companies, hotel companies, livery stables and veterinary companies, and companies for making bricks and tiles'.[42] By 31 December 1864, there had come into existence in Bombay 31 banks, 16 financial associations, 8 land reclamation companies, and 20 insurance companies, when a few years back none had existed.[43]

Intermediaries like drafters and lawyers also made considerable sums from the pickup in market activity. Caught up in the drama of participants who made and lost fortunes, most people forgot that it was the intermediaries who also benefited and, in fact, had the best chance of holding on to gains. Some years before the India run, observers had noticed that fortunes came erratically to the 49ers of the California Gold Rush (the hopefuls who arrived in 1849 to mine gold), but more predictably to dry goods merchants such as Levi Strauss, who supplied the prospectors. Richard Cobden, the English statesman and economist, offered advice along these lines to a friend caught up in Bombay's Cotton and Share Mania:

> My advice to you is to make as much as you can, professionally, during the saturnalia of rising prices, but not to take a part in any speculation, or to invest a farthing in any shares or joint-stock undertakings, or to commit yourself to unpaid-up shares of any kind. I am old enough to have been a witness of the panic of 1825, and of all the crises that have followed, and depend upon it the present state of speculative excitement will

[42] United Kingdom Parliament, *Report of the Commissioners*, 11.

[43] Rekha Ranade, *Sir Bartle Frere and His Times*, 80.

> be followed by its revulsion as sure as the headache succeeds the debauch.[44]

It is also recorded that the recipient never followed that advice.

The peak of market activity in Bombay was from July 1864 to April 1865. By this time, India's first bull market had reached its pathological stage and the usual symptoms of stock market mania had begun to present themselves. The parallels with the Tulip Mania or South Sea Bubble of an earlier age, or the internet mania of more recent times, are remarkable. In financial markets history repeats itself as farce, never giving the more austere idea of tragedy a chance. Many in the business community in Bombay had abandoned their vocations or jobs, and threw themselves into share trading in the belief that they could make money there. Taking their lead from the Bank of Bombay, banks began using shares – with their inflated prices – as collateral, instead of the more conservative bullion or government securities.[45] Advances were often made on the basis of oral assurances or personal guarantees, rather than the collateral-based lending criteria of commonsense banking;[46] promissory notes signed by a single borrower usually proved sufficient to make huge advances to that borrower. The Bank of Bombay's management was found speculating in share allotments.[47] 'Six hundred per cent was a fair return for one's investments in those days…'[48] In the final stages, it was reported that even mattresses and beddings were ransacked and eagerly cut open to collect the cotton.

All this brought about hand-wringing by the authorities but to no avail. Sir Bartle Frere's own personal enthusiasm for the reclamation

[44] James Douglas J.P., *Glimpses of Old Bombay and Western India: With Other Papers*, London: Sampson Low, Marston and Company, 1900, 56.

[45] United Kingdom Parliament, *Report of the Commissioners*, 7.

[46] Ibid., 7–8.

[47] Ibid., 13.

[48] John Russell Young, *Around the World with General Grant*, New York: The American News Company, 1879, 616. John Russell Young, author, diplomat, and a future Librarian of Congress, accompanied Grant on his world tour and published a two-volume account.

projects, while not venal, had initially blinded him to what was going on. By now gloomy and Cassandra-like, he showed shocking prescience on how it would all end but seemed powerless to prevent that end from coming.[49] Sir Bartle would not be the first regulator to realize that in financial markets, you can protect the sheep from the wolves, but there's no one to protect the sheep from themselves.

And so came prosperity of a sort that Bombay had not seen before. The suddenness of it all should have brought some foreboding of its impermanence, but the historical strangeness of the episode – it was India's first bull run – hid that impermanence from all but the most astute. The payments for cotton exports from India had resulted in bullion transfers from England to Bombay, and now the transmogrification of that gold and silver to stocks and paper was taking place. In turn, the prices of those stocks and paper kept going higher and higher at a far greater pace than prices of the more sedate bullion, briefly confirming the wisdom of all those who had made the shift in asset allocation. All this brought sudden and incredible wealth to the city. Bombay's Diwali of 1864 was matchless, a time when a city of prosperous traders and merchants – their judgment and shrewdness momentarily confirmed by that tremendous rise in prices – came out in expansive style to show everyone that it had arrived. An entire city that still lacked gas and electricity twinkled with the flickering light of a million diyas. Sir Dinshaw Eduljee Wacha, an eyewitness to these events, lived to see a further half century of Diwalis and recalled that none came close to that never-to-be-forgotten Diwali of 1864:

> Never was she (Bombay) so widely ablaze from Colaba to Mahim as in those halcyon days when Premchand Roychand was the King of the speculation, the Idol of multitudes, and the Great God of Gold, at whose shrine European and Indian alike paid puja. The Diwali of 1864 surpassed all. Each owner

[49] John Martineau, *Life and Correspondence of Sir Bartle Frere*, 14.

> of a shop or house illuminated his belongings according to his ability, but the pervading religious sentiment was at the bottom of them all. The sentiment of purity – purity in thought, purity in action, purity in all social relations, especially between trader and trader and merchant and merchant. Interchange of trading courtesies were [*sic*] common and are still continued. … In the Fort, Bazargate Street was literally ablaze with thousands of lights from globe lamps, Argand lamps and chandeliers, and the most notable and famous place of such illuminations were the pedhies of Jewraj Baloo, Khatao Makanji, Goculdas Tejpal and Ebrahim Nooroodin, a rich Borah merchant trading with China. … Night was turned into day and without the aid of gas or electricity.[50]

Bombay's Diwali of 1864 also marked a great milestone in social change that has gone unnoticed to this day. It marked one of the first occasions in the modern era when women stepped out as a group and claimed public spaces in India. Till then, the culture of the zenana prevailed, and public spaces were still off limits for women, especially those from better social backgrounds. But after that Diwali it would all change. Women turned out in hundreds on the streets, and while before they had peeped from behind curtains in horse-drawn carriages, they now moved around in open carriages and even on foot.[51] Never before had that happened on a regular basis, but after that Diwali of 1864, it became more common, especially among the Bhatia, Parsi, Katchi, Gujarati Bania, and Baghdadi Jew communities. It would also mark the first time South Bombay saw itself as a little apart from the country's mainstream. As often happens in India, a social event had broken through layers of custom and tradition and done in a brief moment what many social reformers had tried to do over far longer periods with leaflet and pamphlet.

[50] Sir Dinshaw Eduljee Wacha, *Shells from the Sands of Bombay*, 175–77, 180, 182.

[51] Ibid., 182–84.

At the centre of this tamasha was the Pied Piper himself – Premchand Roychand (1831–1906). The son of a Bania Oswal timber merchant, this Surti came to Bombay in the 1850s, at a time when maritime trade and the railways were beginning to usher in a period of economic expansion.[52] After an initial apprenticeship, Roychand started trading in *hundi*s (indigenous bills of exchange) and shares of banks and cotton presses, which were among the earliest shares traded in Bombay.[53] Like Bombay brokers for generations to come, this first dervish of Dalal Street found proprietary trading both lucrative and to his liking; he would broker for others besides trading for his own account, and in doing so, established a pattern of brokers acting as both agent and principal that would cause severe agency issues among his fraternity in later years. So prodigious was his memory that it was said his *chopri* (book) stayed in his head till thc end of the trading day, after which it was dictated to his clerk as a record of that day's transactions.[54]

Dutifully described by his biographer Wacha as 'lithe of limb and sweet of temper, of engaging manners, and free from the pride of riches, who had seen no more than thirty-four summers',[55] Roychand, at the start of the move, sourced cotton from agencies already established in south Gujarat and Kathiawar and quickly amassed a fortune. An English admirer, Sir George C.M. Birdwood, would portray him as devoid of worldly ambition and say that 'his pleasure was in the race run, not the

[52] Like the Marwaris operating out of Calcutta, the Oswal Jains were a trading and mercantile community with extensive networks between Bombay and cotton-growing regions in the interior. These networks were vital in the early years of the cotton trade. Lakshmi Subramanian, *Three Merchants of Bombay*, New Delhi: Allen Lane/Penguin, 2012, 147–49.

[53] *Federal Observer*, Stock Exchange Special Number, Vol. 1, Nos. 36 and 37, 15.

[54] Ibid.

[55] Sir Dinshaw Eduljee Wacha, *A Financial Chapter*, 50. Wacha was an apprentice with the Bank of Bombay and an assistant at Brodie and Wilson, the firm that liquidated Roychand's estate. One of the founding members of the Indian National Congress, he later served as its president and was also the president of the Indian Merchants' Chamber.

prize.'[56] Yet, like many an operator after him, Roychand's prize would come, and go, during the Cotton and Share Mania.

Right from the mania's early days, Roychand acquired a reputation for obtaining information and commercial intelligence. He was plugged into both ends of the trade: his European clientele informed him about Liverpool cotton prices and his family and community contacts in Surat and Kathiawar kept him abreast of crop conditions there. He then started establishing agencies in cotton-growing areas for the purchase and sourcing of short staple. Of the major cotton-growing areas – Kathiawar in Gujarat, Berar in Central India, and Dharwar in the Deccan – it was Kathiawar, where Roychand's agencies were located, that was the best connected to Bombay and consequently benefited the most from the surge. Simultaneous spot and forward transactions on the consignments to Liverpool were always profitable, and often he would buy on spot markets in the hinterland and simultaneously sell forward on the Liverpool market, locking in the price differential.

Then came his appointment as guarantee broker to Ritchie Steuart, a leading firm in the cotton trade[57] (Ritchie Steuart would later merge into Forbes Forbes Campbell, which as Forbes & Company of the Shapoorji Pallonji group is still in operation). The guarantee broker – a peculiar institution in comprador capitalism – was essentially a local broker who found creditworthy small firms and guaranteed to reimburse a British firm from losses made on advances to these small firms. Advances from British agency houses stimulated exports and financed the cotton trade, but guarantee brokers like Roychand were needed to channelize those advances. For a fee (usually 1 per cent), the British firm gained the superior local knowledge of the guarantee broker who, in turn, functioned almost as a one-man credit committee or credit bureau for the British firm (the practice would survive into the modern era as the 'comfort letter' that many of India's banks, usually from the public sector,

[56] Sir George C.M. Birdwood, 'Sett Premchund Roychund', *Sva*, London: Oxford University Press, 1915, 91.

[57] Sir Dinshaw Eduljee Wacha, *Premchund Roychund*, 40–43.

took from parties connected with borrowers). All this put Roychand at the centre of the exploding cotton business, and the guarantee trade, in particular, cemented his grip over it.

Among the first to recognize that in financial markets information is all, Roychand, like some other participants, reportedly developed an ingenious way to obtain news ahead of the majority. The market-moving information of that time concerned the progress of the American Civil War and the condition of the Liverpool cotton market, and its only source was London newspapers. The absence of a telegraph connection between England and India – the first tenuous link was established only in 1864 – meant that the information could only be transmitted via mail ships, bimonthly steamers that carried British newspapers such as the *Home News* or the *Overland Mail* with their news of the war's progress. Alternatively, the London agents of big participants gave mail ship captains sealed letters on market information updated till the last hour of the vessel's sailing. Getting information before the next party and acting on it was advantageous, more so as the stock market had no fixed timings in those days and traded late during the mania, allowing a participant to act on information received well into the night. So, fast-moving country boats would intercept the mail ships at the outer lighthouses of Bombay harbour.[58] In some cases, country boats would even try to outmanoeuvre and out-speed the harbour pilot's vessel as it approached the mail steamers; finally, the one-upmanship resulted in many boats anchoring outside the harbour as they waited to intercept the mail steamers even before they came into sight. Armed with information thus obtained in advance of market participants, Roychand and some others traded to their advantage.

This story, probably apocryphal, is not very different from that of the Rothschild agent who, having observed that Waterloo was won, ensured that the English Rothschild was informed of the victory even before Wellington's own couriers could tell the British Cabinet. What followed

[58] Ibid., 43–45; Sharada Dwivedi, *Premchand Roychand*, 46–47.

became one of the most enduring myths in finance. Aware that the market was watching him like a hawk because he had the fastest access to the best news, Nathan Rothschild – so the story goes – sold instead of buying. 'Rothschild is selling, Waterloo is lost!' rose a cry, and the market for British government consols sold off and collapsed, following which Nathan Rothschild bought heavily into the market that he had just made for himself.[59] When the actual news broke and the market rose again, a fortune was made. The stories seem quaint and yet the underlying principle – getting information before the next player and acting on it – continues to remain relevant for inefficient markets like India.

Like other noted participants associated with market episodes of this magnitude, Roychand acquired an aura about him as the mania unfolded. Here is Wacha's description – effusive, extravagant, and extreme – of a *khiladi*, a player, at the height of his reach and powers in a nineteenth-century stock market coming to terms with its first bull run:

> Of these 'Share Kings' as they were sometimes called, Mr. Premchund Roychund was the most prominent as he was also the most potential [*sic*].[60] He was reputed to be the possessor of an "Open Sesame" which might have been envied by the romantic Ali Baba of Arabian Nights' Tales. No enchanter in Wonderland or Dreamland could have worked greater golden miracles by the magic of his consummate financial skill than Mr. Premchund, the veritable Golden Calf of the glorious days of 1864 at whose shrine the rich and the poor, the young and the old, the official and the non-official alike paid perfervid poojah. To the vulgar in search of sordid silver he was the very incarnation of a hundred Mammons, rolled into one. He was the one Chemiagar (Master Alchemist) who could turn dust into the yellow metal, the one unrivalled magician who could

[59] One version of this story is recounted in Larry Harris, *Trading and Exchanges: Market Microstructure for Practitioners*, New York: Oxford University Press, 2003, 266.

[60] Many contemporary accounts spelt the name as Premchund Roychund.

> by his magic wand transmute the sands of Back Bay into solid nuggets of gold wherewith to pave the way to Paradise.
>
> To myriads of the mad crowds of Bombay of those days he was like unto the Croesus of old-world renown, unsurpassable and unsurpassed. Wherever you went you heard but one cry: 'There is but one Golden God and his prophet is Premchund!' Premchund, Premchund, Premchund that was the name that deafened your ears from morn to eve.[61]

Yet speculative instincts were hidden in an air of cautious probity that encouraged others to trust him. For the multitudes that thronged the early morning durbars at Premodayan, Roychand's bungalow at Love Lane in Byculla, this 'mild Hindu of a most benevolent type'[62] had only kind and encouraging words, words that the crowds hung on to and acted on, words that could lead to wealth.

Most working days would find Roychand going from the Byculla bungalow to another townhouse in the Vithalwadi Kalbadevi area, north of where the present Metro Cinema is located. After dispatching affairs there, he would move again to an office in the Fort area, only to begin his rounds again, starting with the firm of Ritchie Steuart. He would then make his way to the share bazaar, which at that time operated in the open area at the junction of Mahatma Gandhi Road and Nagindas Master Road, in front of the present Central Bank of India building. Roychand cut quite a sight as he went around the Fort area clad in a snow-white *angarkha*, an outer robe, with the bania's turban perched firmly on his head, constantly surrounded by a gaggle of brokers who executed his wheeling and dealing. One among them even held an umbrella reverentially over the share market's *cakravartin* (universal ruler) as protection from the harsh midday sun.[63] As the mania peaked,

[61] Sir Dinshaw Eduljee Wacha, *A Financial Chapter*, 47–48.

[62] Ibid., 49.

[63] Other brokers who figured prominently in the mania included Seth Chunilal Motilal (who later became the BSE's first president), the duo of Jamnadas and Devidas (referred to as Jamna-Devi), and Burjorji Sorabji Lahaiwala. Sir Dinshaw Eduljee Wacha, *A Financial Chapter*, 78.

Roychand's word became associated with such quick profits that he was 'worshipped as such not only by his own fraternity, but by the vulgar mass who floated like geese in the Share Market and willingly chose to be entirely guided by him'.[64] Descriptions of Roychand often came with these inbuilt metaphors of his invincibility. Sir Bartle Frere, who observed the phenomenon up close, would later marvel that Premchand Roychand's position was like nothing he had seen or heard of in any other community.[65]

But the singular feature of his nature was a certain preternatural equipoise, a balance of the faculties that made him take winning or losing with the same phlegm, and it was this quality that drove him to double up his positions or cut them without a hint of fear or regret. It allowed for a certain calm decisiveness in trading and this, rather than any grand conception or vision or skill at execution, was to remain his most intriguing quality. To this must be added a trait that all observers agreed on – congenital good cheer and optimism that went together with a relentless focus on possibilities; the combination meant that this first dervish of Bombay's Dalal Street never allowed an opportunity to pass by that presented some benefit to him. In a society so focused on human limitations, this emphasis on human possibilities seemed like a breath of fresh air to many and was the main reason behind Premchand Roychand's success as a Pied Piper. Of moderate personal habits, in keeping with his *Shravak* (householder of right conduct) beliefs, he reserved his excesses for the stock market and would set a trend for discreet enjoyment of the market's bounty that successive dervishes would follow; in later years, those more ostentatious had to deal not just with the subtle social censure that followed any deliberate display of wealth, but also with the schadenfreude – that discreet delight in the misfortune of others – that followed on the occasions when they stumbled.

[64] Sir Dinshaw Eduljee Wacha, *Premchund Roychund*, 56.

[65] United Kingdom Parliament, *Report of the Commissioners*, 14.

Part of his power and aura also came from the way he distributed stock. Roychand maintained a grip on share allotments and distribution, distributing stock in primitive circumstances as effectively as stockbroker James Keene would in a later generation for the Morgan interests in US Steel. It was a natural gift, exercised by him and him alone – since this was India's first bull run, there was no one to learn it from. From the initial stage of the market's evolution, and without the benefit of any outside experience, he recognized the importance of broad-basing a shareholding when establishing a new company; like later-day investment bankers, he also saw the potential of using hot new issues as currency while returning favours and distributing largesse. As a guarantee broker, Roychand cast a wide net during the mania and was directly involved in many ventures; even when not connected to a venture, he would often receive an allotment and assist in the distribution of the remaining shares.[66] The waiting multitudes then promptly proceeded to realize the premium the shares traded at because of the issue's association with Roychand.

The most remarkable feature of India's first mania was its duration. As the American Civil War reached its climax, any sensible person would have reasoned that the South was a lost cause and that the scarcity premium built into Bombay cotton prices would end, and end soon. In fact, the standard contracts of that time had been falling for some time. Both middling Orleans (the market-leading American grade cotton) and Surats, the Indian contract, had been falling in the period between the mid-1864 peak and April 1865; middling Orleans had fallen from 31 *d.* to 13½ *d.* and the Surats had fallen from 24 *d.* to 9 *d.* over this period[67] (quotes are pence per pound). Yet, market participants in India, the occasional lurch downwards excepted, continued to live in cloud cuckoo land till the very end.

One explanation for this comes from their reading of British newspapers of the day. Many British newspapers were unabashed

[66] Ibid.; Sir Dinshaw Eduljee Wacha, *A Financial Chapter*, 50–51.

[67] Ricky-Dale Calhoun, 'Seeds of Destruction', 408, 422.

supporters of the South during the early years of the American Civil War, and their coverage reflected their sentiments. The expediency of Britain's heavy reliance on Southern cotton clashed with the moral imperative of abolishing slavery, and much of the clash was seen through the prism of the country's ruling class – at that time, inherently aristocratic and instinctively pro-South. But public opinion on the Civil War shifted when thinkers such as Mill and Cobden came out in support of the North; the tide would turn further with Lincoln's issuance of the Emancipation Proclamation. Newspaper coverage reflected these complex interests and sentiments, wavering between supporting the South and its right to secede and siding with the North in abolishing slavery.[68] Later, the *Times of London* was to engage in extensive recriminations and scapegoat-hunting to remedy its biased coverage of the American Civil War, a coverage that exaggerated Southern strengths and gave the perception that the South could actually win, or at least prolong the war.[69] But at that time, the traders in Bombay just got the British newspapers, and their perceptions were coloured by that coverage. Contemporary accounts noted the Bombay traders' exaggerated faith in the South's capabilities in the war, which then led to undue belief in the South's capacity to extend the conflict.[70] This may account for the inability of the market to adjust gradually to the end of the war. Market participants, exposed to the same news, drew the same conclusions.

Remarkably, the Civil War's outcome should not even have mattered to the Indian market. Victory by either belligerent, North or South, would have resulted in the end of the blockade, a resumption of the flow of Southern cotton in world markets, and a collapse in Indian cotton prices. The North's victory – what finally happened – would have removed the need for the blockade, while a Southern triumph –

[68] Alfred Grant, *The American Civil War and the British Press*, Jefferson, NC: McFarland and Co. Inc., 2000, 1–20, 121–34.

[69] Phillip Knightley, *The First Casualty: The War Correspondent as Hero and Myth-maker from the Crimea to Kosovo*, Baltimore: Johns Hopkins University Press, 2000, 34–40.

[70] Sir Dinshaw Eduljee Wacha, *Premchund Roychund*, 140.

if it had happened – would have lifted the Union blockade by force. So, the bet was not on the outcome, but the duration of the American Civil War. Despite that, the fledgling Bombay market refused to adjust to information suggesting an imminent end to hostilities, and there is no evidence of participants thinking through the issue along the above lines. In later years, the maxim would be '*Achetez aux canons, vendez aux clairons*', or buy on the cannons and sell on the trumpets. This phrase – a reference to buying when the uncertainty or risk was at its maximum, and selling when the situation was beginning to resolve itself – was unknown to market participants at that time.

'General Lee surrendered the army of Northern Virginia this afternoon on terms poposed [*sic*] by myself the accompaning [*sic*] aditional [*sic*] correspondence will show the conditions fully.'[71] Grant's telegram, drafted while he sat in mud-spattered breeches on a stone by the wayside, was addressed to Secretary of War Edwin Stanton, and announced Robert E. Lee's surrender shortly after the generals met at the Appomattox Court House on 9 April 1865. Despite the storied place that subsequent history would accord the Grant–Lee encounter, the cable, like its sender, was direct and utterly without flourish or affectation; the message also reflected Grant's 'endearingly erratic' spelling habits.[72] Though the surrender of other Confederate armies and the South's own political capitulation would come later, the telegram, by announcing the surrender of the largest of the South's armies, effectively proclaimed the end of the American Civil War.

Despite the telegraph's influence on life in the West, its effect was less felt internationally in that age. The news from America reached England via mail steamer on 23 April 1865, a good 14 days later.[73]

[71] Ulysses S. Grant to Edwin M. Stanton, telegram, 9 April 1865, George F. Shepley Papers, Maine Historical Society, Available at http://www.mainememory.net/artifact/76625.

[72] John Keegan, *The Mask of Command*, New York: Penguin Books, 1987, 181.

[73] Ricky-Dale Calhoun, 'Seeds of Destruction', 400.

By now, telegraphic communication from England to India had been established – at the height of the mania, in 1864 – but it involved overland lines from Europe to the Persian Gulf, followed by an undersea cable to Karachi, from where the Indian network began. The overland section was highly unreliable, and this accounts for the long lead times in information transmission. Consequently, the news of Lee's surrender at Appomattox reached Bombay on 1 May 1865, a full three weeks after the event.[74] Sir George C.M. Birdwood, editor of the newspaper that later became the *Times of India*, recalled the arrival of the news in Bombay; he was at a business meeting in the Fort area when a clerk arrived and announced the news.[75] Roychand was present. By now his earlier messaging system through the country boats of Bombay harbour had met the fate of all such attempts in the arms race to get information faster than the next participant – unplanned obsolescence.

The spotty telegraph network had ensured that information, the lifeblood of the market, did not transmit quickly. As a result, there was little of the market's tendency to 'discount' – or anticipate – the future before it arrived. That future, in this case, meant the re-entry of the South's cotton onto world markets and an end to the scarcity premium that had led to inflated prices for Indian cotton.

The result was catastrophe.

The dénouement was as sudden as it was unexpected. There was the predictable rush for the exit, all at the same time, resulting in a collapse in prices. This happened first in the cotton futures market and then in the shares of the financial and the reclamation companies that were started during the mania. Contagion moved from the cotton market to the nascent stock market, and as the scarcity premium on cotton prices dropped, the share prices of the big cotton trading houses and reclamation companies also fell. In turn, the banks and financial associations that had loaned money against the shares of those companies

[74] The news was published in Bombay newspapers on 2 May 1865. Radhe Shyam Rungta, *The Rise of Business Corporations*, 86.

[75] Sir George C.M. Birdwood, 'Sett Premchund Roychund', 91.

as collateral, now found the value of the collateral evaporate, which put their own viability at risk and led to a collapse in their stock prices; many held each other's shares as assets, which also fell in value. Credit froze – and in contrast to the expansive Diwali of the previous year – trust simply evaporated.[76] All this was a pattern that would repeat itself in commercial crises well into the modern era.

On 18 May 1865, the first of the substantial business failures was announced as the firm of Behramjee Hormusjee Cama, the largest shipper of raw cotton, was unable to meet its obligations and fell for ₹330 lakhs.[77] This was followed by a string of others. Also caught and almost wiped out in the undertow was a young merchant named Jamsetji Nusserwanji Tata; the experience would lead the future Father of Indian Industry to view financial trading with circumspection for the rest of his life.[78] On 1 July of that year, hundreds of forward contracts – the time bargains – came due on settlement.[79] An overcast day in the peak of Bombay's monsoon, it found the traders frantically closing out their positions in the open, under banyan trees. To the traders, it seemed as if the elements themselves had conspired to end their bull market. Without a clearing house to guarantee settlement, the time bargains carried severe credit and counterparty risk.[80] Enforcement of the contracts would anyway prove impossible because of the pending passage of the bill that treated them as wagers or bets and not commercial contracts.[81]

[76] Sir Dinshaw Eduljee Wacha, *Premchund Roychund*, 145.

[77] Sir Dinshaw Eduljee Wacha, *A Financial Chapter*, 212.

[78] F.R. Harris, *Jamsetji Nusserwanji Tata: A Chronicle of His Life*, London: Oxford University Press, 1925, 5–11.

[79] Between £8 and £9 million of time bargains fell due. Sir Dinshaw Eduljee Wacha, *A Financial Chapter*, 212. See also Rekha Ranade, *Sir Bartle Frere and His Times*, 90.

[80] A clearing house stands between clearing members and ensures the exchange of securities for consideration takes place without settlement risk.

[81] That time bargains were unenforceable anyway is outlined in Iltudus Thomas Prichard, *The Administration of India from 1859–1868: The First Ten Years of Administration under the Crown*, London: Macmillan and Co., 1869, 220. Much of the legal clean-up was left to Justice Chisholm Anstey – 'who combined with great eccentricity of manner much determination of character, and an unusually vehement habit of expression… '. Justice Anstey's references to 'miserable gamblers'

Predictably, commitments could not, or would not be met, resulting in another cascade of failures; prominent among these was the Pied Piper himself.

In a desperate attempt to extricate himself, Roychand approached for the last time his biggest creditors, the Bank of Bombay and the Asiatic Banking Corporation. They had advanced the largest sums to him and consequently had the principal stake in his solvency.[82] As is usual in such crises, rather than the financial condition of the debtor itself, it was the creditor banks' viability if their biggest debtor defaulted that was the main issue under discussion. So, in April 1866 – in one of the earliest documented cases of large-scale loan evergreening in India – both entities loaned Roychand further large sums to keep his account going and prevent an outright default. Jewellery and shares were offered by Roychand as security, but the jewellery was later found to be worth only a fifth of its stated value, and most of the shares were worthless after the crash.[83]

By now, everyone was reduced to betting on the cotton market's recovery, and as the American South took its own time resupplying world markets, cotton prices did briefly oblige with a rally. But this did not last and cotton prices continued to fall.[84] By mid-1866, India's Cotton and Share Mania ran into the Overend Gurney panic in London, and the resulting worldwide recession brought about a further collapse in conditions and confidence. Even the capital to evergreen Roychand's loans went down the drain, and the Pied Piper had his own reckoning barely five months after those dealings. After being 'extremely embarrassed' – the elegiac term used in those days for an inability to meet obligations and pay debts – Premchand Roychand filed for insolvency in September 1866. By now, Act XXVIII of 1865,

---

left little doubt about the thrust of his judgments. The justice made himself so unpopular that public meetings were held in which participants read petitions calling for his removal. 218–21, 261.

[82] Sir Dinshaw Eduljee Wacha, *Premchund Roychund*, 152–53.

[83] United Kingdom Parliament, *Report of the Commissioners*, 37–40.

[84] The Surats almost halved again from their 1865 low and touched 5 *d.* by 1867. Ricky-Dale Calhoun, 'Seeds of Destruction,' 422.

arguably India's first legislation dealing with the stock market, had been passed to deal with the spate of bankruptcies, and Roychand's estate was dealt with under its provisions. Like many an operator after him, Roychand had allowed his wheeling and dealing to get ahead of both his memory and his accounting, and as a result, the estate was a chaotic mess. So numerous were the transactions that the liquidators themselves functioned almost as a sort of clearing house as they sought to decipher and settle Roychand's multiple dealings. The entire process took three years of Herculean effort, following which the estate paid out just 1.5 per cent of its liabilities.[85] Yet the defined, time-bound nature of the process is in contrast to the modern era, when it is possible, despite the advantage of computers and the internet, for zombie companies to limp along for years before a resolution comes in sight.

At company meetings, creditors, directors, and shareholders sat together to try and settle the issues. Resolutions were stormy affairs, with books and chairs and papers flying in all directions, and the choicest abuses heaped on company directors, including Roychand himself.[86] But to no avail. By the end of 1866, of the scores of companies, banks, financial associations, and land reclamation companies that had come up, barely a dozen survived. One land reclamation company, not a single financial association, and only a few banks continued to operate.[87]

The most noted end was of the institution at the centre of it all – the de facto central bank of the presidency, the Bank of Bombay. The evergreening of Roychand's loans had been the last act in its downfall. The bank's capital of a little over ₹2 crores had been eroded, with almost 70 per cent of that the outcome of irrecoverable advances to Roychand and his associates.[88] In an unusual episode of financial history, an individual had brought down what was, in effect, the Bombay

[85] Sir Dinshaw Eduljee Wacha, *A Financial Chapter*, 222; Sir Dinshaw Eduljee Wacha, *Premchund Roychund*, 156–58.

[86] Sir Dinshaw Eduljee Wacha, *A Financial Chapter*, 217; Sir Dinshaw Eduljee Wacha, *Premchund Roychund*, 147–48.

[87] Rekha Ranade, *Sir Bartle Frere and His Times*, 92.

[88] Sir Dinshaw Eduljee Wacha, *Premchund Roychund*, 160.

Presidency's central bank. By now, much of the bank's assets were claims on the estates of insolvents under the just-passed Act XXVIII; most such estates paid out less than 5 per cent of their liabilities on resolution. The bank lived in hope that shares of companies such as Backbay and Asiatic, which it had made advances against, would rally, but that was not to be; by January 1868, the Bank of Bombay was wound up, only to be resurrected in the same year as the New Bank of Bombay[89] (this successor bank would later merge with the Presidency banks of Bengal and Madras to form the Imperial Bank, the predecessor of today's State Bank of India).

In contrast, Premchand Roychand recovered and came back. In the stock markets, as in life itself, it matters not how often a man falls but how often he gets up after he falls. Roychand retrieved his fortune in a second innings, though the historical record is unclear on how he did so. Oddly enough for a bust speculator, Roychand lived the rest of his life by the motto that a man was as good as his word. This was a truism in those days and encompassed the science of risk management at that time. In later years, with changes in commercial morality, the aphorism would still apply but with an adjustment; a man was as good as his word but only till the next margin call.

Surprisingly, despite the public censure in the immediate aftermath of the crash, in later years, Roychand was praised by his contemporaries and held in high esteem. The contrast with latter-day Pied Pipers such as Harshad Mehta and Ketan Parekh is striking. In India's financial markets, a peculiar hell awaits the merchant whose dream turns into a nightmare for the public, and yet, in Roychand's case, that was a fate avoided. Perhaps this was because of a redoubling of his already extensive civic engagement, together with his considerable philanthropy in areas such as education and poverty alleviation.[90] This appears almost

[89] Sir Dinshaw Eduljee Wacha, *A Financial Chapter*, 97–98.

[90] There was a marked focus on education in Roychand's philanthropy. Donations of ₹2 lakhs each went into the construction of the Rajabai Clock Tower of Mumbai University and the university's library; donations also went to endowing scholarships at Calcutta University, and he made contributions

as a sort of atonement, but later observers see it as part of a complex process of engagement between a colonial government that encouraged philanthropy among its wealthier subjects and those subjects whose concern for the common weal was matched by a desire to build social status through charity.[91]

Following his discharge, Roychand lived out the rest of his life at an even tenor, and even Wacha's biography, ostensibly a recounting of a full life, focuses almost exclusively on the events of the mania, without much recorded on the 40 years, all productive, that followed that episode. His life was unremarkable before 1860 and an anticlimax after 1866. Fortunately, Roychand had never claimed to be anything other than a broker and continued transacting as such, besides functioning occasionally as an agent for cotton factories.[92] The obituaries, upon his death in 1906, were as fulsome in their praise as Wacha's earlier description, fulsomeness attributable to the hagiographic style common at that time but also the result of those considerable efforts in philanthropy and good works. *Wisdom before riches* – the motto engraved on the crazy china mosaic of his Matheran mansion – was Roychand's hard-earned takeaway from the entire experience.[93]

The general whose telegram ended India's first bull market visited Bombay some years later. In 1877, Ulysses Simpson Grant – by now the first General of the Army and two-term United States president – exited the stage of history and embarked on a world tour that brought him to Bombay in February 1879.[94] The man of sternly republican sympathies

---

to a Mahim orphanage that later became Bombay Scottish School. A devout Oswal Jain, Roychand's munificence – as much as ₹40 lakhs according to Wacha – was also directed at religious endowments and charities that focused on his community; Jain temples, dharamshalas, and pinjrapoles benefited. Much of his largesse was self-effacing, and the naming of the university tower after his mother, Rajabai, was suggested by the university senate, not Roychand. Fuller recounting is in Sir Dinshaw Eduljee Wacha, *Premchund Roychund*, 165–178; and Sharada Dwivedi, *Premchand Roychand*, 94–99.

[91] Lakshmi Subramanian, *Three Merchants of Bombay*, 182–83.

[92] Sir Dinshaw Eduljee Wacha, *Premchund Roychund*, 180–81.

[93] Sharada Dwivedi, *Premchand Roychand*, 10.

[94] John Russell Young, *Around the World with General Grant*, 605–25.

was taken in by the pomp and panoply of Empire, grudgingly noting, and almost approving of it.[95] But there is not much on record of what the general felt about the bull run he had ended, and it is unclear whether he even realized the consequences of his great victory on far Bombay. This unawareness was reciprocal, and not a single account of the Cotton and Share Mania mentions the visit, some years later, of the person who ended the run. Grant, whose telegram ended one financial mania, saw his own financial life ended by another. Grant and Ward, a firm with which he had little intimate involvement, had used his good name with distressing results; the firm fell during Wall Street's Panic of 1884 and its end effectively bankrupted him. Persuaded by the author Mark Twain to write his memoirs as a sort of comeback, Grant, dying of throat cancer at the time, embarked on the project and finished the book a few days before his death. The *Personal Memoirs of U.S. Grant* was an acclaimed *apologia pro vita sua* on why, and how, the North won its fight for a just cause.[96] A considerable success – Mark Twain had shrewdly marketed the book to Civil War veterans who felt they owed Grant – it rescued his family from financial oblivion.

Here, there took place one last turn in this karmic wheel of events and protagonists. Mark Twain, who played a role in Grant's resurrection from his financial catastrophe, would later witness Roychand's comeback from the earlier speculative debacle that Grant had occasioned. By this time, Mark Twain was also on the run from his own demons; an aborted business venture had left him with considerable debts. Like Grant before him, Mark Twain embarked on a world tour, doing what he did best – lecturing and writing – in an attempt to recover his fortunes and pay back his creditors. This brought him to India in 1896 and occasioned a visit to Roychand's bungalow in Love Lane, Byculla.[97] There had been little diminution in the public's fascination with Premchand

[95] Ibid., 617.

[96] John Keegan, *The Mask of Command*, 202.

[97] Premodayan, the Byculla bungalow Roychand lived in between 1859 and 1906 is presently an orphanage that is part of the Regina Pacis Convent. See Sharada Dwivedi, *Premchand Roychand*, 32–39.

Roychand's wheeling and dealing but Mark Twain does not bear witness to that.[98]

And yet, much good came of all this. It was an age when the business community had a pronounced sense of civic engagement, and much of the wealth that was generated and saved went into civic schemes and building projects, some of which have endured to this day. Roychand's profits from the mania financed a famous Bombay landmark at the University of Bombay (later renamed University of Mumbai) – the Rajabai Tower, named after his mother. The merchants donated parts of their new wealth and grandly endowed the construction of public buildings including hospitals, libraries, and training institutes;[99] some of the buildings in the Fort area, including parts of the building crescent that surrounds the Horniman Circle garden, date back to those years.

The Cotton and Share Mania also spurred infrastructure development, particularly in the railways. By 1863, the Great Indian Peninsula Railway link between Bombay and the cotton-growing centres of the Deccan was thrown open, and a year later, the BB&CI line to Ahmedabad would open up the weaving centres of that city. One of the companies launched during the bubble years would bring gaslight to Bombay for the first time in 1866. The episode also sparked a renewed interest in company law and corporate governance, and shareholder disclosures got their initial fillip after the Cotton and Share Mania;[100] the first steps

[98] Mark Twain, *Following the Equator: A Journey around the World*, Hartford, CT: American Publishing Company, 1897, 380–85. 'And thence we went to Mr. Premchand Roychand's bungalow, in Love Lane, Byculla, where an Indian prince was to receive a deputation of the Jain community who desired to congratulate him upon a high honor lately conferred upon him by his sovereign, Victoria, Empress of India… The company present made a fine show, an exhibition of human fireworks, so to speak, in the matters of costume and comminglings of brilliant color. The variety of form noticeable in the display of turbans was remarkable. We were told that the explanation of this was, that this Jain delegation was drawn from many parts of India, and that each man wore the turban that was in vogue in his own region. This diversity of turbans made a beautiful effect.'

[99] Gillian Tindall, *City of Gold: The Biography of Bombay*, New Delhi: Penguin Books, 1992, 171.

[100] Dwijendra Tripathi, *The Oxford History of Indian Business*, 108.

towards integration of the three Presidency banks into what would later become the Imperial Bank, and still later the State Bank of India, were taken in response to the end of the Bombay Presidency's bank.[101] The financial mania also acted as a catalyst for the creation of Bombay's cotton mills, and that industry's genesis dates back to the 1870s.

The change in the city was apparent for years after the mania ended, but it was not because of cotton alone. Cotton's dominant position would ease as Lancashire did not want Indian cotton after the South's cotton exports resumed, and in just a few years after the Civil War, America would resume its dominant position in world cotton markets. Nevertheless, Bombay would come back as was its wont, and the reestablishment of the cotton trade on sounder lines, the infrastructure investments of the boom years, and the opening of the Suez Canal in 1869 would start a new chapter in the city's history.

Critically, the first undersea cable link between England and India was established on 23 June 1870, going from Bombay to Aden and then on to Suez, after which there was a connection to Malta and Gibraltar, with the cable coming ashore in England at Porthcurno, Cornwall (another submarine cable link had connected England and America earlier, and together these events ushered in a century-long era of international communication via undersea cable). As was the custom of the time, on the day the India–England service was thrown open, noted personalities exchanged pleasantries via telegraph messages. Among them was US President Ulysses S. Grant who, in reply to a message hoping for a lasting union between 'the Eastern and Western hemispheres', congratulated India upon its successful connection with 'the balance of the world'.[102] The connection meant that Grant's own 1865 cable, which had taken a full three weeks to reach India, could now reach in a matter of minutes. The founding episode of India's stock market history may not even have occurred if these connections had been made a few years earlier.

[101] Ibid.

[102] 'A Telegraphic Evening Party', *Illustrated London News*, 2 July 1870.

A by-product of the frenzied activity of those years was the formation of the traders into an association. The Native Share & Stock Brokers' Association was formed on 9 July 1875 with 318 founding members, each joining with an entrance fee of ₹1;[103] subsequent values for this entrance fee – called the 'card' – were ₹5 in 1877, ₹1,000 in 1896, ₹2,500 in 1916, and ₹48,000 in 1920.[104] At its founding, it was the first and only organized market for securities east of the Suez. In a peculiar case of reverse discrimination unusual for those times, The Native, as its name suggested, was a voluntary association that admitted only the locally born. British subjects were initially banned from membership; in later years they were allowed to join, but only if they or their families had been resident in the Bombay Presidency for at least 10 years prior to applying for membership. This was later reduced to five years, but the residency requirement made little difference, and the complete absence of British or European subjects from the exchange's story and records is striking. In fact, the word 'Native' in the title was unneeded, for unlike the managing agencies and merchant associations of Calcutta that had their own exclusively British chambers, in Bombay no parallel British association of brokers existed to set off against a native association. Holding the colonial era responsible for many of India's problems generations after that era had ended would later become a fashion of sorts, but that excuse was not available to the exchange. It had been, and would remain, a local effort all along.

That the exchange's membership was always local was seen as a source of pride by some, and there was a 'swadeshi' tinge to much that the exchange did. The stock market joined the cotton and other wholesale markets in protests during the Independence movement, and there were

[103] K.R.P. Shroff, *History and Present Position of the Stock Market in India*, 6. Roychand was one of the founding members and on the original management committee.

[104] Ibid. There was also an annual subscription that was raised from ₹1 to ₹3 in 1876 and ₹5 in 1877. It would remain at this level for almost half a century before being raised again on the Atlay Committee's recommendations. It remained a token outlay compared to the 'card'. See K.R.P. Shroff, 'The History of the Bombay Stock Exchange', *The Bombay Investors' Year Book 1940*, Bombay: Devkara Nanjee Printing and Publishing Co., 1940, 7.

even calls for ending the forward market in government securities.[105] After Gandhi's 1932 arrest in Bombay, the brokers shut the market for three days in protest and many, including Laxmidas Karkishandas, D.S. Purbhoodas, and Rajender Somnarayan, actively supported the Independence movement; K.R.P. Shroff, the exchange chairman, even returned a government decoration.[106] Yet, all this was seldom exploited by the Association during its existence, and to this day, these facts are not widely known. In later years, hypernationalist assertion by the mob would become the norm, and yet the stock exchange saw little need to proclaim these facts. Perhaps the search for Lakshmi overrode everything else and was too draining in and of itself to deal with jingoistic posturing; besides, for much of the post-colonial Independence era, official India would view that search and the means by which it was conducted with distrust, and in the exchange's case, sometimes with sufficient cause.

On 3 December 1887, the Native formalized itself through an indenture whose Articles of Association would govern operations for the better part of the next century.[107] All this activity had resulted in Asia's oldest exchange, and the Native predates all organized market activity in Asia. Eventually, the formal nomenclature changed to The Stock Exchange, Bombay, with BSE as popular abbreviation. After corporatization in 2005, the official name is the Bombay Stock Exchange Limited.

Till about the 1840s, traders and brokers gathered to trade cotton and stocks at the old Bombay Green, a large and open expanse of land in front of Town Hall (which presently houses the Asiatic Society).[108]

[105] 'The Share and Stock Brokers' Association held a meeting on the 24th (of June 1930) at their Association hall under the presidentship of K.R.P. Shroff. They condemned the conduct of the police in dispersing the share brokers' procession by a lathi charge on the 21st and passed a resolution urging the boycott of British goods. A number of speakers suggested that the best means of protesting against the highhandedness of the police was to put a stop to all forward transactions in Government securities.' *Bombay Congress Bulletin*, 24 June 1930, as mentioned in Head Police Office records, No. 3133/H/3717, Bombay, 25 June 1930.

[106] Sameer Kochhar, *BSE: Journey of an Aspiring Nation*, New Delhi: Skoch Media, 2015, 46.

[107] Sir Wilfrid Atlay, *Report of the Bombay Stock Exchange Enquiry Committee*, Bombay: Government Central Press, 1924, 3–4, 32–39. Appendix 3 of the report contains the original Articles of Association of the Bombay Exchange.

[108] Sir Dinshaw Eduljee Wacha, *Shells from the Sands of Bombay*, 326–29.

Over the years, trading in cotton and stocks moved to separate locations, with cotton stacking and trading moving from the Bombay Green to the area now known as Badhwar Park in Colaba in the 1840s, where it continued till about 1910, after which the activity moved again, first to Cotton Green at Sewree and later to Kalbadevi. The stock traders continued to meet on or near the Bombay Green, but beginning from about 1859, it was laid out as Elphinstone Circle, with buildings laid out in a crescent around a garden.[109] As a result, the share traders made a gradual move to the Fort walls, and between 1855 and 1874 they met at various places around the Flora Fountain area. Wacha, describing these locations of the 1860s, in his 1913 work on Premchand Roychand says:

> Next, Premchund would stroll to the place where his own fraternity of all sorts and degrees congregated and transacted business. It was called the 'Share Market,' but at the time it had no local habitation. The trysting place was under two or three shady fig (banyan) trees the exact site of which it is difficult at this distance of time to fix. But the spot on which the premises of Messrs. Treacher and Co. presently stand and a part of the road as far as the tram lines covered the whole ground where sharebrokers carried on their daily avocation.[110]

In 1913, Treacher and Company, pharmacists, were in the Old Oriental Building, which is still located at the intersection of the Esplanade (now Mahatma Gandhi Road) and Meadows Street (now Nagindas Master Road), and the trams referred to in this passage ran along Mahatma Gandhi Road till 1964. The Central Bank of India building is next door, so the intersection and open area in front of the Central Bank building and the Old Oriental Building was the main location of the Share Bazaar during the mania, though the larger area stretching from St Thomas Cathedral to Flora Fountain also finds

[109] Ibid.

[110] Sir Dinshaw Eduljee Wacha, *Premchund Roychund*, 79.

mention in accounts.[111] During the mania, these areas were the centre of much action and large crowds of brokers and traders gathered there, organizing themselves by trade size and often calling out the names of bigwigs who founded companies when they wanted to trade, rather than the names of companies themselves.[112]

During the boom, brokers were seen as a privileged class but afterwards much changed, and they were seen as a nuisance and obstruction. So, after the Cotton and Share Mania, the crowd moved again, and by 1875, Dalal Street had become the centre of activity. It was on Dalal (or Broker's) Street, just south of Elphinstone Circle (later known as Horniman Circle), that the peripatetic traders settled into rented premises owned by Bai Motlibai Wadia and once occupied by the newspaper *Advocate of India*. But the exchange had no funds of its own, so the initial funds for a trading hall were provided by industrialist Sir Dinshaw Maneckjee Petit, who in 1874 donated to the association shares in the Victoria Manufacturing Company. These were subsequently sold and the amount so raised was reinvested in 4 per cent Government of India bonds, providing the Association's first capital.[113] In consideration, the exchange's trading hall is still named after Petit.

The Stock Exchange Old Building was occupied in 1895, and Broker's Hall was inaugurated there in January 1899, almost a quarter century after the traders had formed their Association. Acquisitions and expansions took place in 1920 and 1928, when an adjoining plot between Hamam Street and Dalal Street was acquired. Here, on the northeastern edge of Dalal Street, where it meets Bombay Samachar Marg, the Stock Exchange New Building was constructed and occupied

[111] K.R.P. Shroff, *History and Present Position of the Stock Market in India*, 5–6.

[112] During the Cotton and Share Mania, trading also took place in the sugar market near Mandvi (north of Victoria Terminus), in the Bazaar Gate area corresponding to Perin Nariman Street, and at the municipal bus depot in front of Victoria Terminus. See J.R. Screwvala, 'Share Bazaar in 1864–65', *Federal Observer*, Stock Exchange Special Number, Vol. 1, Nos. 42 and 43, 30 March 1941. Victoria Terminus was later renamed as Chhatrapati Shivaji Terminus.

[113] Seth Jamnadas Morarjee J.P., 'The Native Share and Stock Brokers' Association: Origin and Growth of the Bombay Stock Exchange', *Federal Observer*, Stock Exchange Special Number, Vol. 1, Nos. 36 and 37, 10 November 1940, 11.

in 1930.[114] Its successor is the present landmark known as Phiroze Jeejeebhoy Towers, named after a BSE president, and the home of the Bombay Stock Exchange since 1980.

After the Cotton and Share Mania of the 1860s that started it all, the public's presence in the stock market was negligible, and a full half-century would lapse before the bull moves towards the end of the First World War in 1918, and its aftermath, produced enough of a public presence to find mention in the historical record. In the public's absence, business was essentially transacted between company owners and brokers. Trading was mostly limited to a select lot of brokers, usually averaging between 250 and 300, numbers that had not changed much from the days of the mania. The firms were all family-run, and it is remarkable – given the extreme volatility in the Indian business environment – that some are still in existence.

Names still around from that era include Jamnadas Morarjee, D.S. Purbhoodas, Harjivandas Nemidas, Brijmohan Laxminarayan, and R.R. Nabar; in many cases, the initialized version of the firm's name became more popular than the full form, and the Morarjee and Purbhoodas firms were typically known by their initials, JM and DSP. Later, some of these firms would form joint ventures with big international names without even realizing that their lineages went further back than those of the foreign firms they ventured with. Seth Jamnadas Morarjee, who founded the eponymous firm that bore his initials, JM, in its name, recounted the arrival of his father, Seth Morarjee Jutha, in 1857 from Mangrol in Junagadh, Gujarat, to 'do business as a broker in shares and stocks'. Jamnadas's own firm, founded before he joined the BSE board in 1915, would form a joint venture with Morgan Stanley, started later in 1935.[115] Similarly, the records show that D.S. Purbhoodas's grandfather,

[114] K.R.P. Shroff, *History and Present Position of the Stock Market in India*, 7–8.

[115] Seth Jamnadas Morarjee J.P., 'The Native Share and Stock Brokers' Association', 11. Harjivandas Nemidas, through its founder Nemidas Hemchand, dates back to 1878. See 'Harjivandas Nemidas Securities Private Limited', *Yugvandna*, Stock Exchange Edition: 125 Years of the BSE, February 2003, 82–83.

Seth Purbhoodas Jeevandas, had founded the family firm by buying a card for ₹5.[116] A card value/entrance fee of ₹5 was recorded for the first time in 1877 and stayed at that level till 1896, so clearly the firm that was later named D.S. Purbhoodas was founded between these dates, both of which predate the 1914 founding of Merrill Lynch, the foreign firm in the tie-up of DSP Merrill Lynch.[117]

In the early years before the establishment of a clearing house, cash settlement took place against the *Tran Kagalia* or the Three Papers, referring to the application form, transfer deed, and share certificate.[118] A big improvement in clearing and settlement came in 1921 with the establishment of a clearing house by the Bank of India. Till recently, the Bank of India was the only bank located on the BSE premises, with special responsibilities on settlement.

Official recognition of the BSE came after five decades of its existence, when the exchange was recognized in May 1927 under the Bombay Securities Contracts Control Act. But formal large-scale issuance of stock through a limited liability joint-stock company was still some time away. The formation of the Tata Iron and Steel Company would give the necessary impetus to the story.

[116] 'Seth Dharamdas Samaldas Purbhoodas,' in *Federal Observer*, 42-43.

[117] K.R.P. Shroff, *History and Present Position of the Stock Market in India*, 6.

[118] Seth Jamnadas Morarjee J.P., 'The Native Share and Stock Brokers' Association', 11.

2

A CENTURY OF MARKING TIME

Interregnum to 1991

Whatever be the legacy and achievements of Jamsetji Nusserwanji Tata, it is a fact that wealth creation during the stock market's early years does not count among them. It is difficult to see this through the sepia-tinged history of the Tata Iron and Steel Company (TISCO), what with its record of obstacles overcome and achievements notched. When the Tatas needed to raise equity capital for TISCO, bankers in London – the first source of capital in the Empire – were wary. Somehow, the business idea of natives moving around in bullock carts in Bihar, as they looked for iron ore to make into steel, did not seem very sound. Besides, the founder visionary had passed on some years earlier, leaving his sons to carry forward his legacy. The bankers said no.[1]

So, the Tatas raised the money locally through a share issue. In early twentieth-century India, with no investor base, no real enabling legislation, and no heavy engineering expertise to complete projects, raising money on this scale would have been difficult, if not impossible. Yet TISCO's 1907 share issue was a triumph, raising ₹2.3 crores (£1.6

[1] Margaret Herdeck and Gita Piramal, *India's Industrialists*, Boulder: Lynne Reiner Publishers, 1985, 314–15.

million) from 8,000 shareholders over 3 weeks, with wealthy participants including maharajas subscribing to the riskier common and deferred shares, while smaller shareholders, mainly drawn from the founder's Parsi community, family, and friends, together with other Bombay residents, subscribed to the preferred stock.[2]

TISCO's float holds great significance in the popular imagination and yet, as seen earlier, issuances had been ongoing for decades prior to 1907. It was not even the largest issuance, as Calcutta's ₹50 lakh Union Bank issuance of 1829 was much bigger (after adjusting for inflation). Nevertheless, TISCO's issuance has come to enjoy a certain prominence in market lore, perhaps due to the survivorship bias that results from Tata Steel still being around. That the issue took place at all was the achievement.[3]

The problem, from this story's standpoint – the vantage of the stock investor – is what happened after that.

Whether the story had a happy ending or not in the long run depends on what your view of the long run really is. The subsequent performance of the stock mirrored the company's early years and was a disaster that lasted decades. A massive expansion program after the First World War was financed through borrowing. Costs spiralled, the capital structure leveraged by debt taken on through the borrowing program had to be serviced, and transport and labour issues plagued the venture. Cheap imports flooded the domestic market, and the final straw was the Great Kanto earthquake of 1923, which hit the company's largest pig iron

[2] See Morris D. Morris, 'The Growth of Large-scale Industry to 1947,' *The Cambridge Economic History of India: Volume 2, c. 1751–c. 1970*, eds. Dharma Kumar and Meghnad Desai, Cambridge: Cambridge University Press, 1983, 590–91.

[3] Four members of the Tata family subscribed to 13 per cent of the issue. Ibid., 591. The low promoter holdings in group companies were a feature of the house for much of the twentieth century; most business houses of that era used the managing agency system to control portfolios of companies with small holdings. After the agency system was abolished in the late 60s, many houses, including Tatas, continued with small holdings. It was only towards the end of the twentieth century that the Tata trusts started increasing their holdings in group companies using cash flows generated by Tata Consultancy Services (TCS), an IT services major that was privately owned by them.

customer at that time – Japan.[4] Things came to such a pass that meeting a payroll became impossible.

It is an enduring part of Tata mythology that the founder's son Dorab mortgaged his personal fortune and staked it on the company's renewal. More poignant, given the emotional attachment Indian women have for their jewellery, is the story of his wife pledging her personal jewellery to keep the venture afloat till good times came again.[5] The collateral pledged with the Imperial Bank – now State Bank of India – seems to have been adequate, compared to later day standards; it included Lady Meherbai Tata's cushion-cut Jubilee Diamond, all of 245 carats, twice as large as the Kohinoor, and for a brief while, the largest diamond in private hands. Unusual also was the support of unlikely allies including Jawaharlal Nehru and Mohammed Ali Jinnah; this would be one of the last occasions they cooperated on a venture.

Lore has it that one railway commissioner said the Tatas were so incompetent at making steel, that he would eat all the steel they produced.[6] The story goes that the Tatas went on to make so much of the metal that one wag at Bombay House commented that the commissioner would have had a mild case of indigestion – if only he had followed through on his promise.

All of this was very dramatic and satisfying and cathartic, and just the sort of stuff designed to give a colonized nation its confidence back. But in all this drama, Tata Steel's share price had begun its long and slow collapse into single digits, reaching a low of ₹8 in 1924–25.[7] It recovered – but over many years – and finally came back on soaring demand for steel on the eve of the Second World War, following which it went on to become a blue-chip stalwart. Pioneering did not pay, as

[4] The early days of the steel saga are recounted in R.M. Lala, *The Creation of Wealth: The Tatas from the 19th to the 21st Century*, New Delhi: Penguin Books India, 2006, 27–29.

[5] See R.M. Lala, *Beyond the Last Blue Mountain: A Life of JRD Tata*, New and Updated ed., New Delhi: Viking, 1993, 41.

[6] R.M. Lala, *The Creation of Wealth*, 20.

[7] K.R.P. Shroff, *History and Present Position of the Stock Market in India*, Bombay: The Stock Exchange, Bombay, 1962, 18.

Tata's contemporary Andrew Carnegie once said. And sometimes it did, but after an awfully long time.

In the long reach of events, most of the twentieth century was a period when the market marked time.[8] The stock markets were a sideshow during the colonial era and for two generations after Independence. When describing India's financial system and structure in 1992 – for *The New Palgrave Dictionary of Money and Finance* – the redoubtable economist K.N. Raj did not find stock markets significant enough to mention them.[9] This indifference is especially obvious in official India's attitude towards the stock market during this Century of Marking Time. Much of the stock market's institutional development took place in telegraphic form in the last decade of the twentieth century, following which there was a steep take-off in indexes and market activity. Both the compressed nature of the reform effort and the take-off are so striking that they overshadow what preceded them, and there is a tendency to deprecate the century and a half of events before the reform era. Yet, this period is significant for its development of habits of the heart and mind in trading and investing that allowed for that later spurt.

Equity markets in the pre-Independence period remained centred on physical trading at exchanges founded in Bombay (1875), Ahmedabad (1894), and Calcutta (1908).[10] But, as seen, market activity in these cities (particularly Calcutta) predated the formal founding of exchanges by many years. India is the world's oldest emerging market with recorded trading going back to the early nineteenth century, and much of this is

[8] Market practices of the pre-Independence era were documented in various reports, among which are those of Sir Wilfrid Atlay (1924), Walter B. Morison (1937), and P.J. Thomas (1948). All reports are now available online at https://www.sebi.gov.in/reports/history-of-indian-securities-market/sep-2010/material-on-the-history-of-indian-securities-market_20513.html.

[9] R. Nagaraj, 'India's Capital Market Growth: Trends, Explanations and Evidence,' *Economic and Political Weekly*, Vol. 31, No. 35/37, September 1996, 2561.

[10] The founding of the early exchanges is outlined in K.R.P. Shroff, *History and Present Position*, 1–7, 8–11.

because of pre-exchange trading in Calcutta. Before physical gatherings of traders created a market, it was convenient to publish quotes for stocks in newspapers, and the early Bengal newspapers performed functions similar to the over-the-counter (OTC) pink sheets of a later era. One of the earliest quotes for a financial instrument in India is from an 1805 edition of the *Bengal Hurkaru and Chronicle*; the quotation is for 1801 government securities with coupons ranging from 6 per cent onwards.[11] The *Bengal Hurkaru and Chronicle* also contains some of the earliest references to share trading in India, and from about the 1820s, its pages are sprinkled with bid-offer quotes for stocks at various prices. Quotations on bank shares were appearing in the *Hurkaru* from the 1820s, and in an 1829 edition of this newspaper, we find one of the earliest share quotes in India – ₹4,400–4,600 as the bid-offer for the Bank of Bengal's stock.[12] From the 1830s, quotes on the Bank of Bengal and the Union Bank's shares appeared regularly in newspapers, together with reports on the proceedings of insurance companies such as the Universal Assurance Society for Lives and the Oriental Life Insurance Company.[13]

Calcutta was also the real progenitor of India's IPO market. Despite Bombay's importance from the early years, Calcutta led Bombay in primary issuance, and significant new issuance started here. In what was the first sustained period of share issuance in India – the two decades starting from the 1820s – various Calcutta businessmen repeatedly used the joint-stock form of organization to capitalize enterprises.[14]

[11] *Bengal Hurkaru*, Volume 11, No. 520, 1 January 1805. Early copies of the *Bengal Hurkaru and Chronicle* are available at the Library of Congress' World Digital Library. See https://www.wdl.org/en/item/16067/view/1/4/#q=bengal%20hurkaru%201805.

[12] *Bengal Hurkaru and Chronicle*, Volume 4, No. 104, 28 October 1829. The high unit prices of shares would have ensured only a wealthy clientele for them.

[13] *Bengal Hurkaru and Chronicle*, Volume 14, No. 122, 19 November 1834.

[14] Even before the 1820s, Radhe Shyam Rungta finds that the joint-stock company form of organization was applied in Calcutta to a trading company in 1756, to a bank in 1786, and to the development of an agricultural estate in 1818. Nevertheless, there are no records of trading in their shares. R.S. Rungta, *The Rise of Business Corporations in India, 1857–1900*, Cambridge: Cambridge University Press, 1970, 10–12.

This, despite not enjoying the protection of limited liability, which came only from the 1850s. Early capitalists such as Dwarkanath Tagore and Rustomjee Cawasjee Banajee raised capital via share issuance and then appointed themselves as secretaries or agents, thus combining the advantages of joint-stock organization with control. In this sense, they were precursors of the managing agency system that was to dominate enterprise in later years, with Rustomjee, Turner and Carr, Tagore being among the first managing agencies in India. Through their exertions, various companies, such as the Calcutta Docking Company and the Bonded Warehouse Association, issued shares. Dwarkanath Tagore, and not Dhirubhai Ambani as later generations assume, was the first businessman to use large-scale equity issuance to finance enterprise,[15] and he found it convenient to raise equity for his enterprises by putting notices in the *Hurkaru*, where he was a part-owner.

Nevertheless, these were small issues compared to the flotation of the Union Bank. The foundational event of India's IPO market was the 1829 issuance of Calcutta's Union Bank, capitalized at ₹50 lakhs with 2,000 shares of ₹2,500 each. The sum raised (it was called up in instalments) was staggeringly large for that time, issued as it was to capitalize a private bank that could take on the government-owned Bank of Bengal as the Bengal Presidency's main clearing bank. To get a rough idea of what such a sum could buy then, consider that in 1846, the Maharaja of Jammu, Gulab Singh, bought the state of Kashmir for ₹75 lakhs, implying that the Union Bank issue was large enough to buy two-thirds of Kashmir.[16] Tata Steel's 1907 issue has entered market lore as India's

[15] Dwarkanath Tagore's firm and its associates were involved in most of Calcutta's commercial and issuance activity and floated the Calcutta Steam Tug Association, the Bengal Salt Company, the Steam Ferry Bridge Company, the Bengal Tea Association, the Bengal Coal Company, and the India General Steam Navigation Company. See Blair B. Kling, *Partner in Empire: Dwarkanath Tagore and the Age of Enterprise in Eastern India*, Berkeley: University of California Press, 1976.

[16] The currency of the Union Bank issue, the Calcutta rupee or sikka, traded at about par with the Nanakshahi rupee, the currency of Ranjit Singh's empire and numeraire of the Kashmir transaction, which makes a relative price comparison possible. I am grateful to Jan Lucassen, editor of *Wages and Currency: Global Comparisons from Antiquity to the Twentieth Century*, for confirming this observation. Jan Lucassen, email message to the author, 13 January 2020.

first significant IPO, but Union Bank's 1829 issuance took place over seven decades earlier and was almost twice as large as the TISCO issue (adjusted for inflation).[17] The bank was founded by Dwarkanath Tagore and other merchants, with bill discounting in indigo and financing of indigo cultivation as its main line of business. Unfortunately for the nascent IPO market, in the absence of limited liability, each shareholder – even if they owned as little as a single share – was legally liable to the full extent of their personal assets for all debts contracted by the firm. When the indigo business turned south in 1847 and the Union Bank went under, several prominent zamindars of Bengal went down with it, and Calcutta's nascent primary market would take many years to recover from the episode.[18]

In 1864, *Roussac's Daily Money Market Report* listed 91 Calcutta companies, of which little over a third were tea-related.[19] Since there was no real national market, Calcutta followed its own market cycles. Bombay's Cotton and Share Mania bypassed the city, though Calcutta had a boom in tea shares about the same time, albeit on a smaller scale.[20] This was followed by booms and busts in jute in the 1870s, further tea booms in the 1880s and 1890s, and a mining and collieries boom that peaked and sold off in 1908.[21] The bust that followed the run on mining shares was so severe that it led to calls for more organized market activity in Calcutta, and the 1908 founding of the Calcutta Stock Exchange Association (CSEA) at Lyons Range.[22] Unlike the Bombay exchange, which explicitly kept out Europeans and confined itself to local interests,

[17] The discount rate assumed is 3 per cent.

[18] Blair B. Kling, *Partner in Empire*, 198–200.

[19] A.K. Sur, 'History of the Stock Exchange,' *The Stock Exchange: A Symposium*, ed. A.K. Sur, Calcutta: Calcutta Stock Exchange Association, 1958, 2.

[20] Liberal government norms on wasteland acquisition, initially passed to encourage cotton cultivation, were used to acquire land for tea cultivation. Led by the Assam Company, only a handful of companies managed to survive the bust. R.S. Rungta, *The Rise of Business Corporations*, 94–108.

[21] Ibid., 3. The Place, Siddons & Gough brokerage played a key role in the foundation of the Calcutta exchange and would dominate its activities in the early years.

[22] A precursor to the Calcutta Stock Exchange Association (CSEA) was the Royal Exchange, founded in 1898 on the premises of the Bengal Chamber of Commerce. See Vera Anstey, *The Economic Development of India*, London: Longmans, Green and Co., 1931, 112.

the Calcutta exchange's first management committee of 1908 had five Europeans and four Indians.[23] Jute, collieries, and tea dominated the lists in Calcutta.[24] In later years, Calcutta would become well known for its *katni* market, a kerb market that was many times the size of the regular market inside Lyons Range.

Till recently, a Calcutta-based company also held the record for the oldest listed company in India. Assam Company is also the world's first tea company. Formed in 1839 and with share certificates dating from that year, trading in its shares has been recorded in Calcutta at least from the mid-nineteenth century. Radhe Shyam Rungta records a price quote of 520 for the stock in November 1863 during the boom in Calcutta tea shares, and the stock has a trading history from that date till October 2019, when it ceased trading.[25]

But Bombay was clearly the leader among the founding exchanges. Most trading activity originated there, and the only national market for stocks in the Century of Marking Time was the BSE. By the late nineteenth century most of the companies that defined the Cotton and Share Mania had gone, but King Cotton still dominated the listings in Bombay. Jamnadas Morarjee, a Bombay exchange pioneer who entered the market in 1896, noted that trading in the late nineteenth century took place mainly in textile mills, cotton pressing and ginning companies.[26]

[23] A.K. Sur, 'History of the Stock Exchange,' 5. Kedarnath Khandelwal was elected the first Indian president of the CSEA in 1931.

[24] Aditi Roy Ghatak, *Down Lyons Range*, Kolkata: P.K. Ray for the Calcutta Stock Exchange Association, 2008, 40–41. Substantial debt trading in 4 per cent Government of India paper and India Generals also took place on Lyons Range in the early years. Ahmedabad, the smallest of the founding three exchanges, focused almost exclusively on cotton textile mills.

[25] R.S. Rungta, *The Rise of Business Corporations,* 102. Presently, the oldest listed company in India is Bombay Burmah Trading Corporation of the Wadia Group, founded in 1863 and with trading dating back to the late nineteenth century. The oldest company in India that is extant and presently traded is E.I.D. Parry. Parry's of Madras (now Chennai) has an unbroken record of operations that goes back to 1788, and as a business entity of recognizable corporate form dates from 1839, though the stock's regular trading on an exchange dates from much later.

[26] Textile mills included Maneckji Petit, Lukhmidas, Sun, Mazagaon, and China, while pressing and ginning companies included Colaba Press, Akbar Press and Fort Press. See Seth Jamnadas Morarjee J.P., 'The Native Share and Stock Brokers' Association: Origin and Growth of the Bombay Stock Exchange,' *Federal Observer*, Stock Exchange Special Number, Vol. 1, Nos. 36 and 37, 10 November 1940, 11.

In the pre-Independence era, the majority of the listed companies came from sectors such as cotton mills, railways, banks, cements, and electric utilities, and of these, textiles and banks dominated the Bombay lists in the early years.[27]

Among the trading favourites of the era were Century, Maneckji Petit, Tata Steel, Howrah Jute, and Kohinoor Mills. In contrast to the modern era, stocks usually went up or down not for any technical or fundamental reason, but simply because operators bought and sold them. Brokers and operators tended to specialize in certain counters. To say speculation was rampant would assume that there was something other than speculation present, but there usually wasn't. The markets were a *satta* (betting) bazaar.

The high unit prices of stocks in the colonial era are noteworthy. A sampling from 2 October 1923 shows prices of ₹1,745, ₹4,100, and ₹3,200 for trading favourites Kohinoor, Morarjee, and Maneckji Petit respectively.[28] Kohinoor's 1923 stock price of 1,745 would be considerable in today's time – about ₹30 lakhs in 2020 prices and adjusted for inflation. This price point would be unthinkable today, and multiple stock dividends (or bonuses) together with stock splits would have taken place to keep the stock in an 'affordable' range for the trading public's benefit. Yet no attempt took place in that age to make the stock 'affordable' to the average investor.[29] One explanation is that physical share certificates were manually cleared and settled. Higher unit prices meant fewer shares for any given capital base, which, in turn, meant fewer share certificates to deal with through cumbersome manual clearing systems. Besides, with fewer shares in absolute numbers, cornering stock would also have been easier, though this reason was never officially stated.

[27] P.J. Thomas, *Report on the Regulation of the Stock Market in India*, New Delhi: Ministry of Finance, 1948, 30.

[28] Sir Wilfrid Atlay, *Report of the Bombay Stock Exchange Enquiry Committee*, Bombay: Government Central Press, 1924, 55.

[29] The earliest suggestions of stock splits and stock dividends ('bonus shares') to deal with the high unit prices of shares and their low number are made in Walter B. Morison, *Report of the Stock Exchange Enquiry Committee*, Bombay: Government Central Press, 1937, 21. The practice would become widespread in later years.

For many years, the exchange conducted the business of a great public market for securities, more to the advantage of its members than to the advantage of the public. Non-disclosure of actual transaction prices meant that some brokers often bought at one price, but quoted the day's high price to the customer and pocketed the difference;[30] the day's high price – part of the daily quote that got printed in the newspapers – set the upper limit for this practice. Brokerage commissions could be as high as 5 per cent, but they were not quoted in the contract note; instead, the extortionate commissions got hidden by clubbing them with the purchase price.[31] Entry barriers to exchange membership were high and effectively membership passed within families for generations.[32] Risk management was poor to non-existent and that combined with the leverage inherent in the forward market to produce periodic payment and settlement crises.[33] So, some market practices of the colonial period were questionable and were to continue into much of the post-Independence era, but it is also clear that the majority of brokers strove to conduct business on honourable terms. As a consequence, in the colonial period at least, outright defaults stayed low, and this is despite the speculation and non-existent risk management systems. The self-enforcing code of the broker club, strong exchange management, and close ethnic and religious ties between members ensured that most cases of default or bad deliveries were settled within the club. Smaller cases were usually settled through processes such as compromise or 'relief', but the larger cases periodically imposed strains on the system.

[30] Some evidence of this practice (in the mid-1980s) comes from L.C. Gupta, *Stock Exchange Trading in India: Agenda for Reform*, New Delhi: Society for Capital Market Research and Development, 1992, 21–22. There is less evidence from the pre-Independence period.

[31] Many early studies called for abolishing the practice of clubbing brokerage with price, but it would prevail till SEBI put an end to it in the 1990s. See Walter B. Morison, *Report of the Stock Exchange Enquiry Committee*, 15–16 and P.J. Thomas, *Report on the Regulation of the Stock Market*, 73.

[32] 'The security business in the country has tended to be in the hands of a few families of stockbrokers whose actions are primarily governed by the need to protect their own interest and bereft of the interests of the investing public…' Ministry of Finance, Department of Economic Affairs, *Report of the High Powered Committee on Stock Exchange Reforms* (G.S. Patel Committee), New Delhi: Controller of Publications, 1985, 10.

[33] P.J. Thomas, *Report on the Regulation of the Stock Market*, 45–51, 68–84.

The unmargined naked forward and the short sale (together with the short's occasional outcome, the squeeze) were the dominant market practices of that era.

The unmargined naked forward contract was the usual trade and allowed on a 'specified list' of the most liquid stocks of the largest companies. The term 'unmargined naked forward' has itself been created for this account, and there is no mention in the historical record of such a trade. In the annals, the contract was usually called the badla trade, though 'contracts for the clearing', 'cleared securities', 'A group', and 'specified list' were also used as innocuous nomenclature over the decades. The unmargined naked forward was a peculiar beast. The position could be initiated without putting up any capital and was therefore an unmargined trade; it was initiated without any pretence at owning the actual underlying stock, hence the term 'naked'; finally, it was a bet on the price of a stock on a forward (or settlement) date and was therefore a forward contract. Buying a stock with cash at 120 and selling at 140 would be the simplest trade, resulting in a profit of 20 (140–120) or 16.6 per cent (20/120 expressed as a percentage). Buying it at the same 120 on a, say, 30 per cent margin and selling it at the same 140 would result in considerable profit; the capital put up was just 36 (30 per cent of 120) and the profit that resulted was the same 20 (140–120). This is leverage, and because of that leverage, the same trade's profit percentage of 16.6 per cent was now a hefty 56 per cent of the capital put up (20/36 expressed as a percentage). For a certain type of trader in a financial market, this leverage is everything.

But the unmargined naked forward, a derivative that was the basic trade of the Indian market for generations, was another league of bet.[34] Without any capital – or margin – put up and without owning the stock, the trader initiated the badla trade and just received or paid the

[34] The badla forward market of the 1950s is briefly described in H.T. Parekh, *The Bombay Money Market*, Bombay: Oxford University Press, 1953, 73–77. Also see P.J. Thomas, *Report on the Regulation of the Stock Market*, 40–51, 68–84.

difference between the initiated price and its future price on the day of settlement (or any day in between). In this example, the stock was bought at 120 and sold at 140 resulting in a profit of 20, but because the capital put up was 0, profits as a percentage of the capital put up were 20/0, or so large as to be undefined (the example ignores taxes and transaction costs that are incurred for every transaction).

This was 'gambling in differences' – the polite term used in multiple reports of that era to describe the phenomenon of forward trading in stocks with settlement in 'marked to market' price differences between one settlement and the next.[35] Needless to say, receiving a profit on the trade was sweet and essentially money for nothing. But paying out on this trade when it led to a loss was another thing altogether, and defaults on the payout routinely generated severe counterparty risk on the entire system. The *dabba* (bucket shop) trading of today – a form of regulatory arbitrage that periodically surfaces whenever participants start viewing regulation as too cumbersome – continues to use trading in differences as its basic operating principle.[36] Notice also that this was not very different from the Roychand time bargain, and in fact, nothing much had changed from Roychand's era. The derivatives-like features of India's cash market were present right from the earliest times, and much of this was because futures trading techniques in commodity markets such as cotton had transplanted themselves into the stock market.[37]

So, a participant initiating a trade on 1 June had till 14 June to decide whether to square up, take delivery of the underlying share, or carry forward the trade. The price move between 1 June and 14 June was profit if the trade worked out, and the majority of traders simply squared up at any time over the 14-day settlement period and made the difference, turning a profit or paying out a loss ('gambling in differences'), all without putting up any capital. If the trader did

[35] Sir Wilfrid Atlay, *Report of the Bombay Stock Exchange Enquiry Committee*, 2, 14.

[36] For a recent example see Debashis Basu, 'Boom in Digital Dabba Trading,' *Business Standard*, 18 July 2021.

[37] Forwards and swaps are typically non-tradable derivatives that are privately arranged between parties. As shown, India's badla system had extensive forward-like features.

not square up by 14 June, they had the option to take delivery of the underlying share – either by paying up the full price of the share or carrying forward the trade into the next settlement. Taking delivery by paying the full price ended the matter, but if the carry forward option was chosen, the trader could carry forward the trade into the next 14-day settlement at an interest rate – the badla rate. This badla rate rose or fell depending on various factors, including the amount of badla finance available, overall call market interest rates, upcoming events, and the all-important technical position of the market, i.e., its net long (buying)/ short (selling) positions.[38]

[38] Badla usually followed a 14-day settlement period that ended on alternate Fridays with a badla session on the following day (Saturday). The duration of the settlement period varied over the Century of Marking Time, with a monthly settlement before 1946 and a weekly settlement after 1994. At the badla sessions, the badla financier (*budliwalla*) lent capital into the market by taking delivery on behalf of the long side that wished to carry forward purchases into the next settlement; in effect, the *budliwalla* paid cash for the long side into the market, following which, at the Saturday badla session, the long side sold and repurchased the same position using the *budliwalla*'s capital, resulting in a long rollover into the next settlement. Alternately, the *budliwalla* lent shares into the market by giving delivery on behalf of the short side party who wished to carry forward his sales into the next settlement; in effect, the *budliwalla* delivered shares for the short side into the market, following which, at the badla session, the short side purchased and resold the same position using the *budliwalla*'s shares, resulting in a short rollover into the next settlement. The market became technically overbought if shares bought were more than the willingness to take delivery, leading to net capital demand and high *vyaj* badla rates; this was *seedha* badla and paid by the buyer to the seller. The market became technically oversold if shares sold were more than willingness to give delivery, leading to net share demand and low *vyaj* (*seedha*) badla rates; occasionally, in severe bear conditions (or when the squeeze was on), *undha* badla kicked in, and these were rates paid by the seller to the buyer. This was almost like the backwardation charge of commodity futures markets. Because of the general pessimism and low growth rates of the badla era, situations where *undha* badla occurred were not uncommon – resulting in the bear operator receiving unusual gains and biasing the system in favour of the short side. More technically (like in the futures markets) the Indian stock market's badla forward system was often in contango; but (unlike in the futures markets) it was in backwardation more than it needed to be.

At the Saturday badla sessions, exchange authorities announced the price – the *havala* rate – at which specified shares could be carried forward on the above transactions; this *havala* rate or board rate had been first proposed by Jamnadas Morarjee in 1916. It was usually the closing price on the preceding day (Friday) but this was not always the case. The *havala* rate was controversial, as depending on the direction of speculative activity, it could be (and sometimes was) used by exchange authorities to impound profits from bulls or bears. A lower *havala* rate reduced profits to the bulls, as it lowered the difference between the price the trade was contracted at, and the *havala* rate used to carry forward into the next settlement; a higher *havala* rate did the same to the bears. Powerful market factions sometimes sought to hijack exchange management and manipulate *havala* rates, but such incidents

The trader who carried forward did not pay for their shares, and so, the balance of financing had to be provided by a *budliwalla* (badla financier). Annualized badla charges in the call market's modern era generally averaged between 18 and 24 per cent and could go even higher in a bull market, but these high rates were not viewed as usurious, and most observers justified them because of the risk involved. The badla financiers, however, benefited from the implicit collateral of the purchased shares (though legal precedent and contract enforcement were hazy on this), and as a result, the risk may have been lesser than was imagined. So, badla returns may have been justified compared to the risk involved, and as proof, consider that the smart money of that era often chose only to be badla financiers, and finance others, as they were the ones who took on market risk. But knowledge of all this was poorly articulated and the system was never fully understood by those on the outside.

For much of the twentieth century, the system operated without margins, and so, the very high unit prices of shares did not act as a deterrent to the public. It was only in later years that the trader had to pay a margin at all (usually between 5 and 15 per cent).[39] Intra-settlement profits also counted towards margin; in the above example, profits on the move between 1 June and June 14 – assuming the trader had bet right – were also applied to the margin, effectively lowering it further. In effect, this capitalized trading profits of those who had bet right, allowing them to bet more on the move, which, in turn, created terrific momentum on short-term market trends. Typically, the decision would be to roll over into the next settlement, either by using the carry forward option, or by squaring up in the closing minutes of the expiring settlement and reopening in the opening minutes of the next settlement. In a bull run, the long traders – consumed with regret if they lost out on

---

were exaggerated and few and far between; after all, there was an opposing faction who had every incentive to make sure such incidents did not happen, and this ensured equilibrium (this analysis had to be pieced together from various sources. The BSE did a good job of managing its own systems but found it difficult to competently describe those same systems, and this was most apparent in the era after K.R.P. Shroff and Phiroze Jeejeebhoy).

[39] In the colonial era, there were repeated attempts to introduce margins but there was no real margining system. See Walter B. Morison, *Report of the Stock Exchange Enquiry Committee*, 12–13.

further upside – would roll over into the next settlement, while the short traders – consumed with regret if they had to take their losses – also rolled over into the next settlement. The market, anyway a boiling cauldron of emotions, saw those emotions magnified by its microstructure. These were traders who didn't even know they were derivatives traders, and it didn't take much for them to get sucked into this system. One study on volumes done towards the end of the badla era estimated that about 65 per cent of trade was squared up at settlement end (usually to be reopened in the opening minutes of the next settlement), about 25 per cent was carried forward on badla into the next settlement, while only about 10 per cent was actual delivery-based buying.[40]

Note also that the trader who bought the stock on 1 June got free two-week options that expired on 14 June, to either: square up (and make or pay the difference), carry forward the trade, or take delivery of the underlying share. Various permutations of these options were also possible, but the most critical option was observing and benefiting from 14 days of volatile price movement before opting to pay cash on delivery or use the forward system. These free options – effectively embedded options on forward contracts – had immense value that went unrecognized in that era mainly because of ignorance about derivatives.[41] In later years, Nehruvian India's bureaucrats would ban options trading without realizing that the entire stock market ran on a system of hidden embedded options on the widely traded forward list! To this day, accounts of those years – while recognizing the similarity between the forward list and futures contracts – are silent on the embedded options on forwards that really drove the system.

Notice also that the length of the settlement period decided the duration of the forward contract and the value of the embedded options;

[40] L.C. Gupta, *Expert Study of Trading in Shares in Stock Exchanges*, Volume 2, Appendices – Working Paper/Note 1, 'The Volume and Nature of Speculation on Indian Stock Exchanges: Regulatory Implications,' New Delhi: The Society for Capital Market Research and Development, 1991, 20.

[41] Options are the right (but not the obligation) to buy or sell an underlying asset at a specific price on or before a specified expiration date. Calls are rights to buy and Puts are rights to sell. Badla's options on forwards were actually second-order derivatives – or derivatives on derivatives – with complex valuation profiles. Nevertheless, little attempt was made in the badla era to disentangle valuation profiles of instruments.

the lengthier the settlement period, the longer was the time period to get price upside, and the higher was the embedded option value. So, 28 June was twice as valuable as 14 June as a settlement end.[42] Naturally, this also guaranteed that any reduction of the settlement period was bitterly opposed by brokers and other participants. Brokers and participants did not think through the issue along the above lines – even if they did, there is no written record of the same – but most instinctively sensed that longer settlement periods benefited them and countered attempts to reduce settlement duration.

Till 1946, traders had a one-month period to settle the trade.[43] After 1946, the monthly settlement was reduced to the fortnightly 14-day settlement, which usually resulted in positions being rolled over to the next period.[44] Obligations could thus be postponed indefinitely or at least till the trade (hopefully) turned a profit, but this indefinite postponement of settlement obligations by rolling them over into the next settlement sometimes led to catastrophic crises on payment of cash or delivery of shares. In later years, attempts were made to limit (to between 60 and 90 days) the period over which such back-to-back rollovers could take place, but this proved difficult to implement.[45] So, for much of the Century of Marking Time, the Indian stock market consisted of unmargined naked forwards with embedded option features and fortnightly two-week tenors that kept getting rolled over on alternate Fridays. In 1994, the settlement period was reduced to a week, which reduced yet again the value of the embedded options but left all other features intact.[46]

[42] Today's options traders will recognize this as the 'time to expiry' feature in standard option pricing models such as Black–Scholes–Merton.

[43] K.R.P. Shroff, *History and Present Position of the Stock Market in India*, 51.

[44] The 1937 Morison committee had also suggested reducing the settlement period from monthly to fortnightly intervals, effectively reducing the value of embedded options granted to traders during the settlement period. Walter B. Morison, *Report of the Stock Exchange Enquiry Committee*, 13–14.

[45] For example, the 1995 G.S. Patel Committee report suggested limiting back-to-back rollovers to four settlements totalling about 60 days.

[46] Reducing the settlement cycle from fortnightly to weekly settlements and standardizing the settlement cycle across exchanges were key recommendations in L.C. Gupta's 1991 study. See L.C. Gupta, *Expert Study of Trading in Shares in Stock Exchanges*, New Delhi: The Society for Capital Market Research and Development, 1991, 6–7, 54–55.

Since there was no separate derivatives market, the above practices, with their extensive derivatives-like features, took place in the cash market. Stocks on which badla was allowed were grouped under the 'specified list' or 'A group' and these constituted the forward market. The remaining stocks, for which full payments were made via cash on delivery, were grouped under the 'non-specified list' or 'B group', and these constituted the bulk of listings. Traders naturally gravitated towards the unlimited leverage of the forward market that came from its non-existent to low margins and embedded options. As a result, most volumes came from the forward side, which made for an unbalanced stock market. Before 1915, there were no restrictions on entry into the badla or specified list, and any stock could be traded on the badla trade. It was only from 1915 onwards, and at the insistence of Jamnadas Morarjee, that the exchange's permission was even required for additions to the forward specified list.[47]

A 1923 register for the BSE noted a total of 132 companies in the cash lists and 40 in the forward (or badla) list.[48] In later years, the forward market's 'specified list' continued to expand, and at the system's height, it usually included 100 to 150 stocks. On the eve of the Mehta Bull in 1990, BSE's M.R. Mayya documented that badla was conducted in the exchanges of Ahmedabad, Bombay, Calcutta, and Delhi with 80, 58, 40, and 18 scrips respectively. So, excluding common scrips across exchanges, about 128 stocks traded forward on an all-India basis at the four exchanges.[49] Yet, this badla list of between 100 to 150 stocks typically accounted for as much as 80 to 90 per cent of total volumes, while the non-specified shares – at one time, they numbered over 5,000

[47] Forward trading in the late nineteenth and early twentieth centuries focused on mills such as Maneckji Petit, Lukhmidas, Sun, Mazagaon, and China. See Seth Jamnadas Morarjee J.P., 'The Native Share and Stock Brokers' Association,' 11, 13. Jamnadas Morarjee was also the moving force behind cheque payments that were introduced from 26 September 1916. Before that date, brokers came by carriage filled with specie and cash to meet commitments, and settlements that sometimes went over a crore of rupees were settled in cash till the early hours of the morning.

[48] Appendix 10 in Sir Wilfrid Atlay, *Report of the Bombay Stock Exchange Enquiry Committee*, 108–09.

[49] M.R. Mayya, 'Regulatory Framework for Stock Markets: The Indian Experience,' *Symposium on Capital Market Development and Privatisation*, Mumbai: Commonwealth Secretariat, 1990, 190.

scrips – accounted for the remaining volumes.[50] In an earlier era, the 1937 Morison Committee had noted that badla's volumes were a similar proportion of total volumes, which meant that badla – the unmargined naked forward – was the dominant historical feature of the market and retained that dominance over the Century of Marking Time.[51]

The absence of margin requirements and resulting improvement in liquidity also meant that badla stocks on the specified list usually enjoyed better valuations than stocks on the all-cash B Group list. Consequently, company promoters (founders) had a built-in incentive to put their stocks on the specified list. In particular, bull markets were not broad-based and usually focused on the heavily traded counters in the badla list. In turn, exchange authorities often added or removed stocks from the forward list, which guaranteed valuation changes irrespective of fundamentals. In later years, the introduction of the National Stock Exchange's derivatives segment would see similar improvements in liquidity for stocks placed on that segment.[52]

In fact, badla was the source of Bombay's standing as a national market that never had to deal with the liquidity and price continuity issues that confronted Calcutta and Madras.[53] Introduced in Calcutta only in 1949, when it was offered on eight scrips, the Calcutta badla list was never as extensive as Bombay's list.[54] In Calcutta's case, even the presence of forward markets did not guarantee liquidity, which continued to remain an issue for most scrips other than Indian Iron and Steel Company (IISCO).[55] Madras did not allow badla or any other version of the

[50] In 1988, out of over 5,000 listed stocks, the 122 badla stocks accounted for over 80 per cent of volumes while the top 25 badla stocks accounted for 60 per cent of volumes. See M.R. Mayya, 'Recent Developments in Stock Exchanges,' *Seminar on Capital Markets: Problems and Prospects*, 4 February 1988, The Stock Exchange, Bombay: BSE, 1988, 9.

[51] The 1937 Morison report also estimated forward badla volumes at between 80 to 90 per cent of market turnover. Walter B. Morison, *Report of the Stock Exchange Enquiry Committee*, 3.

[52] Empirical work is yet to be done on valuation effects when stocks are added or removed from the NSE's derivatives segment.

[53] H.T. Parekh, *The Bombay Money Market*, 68–69.

[54] A.K. Sur, 'History of the Stock Exchange,' 22.

[55] Aditi Roy Ghatak, *Down Lyons Range*, 60–61.

carry forward trade;[56] without forward markets, liquidity remained an issue right from the founding of the Madras Exchange.[57] The Madras Stock Exchange opened in 1920 but was forced to shut down in 1923 due to the absence of liquidity. It would reopen in 1937, following a boom in southern plantation companies and the introduction of trunk telephone facilities that allowed Bombay and Madras traders to get quotes from each other's exchanges, but the liquidity issues remained. Madras's inherent conservatism did not allow for kerb markets, and so, the Madras exchange relied on inter-exchange business to bring in the volumes.[58]

Several factors came together to make badla a mainstay. In a capital-scarce economy where the public had little access to bank financing for market activities, not asking for capital was the ultimate solution to the problem of getting the public into the market. Self-interested brokers would cheerlead the system on, mainly because the unlimited leverage it provided was a deadly drug that was abused by the average trader who overtraded with huge positions, resulting in considerable commissions for the broker. The domestic and foreign buy sides came into existence only from the 1990s, so for much of the Century of Marking Time badla made up for their absence. Finally, clearing and settlement systems were manually operated and cumbersome, so the massive square-up business within the settlement period had the convenient side effect of reducing the burden on clearing and settlement.

Because of these conditions, badla was what was needed for the Herculean task of running a viable stock market in India during the Century of Marking Time. This is a simple but vital fact that is often overlooked by contemporary critics of the system. An earlier era must be looked at through its own lens rather than through the lens of a later generation, but the inability to do so leads to a certain presentism that is a singular feature of the ahistorical Indian environment. At one

[56] Madras Stock Exchange Association Limited, 'Proceedings of the Council of Management,' 5 October 1943.

[57] H.T. Parekh, *The Bombay Money Market*, 70.

[58] P.J. Thomas, *Report on the Regulation of the Stock Market in India*, 11–12.

end, badla was a call market where wealthy individuals loaned funds into the market at badla rates that rose and fell based on the market's demand for funds; at the other end, it was also a lending and borrowing mechanism for stocks that allowed for a short side which contributed to market efficiency. The badla market in unmargined (or lightly margined) naked forwards – the system lasted in modified form till 2001 – provided much-needed liquidity and price continuity to India's stock market at a time when those were scarce commodities. This totally indigenous and locally designed system allowed for the liquidity and price continuity that were the distinguishing features of the Bombay market, even as the derivative-like features and unlimited leverage of the system occasionally proved to be its undoing.

The system was a complex combination of a cash market, a derivatives market in forwards and options, and a clearing/settlement process. In fact, the old BSE had more in common with the derivatives markets of Chicago than with a regular market such as the NYSE, but unfortunately that commonality did not include the careful risk management and margining that went with such derivatives markets. It is also tempting to see badla's forward mechanism as unique to India, but the Paris Bourse had a similar system as its mainstay for many years.

The derivatives-like nature of the badla market did have another advantage that would manifest in later years. As a market in standardized forwards, the badla product was similar to a futures market, and because of this prior familiarity the stock market would transition easily to the derivatives futures segment after it was rolled out in 2000 and 2001. As a result, India is presently (with South Africa and Spain) among the world's largest markets for single stock futures (SSFs).

The short sale was another established market practice, in contrast to the present day when the exercise has almost disappeared. Most people go long in financial markets, i.e., they buy, hope a stock goes up, and then sell at a profit. In a short sale, the opposite takes place – people first sell in the expectation that the stock will fall and then buy (or square up) at lower prices, thereby making a profit by trading for the fall. Selling something you don't own sounds absurd and counterintuitive, and yet in some financial markets it is an accepted practice, usually done by borrowing shares through a market lending/borrowing mechanism and then short selling them. When bought back at lower prices – short covering – the shares are returned to the lending/borrowing mechanism. Often, traders wouldn't even go through the trouble of borrowing before short selling. This was the naked short.

Because of the low liquidity in many stocks, short selling in the Bombay market often led to short corners and squeezes.[59] Short sellers who were trading for the fall and had sold stock without owning or borrowing it – the naked short – would typically buy back and square up after the fall at a profit. In case the stock did the opposite and kept rising, the short sellers would have to buy back at any higher price to meet their obligations; more technically, on settlement day the short seller could be held to ransom if more stock had been sold short than was available for delivery. If the free float – the amount of stock actually available in the market – was low, the stock could get cornered.

In the Bombay market, it was a general rule that stocks were always harder to obtain than money. In fact, high promoter holdings in many Indian companies meant that the free float was low to begin with, making the corner even easier. With little free float available, the price would keep going higher as desperate short sellers bought back at any price to meet their obligations – the corner – thereby reducing the free float even further. In case no stock was available at all – the squeeze – the situation could get out of hand, and the cornered stock's price would skyrocket. In extreme cases, desperate short sellers – on the naked short, cornered, and facing the squeeze – sold their other portfolio holdings to meet their obligations, effectively causing a collapse in the broader market. This state of affairs was remarkably similar to Wall Street's

[59] The widespread prevalence of the naked short and its sometime result, the corner, were repeatedly noted in the pre-Independence era. Sir Wilfrid Atlay, *Report of the Bombay Stock Exchange Enquiry Committee*, 2, 13–17, 24–28.

Northern Pacific Corner of 1901, and the subsequent crash that resulted. The Northern Pacific Corner – an event so uncommon that it became a celebrated moment in America's stock market history – was routinely relived on Dalal Street for much of the Century of Marking Time.

In 1896, led by one Chunidas Dharamdas Saraiya, the first successful corner in exchange history occurred in the shares of Sun Mills. Saraiya was acting on behalf of Sun's managing agency, which explained his motives, and had connections with the Bank of Bombay, which allowed him the financial resources to pull off the move.[60] Bear hammering with the naked short took Sun down, but Saraiya's substantial buying with Bank of Bombay resources first absorbed the selling and then took the stock up. This led to the price rocketing higher, from 200 to 550, and on settlement day, Saraiya put on the squeeze and demanded an astonishing 1,000 from the cornered bears to effect full settlement. Chunilal Motilal, the BSE president at that time, provided 'relief' and arranged a compromise at 500, thereby ending the matter but also setting a precedent for how such issues would be resolved in the future. Corners were also attempted in Maneckji Petit Mills in 1910 and 1913, but they never worked out because of the lack of financing for the bulls who attempted the corner.[61]

Short corners were a regular feature of the Indian market in the badla era that ended in 2001, but the typical manifestation was unusual price movement resulting from factors such as the naked short and the low free float playing out on the technical position of the counter. Such technical forces could have powerful effects on price discovery (particularly around settlement) and, in fact, were all that mattered in a market that typically did not know or care about fundamentals. These were referred to as unintentional corners (and were caused by peculiarities of the badla microstructure), but the motive of deliberate cornering of bears led to intentional corners, and such were the dramatic episodes, including Sun and Petit, that entered the historical record.

[60] Seth Jamnadas Morarjee J.P., 'The Native Share and Stock Brokers' Association,' 12. Queen Mills, Kurla Mills, and Manmad Press were late nineteenth-century corners that did not succeed.

[61] Ibid.

Sometimes the entire market would go through phases when corners appeared like a rash on its visage. One such phase occurred during the 1920s, just after the First World War. Promoters had accumulated substantial funds in the commodity boom brought about by the war, and these surpluses then financed speculative purchases on the stock exchange. Bear elements underestimated the resources available to promoters and continued with their earlier bearish views, attempting to short sell cotton mill stocks such as Standard, Madhavji, Fazulbhoy, Currimbhoy, David, Svadeshi, and Finlay. Against the backdrop of a market that was anyway turning violently bullish – worldwide, the Roaring Twenties were just getting going – promoters and sympathetic brokers tried to corner and squeeze bears in the above stocks. By 1922, there was a rash of such corners and squeezes, but most did not succeed, which prompted the promoter class to ask for an inquiry into the exchange's affairs, which resulted in the 1924 Atlay Committee. In his dissenting opinion to the Atlay Committee report, lawyer Bhulabhai Desai opined that the corner phenomenon was temporary; he went on to say that promoter groups were attempting to squeeze Association members and that both the bullish sentiment and promoter access to resources would soon end.[62] And so it did.

Such market practices caused the periodic settlement crises of that era. Like most settlement crises, they occurred over cash payments or share deliveries, and were amplified both by badla's terrific leverage and the tendency of traders to routinely abuse that leverage. In fact, these recurrent crises dominated discussions in various government committees appointed to look into the exchange's affairs, notable among which were those headed by Sir Wilfrid Atlay (1924), Walter B. Morison (1937), and Dr Parekunnel J. Thomas (1948). During these payment or delivery crises, petitions to the BSE authorities for 'relief' often worked. On the short corner situation, for example, magnate Cornelius Vanderbilt's 1863 cornering of trader Daniel Drew over Harlem Railroad shares had resulted in an immortal stock market rule

[62] Bhulabhai J. Desai, 'Minority Report,' *Report of the Bombay Stock Exchange Enquiry Committee*, Sir Wilfrid Atlay, 21–29.

later attributed to Drew himself: '*He that sells what isn't his'n, Must buy it back or go to prison.*'[63] But implementing Drew's rueful doggerel proved problematic in India, and in this culture of tolerance – where market participants also shared family, ethnic, and religious ties – enforcement could not include such drastic measures.

So, exchange management – run by the brokers anyway – then sat down, provided 'relief' and informally sorted out the affair, helped along by those close ties among members. To do this, the management gave itself the discretion to intervene and arrange compromises. For many years, Rules 26, 26(k), and 26(kh) of the BSE's Articles of Association gave the exchange's management this right of intervention.[64] Often, the exchange even dictated the *havala* (closing) prices at which settlements took place, along with sundry other compromises that were affected to avoid default.[65]

Such arrangements were expedient in a privately governed market without external regulation, operating in a country where contract enforcement was regularly ranked among the worst in the world.[66] In India, legal formalism and a vast corpus of common law, both codified and precedent, did not translate easily into contract enforcement. In those dusty legal tomes that lined courtroom walls, there was a lot of law, but justice took its own time coming, and this made private arrangements necessary. Besides, it was not just the quality of legislation

[63] The incident is recounted in Bouck White, *The Book of Daniel Drew*, New York: Doubleday, Page and Company, 1910, 99.

[64] 'We find, however, that the fundamental cause of all embarrassment in the affairs of the Association is the interference by the Association with the course of free trading in the market.' Sir Wilfrid Atlay, *Report of the Bombay Stock Exchange Enquiry Committee*, 15–16.

[65] In 1952, the *Economic and Political Weekly* (EPW) outlined a typical situation which led to a compromise at between 25 to 50 per cent of outstandings. 'It has taken more than three weeks for the authorities in the Bombay Stock Exchange to solve the settlement crisis by persuading the members to compromise.'; and later, 'Compromise on the basis of four-to-eight annas in the rupee has become the accepted method of settling liabilities.' 'Deliberate Default,' *Economic and Political Weekly, Around the Markets*, 29 March 1952. Sixteen annas made up the rupee in its pre-decimal avatar.

[66] Contract enforcement continues to be a problem well into the modern era. See Franklin Allen, Rajesh Chakrabarti, Sankar De, Jun Qian, and Meijun Qian, 'Law, Institutions and Finance in China and India,' *Emerging Giants: China and India in the World Economy*, eds. Barry Eichengreen, Poonam Gupta, and Rajiv Kumar, Oxford: Oxford University Press, 2010, 125–83.

and laws but their enforcement that was always an issue.[67] In fact, the Atlay and Morison committees would formalize the BSE's by-laws and rules, resulting in codification of exceptionally high quality that would be used in later legislations, such as the Securities Contracts (Regulation) Act (or SCRA) of 1956.[68] Nevertheless, enforcement in a self-regulatory framework demanded a civic sense and discipline that was often missing, leading to situations where parties bargained over the provision of 'relief'.

This sort of petitioning for 'relief' was the Indian version of the 'appeal to Frederick'. In the mid-seventeenth century Frederick Henry, hereditary stadtholder in the Netherlands, issued edicts that prevented contract enforcement of naked short sales through the courts. This was done to discourage and prevent the *windhandel* or 'selling in the wind' trade – essentially the naked short play – by making it unenforceable in a court of law.[69] Under Frederick's decree, the side that wished to relieve itself of an obligation and get out of a losing short trade could simply invoke the provision that rendered impossible contract enforcement through the courts – by appealing to Frederick's edict for 'relief'. But in the BSE's case, appeals for relief to evade obligations also called in play value systems that enjoined moderation and eschewed excess; besides, there was a strong 'we're in this together' mentality that came into play during crises. The hypocrisy was noteworthy, for in all the appeals to the value system that rejected excess, the intemperance and overtrading that had led to the crises were conveniently forgotten. Inadvertent and unrecognized hypocrisy was a common problem in India, almost a defence mechanism against the contradictions and complexities of the country.

[67] The inability to enforce well-drafted by-laws that were based on market practice in London or New York was noted by some observers. P.J. Thomas, *Report on the Regulation of the Stock Market in India*, 107–08.

[68] Besides its head, the Atlay Committee consisted of Sir Fazalbhoy Currimbhoy, Sir Purshotamdas Thakurdas, R. Lindsay, Captain E.V. Sassoon, Bhulabhai Desai, and Pherozeshah Dalal, with G. Davis ICS as Secretary. Besides Walter B. Morison, the Morison committee consisted of S.N. Pochkhanawala and Rahimtoola M. Chinoy, with H.M. Patel ICS as Secretary.

[69] See Geoffrey Poitras, *Valuation of Equity Securities: History, Theory and Application*, Singapore: World Scientific Publishing, 2011, 129.

Normally, reputation effects would set limits to this practice, as other participants rejected dealings with parties who used such appeals for relief to deny their obligations. In fact, in Amsterdam's early share markets, many traders opted not to appeal to Frederick to get out of their obligations because of the resulting loss of reputation and rejection by other players. More generally, reputation effects are critical in privately governed markets without external regulation or contract enforcement.[70] But in the BSE's case, such reputation effects appear to have been secondary and left no real impression on brokers, who seem to have had little compunction in asking for relief. As a result, the appeals for relief also came with a moral hazard – the tendency of participants to repeat the same practice in the belief that they would always get bailed out by the exchange authorities. In later years, the dominant faction in the market during a payment or delivery crisis – bull or bear – would often attempt to hijack exchange management over these appeals for relief.[71] To combat this, numerous attempts were made to restrict the exchange's discretionary powers to arrange such compromises, but most such attempts never went beyond exhorting management to voluntarily give up those powers. Exchange management was reluctant to do this, and so, such exhortations ended up as lectures about the inviolability of bargains.[72]

Finally, with the attempts at self-regulation proving to be a hit-or-miss affair, the state stepped in. The first attempt at regulation of market activity in India took place with the Bombay Securities Contracts Control Act of 1925, in the pre-Independence colonial era. Technically, it was not the first attempt, as the earliest legislation concerning the stock market was the Bombay presidency's Act XXVIII of 1865, which dealt with the insolvencies of the Cotton and Share Mania, but the 1925 act was the first legislation to deal directly with the stock market itself.

[70] See Edward Peter Stringham, *Private Governance: Creating Order in Economic and Social Life*, New York: Oxford University Press, 2015, 50–60.

[71] Attempts to hijack exchange management had been ongoing for some time. See Sir Wilfrid Atlay, *Report of the Bombay Stock Exchange Enquiry Committee*, 3, 16.

[72] One early example is from Walter B. Morison, *Report of the Stock Exchange Enquiry Committee*, 3–5, 9–11.

Among other things, the 1925 act asserted that exchange rules could only be made or changed with government approval and also that the government could grant and withdraw recognition to stock exchanges. But the legislation proved ineffective as it did not apply to forward badla trading, where over 90 per cent of volumes were generated.[73] A bill to replace the 1925 act was drafted in 1939, but it ran into the uncertainty of the Second World War, following which the 1950 Indian Constitution made stock exchanges a Union rather than a state subject. This effectively ended all efforts at provincial legislation, and in 1956, the omnibus SCRA would become the defining legislation for markets.

In the colonial era, the market responded better to international news than it would in the decades after Independence. A noted boom-bust cycle took place between 1914 and 1924, in the period during and after the First World War, followed by another cycle between 1925 and 1933, whose Roaring Twenties up move ended with the Great Depression. In the late 30s, there was a noted steel boom that peaked in 1937, driven in large part by the armaments buildup that preceded the Second World War. A last pre-Independence boom-bust cycle between 1943 and 1946 coincides with the later half of the Second World War and its aftermath.[74] The cycles that coincided with the World Wars were also significant as both resulted in IPO waves that ended in manias.[75]

Post Independence, the stock market continued to be a sideshow for a number of reasons: first, the low growth rates in the decades after Independence were not conducive to equities; second, the deep-rooted misgivings Nehruvian socialists had towards the market, misgivings

[73] The Bombay Forward Contracts Control Act (1947) was later applied to commodities and bullion but was not extended to stock markets because of the BSE's objections. Many of its provisions were subsumed in separate 1952 legislation that dealt exclusively with commodity markets.

[74] The boom-bust cycles that coincided with the World Wars are covered in K.R.P. Shroff, *History and Present Position of the Stock Market in India*, 11–29.

[75] These market highs and the primary side are covered in a later section.

that were unfortunately confirmed by independent India's first financial scandal, the Mundhra–LIC stock imbroglio of the 1950s that caused the resignation of Nehru's finance minister, T.T. Krishnamachari;[76] third, the lack of adequate instruments; fourth, the BSE's tendency to behave like a closed and self-interested club, impervious to outside influence; fifth, the traditional Indian regard for land and gold, which left little space for equity allocation; and finally, the lack of adequate companies to list, as Indian entrepreneurship faced its long black winter of neglect.

More technically, and from the standpoint of corporate financing patterns, well into the 1950s, less than 10 per cent of funds used by large companies came from equities, and as much as two-thirds came from internal generation of funds or private networks such as the managing agency system.[77] By functioning as a private market for capital, the managing agency system in particular competed with and often displaced fledgling public markets, though some people – by pointing out that underdeveloped public markets made the managing agency system necessary – would argue causality from the other side. Managing agents were the venture capitalists of their time, nurturing and building enterprises up before taking them public. At the system's height, a handful of managing agents controlled a large number of companies under long-term contracts and transferred among the

[76] Haridas Mundhra, a small time Calcutta businessman controlling a number of dubious companies, duplicated the share certificates of companies he controlled, pledged them with banks, and raised capital. When Mundhra couldn't repay, the banks followed the standard practice of selling pledged stocks to recover dues, but on delivery, some of the certificates were found to be false; Mundhra was even indicted by the BSE for peddling false share certificates. Mundhra then tried to influence the newly formed LIC to purchase shares of some of these companies from him at inflated prices, following which he would presumably pay back the banks through the capital so raised from LIC. LIC bypassed its own investment committee to purchase Mundhra's shares at inflated prices and the news leaked, despite Jawaharlal Nehru's wish to keep the affair private. In what became known as the Mundhra share scandal of 1958, Feroze Gandhi, a Congress MP and Nehru's son-in-law, made his name exposing much of this. The scandal also caused the resignation of Nehru's finance minister, T.T. Krishnamachari. Justice M.C. Chagla's public inquiry of 24 days that established the above facts was a model for such hearings that subsequent government inquiries should have followed but seldom did. In contrast, the Harshad Mehta proceedings are dragging on 28 years after the scandal. For a profile of Mundhra's colourful character, see Aditi Roy Ghatak, *Down Lyons Range*, 71–77.

[77] George Rosen, *Some Aspects of Industrial Finance in India*, Glencoe, IL: Free Press, 1962, 42, 53.

companies they controlled, funds needed for working capital and other long-term requirements.[78] Such activities displaced external providers of corporate finance and lessened the need to approach public markets such as a stock exchange. This was particularly true of Calcutta's managing agencies, mainly British and with access to sterling capital in the UK, which continued operations till the rupee devaluation in 1966, followed by the currency's subsequent decline, made business unviable for many. By contrast, Bombay's managing agencies were usually local and had limited access to sterling capital; this increased their reliance on local capital and local shareholders, and this is another reason why the Bombay exchange usually led Calcutta in scale of activity.

Contributing to the marginal nature of the market was the inability of world markets to buy into a piece of the action. India was a closed economy in autarky and without capital account convertibility, which in effect meant that foreign capital was barred from accessing Indian stock markets. Autarky, and the resulting divorce from global events, also meant little market response to international news flow. As a result, the market essentially marked time during the first three Five-year Plans and would continue marching to its own drummer for much of the remainder of the twentieth century.

The stock market continued to remain an adjunct activity through the heyday of Nehruvian India and afterwards, tolerated because it had been around for a long time but seldom understood. The brahmin's wariness towards the bania combined with ignorance, to produce an attitude of indifference and suspicion. In turn, the market, with its rampant speculation and arcane practices, did all it could to justify Nehruvian India's lack of confidence in it. Badla – that complex combination of a cash market, a derivatives market in forwards and options, and a clearing/settlement process – continued to dominate trading. In effect, badla blurred the distinction between the cash market, where cash and shares change hands, and a forward derivatives market, where positions are

[78] The managing agency system was abolished in 1966–67 but given a three-year transition period. The system is outlined in Omkar Goswami, *Goras and Desis: Managing Agencies and the Making of Corporate India*, New Delhi: Penguin Random House, 2016.

either settled in the future or rolled over. So popular was badla because of the leverage it provided, that actual cash transactions where shares changed hands for cash were negligible. Badla was periodically offered, banned, and reintroduced, and cracking down on badla's speculation was a favourite activity of Nehruvian India's bureaucrats. Many of these issues were highlighted in the first interaction between Nehruvian India and the stock market, which took place through the P.J. Thomas Report of 1948.[79] That interaction – and it was a difficult and strident one – would foreshadow the next half century of the relationship. But it is from Thomas that we get the first ever estimate of the Indian stock market's capitalization: a figure of ₹404 crores for 1939.[80]

Markets also exist to price growth, but the low 3 to 4 per cent annual growth rates that economist Raj Krishna called the Hindu rate of growth did not generate much interest in the stock market. These were the sleepy Rip Van Winkle years, when operators controlled proceedings, and a stock usually needed a sponsor operator to make it move up or down. Old trading favourites such as Tata Steel, Century, and ACC continued to dominate proceedings, but now Scindia Steam Navigation, Premier Automobiles, National Rayon, and Svadeshi were also frequently traded; BSE trading floor layouts from the early 1960s show that these scrips had volumes large enough to justify having specific areas – or counters – on the trading floor reserved for them. Despite entering the story with a bang during the 1865 Cotton and Share Mania, the public would remain marginal during most of this era, with public participation in the market largely confined to wealthy individuals or an emerging middle class from the big cities. In later years, the public's presence would usually register only at the big tops.

In fact, there was no stock index for the first century of the stock market – an astonishing omission that testifies to the rudimentary state of affairs over much of this period. The first formal attempt to

[79] P.J. Thomas, *Report on the Regulation of the Stock Market in India*, 25–84.

[80] Ibid., 35. Market capitalization at Independence was ₹971 crores. Thomas found that the NYSE's market capitalization at about the same time was ₹20,700 crores, so the Indian market was 5 per cent of the NYSE's market value at Independence, and this proportion is about the same presently. Ibid., Table 5, 28.

construct an index for the Indian stock market dates to the 1914–20 period, when economist G. Findlay Shirras constructed a 'Table of Index figures showing Fluctuations in shares' which was recorded in the Atlay Committee report of 1924.[81] K.R.P. Shroff, the BSE's long-time president, also constructed his own indexes to illustrate market movement. But there was no attempt to translate these early efforts into a regularly calculated index, and so, brokers manually and informally added up prices of key stocks such as Tata Steel, Tata Engineering, ACC, Century, and Scindia to form a picture of the market. For many years, these informal attempts, along with a weekly index brought out by the RBI, sufficed for the market.[82] The BSE Sensex was only created in 1986, with 1978–79 as the base year on an index value of 100.[83] Over a century lapsed between the start of trading under those banyan trees and the launch of an index.

After Independence, much of India's economic development was controlled by a planning process that revolved around the generation and implementation of Five-year Plans. Priority was given to areas such as agriculture, and the public sector was expected to be at the commanding heights of the economy. A financial sector that was small, unsophisticated, and essentially private, now gave way to state-dominated finance, as wave after wave of nationalization and public-sector emphasis ensured state control of areas such as banking, insurance, and fund management.[84]

[81] See Appendix 8 in Sir Wilfrid Atlay, *Report of the Bombay Stock Exchange Enquiry Committee*, 105–06.

[82] Other indexes were also calculated. For some years, the central bank maintained the Reserve Bank of India Equity Index, but this was a weekly calculation based on the price averages of 356 stocks with 1970–71 as the base year. This RBI Equity Index had Bombay and All-India versions. For a few years, the BSE also calculated a weekly Cleared Securities Index for 10 leading scrips on the forward badla market while the *Economic Times* came out with its ET Index of Ordinary Shares. See Bombay Stock Exchange, *Profile of Stock Exchange Activity in India*, Bombay: The Stock Exchange, Bombay, 1970, 58, 61–65.

[83] Indian Rayon was the largest component in the first Sensex computation and weighted in at almost 13 per cent. See Parag Parikh, *Value Investing and Behavioral Finance*, New Delhi: Tata McGraw-Hill, 2009, 97.

[84] H.T. Parekh estimated that by the mid-1970s as much as 90 per cent of investments of ordinary savings were owned or controlled by the government. H.T. Parekh, 'Indian Capital Market: Past, Present and Future,' *A.D. Shroff Memorial Lecture*, Bombay: A.D. Shroff Memorial Trust, 1975, 10–18.

Pernicious as an instrument of state control was an office called the Controller of Capital Issues, or CCI. The CCI had its origins in the first ever central legislation dealing with the stock market – the Defence of India Rules of 1943, which were put in place at the height of the Second World War. Rule 94-C banned the badla forward markets to 'counter speculative operations' but also to prevent investible capital from moving into areas not connected with the war effort.[85] The war's conclusion should have ended these capital controls – and, in fact, the law lapsed in September 1946 – but like many regulations in India, the rules stayed on in alternate forms after their time had passed. Some of the rules that concerned capital markets then morphed into the Capital Issue (Control) Act of 1947. The eponymous CCI that resulted from this act was a grand panjandrum with the magisterial right to price paper and decide issue structure. Lack of knowledge on how to price stocks and the resulting tendency of the CCI to deliberately price paper at face value led to chronic undervaluation of new issues, which in turn worked as a disincentive for promoters to issue equity at all.

Finally, the planning approach to development that commenced in 1951 did not foresee a major role for stock markets as a source of savings channelization from households or capital issuance by firms. As a result, corporate finance, the heavy-duty long-term financing requirement of companies, was dominated by debt issuance, raised usually from public-sector development finance institutions (DFIs) such as IDBI, IFCI, and ICICI.[86] In later years, it would become fashionable to criticize the BSE for the state of affairs prior to the reform effort, but attention must also be drawn to the state's dogma of placing the public sector at the commanding heights. Till the mid-1980s, that dogma ignored or suppressed equity markets and assigned a dominant position to debt financing from DFIs.

[85] In an early case of regulatory arbitrage, Rule 94-C then caused a flare-up in bucket shop activity and moved the formal market to the kerb or *katni* market.

[86] For another overview of the financial sector in this period, see Susan Thomas, 'How the Financial Sector in India was Reformed,' *Documenting Reforms: Case Studies from India*, ed. S. Narayan, New Delhi: Macmillan India, 2006, 174–78.

Strangely enough, the equity markets themselves remained immune to much of this state dominance and continued to retain their private-sector character, largely due to the existence of small family-owned brokerage firms with close ethnic and communal ties to one another. Despite the dominance of public-sector institutions on the buy side, Indian equity markets continued to maintain this essentially private character on the sell side, right through the Nehruvian era. Ironically enough, it was the private character of these intermediaries that would account for the market's dramatic response to state-sponsored intervention in later years. The legal and contractual framework for equities underwent a transformation in the 1950s with the passage of landmark legislation. When the Constitution of India came into effect in 1950, stock exchanges and their activities became a central government subject, as per the Union List of the Seventh Schedule, which defined subjects under the Union of India's purview. As a result, BSE activity came under the domain of the finance ministry, effectively ending its long history as a self-regulating organization, though under K.R.P. Shroff's leadership it would continue behaving as one for many years thereafter.

The SCRA of 1956, based largely on the work of the A.D. Gorwala Committee of 1951, further formalized the enabling legislative framework for securities transactions.[87] It replaced the Bombay Securities Contracts Control Act of 1925 and was to effectively become the parent legislation to all securities market transactions, together with the Indian Contract Act of 1872. Under the SCRA, the BSE was also granted permanent recognition as the first stock exchange in the country. The omnibus Companies Act of 1956, based largely on the work of the Cooverji H. Bhabha Committee of 1952, was another key piece of

[87] Astad Dinshaw Gorwala, *Report of the Committee on Proposed Legislation for the Regulation of Stock Exchanges and Contracts in Securities*, New Delhi: Government of India Press, 1951. Other members of the Committee included K.R.P. Shroff, B.N. Chaturvedi, V.S. Krishnaswamy, Pranlal Devkaran Nanjee, L.S. Vaidyanathan, P.D. Himatsinghka, Jagmohandas J. Kapadia, G.P. Kapadia, and P.S. Nadkarni. The original 1951 report is available at https://indianculture.gov.in/report-committee-proposed-legislation-regulation-stock-exchanges-and-contracts-securities.

enabling legislation passed at the same time.[88] Together, the SCRA and Companies Act would define the legal and contractual framework for equities over the next two generations, till a second burst of legislative activity – dealing mainly with the market's microstructure – would take place in the 1990s.[89]

With the passage of the SCRA, the Municipal Era of the stock market was formalized, and it would last from Independence till the early 1990s. In particular, Sections 13 and 19 had far-reaching consequences that shaped the market for generations after Independence. Section 13 affirmed that all securities contracts in notified areas or States, which were not entered into with, through, or between members of recognized stock exchanges, were illegal. The SCRA then granted permanent recognition to six exchanges in six cities, effectively designating these cities as notified areas (their number would rise over the years). Section 19 of the SCRA then stated that no person – other than on a recognized stock exchange – could organize (or assist in organizing) for the purpose of assisting in, entering into, or performing any securities contracts. Finally, members of one exchange were not permitted to become members of other exchanges, or even to have branches to service clients located in other cities, which further segmented the market at the municipal level and prevented the formation of a national market.[90] It was only from the late 1980s that a member of one exchange was allowed to become a member of another exchange.[91]

In combination, these provisions gave recognized exchanges a monopoly within their notified areas and effectively created a series of municipal monopolies that were to define India's stock markets well

[88] Cooverji Hormusji Bhabha, *Report of the Company Law Committee, 1952*, New Delhi: Government of India Press, 1952. Other members of the Committee included Hussain Imam, M. Shankaraiya, Mohanlal L. Shah, A.D. Vickers, J.J. Kapadia, P.N. Vajpeyi, V.S. Krishnaswami, G.P. Kapadia, Tricumdas Dwarkadas, S.M. Basu, S. Ranganathan, and D.L. Mazumdar. The original 1952 report is available at https://indianculture.gov.in/report-company-law-committee-1952.

[89] This is covered in a later section.

[90] Government of India, *Ministry of Finance*, Stock Exchange Division, Press Note, 14/3/SE/86 Apt.

[91] Ibid.

into the 1990s. Brokers in a city effectively got a monopoly on share transactions within that city's limits, and this ensured that rather than a single market, the country had a series of municipal-level markets resulting from a series of municipal monopolies. This conception of the market had existed right from its founding in the mid-nineteenth century, and the SCRA simply gave legislative endorsement to the existing system.

The SCRA's sanctification of the Municipal Era also had the unfortunate side effect of preventing the BSE, the only exchange with a national presence, from taking the lead in creating a national market. Later it became fashionable to blame the BSE for the pre-1991 state of affairs, but the role of the SCRA in preventing the BSE from creating a national market must also be revealed. More generally, the SCRA – by giving the government wide-ranging and draconian powers to supersede the governing board, take over exchange properties, suspend its business, or withdraw recognition – set up a framework that allowed for pervasive government influence over the market. Despite these draconian powers and its all-important role in financial intermediation in the Nehruvian era, the State was reluctant to interfere in exchange affairs. The stock market's negligible role in intermediation and resource mobilization further reduced the government's need to involve itself in the former's affairs. Dirigisme – directive state control of economic activity – was rampant at the time, and yet the market's marginal role in the plan era actually protected it from that orientation.

But it was not the SCRA as much as the political and social environment in the period immediately after Independence that remained unremittingly hostile to the equities business. In 1957, T.T. Krishnamachari imposed the wealth and expenditure tax, leading to a huge fall in stock markets. The year 1958 brought a freeze on dividend distribution and a tax on stock dividends – 'bonus' shares as they are called in market parlance – which led to another massive sell-off.

If the 1950s looked like the heyday of socialist hostility, the 1960s and 1970s showed up the side effects of wars and misplaced policy. The years between 1962 and 1971 saw three confrontations: with China in

1962 and with Pakistan in 1965 and 1971. Of these, the last was a major regional conflict that saw the map of South Asia being redrawn. The period also saw the introduction of the Gold (Control) Act in 1962, successive droughts in 1965 and 1966, and a major rupee devaluation, also in 1966. A first wave of bank nationalization took place in 1969 – a second wave would follow in 1980 – and artificial restrictions on company expansion were put in place through the Monopolies and Restrictive Trade Practices (MRTP) Act of 1969. Badla was banned twice in the 1960s, following the 1962 China conflict and in 1969, after a wave of speculation in steel. The later ban resulted in a market shutdown for a while, and the ban itself was rescinded only in the early 1970s. OPEC oil shocks in 1973 and 1979 also had disproportionate effects on a country that imported most of its oil. A successful nuclear test in 1974 was followed by Indira Gandhi's declaration of an internal Emergency in 1975.

Situated in this context, growth continued to be low, but inflation – caused by war-related government expenditure, droughts, the rupee's devaluation, and oil shocks – began to rear its head. This environment of limping growth and high inflation is the worst sort for equity markets, and market performance in the 1960s and 1970s was no exception to this rule. Nowadays, participants take for granted the market's majestic upward swing, but it rose just 2 per cent through the 1960s and just 70 per cent through the 1970s,[92] as per a weekly RBI index that tracked movements. Through all this turbulence, the government did not have to worry about the market itself – in later years, policymakers would make foreign policy with an eye on the Sensex and foreign flows, but in those days, there was neither Sensex nor foreign investor.

But in the midst of all this turmoil, a landmark in market development also took place. Spurred on by a news item on Pakistan's attempts to create a mutual fund, Finance Minister T.T. Krishnamachari's desire to do something similar led to the creation of India's mutual fund industry.

[92] M.R. Mayya, 'Recent Developments in Stock Exchanges,' 7–10.

The first mutual fund – the Unit Trust of India (UTI) – was founded in 1963, marking the birth of the organized buy side in India.[93] The founding scheme came out a year later as Unit Scheme 1964 (US-64), and it was to become extraordinarily popular. UTI would have a tortuous history in its early and middle years, alternating between its high-minded mission of being a vehicle for small investors and being a handmaiden of the government and brokerage community. Both roles were dubious and led to unintended consequences. In its handmaiden role, UTI alternated between being used by the government in its misguided attempts to prop up markets and being used by the brokerage community as a buyer of last resort. But it was UTI's high-minded mission as a vehicle for small investors – or as 'an adventure in small savings' as Krishnamachari put it[94] – that really got the fund into trouble. In fact, for years, UTI offered its customers guaranteed fixed dividends and guaranteed redemption prices on its units, while taking customers' capital and investing it in equities that offered no guarantees on either dividends or prices. Naturally, this extraordinary situation resulted in periodic collapses followed by bailouts – most spectacularly for US-64 in 1998 – and UTI lived up to its founding mission of being an adventure in small savings, all right.[95]

But above all, it was an era of high-handed government regulation. The surprise nationalization of Indian Iron and Steel (IISCO) in 1972 dealt a blow to the Calcutta exchange where the stock had been a pillar. The stock went from 50 to 4 at opening, and journalist Aditi Roy Ghatak records how one S. Bhalotia, who had a large position in the counter, collapsed on the floor of the exchange.[96] The IISCO

[93] See V.G. Pendharkar, *Unit Trust of India: Retrospect and Prospect*, New Delhi: UBS Publishers and Distributors, 2002.

[94] Priya Nandkarni, 'Unit Scheme 64: RIP,' *rediff.com*, https://www.rediff.com/money/2008/jun/02uti.htm.

[95] For an outline of the US-64 issue, see ICFAI Centre for Management Research, 'The US 64 Controversy,' *Case Studies in Finance, Volume II*, Hyderabad: ICFAI Centre for Management Research, 2004, 133–39.

[96] Aditi Roy Ghatak, *Down Lyons Range*, 197.

nationalization, together with the flight of industry from Bengal, would lead to Calcutta's long and slow eclipse by the BSE.[97]

In 1974, the government introduced The Companies (Temporary Restrictions on Dividends) Act, through which it actually restricted the right of companies to declare dividends; companies were restricted to dividend payments of 12 per cent of their stock's face value or one-third of their profits, whichever was lower. The markets crashed more than 20 per cent and were closed for almost a fortnight. Socialist-era legislation was now reaching its nadir.

The stock market was caught between a Congress government thrashing around in its own *atmanirbhar* (self-reliance) ideology and a global environment that relentlessly impinged through wars and oil shocks.[98] Yet through all this, the search for Lakshmi continued. In later years, it would become fashionable to criticize the stock market for its methods, without realizing that it should have been eulogized for simply having survived. Lacking a historical account that could shed perspective on all this, the whiz-kids of the 1990s looked at the BSE with scorn, and could not comprehend that the market's survival in this environment was itself an achievement. In turn, the government committees appointed to examine the market's affairs were happy to ignore the government's own responsibility for this state of affairs.

The market could simply have faded away under the onslaught, but it soldiered through it all, building habits of the heart and mind in trading and investing that would flower in later years.

In fact, soldiering through cavalier regulation and the socialist-era mindset sometimes had unintended consequences that later proved beneficial. Continuing his crusade against multinationals, George Fernandes in 1978 forced them to comply with the dilution norms of

[97] Indian Iron's influence on the Calcutta exchange is also documented by Ghatak. Ibid., 60–61, 81–83.

[98] 'Underwriters are undertakers and brokers are broke' was how one observer summarized the view of most participants in a meeting with visiting US SEC staff members. United States Securities and Exchange Commission (SEC), *Regulation of the Indian Securities Markets: A Preliminary Survey,* Norman S. Poser and David Silver, Washington, D.C.: January 1965, 4.

the 1973 Foreign Exchange Regulation Act (FERA); MNCs had to reduce their foreign parent shareholdings to a certain percentage (usually 40 per cent), either through a compulsory sale of shares or issuance of fresh stock.[99] This forced the MNCs (many from the consumer goods industry) to dilute majority stakes in their local subsidiaries in favour of the Indian public. Pricing was decided by the grand panjandrum himself – the Controller of Capital Issues – and predictably, the controller's formula resulted in severe under-pricing of shares.

Rather than comply with this confiscatory legislation, some MNCs (including IBM and Coca-Cola) left India, but the ones that stayed had to offer shares to the public at very low prices. About 123 MNCs ended up offering shares that were priced much lower than their intrinsic value. For the investing public, this was a double windfall – the companies were outstanding and the under-pricing was marked; many years later, participants would look back wistfully on the episode and wish they had bought more. The FERA dilutions were the first real gains for that hardy tribe of long-term investors who were just being born, and the episode would mark the embryonic beginning of an equity culture in India;[100] by some estimates, the move also increased the shareholder base by nearly two million. Despite the market's long history, this nascent equity culture seemed so strange in the early years that many referred to it as an 'equity cult'.[101]

Action on the issuer front gave such activity a boost. Foremost among the issuing companies was Reliance, and its 1977 issuance marked the first case of broad retail participation in the primary markets.[102]

[99] Under FERA, foreign companies in non-priority sectors were allowed to hold up to 40 per cent in their Indian subsidiaries but had to dilute the rest to local shareholders. Those who could establish that at least 60 per cent of their output was for export markets or whose processes involved advanced technology not available domestically were allowed to retain holdings of up to 74 per cent. The ordinance prompted some MNCs to diversify into unrelated export areas such as shrimp farming and garments just to meet the 60 per cent export market criterion.

[100] K.R. Choksey, interview by author, Mumbai, 2018. Choksey entered the stock market in 1961 and was an eyewitness to events of this era.

[101] The phrase 'equity cult' disappears from popular usage by the end of the millennium.

[102] Gita Piramal, *Business Maharajas*, New Delhi: Penguin Books India, 1996, 35–37.

Reliance's share issue – 58,000 people subscribed as shareholders[103] – was a landmark in the stock market's development. Dhirubhai Ambani's success with Reliance, and his realization that a rising share price was the best currency for a growth company, introduced India to the wondrous effects of a continuous compounding machine in the stock market. Pathologically afraid of debt in the early years, Ambani's reliance on equity issuance changed India's stock markets. Unique among promoters of that era, Ambani actually tried to treat his shareholders as partners in his enterprise. As a result, seasoned issues – the follow-up share issues – also went on to become successes. A long series of convertible bonds then followed. The convertibles were a way around the high interest rates on corporate bonds of that era, as convertible bondholders opted for a lower interest coupon in return for the upside potential from later conversion to equity; the resulting equity dilution in the capital structure was less of a concern, offset in large part by the company's tremendous growth. A generation of participants roared their adulation at the packed sports stadium where Reliance's annual meetings were held and kept the faith through a string of controversies that were to dog Reliance during the early years, when it was a young company on the make. The patience paid off, and many went on to buy homes or get daughters married on the strength of Reliance stock. 'I am the bubble that burst' was Dhirubhai Ambani's remark, tinged with grim irony, when he recalled the doubters and naysayers who chattered skeptically about the public issues and the early years of Reliance.[104]

And what effect did all this activity in the market have on the BSE 'card'?[105] Time series data on the value of BSE membership during the Century of Marking Time shows fluctuations with market conditions, and this is not surprising. The card's value technically came from the

[103] 'Reliance Goes Public for the First Time by Announcing Its IPO,' *JioInstitute*, https://repository.jioinstitute.edu.in/concern/images/754450ec-410c-49a0-adbf-4d62f81c0e1c?locale=en#?c=0&m=0&s=0&cv=0&xywh=-1297%2C-82%2C4637%2C1635.

[104] T.N. Ninan and Jagannath Dubashi, 'Dhirubhai Ambani: The Super Tycoon,' *India Today*, 30 June 1985.

[105] The card was called a 'seat' on the London and New York exchanges.

right of nomination that entitled members to transfer their right of membership with the approval of the exchange's governing board. At the BSE's foundation in 1875, the value of that right was all of ₹1. In the exchange's first half century, subsequent values of the card were: ₹5 in 1877, ₹1,000 in 1896, ₹2,500 in 1916, and ₹48,000 in 1920.[106] Card values of 6,700, 64,000, 14,000, and 32,000, for 1932, 1946, 1954, and 1962 respectively were documented in K.R.P. Shroff's account.[107] Remarkably, 1968 shows a card value of 15,000 – so between 1920 and 1968 the value fell by more than half, from 40,000 to 15,000, showing the severe damage of the 1960s and the market's marginal standing in the Century of Marking Time. Yet by the early 1990s, the value crossed ₹1 crore, and an all-time high between ₹3.5 and 4 crores was recorded by the new millennium. This would, in turn, fall to less than ₹1 crore over the next decade for reasons discussed in later sections.

The 1980s marked a stirring in the stock market. It is common to see the period post-1991 as a new beginning for the market, but the historical break from the past actually began in the mid-1980s. Four distinct clusters of activity took place at the government and market level that resulted in a significant change in the tempo of market activity: Rajiv Gandhi's reform efforts, a regional exchange spurt, the G.S. Patel committee meetings that started the Committee Era, and the first post-Independence IPO wave.

First, Rajiv Gandhi's early attempts at liberalization led to an initial increase in tepid growth rates. His finance minister V.P. Singh's 1985 and 1986 budgets were the first occasion when the budget – till then a routine statement of government finances and programmes – was used as a signalling device on reform. Though it was to become a cliché in

[106] K.R.P. Shroff, *History and Present Position of the Stock Market in India*, 6. In 1909, 1917, and 1920, traded card values of 2,500, 7,000, and 40,000 respectively were recorded in the Atlay Committee's report. See Sir Wilfrid Atlay, *Report of the Bombay Stock Exchange Enquiry Committee*, 5.

[107] K.R.P. Shroff, *History and Present Position of the Stock Market in India*, 6.

later years that India only reformed in crises, no crisis triggered these efforts. There was simply the dawning realization that things were not quite right and that both market and planning could be used for resource mobilization.[108] From a market standpoint, for once a government was doing things a little better – but nothing more than a little better – which, in itself, was a huge contrast to the outright hostility of previous decades. As a result, the markets began stirring. The ratio of market capitalization to GDP was usually below 5 per cent during the Century of Marking Time, but 1987 marked the last year in India's history when that ratio stayed in single digits.[109] From the 1980s onwards, the ratio would rise to almost 60 per cent during the Harshad Mehta bull run, which ended in 1992, and this move represents a one-time rerating.

Second, a multiplication in regional exchanges took place in the 1980s, driven in large part by the Municipal Era's mindset and recognition of the market's resource-raising potential. This had happened before; exchanges grew from 3 to 23 between 1933 and 1947, as mushroom exchanges were founded just after the Second World War. But all the new exchanges had faded away.[110] Sections 13 and 19 of the SCRA were now used to foster a second spurt in regionals, and between 1979 and 1983, the number of exchanges grew from 6 to 21. Cities with little connection to the stock market applied for and obtained clearances to start exchanges.[111] Stock exchanges sprang up in cities such as Ludhiana

[108] The actual break with the past came a little later with the eighth Five-Year Plan (1992–97). For the first time, the plan envisaged a larger role for private investment in financing industrial expansion, much of which was to be raised through the stock market.

[109] Bombay Stock Exchange, *The Stock Market Today: 1990*, Mumbai: The Stock Exchange Foundation, 1990, Annexure III, A–3.

[110] For details of these mushroom exchanges, see K.R.P. Shroff, *History and Present Position of the Stock Market in India*, 22–23, 28–29. Attempts had even been made to start alternate exchanges in Bombay and Ahmedabad, but neither took hold.

[111] Of the first three exchanges, Bombay and Ahmedabad were founded as voluntary, not-for-profit associations of persons, while Calcutta was organized as a limited liability company. Later, most of the regionals incorporated as companies limited by guarantee or as public limited companies. Bhubaneshwar, Hyderabad, Kutch (Saurashtra), Madras, Patna (Magadh), and Pune were companies limited by guarantee, while Bangalore, Baroda, Cochin, Coimbatore, Delhi, Guwahati, Jaipur, Kanara (Mangalore), Ludhiana, Meerut, and Uttar Pradesh (Kanpur) were organized as public limited companies. Among these later regionals, Indore was the only exchange organized (like Bombay and

and Patna, which had little tradition of share dealing, raising concerns about further fragmentation of an already small liquidity pool. Thinking in these pre-reform years would also envisage market development as a series of expansions and linkages of these municipal jurisdictions. For a while, this line of thinking would prove influential when the reform effort kicked in.

Third, the mid-1980s marked the start of the Committee Era, and between 1985 and 2002, different committees produced reports on various aspects of the market. The benign neglect of the Nehruvian era was giving way to acknowledgement of the market's potential for savings channelization and resource raising, and the committee reports exemplify the attempt to reorder relations between state and market. Noteworthy among these committees were those headed by G.S. Patel (1985 and 1995), Abid Hussain (1989), M.J. Pherwani (1991), L.C. Gupta (1998), and J.R. Varma (1997, 1998, 2000, 2001, and 2002).

The longest and most substantial of these reports, the G.S. Patel committee report of 1985 was also the first in a series the government commissioned to familiarize itself with the stock market.[112] The near four-decade gap between P.J. Thomas's 1948 report and Patel's meant that the government had to do a fair amount of catch-up with the market. Officially called the *Report of the High Powered Committee on Stock Exchange Reforms*, the Patel report thoroughly documented the market but did not produce any significant recommendations, and its overall tone – perhaps in keeping with its aim of simple familiarization – was cautious and mindful of the status quo. The report's summary of

---

Ahmedabad) as a voluntary, not-for-profit association of persons. Visakhapatnam was the last of the regionals to be recognized in 1996, while the Over-the-Counter Exchange of India (OTCEI), National Stock Exchange (NSE), and Interconnected Stock Exchange of India (ISE) were among the last exchanges to be recognized. This leads to a total of 25 exchanges over the market's history till about the millennium's end, but it does not include mushroom exchanges established in various cities in the pre-Independence era.

[112] Ministry of Finance, *Report of the High Powered Committee* (G.S. Patel Committee Report). The other members of the 1985 G.S. Patel Committee were D.R. Mehta, S.M. Dugar, S.S. Nadkarni, M.J. Pherwani, S.A. Dave, D.H. Pai Panandiker, K.V. Shanbhogue, M.R. Mayya, E.R. Krishnamurti, L.C. Gupta, and Paul Joseph.

recommendations and suggestions came to 26 pages, and much of it focused on exchange organization and management, membership, and new issue listing. The overall impression was less of an attempt to clean the Augean stables and more of a sense of struggle in conceptualizing the market. It was early days yet, and Patel, himself a market insider and former UTI head, could not overcome the Municipal-Era mindset. As a result, the report was tentative in its conclusions, unable to even visualize a national market beyond the municipal monopolies the SCRA had wrought.

The fourth and last cluster of activity that characterized the 1980s was an IPO wave. Two earlier waves had followed the World Wars, and in 1985, again, a deluge of companies approached the markets. Leasing companies were the flavour of this wave, mainly due to changes in tax legislation that favoured leasing.[113] When the wave ended, the number of listed companies had doubled to over 2,000.[114] This had positive effects on market capitalization and, for the first time, increased the company universe the public could choose from. As is usually the case with such booms, the quality of companies left much to be desired, and many went on to become what the trade euphemistically referred to as 'vanishing companies', i.e., companies that took the subscription and disappeared. Like the mushroom companies of an earlier era, vanishing companies presented a dilemma to authorities because the main punitive actions the exchange could take – suspension of trading or delisting of securities – punished the victims (the shareholding public) more than the perpetrators (the dodgy promoters). The leasing boom, in turn, ended with a flood of paper from new entrants that continued till the cessation of favourable tax treatment.

Besides these distinct activity clusters, it is the rise of inflation-beating returns that is noteworthy about the 1980s. From this period, equities started performing their traditional role as a hedge against inflation, and the 500 per cent rise in the market during the 1980s handsomely

[113] H.T. Parekh, 'The Changing Pattern of the Indian Capital Market,' *Seminar on Capital Markets: Problems and Prospects*, 4 February 1988, Bombay Stock Exchange, Bombay: BSE, 1988, 11.

[114] This is covered in more detail in Chapter 19.

beat inflation for the first time;[115] in contrast (and as noted earlier), the weekly RBI Index of stock returns had risen just 2 per cent through the 1960s and 70 per cent through the 1970s, with neither of these returns beating inflation. Here too we see for the first time a significant market reaction to government reform, and the 150 per cent gain in the Sensex between November 1984 and February 1986 marks the first time Dalal Street responded to a reform initiative. The market would now react to reform in Pavlovian fashion, and so profound would be the conditioning in later years that just talk of reform would be enough to send stocks higher. In turn, downsides would trigger cries for reform as a sort of market rescue, but the imploring was usually done without the slightest articulation of what that reform entailed.

The buy side was also evolving. UTI's initial attempts at setting up a buy side saw follow-up action by the State Bank of India, and in 1987, SBI Mutual Fund launched its Magnum scheme, which triggered a wave of other public-sector mutual funds. Initial attempts at investor protection were also made, and an Investor Protection Fund was introduced in the same year.

The number of Bombay brokers transacting in stocks also did not change much, gradually rising from 333 in 1896 to 504 by 1962. They did not go over 600 well into the start of the reform era,[116] with only three-quarters or so active at any given point in time. Private individuals or partnerships were the only entities allowed to hold cards, and corporates were allowed as members only from the late 80s. The investor base was negligible compared to the post-1991 period but was just beginning to make itself felt. Information, that lifeblood of markets, was scarce and – given the tendency to spread rumours or get misleading information published in newspapers – had to be analysed through a filter of extreme skepticism. As television was state-controlled, media coverage was mainly through the pink papers and occasional

[115] M.R. Mayya, 'Regulatory Framework for Stock Markets: The Indian Experience,' *Symposium on Capital Market Development*, 183.

[116] Brokers numbered 333 in 1896, 362 in 1916, 478 in 1920, and 504 by 1962. K.R.P. Shroff, *History and Present Position of the Stock Market in India*, 6.

magazines. Quarterly filings as a practice came much later, so serious value investors had to wait for a company's annual report and obtain it as a shareholder to know what was going on; many people literally bought a single share of a company so they could get its annual report, a practice that continues to this day. Equity research as a field was also non-existent, and yearbooks brought out by brokerages such as Place, Siddons & Gough in Calcutta or Kothari & Sons in Madras had to suffice as sources of information.[117] It is only from the late 80s that certain brokerages offered equity research as a service, and among these early pioneers were CIFCO, Jamnadas Morarjee, and D.S. Purbhoodas.

In today's times, Dalal Street is a state of mind, but in those days, it was an actual physical market. The main market was physically located at the trading ring in Bombay and content to take most of its orders from that city; one study found that of the 600 members, 550 had offices in the BSE building or within a 3 km radius of Dalal Street.[118] Because the liquidity pool remained in Bombay, the rest of the country was at a disadvantage, as order routing from outside Bombay was cumbersome and inefficient. Clearing and settlement took place on alternate Fridays after the two-week badla settlement cycle, but the duration of the settlement period had varied over the Century of Marking Time, with a monthly settlement before 1946 and a weekly settlement after 1994. Often the regional exchanges deliberately had different settlement cycles to allow the Bombay traders to roll their positions over between exchanges; this brought business to the regionals, but the rollovers (particularly those between the largest liquidity pools of Bombay and Calcutta) could indefinitely postpone settlement obligations and

[117] Place, Siddons & Gough brought out the *Investor's India Year-Book*. Place, Siddons & Gough yearbooks start from 1912, just four years after the foundation of the Calcutta exchange, and provide a time series over half a century till the 70s. The usual format is an introductory essay on financial and market conditions followed by company-specific documentation, with much of the focus on Calcutta-listed companies. From 1936, Kothari of Madras came out with the bulkier *Investors Encyclopedia*, which also included much material on rules and regulations. The Calcutta exchange brought out its first yearbook in 1937, followed by Madras in 1952. See A.K. Sur, 'History of the Stock Exchange,' 14–15.

[118] V. Shankar, 'IT Architecture at the Bombay Stock Exchange for the Nineties', *Handbook of Articles from the Stock Exchange Review 1989–1991*, Mumbai: BSE, 1992, 157.

often led to crises. Besides the rollover business, price differentials of as much as 10 per cent between exchanges were the key incentive for interexchange arbitrage in the early years.[119]

The overall impression of the market at the end of the Century of Marking Time is of a closed club of brokers running a marginal sideshow of arcane practices, with little risk management and severe conflicts of interest, who looked out for each other when it suited them. The lack of professional management also translated into a non-existent surveillance or compliance department, and this became an issue when volumes picked up from the 1980s. Order books on the carry forward trade were often known to select people, who then bet on or against the order book in a counter and the operator behind it; the exceptional leverage badla allowed for made such information very valuable. Collusion between brokers and the institutional buy side – which practically meant UTI – was rampant, leading to practices such as front running and paying for order flow; some practices, such as paying for order flow, continue into the present day.[120] Trading hours were leisurely, taking place on the physical floor through open outcry for all of two hours a day between noon and 2 p.m.; it was only well into the modern era that the trading day was gradually extended to its present timing. In the colonial era, the holiday schedule was equally languid, with a long list of bank and Association holidays, besides four to five days for Diwali and a week for Christmas.[121] The list of holidays would reduce over the years.

Yet, it could be a good business if you were on the inside. One market participant from that era who is still around is K.R. Choksey. One of the earliest practitioners of what people would today call value investing, he is a familiar figure on Dalal Street, striding around in his uniform,

[119] M. Narasimhan, *Financial Sector Reform and the Capital Markets*, Fourth Phiroze Jeejeebhoy Memorial Lecture, Bombay: The Stock Exchange, Bombay, 1992, 23.

[120] Front running is buying ahead of a large order, in the hope that the order causes an upward bump in price that the front runner sells into. Paying for order flow usually implies recycling part of the brokerage back to the large customer from whom the order originated.

[121] The complete list of holidays is in Sir Wilfrid Atlay, *Report of the Bombay Stock Exchange Enquiry Committee*, 9, 113; also see Walter B. Morison, *Report of the Stock Exchange Enquiry Committee*, 31.

a dark-coloured, long-sleeved safari suit. Choksey recalls those not-so-distant days; they were, he says nostalgically, 'a royal business'.[122]

The behaviour of traders and the nature of market action were also influenced by the microstructure. The badla mechanism of that era had many flaws, but it did possess one vital attribute of a well-functioning market.[123] While a twisted product, it allowed people to easily take the short side in the cash markets, and constraints against short selling were virtually non-existent. Short selling moderated the bull rise, aided price discovery, allowed for the differences of opinion that are the essence of speculative markets, and prevented one-sided movements.[124] Finally, in a sell-off, the bear who had short sold had to come in and buy to cover up, and this short covering prevented the fall from turning into a collapse. The bear with its short cover buying was an invisible (but inbuilt) pillar of support to the market.

In fact, badla – the unmargined naked forward – went one step further in its facilitation of the short side. The unmargined naked forward, when deployed on the short side, effectively allowed for unlimited shorting without borrowing or ownership during the inter-settlement period – the naked short became a routine affair built into the market's operation. In effect, badla created an infinite supply of stock that depressed prices, incentivized and encouraged the short side, and fed into the pessimism of that era. So badla led to an old market principle, not articulated as such but nevertheless present, that the public was always long and wrong but the professional was often short and right. A stock that went up a lot was instinctively shorted, and some companies, such as Reliance,

[122] N. Mahalakshmi and Rajesh Bhayani, 'How the Indian Stock Market Has Changed in the Past 50 Years,' *Business Standard*, 11 July 2007.

[123] The final years of the badla system are covered in L.C. Gupta, *Expert Study of Trading in Shares*, 21–28.

[124] For one of the few public acknowledgements of the short side's importance, see Basistha Basu, 'History Repeats: Investors Fail to Learn Much from Past Mistakes,' *Economic Times*, 23 January 2008.

struggled with this mentality for years; Reliance's attempts to corner and squeeze the short side would lead to noted encounters through the 80s and early 90s.

Despite the pressure from the short side, the badla system itself proved surprisingly resilient, going through multiple bans but always being reinstated in inventive ways because of the market's unquenchable demand for a leveraged product. Notable bans (together with their proximate causes) took place in: 1933 (Great Depression and the Currimbhoy Ebrahim collapse), 1943 (Defence of India Rules), 1962 (Indo–China War), 1969 (Steel Speculation), 1987 (Overtrading), and 1993 (Harshad Mehta), followed by a final proscription in 2001. The reinstatements usually took place after suitable tinkering with margins, carry forward eligibility, or reductions of settlement periods, but the tinkering always left the derivatives-like features of the system intact. As noted earlier, changing the system's name was vital for acceptability, and so, badla was reinstated or modified as 'A group' share trading in June 1970, as 'specified' share trading in August 1983, as 'unofficial' badla in January 1994, as 'modified carry forward' in January 1996, and as 'revised carry forward' in 1997.[125] As short selling in the cash market was an accepted practice, some people became adept at it.

The activity was also politically acceptable, as the organized buy side's absence in that era meant no long-term constituency in favour of perennially rising markets. It was the age of the bear, and most noted among them was Manu Maneklal Sheth, popularly known in the market as Manu Manek. Reputed at one time to control as many as 12 BSE membership cards, Manek was a noted participant of the 70s and 80s. 'Manek was a legendary personality and a powerful operator who dictated the market,' says Choksey.[126] So influential was Manek, that in some cases, it was difficult to become a director in certain companies without his nod. It was said that on an annual general meeting (AGM)

[125] M.R. Mayya, 'India at 50: Five Decades of Growth,' *Glimpses of Indian Stock Markets*, Mumbai: Indian Institute of Capital Markets, 2010, 10–11.

[126] N. Mahalakshmi and Rajesh Bhayani, 'How the Indian Stock Market Has Changed in the Past 50 Years'.

day, Manek would send out his list of candidates to the companies, and only the chosen ones got elected.

Market memory has Manek as a bear, but the reality is otherwise. On the 10th floor of the BSE is the office he occupied in his heyday – Room 1018. On a desk is a small photo of the man who ruled the markets in that era. Diligently adorned daily with a single fresh hibiscus, the photo shows a serious, portly man with pouting lips and piercing eyes clad in a white kurta pyjama, quite nondescript for a master of the market. Today, the office denizen is Vikram Chandrakant Kenia, Manek's son-in-law. A rotund, perfectly apple-shaped man with heavy jowls who looks like a *sethiya* from Bollywood central casting, Kenia confirms what many in the market have known for years.

Despite his reputation, Manek actually made his name as a badla financier, a sort of intermediary between wealthy individuals on the outside and the arcane financing requirements of the BSE's badla system.[127] As noted earlier, annual badla rates often went as high as 18 to 24 per cent (and could go even higher in a bull market), which made financing another trader's position a better proposition than trading one's own book. Recall that at one end, badla was a call market where wealthy individuals loaned funds into the market at badla rates that rose and fell based on the market's demand for funds; at the other end, it was also a lending and borrowing mechanism for stocks that allowed for a short side, which contributed to market efficiency. Instead of actually taking on market risk as bull or bear, Manek preferred operating at both ends of the badla system. In the 70s and 80s, he reportedly financed up to 5 lakh shares for the long side every settlement fortnight, a considerable number for that time; alternately, he was also adept at arranging shares for delivery into the system on the short side.

The buy side's absence till the 90s, together with the proscriptions on bank financing of brokers, increased the system's reliance on badla financiers such as Manek. They were the only sources of capital needed to bull stocks higher. For a brief while in the 80s and early 90s –

[127] Vikram Kenia, mentioned in an interview by the author, Mumbai, various years.

after the tenures of K.R.P. Shroff and Phiroze Jeejeebhoy and before SEBI's formation in 1992 – this financial influence also translated into political power and a grip on the politics of the exchange.[128] The big badla financiers such as Manek were often able to lead coalitions and alliances of brokers to victory in elections to the BSE's governing board. This political power was to prove a big source of resistance to Indian capital market reform.[129] Much of the BSE's opposition to the reforms of the later period was led by brokers like Manek who reaped immense benefits – or economic rents as the parlance goes – from controlling access to finance under the badla system.

Manek's financing of positions also meant that he had knowledge of which operators were overextended in key counters, information that he used to his advantage. But he was also an astute trader and reportedly, with Debu Bhalotia of Calcutta, one of the finest readers of secondary market movement in that epoch. Often when someone came to Manek excitedly extolling a stock's virtues and asking him to buy it, Manek would smile sweetly, escort the person out of his office, and promptly short sell the stock. His thinking was that if the stock was really strong, there would be little reason to talk it up.

Much of this only lasted till Manek's dispute with Dhirubhai Ambani and Reliance in 1986, which became the stuff of market lore. In the 1980s, Reliance corporate financing was heavily dependent on regular issuances of convertibles, which in turn required a steadily rising share price. This brought Ambani into frequent tussles with the market's short side, and noted clashes took place in 1982, 1986, and 1995.[130] Of these, the 1986 encounter was on the largest scale. Believing a bear cartel led by Manek was operating in the Reliance counter and preventing its

[128] John Echeverri-Gent, 'Politics of Market Micro-Structure: Towards a New Political Economy of India's Equity Market Reform,' *India's Economic Transition: The Politics of Reforms*, ed. Rahul Mukherji, New Delhi: Oxford University Press, 2011, 331–50.

[129] Ibid., 331–34.

[130] For coverage of the 1982 corner, see Chander Uday Singh, 'Reliance Roulette: Bear Speculators Fail to Bring Down Price of Reliance Shares through Large-scale Selling,' *India Today*, 31 May 1982. This episode is also the lead-up to Gita Piramal's profile of Dhirubhai Ambani, *Business Maharajas*, 3–5. For the 1995 incident, see Shekhar Ghosh, 'Breaking a Bear Hug,' *Outlook Magazine*, 1 February 1996.

ascent just as the company was launching its 1986 convertible issue, Reliance complained to the BSE about vested interests at work on the scrip. The BSE, under Manek's influence anyway, gave a tepid response, and things reached a point where Reliance decided to take matters into its own hands. This resulted in Ambani cornering and smashing the bear cartel. The modus operandi, reportedly handled by a trusted Ambani lieutenant named Anand Jain, was the time-honoured market practice discussed earlier: substantial massive buying in the scrip that took it past all previous resistance levels, together with enforced delivery that compelled the bears – many on the naked short, cornered, and facing the squeeze – to square up with huge losses. The entire stock market was shut for a few days (as it had been after the 1982 episode), and the exchange's management struggled to arrange compromises that settled the issue.

In later years, these episodes would capture the popular imagination, even becoming the subject of Bollywood movies and YouTube videos with details that got more colourful and lurid with each retelling. But such fireworks would become uncommon in the modern era, as the creation of derivatives markets and badla's abolition in 2001 effectively removed the short side from India's markets. With little outlet for shorting, the old attitude towards it waned, and in fact, it would go violently into reverse in the modern era, when only the long trade became possible (in historical terms, the talk of 100 baggers and 1,000 baggers dates only from after badla's ban at the millennium's turn).

Corners and squeezes (the parlance was rarely used) would continue well into Dalal Street's modern era. But the Reliance episodes marked the passing of the phenomenon, and badla's 2001 abolition, together with the entry of mutual funds (and their political power), did away with the short side and the corner phenomenon.

Principal agent issues and the absence of professional exchange management often led to severe conflicts of interest. This conflict had been present right from the exchange's founding. After all, Article XV of the BSE's Articles of Association had laid out the primary aim of the exchange as supporting and protecting the '*character, status, and interests of brokers dealing in shares, stock, and other like securities in Bombay…*'[131] There was no reference of any sort to the public and consequently no question of defining or protecting a public interest. It was only in 1924 – after the BSE's first fifty years of business and at the insistence of the Atlay Committee – that the interest of the public in a large market for securities in India was finally recognized.[132] Despite that formal recognition, the earlier attitude prevailed, and the brokers who both owned and ran the exchange, ran it for themselves and their own interests.

Yet, the club could surmount conflicts of interest and even rise above itself on occasion. Self-interest sometimes led to informal coordination attempts during market crises, and one example of this comes from a tragic event in 1984 – the assassination of Indira Gandhi by her bodyguards. Many years later, Basistha Basu of the *Economic Times* Kolkata edition collated this remarkable account – based on the firsthand recollections of market participants – on how it all worked during that crisis:

> 'There were two things that Debu Bhalotia said the moment he arrived at the hastily summoned meeting. He urged the president to keep the CSE market closed for sometime to watch the trend in Bombay and he also gave his personal chopri (the red notebook on which brokers used to scribble their transactions in the days of the open outcry system) to Ajit Day of Dayco Securities, also a board member, saying that whatever was needed to be done, should be done. Those were his exact words,' the member recalled. 'It was crisis time,' recalled Ajit Day, past president of the CSE, when asked about the incident. 'We were pulling out all stops. Ganesh Pyne (a very big institutional broker of those times) got instantly in touch

[131] Sir Wilfrid Atlay, *Report of the Bombay Stock Exchange Enquiry Committee*, 34. This attitude carried over to the regional exchanges, particularly Kolkata. See, for example, Aniek Paul, 'A Requiem for the Calcutta Stock Exchange,' *Mint*, 23 May 2014.

[132] Sir Wilfrid Atlay, *Report of the Bombay Stock Exchange Enquiry Committee*, 4,129.

> with GS Patel, then chairman of Unit Trust. Patel saab passed on necessary buy orders to Pyne and Hemendra Kothari, for whatever was needed to be bought in the Kolkata and Bombay markets, to prevent a landslide. The market started at 12 noon and immediately started falling, some 7–10%. The Securities & Exchange Board of India wasn't born still, so we set manual filters at around 12.40 pm, freezing the price line and inviting all who wanted to sell to offload at those prices,' he recalled.
>
> It was at this juncture that Debu Bhalotia stepped in. 'He stood like a rock in Kolkata, mopping up all that anybody had to offer. Manubhai Maneklal did the same on the Bombay Stock Exchange. Unlike the dementors in Harry Potter's world of Azkaban, he sucked the panic out of the system,' Mr Day said.[133]

The informal mechanisms of that era stand out in this passage, as does the 'we're all in this together' attitude remarked on earlier in the chapter. Some old-timers say that this sense of togetherness – camaraderie almost – that the club felt during a crisis is missing nowadays. The system has become more professional. In an interview, Sevantilal Shah, an old-timer on the Calcutta bourse, who spent over half a century in this era of the game, lamented the lack of comradeship and solidarity in today's market: 'There was then a (*sic*) bonhomie, a spirit of camaraderie among all of us. Girdhari Kejriwal, Bihari Khandelwal, Gokuldass Bangur, Govind Dasji Bangur, D.S. Prabhudas (*sic*) and Jamnadas Morarji (*sic*) in Mumbai, Hemendra himself… anytime, anybody could be asked to stand up for the market.'[134]

Indubitably, the one person who could really stand up for the market was the head of the exchange itself. For most of the first century of its

[133] Basistha Basu, 'Classical Bears in a Tail Spin,' *Economic Times*, 15 June 2006.

[134] Ibid.

existence, the BSE was managed by the brokers themselves through leaders of ability and long tenure. The exchange's governing board consisted of brokers and had no representation from the investing public; government nominees were added only later. BSE cardholders (usually numbering over 400) elected 16 members who, together with two government nominees, constituted the governing board. The board members, in turn, elected a chairman or president, a vice president, and a treasurer. For a long part of the twentieth century, the BSE's head was unanimously elected with little by way of competition, and as a result, the exchange leadership enjoyed longevity of tenure during much of the Century of Marking Time. There were just six presidents in the century from its founding in 1875 to 1980: Seth Choonilal Motilal (1875–96), Sir Shapurji Broacha (1896–1919), Sir Kikabhai Premchand (1920–22), Nusserwanjee P. Karani (1922), K.R.P. Shroff (1923–66), and Phiroze Jeejeebhoy (1966–80). Setting aside the 1920–1922 period (when there were two presidents), the BSE had just four presidents who led the organization for over a century, indicating remarkable stability of tenure. Of these, K.R.P. Shroff and Phiroze Jeejeebhoy cumulatively led the BSE for a 57-year period, with Shroff's 43-year term as chairman and president the longest tenure for an exchange head in the history of the world's stock exchanges.

K.R.P. Shroff (1878–1971) entered the stock market in 1902 and retired as its chairman and president in 1966; this 64-year association with the market is the longest of any participant recorded in this account.[135] When Shroff entered the market in 1902, survivors of the Cotton and Share Mania that Lincoln and Grant had ended over three decades earlier were still around, among them Premchand Roychand, who passed on in 1906. Many readers of this book might well have been around in 1966, at the time of Shroff's retirement, and in that sense his tenure serves as a link between the founding episode of the market and our own time. Shroff became the BSE's head in 1923 and initially ran

[135] Rajendra Somnarayan, 'Welcome Address at the Diamond Jubilee Celebrations of the Bombay Stock Exchange, 24 April, 1936,' Bombay: Bombay Stock Exchange, 1936, 10.

his family firm while managing exchange operations in an honorary capacity, but he gave up business activities in 1939 and devoted himself solely to exchange affairs. His term fell evenly between the colonial period and the Independence era, and he figured prominently in all policy matters pertaining to the market in that age. Government reports and commission findings were written in consultation with him, and even the hostile reports grudgingly acknowledged that issues with the market had little to do with the exchange's leadership.[136] Shroff was consulted extensively on the drafting of the SCRA, and many of its sections owe a debt to him. In contrast to later business leaders who cautiously toed the government line and were *ji huzoor*s (yes men) on government action, Shroff could be outspoken, calling Finance Minister T.T. Krishnamachari's 1957 budget 'no carrot and all stick', which in turn reportedly prompted TTK to say, 'Let them go to hell.'[137]

Shroff's sign-off was essential on all the compromises between parties and bargaining over 'relief' that took place in the badla era, but by all accounts, he never took corrupt advantage of that power and this added to his influence. According to contemporary reports, he was kind but firm, keeping the flock in line, often through the force of his personality and the prestige of his long tenure.[138] By many accounts, the BSE's shenanigans were less of an issue during his term – particularly so in the pre-Independence era – and the shenanigans that did take place were carefully hidden behind his stern visage and Parsi *fetah*. He was known universally as K.R.P. Shroff and always signed as such; he used this version of his name in the committee proceedings that developed the SCRA and even in legal proceedings where he was a party. Consequently, there are few documents in the BSE archives that spell out his initials, and it is only as an awardee in the 1967 Padma Bhushan list that his full name is spelt out as Kaikhushru Ruttonji Pestonji Shroff.

[136] P.J. Thomas, *Report on the Regulation of the Stock Market in India*, 11.

[137] Sameer Kochhar, *BSE: Journey of an Aspiring Nation*, New Delhi: Skoch Media, 2015, 77.

[138] Bombay Stock Exchange, 'K.R.P. Shroff: Patriarch of the Stock Exchange and the Father of the Stock Market in India,' Bombay: BSE, 1966, 5–6.

Shroff's annual salary of ₹50,000 in 1939 was a material part of the BSE's cost structure at that time, and he was a cost centre in his own right;[139] in fact, the amount was remarkable, given the small scale of BSE operations in that era. The inflation-adjusted figure of about ₹2 crores would be commonplace today; nevertheless, consider that the BSE's present incumbent only makes a little over three times Shroff's inflation-adjusted salary, but presides over a market that is 37,000 times larger.[140] Shroff's brief work, *The History and Present Position of the Stock Market in India*, written in 1962 towards the end of his long tenure, remains the key eyewitness account of the market in the twentieth century's first half, composed as it was by the head of the exchange itself. Many accounts referred to him as the Father of the Stock Market, and his annual election by popular acclaim to head a statutory public body as its chairman and president was repeated over 43 years, a feat unprecedented for his own time and never replicated since. On his passing in 1971, the BSE shut shop for two days, the last time a national stock market would close as a mark of respect to its former head.[141]

After Shroff, the chairman and president's roles were split, and the president's position was occupied by a succession of brokers.[142] His successor, the chairman of the exchange from 1966 to 1980, was Phiroze Jeejeebhoy (1915–80). Unlike Shroff, and most others who made up the market in that era, Jeejeebhoy was a highly educated man who held degrees from Bombay, Cambridge, and London. He had entered exchange management in 1946 as BSE secretary, and other than a stint at the RBI, spent his entire career at the exchange, where he commanded the same respect Shroff had enjoyed, both among the broker class and

[139] J.R. Screwvala, 'Mr. K.R.P. Shroff, President of the Bombay Stock Exchange,' *Federal Observer*, Stock Exchange Special Number, Vol. 1, Nos. 36 and 37, 10 November 1940, 26.

[140] The 1939 market capitalization of ₹404 crores is from P.J. Thomas, *Report on the Regulation of the Stock Market in India*, 35. A market capitalization of ₹150 lakh crores is assumed for 2020.

[141] Bombay Stock Exchange, Governing Board, *Minutes*, 28 June 1971. Available at https://www.sebi.gov.in/History/BSE_1971-80.pdf.

[142] They included Kantilal Ishwarlal (1966), Dhirajlal Maganlal (1966–70), Laldas Jamnadas (1971–73 and 1980–85), Jayant Amarchand (1973–77), and Malthardas Samaldas Kothari (1977–79).

the government.[143] But unlike Shroff, Jeejeebhoy had to handle the full impact of official India's attitude to the market, and his era was marked by the effort needed to deal with the government's remarkable ambivalence and hostility towards the stock market. As a result, much of his time went into handling the side effects of government dictates on the market. Badla was repeatedly banned during his tenure, and much effort went into reintroducing badla in other forms so that the market could continue to benefit from its larger volumes.

Besides trying to keep the government out of markets, Jeejeebhoy's other focus was on building the physical infrastructure needed for a private exchange in an age when there was little finance and support. He initiated the BSE's computerized batch-processing of physical floor operations as early as 1972 and conceived important parts of the microstructure-like dematerialization and depositories many years before they were implemented. Jeejeebhoy's monument was the BSE building complex on Dalal Street that was named after him in recognition of his efforts in its financing and construction.[144]

But by the time Jeejeebhoy's tenure ended with his death in 1980, the conflict of interest and strains that arose from both owning and running an exchange were becoming apparent. A gentleman – and perhaps handicapped by that quality – Jeejeebhoy's career ended at a time when the exchange business had become a rough-and-tumble game that had little place for gentlemen. Like Shroff, he kept the show on the road through the force of his personality and presence, and it is a fact that most of the scandals associated with the Bombay exchange arose in the era after both stalwarts.[145] M.R. Mayya, who worked with

[143] Comments of Nimesh Kampani in Sameer Kochhar, *BSE: Journey of an Aspiring Nation*, 18–21.

[144] Ibid. Morarji Desai laid the foundation stone on 16 May 1968, but it would be twelve years before the first phase was inaugurated in 1980; the second and final phase was completed in 1991. The architect for the BSE building was Chandrakant Patel of the Architectural Research Unit.

[145] R.S. Bhatt, former UTI chairman, also recalls a better governed market in the era before Independence. See R.S. Bhatt, 'Revival of the Capital Market,' *35th Meeting of the Standing Committee of the Presidents of the Stock Exchanges in India*, Bombay: BSE, 1988, 17. The one major scandal from their time significant enough to find repeated mention in the historical record is the Mundhra–LIC imbroglio of the 1950s, but that originated in Calcutta.

both for many years, would note Shroff for his ethics and Jeejeebhoy for his vision.[146]

Towards the end of Jeejeebhoy's tenure, the government had begun its involvement in exchange management, with mixed results. By the mid-1980s, the Committee Era had also begun, and starting with the G.S. Patel committee, the government began familiarizing itself with exchange activities through a series of such commissions. Keen on resource mobilization through markets, the state – for the first time ever – started using the extensive powers it had granted itself under the SCRA. This had been Shroff's concern all through, aware as he was of the SCRA, a legislation that he helped draft. The composition of exchange boards and management became a contentious matter at the heart of the main issue of broker ownership and management of exchanges.

The 1985 G.S. Patel committee was the first to recommend that at least 50 per cent of the governing board be made up of outside directors,[147] with an executive director reckoned separately. So, from the mid-1980s, an executive director appointed by the government on the recommendation (nominally) of the governing board, served as the exchange's CEO and effective head. Of these, the first was V.D. Sonde, whose term lasted three years.

Sonde's successor Mangalapadi Ramachandra Mayya's ten-year term as executive director from 1983 to 1993 marks the last appointment of historical significance at the BSE. After Mayya, both the position and the institution were diminished, and the National Stock Exchange (NSE) would become the dominant exchange just two years after his retirement. The brokers continued to bring forth people to lead the exchange, but regulatory changes now called for reducing broker control of exchanges, and Mayya was appointed under these provisions. M.R. Mayya was the First Regulator of India's stock market, acting as such even before the field of stock market regulation came into existence in India in the early 90s. An officer of the introductory cadre of the Indian

[146] M.R. Mayya, *Glimpses of Indian Stock Markets*, 233, 253.

[147] Ministry of Finance, *Report of the High Powered Committee* (G.S. Patel Committee Report), 118.

Economic Service (IES), he spent 18 years at the Forward Markets Commission (which helped him understand the complexities of badla's forward system) and another 10 years at the finance ministry's Stock Exchange Division, before taking on his BSE role.[148] He remains the only regulator to be appointed the head of a major exchange.[149] Appointing a regulator with a regulator's instincts as an exchange head came with its own set of issues. It was not seen as untoward in that informal age but would be unlikely in later years, and it remains an interesting question whether someone with a business background would have been a better choice for the BSE in those crucial times.

Nevertheless, under Mayya's watch, the Sensex was launched on 2 January 1986. Another initiative, the PTI Stockscan Service, the forerunner to all screen-based trading in India, which displayed quotes on an electronic screen in the four metros and Ahmedabad, was launched in August 1987. Price-earnings (PE) ratios were first calculated for the Indian market by the BSE in January 1989, published through Stockscan and mentioned with the daily quotation lists. Another programme with far-reaching effects was the BSE Training Institute, which remains to this day an important centre for education in capital markets.[150] Because of the informal nature of that era, the institute had the benefit of having stalwarts such as C. Rangarajan, S.A. Dave, and M.J. Pherwani on its faculty;[151] in later years, as markets grew and formalized, it would be unthinkable for a central bank governor, the regulator's head, and the chief of the largest mutual fund to serve together on a faculty. Much of the development work on BOLT, the BSE's online trading platform, was also initiated during Mayya's tenure.

[148] 'Shree MR Mayya' *Yugvandna*, Stock Exchange Edition: 125 Years of the BSE, February 2003, 30–34.

[149] S.A. Dave, the first SEBI chairman (1988–90), also served on the BSE board but not as its head.

[150] The BSE Training Institute was founded in January 1989. The BSE's *Stock Exchange Review*, published between 1989 and 2001, is a source of information on the reform period of the 90s. In keeping with its reputation for secrecy, the NSE does not have a comparable record which is in the public domain.

[151] Bombay Stock Exchange, *The Stock Exchange Review: July 1989*, Bombay: The Stock Exchange, Bombay, 1989, 14–16.

Unlike Shroff and Jeejeebhoy, Mayya had the instincts of a Nehruvian bureaucrat, and his articles are full of justifications for elaborate powers to restrict the badla trade, powers that he insisted could be wielded only at his and the exchange's discretion. In a remarkable passage in one of his pieces, he explains:

> These powers include suspending carry forward facility whenever the aggregate outstanding position in any security exceeds pre-announced limits; imposition of price corrective measures; fixing differential rates of making – up (*sic*) prices; prohibiting short sales and long purchases; suspending buying-in and selling out provisions; ordering contractions of outstanding carry forward position; imposition of limits on purchases and sales for speculative business; imposing additional limits on price fluctuations; suspending off-the-floor transactions; fixing minimum and maximum prices; regulating carry forward charges and so on.[152]

He goes on to add that these powers (the above list does not include all-time favourites such as fiddling with margin requirements, or moving scrips in and out of the badla group) were to be exercised proactively rather than reactively. The passage gives the impression that by now badla had degenerated into chaotic interaction between a system that defied risk management and an exchange management that demanded considerable discretionary powers to deal with that risk.

The century-long stability of tenure that had defined the BSE's leadership would end when Mayya's term concluded, and the management entered a period of great turbulence. Mayya's retirement in August 1993 was a little before the NSE went online in November 1994, and in that sense, his departure marks the end of an era and the beginning of another. In his active retirement, which lasted two decades till his death in 2014, he remained a tireless evangelist for open capital markets – by now the zeitgeist demanded it – and was,

[152] M.R. Mayya, *Glimpses of Indian Stock Markets*, 317–19.

in fact, more influential in that role than as a BSE head. Like Shroff before him, Mayya wrote prolifically, and his writings remain an important source of material for the early years of the reform era.[153] He maintained a quixotic interest in the regional exchanges, particularly the Mangalore Stock Exchange, located as it was in the region from which he hailed. In a final posting, he served as chairman of the Inter-connected Stock Exchange (ISE), a system designed to network the regional stock exchanges, but both ISE and the regionals would fade away.

It was an informal and comfortable yet totally self-interested age, and its last hurrah came from an unlikely source: a portly, moustachioed broker named Harshad Mehta. His machinations would lead to a boom-bust cycle with repercussions that would change the market forever.

Mehta started out as a drifter who tried his hand at various odd jobs, including selling hosiery, sorting diamonds, and marketing insurance. He then quit an assignment with the New India Assurance Company and worked at low-level clerical positions with various brokerages, gradually rising to positions of responsibility. Mehta got his break in 1984 when he bid for, and won, a BSE card with the support of his former employers. By 1991 – on the verge of the reform announcements – he was an established player and recognized for his long-side proclivity at a time when the market was evenly divided between long and short sides; even in those early days, he was known for his fireworks in the Associated Cement Companies (ACC) scrip.

Popular imagination attributes the bull market of 1992 almost exclusively to Harshad Mehta's exertions.[154] It is a neat morality play at work: the small-town operator whose knavery allows him to make it big

[153] Most of Mayya's written work is in *Glimpses of Indian Stock Markets*, published by the Indian Institute of Capital Markets.

[154] For an example of early media coverage of the Harshad Mehta episode, see Daksesh Parikh and Lekha Rattanani, 'The Rise and Fall of Harshad Mehta,' *India Today*, 31 May 1992.

overnight, who briefly leads the high life but simply cannot handle it, gets caught out, then pays a price for that flashiness which has offended middle-class mores, and so on. Over the years, the media has gone to town on the episode, and yet the impression of Harshad Mehta being at the centre of it all is far from correct. There were wider and more prosaic factors at work which have not scratched the surface of that popular imagining of the Mehta Bull.

From the early 1980s onwards, a number of developing countries had taken policy measures to develop stock markets and reduce their corporate sectors' demands on financial systems.[155] Nothing much had happened on these lines in India, and the coalition government of P.V. Narasimha Rao was simply playing catch-up when it embarked on a significant reform program in response to a balance of payments crisis and the fall of the Soviet Union. Finance Minister Manmohan Singh's path-breaking budget of 24 July 1991 then began the dismantling of the license raj, together with a host of other measures. All this happened in the early stages of the Mehta Bull, and it was the displacement caused by these world events and reforms, together with Mehta's bulling, that resulted in the movement. Mehta should have been just another operator calling the market right, but the historic nature of the up move – unrecognized at that time and subsequently – together with his ambition, took activities to another level.

And yet that ambition flew in the face of a problem all bull operators had to deal with: the problem of financing that arose from proscriptions on bank lending into the stock market. For this problem, Mehta found a novel solution. Like Premchand Roychand before him, he discovered ways to access the banking system and generate the capital needed to keep his bull move going. This he did by finding loopholes in the interbank market for government securities, or G-Secs.[156]

[155] For a survey, see Ajit Singh, *Corporate Financial Patterns in Industrializing Economies: A Comparative International Study*, International Finance Corporation, Technical Paper No. 2, World Bank, Washington, DC, 1995, 1–34.

[156] Despite its proximity to the events it describes, the best early account of the Harshad Mehta imbroglio is Samir K. Barua and Jayanth R. Varma's work on the subject. See Samir K. Barua and Jayanth R. Varma, 'Securities Scam: Genesis, Mechanics, and Impact,' *Vikalpa*, 18, (1), January–March 1993, 3–12.

The interbank market for treasuries, as murky then as it is now, was a broker-driven, OTC market, and relatively easy to manipulate for someone with a deep knowledge of it. Under India's system of financial repression, banks had to compulsorily buy G-Secs to help fund the government's perennially large fiscal deficits. Mandated amounts of bank deposits had to be invested in G-Secs through a government-set statutory liquidity ratio (SLR) – then at 38.5 per cent. Banks with G-Secs in excess of that ratio sold them on to deficit banks, which bought the G-Secs needed to maintain the ratio. These transactions took place in the interbank market through ready forward deals (RFDs); in effect, banks selling G-Secs accessed funds (or borrowed) from the banks buying G-Secs (who lent). Much of the treasury market's activity took place through these RFDs, which were secured short-term 15-day loans between banks. Effectively, the borrowing bank sold its G-Secs to the lending bank, and then bought them back two weeks later at a slightly higher price that included an implied interest charge. Most treasury markets would recognize the above as a sort of repo transaction or repurchase agreement. This was a repo market in its infancy, and so, it cleared and settled through an antiquated manual clearing and settlement system that was also populated by brokers like Mehta.

Through these ready forward deals, Mehta mediated between banks that had surplus or deficit levels on the SLR. In an RFD, a broker like Mehta brought together two banks on the transaction described above, for which he was paid a commission. Over time and because of the antiquated settlement systems, actual G-Secs were often not even traded in an RFD, and instead a parallel arrangement in bank receipts came up. Bank receipts were instruments parties exchanged with one another in lieu of actual G-Secs when they went about arranging ready forward deals. Since this was an OTC treasury market where the counterparties were usually large money centre banks, all participants simply assumed that the bank receipts so traded were backed by actual G-Secs.

While mediating and market-making between banks that had to maintain the RBI-mandated SLR, Mehta discovered a profitable way to generate working capital in a perpetual money machine. Although the broker was only supposed to be an intermediary, handing over G-Secs and cheques drawn on counterparties to the respective parties, Mehta convinced banks to write cheques to him, which he then wrote a short while later to counterparty banks. The monies entered his account but went out a little later to counterparty banks, which effectively allowed him the float on the huge sums routinely generated by what was (in effect) an interbank wholesale market for treasuries. A loophole in reporting requirements also helped. Instead of daily reporting on SLR requirements, the RBI had mandated weekly reporting – the average holding for the week (and not the daily holding) had to be above the government-mandated SLR. Not many cared about where the funds went between the weekly reporting dates, and this gap aided Mehta's operations. Clearing and settlement systems were manual in those days, which allowed Mehta to play this float and generate working capital, which was then channelled from the G-Sec market into the stock market.

Mehta used the channelled funds to enter the stock market and bull shares higher. The entire market became a roaring four-bagger in short order. Nobody knew what to make of it all. Almost half a century had lapsed between the Second World War boom that ended in 1946 and the bull market that Mehta presided over in the early 1990s. This was a remarkable length of time between bulls – almost two generations had passed – and the market, in effect, had lost its memory of what a real bull run looked like.

Harshad Mehta's exertions had resulted in a wonderful gaga world of soaring share prices. Taking advantage of the rising prices, Mehta and his henchmen periodically sold positions and retired their bank receipts when it was time to return money to the banks. Alternately, payouts to banks were met from fresh pay-ins into the system, as new money entered the treasury market and the antiquated clearing and settlement systems continued to ensure that none was the wiser. In effect and for a brief while, Harshad Mehta was the clearing house for one of the largest financial markets – the wholesale market for government securities.

With the public entering in droves, the bull move was now feeding on itself, and yet the price levels were such that ever-larger sums were needed from the money machine to keep the move going. In the 1865 Cotton and Share Mania, the Bank of Bombay had obligingly expanded its share capital and lent it out to keep the show on the road, but now other methods were required. So, in the second stage of his operations, Mehta found minor banks such as Bank of Karad and Metropolitan Cooperative Bank that issued bank receipts which were not backed by government securities. Mehta passed these bank receipts onto unsuspecting banks in the G-Secs market, who, believing that the receipts were backed by government securities, lent money against them. Funds so generated were also used for stock market operations.[157]

Surprisingly, some of the bull move took place against the backdrop of international markets that were selling off, and heavily at that. The 1990–91 Gulf Crisis brought about by Saddam Hussein's invasion of Kuwait was in full swing. World markets fell between 15 and 40 per cent and oil, on which India was heavily dependent, almost doubled in price. The market initially kept rising through the chaos of soaring oil prices, collapsing world markets, and the general sense of dread brought about by the Kuwait invasion. It would mark the last occasion when the market rose over a considerable period in defiance of international events.[158] The market then sold off severely, losing almost a third of its value, by which time the Gulf War had speedily and successfully concluded in January 1991. So, by mid-1991, the market had the Gulf War behind it and Manmohan Singh's July budget ahead of it, which set the stage for going into the Mehta Bull's pathological phase – when all the crowd wants to do is buy – between late 1991 and early 1992.

By late 1991, Harshad Mehta had become the Big Bull. Like Premchand Roychand, so invincible was the aura of Mehta at his height

[157] For a chronology, see Debashis Basu and Sucheta Dalal, *The Scam: Who Won, Who Lost, Who Got Away*, New Delhi: UBS Publishers' Distributors Ltd., 1993, xvii–xxi. A successor volume is Debashis Basu and Sucheta Dalal, *The Scam: From Harshad Mehta to Ketan Parekh*, Mumbai: KenSource Information Services, 2007.

[158] Wall Street's crash of 1987 also had no effect on Indian markets.

that it was said the market would start rising when his Lexus entered Dalal Street. Amazing also was the rise in the cement company ACC's scrip; it had been Mehta's favourite from the early days, and its rise from 200 to almost 10,000 on 2 April 1992 resulted in a 50-bagger in short order. This was an unreal move for a blue-chip heavyweight in that era. The Mehta run was the first encounter between badla's terrific leverage and modern bull conditions, and the combination resulted in fortunes being made overnight. By end 1991, the move had spread to the regional exchanges, though the real action remained in Bombay.[159]

Critically, the Mehta move corrected in short order the undervaluation in the market that had gone on for generations during the Century of Marking Time. 1987–88 would be the last year when the market capitalization to GDP ratio was in single digits; with the Mehta Bull the ratio would quickly rise to about 58 per cent in 1992, which marks a historic break from the past, following which we enter the modern era when the ratio usually moves between 60 and 90 per cent of GDP. The run also led to the largest decadal move in the market's history, and the Sensex went from its average level of 225 (in 1982) to 4,467 on 22 April 1992. Over this decade the market became a 20-bagger, and on a logarithmic scale, this represents the single largest decadal move – about 1,900 per cent – in the market's history.[160] The Sensex crossed 1,000 for the first time in July 1990, but the bull would reach its pathological stage in early 1992 – repeatedly hitting 1,000-point milestones during the first four months of that year, and doubling in short order before peaking at 4,467 in April 1992. Much of the move followed Manmohan Singh's July 1991 budget, impressing on the market's unconscious mind the connection between reform and market movement. This would be the second time since V.P. Singh's budgets of the mid-1980s that

[159] Later, rumours circulated that the Calcutta exchange did its bit to end the Mehta Bull by leaning on Calcutta brokers who were doing Mehta's bidding and by increasing margins on his favourite scrips such as ACC. Aditi Roy Ghatak, *Down Lyons Range*, 109–10.

[160] The Sensex dates from 1986, with 1978–79 as the base year, and so, the 1982 value is that year's average value as recorded in the BSE archives. Bombay Stock Exchange, *The Stock Market Today: 1987*, Bombay: The Stock Exchange Foundation, 1987, 12.

such a connection was made, following which Pavlovian salivation over pending reforms would become a market norm. Remarkably, the fireworks to the upside had taken place despite the unlimited shorting capacity of the old badla system; in later years – with the short constraint introduced – the 1,000- and 2,000-baggers that resulted would make even the 50-time ACC move seem tame.

This was also the first real break from the valuations of the past. Market capitalization was now on record, and it rose from P.J. Thomas's 1939 figure of ₹404 crores to ₹3,54,000 crores in 1992.[161] But it is the Mehta Bull's valuation that would set a record. The BSE archives show that on 22 April 1992, the Sensex recorded a PE multiple of 57 and a price-to-book ratio of 10, levels that have never been surpassed to date.[162] These were the early days of Sensex computation, but even if the methodology is an issue, consider that later bull markets have topped out at half these levels.

The extent to which this is a break from the past has not been documented before, mainly because relative valuation measures were not widely used, and data on PE ratios before the Mehta Bull is difficult to come by. Nevertheless, one pioneering study from L.C. Gupta that documents changes in the ratio across time is available in the BSE archives. Gupta records a median PE ratio of 6 in 1980, which rose to about 14 in 1985–86 and plateaued at that level through the late 1980s.[163] As the market got more expensive, dividend yields dropped from over 6 per cent in 1980 to less than 3 per cent by the end of the decade, and the price-to-book ratio, usually at 1 in the early 1980s, had risen to about 4 by the end of the decade.[164] As this indicates, some of the valuation break was accomplished even before the Narasimha Rao and Manmohan Singh–led reform initiatives of the early 1990s, which

[161] Bombay Stock Exchange, *The Stock Market Today: 1993*, Bombay: The Stock Exchange Foundation, 1993, 4.

[162] Bombay Stock Exchange, *BSE Books: Financial Ratios of BSE Indices*, Bombay: BSE, 1992, 22.

[163] L.C. Gupta, P.K. Jain, and C.P. Gupta, *Indian Stock Market PE Ratios*, New Delhi: Society for Capital Market Research and Development, 1998, 36–37. The index used is the BSE National 100 index. Gupta's study excludes loss-making firms, which biases the results to the upside.

[164] Ibid., 35, 112–13.

flies in the face of popular perception that reforms and the Mehta Bull are what led to the rerating. The rerating had started in the 1980s itself, and the reforms – together with the Mehta Bull – briefly took the market from that rerating into the stratosphere.

The end of this undervaluation – together with unfolding world events and the displacement of the reform process – also led to *naya daur* (new era) thinking, which, in this case at least, was sound. In later years, the move would be attributed to Mehta – and his exertions in the G-Sec market did provide the liquidity – but these other factors were also at work in the bull run. Yet most accounts of the Mehta Bull tend to be breathless tick-tocks filled with innocuous detail that ignore many of these wider factors. Reading these accounts, one is reminded of the folk tale about the *kupamanduka*, the frog at the bottom of a well, who, when asked what the world looked like, stared up from the bottom of his long tubular dungeon, saw the sky above the well head, and said that the world was a patch of blue.

Something was needed to justify these wonderful price rises, and the obligatory snake oil was found in Harshad Mehta's replacement cost theory. The replacement cost theory basically states that a company's valuation should be based on the amount of money needed to replicate or 'replace' it. The idea itself has a long history in stock valuation and is based on strong theoretical foundations. James Tobin at Yale University had developed its most noted metric – Tobin's q.

Tobin's q, the ratio of the market value of a firm to its replacement cost (or its book value, if the replacement cost cannot be calculated), implies, *ceteris paribus*, that the firm is undervalued if the ratio is less than 1 and overvalued if it is greater than 1.[165] There is little to indicate the public saw the Indian market this way, but constantly rising share prices can justify a lot of theory. There is also nothing in the historical record to indicate that Tobin's q was ever calculated for the Indian market during those years, and in fact, there is no indication that anyone saw the equivalence between Mehta's arguments and the Tobin ratio.

[165] James Tobin, 'A General Equilibrium Approach to Monetary Theory,' *Journal of Money, Credit and Banking* 1 (1), 1969, 15–29.

Subsequently too, no attempt has been made to calculate it for that period, and so, the soundness of Mehta's famous argument has never been empirically tested. In fact, the undervaluation coming out of the Century of Marking Time was so deep that the market would have appeared cheap on any metric, including Tobin's *q*. But it would not have stayed cheap for very long. On the replacement cost argument, even if Tobin's *q* was less than 1 during the move, it is unlikely that it would have stayed that way for long, as the market – the numerator in the ratio – itself became a 4-bagger in short order and eliminated any undervaluation.

The end came on 23 April 1992, after a famous exposé in the *Times of India* by Sucheta Dalal, the redoubtable financial journalist. Some banks discovered they were holding bank receipts not backed by G-Secs; in other cases, Mehta – despite payments to him by banks – could not meet his obligations to those banks' counterparties. The market sold off and lost half its value by early 1993, one public-sector bank chairman reportedly committed suicide, and Mehta was later charged with over 70 criminal offences, while over 600 civil action suits were filed against him. Mehta went to jail, convicted in just one of the many cases against him, and subsequently died there.[166] In mute testimony to the state of India's legal system, some cases are still grinding their way more than a generation after the episode and despite the diligent efforts of court-appointed custodians such as A.K. Menon.[167]

The brokers took it in the neck, and the episode marks the start of a decade of moral panic with brokers as folk devils, seen by the public as responsible for it all. But the RBI managed to quietly glide away, despite the fact that its regulatory failure in the G-Sec market played a key role in the scandal. Like the last Reliance corners of the 1980s, the Harshad Mehta episode captured the public imagination. More generally, the

[166] On the aftermath of the Harshad Mehta scam – and particularly the staggering legal complications – as revisited on its 20th anniversary, see Sucheta Dalal, 'The Harshad Mehta Scam Broke 20 Years Ago. What Has Changed?,' *Moneylife*, 3 May 2012.

[167] For proof that nothing much changed between the 20th and 25th anniversaries of the scam, see Shailesh Menon and Maulik Vyas, 'The Harshad Mehta Case: 25 Years & Counting,' *Economic Times*, 5 July 2016.

decade that ended in the early 90s became the focus of much media attention in later years, and Bollywood would use the incidents of this era to make movies that usually combined breathless schadenfreude with cavalier regard for what actually happened.

The Century of Marking Time ended with the entrance of a party that would dominate proceedings in the years to come. This was the foreign institutional investor, or FII, and the ingress would change the world of Indian stock markets permanently and for the better. As part of the reform effort, FIIs were allowed into the markets from September 1992, well into the Mehta downswing. Their entry resulted in a second dramatic up move, as foreign inflows, the expectation of further foreign inflows, and a newly created private mutual fund industry bid up the limited floating stock available. In fact, this second up move in 1994 took the market back to its previous Mehta top. In a wild roller coaster ride, the market had halved after the Mehta top and then doubled with FII entry, and this doubling took it back to the April 1992 high of about 4,500. Most participants forget this second surge and tend to subsume it under the Mehta move, though the causality behind the two moves was very different. In turn, this level would not be decisively taken out till 1999. The seven-year gap between the Mehta top of April 1992 and its decisive and final takeout in 1999 is the longest such period in the modern era and, as such, a time of prolonged frustration and disenchantment with equities.

One casualty in all this was the firm of Morgan Stanley, a big Wall Street name that grandly rolled into town as part of the FII opening. Its new fund offering was the first by a foreign fund house, and it saw queues extend multiple city blocks; the application forms are said to have had a black market value of ₹10 each. The firm came in towards the top of the second surge when public fervour was at its height. Needless to say, the fund's early investments collapsed in value, and it would be many years before its original net asset values were reached.

But through all the turmoil, a new era was dawning that people could not yet see. The Harshad Mehta Bull and the deficiencies that ended it would act as a spur to the stock market's development. Despite the gloom and doom of the Mehta aftermath, the stock market was on the verge of entering its great era of development, and with it would come all the institutions, markets, and procedures that people nowadays take for granted. It would mark a new beginning for an old market.

3

NEW BEGINNINGS

1991 to 1999

An undervalued achievement of the P.V. Narasimha Rao – and Manmohan Singh – led reform effort that began in 1991 was the transformation of the stock market. Today's market is largely a result of these efforts, and the decade from 1991 marks an era of great capital market reform and development. So total has been the transformation and so complete the break with the historical continuity of the past, that over a century of market activity which preceded the break now appears as a blur, and it is common to find accounts of India's markets starting from the 1990s. Yet, it remains an unsung story with unsung heroes. Perhaps that's because the story lacks the glamour of market movements – much of the story is technical and concerned mainly with the workings of the market's back office – and so, its protagonists don't get the media prominence enjoyed by those chattering analysts and fund managers.

Improving resource allocation by moving from state planning and control to price signalling in clearing markets was the usual and overarching reform objective. Since financial markets cleared better than factor markets for land or labour (and had fewer vested interests), they became part of the low-hanging fruit of reform. But this was never explicitly stated as such and simply evolved as a priority along the way. Also, plan outlays were now throwing up capital shortages, and stock markets could be used to fill resource gaps and meet funding requirements; any improvement in their functioning could prove handy.[1]

Four distinct sets of activities took place during this period. First, a group of politicians and bureaucrats overcame the rent-seeking of a near-monopolist BSE and willed into existence a new exchange – the National Stock Exchange (NSE) – that would take on the old. Second, they uprooted the old microstructure and put in place a new one for the market. Third, that upstart exchange, the NSE, created new markets in derivatives and forward products that would dominate trading in the years ahead. Finally, the politicians and bureaucrats created a new framework for regulation by setting up a regulator – the Securities and Exchange Board of India (SEBI) – who would inaugurate systems on clearing, settlement, and dematerialization that would be the final link to a new market.

The last decade of the twentieth century must therefore rank as the decisive decade of the stock market's existence. The founding of (what later became) the dominant exchange, an entirely original microstructure, whole new markets for derivatives, and the creation of a regulator, all happened at the same time. All this change was distinct from the usual market *dramabaazi* (histrionics) that happens on a daily basis and, taken together, made for an uncertain and volatile period. Little thought appears to have been given to sequencing, that vital strategic prerequisite of economic reform. It was all done in multi-splendoured, typically Indian fashion, all at the same time and with everybody stepping on everybody else's toes, like the jostling and pushing of guests heading to the just-opened bar at a big fat Punjabi wedding.

[1] This was a basic focus of the Abid Hussain Committee. See Planning Commission, *Report of the Working Group on the Development of the Capital Market* (Abid Hussain Committee), New Delhi: Planning Commission, 1989. The other members of the committee were Raja J. Chelliah, S.S. Nadkarni, Nitin Desai, N. Vaghul, A.V. Ganesan, M.J. Pherwani, P.G. Mankad, Mahendra N. Kampani, Amitabha Ghosh, Rashmi Agarwala, and Srinivasa Madhur.

But it was done. Much of it was carried out through the exertions of the novices who founded the NSE, but there were other participants, including politicians, bureaucrats, and academics, who played important roles. Appropriately enough, most of the change was completed by the turn of the millennium, and a market whose basic structure had not changed much in over 100 years found itself suddenly thrust into the twenty-first century. Documentation and academic research on the stock market began now, and it was this surge in documentary and academic activity – ignoring as it did the preceding century of market behaviour – that also accounted for that disjointed historical break. Much of that early activity was done in Delhi – largely because market regulation at that time was the responsibility of the Finance Ministry's Stock Exchange Division – and in 1988, the University of Delhi's Department of Commerce conducted one of the first seminars on the stock market.[2]

Received wisdom has it that Manmohan Singh, fed up with the inability of equity markets to fulfil their role of channelizing savings towards risk capital, and seized of the need to attract capital flows following a 1991 balance of payments crisis, set up the NSE as part of the reform process that followed. The new exchange's initial achievement was remarkable – the BSE, a century-old incumbent operating a statutory monopoly on a liquidity pool, got overturned in less than a year by a rank upstart. Also, much of what is outlined below was accomplished by a minority government, as P.V. Narasimha Rao, the prime minister who gave Manmohan Singh the political go-ahead on all this, headed a Congress government without the required parliamentary numbers; this defied conventional wisdom, which held that only stable governments with parliamentary majorities could push through economic reform. How all this happened should have been an abiding conundrum of

[2] Department of Commerce, University of Delhi (South Campus), *Proceedings of a National Seminar on Indian Securities Market: Thrust and Challenges*, New Delhi: Department of Commerce, University of Delhi South Campus, 1988.

Indian economic inquiry, and yet, no attempt has been made so far to explain what took place.

But first, the politics – or more formally, the political economy of rent-seeking – because it dominates the reform process and also because politics is what Indians do best. Despite that, the only scholarly research-based account that focuses on the politics behind the NSE's founding comes from an American, John Echeverri-Gent of the University of Virginia.[3] Echeverri-Gent locates the events of the reform era in the political economy of a peculiar form of rent-seeking. The battle for economic rents – or rent-seeking behaviour – is a familiar arena to most reformers and economists. Economic rents are what the holder of a resource could get over and above its market price, that market price itself being what the resource would command when used in an alternate opportunity. Seen this way, economic rents are an excess return over and above the opportunity cost of resources.[4]

Under most schematics, economic rents come from two sources: the moat or intervention. In the first schematic – *the moat* – returns from product innovation, or something a company does very well, create a moat around the entity and allow it to earn supernormal profits, or innovation rents; in a perfectly competitive world this would not last, as competition and its handmaiden – imitation – breach the moat, facilitate new entry from rivals, and drive any excess returns down to the cost of capital. In the second schematic – *intervention* – some combination of power and/or government intervention leads to intervention rents, which are distributed exclusively to certain beneficiaries. Often, in attempting to perpetuate the system, these beneficiaries create a dynamic of rent-seeking behaviour that reduces social welfare, which is a polite way of talking about crony capitalism or corruption.

[3] John Echeverri-Gent, 'Politics of Market Micro-Structure: Towards a New Political Economy of India's Equity Market Reform,' *India's Economic Transition: The Politics of Reforms,* ed. Rahul Mukherji, New Delhi: Oxford University Press, 2007, 328–58.

[4] Much of the theory of rent-seeking behaviour was developed by Gordon Tullock. The term itself is attributed to Anne Krueger. An early treatment is found in *Toward a Theory of the Rent-seeking Society,* eds. James M. Buchanan, Robert D. Tollison, and Gordon Tullock, College Station, TX: Texas A&M University Press, 1980.

Echeverri-Gent goes on to create a third category – market microstructure rents. Trading rules and institutions that comprise a market's microstructure create rents, that benefit certain participants who then resist changes towards alternate rules that would create more efficient markets. In contrast to intervention rents, where participants induce state interventions that often restrict competition, market microstructure rents are created by market rules that shape competition in the absence of state intervention. Unlike moat-based innovation rents which are dissipated by competition, market microstructure rents are reinforced by competition, because the winners use their rewards to perpetuate existing institutions through new rounds of competition. In such a situation, any attempt to change the market's microstructure and its rules in pursuit of more efficient markets leads to collective action by the group affected.[5] This dynamic led the BSE to resist the government's initial attempts at market reform. Echeverri-Gent argues that the battle for economic rents with entrenched BSE brokers manifested as conflict over the market's microstructure.

Such conflicts had happened before. In 1925, following up on the Atlay Committee's recommendations, the Government of Bombay had sought to legitimize the BSE's de facto monopoly over the market by giving it a de jure monopoly over share trading. In return, the exchange would have to give up its rule-making powers over the market's microstructure.[6] This was predictably rejected by the BSE; there was little need to legitimize a de facto monopoly when it was the only game in town. Unlike the Atlay Committee report, Morison (1937) and Thomas (1948) were both exhortatory in nature and lacked any specific proposals on rule-making powers. It was only with the passage of the SCRA in 1956 that the government gave itself rule-making authority over the market's microstructure. But that authority was seldom used in an era when raising resources took place through the Five-Year Plans,

[5] John Echeverri-Gent, 'Politics of Market Micro-Structure,' 329–30.

[6] K.R.P. Shroff, *History and Present Position of the Stock Market in India*, Bombay: The Stock Exchange, Bombay, 1962, 16.

rather than the market. This situation continued unchanged till the reform era's onset in the late 1980s.

Brokers of the 1980s fell into two groups: the reform-minded lot who thought they would benefit from increased volumes (particularly from foreign investors) if the markets were opened up, and the remainder whose businesses benefited mainly from badla's speculative fireworks. Crucially, this second group included the badla financiers who had a considerable stake in the status quo, which gave them little incentive to change. At one end, the badla financiers ran a call market for funds and were the vital link between the market's financing requirements and wealthy individuals on the outside who supplied that financing; at the other end, they ran a lending/borrowing mechanism for stocks. Effectively, they mattered to both the long and short sides of the market, using the call market to finance the long side and using the lending/borrowing mechanism to supply stocks to the short side – by making up differences in either funds or stock. In some ways, it was an open and competitive system with interest rates – *vyaj badla* – that fluctuated and rationed credit in the call market for funds. In fact, the balancing of bull and bear sides was quite remarkable, and the system met this key requirement of an efficient market.

The naked forward contracts that formed the bulk of badla volumes allowed the public to trade with near-unlimited leverage, and the huge volumes from this over-trading resulted in considerable commissions to the brokers.[7] The system also depended on lax settlement, so any reform of the settlement system was a direct threat to badla volumes and the commission earnings from them. In fact, the volumes that badla generated were staggering for their time and are not appreciated even to this day. In 1989–90, a blue chip like the cement company ACC turned over its entire market capitalization every month. That meant ACC turned over 12 times its market capitalization that year. In the same period, IBM, the highest velocity share on the NYSE, turned over just

[7] For an early 1973 study that examined the badla era's obsession with liquidity, see L.C. Gupta and J.K. Rohatgi, 'Stock Market Liquidity: How Much? For Whom?,' *Economic and Political Weekly*, 8, 34, 25 August 1973, M85–M87, M89–M96.

1.1 times its market capitalization.[8] Nowadays, it would be unthinkable for, say, the Reliance stock, with its market capitalization of about ₹17,00,000 crores ($220 billion) in 2024, to have a cash market turnover of ₹17,00,000 crores in a single month; even combining the monthly cash and derivatives market turnovers would not produce anything close to such a figure for the Reliance stock. Yet the badla system – because it combined cash and derivatives features with negligible margin requirements – produced equivalent figures in its time.

The restrictions on bank financing into the market only added to the badla financiers' influence, and other brokers usually turned to them to fund and roll over positions. Such financing activity provided information on the order book for carry forward trades, which allowed some badla financiers to estimate which operator was overcommitted on certain counters, and this knowledge proved useful in speculative transactions. Finally, the badla financiers' access to financing and settlement meant that BSE authorities frequently turned to them to sort out payment and settlement crises.

Naturally, all this translated into considerable political power. The badla financiers led coalitions of brokers in exchange elections and effectively controlled the BSE's board.[9] Much of this became apparent only after Jeejeebhoy's tenure as Chairman ended in 1980, and the records are silent on politics before that date. With so much hinging on the status quo, the badla financers had little reason to change things. As a result, the BSE's resistance to reform was led by badla financiers such as Manu Manek, and it was their vague and inchoate opposition to change that was the main source of the BSE's intransigence in the twentieth century.

Reform also ran into traditional problems of collective action among investors and issuers.[10] Conceptually, investors and issuers were the

[8] L.C. Gupta, 'The Volume and Nature of Speculation on Indian Stock Exchanges: Regulatory Implications,' *Expert Study of Trading in Shares in Stock Exchanges*, Volume 2, Appendices – Working Paper/Note 1, New Delhi: The Society for Capital Market Research and Development, 1991, 2, 4–6.

[9] John Echeverri-Gent, 'Politics of Market Micro-Structure,' 331–34.

[10] Ibid., 331.

two participants in a capital market between whom the broker – or the investment banker – intermediated. But investors were too disbursed, and issuers (corporates) often colluded with brokers to manipulate share prices. Investors could not enforce change because of a collective action problem, and issuers simply had little incentive to bring about change. Consequently, a small but determined group of brokers found it easy to resist reform.

Much of this unfolded against a backdrop of extraordinary volatility. The decade of the 1990s was characterized by several scams or settlement crises: in procession, came Harshad Mehta (1993), MS Shoes (1995), Sterlite/Videocon/BPL (1998), and Ketan Parekh (2001). There was also government instability, as successive Lok Sabhas could not summon adequate majorities, leading to national elections in 1996, 1998, and 1999; the first half of the 1990s had Congress-led governments and the latter half had BJP-led governments, with a brief period in between when neither of the two major groupings led governments. Despite that, a bipartisan consensus seems to have emerged on stock market reform and the effort remained remarkably apolitical at the national level. What politics there was over the market always took place at the participant and committee level. So, the overall impression is of a chaotic series of events and actions set against a milieu of remarkable turbulence that somehow worked out in the end. And yet, path dependency in the sequence of events is pervasive, and there is much in today's markets that is traceable to decisions and events of that era.

Initial attempts at reform were met with resistance or rent-seeking behaviour, and this had been a historical pattern in the exchange's reactions to Atlay, Morison, and Thomas. But by the 1980s times had changed, and the BSE was in danger of being bypassed by revolutions in technology and finance. Technology – above all the advent of the computer – was beginning to make the physical floor redundant, while the revolution in finance through risk management and derivatives made the exchange's own procedures seem dated. As part of the 1991 reform efforts, the government had recognized that capital market changes represented the low-hanging fruit of reform. The government also had the authority to make those changes; after all, the Finance Ministry enjoyed broad powers under the Securities Contracts (Regulation) Act but was usually reluctant to use them, and this had also been a historical pattern. So, when the ministry actually exercised that authority during the reform effort, it came as a shock to the exchange.

Meanwhile, the broker club was tone deaf to even token attempts at change. Efforts to register brokers and impose a turnover tax were resisted, as were modest proposals to unbundle the brokerage from the price quoted to the customer.[11]

The BSE then passed into the control of the badla financiers and went through a revolving door of presidents during this crucial period. More generally, the 80s and 90s were a period of management flux that contrasted sharply with the stability of the previous era. After Phiroze Jeejeebhoy's tenure as chairman ended in 1980, much of the remarkable stability that had characterized the BSE's leadership also ended, and a period of management turbulence followed that was to continue through the crucial reform period and into the next century. The government began meddling in the exchange's management with mixed results, and three changes took place that resulted in considerable turmoil in exchange management. These included: the practice of appointing executive directors, the continued splitting of the chairman and president's posts, and an April 1993 decree that severely restricted the president's tenure.

First, after Jeejeebhoy, the government insisted on appointing an executive director who would be responsible for the exchange's day-to-day affairs. M.R. Mayya enjoyed length of tenure over two five-year terms, but after Mayya's retirement in 1993, the Executive Director's post was occupied by government functionaries without business

[11] Encounters over basic issues such as broker registration are recounted by the second head of SEBI in his memoirs. See G.V. Ramakrishna, *Two Score and Ten: My Experiences in Government*, Delhi: Academic Foundation, 2004, 129–72.

backgrounds who held office for limited terms. Mayya's successors into the millennium included A.N. Kolhatkar (1993–95), R.C. Mathur (1996–99), A.N. Joshi (1999–2002), Manoj Vaish (2002–04), and Rajnikant Patel (2004–08). The relationship between the executive director and the broker-run governing board was untenable; the governing board was made up of influential broker members, and for an executive director, enforcing compliance meant enforcing regulations against the same people who determined his terms and conditions of service. As a result, most executive directors after Mayya had issues imposing their writ on the brokers who had appointed them, and self-regulation became a fig leaf in such a framework. It was only after Patel that the executive director's post was abolished and the present arrangement of a president/CEO was established, with Madhu Kannan (2009–12) the first incumbent, followed by Ashishkumar Chauhan (2012–22).

Second, in 1966, the chairman and president's posts had been separated, with Jeejeebhoy as chairman and a broker as president. However, after Jeejeebhoy's tenure ended, both posts came to be occupied by brokers, and this changed the tenor of the exchange's management. Significantly, it had been an iron rule with the earlier heads to never trade their own accounts or run their own businesses, but the brokers who now occupied these posts had brokerage businesses with active proprietary books, which led to severe principal–agent problems. These later BSE heads – drawn mainly from the speculating broker class – lacked the disinterestedness and gravitas of the earlier stalwarts, found their focus diverted by the draining task of trading their own books in a volatile market, and could not devote all their energies to exchange affairs. As a result, many even delegated strategic direction to the executive directors, but after Mayya's 10-year term ended, there was instability of tenure even in that position. During the 1980s and 1990s, exchange leadership was hostage to the politics between the badla financiers and the reformers, and institutional direction kept changing depending on which side could muster enough support at the elections.[12]

[12] John Echeverri-Gent, 'Politics of Market Micro-Structure,' 333–34.

A case in point was Mahendra Kampani, a BSE president. His modest attempts at reform were resisted, as were his proposals on computerization, and Kampani was ousted from the exchange's board in March 1988.

Finally, a SEBI directive of 20 April 1993 required the BSE president to take a year's break after two consecutive one-year terms and led to a revolving door presidency, causing further discontinuity in exchange management in the 1990s.[13] Because of this directive, the BSE's top job rotated almost at annual intervals between various brokers, with petty politics dominating their elections. As a result, there were 11 presidents in the crucial 15-year period between 1986 and 2001, by which time the reform effort had run much of its course.[14] By then, the government was taking explicit steps to end broker control over the exchange – without putting anything sensible in place to replace that control – and so, the exchange's board and its management were both in play. In contrast, such SEBI directives did not even apply to the OTCEI or NSE, as they were founded by government financial institutions, and this was just another example of blatant discrimination against the BSE in the early years of the reform era. Done ostensibly to reduce the brokers' hold over the exchange, the April 1993 directive also put the onus for stability and management continuity on the executive director, but as seen, most executive directors who succeeded Mayya from 1993 also had short tenures. All these factors resulted in a BSE leadership vacuum in the reform era that was now well underway.

Shroff and Jeejeebhoy had jealously guarded the interests of the BSE and its members, but only by reconciling them with a larger public interest. Their attempts at self-regulation usually succeeded in what was a much smaller market. If all else failed, their personal standing, together with the implicit threat of government intervention as the alternative

[13] Securities and Exchange Board of India (SEBI), *Order under Section 8 of the SCRA*, Circular, SMD/SED/6919/93 of 20 April 1993, Bombay: Securities and Exchange Board of India, 1993.

[14] They were Ramdas Lallubhai Dalal (1986–87), Mahendra N. Kampani (1987–88), Govindbhai B. Desai (1988–91), Hemendra M. Kothari (1991–92), Govindbhai B. Desai (1992–94), Bhagirat B. Merchant (1994–95), Kamal Kabra (1995–96), M.G. Damani (1996–98), Jasvantlal C. Parikh (1998–99), Anand Rathi (1999–01), and Deena Mehta (2001).

if the self-regulation framework didn't deliver, kept the show on the road. Being a self-regulating organization allowed for a certain freedom from government regulation, but it also called for a certain discipline while keeping the flock in line and implementing the self-regulation framework. It was a discipline that the later presidents and executive directors could not muster up. The alternative to being a self-regulating organization was regulation by the Indian government, which, in that era at least, was always heavy-handed, often incompetent, and sometimes corrupt. So, the threat of that regulation was a bogeyman used by the exchange's revolving-door management of the 1980s and 1990s to keep the flock in line, but it was used once too often, and by the 1990s, the threat had lost its capacity to frighten the brokers into good behaviour.

Most of these issues came to a head over the plan to automate and computerize the exchange's operations. The process had begun under Jeejeebhoy in the early 70s with centralized clearing and settlement through batch processing of floor transactions, but the trading floor continued to remain manual with bargains struck between traders in a ring.[15] Volumes surged through the mid-80s due to the initial liberalization efforts, which resulted in systems upgrades in 1982, 1985, and 1987.[16] Clearing and settlement cycles were computerized through batch processing by the late 80s, but the vital floor operations continued to remain manual and quote driven.

A BSE study group then undertook a tour of the world's major exchanges in 1989, which further brought out the gap between the

[15] After *saudas* (bargains) were struck, abbreviated details were entered in a *sauda* block book and transferred to a *sauda* sheet, which was then handed to the BSE's computer department for batch processing. The computer processed this to print out statements for each member showing their matched and unmatched transactions. The system was reactive and generated large numbers of unmatched transactions – often as much as 30 to 40 per cent of the day's business – with corresponding increases in paperwork and delays. Computer Maintenance Corporation, *Technical Project Report, Online Trading and Trade Support System: Executive Summary*, Bombay: CMC, August 1991, 1–2. In later years, *sauda* sheets were handed in on floppies rather than physical paper, which reduced the unmatched problem somewhat. See Bombay Stock Exchange, *National Stock Market System*, Bombay: BSE, 1992, 14. The system was also Bombay-focused with no upcountry facilities available.

[16] V. Shankar, 'Automation Plans of the Bombay Stock Exchange,' *Handbook of Articles from the Stock Exchange Review 1989–1991*, Mumbai: BSE, 1992, 27–35.

exchange and international best practice. But the group reached the conclusion that only non-badla shares should move to a quote-based computer network similar to Nasdaq.[17] Depending on the experience in non-badla stocks, the badla list in forwards that accounted for the bulk of volumes was to move to screen-based trading at an undisclosed future date; since badla shares on the 'specified list' accounted for between 80 and 90 per cent of volumes, this left the majority of volumes unaffected by the proposal.

But volumes continued to soar with the Harshad Mehta bull market, rising from 4,000 daily bargains in the early 1980s to about 1,00,000 daily bargains in the early 1990s. The manual floor operations were less of an issue, mainly because operations are highly scalable on the trading floor – a simple matter of executing an order for 1,000 as opposed to 10 shares. But the back office was less scalable, and problems arose when floor trading volumes far outpaced the back office's capacity in clearing and settlement. Despite computerized batch processing of settlements, the BSE's back office could not keep pace with the volume increases of the Mehta Bull. Wall Street's 'tronics' boom during the 'Go-G' Bull of the late 1960s had also led to a similar breakdown in back-office operations and required a complete market shutdown to get operations back on track.[18] But the BSE was unaware of this and could not draw on any lessons from the episode, despite its obvious parallel with the BSE's own predicament. Further, the brokers who ran the BSE – and made their money through commissions generated from trading volumes – had little incentive to invest heavily in the unglamorous back office, always seen as a cost rather than a revenue centre.

The focus on maximizing 'card' value also had consequences. Transactions and volumes grew, placing new demands on the brokerage fraternity, but membership continued to stay cartelized to maximize the value of the BSE 'card'. As a result, the brokerage community stayed

[17] V. Shankar, 'IT Architecture at the Bombay Stock Exchange for the Nineties,' *Handbook of Articles from the Stock Exchange Review 1989–1991*, Mumbai: BSE, 1992, 156–62.

[18] The episode is outlined in John Brooks, *The Go-Go Years: The Drama and Crashing Finale of Wall Street's Bullish 60s*, Wiley Investment Classics, Hoboken, NJ: John Wiley and Sons, Inc., 1999.

small in absolute numbers and 'card' values soared, but the market was growing to levels unseen in the Century of Marking Time. By 1990, computerization was still a pipe dream and the issue had got entangled with the real problem – the exchange's politics and the inability to conceptualize the broad microstructure of the market.[19]

A Computer Maintenance Corporation (CMC) project report of 1991 then made the mental break with the past by envisaging a move to a screen-based, order-driven system in four phases between 1992 and 1995, with non-badla scrips entering the system first, followed by badla scrips at a later date.[20] But the inability to conceptualize the market in quote versus order-driven terms was still apparent, as was the BSE's attempt to hold on to its physical floor/quote-driven format for the all-important badla list. Consequently, most of the CMC effort focused on capture of deal information from the physical floor with its quote-driven system, rather than on a totally new system – either quote or order driven – that automated the trading process itself. The physical concentration of the market also led to this mindset; of the 600 members, 550 had offices in the BSE building or within a 3 km radius of Dalal Street, which contributed to the emphasis on electronic capture of geographically concentrated manual operations.[21]

The resistance to automating the trading floor was understandable; in all probability, it would have ended the practice of overcharging on which the system rested, reduced the profitable opportunities for inter exchange arbitrage, and done away with the practice of end-of-day 'adjusting entries'. In short, it would effectively end the murkiness and lack of transparency that the system thrived on earlier, besides leaving an audit trail for government agencies. Understandably, computerization was seen as a threat and resisted by the brokers who governed the exchange at that time. So, nothing much came of the CMC report,

[19] Bombay Stock Exchange, *The Stock Exchange Review: July 1989*, Bombay: BSE, 1989, 15. Remarkably, even at this late date, there is still little debate in the records on the basic choice between quote-driven and order-driven markets.

[20] Computer Maintenance Corporation, *Technical Project Report*, 1–2.

[21] V. Shankar, 'IT Architecture at the Bombay Stock Exchange,' 157.

mainly due to continued broker resistance but also because of the inability to gauge the tide of events brought about by the reform effort.

By now, all this resistance persuaded the government to think in terms of a National Stock Market System (NSMS). This was first articulated in a 1991 document commonly known as the Pherwani report, after the chairman of the committee that produced it.[22] The Pherwani report is important because one of its lesser recommendations would decisively change the market.

The Municipal Era – that came into being through sections 13 and 19 of the SCRA – was now at its peak, and the Pherwani Committee was originally set up to evolve policy that could deal with the waves of proposals for new exchanges that were inundating the finance ministry. The seven exchanges of the Independence era had grown to 19, with further proposals for another 13, and there was a strong possibility that the country would have 32 stock exchanges if all the proposals were accepted.[23] Consequently, the Pherwani Committee wavered on whether more exchanges or a better network of the existing system would best serve the needs of investors. It reached the conclusion – rightly enough, given the massive spread of regional exchanges since the early 1980s – that more exchanges would only add to the confusion and not serve any purpose. Conceptually, it settled on closer linkages between existing exchanges through the creation of the NSMS. Yet, inexplicably, it also recommended the addition of five new exchanges at New Bombay, Nagpur, Gwalior, Chandigarh, and Shimla – this despite

[22] Government of India, Ministry of Finance, *Report of the High Powered Study Group on Establishment of New Stock Exchanges* (Pherwani Committee), New Delhi: Ministry of Finance, June 1991. Besides M.J. Pherwani, other members of the Pherwani Committee were K.U. Mada, D.K. Bhatia, and L.C. Gupta, with Vibhav Kapoor as Member-Secretary. M.J. Pherwani, a former UTI chairman, headed Infrastructure Leasing and Financial Services Ltd (IL&FS) at the time when the report was prepared.

[23] Ibid., 38, 89. Annexure 19 of the report lists the additional proposals.

the committee's own recognition of the severe overcrowding in the exchange space. The reasoning behind this contradiction has never been fully explained, neither by the committee in its report nor subsequently.

The Pherwani report recommended a three-tier NSMS of principal exchanges (the four metros of Bombay, Delhi, Calcutta, and Madras that, together with Ahmedabad, accounted for over 85 per cent of extant volumes), regional exchanges, and additional trading floors.[24] A second set of recommendations dealt with back-office issues, including a national clearing and settlement system and the creation of a depository trust that could be used in common by the exchanges. Finally, a third set of recommendations dealt with setting up the five new exchanges.[25]

The Pherwani report had a number of issues that are apparent with the passage of time. In keeping with that era's primitive knowledge of market microstructure, the report did not make reference to even basic distinctions such as those between quote-driven and order-driven systems. The NSMS was a hazy concept, and the report did not deal with the technicalities that would be needed to make the idea functional; what networking entailed was left open and vague. It is hard not to draw the conclusion that the NSMS itself was basically an attempt to throw technology at the Municipal Era's mindset. The committee's first (and main) recommendation on the three-level NSMS would be consigned to history's dustbin. The second set of recommendations on the all-important back-office infrastructure was unobjectionable in itself and would be adopted but not in the form envisaged – rather than developing common market infrastructure, surviving exchanges would evolve their own clearing and settlement.

And what of the third set of recommendations on the new exchanges? Pointing out badla's tendency to build volumes in big companies while leaving the rest illiquid, the report had recommended a new exchange that would focus on mid-sized companies and debt trading. This was to be located not in the island city of Bombay but in the extension of

[24] Ibid., 10–26, 115.

[25] Ibid., ix.

New Bombay that was coming up on the mainland and where many wholesale markets were due to be shifted. This new exchange would provide access to investors all over the country on an equal footing. Its mid-sized company listings would simply be a complement to the large companies listed on the BSE, and in fact, the report saw many of them graduating to a BSE listing, just as many companies listed on the American Stock Exchange graduated to the NYSE.[26] Public-sector firms would also be a focus area of this new exchange. The report noted, but only in passing, what was to become the new exchange's biggest advantage: the chance to bypass existing systems and market practices.

The proposals were modest and instinctively kept the BSE's interests in mind. The focus on mid-sized companies effectively allowed the BSE a continued monopoly on blue-chip trading through the all-important badla list; besides, the new exchange was also to focus on debt instruments, a worthy objective given the parlous state of debt markets, which had the incidental advantage of not upsetting the BSE's dominance of equities. In and of itself, the Pherwani report simply could not, and did not, make the mental break from the existing BSE-dominated setup, which was required to create an entirely new market.

So intransigent was the BSE that even these modest proposals were viewed as a threat. By the time the report came out in June 1991, the BSE had reached the peak of its ascendancy. Because of the multiplicity of exchanges, an exchange's share of market capitalization rather than turnover was a better indicator of its position, and BSE-listed stocks accounted for about 93 per cent of Indian market capitalization in 1990.[27] In fact, this was well into the Harshad Mehta bull move, and almost all the resulting expansion in volumes and market capitalization went to the BSE instead of the other principal or regional exchanges, further cementing its dominance. So, for the BSE, the optimal solution was a

[26] This analogy was explicitly drawn by the committee. Ibid., 48.

[27] Bombay Stock Exchange, *The Stock Market Today*, Bombay: The Stock Exchange Foundation, 1990, 5. Of capital listed on all exchanges, the BSE accounted for 82, 92, and 51 per cent of equity, debentures/bonds, and preferred stock categories respectively. All figures are reckoned as of 31 March 1990.

status quo that entailed linking existing exchanges rather than setting up new ones.[28] Taking the example of the United States' Intermarket Trading System that had been developed at the initiative of the NYSE, the BSE envisioned the market as an interlinked quote-driven system through composite quote displays. It consequently had no issues with the first and second set of Pherwani report recommendations, but it stridently objected to a single part of the third set of recommendations – the exchange at New Bombay.

The exchange proceeded to hire a consultant, Arthur Andersen, ostensibly to review international best practice on the NSMS, but actually, this was done to counter the third set of recommendations espousing a new exchange in its backyard.[29] Andersen – clueless about the historical and political background – pointed out in a December 1991 report that in most international markets, the NSMS had developed by improving systems for linking existing exchanges and not through the creation of a new exchange, so setting up another exchange would amount to further fragmentation of an already small and fragmented liquidity pool.[30] This was a strong argument, though it is difficult to conceive of fragmentation beyond what the SCRA's municipalization provisions had already wrought.

More crucially, the report emphasized that (by 1989) over 70 per cent of BSE-listed companies had less than ₹3 crores in paid-up capital and fewer than 10,000 shareholders. The first post-Independence IPO wave of the mid-1980s in leasing companies and mini cement/steel plants had led to this situation, but the report was too close to events to notice that. Many of these companies were undercapitalized and under-owned, with no real financial performance to speak of; most had no business being listed, and so trading or market-making on a new exchange would not solve any issue for these companies.[31] The Andersen report pointed

[28] Bombay Stock Exchange, *National Stock Market System*, 4.

[29] Arthur Andersen & Associates, *Review of International Experience of National Stock Market Systems*, Bombay: Arthur Andersen, 1992, 1–12.

[30] Ibid., 10.

[31] Ibid., 34.

out that this effectively ended the rationale for small and mid-sized company listings at the New Bombay exchange.

Andersen's report had further forceful arguments against the new exchange. At that time, nowhere in the world – but for one exception – were there two stock exchanges in the same city. That exception was New York, which besides the NYSE also had the American Stock Exchange – an exchange that had come off the kerb and was never a real rival to the Big Board. So, there was the appeal of aligning with international best practice that also went in the BSE's favour. Finally, the new Over-the-Counter Exchange of India (OTCEI) was already tasked with listing small and medium companies, further calling into question the basic rationale behind the new exchange's listing of mid-sized enterprises.[32] Rather than a new exchange, the Andersen report called for resources to go into infrastructure and technology that could facilitate the NSMS, together with further development of the BSE's trading systems.

These were compelling arguments, and for a while, it appeared as though Andersen was recommending the right deed for the right reasons. The report's findings found an influential ear in Ashok Desai, the chief economic advisor of that time and a member of Manmohan Singh's team during the reform years of the early 1990s. Like other colleagues, Desai had been ambivalent about the creation of an entirely new exchange. Echoing Andersen, his concern was that such a move would divide and fragment the market even further, lead to the promotion of a *sarkari* (government) stock exchange, and kill Asia's oldest exchange.[33] As a result, the file dealing with implementation of the Pherwani report would remain with Desai for a considerable period. In one of those supreme and unrecognized ironies that India abounds in, all of Desai's concerns would come to pass and play out exactly as he had foreseen – but only as a prelude to one of the successes of Indian economic reforms in that era.

[32] Ibid.

[33] Shaji Vikraman, 'How Untested Ideas Proved Transformational in Building India's Biggest Exchange: NSE,' *Economic Times*, 13 December 2013.

In April 1992, the Harshad Mehta bull peaked and turned to the downside. Revelations that Mehta had manipulated the government securities market only to divert funds into the stock market led the market to lose almost half its value. The sell-off and the scam's revelations put the BSE and its brokers on the defensive. After the eponymous scam broke, it became difficult for the BSE to claim that a government-run stock market would not work, as evidently a privately run market also had systemic issues. Remarkably – and despite all this – the obduracy of the BSE continued, fuelled in large part by its dominance of the Mehta bull market's colossal volumes. But the scandal that followed and the broker club's inability to consider even modest change, transformed the government's attitude to the stock market. By now, the reform efforts set in motion by Manmohan Singh's June 1991 budget were gathering momentum, and financial markets were an important part of those efforts.

A crossroads was reached when Ashok Desai visited BSE and was assured by its board that efforts on automation and computerization were on track. A visit to the computer room where he observed the BSE's intermittent efforts convinced him otherwise;[34] the BSE was still wavering on the introduction of screen-based trading for the physical floor badla scrips that made up the bulk of volumes. Half-hearted efforts were producing half-hearted results. Desai finally changed his mind on the need for NSMS. Losing his support would prove decisive. Policymakers had begun to realize that any sort of incremental approach to reform was no longer feasible. The focus then shifted to the Pherwani proposals and the opening provided by the New Bombay exchange suggestion. The recommendation – slipped in almost as an afterthought and contrary to the vision of linking existing exchanges in a national system – would change the market forever. The New Bombay exchange was to become the NSE.[35]

[34] Ibid.

[35] Chapter VI of the Pherwani report contains the original NSE proposal. Ministry of Finance, *Report of the High Powered Study Group*, 45–48. Recommendations 15 to 17 deal with the NSE's formation.

Events now began to take on some momentum, and Finance Minister Manmohan Singh provided the political will to get the project going. He leaned on Y.V. Reddy, the bureaucrat in charge of capital markets, who, together with his fellow IAS officer from the Andhra Pradesh cadre, G.V. Ramakrishna (now head of the newly created regulator SEBI), provided the necessary impetus. At an August 1992 meeting in the finance ministry, the decision to create a new exchange was taken, which makes the period between that date and November 1994 (when NSE trading went live) important to the market's story.

Convened by Montek S. Ahluwalia, a key member of Manmohan Singh's reform team, the meeting included G.V. Ramakrishna, S.S. Nadkarni, P.J. Nayak, and R.H. Patil, among others. In a crucial decision, the Industrial Development Bank of India (IDBI) was chosen as a nodal institution for the new exchange's founding.[36] Nadkarni, who headed IDBI, then selected another IDBI veteran R.H. Patil to shepherd the project. In turn, Patil deputed a team of five – Ravi Narain, Chitra Ramkrishna, Ashishkumar Chauhan, Raghavan Putran, and K. Kumar – who, with him, would make the NSE's founding group.[37] All were novices, with little experience in equities or capital market operations, which was not surprising as the BSE had the monopoly on exchanges and expertise at that time. Other than Chauhan, who was a Gujarati, none came from a community traditionally regarded as having a presence in India's stock market.

Given their inexperience, it is astonishing that the tyros got all the early decisions right. First, the Pherwani-conceived New Bombay entity – confined as it was to small companies and debt instruments – was rejected as an exchange of shreds and patches; at an unconscious level, the exchange had been conceived only with the BSE's interests in mind. Second, the group even rejected a competing exchange idea that had a head start; this was the OTCEI, which was inspired by Nasdaq's system

[36] At that time, IDBI was one of a trio of development finance institutions that also included ICICI and IFCI.

[37] Patil's own recollection of these events is in R.H. Patil, 'Current State of the Indian Capital Market,' *Economic and Political Weekly*, 41, (11), 18–24 March 2006, 1001–11.

of multilevel market makers. Competitive considerations may have been responsible for this decision, as OTCEI had been co-promoted by ICICI, generally regarded as IDBI's rival in the development banking space. Third was a key decision that solved the problems of agency and ownership that had plagued the BSE, an exchange owned and run by brokers. The new exchange would be owned by institutions and managed by professionals, with brokers separated from exchange ownership and operations.

The NSE's founding group got important pointers on what to avoid from the Pherwani and Andersen reports. The group selectively picked or rejected recommendations from the Pherwani report – they selected the exchange marked for New Bombay and named it the National Stock Exchange, but rejected as too limiting the Pherwani proposal that the new exchange be confined to small companies and debt instruments. Ironically enough, from the BSE's Andersen report came the realization that smaller companies had deeper problems with viability that liquidity provision on a new exchange could not resolve, which made the NSE founders reject being confined to such small and mid-sized entities. What was left out of the reports proved as pivotal to the NSE's success as what was let in – Pherwani had been silent on the distinction between quote- and order-driven markets, which left the novices free to stumble on a screen-based market that happened to be order-driven. Crucially, rather than linking the SCRA-sanctioned municipal monopolies using a network as the Pherwani NSMS had originally planned, the NSE chanced upon the market as a nationwide electronic communication network that was order-driven and that bypassed the municipal monopolies. In this they were unlikely pioneers, though L.C. Gupta had first mentioned the idea in a 1991 study.[38] Avoiding the smaller companies and rejecting Pherwani's municipal mindset meant conceptualizing a new exchange from scratch, and this start from a clean slate, free from the burdens of the past, was to prove fundamental to the NSE's early success.

[38] L.C. Gupta, *Expert Study of Trading in Shares in Stock Exchanges*, 7.

The Pherwani report was not the group's only point of reference. They extensively studied international best practice while making the early decisions – the BSE's monopoly on exchange expertise had left the founders with little choice but to do this. The NSE took the large-company focus of New York's NYSE, Nasdaq's nationwide network of trading terminals, the computerized order-driven books of Paris and Vancouver, and the settlement guarantee of Chicago's futures market, and combined them into its own unique model, as noted years later by R.H. Patil.[39] For advice on a business model that could combine these features, the founders also hired noted Hong Kong–based capital markets consultancy International Securities Consultancy.[40] The NSE would be the penultimate among the world's major exchanges – Moscow followed it by a few months – so taking the best from the rest was easy. The exchange's founding reflected the remarkable assimilative and absorptive powers of Indian civilization, but in the high-tech, future-obsessed atmosphere of today's stock exchanges, no one sees it as such.

The NSE's founding is providential when one considers the evil fairies present at its birth. It was understandable that an inefficient and threatened near-monopoly like the BSE wished to see the NSE stillborn. Less explicable is the singular fact that the only people who could will the NSE into existence – the finance ministry and the recently created SEBI – were themselves initially opposed to its creation; as seen, key actors at the Finance Ministry and SEBI were initially wary about implementing the Pherwani report. The Pherwani Committee's timing was also unfortunate. It had its first meeting on 22 January 1991 and published its report in June of that year – the same month as Manmohan Singh's path-breaking budget that started the reforms – by which time most of its recommendations seemed dated. Perhaps this accounts for the report's most glaring contradiction – it noted an already crowded exchange space on the one hand, and yet recommended five more exchanges on the other hand. In fact, some of the proposed locations such as Shimla and Gwalior were so farfetched

[39] R.H. Patil, 'Current State of the Indian Capital Market.'

[40] Ibid.

that the temptation is to see them as far-out alternatives that had to be suggested only to provide some company to the real objective of the New Bombay exchange, which became the NSE.

In later years, the Pherwani report was seen as instrumental to the NSE's foundation, but it was a half-hearted report – a prisoner of its time – that subconsciously kept the BSE-dominated setup in mind. The report's suggestion on the five new exchanges was a nod to what had happened previously in the Municipal Era, and the NSMS proposal was a window to the future – and yet neither would fructify as the committee proposed. It was the subsequent development work done independent of the Pherwani committee that was to prove decisive to the NSE's foundation and later success.

Also decisive to the NSE's foundation was the BSE's own attitude. The BSE of that era was a closed club with a municipal monopoly and therefore something of a *kupamanduka* – a frog in a well. Those superficially clever market readers and stock traders never thought deeply about change, and history and its tides were beyond their ken. Besides, whenever the government made noises about market practices, the BSE fobbed it off by claiming a monopoly on stock market expertise. Consequently, the BSE saw 1991 as the latest in a long series of such noises by the government, and the exchange simply could not recognize the surge of events produced by the reform effort of the early 90s. This insouciance was the dominant institutional ethos for generations and a consequence of the BSE's long monopoly of the stock market. In fact, K.R.P. Shroff in his *History and Present Position of the Stock Market in India* makes no mention of the market practices that were the concern of various commissions of that period. Written in 1962 and towards the end of his long innings, the book is a robust defence of the stock market without the slightest acknowledgement of the need for any change. The focus is simply on the ebb and flow of external events and the market's reaction to them; practices of that age (many of which continued into the modern era) are simply ignored or taken for granted.

But Shroff's position is understandable, as he was writing a generation before the computer's advent changed financial markets; besides, in that pre-computer age, there were fewer glaring differences between the Bombay market and international best practice. Consider that even as late as 1989, H.T. Parekh, another seasoned market participant and founder of HDFC, was also silent on market practices and the need for any change. Speaking at the Phiroze Jeejeebhoy Memorial Lecture – and on the absolute brink of the most transformative period in Indian stock market history – Parekh did not offer even a hint of its approach.[41]

It must also be noted that around the time of the NSE's founding, the BSE management was caught up in other events, some of which bordered on the tragic. In fact, 1992 and 1993 were the worst years in the BSE's history and a portent of things to come. The Mehta aftermath had resulted in the market falling by half between April and August 1992; one noted participant reportedly had made plans to sell a chunk of his portfolio to buy an apartment in a prominent part of town, only to get caught in the sudden sell-off, and that experience was common to many. The bomb blasts followed on 9 March 1993, and the BSE was at its epicentre. Starting from 1.25 p.m., explosions took place in the underground car park and on the streets around the exchange. Yet the BSE never lost a single trading session – the blasts took place on a Friday, and the market opened for trading on the following Monday, with the opening seen as emblematic of Bombay's ability to come bounding back. M.R. Mayya led it all, and the brokerage community rallied around him. But the events – coinciding as they did with the NSE's formation – proved to be severely disruptive to the BSE's management and may also have been responsible for its slow response.

Even if BSE management had been far-sighted enough to see the need for change, the interests of the badla brokers who ran the BSE simply made them impervious to adjustment.

The badla financiers had their own reasons for resistance, but as brokers, they lacked the political muscle that public sector bank unions or workers had. Reform required their cooperation but only up to a point. Beyond that point, the finance ministry had powers under the

[41] H.T. Parekh, 'The Capital Market,' Phiroze Jeejeebhoy Memorial Lecture 1989, Bombay: BSE, 1989, 1–32.

SCRA that had never been used but could be if it came to the crunch. That point had now come, and so, faced with the BSE's continued intransigence, the finance ministry stepped in and, in one of those occasional cases of successful government intervention, helped found the NSE.

The National Stock Exchange

Its detractors began by saying the NSE was doomed because 'exchanges are not about technology, they're about people,' and the NSE had no people behind it.[42] Then they said the NSE was damned because it started off as a *sarkari* – or government – stock exchange. This reference to a *sarkari* exchange is a final incongruity in the story. The 1991 reform effort that resulted in the NSE's creation was about dismantling the license raj and rolling back the government's influence on economic activity. So, it is paradoxical that a key achievement of that period – the NSE itself – took place through an act of government intervention. In fact, as seen, some of the reformers themselves did not wish to will into existence a singular achievement of that era, simply because it would have been an act of government intervention in a reform effort whose philosophy was getting the government out of business. It is also surprising that few have noted this incongruity, and many years after the event, it is an unsettling fact that many of the reformers still did not see the irony of it all. But then, this is a society with little concept of the ironic. What Reinhold Niebuhr called 'apparently fortuitous incongruities in life which are discovered on closer examination, to be not merely fortuitous' simply do not exist in a country where the idea of karma dominates.[43]

The NSE started as one of the first public-sector exchanges in the world; then it took on a century-old incumbent operating a monopoly on

[42] 'People told us, "Exchanges are not about technology, they are about people."' As quoted by Ravi Narain, in Tarun Khanna, *Billions of Entrepreneurs: How China and India Are Reshaping Their Futures*, Boston, MA: Harvard Business School Press, 2011, 96.

[43] Reinhold Niebuhr, *The Irony of American History*, Chicago: University of Chicago Press, 2008, xxiv.

the country's only major liquidity pool and overtook that incumbent in short order. Even R.H. Patil, who had the mandate that started it all and who always knew he would succeed because of the BSE's complacency, got the time frame wrong. He thought it would take between five and ten years to overtake the incumbent, but the NSE became India's largest exchange in its first year of operation.[44] How did they do it?

Knowing nothing about starting or running an exchange might have been an advantage, as it entailed studying the BSE, understanding what was wrong there, and deliberately avoiding those errors. This recognition of the chance to start from scratch and free from the weight of legacy allowed the founders the freedom to conceptualize and execute as they saw fit. These were novices starting from a clean slate who used that advantage to the hilt.

Getting the big decisions right on ***ownership***, the ***business model***, and ***technology*** proved crucial.

The BSE's intermingling of ***ownership***, exchange management, and trading had led to severe principal–agent problems and conflicts of interest. By contrast, the NSE was founded on two separations: the ownership of the exchange and its management were separated from each other, and both were, in turn, separated from the right to trade on it.[45] Ownership vested with (and continues to vest with) a group of financial institutions, banks, and other intermediaries, many of whom had a direct interest in capital markets.[46] The NSE's major founders, such as IDBI and UTI Bank, were large buy side users of securities markets,

[44] Veena Venugopal, 'Meet the Man behind NSE's success,' *Outlook Money*, November 2007.

[45] On some of the policy and technical issues behind the NSE's formation and the difficulties involved in displacing existing liquidity pools, see Ajay Shah and Susan Thomas, 'David and Goliath: Displacing a Primary Market,' *Journal of Global Financial Markets*, 1(1), Spring 2000, 14–16.

[46] The NSE is owned by a set of leading financial institutions, banks, insurance companies, venture capital firms, other financial intermediaries, and some individuals. A private market exists for its shares, and shareholders discreetly enter and leave in a tightly scripted valuation game. Presently, major domestic shareholders are LIC, SBI and its subsidiary SBI Capital Markets, IFCI, and Stock Holding Corporation of India. Foreign shareholders have included Aranda Investments, Gagil FDI, SAIF II SE Investments Mauritius Limited, Veracity Investments, Goldman Sachs, Morgan Stanley, and Citigroup. Periodically, NSE shareholders have had discussions with the exchange about going public and the media has reported on its IPO plans.

and so, their incentives were aligned with the purpose of the institution, which was to create a well-functioning capital market intermediary. Still notable among the founder-owners is IDBI, the institution that gave the NSE its founding team. The NSE was structured as a for-profit company, as opposed to the BSE which – like most exchanges of its era – was structured as a not-for-profit voluntary association of persons. NSE management is kept professional, and it still enjoys the legitimacy of being led by the founding generation.

In particular, the second separation – removing the broker/trader members from the exchange's ownership and management – minimized the conflicts of interest that had plagued the BSE. These conflicts were most apparent on issues such as expansion of the membership base, adoption of customer-oriented market practices, and introduction of new technology. So, the NSE's management has no trading interests of its own, and reportedly, it doesn't trade the markets. This separation of ownership interests from trading interests – called demutualization – effectively solved much of the principal–agent problem and was, in fact, later adopted by the BSE.[47]

The NSE's first CEO, R.H. Patil, would say many years later:

> Since I had an opportunity to create a new thing, I looked at what was the most desirable thing – why not bring the best of the things that will help the market. We looked at the existing exchange and thought, let's look at its deficiencies and correct them. The first major deficiency was that brokers owned and ran the exchange. It was unjust to small brokers and investors. We said if we have to set up an exchange, it has to be for the whole country. That's why we set up the satellite communication model. We can go to any place and set up a terminal in three days. The second aspect was that brokers should not have any room in the exchange – neither ownership room nor management room. We

[47] For an early account of issues involved in exchange demutualization that also illustrates the wide range of possible outcomes, see Jennifer E. Elliott, 'Demutualization of Securities Exchanges: A Regulatory Perspective,' *IMF Working Paper*, WP/02/119, July 2002, 1–30.

> gave ownership of the exchange to institutions, management to professionals and trading operations to brokers.[48]

Paradoxically, the separation of ownership and management could lead to its own set of agency issues and thus called for particular attention to incentives.[49] The attention paid to incentives at the founding was unusual, when one remembers the public-sector origins of the NSE and the cavalier regard the public sector usually has for incentives. This attention evidenced itself in the issue of management compensation, and at the time of founding, a lengthy debate ensued over giving stock options to management. The idea was rejected, as giving shares would incentivize management to maximize profits and take away from the fledgling organization's regulatory and institution-building role. As a result, the considerable salaries of NSE management reflect the fact that stock options and other incentives are not available to them. This sort of balance between the NSE's regulatory and profit-making roles was seen as vital at the founding itself, but it was a balance that would be kept to varying degrees in later years.

The high compensation also avoided the *karmayogi* trap that is so common in India, particularly in areas such as the public and not-for-profit sectors. The *karmayogi* trap happens when the powerful cultural ideal of selfless, non-attached action as practised by the *karmayogi* is seen by society as a substitute for incentives such as money and options. It is prevalent in areas such as education or journalism, and other areas like medicine are only now beginning to escape its hold. So, the teacher gets paid next to nothing but still has to be 'dedicated', and in return, society gives them prestige and respect instead of money. But after all this, that same society subtly views any of the teacher's attempts at furthering their financial position as somehow unworthy and unbecoming of a

[48] Veena Venugopal, 'Meet the Man behind NSE's Success.'

[49] Principal–agent problems deal typically with how a principal/owner incentivizes an agent/ employee to act in a manner consistent with the principal's interests rather than the agent's interest. The attention to incentives as a way around the principal–agent problem owes much to Stephen A. Ross and his 'The Economic Theory of Agency: The Principal's Problem,' *American Economic Review*, 63 (2), May 1973, 134–39.

guru and *karmayogi*, effectively trapping them in that position. Because of the *karmayogi* trap, monetary incentives get deemphasized and therefore cost less, which is convenient for the organization meeting a payroll but less convenient for the person whose higher values are being appealed to.

The strategy and ***business model*** the NSE chose relied heavily on enfranchising groups traditionally shut out from the markets. Consequently, membership issues received the keenest consideration during the initial discussions. The overall objective – never stated as such but always kept in mind – was to end the Bombay-focused nature of the business, thereby giving it a more cosmopolitan and pan-national character.

The BSE had been a closed club, with informal yet binding ethnic and religious ties between members; you threw a stone from the top floor of the exchange and it landed on a Shah or a Sanghvi. For most of the twentieth century, only private individuals and partnerships with unlimited liability were allowed cards, and this brought its own discipline. In later years, the BSE's membership restrictions were seen as Luddite, but it is important to remember that volumes during the Century of Marking Time were hardly sufficient for the membership roster of that era.[50] Nevertheless, even when business picked up during the late 1980s, the members continued with the earlier restrictions and were reluctant to expand membership to deal with the increased volumes. These restrictions effectively cartelized membership and raised the price of membership cards to the benefit of existing members.[51] In contrast, the NSE, with its liberal membership norms, encouraged corporate membership, though only after due attention to risk management and the professional qualifications of potential members.[52]

[50] H.T. Parekh, *The Bombay Money Market*, Bombay: Oxford University Press, 1953, 66.

[51] Ajay Shah and Susan Thomas, 'David and Goliath,' 15–16.

[52] Initially, corporations or individuals could become NSE members by making a ₹10 million interest-free deposit with the exchange and agreeing to pay a fee that varied based on their trading volume. The ₹10 million deposit was substantially less than the price of a BSE membership card at the time. Presently, membership is based on elaborate combinations of trading and clearing privileges, with special provisions for big proprietary traders. Besides meeting deposit and net worth requirements,

Before the NSE, the liquidity pool – despite the presence of regional exchanges – remained at the physical floor in Bombay, particularly in the case of large orders. As a result, outside investors had to route orders through a series of correspondent brokers to the appropriate exchange, which usually meant the Bombay floor. This resulted in a great deal of uncertainty on execution, together with high transaction costs. Unlike the Bombay-focused BSE, the NSE's membership had a pan-national character from the get-go, which allowed for an easier market roll-out. Further, all investors had simultaneous, real-time access to the same screen-based order book, which seemed like a miraculous development when compared to the chaos and murkiness of the Bombay floor. As a result, the NSE essentially discovered the market for securities outside Bombay, which it did by connecting the fragmented liquidity pools and trader communities that had resulted from the SCRA's Municipal Era.

The response to all this – and particularly from the non-traditional trading communities located outside Bombay – was dramatic. The NSE's liberal membership norms and the possibility of pan-national trading allowed many big traders and investors to disintermediate the broking community and get their own memberships. This pent-up demand allowed the NSE to become the dominant exchange in its first year of operation, even without the advantage of a leveraged product that could appeal to traders.

On Day One of any new exchange's existence, its volumes are generally much lower than those of an incumbent favoured by networking effects, and it was understood that the incumbent BSE's liquidity and volumes would be far larger than the fledgling NSE. Besides, finding companies to list – and then getting them to sign complex listing agreements – would have meant overcoming the inertia of firms happy to continue with their BSE listing alone. The NSE solved these problems by automatically allowing the 1,200 most liquid scrips on the BSE to list without any further ado on the NSE.[53] Because of this arrangement,

members pay a one-time admission fee, annual subscription charges, and minimum transaction charges.

[53] Ajay Shah and Susan Thomas, 'David and Goliath,' 17.

the NSE initially had to forsake a key revenue source for any stock exchange – listing fees. Consequently, in the early years, interest from member deposits pledged with it rather than listing fees was the major source of revenue. The NSE would then shift to a transaction-based revenue model, where user charges were imposed on transactions, effectively binding the organization's financial well-being to its ability to attract transactions.[54]

Technology played a big role in all this, in keeping with all the new activity in the exchange space. More than anything else, screen-based order books are collections of telecom networks and equipment. India's telecom infrastructure – abysmal at that time – militated against using land-based technology for the fledgling exchange's technical backbone, and so, the NSE used satellite-based communications through VSATs (very small aperture terminals) for its trading network. Like decisions on market design, this was also inspired by an international example, namely the VSAT satellite networks that US department stores like Walmart used for tracking inventory and settling cash transactions.[55] For the first time in the country's history, all traders – linked to the VSAT network through computers in brokers' offices – had access to the same market at the same time on a pan-India basis.[56] This reduced transaction costs and lowered the uncertainty on order execution that had characterized the Municipal Era's system of order routing through regional brokers to the BSE floor. The BSE would respond with its own system, the BSE Online Trading System (BOLT), but its national rollout was mysteriously delayed, and this allowed the NSE a monopoly on all-India trading for a short but crucial time (a technological arms race between exchanges that once seemed like a novelty would become the norm after the NSE's founding). In later years, with improvements

[54] Ibid., 17, 19–20.

[55] Ibid.

[56] Equipment and software from vendors in the US, Canada, France, and Israel were put together in a consortium led by Tata Consultancy Services. Hong Kong-based International Securities Consultancy also assisted with the project. The NSE initially used the TCAM system that was developed in the United States for the Vancouver Stock Exchange as the basis for its trading system.

in telecom infrastructure, VSATs would be just one of the connectivity options offered by the NSE, and leased-line terrestrial-based systems would also be used.

Microstructure

But the real revolution the NSE wrought was in market microstructure – the processes and outcomes involved in exchanging financial assets under a specific set of rules.[57] The subject deals with how specific trading rules affect the price formation process. Though an important and highly technical area, the setting up of these trading rules and their daily implementation is usually taken for granted by most participants. Think of microstructure as a combination of unseen rules and computers that enforce those rules – the plumbing and pipes behind the flickering prices. In fact, a precise definition of the stock market borrows heavily from the field, and if one were to describe today's stock market in technical terms, it might go something like this: *the Indian stock market is an order-driven, screen-based, continuous time, non-specialist market with an electronic limit order book, price/time priority, and a pre-open call auction.* All these terms come from the sub-field of financial economics dealing with microstructure, and what the terms describe came into existence in the 1990s, when the NSE essentially remade the market's microstructure.

The NSE essentially upturned all notions of microstructure in India, and here too, so thorough has been the change and so indifferent the environment to what came before, that little attention has been paid to this transformation. There are only scattered references to the old market in most accounts, and the whiz kids of the 1990s made little attempt to understand what they were replacing.

In contrast to today's screen-based, order-driven market, for much of the twentieth century, the BSE had been a floor-based, quote-driven market that restricted itself to Bombay, in keeping with Sections 13 and

[57] Comprehensive treatments of the subject are found in Larry Harris, *Trading and Exchanges: Market Microstructure for Practitioners*, New York: Oxford University Press, 2003 and Maureen O'Hara, *Market Microstructure Theory*, Cambridge, MA: Blackwell, 1995.

19 of the SCRA.[58] As was the custom since Premchand Roychand's time, brokers could be both principal and agent, transacting their proprietary books as principals, or buying and selling on behalf of their clients as agents. Besides being both principal and agent, Bombay brokers could also be market makers or jobbers. There were no prescribed distinctions between brokers and jobbers in Bombay. A similar situation had existed on the London Stock Exchange (LSE) till 1909, following which London switched to a 'single capacity' system that laid down formal distinctions between the two roles.[59] Bombay however continued with the informal system with no clear distinctions between brokers and jobbers.

In their capacity as market makers or jobbers, Bombay's brokers stood at specific spots on the BSE trading floor and announced continuous two-way quotes in a stock.[60] Many of these brokers who doubled as jobbers had no contact with the public and only dealt with other brokers; brokers acting as agents for the public usually dealt with these 'brokers as jobbers' for order execution, and the latter tried to keep their books balanced by day's end, selling all they had bought and vice versa.[61] During market hours when there were more buyers than sellers, jobbers raised their quotes to discourage buyers and encourage sellers, causing the price to move up; the reverse happened to the downside.

These BSE jobbers were similar to market makers such as London's jobbers or the specialists employed by the NYSE, except for one crucial distinction. On those exchanges, jobbers or specialists had formal rights and obligations, while BSE jobbers had neither rights nor obligations and exercised their functions in an informal fashion. This resulted in important differences between the BSE and those markets. First (and

[58] The market's microstructure in the pre-Independence era is surveyed in P.J. Thomas, *Report on the Regulation of the Stock Market in India*, New Delhi: Ministry of Finance, 1948, 42–54; the trading floor of the 50s is described in H.T. Parekh, *The Bombay Money Market*, 66–69.

[59] Ranald C. Michie, *The London Stock Exchange: A History*, New York, NY: Oxford University Press, 2001. London's 'single capacity' system itself ended with the exchange's Big Bang reforms of October 1986.

[60] Bombay Stock Exchange, 'How the Stock Market Functions,' Bombay: BSE, Undated, 3–5.

[61] Ibid., 3.

taking the NYSE by way of comparison), the specialist in (say) IBM was a designated party with the exclusive right to make the market in IBM, a right that came with the dual obligations of keeping IBM stock as inventory, besides standing ready to buy or sell IBM to prevent market imbalances. By contrast, the BSE did not give exclusive transaction rights in a counter to jobbers, and so, it did not take from them any obligation to make the market in that counter. Second, there was usually an exclusive specialist per stock arrangement on the NYSE, as opposed to the BSE, where there were several jobbers who made the market in pivotal players such as Reliance and Hindustan Lever.[62] Third, and because of that exclusivity, the NYSE specialist could not refuse to buy or sell IBM, unlike India where the informal jobber had the right to refuse a Reliance order. Finally, the NYSE specialist's spreads were closely monitored by exchange authorities, but on the BSE, the jobber quoted as he pleased.

This situation raised agency issues and came with inbuilt conflicts of interest. Critically, as jobbers, brokers knew the order book – after all, they had created it – and so, they knew the direction in which the market was headed. In huge bull markets, they gave up their jobbing activities and speculated profitably for their own account, thereby increasing the order imbalances on the buy side when those imbalances were least needed. As a result, in times of market stress, the BSE restricted jobbers' activities, but this was the opposite of the required course of action – if they were really performing their market-making functions, jobbers' operations should have been almost unrestricted on such occasions. Market microstructure as a field of knowledge did not exist in those days, which led to such situations.

Misunderstanding about the jobber's role also caused misunderstanding about BSE operations. For example, illiquid counters usually had high jobber spreads, and so, a jobber could quote (say) 212–29 as *his* buy-sell spread on a stock. Since the jobber was the market,

[62] Ibid. The NYSE gave exclusive rights to the specialist to make the market in a stock; by contrast, London's market had competing market makers (often as many as three or four) for each scrip. On the NYSE, specialists are now known as 'designated market makers'.

this was the market quote. A client's broker would have to buy for his client (and from the jobber) at 229, followed perhaps by another client's broker executing a sale for his client at 212; assuming (only for the sake of clarity) there were no other transactions in that session, this resulted in 229 being recorded as the day's high price in the next day's newspapers. This gave the impression that the client's broker was fleecing the buy side client by quoting the day's high price, but it was often the jobbers' high spreads and the resulting bid-ask bounce (the client's constant buy at 229 and sell at 212 as the client's broker executed with the jobber) that led to the phenomenon.[63] But other market practices could not be put down to misunderstanding, and among these was the practice of clubbing the brokerage commission with the price, which effectively hid the commissions and made it difficult for the customer to shop for lower rates.[64]

In keeping with accepted practice at that time, the trading floor was laid out by counter, and key stocks or 'pivotals' had designated areas where brokers who worked those counters tended to gather and trade. Jobbers stood on a raised ledge against the wall of the trading floor while brokers and dealers jostled in the centre.[65] The floor may not have been an efficient way to trade, but the dull, powerful roar of the BSE ring during trading hours was a memorable experience for the outsiders who observed it. In the 1950s, H.T. Parekh records that there were about 800 traders in the ring, but in later years, each BSE cardholder got 7 passes to enter the ring, which allowed for about 4,000 passes in

[63] In early surveys, customers often complained about being charged the high prices of the day's trading. See L.C. Gupta, *Expert Study of Trading in Shares in Stock Exchanges*, 31.

[64] Clubbing brokerage with the price was an established market practice and noticed for the first time in 1937 by Morison. See Walter B. Morison, *Report of the Stock Exchange Enquiry Committee*, Bombay: Government Central Press, 1937, 15–16. For a catalogue of market practices on the eve of the reform effort, see L.M. Bhole, 'The Indian Capital Market at Crossroads,' *Vikalpa*, Vol. 20, No. 2, April–June 1995, 29–38.

[65] The trading floor and market practices of the post-Independence era were also outlined by US SEC staff on consulting assignments. See United States Securities and Exchange Commission (SEC), *Regulation of the Indian Securities Markets: A Preliminary Survey*, by Norman S. Poser and David Silver, Washington, D.C.: January 1965, 22–30.

all.[66] Women were absent from the exchange floor for most of the market's history till Deena Mehta came along in the late 80s and breached that bastion.[67] By 1995, the floor itself was gone, and so, female floor traders from this period remained a very small and exclusive group of pioneers that included Ila Gupta and Aarti Kotak.[68] On an average day in the early 90s, well over 3,000 traders thronged the ring, shouting and gesticulating in a single enclosed space.[69] In fact, the old BSE ring had one of the world's largest crowds on a stock market floor, in line with what the Chicago pits or the Big Board floor had accommodated in their heyday. Noise levels were incredibly high which made verbal communication difficult, so eye contact followed by hand signals was the usual practice while consummating a trade.[70]

In 1968, Louis Malle, the noted French *auteur*, filmed the BSE trading floor and captured the sheer physicality of floor trading in that era. During bull moves (unknown to Malle, the steel speculation of the late 60s was in full play during his shooting), floor trading became a contact sport, and traders could be seen grabbing other traders by the face to move them into each other's lines of sight; to prevent being swept away by the surging throng, some traders (most likely jobbers) clung onto their posts by inserting one arm through a leather strap.[71]

Members with extra passes usually handed them on to *taravaniwala*s. These were small-time jobbers – numbering about a 1,000 – who quoted both sides of the trade for the non-pivotals and worked inside

[66] H.T. Parekh, *The Bombay Money Market*, 67.

[67] Sameer Kochhar, *BSE: Journey of an Aspiring Nation,* Gurugram: Skoch Media Pvt. Ltd., 17–18.

[68] Ila Bharat Gupta, interview with the author, Mumbai, August 2021. Ila Gupta also figures in another incident in the exchange's history. In those days, BSE cards were transferred to sons free of charge, while daughters inheriting the card were treated like outsiders and had to pay transfer charges of ₹50,000. Gupta interceded with M.R. Mayya on this issue and got BSE bylaws changed to bring inheritance rights on par.

[69] M.R. Mayya, 'Regulatory Framework for Stock Markets: The Indian Experience,' *Symposium on Capital Market Development and Privatisation*, Bombay: Commonwealth Secretariat, 1990, 190.

[70] BSE floor operations of the 80s and early 90s are recounted by Deena Mehta in Sameer Kochhar, *BSE: Journey of an Aspiring Nation,* 99–100.

[71] The film is available on YouTube. See *Phantom India,* Episode 7, Bombay-The Future India, directed by Louis Malle (1969; Paris: Nouvelles Éditions de Films), Documentary. (51:50)

the spread.[72] They were supposed to transact only in their member firm's name and not for their own account, but this rule was often ignored, which led to frequent problems with order matching and confirmation.

Jamnadas Morarjee recorded that markets in the late nineteenth century commenced at 1 p.m., but by the 1920s the exchange's rules called for trading between 12 p.m. and 2 p.m. for badla 'specified list' shares, with cash list shares allowed to trade a little longer.[73] The 12 to 2 timing continued well into the modern era. Trading hours were subsequently extended to 3 p.m., but it was only with the introduction of screen trading in 1995 that the familiar trading day between 10 a.m. and 3.30 p.m. emerged. In later years, the opening was advanced to 9.15 a.m., where it remains to the present day (the NSE had a longer trading day right from inception, and it was only in recent years that trading hours were synchronized across exchanges).

Yet the number of transactions that resulted from all this was astonishing and has not been fully appreciated to this day. In 1980, average bargains per day came in at about 4,000, but with the onset of the Harshad Mehta bull of the early 90s, daily bargains rose to about 1,00,000.[74] By contrast, around the same period of the early 90s, the NYSE traded about 80,000 bargains a day. Note also that the NYSE had a full 6.5-hour trading day to do so, as opposed to the 2-hour trading period on the BSE.[75] So the per hour volume of transactions was much higher on the BSE – perhaps the highest in the world for that time –

[72] L.C. Gupta, *Stock Exchange Trading in India: Agenda for Reform*, New Delhi: Society for Capital Market Research and Development, 1992, 96; L.C. Gupta, *Expert Study of Trading in Shares in Stock Exchanges*, 32–33.

[73] Seth Jamnadas Morarjee J.P., 'The Native Share and Stock Brokers' Association: Origin and Growth of the Bombay Stock Exchange,' *Federal Observer*, Stock Exchange Special Number, Vol. 1, Nos. 36 and 37, 10 November 1940, 11; Bombay Stock Exchange, 'Draft Rules of the Native Share and Stock Brokers' Association,' Bombay: BSE, 1937, 69.

[74] Bombay Stock Exchange, *Settlement, Share Depository, and Trading Systems*, Bombay: BSE, 1991, 1.

[75] Computer Maintenance Corporation, *Technical Project Report*, 9; Bombay Stock Exchange, *The Stock Market Today*, Bombay: The Stock Exchange Foundation, 1993, 6; M.R. Mayya, 'Reflections on the Changing Scenario of the Indian Stock Markets,' A.D. Shroff Memorial Lecture, 1994, in *Glimpses of Indian Stock Markets*, Mumbai: Indian Institute of Capital Markets, 2010, 21. NYSE trading hours (since 1985) are between 9.30 a.m. and 4 p.m.

though the value of individual transactions was much lower. The limited trading hours were also a key causal factor behind the kerb market – the street market outside the exchange – and so, for decades, the kerb served as a key market institution.[76] *Khangi bhao* or *band ke bhao* were terms often used for kerb trading. Lore has Indian kerb markets as a public phenomenon, but because of the limited trading hours, one party on the kerb was often a broker trying to meet a client order that came in after the two-hour trading period. Closing quotations on kerb transactions that took place till late in the evening influenced the next day's opening prices, and some participants manipulated closing quotes on the kerb to influence market opening prices.

Margining was an important part of the microstructure. In the pre-reform era, its significance grew over time, and its import continues to resonate in today's margin-driven derivatives markets. As seen earlier, for much of the twentieth century, the badla system had no margin requirements and business usually meant receiving or paying differences in unmargined naked forwards. Later, margining's importance arose from the absence of brokerage capital requirements; surprising though it may seem today, in the early days there were no capital requirements that linked a brokerage's volume of business with the capital it commanded.[77] Later such requirements were introduced, but they were quite nominal, and the exchange preferred enforcing margin limits on positions to imposing capital requirements, on firms. As a result, brokerages undercapitalized to begin with, continued to be so, and often lacked the capital to fund client positions; in turn, brokerages were predisposed to demanding ever lower margins for their clients, which meant greater leverage and risk for the broader market. Crucially, exchange governing boards were dominated by brokers anyway, who were also predisposed to lowering margin requirements, and this exposed the system to further risk.[78]

[76] Ministry of Finance, *Report of the Study Group to Examine the Issue and Problems Relating to Unregulated Share Trading Counters and Other Dealers in Securities*, Ajit Day (Convenor), New Delhi: Ministry of Finance, 1991, 28.

[77] M.R. Mayya, 'Regulatory Framework for Stock Markets,' 193.

[78] Even when BSE management raised margins, regulatory arbitrage took place through *chalu upla* transactions – a sort of unofficial squaring up and netting between parties.

The margin regime changed over the years, but at the peak of the badla era, it usually consisted of three types – daily, carry forward, and ad hoc margins – with the combined total rarely going beyond 10 or 15 per cent.[79] Notional intra-settlement profits over a monthly (and later fortnightly) settlement period were also applied towards margins, reducing them even further; the length of the settlement period, market volatility, and very high leverage meant that the side that had bet right and made substantial intra-settlement profits could avoid paying up margin through this provision alone. As a result, margins were rarely enough for the price volatility of that time, which left the system open to repeated crises that were usually settled by compromises and bargaining over 'relief'.[80]

Remarkably, the BSE's margining system of the 1980s was contrarian, so in a falling market, bulls paid half the margin bears paid, effectively doubling their speculative capital; in a rising market, the opposite took place.[81] This instinctively contrarian position was extraordinary for an institution and one of the few cases in financial history when an exchange officially leaned against the market as a matter of policy. In effect, this made the BSE management a party to market conditions, another unprecedented move that explains the extreme discretion the management gave itself in regulation. The tendency towards dirigisme and interference that would characterize Indian regulation in the modern era was apparent from its early years, and margining itself became another instrument of regulation rather than a routine of microstructure.[82]

[79] Ibid.; L.C. Gupta, *Expert Study of Trading in Shares in Stock Exchanges*, 15, 23. In 2000 – during the final days of the badla system and against the backdrop of the IT bull run – the complex margining arrangements included: daily margins, mark to market margins, additional carry forward margins, and additional volatility margins. See The Stock Exchange, Mumbai, *Inspection Manual: Revised Edition*, Mumbai: BSE, 2000, 16–18.

[80] L.C. Gupta, *Stock Exchange Trading in India: Agenda for Reform*, 44. Value at Risk (VAR) methodologies were unknown at that time.

[81] M.R. Mayya, 'Regulation of Stock Market and Investor Protection,' in University of Delhi, *Proceedings of a National Seminar*, 131–32.

[82] According to Mayya: 'Calling for stability in these rates, as is being done by a section, is displaying ignorance of the objective of the margin requirement.' Ibid., 132.

Yet the BSE badla system – the unmargined (or lightly margined) naked forward – produced remarkable liquidity for the big counters, and it is crucial to remember that for much of the Century of Marking Time, this liquidity came despite the absence of a domestic and foreign buy side, and despite proscriptions on bank financing of market activity. The liquidity and thick order books on pivotals such as ACC have been noted earlier. Spreads on pivotals in the badla 'specified list' remained among the lowest in the world for that time and ranged between 0.1 and 0.25 per cent.[83] Spreads on badla stocks were often lower than spreads for the most liquid scrips on the London exchange, a remarkable feat considering the primitive market infrastructure of that era. The real issue was with the 'non-specified' B group shares outside the badla list that traded fully for cash. On these, spreads were often as high as 15 per cent, so high that there was practically no liquid market in such stocks.[84] The aforementioned study also found spreads on Bombay's illiquid stocks much wider than on comparable stocks on the London exchange. Badla, therefore, concentrated liquidity and market action in its own list but at a cost to the broader market. As seen earlier, the specified badla shares usually numbered not more than 150 out of over 5,000 scrips, yet this 3 per cent of badla stocks usually accounted for between 80 and 90 per cent of traded volumes.[85]

Nevertheless, in later years, the narrowness of the market's liquidity was exaggerated by the excessive breadth of market listing. After all, 150 out of over 5,000 companies cornering liquidity looks disconcerting, but if the base's larger number was (say) 800, the excessive concentration of liquidity in the badla list would not look so alarming. In fact, the IPO waves between 1985 and 1995 had resulted in a large increase in listed scrips, but many among the 5,000 were poorly capitalized companies

[83] M.R. Mayya, 'Regulatory Framework for Stock Markets,' 190.

[84] M.R. Mayya, 'Reflections on the Changing Scenario,' 22.

[85] Various accounts emphasized this tendency of the badla system to concentrate volumes in its own stocks. See M.R. Mayya, 'Recent Developments in Stock Exchanges,' *Seminar on Capital Market–Problems and Prospects*, 4 February 1988, Bombay: BSE, 1988, 7–10; M.R. Mayya, 'Regulation of Stock Market and Investor Protection,' 131; the lack of market breadth is also noted in L.C. Gupta, *Stock Exchange Trading in India*, 55–62.

with little liquidity that had no business being listed anyway; many were also bankrupt companies that lingered on due to an inadequate insolvency regime. So, though badla had a tendency to concentrate liquidity in the pivotals, many of the counters that remained illiquid were so for reasons that had little to do with the badla system. Badla concentrated volumes in the blue chips and narrowed market breadth, but the vast number of small scrips with no volumes – which should not have been listed anyway – made the market breadth seem narrower than it actually was. In their eagerness to make a reform case, the whiz kids of the 1990s simply did not take this into account, and the BSE did not do a good job of explaining its own case. But the BSE's inability to do so was to have consequences, as the artificial narrowness of the market's liquidity pool was a key reason behind the NSE's founding.

Few of the conferences of the 1990s made an attempt to document and analyse the extant microstructure along the above lines, and little effort was made by the whiz kids to even understand the BSE's procedures. In the conference papers, surprisingly little is available on the basic distinction between quote- and order-driven systems, and much of the discussion focuses on the merits of floor- vs. screen-based trading. The implicit assumption was that such screen trading would be through an order book, and the biggest advantage of such a system – that it did not have to monitor market intermediaries – was occasionally mentioned.

The biggest change from the past was precisely in this, that the NSE's trading system – the National Exchange for Automated Trading (NEAT) – was screen-based and without a physical floor. Significantly, it was an order-driven system, as opposed to the BSE floor, which was quote-driven. The NSE used an electronic limit order book (ELOB) to aggregate orders and then match buyers and sellers on a computer using a price/time priority rule.[86] Orders were first ranked on price, and then orders bunched at the same price were ranked according to the

[86] Ironically, the BSE had been the first to recommend an ELOB – but only for thinly traded shares. See R.R. Nair, 'A Computerized System for Improving the Liquidity of Thinly Traded Securities in the Bombay Stock Exchange,' in Bombay Stock Exchange, *35th Meeting of the Standing Committee of the Presidents of the Stock Exchanges in India*, Bombay: BSE, 1988, 69–72.

time they were entered.[87] The top 'bid' on the buy side of the order book (usually the left side) was the highest rate at which an anonymous trader (or the market) would buy, and the top 'ask' on the sell side of the order book (usually the right side) was the lowest rate at which an anonymous trader (or the market) would sell.

So, on the buy side, the ELOB might rank anonymous buy orders (the bid) at 393.15, 392.8, 392.4, and 391.9 with various buy quantities against each price (buy bids are ranked in descending order). On the sell side, the ELOB might rank anonymous sell orders (the ask) at 393.2, 393.6, 393.9, and 394.1, with various sell quantities against each price (sell bids are ranked in ascending order). In this example, the highest buyer and lowest seller would come in at the market rate of 393.15/393.2, and if the buyer reaches out, the trade would take place at 393.2. Impatient buyers wanting to fill orders would then have to reach for the next ask at 393.6, and so, the stock price would tick higher. At the market clearing price, Trader X would (typically) have to buy at the ask (393.2) and sell at the bid (393.15). So, Trader X always loses by buying high and selling low, and this bid-ask spread together with brokerage, taxes, and impact cost is what Trader X pays to the anonymous trader/market for the liquidity they are providing Trader X. The moment Trader X accesses the market – and trades by reaching for price – he loses all this, and that is just the way life is in the markets. Alternately, instead of taking liquidity, Trader X can be the anonymous trader/market and provide liquidity by just entering his quote in the ELOB, but that means facing execution risk, especially if the quotes are distant from the market rate.

This screen-based and computerized trading had the advantage of being transparent and open to surveillance; it also improved price discovery and removed the inefficiencies of the open outcry system.[88]

[87] The market opens with a call auction which runs for 15 minutes, following which trading takes place on price-time priority through the matching system of the limit order book. Traders can view the best five bid-ask prices at any given point in time.

[88] The BSE's open outcry system sometimes had conversion rates as low as 30 per cent, in contrast to the NSE's limit order book which resulted in conversion rates exceeding 90 per cent from the early years itself.

Critically, it promoted equal market access by allowing participants across the country to simultaneously view the full market (the ELOB across stocks) on a real-time basis; this improved the position of investors outside Bombay, who previously had to work through multiple intermediaries to access the BSE's physical floor.[89] It was a change that effectively ended the Municipal Era. Tick sizes – the amount prices were allowed to move in a single step – were also kept at a standard 5 paise or ₹0.05.[90] By contrast, in earlier times, tick sizes on the BSE ranged from ₹0.25 to ₹1.00, and *taravaniwala*s who operated within the spread often lobbied for even higher tick sizes.

Noting the advantages of a screen-based order book, the BSE launched its own system called BSE Online Trading (BOLT) within a record 50 days, and the system went online in March 1995. By now, the NSE was running away with the market, and any debate on badla vs. non-badla or quote- vs. order-driven systems was redundant. The BSE opted for a near replica of the NSE's system, and so, the NSE would decide for the BSE what the BSE could not decide for itself. But the BSE's attempt at catch-up was hampered in the early years by BOLT's restricted use to its home city – now Mumbai, after the 1995 name change – and it would be some time before the system spread nationally. In fact, in the crucial early years, Bombay and the regionals were anyway barred from setting up terminals outside their geographic municipal areas, while the NSE with its national mandate had no such restrictions.

Later, allegations would surface that SEBI's withholding of permission for BSE BOLT expansion during this crucial period allowed the NSE to clean up the trading markets outside Mumbai. Earlier, approval of the BSE's request for membership expansion had also been delayed for a considerable period, and it would take almost two years for that approval to come through (the membership expansion would have allowed the

[89] The BSE trading floor had tried to improve access by allowing members' staff and remisiers on the floor, but this raised issues of manipulation and bad trades. United States Securities and Exchange Commission (SEC), *Regulation of the Indian Securities Markets,* 24–25.

[90] Ajay Shah and Susan Thomas, 'David and Goliath,' 17. The NSE's uniform tick size of ₹0.05 for all stocks would also become a standard market practice.

BSE to raise the resources necessary to take on the NSE). M.R. Mayya, the BSE's effective head at the time, would later openly claim that the BSE was a victim of SEBI's machinations.[91] None had noticed that both the second and third SEBI chairmen – G.V. Ramakrishna and S.S. Nadkarni – had been present at that April 1992 finance ministry meeting that effectively founded the NSE and were closely involved in its early setup. In a fast-changing environment – when the market's entire microstructure was up for grabs for the first and only time in its history – withholding permission was all that was needed to sabotage one side's effort.[92]

This sequence of events was to set a pattern for the future. In fact, this would mark the start of a long period when the finance ministry and SEBI would instinctively favour the new exchange in its endeavours, often at a severe cost to the BSE.[93] Unfettered by custom or tradition and with a professional management team, the NSE would continue setting the agenda on Indian capital market reform for years to come, with the century-old incumbent BSE always playing catch-up. Another end result was the rather neat duality in the Indian stock market today – two major exchanges, two clearing and settlement systems, two depositories, and two derivatives markets. This symmetry also makes future empirical research on Indian equities a lot easier, as having a non-fragmented microstructure with only two exchanges makes it easier to gather and analyse empirical data. Large amounts of electronic data are out there, waiting to be analysed for insights.

Though the NSE's screen-based, order-driven system was to become a standard for the stock market, the move was not without its drawbacks.[94]

[91] M.R. Mayya, *Glimpses of Indian Stock Markets*, 235, 262.

[92] A generation later, Jignesh Shah, a commodity exchange founder, would also claim that SEBI was delaying various approvals to favour his NSE-sponsored rivals.

[93] Sameer Kochhar, *BSE: Journey of an Aspiring Nation*, 97.

[94] For surveys of the market's early microstructure, see Ajay Shah and Susan Thomas, 'Developing the Indian Capital Market,' *India: A Financial Sector for the Twenty-first Century*, eds. James A. Hanson and Sanjay Kathuria, New Delhi: Oxford University Press, 1999, 205–65. Also see Ajay Shah, Susan Thomas, and Michael Gorham, *India's Financial Markets: An Insider's Guide to How the Markets Work*, Noida: Elsevier, 2008, 55–80.

Quote-driven markets such as the old BSE had one advantage. Order execution was usually guaranteed, as the market maker – the jobber or specialist – quoted on both sides and made his money from the spread; quote-driven markets therefore reduce the risk of buyers and sellers not finding counterparts in a timely fashion in illiquid securities. So, the advantage of a quote-driven, specialist-led market is the liquidity it presents, as market makers are obliged to either match an incoming order with another order or fill it from their own inventory. Hence the continued prevalence of modified quote-driven exchanges such as New York, London, and Nasdaq. The NYSE, for instance, is a hybrid market that still uses a modified quote-driven system through its specialists (now called designated market makers). These market makers, in return for being given the right to deal in a blue-chip security, are obliged to maintain inventories of that stock and stand ready to create an orderly market in the counter by buying and selling. Specialists are particularly important for large orders that can impact price, as they use both their inventories and order books to smooth over the discontinuous price moves that can take place when large orders hit the market. The old BSE did not have a formal specialist system, but informally, the quote-driven system allowed many floor traders to double up as specialists. When small, they were the *taravaniwala*s and often viewed as parasites, despite the importance of their market-making functions.[95] When large, they were jobbers, and functioned as informal specialists while making the market in big counters.[96] Poor liquidity was also a complaint in the old BSE system, but that was caused as much by the low number of brokers as by the structural flaws in the quote-driven system.[97]

In contrast to quote-driven markets, order-driven non-specialist markets – India's present format – simply aggregate orders in the

[95] Rather than a few big jobbers or specialists, there were many *taravaniwalas* who functioned like the former but without any obligation to make markets. H.T. Parekh, *The Bombay Money Market*, 68; Walter B. Morison, *Report of the Stock Exchange Enquiry Committee*, 28–29.

[96] Floor operations of jobbers are outlined in some detail in Santosh Nair, *Bulls Bears and Other Beasts*, New Delhi: Pan Macmillan, 2016, 17–25.

[97] For generations, the BSE cartelized membership and restricted the number of brokers to maximize the value of its 'card' at auction, which kept the number of brokers artificially low.

ELOB and don't have designated market makers or specialists.[98] As a result, liquidity can be an issue. In our example, with the market rate at 393.15/393.2, the buyer reaches out and consummates the trade at 393.2, but if the market rate is, say, 385/398 with a ₹13 spread and neither side is willing to trade because of that, the order book freezes and liquidity vanishes. So, the present NSE/BSE order-driven system, while transparent and guaranteeing that all investors see the same market, has the disadvantage of not having specialists or market makers. As a result, order execution is not guaranteed, and this is an issue with ELOB-driven markets. The absence of market makers is especially felt during bear sell-offs such as that of 2008, when liquidity dries up only to turn the sell-off into panic. It also becomes difficult for the buy side to accumulate big stakes discreetly, i.e., without driving up the price and increasing impact cost. The problem gets exacerbated by the wide range of stocks in Indian markets; the top 150 stocks benefit from arbitrage-driven volumes between cash and derivatives markets, but for the remaining stocks, liquidity can be an issue, and this problem has carried over from badla's time.

And yet, the key advantage of the present system is transparency, as it clearly shows all market orders and the prices at which participants are willing to buy and sell.[99] The elimination of market makers has also removed the need for their complex surveillance, which would have placed considerable demands on regulatory bandwidth, and this elimination was an important advantage. Finally, eliminating specialists has improved symmetry among participants. Surprisingly, there is little in the record on the above trade-offs between quote- and order-driven systems, and it was the 'electronic' in the electronic limit order book (or screen-based trading, as the popular nomenclature went) that was the focus of the many debates of that era.

[98] For a technical discussion on the differences between quote- and order-driven markets, see Larry Harris, *Trading and Exchanges*, 92–94, 112–38.

[99] The system allows for iceberg orders, where a trader can disclose a fraction, or more, of order quantity.

New Markets and Derivatives

By the 1990s, the earlier raison d'être – running a stock market without an organized buy side and proscriptions on bank lending into the market – for badla was waning and systemic issues came to dominate discussions. Financial futures – first launched in Chicago in the early 1970s – were reaching the peak of their worldwide popularity at about this time, and references to that experience with derivatives had started taking place in Indian stock exchange reviews.[100]

Nevertheless, a new derivatives segment would exist alongside an extant market that had extensive derivative-like features. This presented a dilemma. One solution was to separate the cash from the forward market while doing away with the derivatives-like features of badla. This separation called for a derivatives segment to deal with the market's perennial need for a leveraged product that built trading volumes. The other alternative would have been a straightforward system to buy stocks on margin, but that was not really considered. Even if considered, such a system would have overlapped with badla's features, and more crucially, it would have lacked the hedging properties offered by a full-fledged derivatives market. Complicating matters was the singular fact that badla's carry forward aspects were also a settlement system, which meant that decisions on badla were effectively decisions on the settlement system. This in turn meant decisions on badla and the settlement system could not be made independent of decisions on derivatives, and L.C. Gupta and M.R. Mayya document it as such.[101]

Naturally, all this met with opposition from the BSE, as any new system would compete with the badla system that accounted for the bulk of BSE volumes. For some time, the BSE fobbed off any attempt to reform badla by setting as a precondition this simultaneous introduction of a settlement system with a derivatives segment. Taken together, all

[100] See Leo Melamed, 'The Rise of Financial Futures: The CME and Beyond,' *The Stock Exchange Review: May 1998*, Mumbai: The Stock Exchange, Mumbai, 1998, 5–8.

[101] L.C. Gupta, *Stock Exchange Trading in India: Agenda for Reform*, 88; M.R. Mayya, *Stock Exchange: Developments and Regulation*, Mumbai: The Stock Exchange, Mumbai, 1993, 156.

this looked like a distant pipe dream, so what better way to fob off reform efforts than by setting as a precondition a pipe dream that could not be met. And so it went for some years, till in 2001 that pipe dream suddenly became a reality.

The 1990s had been a period of severe market volatility that led to repeated payment and settlement crises. By now, and because of the repeated crises, bans, and reinstatements, the belief grew that badla could not be reformed. Crucially, by now, the NSE had completed its first year of operations and even overtaken the BSE on volumes. In December 1995, the NSE put out its first request to start a derivatives segment. Yet, it would be a good five years before a derivatives market actually came into being, and in that hiatus, extensive politicking took place over the segment.

In this hiatus, two committees first recommended derivatives markets and then outlined their basic features, particularly on risk management (since it was the Committee Era, much action on market design took place through them). The March 1998 L.C. Gupta committee, influenced in large part by the intervening crises on Harshad Mehta and MS Shoes, was the first to recommend derivatives markets, following which the October 1998 J.R. Varma committee worked out the technical details of the methodology that produced risk management protocols. There followed a confusing and yet significant period when the carry forward mechanism, the settlement cycle, and derivatives markets were worked on simultaneously. Both exchanges competed in launching carry forward products with lending/borrowing mechanisms for stocks, the settlement cycle was progressively reduced, and steps were taken for the launch of derivatives markets. The BSE's badla was seen as coexisting with nascent derivatives markets, and in fact, a last and final expansion of the badla list took place in 1998, when 50 scrips were introduced; this took the badla list to about 150 stocks, a number that was among the highest ever.[102]

[102] Bombay Stock Exchange, *The Stock Exchange Review: March 1998*, Mumbai: The Stock Exchange, Mumbai, 1998, 24.

In line with the Gupta and Varma reports, derivatives markets were introduced in options and futures across stocks and indexes between mid-2000 and late 2001. The coexistence with badla continued, but in March 2001, the Ketan Parekh IT stock crisis broke which, following as it did the earlier crises of the 1990s, changed views on the badla product. In April 2001, a crucial J.R. Varma committee report recommended the end of the century-old badla system and a migration to derivatives trading.[103] This was subsequently adopted by SEBI, and between March and December 2001, badla carry forward systems were banned, all stocks were moved to rolling settlements, and single stock futures introduction was accelerated to give the market a leveraged product for stocks.

The introduction of derivatives gives the impression of a chaotic series of events and actions set against a milieu of remarkable turbulence that somehow worked out in the end. In later years, it became fashionable to claim that the NSE's runaway early success was somehow connected with its dominance of derivatives markets, but that is not the case. As we have seen, the NSE commenced trading in 1994 and achieved leadership in the cash market shortly after that, but its derivatives products were introduced much later. So, the reasons for the NSE's early success lay elsewhere: in the introduction of screen-based trading with a transparent order book, in the creation of a pan-Indian market for the first time, and in the discovery of new trading communities outside Mumbai. Nevertheless, the 2001 badla ban put an end to the BSE's position as an exchange that could compete with the NSE for order flow. The NSE would then go on to monopolize derivatives markets despite being briefly, but unsuccessfully, challenged by the BSE. Measured by number of contracts traded or cleared, the NSE is now the world's largest exchange for derivatives.[104]

[103] Securities and Exchange Board of India (SEBI), *Report of the Group on Deferral Products in Rolling Settlement*, Mumbai: Securities and Exchange Board of India, April 2001. A later chapter on derivatives has a detailed treatment of these events.

[104] Staff Writer, 'NSE Is World's Largest Derivatives Exchange for 2nd Consecutive Year,' *Mint*, 21 January 2021.

SEBI and the Final Links: Clearing and Settlement, Dematerialization

A new sarkar emerged to regulate this new world – the Securities and Exchange Board of India (SEBI). It was a little late in coming. Successive commissions – Atlay (1924) and Morison (1937) – had used government intervention as a veiled threat to get the BSE, a voluntary self-regulating association of persons, to reform itself.[105] After Independence, that pretence was dropped, and the Thomas report of 1948 called for a regulator similar to America's Securities and Exchange Commission (SEC). It even gave that regulator a name, the National Investment Commission, nomenclature that was more appropriate for a public investment body than a regulator.[106] A few years later, Cooverji H. Bhabha, the first Commerce Minister, made another pitch for an SEC-type regulator but to little effect; the brokers' club continued to have its way here, and things proceeded unchanged for a long time. SEBI's establishment would take place a full two generations after the Thomas report that first called for its creation.

Besides regulation, SEBI's founding objectives were investor protection and market development. There was no mention of issuers in its founding mission, itself an unusual declaration of intent in favour of investors. At the regulator's creation in the early 1990s, there was no organized buy side of mutual funds, and so, investors meant the little guys, the trading and investing public. As SEBI's remit is only securities regulation, India is among a handful of countries – besides the US, France, and Italy – that continue to believe in separate regulators for the securities, insurance, and banking businesses.[107] In other countries, the above businesses are regulated through a variety

[105] Sir Wilfrid Atlay, *Report of the Bombay Stock Exchange Enquiry Committee*, Bombay: Government Central Press, 1924, 2, 19.

[106] P.J. Thomas, *Report on the Regulation of the Stock Market in India*, 102–12, 122–26.

[107] For an overview of early Indian securities market regulation see Zia Mody, 'Securities Regulation,' *Capital Markets in India*, eds. Rajesh Chakrabarti and Sankar De, New Delhi: Sage Publications, 2010, 343–74.

of combinations and occasionally through an umbrella regulator for all.[108]

SEBI was created by administrative fiat as a non-statutory body in 1988, with S.A. Dave as its first chairman. It became operational as an autonomous body with statutory powers in 1992, through the passage of an eponymous act of that year. Simultaneously, the Controller of Capital Issues, the panjandrum that controlled equity issuance and pricing, was shut down – its approvals, in any case, were a formality by the late 1980s – and the Capital Issues (Control) Act of 1947 was repealed. SEBI's independence and its clear and sole focus on securities markets regulation were unique features in India's financial architecture at that time.

SEBI's founding in the 1990s also marked the start of a second round of legislative activity that shaped the market. The first round in the 1950s was defined by the Companies Act and the SCRA, but this second bout of legislation focused on the market's regulation and microstructure. Between 1992 and 2003, nine major legislative interventions – of which the SEBI Act and the Depositories Act are key – would lay the legal groundwork for a new regulatory framework and microstructure.[109] Much of the finance ministry's regulatory authority over the market, which under the SCRA existed on paper but was seldom used, was now transferred to SEBI, where it existed on paper and was repeatedly used.

In the early years, like other fledgling regulators, the organization had to show people it meant business.[110] One early and memorable

[108] Suchismita Bose, 'Securities Market Regulations: Lessons from US and Indian Experience,' *ICRA Bulletin: Money & Finance* 2, No. 20–21 (2005), 83–122.

[109] Pertinent among these acts and amendments are: the Repeal of Capital Issues (Control) Act; the SEBI Act, 1992; the Securities Laws (Amendment) Act, 1995; the Depositories Act, 1996; the Depository Related Laws (Amendment) Act, 1997; the Securities Laws (Amendment) Act, 1999; the Securities Laws (Second Amendment) Act, 1999; the SEBI (Amendment) Act, 2002; and the Securities Laws (Amendment) Bill, 2003. For a more detailed treatment see M.S. Sahoo, *Historical Perspective on Securities Laws*, (n.p., n.d.), Available at http://citeseerx.ist.psu.edu/viewdoc/download?doi=10.1.1.603.559 1&rep=rep1&type=pdf.

[110] For an overview of SEBI's role in the first two decades of its existence see G. Sabarinathan, 'SEBI's Regulation of the Indian Securities Market: A Critical Review of the Major Developments,' *Vikalpa*, October–December 2010, 35, 4, 13–27.

tussle took place over the basic matter of unbundling the brokerage on a stock trade from the stock's price. For the brokers, it was a traumatic adjustment from the easy-going tolerance and compromises of earlier days to the heavy-handedness of government regulation, a transition that would have been unnecessary if only the exchange had done a better job as a self-regulating organization. Later, face-offs with the BSE or the broking community were precipitated by a succession of early SEBI chairmen.[111] Of their tenures, D.R. Mehta's term between 1995 and 2002 was the longest and, coinciding as it did with most of the critical reform period, also the most significant. Many of the changes mentioned in this chapter took place on his watch.[112] More generally, the creation of a new and independent regulator also shifted the locus of market reforms from the finance ministry to SEBI itself, and it was at SEBI's initiative that the final links to a new market – clearing, settlement, and paperless dematerialization – would be made.

Clearing and Settlement

Clearing and settlement, the place where cash and shares change hands, is an important but unglamorous part of the securities business. Trades are first confirmed; confirmation is the assurance to the customer – often on the phone and now increasingly through a computer – that the trade has gone through. Following confirmation, clearing and settlement take place. When clearing, all parties determine their obligations and agree on them, following which they match their records with those of the exchange and its clearing house. Then, settlement takes place where buyers pay-in cash and sellers 'pay-in' shares, all of which is reconciled. Following this, buyers receive shares and sellers receive cash during the pay-out. The pay-in for both cash and shares precedes the pay-out, after

[111] SEBI chairmen include: S.A. Dave (1988–90), G.V. Ramakrishna (1990–94), S.S. Nadkarni (1994–95), D.R. Mehta (1995–2002), G.N. Bajpai (2002–05), M. Damodaran (2005–08), C.B. Bhave (2008–11), U.K. Sinha (2011–17), and Ajay Tyagi (2017–22). In 2022, Madhabi Puri Buch became the first woman to head SEBI.

[112] Post-retirement, Mehta built a second calling in social work and service. He set up the Bhagwan Mahaveer Viklang Sahayata Samiti (BMVSS) to provide artificial limbs and prosthetics to the handicapped.

which all trades are then said to be settled. Since brokers have clients buying (for which brokers make a payment to the clearing house) and selling (for which brokers receive a payment from the clearing house) at the same time, some 'netting out' can take place at the broker level, resulting in a net payment to or from the clearing house; since money is fungible and company scrips are more unique and less numerous, netting applies more to cash than to shares. Finally, the process has a legal component as shares represent an ownership stake in an enterprise, and such changes in ownership have to be registered.

The back office where all this happens is tedious and yet vital. Stock market crises become apparent only when trades clear and settle, and most of the badla system's *hera pheri* (hanky-panky) became obvious only when parties could not meet their obligations on clearing and settlement. Badla's 14-day periods between one settlement and the next allowed crises to simmer undetected for a full fortnight. Together with badla's unlimited leverage, this time gap gave hapless parties caught in a crisis every incentive to bet the ranch, double up on their bets, and desperately try to trade their way out of their predicaments, which more often than not, worsened the situation.

The euphemism for all this is counterparty risk, which is the inability of the broker to meet his obligations on either side of the trade – either because his client went on the lam and ran away, or because the broker himself got blown up on proprietary trades. In either case, those close community and religious ties came into play, and the exchange sat down with defaulting parties to sort things out.[113] Nevertheless, these arrangements imposed significant systemic risks on everybody. They also made risk management a question of sizing up the other party, something old-style brokers in India instinctively do to this day.

In 1995, the NSE's formation of the National Securities Clearing Corporation Limited (NSCCL) changed all this. The NSCCL was actually structured like a futures clearing house, mainly because badla's forward trading and the similarity between forwards and futures meant

[113] For a description of the clearing and settlement system in the pre-Independence era, see P.J. Thomas, *Report on the Regulation of the Stock Market in India*, 45–54.

that stock clearing and settlement at that time had futures-like attributes. Its most significant reform was taking counterparty risk on itself by becoming the legal counterparty to all trades, in effect interposing itself between parties; the practice was called novation, and it was a feature of derivatives clearing houses that was adapted to the stock market. So, the clearing house guaranteed all trades of its members, becoming the buyer to every seller and vice versa, which effectively removed counterparty risk. This allowed for anonymity and removed the need to size up or gauge counterparties.[114] But in return, the NSCCL also took its pound of flesh, through collateral and margin requirements. The BSE's clearing house, Indian Clearing Corporation Limited (ICCL), also handles similar responsibilities since 2007. In contrast to international practice, both clearing houses are still owned by their sponsoring exchanges.

Settlement posed its own challenges. The old BSE system had centralized pay-ins and pay-outs for barely 200 stocks of the 5,000 in the mid-1990s listed universe. For the remaining stocks, bilateral settlements between broker/members took place, but this was a system of hideous complexity.[115] It sometimes took as long as two months for a public shareholder to get cash for the shares sold. Cumbersome payment systems meant that funds were in transit for long periods, and during periods of severe market stress, the clearing house was forced to decide whether funds – even when put up – were sound or not. But these challenges were still organizational, and the real settlement tests came through the badla system. As seen earlier, the badla system allowed for two-week settlement periods (earlier it had been a full month), and transactions were squared up over those two weeks, effectively making the trade similar to a two-week forward contract. For many years, even margin was not required, and traders used this to get unlimited leverage over the settlement period; many took large positions with no capital put up and then squared up or netted the difference within the two-week settlement period. Loss-making trades were usually rolled over between

[114] Susan Thomas, 'How the Financial Sector in India was Reformed,' *Documenting Reforms: Case Studies from India*, ed. S. Narayan, New Delhi: Macmillan India, 2006, 180–82.

[115] P.J. Thomas, *Report on the Regulation of the Stock Market in India*, 45–54.

settlements till they turned profits; sometimes that never happened, and the resulting losses that ballooned through the constant rollovers often led to payment crises. All this encouraged high levels of speculation and overtrading that the system could not manage.

By contrast, rolling settlements fix the net position of all traders after the daily trading session, and require them to settle each position daily, as opposed to fortnightly or weekly. Pay-in and pay-out happen a fixed period after each trading day – under a (say) T+3 rolling settlement, a net position at the end of any trading day (T) must be settled by the third working day after the trade.

The introduction of rolling settlements would prove tortuous. Since badla was both a settlement system and a derivatives product, it was only after badla's abolition and the creation of derivatives markets that rolling settlements could be introduced.[116] All this happened over a few chaotic months in 2001. Settlement was also a function of banking efficiency, so changes meant involving the RBI. A five-day settlement period was initially adopted, but the clearing and settlement reforms were way ahead of the RBI's systems. By the new millennium, the market was ready for real-time settlement, but it was only after the RBI introduced the Real Time Gross Settlement (RTGS) that the banking system caught up with the stock market, and T+5 settlements were shortened to T+2.

Presently, all spot trades are cleared with netting by novation at the NSCCL and then settled on a T+2 basis. Finally, because of the high presence of day traders and arbitrageurs, a sizeable percentage of transactions settle through intraday squaring up and don't even make it to the clearing corporation.

Dematerialization

Related to settlement was the question of final proof of stock ownership: did it have to be evidenced in physical form through share certificates,

[116] Ajay Shah and Susan Thomas, 'Policy Issues in Indian Securities Markets,' *Reforming India's External, Financial and Fiscal Policies*, eds. Anne O. Krueger and Sajjid Z. Chinoy, Stanford Studies in International Economics and Development, Stanford, CA: Stanford University Press, 2003, 129–47.

or was another system possible? Transfers of stock ownership in physical form usually involved complex paperwork, numerous endorsements, and a multiplicity of signatures.[117] Sometimes it led to bad delivery – the risk of a buyer not having shares delivered to him – typically because of signature mismatches on the sell side of the trade. So complex and tedious was the transfer process that many participants, rather than take delivery and initiate the transfer, simply preferred to square up or keep rolling over positions in the badla forward market; in fact, the cumbersome transfer process was an important hidden factor behind badla's popularity. One solution was blank transfers – transfer deeds that were signed by parties as sellers but left blank for particulars on the buyer's name. The buyers often passed on these blank transfers to the next person they sold to. Doing this multiple times left shares registered in the names of parties far removed from, and therefore unknown to, the latest holder.

Blank transfers seem like a curiosity today, but they were an important practical consideration in their time, and committees from Gorwala onwards devoted substantial attention to them. By avoiding the necessity of constantly updating shareholdings at the company register level, the practice facilitated the extremely high transfer velocity generated by the badla system, but in doing so, it also helped avoid high registration and stamp duty charges on share transfers.[118] Physical share certificates could also lead to forgeries. The most spectacular of such cases was reported in 1995 and concerned the certificates of Reliance Industries, at that time the company with India's largest shareholder base; rumours of underworld involvement in such cases were also rampant.[119]

[117] For a detailed description of early share transfer, see Mahendra Kampani, 'Share Transfer Simplification Through Stock Holding Corporation,' The Stock Exchange, Mumbai, *35th Meeting of the Standing Committee of the Presidents of the Stock Exchanges in India*, Mumbai: The Stock Exchange, Mumbai, 1988, 1–5.

[118] Walter B. Morison, *Report of the Stock Exchange Enquiry Committee*, 17–19. Also see H.T. Parekh, *The Bombay Money Market*, 79–82.

[119] R.H. Patil was to say later: 'At that time, the underworld was also investing in the market, not directly, but through brokers. In the first couple of years, before depositories became a reality, printed fake securities used to be delivered. They were so well made that you could not tell the original from the fake. It got a bit scary when we discovered who was behind this. Our security advisor, D.S. Soman,

Moving to a system of paperless trading could eliminate the above issues. Such a system had been first envisioned in detail by Phiroze Jeejeebhoy in 1979, but he was at least two decades early.[120] In the early years of the reform effort, paperless trading was the one element of the market that resonated with the public. A depository – a sort of centralized electronic share bank – where every shareholder had an account in which shares were held as entries in electronic form would eliminate the need for physical shares and prevent problems like forgeries. Once physical shares were registered at the depository, their material form could be extinguished, and all that would remain is the account entry. The entire process would be 'dematerialized' – or 'dematted', as market jargon goes (to this day, shareholding statements are called 'demat' statements). Ownership transfers would then get registered through entries between the buyer's/seller's account and the company's register with the depository, with the transactions intermediated through a depository participant, who would usually be a bank or a broker.

One of the fledgling regulator's first major initiatives concerned this 'dematerialization' and paperless trading. The NSE and BSE used the passage of the Depositories Act of 1996 to set up the National Securities Depository Ltd (NSDL) and the Central Depository Services (India) Ltd (CDSL) respectively.[121] Because the idea took its own time catching on with the public, SEBI moved the process along by making it progressively more difficult to trade shares in paper form. Chief among these measures was the rule that shares could only be sold in dematted form, which effectively prompted legacy shareholders into

---

the then director-general of police, took care of it, but there was a lot of fear.' As quoted in Veena Venugopal, 'Meet the Man behind NSE's Success.'

[120] Phiroze J. Jeejeebhoy, *A Blueprint of Economic Democracy: A People's Stock Market and People's Joint Stock Enterprise*, Bombay: Bombay Stock Exchange, 1979, 1–25. The scheme did not make allowance for an additional layer of depositary participants, perhaps because of the small shareholding population of that time. The share transfer process of that era (using physical certificates) is explained in some detail.

[121] Depository ownership was usually vested in stakeholders, who (besides the exchanges) included banks, financial institutions, custodians, brokers, and depositary participants. Some stakeholders belonged to all the above categories. Multi-depository environments were unusual in developed markets at that time, and to this day, they are also unusual in emerging markets.

dematting their holdings before they could do anything with them.[122] In later years, 'nudging' would become a fashionable term in behavioural economics for this sort of policy move, but SEBI had stumbled on a way to do just that many years before Western academics made the term fashionable. Making dematerialization a prerequisite on the sell side of a trade made the whole market move to paperless trading, and much of this was accomplished in a wave between 1998 and 2000.[123] By 2022, there were 100 million demat accounts in which shares were held.[124]

And What Finally Happened

In another twist, the exchange that would dominate equities actually began with debt trading in June 1994, and this date also marks a first for screen-based debt trading in India. Led largely by the NSE's creation, India's stock markets were transformed over the next ten years and effectively thrust into the twenty-first century. The NSE surprised even its founders and went on to become the country's largest stock exchange in its first year of operation – going live for equity trading in November 1994 and surpassing the BSE in turnover and other metrics by October 1995. Much of that turnover came from nationwide trading, and by 1997, almost 60 per cent of the NSE's trading volume came from outside Mumbai. By its tenth anniversary, it was the world's third-largest exchange on some measures, such as the number of transactions handled. At a macro level, India's ratio of market capitalization to GDP saw a one-time increase from the low single digits of the Century of Marking Time to a range that was usually between 60 and 90 per cent of the country's GDP.

With the passage of time, the response of the BSE brokers seems Luddite, and in later years, it would become a fashion of sorts to criticize

[122] L.C. Gupta (ed.), *India's Financial Markets and Institutions*, New Delhi: Society for Capital Market Research and Development, 1999, 145.

[123] Securities and Exchange Board of India (SEBI), *Annual Report for the Fiscal Year 1999–2000*, Mumbai: SEBI, 2000, 95.

[124] 'Demat Accounts Cross 100 Million for First Time, Steep Rise in Last Four Months,' *Economic Times*, 6 September 2022.

them. Yet, too much must not be drawn from their behaviour, and it is a historical fallacy to brand all their reactions as antediluvian. For two generations after 1956, Section 13 and related provisions in the SCRA had limited stock markets to narrow municipal jurisdictions. By restricting market location, the provisions also constrained the mindset of an incumbent BSE that had built its business model around them. Further, the rapidity of the reform programme's onset took the BSE by surprise, even as legacy processes, erratic leadership in the era after Shroff and Phiroze Jeejeebhoy, and complacency brought about by over a century of market dominance dulled the keenness of its response.

At the same time, there was nothing inevitable about the NSE's rise, and it is teleological to assume that there was something predictable and triumphant about its subsequent ascent. Yet, it is also true that even the most minimal of market redesign and reform on the BSE's part would have stymied and perhaps even ended the NSE's progress, but that did not happen. What measures the BSE did take were also hindered in mysterious ways by SEBI, whose delays of BSE proposals for membership expansion and BOLT rollout benefitted the NSE. Remarkably, and despite the market's obsession with leverage, it is noteworthy that the NSE overtook the incumbent without the advantage of a leveraged product. It was only after the introduction of derivatives markets in 2000 that the NSE further extended its lead over the BSE through volumes generated from arbitrage between the NSE's cash and derivatives segments.

As a result of all this, the BSE, a century-old liquidity pool with established relationships, got tipped over by a bunch of tyros within a year. Talk about the low-hanging fruit of reform. Ajay Shah and Susan Thomas, who worked on capital markets in those years, would say: 'The synthesis is that the governmental intervention in this inefficient market was successful because of BSE's weaknesses and because of visionary market design, technology, and governance innovations implemented by a strong NSE management.'[125]

[125] Ajay Shah and Susan Thomas, 'David and Goliath,' 20–21.

The NSE also acted as a catalyst for financial market reform, and much of the hectic pace of reform during the 90s is due to its catalytic role in the markets. L.C. Gupta had foreseen this some years before.[126] The compressed and telegraphic nature of Indian equity market reform in the twentieth century's last decade – in a country not known for drastic moves – is noteworthy, in and of itself. All this took place without the self-imposed urgency that reformers in communist countries of the former Soviet Union would put themselves under, and this makes the pace of change all the more remarkable. Those changes included overturning and reordering the market's microstructure, setting up new markets for derivatives and forward products, reforming the back office through paperless trading, and changing practices in clearing and settlement.[127]

From 1996, there was a new index, the Nifty 50, to compete with the Sensex 30. By some measures, moving from the physical floor to an electronic environment led to post-trade costs falling from 200 basis points to about 40 basis points, following which they would head even lower.[128] Inter-exchange rollovers (between the national exchanges and the regionals) and inter-settlement rollovers were gradually eliminated, and this closed a loophole that participants had used to postpone obligations indefinitely. All this led to improved liquidity, reduced transaction costs, condensed bid-ask spreads, and increased transparency.[129]

The NSE created a pan-national market for securities, essentially discovering and cleaning up the market outside Mumbai. But in

[126] In 1991, L.C. Gupta was among the early few who foresaw the enabling role a new exchange could play in equity market reform. L.C. Gupta, *Expert Study of Trading in Shares in Stock Exchanges*, 59.

[127] Chitra Ramkrishna and Madhu Sudan Sahoo, 'Equity Markets,' *Capital Markets in India*, eds. Rajesh Chakrabarti and Sankar De, 105–06.

[128] Transaction cost reductions that resulted from the move to an electronic environment and other depository issues are discussed in *The Future of India's Stock Markets*, ed. Tushar Waghmare, New Delhi: Tata McGraw-Hill, 1998, 75–81.

[129] The NSE – founded on the principle of transparency in market practice – could apply different standards to itself. Together with other exchanges, the NSE has repeatedly resisted attempts to bring the exchange under the purview of the Right to Information (RTI) Act.

Mumbai, the old relationships between the buy side and the BSE brokers held and allowed the BSE to continue. The BSE, in turn, had to change, and it did. What decades of government commissions and reports from Atlay to Pherwani exhorted and what generations of brokers ignored got done in a few years as competitive forces between the exchanges were unleashed. The formation of a national market also hastened the end of the regional exchanges, and most are at various stages of being wound up.[130] Stock exchanges fell from 23 in 1993, to just the two major exchanges.[131]

Initially, volumes were helped along by price differentials between the two exchanges that attracted arbitrage traders; these supported liquidity at both exchanges through manual keyboard-operated arbitrage, but in later years, algorithmic trading would arbitrage away differentials. More than arbitrage-generated volumes, it was rollover volumes from differences in settlement cycles between both exchanges that helped. For some years, the NSE deliberately kept a Wednesday to Tuesday weekly settlement cycle against the BSE's Monday to Friday cycle; the NSE's settlement cycle started exactly in the middle of the BSE's settlement cycle, and this could not have been a coincidence. Traders of the late 1990s, who took advantage of the free one-week naked forward contract that badla's weekly settlement provided, took further advantage by rolling over positions between the exchanges – the BSE's traders could initiate a position on Monday, roll over their positions to the NSE on Friday, keep the NSE position open from Friday to the following Tuesday, and on that following Tuesday roll it over back to the BSE. This brought speculative volumes to both exchanges but also allowed for indefinite postponement of settlement obligations and was, in fact, a replay of the badla situation from an earlier era; the loophole would be plugged in later years.[132]

[130] Aniek Paul, 'A Requiem for the Calcutta Stock Exchange,' *Mint*, 23 May 2014.

[131] Officially, there are six exchanges in the cash segment; besides the NSE and BSE, they include the Calcutta Stock Exchange, India International Exchange, the Metropolitan Stock Exchange, and NSE IFSC. Other than the NSE and BSE, all have negligible volumes.

[132] Ajay Shah and Susan Thomas, 'Policy Issues in India's Capital Markets in 2000,' Working Paper Indira Gandhi Institute for Development Research, Mumbai, 2000, 2–5.

Subsequently, for the NSE at least, there would be little need for rollover business, as the volumes generated by arbitrage between the NSE's cash and derivatives segment would give the exchange an overwhelming advantage. By 2022, NSE cash volumes would exceed the BSE's sometimes by as much as 20 to 1. By now, the NSE's domination was complete, and this was just a return to the previous era when a single exchange had monopolized the situation. Now, as traders congregate at the largest liquidity pool, the situation takes on the effect of a self-fulfilling prophecy, and that effect is doubly so in a market with such a speculative orientation.

The change in equities was in sharp contrast to the debt market situation. The money and debt markets did not have the historical overhang of the stock markets and should have developed faster, and yet India's stock markets today are more aligned with international best practice and have surged ahead of debt markets across multiple parameters. Examining the history provides some clues to this dichotomy. First, unlike stock markets where the dominant participants – brokers – were from the private sector, India's bond markets had sluggish state-owned banks as the main players. Second, bond markets never had an insurgent like the NSE to shake things up, and their development remained broadly in the hands of bureaucrats at the central bank. Finally, retail participation in the stock market created an obvious political constituency for reform that was missing in institution-driven debt markets that continue to remain murky, non-transparent, and over-the-counter.[133]

Besides the debt markets, reforms of this period also bypassed the equity buy side, and it would be another decade before a raft of measures was declared. Pension fund participation, for example, continued to be low after this period and would only pick up many years later.

[133] Susan Thomas, 'How the Financial Sector in India was Reformed,' in *Documenting Reforms: Case Studies from India*, ed. S. Narayan, 189–93; former Union Finance Minister P. Chidambaram, remarks at the 20th Anniversary Celebrations of the National Stock Exchange of India, Mumbai, 14 December 2013. Also see John Echiverri-Gent, 'Why Do Some Financial Markets Develop and Others Do Not? Politics of India's Capital Market Reform,' Paper presented at The Workshop on States, Development, and Global Governance, University of Wisconsin Law School, Madison, Wisconsin, March 2010.

Later, the NSE, an exchange that was founded on better corporate governance practices, would itself get involved in various controversies over preferential access to co-location servers, sweetheart appointments, and suchlike.[134] But these were trifling, and most troubling of all were attempts at using the murky cesspool of Indian regulation to stymie competitive entry into the exchange space, thereby making it less contestable.[135] In all this, a relevant and unanswered question is whether the NSE's monopoly over the Indian exchange space is generating rents that are being used to finance a vast network of patronage in the market-wide ecosystem. Always a political animal and with political instincts honed from its very founding, the NSE would see those instincts dulled in later years, and multiple reports would come out on its stumbles with the powers that be. The mysterious delays in approving the national rollout of BSE's BOLT, the delays in approving BSE membership expansion, and badla's sudden and total abolition, had all proved decisive in establishing the NSE's dominance, but these later reports implied that the free run that the youthful NSE enjoyed with both the Finance Ministry and SEBI had run its course by middle age.

Much of this was unavoidable as the NSE inexorably got trapped by its own success. By 2020 and for equities at least, the NSE had almost 95 per cent of the cash market and 100 per cent of the derivatives market all to itself.[136] The NSE has tried to disguise this simple fact, and the organization's secrecy, together with the dense and incomprehensible jungle of numbers in the SEBI reports, makes that cover-up easy. In turn, SEBI aids that concealment by fretting about how the Indian market

[134] For an account of corporate wrangling in the NSE, see 'How Ravi Narain Built the NSE, and Then Lost His Grip,' *Moneycontrol*, 4 June 2017, https://www. moneycontrol.com/news/ trends / features-2/how-ravi-narain-built-the-nse-and-then-lost-his-grip-2296629.html.

[135] Much of this is outlined in an exposé by Sucheta Dalal and Debashis Basu. See Sucheta Dalal and Debashis Basu, *Absolute Power*, Mumbai: Kensource Books, 2021. The NSE even filed a ₹100 crore defamation suit against Sucheta Dalal and her site *Moneylife*, but Justice Gautam Patel's order threw out the NSE's case and awarded ₹50 lakhs in damages, which went to the authors and other charitable institutions. The NSE appealed but later withdrew the case.

[136] National Stock Exchange, *Annual Report 2018–2019*, Mumbai: NSE, 2019, 23, Available at https://www1.nseindia.com/global/content/about_us/NSE_AR_2019.pdf.

is turning into an oligopoly, but the figures indicate a market that is, in fact, dominated by a single exchange.[137] For the NSE at least, the balance between its public interest role and commercial considerations is complicated by this de facto monopoly of the Indian market. An exchange that now has a near monopoly on the stock market and that sees itself as a self-regulating organization, would naturally have its own run-in with the organization tasked with regulating that market – SEBI. If an organization that monopolized India's markets practised self-regulation, what role was there for an actual regulator?

The solution lay in introducing a semblance of competition for order flow by rebuilding the BSE as a counterweight, and perhaps here was the reason behind those media reports on the NSE's sudden loss of touch. In recent years, the NSE had also begun to realize all this. If nothing else but to avoid the monopoly tag, it dawned on the NSE that it needed the BSE more than the BSE needed itself. The NSE's 'take no prisoners' approach to the BSE would then moderate, and this allowed the BSE some breathing space, which it used to claw its way back into the derivatives segment.

The NSE's founding team would also move on within a generation to other ventures. Some even tried to replicate the NSE's success in their new ventures – the founding team was fertile recruiting ground for others in the exchange space – but those endeavours would not come close to matching the achievement of the original.[138] By now the historic concatenation of events that allowed for the NSE's success had run its course, and the small postern gate of fate that allowed the NSE to storm fortune's fortress had slowly swung shut. But none of the founding team realized this as they went on with their lives. Ravi Narain and Chitra Ramkrishna, two founding team members who went

[137] Jayshree P. Upadhyay, 'NSE Asks FM, SEBI to Lower Taxes on Market Trading,' *Mint*, 5 November 2019.

[138] The post-NSE careers of some members of the founding team are outlined in the following articles. Palak Shah, 'Geojit's Kumar to Head Troubled USE,' *Business Standard*, 3 January 2012; Pravin Palande, 'How Ashish Chauhan Is Reviving BSE,' *Forbes*, 19 July 2013.

on to lead the NSE, would leave under mysterious circumstances.[139] Ashishkumar Chauhan, almost in an act of historical repentance, went on to head the exchange whose reign he ended – the BSE – but was not able to stop the fall in its business; in 2022, Chauhan moved back to head the NSE, making him the only person to head both exchanges. K. Kumar tried to do an NSE at the OTCEI and the United Stock Exchange (a currency bourse) but both would fade away from the exchange space. Raghavan Putran initially opted out of corporate life to join the Yogananda Mission but returned to briefly head NCDEX, an agri-commodity exchange that never really took off.

And R.H. Patil, who founded the NSE, would recall the idealism that started it all. Before he died at 74, consumed by the lung cancer common in the sugarcane growing areas of Nandgad and Belgaum from which he hailed, Patil would rue that exchanges were no longer for retail participants. 'Exchanges must be for the retail investor, the little fellow. I looked at the exchange as social infrastructure, that purpose is distorted now,' he had said.[140] Later inquiry will establish whether that comment is valid or just the result of an old man's sentimentalism.

[139] Besides R.H. Patil, NSE managing directors include: Ravi Narain (2001–13), Chitra Ramkrishna (2013–16), Vikram Limaye (2017–22), and Ashishkumar Chauhan (2022–present). But for Limaye, all were members of the founding team.

[140] Veena Venugopal, 'Meet the Man behind NSE's Success.'

4

SOFTWARE BOFTWARE

The 2000 Blowout

The previous chapter focused on reforms to the internal composition and structure of the market, while ignoring the index's actual movements. This is partly by design, for with changes to the microstructure falling into place by the late 1990s, the stock market was all dressed up with nowhere to go. The reforms at the millennium's turn had created a new market through a period of wrenching change, and yet that disjointed transformation took place against the backdrop of a meandering index. The stock market essentially went nowhere after the Harshad Mehta mania in the early 1990s, as though to say that the reforms to its structure were too much to handle, and it could not be bothered with the basic task of going up or down. The market kept bumping against the 1992 Mehta top of about 4,500 before falling back. It did this till 1999, making this seven-year period the longest period of below-normal returns in the modern era.[1]

Despite the sluggish index, the 1990s were not a quiet time, and substantial global news broke during this period. Both the Gulf War crisis of 1990 and the East Asian crisis of 1997–98 are significant. The

[1] From 1996 onwards, the Nifty 50 also captures market movement.

stock market dipped and then roared upward through the Gulf War and did nothing during the latter, and more serious, East Asian crisis. Both events remain the last historical instances of dramatic capital market segmentation, when the Indian market could do its own thing, ignore global events, and behave like it was in autarky. After the East Asian debt crisis, markets would find it impossible to ignore global events, and the move out of autarky would become evident. In later years, global conditions would impinge on domestic movements, usually through the ebb and flow of foreign portfolio flows. Consequently, this also marked the final time when Indian foreign policy was made without any regard to markets; subsequently, foreign policy was made with an eye on the Sensex, and FIIs flows became a policy concern (though this concern has been mitigated in recent years by the domestic buy side's access to capital generated by rupee cost averaging plans).

This period is also unusual as it represents the only decadal period when the primary side trumped secondary operations. As seen earlier, the 1985–95 decade saw two IPO waves, with a mid-1980s issue wave followed by a second wave in the early and mid-1990s. This is the only period in India's stock market history when market records mention a buoyant primary side as a bear factor in market operations, perhaps because participants overextended their commitments in the primary market, leaving less capital for secondary operations. Taken together, the two waves resulted in BSE listings crossing 6,000, a record of sorts. Nevertheless, the large number of listed companies would prove to be a mixed blessing. Many had no business being listed in the first place; they were little more than candidates for private equity funding, but the absence of a private equity industry at that time made them approach the public markets. Several were bubble companies with no liquidity or trading volumes. Crucially, the buy side was still finding its feet at that time, so it was the retail public that digested all this dubious paper.

The aftermath of the IPO mania, market scams, settlement crises, and government instability all led to investor disillusionment, and records from the period are eloquent in detailing this disenchantment with stocks. The section on equities from one 1999 account is full of chapter headlines that illustrate this: 'How and Why Investors' Dreams Went Sour and What Needs To Be Done', 'Investors' Confidence: Where the Real Problem Lies', and 'Investors' Disenchantment with Equities'.[2] But much of this existential hand-wringing was an attempt to deal with the hangover from the binges of the Mehta Bull and the two IPO waves. In fact, despite the *hai hai tauba tauba* (alas and God forbid) routine, the market was now on the verge of two of the most significant bull markets ever: the IT Bull and the Rate Bull.

The historical significance of this IT Bull market that peaked at the millennium's turn in 2000 has not been fully appreciated. Largely associated as it was with the software, media, and telecom sectors, the IT Bull was the most one-sided of India's market runs. Despite that, it marks a big break in the market's history and is therefore given its own chapter in this work. It was the last bull to be associated with a single personality – Ketan Parekh – and was the first bull since Independence to coincide with international trends. The end of personality-driven runs and global correlations have come to characterize market runs ever since. The bear market that followed was also to carry its own distinctions (to date at least): lasting as it did from 2000 to 2003, it is both the longest bear in the new millennium and the last bear to end in a market scam.

The proximate cause of the dot-com boom was a worldwide reappraisal of the technology, media, and telecom sectors, brought about in large part by the discovery of the internet. Major technological innovations – particularly those that influence people's lives on a day-to-day basis – tend to have displacement effects in the stock market.[3] The consequences

[2] L.C. Gupta (ed.), *India's Financial Markets and Institutions*, New Delhi: Society for Capital Market Research and Development, 1999, 113–26.

[3] The idea of a displacement as the first stage in a speculative market movement that can develop into a bubble owes its origins to economists Hyman Minsky and Charles Kindleberger. See Hyman P. Minsky, *Stabilizing an Unstable Economy*, New Haven: Yale University Press, 1986; Charles Kindleberger, *Manias, Panics and Crashes*, New York: Basic Books, 1978.

are especially potent if that technology enters the living room or has effects that can be touched and seen by most people.[4] Just as an earthquake on an ocean floor causes only ripples on the surface above it but results in a tsunami as those ripples approach land, so too does deep seismic change at tech Ground Zero cause a wave as it approaches the stock market. The internet was one such technology and displacement, but it had happened before – with railways in mid-nineteenth-century England, radio in 1920s Wall Street, and the 'tronics' boom in the Go-Go 1960s. Something happens to participants when they see the future through these displacements, and the situation is fertile ground for that manic combination which produces a multi-bagger stock – a firm foundation of value on which you can build a castle in the air.[5]

The worldwide move in tech arrived late on Indian shores. It was only in 1998 that tech started attracting any attention in India, though the dot-com boom had been ongoing since the mid-1990s globally. India was in a good position to capitalize on the tech boom when it came. Comparative advantage in the IT space – and particularly services – came from the English language, a large pool of technically skilled manpower, cost-effectiveness, convenient time zone differences, together with an emerging ecosystem in areas such as back-office services. A proximate trigger for the boom was the millennial change to the year 2000 which led to the Y2K scare; there was concern that the change would mess with computers' internal clocks, and the necessary recalibration of those systems was good business for service companies. So the global up move played to inherent domestic strengths, leading to a surge in IT services and related stocks. Many service companies had been floated in the early 1990s and were well placed when the trend arrived.[6]

[4] Robert J. Shiller, *Irrational Exuberance*, 2nd ed., New York: Crown Business, 2006, 38–39.

[5] Burton Malkiel, *A Random Walk Down Wall Street*, 11th ed., New York: W.W. Norton, 2015, 33–36, 394–95.

[6] Satyam and Infosys would go public in 1991 and 1993, respectively. Wipro, the third of the heavyweight listed IT service companies at that time, had a history dating back to 1945 but in different business lines.

The subsequent boom in tech stocks resulted in the most one-sided bull market ever – any stock associated with these sunrise sectors took off, while most of the old 'bricks and mortar' stocks languished. Dalal Street had to explain the phenomenon, and it did so by creating a false dichotomy between 'new economy' and 'old economy' scrips. Nothing moved except the new economy.

Infosys, Satyam, and Wipro were the stars of this bull market, though some lesser lights also took off. As was their wont, analysts had started discounting the happily ever after; they cannot be blamed, as IT companies were in a sweet spot. Earnings growth was tremendous in percentage terms, and the market's capitalization of those expanding earnings through an expanding PE ratio was equally swift. As a result, stock prices exploded upwards. It was a period of extraordinary madness that was apparent only in retrospect.

Appropriately – since the internet was what it was all about – stock trading on the internet took place for the first time in 2000.[7] For generations before that, the market in India had been a physical crowd clustered around the BSE's trading floor on Dalal Street, but the absence of a physical market and trading floor now meant that – for the first time – all the action was taking place online. The market was now a psychological crowd rather than a physical one, and this psychological crowd with a mental unity all of its own had congregated around a wonderful fantasy. But that fantasy had its bedrock in a firm foundation of value. After all, Infosys – in its December 1999 quarterly announcement just before the great Nasdaq crash of March 2000 – had reported almost 100 per cent earnings growth year on year, and that was just the latest in a string of equally successful quarters.[8] Projecting those growth rates another year or two into the future made the stock look reasonably cheap, even at expensive valuations.[9] The market was

[7] Chandana Goswami, 'How Does Internet Stock Trading in India Work?' *Vikalpa*, Vol. 28, No. 1, January–March 2003, 92.

[8] Infosys, 'Reports and Filings Quarterly & Annual Reports,' *Infosys*, Accessed on 20 January 2017, 2–3, 7, https://www.infosys.com/investors/Documents/QR6k/Q3-1999-00.pdf.

[9] Infosys' price-to-earnings ratio ranged between 150 and 300 during the boom years. Parag Parikh, *Value Investing and Behavioral Finance*, New Delhi: Tata McGraw-Hill, 2009, 107.

building a castle in the air based on a firm foundation of value. This is also the first run where India's market moved almost one on one with world markets – and particularly the Nasdaq; anxiously watching the Nasdaq well into the early morning was a ritual followed by many a trader in those years. The Sensex peaked at a little over 6,000 in early 2000, with 1,750 as the corresponding Nifty level. At the top, the index committees charged with maintaining the indexes predictably loaded them up with IT and related sectors, and as a result, when the selloff came, the corresponding effects on the indexes were disproportionately severe.

At the bull run's height, even the familiar name change scam was common. Adding 'Cyber' to a name doubled the price, and adding some variant of the magical 'Infosys' doubled it again. There really was a Cyberspace Infosys, but at least that was a conscious fiddle by the promoters. More intriguing was the case of Softwear – a hosiery company that made socks – which found itself doing very well in the software boom, thank you very much.[10]

Some stocks became 60-baggers or more in a little over a year: Himachal Futuristic went from 20 to almost 1,300, while Aftek Infosys moved from 30 to 2,400. Shorting Himachal Futuristic at 200, after it had quadrupled from 50, might have cleaned you out long before its final level. At a conference to explain this wonderful new world of the internet, there were not many people on the short side; presumably, they did not have any clothes to wear and so were not attending.

Many of these multi-baggers were in the 'K-10' – the 10 stocks that were supposedly the favourites of Ketan Parekh, the bull operator most associated with the run.[11]

A tall broker with a straggly moustache, Ketan Parekh was on the right side of a historic trend but overstayed his market – not the first time this was to happen. That the Parekh-led move happened almost a decade after the Mehta Bull run, and that both ended in tears was

[10] Santosh Nair, *Bulls, Bears, and Other Beasts*, New Delhi: Pan Macmillan, 2016, 178.

[11] Joint Parliamentary Committee, *Joint Committee on Stock Market Scam and Matters Relating Thereto*, Thirteenth Lok Sabha, Volume I - Report, New Delhi: Lok Sabha Secretariat, 2002, 188.

not lost on participants, and comparisons are frequently drawn between the two personalities. Both started out as nonentities who later became shooting stars that flamed out. But the similarities hid many differences. Unlike Mehta, Parekh came from a family of brokers and had long-standing links to other participants; in contrast to the more flamboyant Mehta, he was a professionally qualified accountant and known for keeping a low profile. Yet again, the differences in personal attributes concealed essential similarities in their approaches – both accessed the banking system to keep the moves going, generated research to sell 'stories', and used the buy side as a buyer of last resort.

Remarkably, the person at the centre of it all did not attract much media attention during the main phase of the dot-com boom. The little attention Parekh generated remained confined to hushed whispers about his prowess. Media attention started building in late 1999, towards the end of the boom, and the early coverage was guardedly respectful, as was to be expected. But as the run continued, the sobriquets grew more extravagant, and Parekh would become known as the 'Pentafour Bull' (for his bullishness for specific technology stocks) or the 'One-Man Army'. Later, even the BBC succumbed:

> Parekh is no ordinary stockbroker. In the last couple of years of bull run on the Indian markets, he has made a formidable reputation for himself as the biggest mover and shaker on the Indian bourses.[12]

The handles stuck to Ketan Parekh despite his desire to stay under the radar.[13] The low profile was necessary as it allowed him to conceal his operations while building positions. This cover-up was essential, as Parekh's association with counters often led them to skyrocket higher simply due to the association – because of his 'hot hands', participants kept track of his every move and loaded up, which took the price up

[12] Sanjeev Srivastava, 'Kerry Packer's Indian Venture,' *BBC News*, 27 March 2000.
[13] Clifford Alvares and Shilpa Nayak, 'The One-man Sensex,' *Outlook*, 24 January 2000.

and made it difficult for him to accumulate positions.[14] Nevertheless, the hot-hand effect could be to his advantage if he already had a position in the counter. The idea was to keep his association with the counter private till the position was accumulated, following which the news could leak to a watching world. This was a difficult task in an activity prone to massive rumour mongering and hearsay, and so, he would alternate between being inconspicuous to conceal his operations and maintaining a media profile in the hope of a halo effect that rubbed off onto his counters. It would prove to be an unstable dynamic.

There was nothing exceptional about the rise of Ketan Parekh. Whether by accident or design, he was simply the right person at the right time in the right stocks. There were others like him, and it is unclear how he alone got associated with a move in which many other traders also took part. Yet Parekh's personal ability to move stocks may have been an exaggeration, for like any major movement in the financial markets, it was the public that had the bit between its teeth in the final stages. In what had become a moderately large market, movements on this scale would have been impossible without massive crowd buying and mania.[15] In all likelihood, it was Parekh's 'hot hands' association with the tech counters that was getting the crowd into them. The tendency of participants to hang on to every word or move of the Pied Piper is noteworthy and reminiscent of the crowd's connection with earlier characters such as Roychand and Mehta. Rarely does crowd contagion or imitation in financial markets get as blatantly and publicly acknowledged as it does in the Indian share bazaar. These were people who wanted to be led by the nose, as this breathless passage suggests:

> The market loves discussing him. The Sensex does get linked to Parekh's acquisitions of a jet (false) and a new car (true). Day

[14] 'What is universally respected, though, is his purchases. A broker says that "when people say 'that's Ketan Parekh's counter', we watch it very closely and none of us would rather go against it".' Ibid.

[15] For reports that Indian equity markets were second only to Nasdaq in speculative measures such as the turnover to market capitalization ratio, see B.G. Shirsat, 'Indian Bourses Second-most Speculative after Nasdaq,' *Business Standard*, 5 April 2001; and Rishi Chopra, 'Excessive Speculation Plagues Capital Markets,' *Economic Times*, 8 May 2001.

> traders also monitor Parekh's travel plans and keep a track on his business meetings and holidays abroad... He makes day traders feel ecstasy and paranoia. 'KP's in it,' is often the only reason to buy a stock.[16]

India's IT service companies – particularly the pioneers that had listed in the early and mid-1990s – were good candidates to be stars when the worldwide IT Bull run hit the country's bourses. In its IPO section, SEBI's 1995 annual report showed a small sector – called Infotech – making its debut fifth from the bottom, just ahead of Rubber, Leather, Transport, and Power. It raised just ₹272 crores that year, but that was only a sign of things to come.[17] The larger IT service companies had years of track record behind them and had attained a certain scale. Despite that, it was mainly the smaller companies and the newbies that ended up being Parekh's stomping grounds.[18] Many of these minnows were showing high growth, often on a small capital base, which is not surprising as IT services are not a capital-intensive industry. But small capital bases went together with high promoter holdings, which in turn meant a low free float – the outstanding shares available to the public. Cornering that free float was not a difficult task, and in some cases, it was later reported that as much as a quarter of the free float was controlled by Parekh. Once the position was accumulated, substantial research was initiated, following which the stock was aggressively marketed to institutional investors. This sort of touting and market making is a legitimate exercise that routinely takes place in any market and is seen

[16] See The Money Bureau, 'Mystery Man: Who Is Ketan Parekh, Really,' *Rediff*, 13 January 2000.

[17] Securities and Exchange Board of India (SEBI), *Annual Report for the Fiscal Year 1994–1995*, Mumbai: SEBI, 1995, 16.

[18] 'The phenomenal rise of the securities market and the enormous trading volumes in certain specific scrips referred to as "K-10 stocks" (Aftek Infosys, DSQ Software, HFCL, Global Tele-system, Pentamedia Graphics Ltd., Ranbaxy Laboratories, Silverline Technologies, Satyam Computers Ltd., SSI Ltd., and Zee Telefilm Ltd.) was a phenomenon peculiar to the Indian securities market.' See Joint Parliamentary Committee, *Joint Committee on Stock Market Scam*, 188.

as normal, as long as it stays confined to such activities. But the next stage of Parekh's operations – involving the promoters, the buy side, and the banking system – was to prove his undoing.[19]

Naturally a 'hot hands' operator was deemed useful to promoters and any others hoping to increase the value of their publicly traded stock. As with Roychand or Mehta, just the association with the operator caused a surge in prices. The 'hot hands' association was enough for the feeble-minded and the astute – the former could not be bothered to make a decision, while the latter were happy to piggyback on the surge. Soon a long string of entities – among them investment companies controlled by promoters, overseas entities, and cooperative banks – queued up to hand over capital to the Pied Piper, often through the inter-corporate deposit route. The funds were then used to buy into the K-10 counters.[20] Networks of sympathetic brokers in places such as Ahmedabad and Calcutta (now Kolkata) often provided the necessary anonymity required to build positions. Typically, Parekh's association with the counter was enough, following which the market took the stock up. Overlapping settlement periods at different exchanges allowed positions to be rolled over between them, thereby postponing settlement obligations indefinitely.

As expected, all this led to stunning price increases and commensurate rises in share trading volumes. By now the move had spread from the frontline blue chips to the smaller second-rung counters, where the real killings were made. Parekh's role was to load up on these counters and then market them to the buy side. Spectacular were the price increases in the K-10 scrips, and many of them became 40 to 60 baggers in short order. Volume increases were equally striking as the public got the bit between its teeth – during the boom, the K-10 scrips regularly

[19] 'Diversion of funds allocated to specific projects for use in the stock market for the purchase of specific scrips, investment companies operating in the stock market through brokers, nexus between brokers and corporate entities in the context of the interests of brokers in specific corporate entities, which facts have now come to light, establish the nexus between brokers and corporate entities.' See Joint Parliamentary Committee, *Joint Committee on Stock Market Scam*, 146–47, 148–64.

[20] Ibid., 22.

featured in the top ten lists of stocks as ranked by traded volumes.[21] Besides Himachal Futuristic, other scrips deemed by the public to be part of this group included Global Telesystems, Zee Telefilms, Crest Communications, Silverline, Aftek Infosys, DSQ Software, and PentaMedia Graphics. In later years, the brokerages would develop a wonderful euphemism for such scrips – the 'transitory multi-bagger'.

Mutual funds piled on – buying 'hot hands' and performance – by loading up on the K-10 Parekh counters, and for a brief while, the strategy worked as many saw their net asset values soaring.[22] Not loading up on the 'new economy', and the K-10 in particular, would have resulted in serious underperformance for a substantial period. In fact, this was the most lopsided bull in India's stock market history, as the 'old economy' went nowhere and languished, while the 'new economy' took off. Unsurprisingly, some mutual funds, particularly those from the public sector, came late to the party. In June 1999, UTI started selling those fuddy-duddy PSU scrips in its portfolio that were simply not moving and proceeded to load up on exciting stocks from this brave new world of the internet.[23] Predictably, the reallocation worsened the already abysmal performance of the old economy scrip and fuelled the bull run and outperformance in the new economy stocks even further. This was literally throwing fuel on a roaring fire. By September 1999, close to the coming top, UTI was all dressed up and ready to go; by now, its flagship fund US-64 had diligently completed its asset reallocation, and 'new economy' counters were among its largest holdings. Whether UTI simply came late to the party or whether rigged counters were dumped on it will always remain an interesting question.[24]

[21] The 10 counters with the largest traded volumes – mainly K-10 stocks – usually accounted for between 60 and 80 per cent of market-wide turnover, indicating narrow market breadth. Likewise, delivery volumes on such counters were usually in the low single digits between April and December 2000. See Ibid., 188.

[22] John Echeverri-Gent, 'Political Economy of India's Fiscal and Financial Reform,' Working Paper No. 105, Stanford University, Centre for International Development, August 2001, 17–18.

[23] An extensive recounting is in Joint Parliamentary Committee, *Joint Committee on Stock Market Scam*, 339–437.

[24] 'Silence of the Bulls,' *Outlook*, 6 August 2001.

All this bulling of stocks ran into the issue of financing, a perennial concern of the buy side in India until recently. In this case, the financing came primarily from two sources – the promoters themselves and the banking system. Unlike Mehta, who had to rely almost exclusively on the banking system, Ketan Parekh, in some cases, was actively financed by the promoters themselves.[25] Information provided by the RBI to a Joint Parliamentary Committee (JPC) during later investigations revealed that companies close to Parekh had provided him substantial financing, usually by recycling borrowings from development finance institutions. But the banking system also had to be directly accessed to keep the bull move going, which had been the pattern with Roychand and Mehta as well. The banking system was accessed through the LAS – or loans against shares – product. But the shares were pledged towards the higher end of their moves, which resulted in raising considerable amounts but left the pledge vulnerable to the downside. Particularly controversial were transactions with Global Trust Bank (GTB) and the Madhavpura Mercantile Cooperative Bank (MMCB), both of which later came under investigation. Parekh also happened to be on the board of MMCB. Meanwhile, in GTB's case, exposure was in excess of prudential norms, and allegations surfaced that the bank's share price was rigged upwards for a favourable swap ratio prior to a scheduled merger with another bank.[26] In the MMCB episode, pay orders issued by MMCB in favour of Ketan Parekh were presented by him to the Bank of India and funds obtained, but subsequently the pay orders bounced when presented by Bank of India to the clearing house.[27]

[25] See the JPC's conclusions. 'The Committee note[s] that Ketan Parekh who emerged as a key player in this scam received large sums of money from the banks as well as from the corporate bodies during the period when SENSEX was falling rapidly. This led the Committee to believe that there was a nexus between Ketan Parekh, banks, and the corporate houses.' Joint Parliamentary Committee, *Joint Committee on Stock Market Scam*, 9. For media comment on this issue, see Clifford Alvares and Shilpa Nayak, 'The One-man Sensex.'

[26] SEBI, *Order Under Section 11 And 11B Of SEBI Act Against Promoters of Global Trust Bank and Others*, Mumbai, 2002.

[27] Joint Parliamentary Committee, *Joint Committee on Stock Market Scam*, 22, 28, 29, 54–69, 155–57, 266. Ketan Parekh was also a director of MMCB.

In March 2000, the Nasdaq peaked and broke. The corresponding Sensex break was 23 per cent, but trading favourites – including many of the K-10 – lost as much as two-thirds of their value. Many were pledged at high values or held through the leveraged badla market, and so, the fall triggered margin calls on the counters, which led to the first signs of financial distress among participants. Most of the margin calls were met through additional financing, often raised through dubious means, which prevented the situation from getting out of hand. Markets also provided some respite, as the first big Nasdaq break was followed by a strong pullback in the middle of the year. But the second Nasdaq break in December 2000 would prove decisive, leading to worldwide reappraisals of the tech sector and substantial mutual fund selling. Financial stress increased massively, caused in large part by margin calls on participants operating with leverage. 'Never meet a margin call' is a truism among astute participants that was repeatedly violated in this case.

The financial stress caused Parekh and other participants to turn to Kolkata. The Calcutta Stock Exchange had certain advantages as compared to other exchanges; besides generating the third-largest volumes after the NSE and BSE, it provided some anonymity for Parekh and his co-participants. A holdover of a certain type of stock market – relatively self-regulated and unsupervised – the Calcutta exchange operated just the sort of system that had recently been displaced at the BSE.[28] It too lacked the discipline and judgment needed to implement a self-regulating framework, and a considerable portion of its operations were 'kerbside' and oral, with no records or margin money. Calcutta's badla financiers on the outside reportedly financed Parekh's positions at high interest rates using informal arrangements; dealings in cash were also not problematic because of the city's proximity to traditional industries such as tea and jute, which had a preponderance of cash transactions.

[28] The Kolkata exchange's systemic issues are noted in Joint Parliamentary Committee, *Joint Committee on Stock Market Scam*, 17.

But, led by Nasdaq, the worldwide sell-off continued into 2001. After all, what was happening was just the Indian manifestation of a global phenomenon, though many participants recognized that simple fact only with difficulty, mainly due to the economic isolation caused by India's autarky between 1947 and the century's end. So, when world markets moved further to the downside, Indian markets – by now disproportionately weighted by the index committees in favour of tech stocks – also sold off heavily. Despite the anonymity that Calcutta provided, it was difficult to hide this level of financial distress, and like in Roychand's and Mehta's times, the leveraged positions generated margin calls that resulted in unsustainable pressures on certain participants. In such a volatile market, the leverage was like walking on tiptoe all the time.

In March 2001, just after the presentation of the Union Budget, massive selling took place in the new economy counters, many of which were associated with Parekh. The sell-off after the Union Budget was extraordinary, as the actual budget had seen positive industry response.[29] Both profit-booking and initiation of short positions were responsible for the selling wave. Later, it was disclosed that some BSE brokers had misused their surveillance mechanism to obtain information on counters where Parekh and his allies were overstretched. There followed another bout of panic selling, this time from the buy side and financial institutions who were holding stock as collateral. As leverage was wrung out of the system, this collateral-based selling led to another down round that convulsed the market. Even Parekh's financier, the MMCB, was forced to offload stock it had accepted as collateral to recover its outstanding loans.

This, in turn, precipitated a payment crisis in Kolkata.[30] Parekh's desperate attempts to access funds necessary to help his Kolkata brokers

[29] For a tick-tock of market movements in March 2001, see Oommen A. Ninan, 'Systemic Failure Behind Stock Market Turmoil,' *The Hindu*, 22 March 2001.

[30] 'The funds have gone from Ketan Parekh entities to brokers at Calcutta and Mumbai, the three major broker Groups being the Sanjay Khemani Group, the D.K. Singhania Group and the A.K. Poddar Group. The bulk of funds have been used by Singhania Group and Poddar Group for taking deliveries on behalf of the Ketan Parekh entities.' The Calcutta Stock Exchange payment crisis is documented in Joint Parliamentary Committee, *Joint Committee on Stock Market Scam*, 23, 26, 28, 29–34, 114–36.

did not yield results, and substantial defaults took place in the unofficial Kolkata kerb market that then spread to the formal market. Much of the payment crisis was later conveniently blamed on issues such as 'faulty software' and the like.[31] Three controversial settlements of the Kolkata bourse were declared completed by retaining a sizeable proportion of the payout of operators who had allegedly gotten together in collusive deals.

This sort of volatility sometimes provokes regulatory response, and so it did. The regulatory response brought about a further unravelling in the market, together with the first indication of a scam that had GTB and MMCB at its centre.[32] The Pied Piper was arrested on a complaint from the Bank of India and spent 53 days in police custody.[33] The fall from grace had been dramatic; some days prior to the arrest, the mainstream media had eagerly been seeking his views on the Union Budget. Parekh's arrest prompted a further – and final – selling wave in the K-10 scrips associated with him. The scam prompted intense media coverage and the sacking of the BSE's president, on allegations that he had accessed market surveillance information on other participants.[34] When it all ended, price declines of between 95 and 99 per cent in some of the K-10 counters had taken place, and this was seen as normal. The crowd's mood had changed, and violently. Ketan Parekh's 'hot hands' had prompted the crowd to flock to the K-10 counters, but now there was guilt by association, and the same counters were seen as 'operator driven'. In line with market history, price declines of this magnitude also brought forth public recrimination and calls to the regulator for action. Yet the shenanigans of some participants hid the stupidity of the majority – most had no business being in these stocks in the first place.[35]

[31] 'CSE Crisis Unique,' *Business Standard*, 11 July 2001. Also see Joint Parliamentary Committee, *Joint Committee on Stock Market Scam*, 120–25.

[32] SEBI, *Order under Section 11 and 11B of SEBI Act 1992, against M/s Triumph Securities and Others, in the Matter of Global Trust Bank*, Mumbai, 2003.

[33] Special Correspondent, 'CBI arrests Ketan Parekh,' *The Hindu*, 30 March 2001.

[34] Joint Parliamentary Committee, *Joint Committee on Stock Market Scam*, 136–39.

[35] Many retail investors and HNIs who found the stock market 'very risky' – but who financed the badla system from the outside and received rates of up to 18 per cent because it was 'very safe' – found their funds diverted and lost to unofficial markets. See Sheela Raval, 'Revenge of Badla,' *India Today*,

Accusations of regulatory complacency had by now become routine, and the meltdown's reaction led to the usual finger-pointing at SEBI and the RBI.[36] But protecting the sheep from themselves was not part of any regulator's job, as governor Sir Bartle Frere had realized in an earlier age.

Later investigations would reveal that Parekh had used both the banking system and promoter financing for his operations. SEBI also found evidence of circular trading and rigged prices in several scrips, including HFCL and DSQ Software.[37] GTB and MMCB were driven to bankruptcy as the money they lent Parekh went into the abyss together with his K-10 stocks. Taking advantage of low share prices, several multinationals turned the crisis into an opportunity and bought back shares in their local subsidiaries through open offers; some, including Sandvik, Höganäs, and AkzoNobel, enhanced their stakes only as a prelude to going private. So indiscriminate sell-offs on this scale had the unfortunate side effect of reducing the number of quality companies available to the shareholding public.

SEBI responded to all this by fiddling with margin requirements, following which there was a round-up of the usual suspects – in this case, the sellers whose volumes led to the post-budget crash of March 2001. But some of the regulatory response was to have lasting and historic consequences, as loopholes that had resulted from the market's big reform push of the previous decade were plugged.[38]

It was also the last hurrah for badla. That twisted product – peculiar in its operation and deleterious in its effects – was shown the door,

---

6 August 2001. Nevertheless, retail confidence was not misplaced, as defaults on badla funds were rare in previous eras.

[36] Various government agencies including the Finance Ministry and SEBI (together with other investigative agencies) came in for criticism in the Joint Parliamentary Committee's unanimous report, submitted to Parliament in December 2002. See Joint Parliamentary Committee, *Joint Committee on Stock Market Scam*, 10, 187–221, 222–51. Some of this ritualistic 'looking for the fall guy' would provoke the agencies into the next bout of regulatory *dirigisme*.

[37] Securities Appellate Tribunal (SAT), *SEBI vs. Shri Ashok Kumar Poddar*, Mumbai: Securities Appellate Tribunal, 2002.

[38] The policy response of this period is also outlined in Ajay Shah and Susan Thomas, 'Policy Issues in Indian Securities Markets,' *Reforming India's External, Financial and Fiscal Policies*, eds. Anne Krueger and Sajjid Chinoy, Stanford Studies in International Economics and Development, Stanford University Press, 2003, 129–47.

and a long overdue schism was driven between the cash and derivatives segments of the market. The badla system was banned in July 2001, the Automated Lending and Borrowing Mechanism (ALBM) that was needed to borrow and short stocks was done away with, rolling settlements were introduced, and the move to derivatives trading in specialized markets was accelerated.[39]

The ban on badla effectively removed the short side from the cash segment of Indian equity markets with attendant consequences, and in fact, the March 2001 budget sell-off was the last bear raid in Indian stock market history. By now, the ease with which badla allowed for a short side was becoming a liability in an age when the little guy was heavily in the market through mutual funds. The IT bear's lasting historic significance – unrecognized to this day – is that it ended the short side, which was momentous for the market. This reduced market efficiency and led to a one-sided market that allowed for those spectacular 1,000- and 2,000-bagger moves in later years. SEBI would go even further and impose restrictions that did away with the naked short play; only delivery-based short selling was allowed, though this was a redundant move, given the badla ban and the absence of a market-wide lending/borrowing mechanism.

The brokers took it in the neck and were seen as largely responsible for it all. As seen, the 1990s were a period of scams and settlement crises – Harshad Mehta (1992), MS Shoes (1995), Sterlite/Videocon/BPL (1998), and Ketan Parekh (2001) followed in quick succession. These crises impacted a broad public and often led to moral panic: 'the process of arousing social concern over an issue – usually the work of moral entrepreneurs and the mass media.'[40] During a moral panic, social concern is usually aroused over groups – called folk devils – who 'threaten' established social norms or community interests; much of this is done through the mass media. The threat to established social mores and norms by the folk devils arouses public concern and brings about a

[39] The chapter on derivatives contains a detailed treatment of these events.

[40] 'M: Moral panic,' *A Dictionary of Sociology*, ed. John Scott, 4th ed., New York: Oxford University Press, 2014, 492.

policy response like reform, resulting in social change. Bracketed as it was between the Mehta and Parekh scams, the stock market's decade of the 90s featured one such moral panic. Rebellious teenage gangs as folk devils were the original subject of Stanley Cohen's work on moral panics, while stockbrokers in the scam-tainted markets of the 90s also easily qualified as folk devils.[41] Deviancy and disproportionality are key here. There is a belief that the folk devils are pursuing deviant behaviour that violates societal norms, following which the mass media attempts to build the case against such deviancy and arouses public concern. So effective is the mass media's arousal that the public's response is usually disproportionate to any sort of actual 'threat' the folk devils pose to the established order. Public policy in India often got formulated through a series of responses to such crises-induced moral panics, and it was the resulting outcry, fuelled by a howling media, that led to change.[42]

Because of all this, the crisis was also the last gasp for broker control over exchanges. Broker directors of the Bombay and Calcutta exchanges were removed, as was the BSE's president.

The IT Bull's rise in trading volumes also prompted calls – later heeded – for Tobin tax-type levies, and a securities transaction tax (STT) on share transactions was subsequently introduced.[43] As with all government levies and taxes, once introduced, it took on a life of its own, and the levy continues into the present day. Like Colbert's goose, the

[41] The classic treatment of a moral panic can be found in Stanley Cohen, *Folk Devils and Moral Panics: The Creation of the Mods and Rockers*, 3rd ed., London: Routledge, Taylor and Francis, 2002.

[42] Sometimes you don't even need a crisis to generate a moral panic. In later years, India's right-wing political movements and online mobs would use mass media to take Cohen's idea of a moral panic to its extreme. Typically, 'urban Naxals, anti-nationals, *tukde tukde* gangs and Khan Market gangs' would be seen as folk devils, when in reality they were just groups on one side of a political spectrum. Uglier still was the attempt to brand religious minorities as folk devils, and sometimes even Bollywood insiders were labelled as such. A compromised and suborned media would then be used to set the agenda, transmit the imagery, and make bizarre claims on a range of issues from *ghar wapsi* (reconversion) to love *jihad* (religious miscegenation). This disturbed the social equilibrium, and the country lurched from one moral panic to the next.

[43] Kavaljit Singh, *Tax Financial Speculation: The Case for a Securities Transaction Tax in India*, New Delhi: Public Interest Research Centre, 2001. James Tobin proposed a tax as a disincentive on short-term spot currency transactions that were inherently speculative.

market got plucked on billions of its transactions without squawking too much.[44]

Unlike the Mehta affair, the IT bear did not draw much of a regulatory response from the RBI. The affair – particularly the GTB part – had raised questions about the capital market's exposure to commercial banks,[45] but despite that, the RBI did not tamper with the framework that governed the banking system's exposure to the capital market.[46] It concluded that the issues were not systemic, but concerned the behaviour of certain participants. The inspection regime for cooperative banks – once in two years – also came in for criticism from the chattering classes, as it had been the loophole that allowed MMCB to continue with its operations without detection.

Later, there was much misguided criticism of SEBI's regulatory response. Many believed that earlier regulatory action could have prevented an erosion in values, that somehow the fiasco could have been avoided or at least controlled.[47] But it is clear that that belief was untenable in the light of what happened on Nasdaq and globally. A related criticism was that SEBI did nothing on the upside and only stepped in when the sell-off reached severe proportions.[48] But if the regulator had done something that dampened and reduced the upside, it would have been argued that the SEBI was ending a legitimate market up move with heavy-handed tactics. A fairer criticism is that SEBI's claimed ignorance of Kolkata's *katni* (kerb) market – basically a gambling hell on the street outside the third largest exchange in the country – doesn't ring true.[49]

[44] 'The art of taxation consists of plucking the goose so as to obtain the most feathers with the least hissing,' Jean-Baptiste Colbert (finance minister of Louis XIV). 'Jean-Baptiste Colbert: Quotes,' *Britannica*, *https://www.britannica.com/quotes/Jean-Baptiste-Colbert.*

[45] Joint Parliamentary Committee, *Joint Committee on Stock Market Scam*, 60, 50–113.

[46] Ibid., 245–51.

[47] Ibid., 8.

[48] See Mani Shankar Aiyar, 'Stock Market Scam and UTI Imbroglio: JPC Report X-Rayed,' *Economic and Political Weekly*, Vol. 38, No. 10 (8–14 March 2003), 969–80.

[49] The kerb's importance to Calcutta's operations had been known for many years. Norman S. Poser and David Silver, *Regulation of the Indian Securities Markets: A Preliminary Survey,* Washington, D.C.: United States Securities and Exchange Commission (SEC), January 1965, 40–41.

In any case, the Ketan Parekh episode spelt the end of the Calcutta exchange, but it had been some time coming. The biggest exchange among the regionals, Calcutta (or Lyons Range as it was often called) saw itself less as a regional exchange and more as a competitor against Bombay to become a national exchange. During the Century of Marking Time, its listings – in terms of number of companies and capital – rivalled and occasionally surpassed Bombay. Cotton was the single sector that dominated Bombay, but Calcutta had a wider range of listings that included tea, jute, and collieries; even in 1908, its founding year, the Calcutta general list included 236 companies.[50] It was also the first exchange to produce better data for investors through its yearbooks.[51] Badla's powerful speculative influence on the Bombay market was less felt in Calcutta (or Madras), and as a result, the latter acquired a reputation for investment rather than speculation. Though its badla operations were negligible compared to Bombay, Calcutta offered cash trading at margins that were sometimes as low as 5 per cent, which made it attractive not just to the public but also to institutions, who benefited from the increased volumes.

Nevertheless, even before Independence and especially from the 1960s, Bombay had begun to pull ahead for reasons that had as much to do with the national environment as with local ones. First, Gandhi's boycott announcements against British companies during the Independence movement had disproportionate effects on the Calcutta exchange-listed companies, many of which were British owned, in contrast to Bombay-listed companies which were mainly Indian owned;[52] second, after Partition, many jute-growing areas found themselves in East Pakistan (later Bangladesh);[53] third, industries had

[50] Ibid., 5. A.K. Sur, 'History of the Stock Exchange' in A.K. Sur, ed. *The Stock Exchange: A Symposium*, Calcutta: Calcutta Stock Exchange Association, 1958. As late as 1986, Calcutta had more listed companies than Bombay, though the capital listed in Bombay was much larger.

[51] A.K. Sur, ed. *The Stock Exchange: A Symposium*, Calcutta: Calcutta Stock Exchange Association, 1958, xvi.

[52] The Editors, 'A Century and a Half Since the Neem Tree,' *Himal Southasian*, 1 September 2008.

[53] Aditi Roy Ghatak, *Down Lyons Range*, Kolkata: P.K. Ray for the Calcutta Stock Exchange Association, 2008, 67.

started migrating out of Bengal by the 1970s, though the communists at Writer's Building always maintained polite but distant relations with the capitalists at Lyons Range, located a short walking distance away; fourth, Bengal-based IISCO had been a pillar of the Calcutta exchange, and its surprise nationalization in 1972 dealt a blow to the exchange's operations and volumes, as did the nationalization of collieries in 1972; fifth, after mutual funds were opened up to the private sector in the early 1990s, the buy side's establishment in Mumbai meant that it was the BSE and not Calcutta that benefited from their volumes. Finally, during the Ketan Parekh imbroglio, much of the Calcutta exchange's trade guarantee fund got applied toward meeting the obligations of its defaulting brokers. Calcutta's turnover had surpassed even Bombay's in 1995–96, though its volumes were a little more than half of Bombay's during the IT mania. This turnover plunged more than 90 per cent after the Parekh imbroglio and the IT bear of 2001–02. By 2010, Kolkata's volumes were negligible, and it would later get into a legal tussle with SEBI over its continued existence.[54]

Similar existential issues awaited UTI. The country's largest public-sector fund had completed its asset reallocation in favour of tech stocks by September 1999, following which they all went off a cliff. UTI's flagship scheme, US-64, then suspended redemptions and effectively collapsed under the weight of its wrong investments.[55] After the 2001 sell-off, UTI went so far as to briefly suspend redemptions of its US-64 units.[56] The scheme would later get bailed out by the government, but the crisis marked the end of UTI's dominance of the buy side.

[54] N. Sundaresha Subramanian, 'HC Backs Forced Exit of Calcutta Stock Exchange,' *Business Standard*, 13 April 2016.

[55] V. Shankar Aiyar, 'UTI Flagship Scheme US-64 Pauperised by Former Chairman by Gambling on High-Risk Shares,' *India Today*, 23 July 2001; Government interference in UTIs operations is discussed in V. Shankar Aiyar, 'UTI Crisis: Political Parties Use and Abuse India's Largest Mutual Fund,' *India Today*, 13 August 2001.

[56] S. Vaidya Nathan, 'Behind the UTI Mess,' *Frontline*, 21 July 2001. UTI offered fixed dividends and administered redemption prices on its units, despite investing in equities that offered no guarantees on either dividends or prices. This extraordinary situation continued for years till the IT bust exposed its contradictions.

There was much caterwauling among participants during the IT bear, but this was the usual grumbling about issues that directly impacted their interests. Complaints were especially vociferous in any move that was seen to reduce volumes, and playing the volume card was a standard move by market participants. Sometimes the arguments could be ingenious. For example, some who opposed the badla ban argued that the injunction would reduce volumes and increase volatility in the markets; others argued that uneven access to finance among participants would enable the few parties who were able to get funds from the banking system to have an undue influence on the markets. But none of this proved influential in the wider scheme of things – badla would end and volumes would come back twice as strong in the next bull move.

The tech cycle would mark a coming of age for many Indian market participants. The 2000–03 bear market that resulted would continue till the onset of the Second Gulf War, a three-year stretch that is the longest-running period of declining prices in the modern era. Subsequently, distortions caused by factors such as the absence of a short side and global quantitative easing would ensure price corrections but never time corrections.[57] It was common in later years for top fund managers to look back on the episode with that peculiar combination of bitterness and nostalgia that comes from a hard lesson well learnt.

The Ketan Parekh scam that ended the episode proved to be the last market crisis in a long series. The tech cycle and the Parekh scam came at the end of the great reform period of the twentieth century's last decade, essentially bracketing that era with the Harshad Mehta episode of the early 90s. The Mehta imbroglio provided the opening impetus to a burst of reform measures, following which the reform process waxed and waned, hijacked as it was by the self-dealing of various participants. In fact, beginning in 1996, there had been a four-year hiatus in the reform momentum, and this inertia was overcome only by measures taken in the wake of the IT bust and the Parekh crisis. The latter gave regulators

[57] Quantitative easing is a monetary event that increases systemic liquidity through large purchases of government bonds or other financial assets, usually to drive down interest rates and stimulate economic activity. It was used extensively in the new millennium.

and others the necessary motivation to end the last remnants of the old system – of which the most important was the badla mechanism – and this was done away with in July 2001.[58] The microstructure was now in place, though it was not apparent through all the sound and fury of collapsing prices and a howling media.

[58] The badla system on the eve of its abolition is documented in Bombay Stock Exchange, *One Day Training Programme on the Carry Forward System (Badla)*, Mumbai: BSE, 1999.

5

RISE AND FALL IN THE RATE CYCLE

2003 to 2009

After the big reform push, the Indian stock market made a rather late entry into the modern era. From about 2003, dimly perceived through all the daily histrionics, we see for the first time the more settled cadence of a developed market. There was no more talk of settlement issues or delayed payments or party defaults. From now on, the focus was on the economy, valuations, fund flows, international or domestic events, and the usual babble of markets everywhere. The big clash between the state and the market had been settled. The indifference of the Nehruvian era was followed by a frenetic burst of state-sponsored reform, and then both gave way to a more established cadence. The institutional side started settling down to the point where it was taken for granted, and the action moved to the market cycle itself.

Contemplating this period between 2003 and 2009 is satisfying for a participant who believes in market cycles, encompassing as it does, within a defined and compressed time span, a pronounced cyclical rise and fall in the market. The powerful bull surge between 2003 and 2007 moved the market from sub-3,000 levels to almost 21,000, making it a seven-bagger (the comparable Nifty move was from 900 to 6,300).

From January 2008, the cycle violently reversed, and in the ensuing sell-off, the markets more than halved in a little over a year, falling below 9,000 by March 2009. This was the first big move after the modern microstructure was put in place, which makes this a fertile period for the study of markets. A closer look at this period brings out the stylized factors[1] that drive the stock market as it moves through its cycle – and that will be the focus here – but there remains the usual caveat that it is unclear if accurate analysis of the cycle is at all possible, except in retrospect.

This cycle has other firsts to its name. Unlike the Mehta and IT runs, both of which were associated with individuals, this was the first move not to be associated with a personality. Perhaps the operator class had learnt its lesson and saw media attention as problematic, but a more plausible explanation is that by now the markets had become too big to be influenced by a single person. Other firsts lay in the all-time records for stock moves within a single bull run, with some stocks going up between 1,000 and 2,000 times, driven in large part by the abolition of the short side.

Similar to the IT boom–bust, this cycle coincided almost exactly with international trends, and its beginning and end were part of worldwide moves. Most markets, including India, took the end of the second Gulf War in May 2003 as their cue to start an up move, with most ending their up moves around the time America's S&P 500 index peaked and rolled over in October 2007. Indian markets, too, topped out three months later. Despite all the *garam hawa* (hot air) on 'decoupling' that periodically bubbled up from the brokerages, the Sensex moved almost in lockstep with global markets. Since then, these two features of the move – the disassociation from a single personality and international correlation – have come to characterize the behaviour of India's markets.

---

[1] Entities or phenomena that influence (or are impacted by) the market cycle are marked in bold in this chapter.

Unlike previous runs, this bull run had a conventional **displacement**. The 1991 opening up had displaced the Mehta Bull (though the move was also associated with his treasury market exertions), while the internet had displaced the IT Bull that peaked in 2000. In this bull, the displacement was the **interest rate**, which is in keeping with textbook market lore. Yet, despite its obvious importance – this is the first move with the entire microstructure in place and the largest up move of the modern era (to that date, at least) – the bull move between 2003 and 2007 has no nomenclature attached to it. Given the displacement, it is appropriate to name this the Rate Bull, after the singular causal factor behind the up move.

Interest rates had remained low and stable from the RBI's 1935 founding all the way through to the early 1960s.[2] But from about the late 1960s to the mid-1990s, rates had accelerated considerably, driven in large part by inflation caused by devaluation, wars, droughts, and other calamities; towards the end of this era, blue-chip companies offered fixed deposit returns as high as 15 per cent with little risk, which presented the stock market with high hurdle rates and competition for a limited capital pool.

Only from the mid-1990s did this long-term rate cycle shift downward, and much of that effect was felt during the Rate Bull. 10-year G-Sec yields, or what in India passes for the long-bond yield, fell 900 basis points, or 9 per cent, from 14 per cent in September 1996 to a little over 5 per cent in September 2003 – and both data points are records for interest rates in the modern era.[3] The reduction was staggering and marked a historic and decisive break from the high interest rates of the 1970s and 1980s. A rate reduction of this magnitude had never happened before and has never been replicated since. Creaky monetary transmission – the process by which the RBI's monetary policy influences both the real and financial sectors of the economy

[2] H.T. Parekh, 'Indian Capital Market-Past, Present and Future,' *A.D. Shroff Memorial Lecture*, Bombay: A.D. Shroff Memorial Trust, 1975, 17–18.

[3] Between September 1996 and September 2003, G-Sec yields fell from 14.3 per cent to 5.08 per cent. See: 'India 10-Year Government Bond Yield,' *Trading Economics*, accessed January 2018, https://tradingeconomics.com/india/government-bond-yield.

– reduced the benefits of falling rates in India, but the magnitude of this decline was enough to overcome the tardiest transmission, albeit with a substantial lag. In fact, interest rates had fallen right through the IT boom–bust between 1998 and 2002 but had been ignored by participants, caught up as they were in the fireworks of IT stocks. Tech stocks are not sensitive to interest rates and this explains the disregard, but most Indian equity research also focused on the immediate past and did not go back far enough in time, which made it difficult to gauge displacements of this magnitude as they happened. That ignorance of causality has continued into the present, and the displacement caused by this one-time downward adjustment of rates that ended in 2003 has typically not been associated with the stock market move that followed.

Global and domestic **economic conditions** were also unusually conducive to growth. A multi-year surge in the US housing market was entering its final stages, and this led to an expanding wealth effect, together with substantial consumption-driven growth that spilt over into the world's economies. Seismic technological change had also resulted in productivity growth, reductions in unit labour costs, and reduced inflation.[4] China's admission into the World Trade Organization (WTO) brought some reduction in global consumer prices, albeit offset in part by that country's bullish influence on commodity prices. All these factors combined to produce a prolonged period of growth with low and stable inflation, and the falling interest rates that led to excellent conditions for equities. The effect was felt worldwide, and even places often regarded as growth laggards, like sub-Saharan Africa, grew at 5 per cent or more during these years, primarily due to a global commodity surge. [5]

Towards the end of the cycle, India's economy grew at 9 per cent, leading to the widely held belief that the country had 'arrived' and that this rate of growth was the new normal. Much of this growth came from

[4] US Congress, Joint Economic Committee, *The Economic Outlook (Statement of Hon. Alan Greenspan),* 109th Congress, First Session, 3 November 2005, 3–26.

[5] International Monetary Fund, World Economic and Financial Surveys, 'Regional Economic Outlook Sub-Saharan Africa,' Washington, DC: International Monetary Fund, April 2007, 3–4.

domestic consumption, services, and exports.[6] Nevertheless, increased domestic absorption and rising oil prices fuelled current account deficits that were financed by capital inflows from external corporate borrowing, interest differentials, and portfolio flows into the stock market. The flows into the stock market, in turn, stoked a substantial market boom. Inflation remained moderate through the first half of the move and rose only towards its end, driven by domestic demand and higher oil prices, though the oil impact was moderated as the government resorted to various contortions including oil bonds to avoid the pass-through.[7] As a result, the RBI commenced its rate-tightening cycle by late 2005, but the market would ignore it and keep chugging ahead for a good two years into the tightening. During this cycle at least, the stock market would lag interest rate movements on both sides.

By mid-2003, these favourable conditions had started playing out, but the market was in a slump. The market was at the bottom of the IT boom–bust cycle, and the tech-related new economy sectors had had the stuffing knocked out of them, while the old economy sectors had been neglected all along. In both cases, substantial value was beginning to manifest itself. So, by mid-2003, the market was in a sweet spot – coming off the bottom caused by the IT bust with liquidity conditions turning favourable, and the huge displacement of falling interest rates still to be factored into stock prices. At stock market bottoms, the trinity of Value, Liquidity, and Sentiment kick in at the same time and play on one another. At the bottom, Value begins to manifest itself, Liquidity chases Value and starts the market on its upswing, which improves Sentiment. The improvement in Sentiment, in turn, brings about a crucial psychological change in the crowd's mood as the market chatter shifts from 'sell on rallies' to 'buy on dips', and this gets the cycle going. The extreme violence of this mood change in late 2003 is noteworthy.

[6] Ministry of Finance, *Economic Survey 2005–2006*, New Delhi: Ministry of Finance, Department of Economic Affairs, 2006, 1–4, 9–10.

[7] The government subsidized global oil prices to cushion the public from their volatility. Initially, cash subsidies were used to compensate public sector oil companies, but from 1998 or so, oil bonds were issued instead. This off-budget subsidy financing later became a habit, and food and fertilizers were subsidized in similar fashion.

Domestic **liquidity** conditions – already turning favourable because of the rate reductions – were also aided by a surge in inward remittances from sizable Middle East diasporas on the eve of the Second Gulf War in 2003.[8] But more than domestic liquidity, it was global liquidity that favoured the markets, and this bull brought out the key role of foreign investors in an up move.

Foreign Institutional Investors (FIIs) had been present since 1992, but the Rate Bull confirmed their importance like never before. Participants obsessed over foreign inflows more in this bull than in any other, and the figures were prominently mentioned in the media's daily coverage of the market. The reasons for this obsession became obvious as the market started mirroring the flow of foreign money, surging or selling off as FIIs invested or withdrew funds. From the FII standpoint, the interest was despite the reduction in diversification benefits brought about by high correlations; unlike in the days prior to and just after liberalization, high correlations between India and world markets were now becoming the norm.[9] As a result, for FIIs, diversification benefits from investing in India (and other emerging markets) were gradually reducing – but were still substantial enough to be used as a *raison d'être*.[10] Nonetheless, that was always in the background, and it was usually yield or return that really mattered.

The pattern of FII buying being offset by **Domestic Institutional Investors (DIIs)** selling (or vice versa) also started becoming apparent with the Rate Bull, and both sides started crossing each other with regularity in the markets. FII inflows were tied to global liquidity and

[8] For a view (by the NSE's founding head) of market conditions on the eve of the Rate Bull, see R.H. Patil, 'Interest Rates and Equity Markets,' *Economic and Political Weekly*, Vol. 38, No. 12/13, 22 March–4 April 2003, 1105. There is not even a hint of the roaring bull conditions that lay just ahead.

[9] For correlation calculations from the early years, see Roger Ignatius, 'The Bombay Stock Exchange: Seasonality and Investment Opportunities,' Discussion Paper 29, *Discussion Papers*, Bond University School of Business, 1992, 21.

[10] Five-year rolling correlations between regional and developed stock markets fell after the Asian crisis of 1997–98 but began to rise again after the technology bubble burst in 2001–02. Cyclical variations in correlations (and diversification benefits) are also apparent from this period onwards; markets rise at different paces but tend to fall together, and as a result, correlations tend to fall over long bull phases but rise over an entire cycle of data.

asset allocation trends, but the domestic buy side was only invested locally and had the incentive to smooth out volatile foreign flows that affected local performance. Earlier, the domestic buy side had usually meant LIC, but this was the first bull market where mutual funds started coming into their own, driven in large part by private-sector entry into the fund space and favourable tax treatment for mutual fund products. Despite that, DII efforts at counterbalancing foreign flows would not be enough, as the sell-off in 2008 and 2009 demonstrated. Yet, the Rate cycle is the last occasion when DIIs were overwhelmed by FII selling. In later years, access to rupee cost averaging products such as the Systematic Investment Plan (SIP) would give the domestic buy side the ammunition to counterbalance FIIs and reduce somewhat their influence on the markets. In doing so, the domestic buy side informally reinforced capital market segmentation, but no one really noticed.

The rupee–dollar **exchange rate**, the only pair that really mattered in India's foreign exchange markets, strengthened through most of the Rate Bull. In one of the longest sustained periods of rupee appreciation, the exchange rate moved from 47 to 39 between 2001 and January 2008. It was driven in large part by record portfolio inflows into the market, remittances from non-resident Indians (NRIs), or direct (usually brownfield) investment. The appreciation was a rare reversal in the secular decline of the rupee, and it briefly resulted in a double whammy to the upside for FIIs – they benefited both from the Rate Bull's up move and the conversion to dollars when they exited[11] (when they entered, for instance, they gave up a dollar to buy 47 worth of stock, but on exit they got higher stock prices and gave up only 41 to get back that same dollar). It was the first and only time this would happen in the modern era, and the appreciation fuelled further inflows from FIIs.

However, the strengthening rupee raised concerns about export competitiveness and, along with the expanding domestic liquidity that followed from the central bank's intervention, was another causal factor behind the early onset of monetary tightening. So, for a brief

[11] Exchange rates on INR/USD are available at https://tradingeconomics.com/india/currency.

while, the RBI found itself caught in the familiar policy trilemma of managing the exchange rate, monetary independence, and allowing for some freedom on capital flows. Allowing for capital flows and monetary independence meant giving up on fixing the exchange rate, and this was anyway official policy with the dirty float. But the capital inflows continued, and the rupee continued to appreciate, putting pressure on export competitiveness. As a result, the RBI tried to intervene and prevent the appreciation by selling rupees and buying dollars, in effect, trying to manage or 'fix' the exchange rate; this added to the monetary base and could be inflationary, and so, it sterilized the intervention by selling bonds, which reduced the monetary base by the extent of the intervention. Intervening and sterilizing flows became a pattern, but this complicated monetary policy and was expensive.

As FIIs continued to benefit from rising markets and an appreciating currency, the inflows kept coming. The key point was that neither debt nor equity markets in India had the absorptive capacity to deal with such surges. The G-Sec market was negligible, corporate debt markets were practically non-existent, and the stock market had a peculiar problem: it could absorb inflows – and welcomed them with folded hands as the inflows moved prices to bubble levels – but did not have the capacity to generate outflows. The presence of severe capital market segmentation and domestic bias meant that most participants did not invest outside India. If they had invested internationally, the resulting outflows would have moderated surges and reduced the RBI's need to intervene on inflows. The pattern of heavy inflows – because of unorthodox Western monetary policy and quantitative easing – would repeat itself from 2009 onwards, but this time the RBI would intervene and move the exchange rate downwards to preserve export competitiveness.[12]

The colossal decrease in policy rates between 1996 and 2003 also reduced interest expenses for **companies** and lowered corporate borrowing costs, making future investments cheaper; inefficient monetary transmission usually prevented the pass-through of lower

[12] In this period, India would briefly enter (and then leave) the US Treasury's watch list of potential currency manipulators. The rupee–dollar pair would touch 80 by 2022.

policy rates, but such was the extent of this reduction that it still allowed companies to benefit substantially. Consequently, companies announced massive capital raising plans as capacity utilization increased with rising demand. Working capital – unglamorous yet vital, given the long working capital cycles of most Indian companies – also got cheaper, and inventories and receivables cost less to finance. Domestic consumption, particularly in areas such as white goods and automobiles, rose substantially, and real estate prices also took off. The effect of these changes on corporate earnings had been building for some time but was ignored by a market focused on the tech boom–bust cycle. Inventories remained reasonable through the expansion, but corporate debt would rise in later years.[13] Companies raised considerable amounts of debt, and corporate financing was dominated by issuance of foreign currency-denominated convertible debt with embedded options for equity conversion at high conversion prices; though the coupons were low, the exposure was usually unhedged and effectively a bet on continued stock and rupee appreciation. This did not happen after 2008, which led to financial distress.[14]

Most of the proceeds raised from such financing went into domestic investment, but some of the proceeds were also used to fund overseas acquisitions, often at inflated prices. Overseas expansion for many companies became de rigueur. Towards the end, even Tatas succumbed, buying steel giant Corus at the 2007 top, after rationalizing that this sort of capacity came rarely at one stroke. Whether this worked out in their favour is debatable, as the digestion of Corus was still in progress over a decade later. Discounting the labour arbitrage of IT service companies, most Indian companies would have a poor track record as MNCs.

It was the heyday of the **strong-arm promoters,** many of whom came from the infrastructure space. In keeping with the nature of the

[13] Ashish Gupta et al., 'House of Debt,' *Credit Suisse*, Asia Pacific/India Equity Research, 21 October 2015.

[14] Company strategies for dealing with busted convertibles are outlined in Tanuj Khosla, 'Challenging Times Ahead for Indian Foreign Currency Convertible Bonds,' *Institutional Investor*, 3 June 2011.

displacement, rate-sensitive sectors such as infrastructure and real estate dominated the Rate Bull as much as software had dominated the previous run. As a result, the market became enamoured with the strong-arm promoters of such companies. Many of these strong-arm promoters demonstrated aggressive risk-taking appetites and the capacity to get things done, which went together with that most important of capabilities – the ability to 'manage the environment'.[15] This was a euphemism for the *hera pheri* (hanky-panky) and 'compromises' deemed essential for interaction with the bureaucracy or government, and anything to do with infrastructure required extensive interaction of that sort. Some of the strong-arm promoters were both businessmen and politicians and used political connections to help themselves to the banking system, a full three-quarters of which was anyway government-owned. It was common to find boards of companies owned by strong-arm promoters packed with retired bankers from public-sector banks.

The absence of substantial creditor rights and a government-owned banking system with its own agency issues allowed the strong-arm promoters to abuse the debt contract in their corporate financing. Large sums were raised, mainly from the public sector banking space, and in many cases, chunks of loan proceeds were recycled by the strong-arm promoters back to the banks. Corrupting a bank could be done with the bank's own money and usually involved recycling part of the loan proceeds back to the bank's loan sanctioners. Colossal amounts were borrowed in this fashion, with 'quid pro quo' – the polite euphemism for such a transaction. External shareholders in such companies thought such debt financing was going into investment, but 'managing the environment' in this fashion left fewer debt proceeds for actual investment in fixed assets. Carried out on a large scale, it simply meant fewer fixed assets to service the officially stated debt/equity ratio, effectively making it as difficult to service as a higher debt/equity ratio, and this hidden leverage was a burden unwittingly borne by external shareholders. In many cases, a project's equity component was also borrowed as debt in

[15] 'Managing the environment' is double entendre for a broad swath of activity – usually involving some type of rent seeking – that takes place when the Indian state interacts with businesses.

a roundabout fashion, further adding to the hidden leverage borne by external shareholders.

Big hazy bets on the future were easy with other people's money, and for a while, this debt-fuelled growth led to massive rises in these stocks. Later, many such investments would get mired in that peculiar Indian combination of incompetence, corruption, bad karma, and self-interested dealing, leading to bad debt levels that the banking system might have succumbed to, had it not been backstopped by the implicit guarantee of government ownership. When the inherent unviability of many projects was exposed, the servicing of the debt became impossible, and yet the companies involved limped along for many years after, as part of the undead – zombies that continued because of the country's lack of a bankruptcy code. In turn, the zombie companies led to zombie banks and a dysfunctional banking system that lumbered on through crisis conditions but without an outright blow-up because of the implicit government backstop. Exit would be facilitated in later years by the passage of an insolvency code, but the share prices of many of these companies would move to single digits.

During the bull surge, the Sensex went from its May 2003 low of 3,000 to almost 21,000 in a little over four years, with two major sell-offs in between. The first took place in 2004 when the first Congress-led United Progressive Alliance (UPA) government came to power, but with the support of Communist parties; this was followed by a 2006 crash that was part of a broader emerging market correction. But the market kept pulling back, and the up move continued. The market was inclined to the 'buy on dips' trade – purchases made in the 2004 and 2006 sell-offs yielded substantial profits irrespective of which stocks were bought – and the psychological continuity provided by this line of thought would prove crucial to the bull market's integrity.

Despite the substantial up move, valuations remained sensible except towards the end of the run. Driven mainly by the interest rate displacement, **earnings** grew faster than market prices for a substantial period and this – the most basic of bull market criteria – allowed the move to continue for a substantial period. Corporate profits grew between 15 and 30 per cent every year in those heady days.[16] The market then got comfortable with capitalizing those fast-growing earnings at ever higher multiples. Earlier, the market had valued stocks at, say, 12 times earnings, but now 22 times seemed reasonable given the higher growth rates, and stock prices soared as the higher multiples were applied to higher earnings. This multiple expansion kept the market going on its bull run, and the earnings expansion kept stocks from being exorbitantly priced, except towards the very end. At the run's end, the market, at about 28 times earnings, was reasonably enough at the high end of its valuation band. It was the sweet spot that all bull markets need for take-off and sustenance.

The market took off on the back of economic growth and earnings accretion from the interest rate displacement, but all this happened despite the **government** and not because of it. The entire Rate Bull cycle coincided almost exactly with the Congress-led UPA's first term between 2004 and 2009, and never before or since has such a tremendous rise and fall coincided with a single Lok Sabha term. This first UPA government (it would win a second term in 2009) even had a substantial Communist presence, and it remains an awkward fact that the run took place with a Communist-influenced and supported government in charge of the economy. With a left-of-centre coalition, reform efforts and announcements were negligible; the Securitisation and Reconstruction of Financial Assets and Enforcement of Securities Interest Act, 2002 (SARFAESI), which provided additional powers to banks on loan recovery, was the last major reform initiative, and that was two years old by 2004. So, despite the complete lack of reform initiatives, the market had its best period ever in the years from 2003 to 2007.

This lack of correlation between reform efforts and up moves was now an enduring trait of Indian markets and amply demonstrated in the Rate Bull. Yet the brokerages remained tone-deaf to this absence of correlation. In fact, the only bull market of the modern era to have

[16] Arvind Subramanian and Josh Felman, 'India's Great Slowdown: What Happened? What's the Way Out?,' CID Faculty Working Paper, 370, Centre for International Development, Harvard University, December 2019, 9–11.

a reform underpinning was the first Mehta Bull that was underwritten by Manmohan Singh's 1991 budget. In subsequent years, participants would howl periodically for 'reform', and the howling would reach its peak during lean market phases. When markets did well, there was little need to go on about the need for reform, but when markets did badly – or better still, when they crashed – the urgency and drama of the fall led to the howling.

The UPA government never took credit for the huge bull move, perhaps because of the BJP's dismal experience with the 'India Shining' campaign. Carried away by the up move's initial stage and by a general sense of urban prosperity, the previous BJP government had coined the term 'India Shining' to describe the phenomenon, only to take it in the neck in the 2004 elections.[17] Since then, the term has become a byword for a Pollyannaish view of the country's progress, but it is also a reminder that the world's largest democracy is also one of the poorest, which makes it politically expedient to appeal to the vast majority of have-nots rather than the haves.

In fact, by early 2008, the Rate Bull was just reflecting considerable economic expansion, but the Congress-led UPA still let the market be. Uncertain about the length of such moves and wary after the BJP's experience with India Shining, the UPA government simply did not pay much attention to the market's upsurge. This was wise in hindsight. Because the government did not take credit for the rise, it was not pilloried for the debacle of 2008 that followed. Yet the government couldn't get away scot-free; despite not taking credit for the upside, the state had to deal with the market's howling for 'reform' when things turned to the downside. Dalal Street could be as irrational in its view of the government as in its pricing of a momentum-driven small-cap stock.

Naya daur thinking was also most apparent in the Rate Bull. The sudden acceleration in growth from the interest rate displacement and the inability to see that as part of a worldwide expansion were the main

[17] Advertising agency Grey Worldwide developed the campaign that used the phrase.

causes behind the fallacy. Also contributing to *naya daur* thinking was talk of Chindia, a China–India growth pole in the world economy, and Jairam Ramesh's coinage of the portmanteau in 2004 coincides with the early days of the Rate Bull.[18] Much of this talk was picked up by the international media and echoed back to the country's policy elite, promoter class, and domestic media. Yet, none of the country's well-known development problems – particularly with infrastructure – were addressed during this period, and there was little momentum on reform. But issues of infrastructure and reform were inconveniences the real economy had to deal with. This was the stock market, and it was simply going up. Nothing else mattered.

The amount of capital raised in the Rate Bull's last year came in at ₹42,000 crores, setting a record.[19] Yet, the **IPO** market remained sedate by the standards it had set in the 1990s, bereft of the boom in new issues that had otherwise characterized market tops. To most participants, the primary side did not feel as euphoric as it had in previous IPO waves. One explanation is that issuances were fewer in number but larger in size. Much of the IPO action came towards the end of the bull run, and issuers faced the same problem as brokerages – a lack of conviction on how long the move would last. Reliance Power was the big issue that came in at the top, timing the market perfectly in January 2008 and subsequently losing most of its value.

The Rate Bull's contrast with the IT Bull on **market breadth** is also striking. The IT Bull had been the narrowest of up moves, with all the action concentrated on a small segment of IT, media, and telecom stocks; by contrast, the Rate Bull was the broadest of bull markets, characterized by stable market breadth and extensive sector rotation. Most bull markets have standout sectors that are stars and where the momentum action tends to cluster, but the Rate Bull was characterized by an expansive

[18] Jairam Ramesh, *Making Sense of Chindia: Reflections on China and India*, New Delhi: India Research Press, 2005.

[19] Securities and Exchange Board of India (SEBI), *Handbook of Statistics of Indian Security Market 2010*, 16, https://www.sebi.gov.in/reports/handbook-of-statistics/jul-2011/handbook-of-statistics-on-the-indian-securities-market-2010_20167.html.

move across the general list. This is because the displacement was the interest rate which, by definition, has a broad effect on all sectors. As a result, the move in the general list took all sectors up, though over different time periods. So, the average of the monthly ratio of advances to declines was at 0.98 in 2004, and that ratio stayed at the same level in 2007, the last year of the bull move.[20] The stable market breadth and the tendency of sectors to flare up at different times led fund managers to practice the art of sector rotation; this they did by trying to outguess the market crowd and where it would be next, often with mixed results.

Styles such as 'buy and hold' were rewarded, and the traders had egg all over their faces. Whatever the too-clever-by-half traders sold kept going up, and so they had to be content with limited percentage gains. In contrast to earlier times, when trading markets were the dominant experience, the Rate Bull's steadily trending market – aided in large part by the abolition of the short side – rewarded the more patient investor types. From now on, 'buy and hold' would become the dominant ethos for the domestic buy side, and the Rate Bull was the first golden age for mutual funds. They needed a trending market with stable breadth to match their philosophy, and for the first time ever, the Indian market had simply swung around to reward their investing style. In later years, the distortions caused by quantitative easing would lead to continuously trending markets, and Dalal Street would lose its memory of what a trading market really looked like.

The **public** did not physically come to Dalal Street during the Rate Bull, a first in the Street's long and turbulent history. Old-timers needing that personal connect with a broker to execute their orders and manage their funds still came by, but the order book had been online at least since 2000. Because of internet trading, the market could now be in your living room. The crowd had gone virtual, and for the first time, there was little geographic focus to the euphoria. The public's presence had been an important part of Street lore, supposedly because it indicated

[20] *NSE*, https://www1.nseindia.com/products/content/equities/equities/historical_advdeclines.htm. The NSE's advance-decline ratio is a more accurate indicator of market breadth because it includes fewer penny stocks that are legacies from the IPO booms of the 1980s and 1990s.

a market top. Some years back, Harshad Mehta's Lexus entering Dalal Street had been enough to send the market higher – now *that* was a bull market – but during this move, some old-timers were wont to ask, 'Where's the euphoria?' From their offices on Dalal Street, there didn't seem to be much of it around. In reality, the euphoria was everywhere, but most couldn't see it, not just because the order book was online, but also because they simply didn't want to see it. For many participants, becoming cognizant of the public's euphoria and accepting its portent would have meant calling the top right, which also meant making the painful decision to exit their beloved positions. Far better, therefore, to avoid that decision and insist – all the way into the next bear market – that the public's presence was expected and just around the corner.

Brokerages benefited from the bull surge, as the expansion in volumes helped their top lines while their cost structures remained essentially unchanged. The Rate Bull was the last run when fee-based income streams such as brokerage really mattered to the big wire houses; in subsequent years, annuity-based income streams from housing finance, financial distribution, and other such areas also became their focus.[21] Unconvinced about the move's duration, most made do with existing resources and held off expansion and recruitment till the final stages of the bull run; they had been down this road before and were cagey about the violently cyclical nature of the market. The brokerage commission pool would reach a historic high of about ₹14,000 crores during the Rate Bull top in 2007; subsequently, structural changes – including the public's shift to the low-yielding derivatives markets, the move to online trading, the rise of discount brokerages, and the general commoditization of the brokerage business – would reduce the industry top line, though pool levels would again be reached, and then exceeded, during the SIP Bull that followed.[22]

Many wire houses took advantage of industry conditions, with some selling stock in themselves, while others sold themselves outright. Motilal Oswal went public, while the founding families of D.S. Purbhoodas and

[21] Pravin Palande, 'Why Indian Brokerages are Looking Elsewhere,' *Forbes*, 9 May 2013.

[22] ICRA Research Services, 'Indian Brokerage Industry,' Mumbai: ICRA, September 2017, 4–5.

Jamnadas Morarjee sold out to their foreign partners, bringing to an end presences that had exceeded a century, though both would continue their existence in other areas of the market. This was also the first bull market where regional exchanges and their dominant brokers did not play a substantial role.[23] Till the IT Bull, Calcutta had a role in the interexchange rollover and arbitrage trade, but now all market action would be confined to the NSE and BSE.

Most wire houses were abundantly cautious in the early stages of the move, but by 2007 (and in keeping with market lore), they and the chattering classes had thrown in the towel; most were on the same side of the trade, uniformly long in the market, and generally along for the ride. Many people had to buy at a top for it to happen in the first place. Across the board, brokerage forecasts – and for that matter, all market forecasts – fell victim to the hockey stick phenomenon that happens at turning points; with the market nearing 21,000 in early 2008, the usual tendency was to move along the long end of the hockey stick and forecast a year-end Sensex target of, say, 25,000, but the actual result was an inverted V, and the market went almost to 8,000 during that year.

In later years, **private equity's** concerns with the market could usually be summarized in one word – exits. It desperately needed the 'exits' provided by a heated IPO market, but during the Rate Bull, private equity was going through its first ever fund-raising cycle, and so its concern was entry rather than exit.[24] Private equity had been a five-star industry all along, raising money in the West and deploying it in India while taking on severe currency risk in the process. Private equity came in at the top. Most of the private equity types still lacked the feel for ground-level market movement possessed by the dervishes (the big professional traders) of Dalal Street or by the older brokerages, and as a result, many overpaid for equity in Indian companies. 'The game taught me the game. And it did not spare the rod while teaching,' is

[23] The big regional exchanges had brokers with standing in those markets: Kolkata had Place Siddons & Gough, Stewart Mackertich, and Dayco, while Chennai had Paterson and Co.

[24] Ajay Shah, Susan Thomas, and Michael Gorham, 'Private Equity and the IPO Market,' *India's Financial Markets: An Insider's Guide to How the Markets Work*, Amsterdam: Elsevier, 2008, 45–54.

what Edwin Lefèvre made his fictional character Larry Livingston say in *Reminiscences of a Stock Operator*.[25] For most of the private equity industry it would be a difficult first cycle as well, and Lefèvre's rod was waiting for many of them.

But the most significant cause of the Rate Bull was the **long corner**. The short corner had been a defining feature from the Century of Marking Time, usually coming to a head when on settlement day it was discovered that more stock had been sold short than was available for delivery – a common situation in those days, because badla allowed for the naked short and also because shares were (as a rule) more difficult to obtain than money. As a result, short sellers who had bet wrong would find the price rocketing even higher as they bought back to meet their obligations, which led to the short corner and squeeze. But the Rate Bull marks the first time in Indian stock market history when the long corner – the upside bias to price that results from systemic factors that lower market-wide free float – became first a possibility and then a norm. Unlike the short corner, which was a temporary phenomenon resulting from the technical setup of the market, the long corner resulted from systemic factors: the ownership structure of Indian capitalism, changes in the market microstructure that eliminated the short side, and the absence of international diversification. Because the causes of the long corner were systemic, its effects were pervasive and permanent, and sometimes it felt like the entire Indian market had been cornered long. And yet despite its importance, the term 'long corner' itself does not exist, and this is the first work to define and apply it as such to the market.

The ownership structure of Indian capitalism played a big role in creating the long corner. To understand this structure, it is best to start with its antithesis, as outlined in *The Modern Corporation and Private Property*, a seminal 1932 work on company ownership. In the book,

[25] Edwin Lefèvre, *Reminiscences of a Stock Operator*, New York: John Wiley and Sons, 1994, 37.

Adolf Berle and Gardiner Means postulate a world in which ownership of corporations is widely dispersed, with management control in the hands of a professional managerial class acting through a board.[26] The emergence of the corporation, the basic unit that traded on a stock market, had broken property relationships, as widely dispersed shareholders surrendered control to a stewardship class of managers, who often acted in their own interest rather than that of shareholders. For example, shareholders might prefer firm profits returned to them as dividends, but managers might prefer reinvestment in the firm to increase the size of their kingdoms; alternatively, managers might even take out the firm's profits through higher salaries. After Berle and Means, a long and distinguished line of work further defined and analysed a similar array of problems that clustered under the rubric of corporate governance and agency.[27]

Without going into details, it is sufficient to state that this Anglo-Saxon model of ownership in a Berle and Means world was diametrically opposed to Indian conditions; here, both ownership and control rested with a promoter group, usually a founding family and their related parties, who held significant stakes in companies. In fact, companies with promoter stakes as high as 80 to 90 per cent were not uncommon at one time, and most large surveys found promoter holdings of about 50 per cent (which holds true even in 2025).[28] Ironically, markets tended to reward such companies with better valuations under the rationale that their promoters had more 'skin in the game'. The concentrated ownership of the promoter class allowed for better alignment of cash

[26] Adolf Berle and Gardiner Means, *The Modern Corporation and Private Property*, New Brunswick and London: Transaction Publishers, 1991.

[27] For a survey of corporate governance issues from an agency perspective, see Andrei Shleifer and Robert Vishny, 'A Survey of Corporate Governance,' *Journal of Finance*, Vol. 52, No. 2, June 1997, 737–83.

[28] Melvin Jameson, Andrew Prevost, and John Puthenpurackal, 'Controlling Shareholders, Board Structure, and Firm Performance: Evidence from India,' *Journal of Corporate Finance*, Vol. 27, 2014, 1–20. In a sample size of 1796 firms, close to two-thirds had promoter families, with an average shareholding of about 50 per cent. In contrast to prevailing market opinion, this study found a statistically significant negative association between promoter ownership and firm valuation as measured through Tobin's *q*, irrespective of independent director presence, firm size, or institutional ownership levels.

flow and control rights, which was a cardinal principle of corporate governance, and yet corporate governance continued to remain an issue in the country, primarily because of a cumbersome legal framework that allowed for protection of minority shareholder rights on paper but less so in practice.

High promoter holdings were not confined to the private sector; in public-sector companies, government ownership through the President of India holding was usually over 51 per cent, and such levels were considered necessary for entities like government-owned banks. Primary markets also encouraged the long corner, and for a considerable period, regulations made it possible to get away with selling as little as 10 per cent of issued capital.

So, the ownership structure of Indian capitalism led to high promoter holdings, and the resulting low free floats allowed for the long corner. In fact, the pendulum on free floats and offer amounts had swung in both directions. Following the mania of 1920, the Bombay exchange had insisted that 33 per cent of equity had to be sold for a company to qualify for an official quotation and listing; the BSE would subsequently raise that requirement to 50 per cent, which became irrelevant with the enactment of the 1956 SCRA regulations that prescribed 49 per cent.[29] But in later years, the pendulum swung towards ever lower floats and offer amounts, and as recently as 2001, large companies, according to Section 19 (2) (b) of the SCRA, could get away with offering as little as 10 per cent of their equity to the public. The swing itself has not been highlighted before – hidden as it is behind those bizarrely convoluted IPO regulations – and so, the reasons behind it have never been explained. As a result, there are no real explanations for the phenomenon other than casual ones involving investment bankers and promoters. Investment bankers claim small amounts are offered because of the perennially fragile state of IPO markets; because of regulatory capture, regulators listen to these views. In turn, promoters naturally try to get the long corner to work to their advantage, as the scarcity

[29] K.R.P. Shroff, *History and Present Position of the Stock Market in India*, Bombay: The Stock Exchange, Bombay, 1962, 34.

premium on a stock that is cornered long leads to valuations having second order effects on prices.

In recent years, the pendulum has swung back towards higher free floats, and attempts have been made to get the promoter class to reduce its holding. As of 2022, companies are required to maintain minimum public holdings of 25 per cent. This still leaves considerable holdings with promoters, and it is not uncommon to find companies with nearly half to three-quarters of the shareholding with the promoter group. In a twist that is a common outcome of India's ever-shifting and convoluted regulations, companies issuing a lower amount are given large time periods to raise it to the 25 per cent threshold; in effect, this allows for the continued issuance of tiny amounts of equity while pursuing the benefits of a public listing.[30] For the entire market, about 45 per cent of equity is held by promoters.[31] Empirical work indicates that between two-thirds and three-quarters of listed firms have controlling interests resting with an individual or family – the promoter group.[32] Given the socialist origins of the Indian state, there are anyway numerous government-owned firms, and removing them from the calculation raises the proportion of promoter firms even more than the two-third to three-quarter estimate. One study found that only 3 per cent of firms were widely held – where widely held was defined as a situation in which no single shareholder held more than 10 per cent of equity.[33]

The combined effect of all this reduced the free float, and this reduced free float meant that even a cursory accumulation and holding of stock diminished even further the outstanding shares available in the market. Bull market conditions acting on low free floats then drove up prices of the limited stock available, often to stratospheric levels –

[30] The main legislation for IPOs is the Securities and Exchange Board of India (Issue of Capital and Disclosure Requirements) Regulations of 2018 (the ICDR Regulations), which superseded a 2009 version.

[31] NSE, *India Ownership Tracker*, 11 April 2022. Vol 3, Issue 3, Mumbai: NSE, 2022, 1.

[32] Franklin Allen, Rajesh Chakrabarti, Sankar De, Jun Qian, and Meijun Qian, 'Financing Firms in India,' *Journal of Financial Intermediation*, 21 January 2012, 425; Melvin Jameson et al., 'Controlling Shareholders, Board Structure,' 2, 14.

[33] Ibid.

and this resulted in the long corner. By way of example, consider that IBM would have 0 per cent locked up with a promoter group, while a comparable Indian company, such as Wipro or TCS, would have close to 75 per cent locked up with a promoter group who never really sold or traded the stock, and the long corner acquires some clarity. The years of unconventional Western monetary policy, first in response to the Great Recession and later in response to the COVID-19 pandemic, brought liquidity surges that further heightened the long corner and drove valuations to bubble levels.

A second reason for the long corner arose from a decision made during the microstructure revolution – the July 2001 abolition of badla that also did away with the short side. Before 2001, the ability to short stock was seen as a sine qua non for the market, a natural corollary of the view that differences of opinion were the essence of activities like horse races and stock markets. Perusing the historical record from the early years and reading comments from the likes of K.R.P. Shroff and M.R. Mayya shows a striking and powerful regard for this view.[34] Badla took this view to an extreme by allowing for the naked short; this resulted in an unlimited supply of stock for shorting, which in turn depressed prices and fed into the pessimism of the age. But with the 2001 abolition of badla, the short side was effectively abolished, and the pendulum now moved to the other extreme. The naked short play went from being baked into the market's microstructure to abolition. Without the ability to short and without a real lending/borrowing mechanism for stock, there was no bear side to the market and no countervailing force to deal with the optimism of the bulls. India has no bears nowadays – the only bears are bulls who have liquidated their positions and who are looking to get back in at lower prices. As a result, prices get set by the most optimistic buyer at the margin. The Rate Bull was the first bull market without a short side, and it showed in the price moves. For the first time,

[34] See for example, 'Short Selling Can Go a Long Way in Steadying Prices,' in M.R. Mayya, *Glimpses of Indian Stock Markets*, Mumbai: Indian Institute of Capital Markets, 2010, 337–38. On page 239, M.R. Mayya says, 'Any attempt to disrupt total neutrality between bulls and bears will not work.'

the word 'multi-bagger' entered the market lexicon in India, and price appreciations of 1,000 and 2,000 times were now seen as normal.

Despite the fact that India has no short selling, talking heads in the media often go on about 'short covering' and routinely and reflexively mention it as the reason behind a price increase. The issue is complex and subject to widespread misconceptions. Indian markets allow unlimited intraday short selling, but inter-temporal short selling – across time – is rare because of extensive restrictions that make the short side impossible for most traders.

Intraday short selling is allowed without any price test restrictions similar to America's Rule 10a-1(a)(1). Also known as the uptick rule, the SEC's Rule 10a-1(a)(1) creates a price test for short sales by allowing US traders to short a share only at a price higher than the security's last trade; first enacted in 1938, the idea was to prevent the buildup of catastrophic momentum to the downside during a single trading session.[35] (The rule was eliminated in 2007, brought back in modified form in 2010, and now kicks in only if stocks have lost 10 per cent or more of their value from the previous close.)

Without an uptick rule, traders in India can short unlimited stock during a trading session, subject to the usual margining requirements and without waiting for a price uptick (the price test) to initiate the position. This can sometimes have frightening consequences, especially for blue-chip stocks that are the underlying for derivatives contracts – these counters are anyway not subject to intraday price limits. In January 2009, Satyam's chairman confessed to widespread accounting manipulation and fraud in a letter whose contents were released just before trading hours, and as a result, the stock fell almost 90 per cent within minutes.[36] In 2020, the situation would repeat when the RBI imposed a moratorium on Yes Bank and suspended its board, which also led to a near 90 per cent intraday fall. Derivatives traders

[35] For an overview of the issues involved in abolishing a price test for short sales, see: https://www.sec.gov/rules/final/2007/34-55970.pdf.

[36] PTI, 'Satyam Shares Tank 85% at Rs 6.30 on NSE in Early Trade,' *Economic Times*, 9 January 2009.

operating on margin – and there are millions in India's retail-dominated derivatives markets – risk losing their entire margin capital in minutes (or sometimes even in seconds) when this happens.

Nevertheless, all such intraday trades have to be squared up during the trading day itself because of the short constraint, resulting in a wash transaction from a systemic standpoint; the short drives down the price, and the square up cover on the long side takes the price up, with no real change during the session. Transactions not squared up have to be settled at an auction the next day, but this rarely happens. So, in the uptick rule's absence, the intraday short is often executed by traders and speculators, making for a very volatile intraday market and adding to market momentum to the downside when there is a big break. This sometimes gives the impression that the short trade is allowed, but because the transaction is a wash, intraday short selling has no impact on price. It is the buyer's strike and real delivery-based selling that account for most of the intraday fall.

By contrast, actual inter-temporal short selling in the cash market – across time periods of weeks or months – by using a borrowing/lending mechanism is what impacts price discovery, but this is effectively non-existent since the badla product was banned in 2001. This is the only type of countervailing force that drives down an overvalued stock, moderates the bulls, and allows for the differences of opinion that are the essence of a stock market. The short side was reintroduced in 2008, but the absence of an efficient lending/borrowing mechanism for stock means that it is practically non-existent.[37] Attempts have been made to improve the borrowing/lending mechanisms needed for a short side, but none have really taken off.[38]

Further misconceptions about the short side are generated by the presence of single stock futures (SSFs) in India's vast derivatives

[37] The securities lending and borrowing product is outlined in https://www1.nseindia. com/invest / content/SLB_brochure.pdf.

[38] Use of the securities lending and borrowing mechanism is typically confined to the few occasions when reverse arbitrage presents itself in the derivatives markets. When futures prices fall below spot prices, arbitrageurs can use the mechanism to borrow and sell in the spot cash market, followed by a simultaneous purchase in the futures markets. On settlement, the position is reversed and the basis is captured.

market, and somehow the ability to sell a TISCO futures contract is seen as short selling. But here, the seller is simply selling to a trader who has an opposite view on price and who is consequently buying the TISCO contract – the transaction only results in open interest (the total number of outstanding contracts) increasing by one contract while price discovery in the cash market continues to remain unaffected. In fact, the extreme ease of short selling in India's huge futures markets, together with the liquidity and low transaction costs of these instruments, makes it unnecessary and cumbersome for participants to move to short selling in the cash market through a lending/borrowing mechanism.[39] This is another reason why the lending/borrowing mechanism necessary for a short side has not taken off.

So, today's markets – by not allowing for both sides – are paradoxically less efficient than the markets of the badla era. Yet, there are compelling market efficiency arguments for a short side, and doubly so when one considers the low free floats that anyway bias the market upward. But large publics created by the reform effort – among them the middle class *aam aadmi* (common man), the buy side, and the financial advisors – clamour for perennially rising markets. Premchand Roychand in portrait and the BSE's bronze bull only stare silently at each other in cosmic agreement on the need for steadily rising prices, but these restive publics are more voluble on that need. Compared to their political power and voice, any market efficiency argument for a short side seems laughably weak nowadays. So, despite the widespread presence of the unrestricted intraday short in the cash market and short selling using futures in the derivatives market, actual inter-temporal short selling in the cash market does not really take place in India. Some of the short side may have moved offshore due to regulatory arbitrage – foreign institutional investors tend to be 'buy and hold' investors and may have lending/borrowing mechanisms among themselves that hedge funds can quietly access – but the extent of such offshore mechanisms is unclear.

[39] The single stock futures list peaked at almost 270 in 2008–09 before falling to about 150 by mid-2020.

A third and final reason for the long corner lies in the absence of international diversification. During the Rate Bull years, India's market accounted for less than 3 per cent of world equity capitalization, but for most folios, fully 100 per cent of assets were invested in the country's equity markets.[40] (These proportions would be maintained in later years as well.) For a long time after Independence, capital market segmentation had been de jure, but some of this was done away with during the reform effort; in later years de jure segmentation continued in muddled form, but it was the de facto segmentation that was more invidious. Collectively they led to severe domestic bias, with all investment directed only towards the Indian market. This staggering level of domestic bias was bizarre, and yet not even seen as bias because of its all-pervasive nature.[41]

A number of factors were responsible and they included: a buy side with no experience or competence in global investing, a cultural bias towards the home market, and a marked tendency to think in terms of local stock picking rather than global asset allocation.[42] In turn, the corporate outperformance of the Rate Bull years briefly confirmed these biases towards the home market; the outperformance would not persist in later years, but domestic bias continued to be all-pervasive. This, despite the singular fact that global investing carried substantial benefits, and more so in India.[43]

Because of domestic bias and the lack of global diversification, domestic flows got socked away by the local buy side mainly into the local market. During the Rate Bull, the Indian market had to absorb local inflows from its own publics that were directed exclusively towards it, together with foreign inflows from global liquidity surges. As a result,

[40] India's market usually comprised between 2 and 3 per cent of world equity capitalization.

[41] A later chapter on speculation and investment examines the reasons behind domestic bias and the benefits of international diversification to Indian shareholders.

[42] Constraints on foreign investing were not so much numerical as cultural. RBI rules – framed against the backdrop of the capital account convertibility debate – allowed (as of 2019) up to $250,000 to be invested annually outside India. As usual, the relaxation was subject to an industry-wide limitation.

[43] The diversification benefits to global investing are outlined in Burton Malkiel, *A Random Walk down Wall Street*, 11th ed., New York: W.W. Norton, 2015, 201–08.

both the domestic and foreign buy sides bid up the same limited pool of floating stock, further exacerbating the long corner. Over time, domestic bias became so pervasive and the long corner got so acute that the Indian buy side – 100 per cent invested in their own market – saw investing as turf protection. As a result, they repeatedly and deliberately crossed the FIIs during the Rate Bull, selling when the latter were buying and vice versa, in the process effectively making the market for FII exit.[44] This pattern would first manifest during the Rate Bull but would continue in the quantitative easing years, and in fact, it became more pronounced as the domestic buy side accessed capital from rupee cost averaging plans.

The long corner led to some stunning price moves, and the best part was that it was impossible to prove – this was just a promising company in a promising country whose stock was going up, and that it went up 1,000 times indicated that promise. Moves of 100 to 200 times were common during the Rate Bull and the phrase '**multi-bagger**' – referring to a stock that went up many times – became widespread in this period. In fact, the term's use in Indian markets first dates from the Rate Bull era, and before that, there is little trace in the record.[45] One thousand baggers – stocks that went up a 1,000 times – actually happened, and some stocks, such as Unitech, went on to set records for up moves by rising over 2,000 times. Of all market epochs, it was the Rate Bull, with its huge interest rate-induced corporate outperformance acting in tandem with the long corner, that was the Age of the Bull, and no other situation seemed possible.

Attempts to disguise the multi-bagger's rise frequently took place, usually through stock splits or stock dividends ('bonus shares').[46] In an earlier era, the high prices of Kohinoor or Maneckji Petit were an

[44] A later chapter on foreign investors looks at their interaction with the domestic buy side.

[45] Peter Lynch is credited with coining the term in his book *One Up on Wall Street*, New York: Simon & Schuster, 1989.

[46] More technically, stock dividends (bonus shares) are a nonreciprocal issuance by a company of its own stock to shareholders on a pro rata basis, and usually done by reclassifying amounts from earned capital (retained earnings) to contributed capital (common stock). This 'capitalizes' a part of retained earnings by retaining it in the business on a more permanent basis through the capital stock. No assets or cash flows leave the enterprise, and no valuation effects accrue. Nevertheless, stock dividends can be market-moving in India.

astonishing feature of the market, and prices of ₹5 to 10 lakhs per share (adjusted for inflation) were not uncommon in that age. But now market practice was the reverse, and attempts were made to disguise the up moves and make stocks 'affordable' to the average investor by some combination of rampant splitting and/or issuance of stock dividends.[47] Indulged in enough times, the splits and stock dividends hid the up moves from the public and sometimes even from the pros. The long corner also called into question the bedrock belief that the market was rewarding promoters for skin in the game. Perhaps, but it could also simply be bull conditions acting on an entire market that was cornered long.

In summation, the combination of low free floats caused by the ownership structure of Indian capitalism, the short constraint, and domestic bias made the long corner a daily reality during the Rate Bull. The high promoter holdings of Indian capitalism substantially reduced the free float of stock that was available, and so liquidity surges into the market acted on low free floats and drove up prices. Despite widespread misconceptions, any sort of contrarian or short side to moderate the price rise was impossible at least since 2001 (and practically ever since), and prices got set by the most optimistic buyer at the margin. Finally, because of severe domestic bias, all domestic flows exclusively entered the local market and ended up competing with massive foreign inflows for the same limited pool of floating stock, bidding stocks higher in the process. In later years, quantitative easing from central bank bond buying programs would result in further foreign inflows from liquidity surges, exaggerating the above effects and aggravating the long corner even further. The all-pervasive nature of the long corner – it was a market-wide systemic phenomenon – blinded participants to any other alternative, and vertiginous price rises were often attributed to

[47] For a list of high stock prices from the pre-Independence era, see Sir Wilfrid Atlay, *Report of the Bombay Stock Exchange Enquiry Committee*, Bombay: Government Central Press, 1924, 55. For academic studies on managerial motives behind the phenomenon, see Chhavi Mehta, Surendra S. Yadav, and P.K. Jain, 'Managerial Motives for Stock Splits: Survey Based Evidence from India,' *Journal of Applied Finance*, Vol. 21, No. 1, 2011; Kent H. Baker and Sujata Kapoor, 'Why Indian Firms Issue Stock Distributions,' *Managerial Finance* Vol. 41, No. 7, 2015.

fundamental causes. More crucially, valuation considerations became secondary. That a stock could get cornered was plausible, but that an entire market could get cornered to the point where valuation became a second order issue was beyond the comprehension of most participants.

On 14 January 2008, the Rate Bull reached its final glittering peak. The S&P 500 had topped out and rolled over the previous October, while the Indian market had survived its own scare (over participatory notes) that month.[48] The January 2008 **break** took the market down almost 30 per cent over a matter of days.[49]

Yet there was no proximate cause, and this is a singular feature of the crash. Irregularities in G-Sec settlement had led to the Mehta break, and the IT break took place in lockstep with the Nasdaq sell-off, but the Rate Bull ended in a crash with no discernible cause. It is tempting to think the market was anticipating the acute phase of the global financial crisis nine months later, but this is a fallacy.

Finding proximate causes was also difficult because leading economic indicators (LEIs) were mostly absent in the Indian market; reading tea leaves – a difficult task anyway – was impossible when there were few tea leaves to read. In fact, the available indicators were all flashing bright green rather than red. The real economy was soaring, with growth at 9 per cent, the last published figure before the crash. There were no major signs of corporate excess either; leverage was modestly high, as were inventories, and there was some excess capacity built up, but much of it was not yet on stream. The only real sign of excess was in the market for convertibles, particularly Foreign Currency Convertible

[48] Participatory notes are financial instruments used by foreign investors or hedge funds to invest in Indian securities without having to register with SEBI. Issued by a local broker or other intermediary, they give the foreign holder anonymous exposure to the underlying share, and are a form of offshore derivative contract. Curbs on them resulted in a market wobble in October 2007. Their importance to the market would reduce in later years.

[49] 'Historical Data,' *BSE*, https://www.bseindia.com/Indices/IndexArchiveData.html.

Bonds (FCCBs).[50] Besides, all this was secondary to the main concern of earnings; after all, the market priced itself off corporate profits. Earnings were also on fire and had been compounding at between 20 and 25 per cent for some time; earnings for the December 2007 quarter just before the break had continued that strong streak.[51]

So there was no immediate cause for the crash, and yet this is also in keeping with classic market lore – perhaps it was simply that the last buyer had come in, and there was no one left to buy. It was like adding grains of sand to form a sand-pile on a tabletop; you kept adding grains a few at a time, till a small addition caused one side of the pile to collapse. After the collapse, the talking heads went looking for that last small addition, the proximate fundamental cause that was usually available, but in 2008 even that was not around.

Rather than proximate causes, we must look at the technical composition of the market for the role it played in the crash.

The 'stop loss' **honeycomb** was a key feature of the market's technical composition that contributed to the crash, and its importance was proportionate to the duration of the bull move that preceded it. The market's speculative orientation, coupled with the vast presence of trend-following traders, caused the honeycomb. Many traders who use technicals and follow trends buy a stock on an uptrend and then put in place a 'stop loss' sell order after the purchase. If a stock is bought at 43 and moves up to a market price of 65, the 'stop loss' sell order is set at maybe 57 to lock in profits made from the 43 entry point. As the stock heads higher, the technical trend follower keeps raising the 'stop loss' order behind the market price. As the stock gathers momentum, astute traders start moving their stops even closer to the market price to lock in profits; in this example, at 397 the 'stop loss' would be set at 391.

[50] FCCB issuance usually peaks in the final stages of a market boom. Buyers are happy with a lower coupon, as the option to convert to equity has value in a rising market; issuers not wishing to issue equity at present price benefit from lower interest costs. If the markets don't oblige, as in 2008, the issuers usually refinance, restructure, or buy back the bonds; injecting fresh equity to do this is also an option.

[51] Arvind Subramanian and Josh Felman, 'India's Great Slowdown,' 9–11.

By January 2008, the trading public had been doing this for many years and right through the bull move; as a result, the market at the 2008 top was honeycombed with 'stop loss' sell orders set behind the price. At that final glittering peak in January the market looked its strongest, but because of the honeycomb of 'stop loss' sell orders hidden beneath the price, it was actually at its weakest. What started as a small sell-off then snowballed, triggering vast sales as the market crashed through the accumulated 'stop loss' sell orders.

As the market crashed through the honeycomb, the **derivatives** segment came into focus. Since its founding in 2000, the derivatives market had grown dramatically, and by 2008, the NSE had created one of the world's largest gambling casinos. The stock market now had two clear segments – cash and derivatives – and the position buildup in derivatives worsened the crash by throwing up anomalies between the two segments. At turning points to the downside, the derivatives segment impacted the cash market in two ways.

First, the wringing out of excess leverage was the usual driver behind market crashes, but the cash market now carried negligible leverage, as the loans against shares product was not large, and margin trading was negligible. Most leverage now originated in the gigantic derivatives markets, and the resultant wringing out was done in roundabout fashion. As stocks fell, many traders in the derivatives segment received margin calls. At the top of a massive four-year bull, the natural – and wrong – belief was to think stocks had fallen so far and so fast that they simply had to recover; better, therefore, to keep the position open to benefit from that rebound and then exit. So, rather than cutting losses, positions were kept open and margin calls were met from cash balances. These, however, proved insufficient as the fall accelerated through the honeycomb. Traders then had to sell positions in the cash market to raise margin for their derivatives positions, and this indirect wringing out of leverage – exacerbated by the colossal size of the derivatives markets – further intensified the sell-off. All this resulted from a fatal violation of that cardinal trading rule: 'Never meet a margin call'.

Second, the great arbitrage engine between the cash and derivatives segments briefly went into reverse. The usual first leg of an arbitrage transaction was *buying* in the cash market and *selling* in the futures market, as futures prices were always a little higher due to the spot-futures parity theorems or the 'cost of carry' relationship; on settlement day, the position was reversed and the basis locked in as arbitrage profits.[52] But January 2008 was one of those rare occasions when prices fell so far and so fast, that futures prices were often lower than their corresponding cash prices; traders initiating fresh shorts in the futures segment may have been responsible for this backwardation. So, the first leg of the arbitrage transaction became *selling* in the cash and *buying* in the futures to capture the basis. This trade (usually done intraday, as inter-temporal short selling was difficult) further accelerated the intraday selling and led to the crash. An uptick rule that allowed for a sale in the cash market only after a price test on the uptick would have made this difficult – but the absence of a rule similar to the SEC's Rule 10a-1(a)(1) has been noted earlier.

Further, in countries without single stock futures (SSFs), this arbitrage was possible only between the index futures contract and baskets of stocks that made up that index, which – despite the availability of the computer and its programmed execution – could be cumbersome. But India's huge SSF market – there were close to 150 blue chips where the above trade was possible – meant that the arbitrage could easily take place on individual counters rather than through a cumbersome index basket, and this magnified the impact of reverse arbitrage on the market. The 30 (or 50, if considering the NSE) stocks that made up the indexes were all included in the SSF group of 150, which also exaggerated reverse arbitrage effects.

After the crash came the familiar three-stage downward lurch of an Indian **bear market**, and by October 2008, the market had lost over half its value.[53] The market's four largest point declines till 2008 all happened in that year, a reflection both of absolute market levels and the decline's

[52] Later chapters on derivatives and market highs and lows have a detailed treatment.

[53] 'Historical Data,' *BSE*.

extent.[54] The severity of the fall was proportionate to the extent of the rise, and many of the multi-baggers were down as much as 90 per cent. What went up the most came down the most. The crucial psychological continuity provided by the successful 'buy on dips' trade was now broken, but it had happened too fast, and so the mental shift to 'sell on rallies' was made by only a handful of participants. Just as the advance had been across the general list, so too was the decline, and even sectors such as pharmaceuticals – traditionally seen as immune to such swings – were not spared. Other aspects of market microstructure intensified the sell-off; specialists could have made markets for key counters, but in their absence, there were no parties who stood ready to meet orders from their own inventories. Liquidity always dried up in India during a down move, and without liquidity from specialists to smoothen price impact, even small sell orders in the order book disproportionately impacted prices to the down side and intensified selling momentum. Critically, if there had been a short side, bears who had sold short would have had to take their profits by buying to square up. Bears, with their short cover buying, were an inbuilt pillar of support to the market, but in their absence, the 2008 rout turned into a collapse.

Despite sector rotation during the run, most **sectors** topped out at about the same time in January 2008 – sugar was an exception – which was another unusual feature of the Rate Bull. Likewise, most sectors fell at the same time during the 2008 sell-off, and this is one of those few (but telling) occasions when the well-worn myth of a stock picker's market stood exposed. Stock picking works but only up to a point; at that point, market risk also intrudes on the calculation, and the sell-off that followed the Rate Bull brought home the lesson with some violence. Finding stocks that defied a fall of this magnitude was difficult – you simply needed a bull market, or at least a range-bound market, for stock picking to work. The myth had been exposed before, but the absence of historical records makes this difficult to see. Nevertheless, the sell-off's compressed span, together with the roaring pullback that followed

[54] Sensex losses on the big days of 2008 were: 1,408 points on 22 January; 1,071 points on 24 October; 951 points on 17 March; and 875 points on 22 January.

from 2009 onwards, reduced somewhat the pain of this lesson, and it would not be well learnt. But this did not matter either, as over the years, Indian bear markets kept getting shorter and shorter, and it was price corrections rather than time corrections that took place.

The Congress-led UPA had discovered the discreet joys of manipulating the **political business cycle**, and it remains a singular fact that the sell-off in 2008 and 2009 happened despite massive fiscal and monetary expansion. In the political business cycle, elected governments routinely bribe populations for political gain to win elections, typically by increasing government expenditure on giveaway programs. This sets the stage for fiscal dominance and large deficits that come with inflationary consequences. The party that does this well wins at the ballot box, and as a result, political parties try to outdo one another, leading to a political economy of competitive populism. As tax revenue soared during the boom years, the Congress-led UPA got busy deciding how to blow up the tax gains on welfare schemes to win the Lok Sabha election coming up in April 2009. Budgetary laws such as the Fiscal Responsibility and Budget Management (FRBM) Act had been passed to limit and end fiscal dominance but were abrogated by the Congress to manipulate the political business cycle.[55] Consequently, Finance Minister P. Chidambaram's budget of February 2008, with its farm loan waivers and other sops, later took the fiscal deficit – Centre and states – to over 9 per cent of GDP.[56] This percentage was even higher if off-budget fudges such as oil bonds were considered.

Usually, central banks try to counteract this tendency towards competitive populism by running countercyclical monetary policies with higher interest rates, which prevents the situation from getting out of hand and becoming inflationary. But in India (and worldwide), the script did not play out as planned this time. The Lehman bankruptcy of

[55] Deadlines for FRBM targets were first suspended due to political economy reasons and later postponed in 2009.

[56] Ministry of Finance, *Economic Survey 2010–2011*, New Delhi: Ministry of Finance, Department of Economic Affairs, 42–45, 65–66. This took place much before the global financial crisis that was to break seven months later.

October 2008 – seven months after the budget presentation – brought about the acute phase of the global financial crisis. The RBI reversed the tightening policy it had commenced in 2005, eased monetary policy in line with other central banks, and reduced rates by 400 basis points over a period of months. In the modern era, this would prove to be the steepest cut over the shortest time frame, and rates would revisit their 2003 lows. Further fiscal stimulus over and above the February 2008 budget sops then followed in late 2008 and early 2009. All this massive fiscal and monetary expansion resulted in temporary stimulation and an expansion of aggregate demand, on the basis of which the government won a second term in the 2009 elections and came back as UPA-2. But without supply side responses – India's infrastructure constraints are a perennial causal factor here – and with a positive output gap,[57] much of the expansion fed into the price level, leading in turn to an inflationary surge in the years that followed.

Yet what is pertinent to this discussion on the stock market is that it collapsed in 2008 and early 2009 – right through the unprecedented fiscal and monetary stimulus generated by the political business cycle and central bank response. Contagion effects from the worldwide sell-off caused by the financial crisis, coupled with FII outflows, may have been largely responsible for this. Getting up every day and seeing the global sell-off proved too much for most local traders, who sold along with the rest. So, the up move had occurred despite the Communist presence in the government and the complete absence of reform efforts, and the down move had taken place despite the tremendous stimulus that was in play at that time. Forecasting the stock market from fundamental and logical facts is always a difficult exercise, and the Rate cycle provides another example of this. Nonetheless, the stimulus ensured that the market would come back with considerable force when the time came.

At the **bottom** in October 2008, the Sensex traded at less than nine times earnings. There was a giant flushing sound in October, with that

[57] Output gaps measure the cyclical deviations between actual output and trend/potential output. Positive output gaps tend to be inflationary, as enterprises bid up prices and wages while trying to meet the excess demand.

distinct feeling of good stocks being thrown out with the garbage. News came of a major international bankruptcy – that of Lehman Brothers – and this coincided with the market's low. There followed a distinct limping along the bottom till March 2009, but General Motors's bankruptcy filing around that time had no effect on the markets, indicating that much of the bad news had been priced in and that a bottom was in place by then. Except for banking stocks, most of the damage to the Indian market had already been done by the previous October. At the bottom, many of the analysts had egg all over their faces – some had 6,000 Sensex predictions for end 2009 but the market would go to 21,000.[58]

Forecasts, especially of the future, had to be made with caution.

The public bought on the way down and would have been early. Buying on the way down was like catching a falling knife, as the adage went. It was possible to lose a lot as a value buyer in India, but at least the ones buying in cash were okay. Intrepid souls – and there were many in India's retail-dominated derivatives markets – who bought in the derivatives segment with leverage would have got cleaned out long before the bottom; on the way down, many became investors by temperament but were still speculators by habit, and this confusion of purpose usually proved fatal. Timing was everything, and buying at the bottom or selling at the top was possible, but only by lucky fools or liars. At every stage in that fall, it seemed as though the bottom had been reached, only to see stocks go lower, and sometimes it seemed like buying on the way down was not catching a falling knife so much as stopping a guillotine with a little finger. A stock market whose founding episode – the Cotton and Share Mania – was a bull-bear cycle should have had better sense when it came to judging them, and yet that was not the case. The Indian market perennially forgot and relived its hazy past, and the temptation is to trot out Santayana's hoary dictum as an explanation, but that will not suffice. It was not just that the market was condemned to repeat its history because it had forgotten it; perhaps there was something deeply embedded in human nature itself that caused these repetitions.

[58] 'Historical Data,' *BSE*.

Nevertheless, the chaos and damage hid achievements that participants took for granted. Previous sell-offs of this magnitude had exposed systemic inadequacies, but despite the compressed and telegraphic nature of the 2008 down move, there had been no major cases of broker defaults or scandals. The Satyam scandal doesn't count because it was a corporate event rather than a market event and consequently carried no systemic implications. The historical pattern would now shift away from market events involving the microstructure or its intermediaries and towards corporate events involving the strong-arm promoters or the banks that funded them. More crucially, and for the first time, the clearing and settlement systems had held up through the sell-off, an achievement that participants took for granted. The unglamorous and often neglected back office had come through for the first time, but no one really noticed.

The absence of market events was also due to the cultural change from *sākh* to systems that reform to the microstructure had wrought. *Sākh* to the bania was like honour to the Rajput or learning to the brahmin. It is tempting to see it as reputation, but it meant a little more than that. At an obvious level, it stood for a participant's creditworthiness and financial standing in the market, and it was usually acquired through a track record of meeting commitments.[59] Wider subtexts had to do with meeting community or religious obligations like charity or helping the needy, but above all else, *sākh* reflected a participant's standing in the market – it was the Indian version of '*He's good for 10,000*'. In a world with shaky contract enforcement, inadequate risk management, and no credit ratings, *sākh* performed all these functions. Later generations would elevate *sākh* and look at it with nostalgia, particularly because the alternative was government regulation that was usually a heavy-handed and hit-or-miss affair.[60]

[59] Rahul Bjørn Parson, 'The Bazaar and the Bari: Calcutta, Marwaris, and the World of Hindi Letters,' Berkeley, CA: Unpublished PhD dissertation, 2012, 17–19, https://escholarship.org / content/qt7ng958qz/qt7ng958qz.pdf.

[60] Gurcharan Das, 'Introduction,' Thomas A. Timberg, *The Marwaris: From Jagat Seth to the Birlas*, New Delhi: Penguin Books, 2014.

Yet in the stock market, *sākh* was an imperfect way of doing things and meeting commitments. More technically, *sākh* might have worked in the commodity market for (say) a transaction on 10,000 bales of jute, itself one of a series of relatively infrequent bargains. But even in the pre-reform era, the Indian stock market was a continuous time, quote-driven auction market with millions of leveraged transactions struck every month, and relying on *sākh* for risk management and contract enforcement proved inadequate. Besides, in the stock market, a man was as good as his word but rarely beyond the first margin call. Many of the stock market's crises had been due to this cultural tendency to view risk as a violation of *sākh* rather than as a problem of risk management. The reforms to microstructure that introduced proper margining and risk management ensured that defaults and counterparty risk were effectively eliminated and reduced the need to rely on *sākh*. So, besides the actual changes to the microstructure, it was this cultural change in emphasis from *sākh* to systems that was to be a lasting legacy. A relationship-oriented society – in the stock market at least – was making its painful transition to a more rules-based order.

6

THE SIP BULL AND A VIRUS

From 2009 to the Present

At the 2009 bottom, Value had begun to emerge, the Liquidity surge from considerable domestic and international stimulus was waiting to happen, and as the market came roaring off the low, the Sentiment change would prove dramatic and decisive. The pullback from the March 2009 bottom was the sharpest in the history of India's stock market. In the six-month period between March and September of that year, the market doubled, making a perfect 'V' on the charts as it came off the 8,000 low to almost 17,000. This pullback then developed into another bull market that continued through 2010. But the market sold off in 2011, dominated as it was by the Eurozone's political instability and sovereign debt crisis; it drifted sideways through most of 2012 and wobbled again on concerns over monetary tapering in mid-2013. By late 2013, the market began sensing a BJP victory in the upcoming general elections and started pricing that in with another strong uptrend. It was not disappointed, and the 2014 victory of Narendra Modi and the BJP-led National Democratic Alliance (NDA) was greeted by a substantial up move.

As the ramifications of the BJP's absolute majority began to sink in, this upsurge developed into the bull market's second stage. The bull move would expand through various policy missteps by the government. Helped along by a second BJP victory in 2019 with a larger majority, the market's rise, in the absence of economic growth or corporate profits, was baffling to many knowledgeable observers.

In the later stages, the move was driven by the domestic buy side's increasing access to averaging products such as the Systematic Investment Plan (SIP) and by foreign inflows resulting from quantitative easing by Western central banks. The buy side – without the slightest attempt at global diversification – invested the SIP flows in the domestic market and, together with FIIs, bid up the limited pool of floating stock that resulted from the long corner. The corporate sector did not oblige with profit growth, but that did not matter, and so, valuation concerns became secondary as the market got progressively expensive; by January 2020, the Sensex had crossed 42,000, trading at almost 30 times earnings. It had been an 11-year upsurge from early 2009, and the bull was already long in the tooth when the 2020 coronavirus pandemic led to a substantial down move. That developed into a sell-off every bit as violent as 2008, and in a short while, markets had again lost almost half their value. This loss was retrieved in another liquidity-driven pullback off the bottom, and by early 2022, markets had recovered their lost value and gone on to new highs of over 60,000. Vast tides of global liquidity were distorting markets worldwide, and the Indian market was no exception to the asset price inflation that resulted. Significant price rises took place despite the damage caused by recurrent waves of virus-induced lockdowns and increases in political and social unrest. Nevertheless, Russia's invasion of Ukraine in 2022 and the return of inflation brought a sudden end to years of unconventional monetary policy; the distortions caused by years of liquidity ebbs and flows from global capital markets were now coming to an end.

At the March 2009 bottom, countervailing forces were already in play for a recovery from the Great Recession, though this was not apparent in all the din and chaos of falling prices. Two factors – quantitative easing and the political business cycle – led the dramatic pullback.

First, unconventional Western monetary policy through quantitative easing (QE) improved liquidity flows to markets worldwide. Led by the US Federal Reserve Board, this unorthodox policy was a definitive response to the 2008 financial crisis and considered necessary as US interest rates had reached their lower bound of near zero, which effectively rendered rate policy unworkable. Under quantitative easing, the Fed bought bonds from the banking system and paid for them by crediting the reserve accounts of banks that maintained accounts with it, thus adding liquidity to the system. This purchase of treasury and mortgage securities was to result in a fivefold expansion in the Fed's balance sheet between September 2008 and late 2014.[1] Fed Chairman Ben Bernanke, a keen student of its misjudgements during the 1929 Wall Street crash and the Great Depression that followed, was implementing one type of central bank response to a financial crisis. Its basic template had not changed much since first articulated by journalist Walter Bagehot, and in essence, it involved lending freely to basically solvent institutions (against decent collateral, or even without it, if circumstances warranted), flooding the system with liquidity, and leaving the consequences for later.[2] When the Fed left off, other central banks took turns picking up the slack, and there were strong bond-buying programs from the European Central Bank, the Bank of England, and the Bank of Japan.

Much of this expansion ended up with Western banks in the form of reserves, but some of it also found its way into financial markets, which started moving in response to the vast tides of liquidity unleashed. Aided by the easing, markets took off, and a singular feature of these years was the time and energy participants spent in guessing when

[1] Total assets increased from $900 billion to about $4.5 trillion between 2008 and 2014. United States, Board of Governors of the Federal Reserve System, *102nd Annual Report, 2015*, Washington, D.C.: Government Printing Office, 2016, 20–21. The response to the COVID-19 pandemic led to another increase – from about $4.2 trillion to almost $9 trillion between 2020 and 2022.

[2] Walter Bagehot, *Lombard Street: A Description of the Money Market*, Wiley Investment Classics, Hoboken, NJ: John Wiley and Sons, Inc., 1999.

central banks would end their bond-buying programs.[3] The obsession was understandable as quantitative easing changed the composition of financial assets held by the private sector worldwide. Consequently, some of the expansion ended up chasing yield in risky assets such as emerging markets, of which India was a beneficiary. This quantitative easing translated into heavy flows from FIIs, and the dramatic outflows of 2008 now turned into inflows from 2009 onwards, which piled into undervalued equities and took the markets back up.

Second, the UPA's manipulation of the political business cycle and an expansive RBI policy stimulated the demand side and improved domestic liquidity. There was little need for either of these countervailing forces as India's economy continued to grow through the global financial crisis, with 6.7 per cent as the worst GDP print in the crisis's aftermath.[4] As global easing and liquidity, domestic policy overreaction, and local resilience came together in 2009 and 2010, the market rocketed off its lows and kept going on a strong up move. India was only echoing global moves, and on this occasion at least, the correlations between markets were so strong that both the S&P 500 and the Sensex bottomed out together in the first week of March 2009 before beginning their dramatic reversal. The market got a further boost from the Congress-led UPA-2 election victory and melted up on 18 May 2009, marking the only time it would hit two up circuits on the same day. Down circuits in the market were a given – like everything else, stocks went down with gravity and so markets fell faster than they rose – but up circuits for an entire market were a rarity, back-to-back up circuits more so, and this was the only such occasion.[5]

The market went on to double off the 2009 bottom and continued that momentum through 2010 as it tested the 21,000 Rate Bull high. But the period between 2011 and 2013 was spent dealing with a UPA-2

[3] Editorial, 'Taper Tantrums,' *Financial Times*, 16 August 2013.

[4] Ministry of Finance, *Economic Survey 2009–2010*, New Delhi: Ministry of Finance, Department of Economic Affairs, 2.

[5] Mary Ercilia Gayen, 'History on Dalal Street; Markets Hit Final Upper Circuit,' *Mint*, 18 May 2009.

coalition that had already begun unravelling from its own contradictions. The Congress-led UPA had won a second term but without a clear majority, so while the Communists were out, regional satraps such as Mamata Banerjee of Bengal were in. Banerjee withdrew her party's support in 2012, which resulted in UPA-2 entering a period of prolonged instability. Other regional parties, including the Samajwadi and Bahujan Samaj parties from Uttar Pradesh, then provided something called 'outside support', which was nothing but power without responsibility. They proceeded to acquire disproportionate influence in a government that simply did not have the numbers.[6] A consequence of all this was what participants called 'policy paralysis', but it might also have been the second-term tiredness that sets in after running a country of India's size and complexity for a long stretch. Faced with this limbo, Dalal Street took to howling for reform. But reform was a political process the coalition government found difficult, bogged down as it was by the terrible task of clinging to power for its own sake and without the numbers. In the public's perception, corruption had also gone up, as even small coalition partners felt they could get away with it by promising coalition support in return; Congress tried to turn a blind eye to it all in return for the promise of staying in power, but it would pay heavily for that attitude in later years.

Wobbles also took place in 2011 and 2013 over the Eurozone and the end of quantitative easing policies, but by 2013 the market was effectively at the same 21,000 level it had been at during the 2008 high. In retrospect, it is clear that these years were spent dealing with the Great Recession's aftermath, political uncertainty, and the yo-yo effects of monetary and fiscal stimulus. India's monetary aggregates, in particular, were coming out of a period of extraordinary volatility, and the 1996 to 2012 period – with its dramatic swings in monetary measures – stands out from the time that came before and has never been replicated since. Rates had fallen drastically between 1996 and 2003, risen between 2004 and 2008, and collapsed in 2008 and 2009. Then they climbed quickly

[6] C.P. Bhambhri, 'Poke Me: India Has No Coalitions, Only Marriages of Inconvenience,' *Economic Times*, 29 November 2012.

from 2010 to 2012 – on this occasion, policy tightened at first and then not fast enough, so inflation rose while expectations became entrenched.

In late 2013, the market started surging again in anticipation of a BJP victory and an end to years of coalition politics. Congress-led UPA-1 had benefited from a worldwide economic expansion, the rate displacement, and a strong domestic economy, which it had the good sense not to meddle with. By contrast, UPA-2 got caught up in its own internal contradictions, which played out against the backdrop of the Great Recession's aftermath, and the coalition limped along till the 2014 election put it out of its agony. A forty-year period of single-party Congress rule (with one brief exception) had ended in the late 80s, followed by a quarter century of coalitions and 'outside support' that now came to an end in 2014. The Modi-led BJP victory on a plank of *vikas* (development) was especially well received by the Gujarati community, who were well represented among market participants, and the market soared on election announcements in May 2014. This 2014 upsurge then expanded into the second stage of the bull move, which took the market higher, right through the BJP's first term from 2014 to 2019.

The bull move's second stage from 2014 onwards was unusual not for what happened but for what did not happen.

What happened were policy initiatives driven by a majority government, and in this sense the market's hopes were not belied. The universal identification system of Aadhaar was taken to its logical conclusion as a scheme for transfer of direct benefits; programs in road building, sanitation, and rural electrification were accelerated; low-cost bank accounts were opened through a Jan Dhan financial inclusion scheme; gas cylinders were distributed, health insurance introduced, and a Real Estate Regulation Act addressed the balance between home buyers and builders.[7] In particular, the JAM trinity – banking access

[7] For a detailed recounting of the government's reform efforts till 2020, see Arvind Panagariya, 'Six Years of Reforms: Modi Has Established His Reformist Credentials Alongside PMs Like Rao and Vajpayee,' *Times of India*, 15 October 2020.

mandated through the Jan Dhan scheme, together with Aadhaar and the now ubiquitous mobile phones – improved subsidy transfer, plugged leakages, and offered the masses a path to financial inclusion. The JAM trinity components were seen as the building blocks of a digital stack that was now reckoned a game changer.

But three other initiatives were subject to the law of unintended consequences: demonetization, indirect tax reform, and insolvency legislation. Demonetization had been tried previously in January 1946 and January 1978 when high-value currency notes were banned – ₹500, ₹1,000, and ₹10,000 notes were demonetized in 1946, while ₹1,000s, ₹5,000s, and ₹10,000s were demonetized in 1978.[8] These early efforts had proved ineffective in curbing tax evasion but were less dislocating because the note denominations were large compared to the scale of economic activity at that time; as a result, these prior demonetizations impacted only a wealthy few.[9] But the 2016 demonetization move encompassed smaller denominations, removed 86 per cent of the currency in circulation,[10] and, besides being severely dislocating, also left everyone confused about its purpose. Troubling also was the amorality of a government that reneged on that promise it had printed on every currency note to pay its citizenry a certain sum of money; equally disturbing was the absence of any discussion on this amorality in the reams of chatter that analysed this quixotic move.

The second initiative that did not go as planned was an indirect tax reform through the introduction of the Goods and Services Tax (GST). It would be lauded for its necessity but pilloried for its complexity and convoluted implementation. Together with demonetization, the GST was hard on small and medium enterprises, usually regarded as a lynchpin of much-needed employment generation.

[8] Both episodes are recounted in the official RBI history. See Reserve Bank of India, *History of The Reserve Bank of India: Volume 1, 1935–1951*, Mumbai: RBI Central Office, 2005, 706–09; *Volume 3, 1967–1981*, Mumbai: RBI Central Office, 2005, 450–53.

[9] Ibid. *Volume 3, 1967–1981*, 451, 453. The RBI had misgivings about the exercise on both previous occasions.

[10] Justin Rowlatt, 'Why India Wiped out 86% of Its Cash Overnight,' BBC News, 14 November 2016.

The third initiative on insolvency reform was more promising. In most economies, the freedom to succeed implies the corresponding freedom to fail. But in India, companies did not fail but got 'sick' instead. The bankruptcy code ended this little fiction for a while, at least till it got bogged down over multiple challenges in the courts.

What did not happen was earnings growth, which had been the Rate Bull's sweet spot. Bull markets take place on the back of surging profits and earnings. Ideally, this happens as the market gets comfortable, capitalizing growing earnings with higher multiples. But by the SIP Bull's second half, it became apparent there was no real earnings growth. Corporate sales and profits stayed low or flat, with profits compounding at less than 5 per cent annualized during these years, in contrast to the 20 to 25 per cent growth rates of the Rate Bull. As a result, corporate profits as a share of GDP dropped from over 7 per cent in 2007 to below 3 per cent by 2018.[11] The earnings degrowth had preceded a slowdown in GDP, and to some, the severe dislocations of demonetization and the GST's introduction had contributed to this situation. Much discussion took place on whether the slowdown was cyclical or structural.[12]

Perhaps there was little need for all this handwringing, and the anchoring effect of the Rate Bull years had simply created an illusion of growth. The decades of 2 to 3 per cent growth rates had given way to a steady canter of about 4 to 5 per cent in the immediate post-reform period of the 1990s, which had, in turn, led to a burst of 8 to 9 per cent growth – driven in large part by the interest rate displacement – during the Rate Bull. What was now happening was simply a return to the more sustainable growth rates of the 1990s, but the country's elites

[11] Arvind Subramanian and Josh Felman, 'India's Great Slowdown: What Happened? What's the Way Out?,' CID Faculty Working Paper, Vol. 370, Center for International Development, Harvard University, December 2019, 9–11.

[12] Ibid. Subramanian and Felman document how financial distress in the aftermath of the mid-2000s infrastructure lending boom spread from banks and infrastructure companies to the shadow banks (non-banking financial companies), precipitating falls in investment/exports and consumption. Much of this was masked in later years by a fall in oil prices and the stimulus effects of fiscal deficits that were higher than officially stated.

had too much invested in the Rate Bull's momentary growth spurt and could not deal objectively with the issue.

Behind the low earnings and GDP growth was a financial system that had gotten progressively dysfunctional, while managing to hide that condition behind the backstop of government ownership.[13] The banking system had emerged intact through the 2008 Great Recession, leading many observers and bankers to congratulate themselves on how resilient it was. But the consequences of the Rate Bull's lending binge to the strong-arm promoters now began to manifest themselves. Much of the corporate side of India's banking system had fallen victim to a protean sequence of predatory borrowing, evergreening, delayed bad loan recognition, and blowup. Predatory lending was a familiar concept, taking place when unscrupulous organizations shovelled money at borrowers who had no capacity to repay, leading to defaults and repossession. But the banking system's problem of predatory borrowing occurred when promoters borrowed under dubious circumstances from banks, often corrupting them in the process; corrupting a bank was relatively easy and usually done by recycling part of the loan proceeds back to the bank. Evergreening was the next stage, as the bank shovelled more money at the borrower to ensure the loan stayed current and performing. Delaying recognition of the bad loans that were an inevitable result of this process then followed, and this continued till RBI governor Raghuram Rajan tried to put an end to it. Finally, when the situation became unsustainable, a blowup took place. Repetitions of the above sequence, with some of the banking system's biggest players at the centre of it, all led to a long-simmering banking and NBFC (non-bank financial company) crisis.

Yet, through all this, the market went higher, and it seemed like a miracle had taken place in a twilight zone where the market kept going up irrespective of inconveniences such as the real economy and corporate profits. On the real economy, there were concerns about the steady 6 to

[13] For an early 2013 report on financial repression and the banking system by the author, see Adil Rustomjee, 'Dr. Rajan, Your Next Crisis Is Coming up in Banking,' *Firstpost*, November 2013, accessed 10 April 2020.

7 per cent GDP growth figure put out quarter after quarter.[14] In fact, demonetization and GST, which were universally regarded as disruptive, were introduced between late 2016 and mid-2017, and yet official figures pegged the economy to grow at a reasonable clip for over two years after that, before magically worsening from the March quarter of 2019. That March quarter's results came out in May – just after the results were declared for the 2019 election the BJP won – following which there was a steep fall-off in the growth rate. Much head scratching on GDP numbers took place because of all this, especially among the eminent economists and the chattering classes. The GDP controversy was a stomping ground for clever, opinionated, and argumentative economists – of which the country had no shortage. In fact, the controversy was tailor-made even for those among the chattering classes who wanted to pass off as clever, opinionated, and argumentative economists – of which there was no shortage either. But there was no head scratching among the brokerages, and they were quite happy to play along and take the numbers for granted.

Of concern to many was the gap between nominal GDP, which is not adjusted for inflation, and high-frequency data like corporate top lines. Given the high inflation the country was prone to, nominal GDP growth usually came in at between 12 and 15 per cent, and the gap between this nominal GDP growth rate of 12 to 15 per cent and corresponding high-frequency data like top lines (which also came out in nominal terms) was often stark. Much print and broadcast time was then spent in explaining these gaps. The dialectic between stress and stimulus – between the stress caused by downward lurches in economic growth getting papered over by demand-side stimulus, rather than through more enduring changes to productivity – should have been an enduring theme of these debates, but it was rarely articulated as such.

Nevertheless, the stock market's only concern was the corporate earnings that the market priced itself off through the price-earnings

[14] Arvind Subramanian, 'India's GDP Mis-estimation: Likelihood, Magnitudes, Mechanisms, and Implications,' CID Faculty Working Paper, Center for International Development, Harvard University, June 2019, 354.

ratio. Here, the picture really flickered into a twilight zone. Based on the logic that corporate bottom lines could be expected to grow at the levels of nominal GDP growth, most analysts applied a nominal growth rate of between 12 and 15 per cent to corporate earnings to arrive at a projection. But similar to the other high-frequency data, profit growth was much lower than nominal GDP growth. Strikingly, brokerages continued to overestimate profit growth, and this happened right through the 2014 to 2019 period. Every year, year after year, the analysts overestimated earnings this way – like Hazlitt's sundial, they counted only the sunny hours – and every year, the corporate sector refused to oblige them by producing those earnings.[15] At some point, the analysts should have corrected expectations, but they did not, and the gap between their projections and actual earnings continued.

Finally, the analysts gave up and went along for the ride – this was the stock market, and it was simply going up. So, the market kept rising, and as it rose, the disconnect between corporate bottom lines and the market kept increasing. During the Rate Bull, valuations had stayed sweet and reasonable except towards the very end, but during this bull run an already expensive market started getting more so, and most people simply rationalized and sleepwalked through it all. As the disconnect widened, the market started getting more expensive as it rose. By late 2019, the market traded at almost 30 times earnings, which was a higher multiple – on much lower earnings growth – than the 28 multiple it had traded at during the 2008 Rate Bull top.[16]

In 2019, the BJP returned to power for a second consecutive term with an enhanced parliamentary majority, aided in large part by a wave of jingoistic sentiment generated by air strikes against Pakistan that were launched in retaliation for a bombing that killed 40 Indian

[15] *Horas non numero nisi serenas* or 'I count only the hours that are serene'. William Hazlitt, 'On a Sun-dial (1827).'

[16] Sensex and Nifty valuations are routinely calculated on the exchange websites.

paramilitary personnel. The party's return to power introduced a new political dynamic to economic events. It remains unclear whether the electorate gave the BJP a second majority – albeit with only 37 per cent of the popular vote[17] – to pursue its 'development for all' agenda, or for something else. But that did not matter for, emboldened by the second victory and a wave of adulatory media coverage, the BJP went ahead with implementing its right-wing manifesto. In doing so, it expended large amounts of political capital on its cultural and religious nationalism agenda, which left less to spend on substantive economic and financial issues. This, in turn, raised social, cultural, and religious tension to the point where some thought it would start affecting economic growth and commercial activity.

But the stock market kept rising through all this turbulence and turmoil. After roaring back in 2009, the market stayed high and for the next 10 years kept edging upward into the twilight zone. It rose through the aftermath of the Great Recession and the instability and policy paralysis of the Congress-led UPA-2 that ended in 2014. It continued rising through the severe dislocation of demonetization and GST that were introduced in the BJP's first term between 2014 and 2019. It rose in the absence of fiscal stimulus – for unlike the Congress, which used the political business cycle and giveaways for electoral gain, the BJP relied on its appeal to majoritarianism to get in the vote, and this fiscal conservatism was an unlikely economic benefit of having the BJP in power. It kept rising through the political and social turmoil that occurred in the BJP's second term post-2019, and it also kept rising through the BJP's occasional inability to win state elections.[18] It rose through the GDP growth rates that many said were inaccurate when they were close to 8 per cent, and it rose when that supposedly inaccurate number fell closer to 4 per cent. And it kept rising through the absence of corporate profit growth. There had been little profit growth through

[17] Srinivasan Ramani, 'Analysis: Highest-ever National Vote Share for the BJP,' *The Hindu*, 23 May 2019.

[18] Swaminathan S. Anklesaria Aiyar, 'India Less Secular but Far from a One-party State,' *Times of India*, 20 December 2020.

much of this run, and the non-existent profit growth coincided with one-time write-offs in sectors including telecom and banking. As a result, between FY 2008 and FY 2020, corporate profits as a per cent of GDP dropped from over 6 per cent to under 2 per cent.

The market's rise in the absence of profit growth was baffling to some astute observers, but after a point, most were simply happy to go along for the ride. Without corporate performance to generate a value-buying argument, the only other rationale for this up move came from that old perennial – liquidity. Reform efforts, technological change, and interest rates had displaced the Mehta Bull, the IT Bull, and the Rate Bull, respectively, but the displacement behind the 2009–20 bull run was financial innovation. The central feature of this bull was the rise of the domestic investor through rupee cost averaging products such as the Systematic Investment Plan (SIP). So prominent is the SIP as a market innovation and source of liquidity that it is appropriate to name this up move the SIP Bull. At the top of this SIP Bull move in 2019, the industry was signing on almost a million new SIP accounts a month, with monthly inflows of ₹8,000 crores from the product.[19] It was this growth in SIP flows that provided the domestic buy side with a massive and ongoing source of liquidity that kept the bull move going even after the market got overvalued.

For generations, the Indian buy side had fantasized about access to the household sector's savings. Brokerage reports routinely salivated over the consequences of a doubling of household savings that went into equity; the argument went that a move from allocations of 2 per cent to 4 per cent would result in a doubling of flows, and that was just the take-off from a low base. Through the SIP, mutual fund fantasies were fulfilled, in fact exceeded, and large sums entered the market.

Averaging products had been around for a long time. Benjamin Graham, the patron saint of the Indian buy side, had forcefully recommended them in his writings, which perhaps accounts for their

[19] Association of Mutual Funds of India (AMFI) and Crisil, *SIP-shape: Retail Investors Catalysing Growth of Mutual Funds in India*, August 2019, 5, 14, accessed 10 April 2019, https://www.amfiindia.com/Themes/Theme1/downloads/SIP-Shape-Banner6.pdf.

popularity. Graham advocated dollar cost averaging because regular resort to the product captured the nominal upward swing of the market over the long run and eliminated the need to pick stocks.[20] Nevertheless, his recommendation applied to the US – a market with few government-sponsored fixed-income products like small savings schemes or post office schemes, and so a market where the opportunity cost of equity investing was low. By contrast, in India, the government distorted the fixed income side of the market with schemes such as post office savings products and national savings certificates, which, besides offering reasonable returns, also carried tax benefits. Like the SIP, these schemes were targeted at small savers, and they raised the opportunity cost of investing in equities.

SIP flows were sticky by philosophy and design, as their entire raison d'être revolved around socking away a monthly amount into the markets irrespective of market levels. When markets fell, the standard refrain was to stick to the plan because the same monthly amount bought a little more stock at lower prices. For fund managers, this stickiness was an important part of the product's attraction, as it counterbalanced the redemption pressures they had historically faced. Even occasional periods of market downturn made the SIP unattractive compared to the competing fixed income schemes, and handholding a fickle public through the downturn then became important. So, an industry of financial advisors pounded away at the message that SIPs were good for financial health. '*Keep SIPping*' became their mantra.

With the SIP, the democratization of finance had begun. It is tempting to see this as inevitable in the world's largest democracy, but it was actually a process of hesitant evolution and response to the market's possibilities. T.T. Krishnamachari, the finance minister who created India's mutual fund industry, portrayed the mutual fund as 'an adventure in small savings,' and there is a continuity between that

[20] See Benjamin Graham, *The Intelligent Investor*, New York: HarperCollins, Revised Edition, 2006, 118.

early 60s description and the success of the SIP.[21] When founded in 2006, the minimum monthly investment in the early SIPs was ₹500 (about $10); in early 2009, SBI launched a pilot scheme in Alibaug that lowered the bar even further by having ₹100 ($2) as the minimum amount.[22] Accessing Wall Street for between $2 and $10 a month was unheard of in the US and most other countries – just transaction and intermediation costs would ensure that it was impossible – and yet in India it developed into a profitable business that came to be regarded as the market's saviour. By 2019, the product accounted for 12 per cent of the industry's assets under management.[23] Successful business in India often involves using technology to process huge volumes over small values, and the SIP is another example of that.

But be careful what you wish for; you might get it. Mutual funds now had access to a steady source of liquidity through the SIP, and the fundies proceeded to do the only thing they were supposed to do with it – they invested it in the market and brought about the SIP bull run. But as seen earlier, the corporate sector did not play along. Corporate earnings refused to grow in this period, and yet the SIP money poured into stocks, taking the market higher and making it more expensive. The usual bull market formula was that earnings grew faster than prices, and as a result, the market got cheaper as it went higher, or at least it did not get more expensive. This had happened during all previous bull runs and was most apparent in the Rate Bull. But in the SIP Bull, earnings grew slower than prices – in fact, earnings did not grow much – and as a result, the market got steadily more expensive, reaching 23 times earnings in 2017 and almost 30 times earnings by late 2019.

Like the Rate Bull, the SIP Bull was exaggerated by the lack of global diversification and the continued presence of the long corner. Without global diversification, the default asset allocation was only in India, and

[21] The early days of the mutual fund industry are outlined in the memoirs of the first executive trustee of UTI. See V.G. Pendharkar, *Unit Trust of India: Retrospect and Prospect*, New Delhi: UBS Publishers and Distributors, 2002.

[22] ET Bureau, 'SBIMF Launches Micro SIP,' *Economic Times*, 15 April 2009.

[23] AMFI and Crisil, *SIP-shape*, 16.

almost 100 per cent of portfolios were invested in the country; as a result, the tidal wave of SIP money found its way only into the domestic market, often chasing second-rate paper and driving valuations higher. Another feature of the Rate Bull, the long corner, also continued to manifest itself as a result of the constraints on short selling and low free floats. As a result, that wave of SIP capital remained condemned to a domestic market whose listed companies refused to oblige with high earnings growth, whose buy side refused to invest overseas, whose microstructure exacerbated the situation with the short constraint, and whose promoters allowed for only low free floats. With the SIP, the fundies were hoist with their own petard and in danger of being bomb makers blown up by their own bomb.

In fact, SIP flows were so strong they even compensated for FII flows that abated when the global quantitative easing program wound down after 2014. The reverse happened when FII flows surged (as when quantitative easing resumed during the coronavirus pandemic), and the fundies then sold into such surges. Instead of diversifying globally, the DIIs used the SIP flows as a counterweight to the FIIs, and both sides crossed one another with uncanny regularity in the markets. Rather than compete with everyone else in an international asset market for returns, the DIIs saw themselves as defenders of a domestic market that had to be propped up at all cost when everyone else left.

Of course, the fundies and brokerages had to rationalize it all. A Bloomberg analysis showed that analysts consistently overestimated earnings for much of the SIP Bull. More disconcerting was that the gap between earnings and analysts' estimates widened over the years.[24] After consistently overestimating earnings, at some point, the analysts should have moderated their estimates in accordance with reality, but they did the opposite and kept raising estimates. The corporate sector also did the opposite of what was expected and kept underperforming. So, when the gap between the analysts' perceptions and reality widened, they should have changed their perceptions – but no, they changed reality. This

[24] Deep Narayan Mukherjee, 'Why Are Consensus Earnings Estimates Often Off the Mark?,' *BloombergQuint*, 7 August 2017. Overestimates of between 15 and 20 per cent became routine.

cognitive dissonance seems impossible, and yet they did it through the device of 'forward earnings', which became their new reality. A typical statement, irrespective of market levels, would be: 'The market trades at 19 times forward earnings and is fairly valued.' In December 2019, towards the end of the SIP move (and before the pandemic-induced distortions), triangulating between the 29 times trailing earnings[25] of that time and the 19 times forward earnings implied an earnings growth rate of 53 per cent.[26] How earnings would magically grow over a year from the low single digits of that time to this 53 per cent figure was left unexplained. Few among the public even thought of doing a reality check with this simple calculation. So, the fundies and brokerages got away with it all, and the market kept moving into the twilight zone.

Consequently, even though the real economy stumbled along, the market was kept up, first by quantitative easing and then by the SIP. By the time QE started tapering off in 2014 or so, the SIP was firmly in place and carried the market in the following years, despite evidence that the India growth story had stalled for the medium term. Sometimes, this disconnect between a rising market and the factors working against it seems like a miracle, yet it happened. Perhaps this was just more evidence that the market, as Nobel Prize–winning economist Paul Samuelson once remarked, was micro-efficient but macro-inefficient – that is, the incorporation of information into price happened better for individual stocks than for an aggregate market. Or perhaps, all this was connected to prevailing definitions of the 'market' itself.

Factors such as the SIP, the short constraint, domestic bias, and the long corner were not the only reasons for the twilight zone. The 'market' itself posed definitional issues.

[25] Trailing earnings refer to a company's earnings in the previous 12 months; forward earnings refer to a company's earnings over the coming 12 months.

[26] Yagnesh Kansara, 'Nifty to Touch 13,400 Level in 2020: Kotak Securities,' *Outlook Money*, 20 December 2019.

What is the market anyway? This is not a rhetorical question. What is considered the market is actually a narrow index number that is defined by a bunch of buy side and exchange bureaucrats to the point where it gets divorced from economic reality. In turn, the index's narrowness allows for factors such as SIP liquidity, the short constraint, domestic bias, and the long corner to have disproportionate effects on what people usually call the market.

India has two indexes that measure the stock market. The BSE's Sensex, the public's favourite – like the USA's Dow Jones Industrial Average – is an index of 30 stocks, while the NSE's Nifty is a 50-stock index. Besides the slightly wider coverage of the Nifty, there is little to distinguish one from the other, and both measure the traded equity value of the high table of India Inc., the biggest blue chips. But India has no broad-based benchmark like the US S&P 500 which – by common consent and public acclaim – represents the market. The key point is that such indexes do exist but are not by common consent or public acclaim referred to as The Market, and one would be hard-pressed to even find a pro who can reel off the level of a broad-based index such as the Sensex 500 or the Nifty 500.[27] As a result, the extreme narrowness of India's market indexes – just 30 or 50 stocks – stands in contrast to the country's universe of over 5,000 stocks, more than half of which are traded at any given point in time. This has always been an issue.

There are two levels to the problem. The real economy is sized up by the stock market, while the stock market itself is measured by that handy tool, the market index. In India, there are issues with both appraisals. On the first appraisal – the extent to which the real economy is sized up by the stock market – one finds that large sectors of the real economy have no representation in the stock market. The most glaring example is agriculture, but other sectors such as mining are also underrepresented. Further, unlike a developed economy (like the US) where up to 70 per cent of economic activity is derived from the corporate sector, in India

[27] The Sensex 500 and Nifty 500 are available on their exchange websites.

barely 20 to 25 per cent is derived from a private corporate sector;[28] large unorganized and household sectors are responsible for this, besides that extensive agriculture complex, which is also unrepresented in corporate form. A standard industrial classification (SIC) of a large modern economy would include over 400 industries, and ideally most would be included in a stock market. By contrast, only a few such sectors find representation in India's aggregate stock market, and fewer still make it to the indexes.

On the second appraisal – the extent to which the stock market is measured by the market index – the Sensex and Nifty account for about 48 per cent and 54 per cent of BSE and NSE traded equity values, respectively.[29] In 1998, the Sensex accounted for about 35 per cent of the BSE's market value.[30] This percentage should have fallen over time as the IPO pipeline added to the number of traded companies in the broad market, but its rise to the present 48 per cent level shows how valuations of index components (mainly ultra large blue chips) keep going up relative to the broad market. The preponderance of these limited values is also in contrast to the broad-based S&P 500, which accounts for about 80 per cent of US market value. Another way of looking at the indexes' narrowness is through their sectoral composition. Taking the broader index – the Nifty – by way of example, just four sectors account for almost 80 per cent of the Nifty's value. These four sectors are: banking and financial services, information technology, fast-moving consumer goods, and oil and gas.[31] Unsurprisingly, all four

[28] R. Nagaraj, 'Size and Structure of India's Private Corporate Sector: Implications for the New GDP Series,' *Economic & Political Weekly*, 7 November 2015, Vol. l, No. 45, 43. This share has increased to 35 per cent based on a contentious new series calculation. Unsurveyed data on private companies reportedly contains details on shell companies set up for purposes other than legitimate commercial activity, which exaggerates the impact of the data series.

[29] 'Home,' BSE, https://www.bseindia.com/index.html; 'NIFTY 50 Index,' *NSE*, https://www.nseindia.com/products-services/indices-nifty50-index. All values are computed before taking free floats into consideration.

[30] Bombay Stock Exchange, *The Stock Exchange Review: November 1998*, Mumbai: BSE, 1998, 28.

[31] As of March 2020, the sector weightings (in percentages) are: Banking and Financial Services (36.5), Information Technology (15.03), Fast Moving Consumer Goods (14.46), and Oil and Gas (12.44). The NSE's website has an Indexogram, which provides periodic updates on sector weightages.

sectors are doing very well and playing either to India's comparative advantage (software/tech) or to its large domestic market (banking and consumer goods). But how much do these four sectors contribute to overall GDP? Clearly, they don't account for 80 per cent of economic activity, and by some estimates, they collectively account for less than a quarter to a third of economic activity. This brings up the obvious discrepancy between their economic importance and their weights in the indexes.[32] The gap becomes glaring if one goes back to that 400 industry SIC classification; a broad index should include a chunk of those industries to reflect an economy, but just four from that SIC universe – or about 1 per cent – make up almost 80 per cent of the Nifty index. Clearly, there is scope for wider industry representation in the indexes.

As the real economy was not reflected in the market and as the market was not reflected in the index, the combined effect led to the indexes' divorce from the real economy. This situation became glaringly obvious during the final years of the SIP Bull move. The index committees responsible for the indexes' construction and maintenance had turbocharged and packed them with high-performing sectors.[33] This is not surprising, as most committee members were themselves from the fund management industry and so had a strong interest in defining a market line that kept going up. The NSE's index policy committee, for example, consisted of representatives from mutual fund, pension, and insurance companies.[34] But in defining a line that kept going up, the index committees had, by their own admission, become stock pickers – unconsciously packing the narrow indexes with high return on equity

[32] Estimates of sector contributions to GDP (in percentages) are: Banking and Financial Services (6), Information Technology (8), Fast Moving Consumer Goods (4), and Oil and Gas (15). See IBEF website.

[33] In the early years, continuity and industry representation were the two major criteria for index inclusion. Bombay Stock Exchange, *The Stock Exchange Review: February 1999*, Mumbai: BSE, 1998, 18–19.

[34] As of April 2020. 'NSE Indices Committees,' *NSE*, https://www.nseindia.com/nse-indices/nse-indices-committee.

(ROE) stocks from high-profile sectors, rather than from sectors that offered broad representation of the economy.[35]

One consequence of all this was strategic behaviour by participants. Critically, selective buying in high ROE heavyweights such as HDFC Bank, Reliance, or HUL, which made up a big chunk of a narrow index, was easy to justify as stock picking or investment management, but this also propped up the index – and in doing so, allowed for the entire market to be propped up. Participants called this index management, and it was blatantly acknowledged by many as accepted market practice. With a rising pension fund presence through the Employees' Provident Fund Organisation (EPFO), index management wasn't even necessary as the EPFO was mandated to pour money into exchange-traded funds, which in turn were usually mandated to buy the narrowly defined indexes, taking them higher in the process.

Benchmarking and measurement also become a muddle with a narrowly defined index. All other things being equal, a 100-stock mutual fund should be less risky than a 30 (or 50)-stock index, simply because the mutual fund is more diversified. So, when that fund underperformed a narrowly defined index, was it because of genuine underperformance, or was it because the 100-stock fund was taking on less risk compared to a concentrated index? Adjusted for risk, maybe the 100-stock fund was actually outperforming the index, though it seemed to be underperforming, so calculating risk-adjusted returns also became a muddle. It is a commonplace in India's stock market that all sorts of fireworks and mayhem take place behind the Sensex/Nifty duo, and the narrowness of the indexes explains that.

The tech boom of the late 1990s illustrates some of these issues. The mutual funds loaded up on tech, but the index committees were late in introducing tech into the narrow Sensex, and so, when tech became red hot for a while, fund managers handily beat the Sensex-defined market. The index committees then scrambled to catch up with market fashion and loaded tech onto the Sensex, and so, when tech stocks collapsed, the

[35] Ashutosh Shyam, 'High RoE Cos Dominate New-look Nifty 50,' *Economic Times*, 24 February 2016.

Sensex gave the impression of a market falling a lot more than it actually did. Whether the fundies still outperformed the tech-loaded index as it fell is not clear and would have depended on their strategies, but the episode illustrates the complications in benchmarking to a loaded and narrow index.

Having a turbocharged index to measure the market is well and good for an overall market level, but sometimes the disconnect between that index-calculated market level – that barometer which everybody focuses on – and the real economy becomes apparent. The market simply cannot perform its traditional role as a leading indicator, soaring and swooning in advance of the real economy, when it is conveniently packed with sectors that account for such a small part of that real economy. If the market as a barometer for the real side is to be taken seriously, more attention will have to be paid to defining that barometer. What everyone calls 'The Market' has to change to reflect both the market and the economy.[36] Getting the stock market to reflect the real economy is a tall order and will depend on a multitude of factors that play out over time; more doable is getting the index – through that process of common consent and public acclaim – to reflect the market a little better.

One solution is for either of the exchanges to do away with their benchmark index and simply move to their preexisting broader index, effectively establishing that broader index as a market index by popular consent. Either the BSE or the NSE could do this. But let us assume the NSE makes the shift by eliminating the Nifty 50. This would leave a Sensex 30 (similar to a Dow 30) and a Nifty 500, which would be the equivalent of an S&P 500.[37] Except that the NSE might be wary of losing a generation of Nifty values dating back to the mid-1990s and would be unwilling to make the shift. So, an alternative is to retain the Nifty 50 at its present level, while recalibrating it to the 500-stock universe of

[36] Proposals for a broader-based index date back to the G.S. Patel report of 1995. Securities and Exchange Board of India (SEBI), *Report of the Committee on the Review of the Present System of Carry Forward Transactions*, Mumbai: Securities and Exchange Board of India, February, 1995, 100–01, 152–53.

[37] An index with fewer stocks also suggests itself, as many fundies say that the investible universe in India is less than 500 companies.

the NSE 500. This would maintain price series continuity with earlier market levels, but with greater representation and relevance. Volatility would be lower with a larger and more diversified index, which would have major (and highly technical) implications for derivatives markets where the Nifty is an important underlying for options and futures; the derivatives traders might not caterwaul as the lower volatilities would require them to pay lower margins, but the NSE might have to live with a lower margin float from traders' margins which, in turn, will affect its valuations. Index funds will also have to adjust, but note that India is a stock picker's rather than an indexer's market, so the switch will have fewer ramifications for index funds that represent a very small percentage of the buy side anyway. Selected companies might benefit the most from the prestige of a Nifty 500 inclusion, like how companies go around saying they are S&P 500 components.

There will be policy trade-offs, but the benefits will be significant – the index will reflect the real economy better, the numbers will jump around a lot less, there will be less index management and manipulation, and there will be two distinctive indexes rather than two very similar ones.

The end of the SIP Bull was subtle.

On 20 January 2020, the market again reached a glittering peak and touched 42,200 (Nifty level 12,400). Previous bulls had ended in a crescendo of buying that immediately broke to the downside, and to many astute participants, the tops of 1992, 2000, and 2008 were remarkably similar in look and feel. Here the end was a little different. Since about June 2019, the market had been in a tight range not far removed from its peak, which tightened even further towards the year's end; a technical indicator, the 200 day moving average (DMA), showed this tightening.[38] The indicator was important in India because of the

[38] On the 201st day, that day's value was added while the first day's value was dropped and the average recomputed, and doing this daily resulted in the 200 DMA. Removing the weekends' 104 days, and the 20 or so religious and state holidays, led to about 240 trading sessions in a year, and so the 200 DMA approximated a year's trading sessions.

large mass of traders who followed charts and technicals – breaks below it were seen as significant, and now the indicator was right next to the market line itself. As the market levelled out, the 200 DMA, which had been steadily rising till then, flattened out and began hugging the market line like a softly leaping jaguar. Between November 2019 and January 2020, the market kept bobbing and weaving around the DMA, trying to make up its mind about what to do. Sometimes it went above the indicator, and then it went below. This had happened before during the SIP run, but on each occasion, the bull move had resumed, and participants were lulled into ignoring the phenomenon. Unlike the previous highs, the SIP top formed in slow motion, and till about 12 February of that year, the market continued to trade in a tight range just a little below its 20 January high.

Then along came a virus.

Besides the human casualties from the coronavirus pandemic, it was the dislocation to civilization worldwide that took its toll on the markets. A new word entered day-to-day vocabulary – lockdown – and entire countries were impacted by it. To financial markets, the future that they had to discount suddenly looked precarious, and markets collapsed as a result. Predicting recoveries from such an event is a hazardous exercise, but it is noteworthy that the end of the influenza pandemic in 1921 was followed by the start of Wall Street's great bull move of the Roaring Twenties in 1923 – and such is the immediacy of market action and rising prices, that many accounts of the Roaring Twenties bull run don't even mention the pandemic that preceded it. Likewise, in 2020, the market went through a collapse in March, followed by a liquidity-induced pullback, which took the market to another lifetime high of 60,000 by early 2022.

The coronavirus crash of March 2020 generated a number of historic firsts that have been obscured by the steep rise that followed. The market fell 37 per cent over five weeks – technically, a 10 per cent fall qualified as a correction and a 20 per cent fall became a bear market, but a fall of this magnitude had never happened before within such a compressed time frame. The fall was too large to be called a correction, and yet the time correction of about five weeks was too small to be called a bear market. Bear markets, a prolonged period of falling prices, imply both price and time corrections, but the time corrections had stopped happening in India. In the two decades between 2003 and 2022, there had been just one time correction of a little over a year – between 2008 and 2009. Crucially, the coronavirus crash happened so fast and was so severe that it did not allow for a switch from 'buy on dips' to 'sell on rallies' mode – there was no rally to sell into during this down move.

The drop from the 20 January top of 42,200 to the 24 March level of 25,800 came to 39 per cent, the largest sell-off (in point or percentage terms) over a two-month period; most of the damage was also compressed between a 20 February level of 41,100 and the 24 March level of 25,800, which amounted to a fall of 37 per cent in 5 weeks, also a record.[39] The 3,900 point sell-off on 23 March was the largest single-day fall (both in point and percentage terms) and, at 13.2 per cent, outranked the 12 per cent fall on the worst day of the Mehta crash in April 1992. Finally, the 13 March intraday swing of 5,000 points, or 17 per cent, was also the largest intraday move ever, in point and percentage terms[40] (because of the volatility, all values are intraday rather than closing levels).

Microstructure exacerbated the coronavirus crash just as it had increased the intensity of the 2008 sell-off. It had changed little in the intervening years, so this is not surprising. Like in the Rate cycle, the bear's absence magnified the SIP up move, violating all valuation parameters in the process and allowing the buy side and policy elites to proclaim that all was well; it also magnified the crash, as markets were bereft of the bear with its inbuilt pillar of support through short cover buying. The lack of specialists was especially felt – without specialists to provide liquidity to the order book, volumes dried up to the downside as they had in previous downturns. The 'stop loss' honeycomb had built up to full effect; over the SIP Bull's 11-year move, technical traders had trailed the market price with their 'stop loss' sell orders, leading to a

[39] 'Historical Data,' *BSE*, https://www.bseindia.com/Indices/IndexArchiveData.html.

[40] Ibid.; Surajit Dasgupta, 'Sensex Stages Biggest Intraday Recovery: From 3,300-point Fall to 1,300-point Gain,' *Mint*, 13 March 2020.

honeycomb of sell orders through which the market crashed. Finally, the presence of the intraday short without an uptick rule allowed for terrific intraday moves. That historic 5,000-point and 17 per cent upswing of 13 March resulted from day traders who collapsed the market by pressing the naked intraday short all together first thing in the morning, following which value buying and institutional support took the market up during the day, which made the day traders reverse the naked short with the square up buy, following which they doubled up by buying again, and this blew out the market to the upside. And yet all this was normal and simply how markets moved in India.

In the huge options market, wealth transfers took place from option sellers to option buyers; with massive volatility, option buyers – whose downsides were anyway protected from volatility – saw the value of their options increase substantially through all this movement. Buying volatility directly had just started to happen in India, and it would have been an excellent trade, involving a bet not on direction but on the quantum of movement in any direction; the India VIX rose over 700 per cent within 3 months.[41] Most participants experiencing the crash found its volatility frightening, but this sort of movement had happened before, especially in the Harshad Mehta aftermath; nevertheless, there are few accounts from that era, and the events had faded away even from the memories of those who were active participants in those times. Yet, it has become a general rule that the Mehta market remained unrivalled for its volatility till the coronavirus crash came along.

Paradoxically, the lockdown ended much commercial activity but increased the public's presence in the markets. The market itself had stayed open right through the world's largest lockdown, a back-office feat that participants again took for granted. There were winners and losers as the lockdown changed the way civilization functioned, and one winner was the market itself. Large numbers of people working from home – among whom the young and tech-savvy were disproportionately represented – saw their fancies turn lightly to the market, and many became traders through 3-in-1 accounts. Despite the dismal economic

[41] https://www1.nseindia.com/products/content/equities/indices/historical_vix.htm.

situation, trading volumes bumped higher; June 2020 was a record month (and the first of many such record months) for the big wire houses, especially those with large online presences.

The public also came back because of an extraordinary rally from about April 2020. This rally from April 2020 to early 2022 rivalled in magnitude and intensity the pullback from the Rate cycle's 2009 bottom. The market more than doubled off the 25,800 level it had touched during the sell-off and came roaring back to cross 60,000 (Nifty: 18,000). Like the previous occasion, the proximate cause was quantitative easing from the US Federal Reserve and other central banks through a revival of bond-buying programmes. The quantitative easing program started in September 2008 – whose taper down was well under way – was now given a second lease of life, and by some estimates, the Fed's balance sheet crossed $10 trillion in early 2022, or a little more than twice the peak it had touched in the first round of easing.

The index's largest component – Reliance – used the rally to monetize its telecom operations, by allowing some of the digital world's biggest names to buy into the business. A big part of the market pullback was led by action in its counter; the Reliance stock made up about 12 per cent of the Sensex, and its doubling in the early stages of the market move gave the rally considerable momentum.

But the real economy had collapsed, and the disruption further exposed the elaborate guesswork that went into GDP estimates. In one case, a brokerage guessed the output drop at 45 per cent for the June 2020 quarter, but the day the actual GDP figures came out that brokerage's guess was a drop of 10 per cent – a swing of almost 35 per cent. Between brokerages, guesses on the output drop varied by as much as 20 per cent; all this in a game where even a 2 or 3 per cent swing is considered extraordinary. The herd's charade of guesswork based on guesswork had broken down because their common assumptions had ceased to hold in a coronavirus-hit world. The official figure of a 24 per cent drop for the June 2020 quarter may have underestimated the contraction, as informal sector output was not surveyed, resulting in the better formal sector parameters being applied to the much larger informal sector. The brokerages now had the unenviable job of guessing at the growth rate, besides guessing at how much the government would massage the growth rate.

But after the lockdown gradually eased in August 2020, pent-up demand was considerable and coincided with the year-end festival season. This combination led to a surge in high-frequency indicators and gave the impression that the real economy had rebounded. By now, a vaccine had also been discovered and distributed, following which the mood swung violently and the chattering classes were off to the races again. More critically, SIP flows combined with the global inflows from the quantitative easing program. Nevertheless, the 2020 lockdown had temporarily decimated the same household balance sheets that had remained unaffected by the 2008 crisis, and it was unclear how this would influence SIP flows.

A second wave of the pandemic, more terrible than the first, then hit in the first half of 2021, and daily case counts crossed 400,000. But the market kept going higher based on liquidity flows from abroad that continued unabated. As the market doubled off the 2020 bottom, multiples rose to between 35 and 40 times earnings; from April 2021, earnings were computed on a consolidated rather than a standalone basis, and this one-time event raised earnings and lowered multiples somewhat.[42] Nevertheless, the market's pullback in the face of a collapsing economy only reinforced the divorce between the real and financial sides; calendar year 2020 is the worst year in India's financial history, but the market rises 12 per cent.

Strangely, some profit growth came back despite the chaos. In a remarkable stroke of accidental good timing, the effects of a 2019 corporate tax cut first came into play during the pandemic slowdown, and this stimulus coincided with substantial rate cuts (of almost 300 basis points) that took place despite inflation going beyond the

[42] From April 2021, the NSE shifted to reporting consolidated earnings (i.e., including subsidiaries) for the Nifty's 50 component companies, rather than the stand-alone earnings it had been using till that date. This raised their earnings somewhat and lowered the market multiple.

RBI's threshold.[43] Lacking growth or acquisition opportunities on a large scale, companies chose to return some of the tax savings to shareholders, and dividend payments to the existing shareholder base soared. Formalization through indirect tax (GST) reform would also disproportionately benefit the listed company space, though this effect is difficult to quantify; an end to one-time sector write-offs in telecom and banking also helped. So, such is the noise in the Indian environment that despite severe distortions caused by the pandemic and resulting policy response, the corporate profit/GDP ratio would bounce back after 2020, driven in large part by these effects.

Russia's 2022 invasion of Ukraine then caused a surge in energy and food prices that tipped over inflationary pressures. Till then, the market had settled into an edgy dynamic between the buoyancy caused by liquidity flows from central bank easing and the uneasiness caused by the absence of growth in the real economy; the Value leg of the trinity had broken down, Liquidity simply chased stocks and moved them up, and a change in Sentiment took the markets yet higher. Inflation had not been a problem in the first round of quantitative easing that started in 2008, but this time it came back with a vengeance, causing a hasty end to unconventional monetary policy. In effect, the entire period from 2008 through to 2021 had featured distortions caused by liquidity ebbs and flows from global capital markets, and this was a new normal that markets started taking for granted. Those liquidity flows were now turning into reverse, and presumably, there was pain in the future, as asset bubbles deflated. But it had all happened before.

This story is still unfolding, and yet the account must come to a conclusion. Three themes that conclude and bring the account into the present are: the shift in the market's size and valuation range, the

[43] For an argument that much of this was offset by rising oil taxes that hurt the economy more generally, see Gurbachan Singh, 'Booming Stock Market and Ailing Economy,' *Business Standard*, 16 November 2021.

dominance of the NSE, and the Municipal Era's end, together with that of the regionals who defined it.

The first theme concerns shifts in the market's size and valuation, together with their estimation. The earliest measure of Indian market size (or capitalization) is from P.J. Thomas's 1948 report – ₹404 crores in 1939.[44] This figure rose to ₹22,343 crores in 1986 and touched ₹15,000,000 crores ($2.1 trillion) by January 2020,[45] representing an annualized growth rate of 14 per cent in market value over the 80-year period between 1939 and 2019. This 80-year span is the longest over which a growth rate has been computed for India's market. The growth rate in dollars was less spectacular as it has had to reckon with the long-term depreciation of the rupee. Thomas recorded a market capitalization of ₹971 crores at Independence, but the rupee traded at ₹3.3 to the dollar in 1947, leading to a dollar market value of about $2.9 billion.[46] Market capitalization in dollars was $2.1 trillion in early 2020, implying a growth rate of 9.4 per cent in dollar terms since Independence, which is far less than the 14 per cent recorded in rupee terms (over long time periods, even small differences in compounded returns are highly significant to ending values). Because of currency effects, the market's dollar returns have continued to be catastrophic in recent years, and the Nifty in February 2020 – just before the onset of distortions caused by the coronavirus collapse and liquidity-induced pullback – was still below its early 2008 level. For foreign investors, India is in a long-term bear market with most returns eaten up by the rupee's depreciation, and their TV eulogies of the India Shining story are usually between clenched teeth. Finally, both rupee and dollar returns over these long periods are distorted to the upside by the extremely low values recorded in the Century of Marking Time.

[44] P.J. Thomas, *Report on the Regulation of the Stock Market in India*, New Delhi: Ministry of Finance, 1948, 35. Cotton mills were the largest sector, followed by banks, engineering, electric, and jute mills. Market capitalization stood at ₹971 crores in 1947.

[45] The 1986 figure is from BSE. *The Stock Market Today: 1987*, Bombay: BSE, 1987, 3.

[46] P.J. Thomas, *Report on the Regulation of the Stock Market*, 35.

Another basic measure of market size – the ratio of market capitalization to GDP – was at 9 per cent in 1948, touched a historic low of 3.8 per cent in 1978, and was still at 9 per cent in 1988. It had remained virtually unchanged for almost half a century.[47] From the early 1990s onwards, the ratio made a one-time upward move into a higher range, driven in large part by the reform effort and the entry of foreign investors into the market. This corrected a century of undervaluation brought about by autarky. The surge in valuations is now seen as triumphantly inevitable, but the Century of Marking Time points to how teleological that view really is. The ratio now moves between 50 and 150 per cent of GDP, driven in large part by international norms and the market cycle; in fact, the range's extreme values are outliers, and practically most observations are in the 60 to 90 per cent range. Observations towards either end of this 60 to 90 per cent range will be interpreted by most value participants as occasions to load up or lighten up respectively.

A similar one-time rerating has taken place on valuation. Valuation measures such as PE ratios were first calculated on a regular basis only from about 1989–90, and before that we have to rely on studies by pioneers such as L.C. Gupta. Gupta's work points to PE multiples as low as 6 for the aggregate market in the pre-reform period of the early 1980s, far lower than the long-term average of 15 to 18 that today's participants take for granted.[48] Most studies of long-term averages do not include this pre-reform period, mainly due to lack of awareness but also because including this period would drop the average – perhaps into the 13 to 15 range. So, the valuation range has also clearly shifted, from between 5- and 7-times earnings for the period that ended in the early 1980s to between 10 and 30-times earnings in the decades that followed[49] (the Mehta Bull multiple of over 50 remains a unique

[47] Bombay Stock Exchange, *The Stock Market Today: 1990*, Bombay: BSE, 1990, Annexure III, A-3.

[48] L.C. Gupta, P.K. Jain, and C.P. Gupta, *Indian Stock Market PE Ratios*, New Delhi: Society for Capital Market Research and Development, 1998, 36–37.

[49] 'Indices and Ratios,' *BSE*; https://www1.nseindia.com/products/content/equities/indices/historical_pepb.htm.

outlier). In the pullback following the coronavirus sell-off, valuations entered bubble territory and multiples in the 35 to 40 range were reached; the long-term average multiple now rises to between 18 and 22, in large part due to the quantitative easing–induced distortions for the 2008–22 period.[50]

Until the mid-1980s, price-earnings ratios remained in single digits, and so the market routinely offered dividend yields of up to 6 per cent, but later yields shifted downwards as the market priced growth more aggressively.[51] At present, dividend yields are typically between 1 and 2 per cent. On aggregate, the Indian market is now perennially priced for growth and not value.

The number of listed companies rose from 1,125 in 1946 to about 6,000 in the early 1990s, before dropping to today's figure of a little over 5,000; the actual number of traded companies on any given day is much lower and usually half of this latter figure.[52] (The daily count of traded issues tends to be larger on the BSE because of the large number of legacy companies from the IPO booms of the 1980s and 1990s.)

More generally, in the pre-reform era that ended around the early 1980s, there was a distinct pattern of small increases on small bases. A remarkable time series from a 1970 BSE study covering part of the Century of Marking Time shows how little the market actually moved in that era. Over a period of 40 years between 1927 and 1968, a roughly calculated price index (with 1950 as the base year) rose from 69.4 to 120, implying an annualized growth rate of about 1.3 per cent over four decades.[53] From the early 1980s till about 2010, the pattern shifted to large increases on small bases. Between 1982 and 2010, the Sensex average value moved from 225 to 18,200, which is an annualized growth rate of 17 per cent.[54] As a result, the dominant attitude among many

[50] All observations are based on trailing 12-month earnings.

[51] Since dividend yield is the dividend amount/price, as prices increase, the same absolute value of dividend has a lower percentage yield.

[52] Bombay Stock Exchange, *The Stock Market Today: 1987*, 3.

[53] Bombay Stock Exchange, *Profile of Stock Exchange Activity in India*, Bombay: BSE, 1970, 75.

[54] The 1982 average level is from Bombay Stock Exchange, *The Stock Market Today: 1987*, 12.

participants becomes: '*This is big, but guess what, it's nothing compared to what is yet to come.*' Three major bulls – the Mehta Bull, IT Bull, and Rate Bull – take place during this period, and each drives the market into a higher range; just during the Rate Bull years from 2003 to 2008, the market compounded at 54 per cent.[55] But from about 2010 onwards, the pattern has shifted again, to small increases on large bases. As the global financial crisis ended and the SIP Bull commenced, movements and phenomena matured, and slowing growth on a large base made things a bit of a slog.

But seeing these patterns takes effort, as the violent moves of recent times mean that picking and choosing end points can drastically change results. The growth rate from the Sensex's 2010 average value of 18,200 to the 30,000 level the market stabilized at after the coronavirus crash in April 2020 is just 5 per cent, but the growth rate to the 50,000 level of early 2021 is 9.5 per cent.[56] Consider also that growth from the average 1992 level of 3,050 to the 50,000 level of early 2021 is 10 per cent, which is less than the 14 per cent computed over the 8 decades since the Thomas data.[57] But starting the same calculation a decade earlier – from that 1982 average level of 225 and concluding at the same 50,000 level of 2020 – again gives a long-term growth rate of 15 per cent. So, the large one-time up move of the 1980s and early 1990s distorts calculations, and including or excluding this period leads to different conclusions on long-term returns. This explains the gap between the triumphalism in official reports or brokerage analyses and the actual experience of many participants; brokerages pick and choose Low to High data points to make their case, and fragmented long-term data, together with the disjointed nature of change inadequately recorded over time, allows them to get away with it.

Much of this volatility is itself a product of recent times. As that 1970 BSE time series indicates, the market could not even double over almost two generations during the Century of Marking Time – which simply

[55] 'Historical Data,' *BSE.*

[56] Ibid.

[57] Ibid.; P.J. Thomas, *Report on the Regulation of the Stock Market*, 35.

points to the suitability of that moniker. But coming off lows in 2003, 2008, and 2020, the market essentially doubled in a few months, doing in those few months what could not be done over two generations. So, the market's rate of change was accelerating drastically, broadly mirroring the acceleration in the rate of change that characterizes modern times.

When all is said and done, it is the founding episode of the modern era that still remains the most spectacular of market events. During the Harshad Mehta bull, the Sensex moved from 225 in 1982 to 4,467 at the bull top on 22 April 1992; the market became a 20-bagger, and this 1,900 per cent surge between 1982 and 1992 represents its largest ever decadal move on a log scale. The PE ratio of over 50 in April 1992 also remains a record that has never been surpassed. The upshot of all this was the one-time rerating from the 5 and 6 multiples that L.C. Gupta had noticed, towards the long-term average multiple of between 15- and 20-times earnings. As shown, such periods are responsible for those spectacular long-term growth rates the brokerages put out when they extol the virtues of long-term investing, but a key historical question is whether such periods will repeat – and the answer is that they almost certainly will not. These are one-time reassessments that are the outcomes of a unique combination of events; in this case, it was the euphoria of the Manmohan Singh–led reform move, together with the entry of foreign investors, all helped along by Mehta's machinations in the G-Sec market, that corrected generations of undervaluation and led to the rerating. To put this in perspective, consider that the second-largest decadal move between 2003 and 2013 led to a 7-bagger, while the third-largest move between 2009 and 2019 was a 5-bagger, and this despite the fact that – for maximum effect – both these calculations start from the bear market lows of 2003 and 2009. Thus, trough to peak bull moves in the modern era appear to be settling in the 5- to 7-times range, while peak to trough bear moves are usually cuts between half and two-thirds off.

A second theme is the NSE's dominance, which seems complete at the present moment. The NSE's founding was momentous for the Indian market. Only the next to last of the 25 exchanges to be recognized by the millennium's end, it would still end up being the leading exchange.[58] In the process, the exchange has effectively monopolized the stock market with market shares of 100 per cent and 95 per cent in the derivatives and cash segments respectively.[59] While much of the early success was driven by its technology and market design, in later years its dominance has come from leadership in derivatives. The derivatives segment allowed the NSE to corner the arbitrage volumes on all arbitrage between the cash and derivatives markets; in most countries, the arbitrage trade takes place only between the index and a basket of stocks underlying the index, but in India, the extensive presence of single stock futures (SSFs) allows for the arbitrage trade on individual counters too.[60] In turn, this has substantially increased cash market volumes (more so for the blue chips) and allowed the NSE to turn its derivatives supremacy into leadership in the cash segment, thereby dominating the stock market. The derivatives segment also gives the NSE a substantial float from the margins that traders deposit with the exchange, and controlling both the cash and derivatives segments gives the NSE an organizational and cross-margining advantage on the arbitrage trade that no other exchange can match.

The exchange space had moved from 25 exchanges to the BSE/NSE duo and then effectively to just the NSE. Trapped by its success, the NSE had monopolized the Indian market but was afraid to say so and kept hoping no one else would notice. The contrast between the environs that housed the two exchanges makes this a little clearer. The BSE's Phiroze Jeejeebhoy Towers and the historic Fort area that houses it are all of a piece, and the building towers above the little structures around it, almost indicative of its soaring self-worth when it was completed in the early 1980s, a time when the BSE was the only game in town. By

[58] Subsequently, recognitions were granted to the India International Exchange and the Metropolitan Stock Exchange of India.

[59] National Stock Exchange, *Annual Report 2018–2019*, Mumbai: NSE, 2019, 23. The BSE has re-established itself very recently in the derivatives segment.

[60] Despite being handled by computers, index arbitrage can seem cumbersome compared to the smooth execution on SSF arbitrage.

contrast, the NSE building in the Bandra Kurla Complex looks like a layered squat monolith, a modern grey ziggurat with its successively receding levels and stories; almost designed to be low profile to a fault, its design philosophy reflected the attitude of the organization itself. The difference in the exchanges' surroundings and ambience is also striking. The BSE's Jeejeebhoy Towers still houses the brokers, and a steady stream of people entering and leaving their offices – either as clients or employees – ensures the hustle and bustle of a bazaar. The students at the BSE Training Institute also allow for a youthful feel. Despite the security, there is nothing guarded about the BSE's building, and it remains an iconic and much beloved landmark, always milling with people. By contrast, the NSE's building mainly houses its staff, and the absence of the bazaar's bustle is striking. Far removed from the lively anarchy of Indian cities, the most distinctive feature of the setting is the absence of people coming and going, and in this, it feels like a near-empty suburban office park in an American city.

The NSE's emphasis on transparency applies more to the parties who trade on it but less so to its own actions, and the exchange's leadership has always been guarded and secretive about its activities. (The exchange has no publicly accessible archives or library.) It is an attitude that has intensified with the exchange's progressive monopoly of the markets.[61] Like that other ambiguity, the Tennessee Valley Authority (TVA), the NSE also professes to be run as a private corporation. But unlike the TVA's shares that are held by the US government, the NSE's shares are held by various public and private sector entities, with ownership changing at constantly higher valuations in a discreet game of musical chairs orchestrated by the NSE itself.

The NSE's history and early years are perfunctorily recorded on its website, in stark contrast to its own historic role in the market's evolution. The website itself is packed with numbers and figures that would make the eyes glaze over, and this is perhaps because the NSE has both cash

[61] The NSE repeatedly resisted attempts to bring it under the Right to Information Act. See Sucheta Dalal and Debashis Basu, *Absolute Power*, Mumbai: Kensource Books, 2021.

and derivatives segments to deal with. The vast information on the website – the options chain alone runs into many screens – perfectly hides the secretive nature of the organization behind it all. With so much information to disclose on the market, there is little space for information about an organization that *is* the market.

The NSE's monopoly position sometimes leads to complicated conflicts of interest. Every stakeholder has to deal with the NSE because it is effectively the only game in town, and so, the exchange has often found itself at the centre of webs of interlocking relationships that blow up into controversy. As algorithmic trading catches on and as research expands, the NSE has found itself in the middle of attempts to extract advantage from the masses of electronic market data that the exchange generates – data that is mined by an assorted group of quant jocks, data cowboys, and algo traders. Rather than the old-fashioned idea of buying low and selling high, many from this group are predisposed towards esoteric stuff like computational finance or statistical arbitrage; in fact, given the large number of engineer/MBA types on the Indian buy side, it is surprising that there are not more cowboys around.

It is a complex and deliberately low-profile ecosystem, with some in the system even connected by marriage or kinship to senior NSE staff. As by now, the NSE is the market, the terms under which this ecosystem engages with the market are governed by the NSE, rather than by a befuddled regulator. In fact, SEBI has alternated between being in the NSE's thrall and trying to show that it isn't. Sometimes it appears like the NSE is simply more competent and with too storied a track record for anyone, including the regulator, to question it. Recently, all the above issues have come together in a colocation scandal that revolves around the NSE's management and its role in giving some parties preferential access to the exchange's premises to locate their servers.[62]

The NSE's de facto monopoly over the market should have posed policy questions but never has because of a complex conspiracy of silence

[62] 'How Ravi Narain Built the NSE, and Then Lost His Grip,' *Moneycontrol*, 4 June 2017, https://www.moneycontrol.com/news/trends/features-2/how-ravi-narain-built-the-nse-and-then-lost-his-grip-2296629.html. Also see Sucheta Dalal and Debashis Basu, *Absolute Power*.

around the issue. The incumbent possesses formidable advantages, and network effects are simply too strong and clearly in the NSE's favour. It is understood that competition for order flow among exchanges is preferable to a single exchange monopoly, but there is little discussion on the same. By way of remedy, one obvious solution lies in rebuilding the BSE as an effective counterweight that could introduce an element of competition in the exchange space; informally getting the buy side to split its orders by placing 1 or 2 in every 10 shares on the BSE is a good way to make a start in the cash market. Another alternative – lodging the cash and derivatives segments of the NSE with separate companies – would end the NSE's cross-margining and organizational advantage over both markets, but it would still leave the new entities with separate monopolies over their respective segments.

A third theme in all this is the end of the Municipal Era and of the regional exchanges that defined it. With the passage of time, it is tempting to see the regionals as a historical curiosity, but they had been an important part of the market's story. Much of the 1991 Pherwani report – with its decisive recommendation on the NSE's creation – had in fact revolved around the role of the regional exchanges, and the report could have resulted in an equally likely, but radically different, outcome for the microstructure.[63] In all likelihood, that outcome would have involved a national market system consisting of a computer network of national and regional exchanges, held together by a common depository and clearing corporation. It would not have been very different from what evolved in the US, and yet it did not happen.

For much of the market's Municipal Era that ended at the millennium, equities had been a business where every major municipality had its own exchange with a monopoly on transactions in that area. Section 13 of the 1956 SCRA further sanctified the municipal monopolies that provided much of the raison d'être for the regionals. Since SCRA

[63] The Pherwani committee dealt at great length with regional exchanges and would make repeated references to building a market with them. Ministry of Finance, *Report of the High Powered Study Group on Establishment of New Stock Exchanges*, New Delhi: Ministry of Finance, June 1991, 106–10, 115. Annexures 5, 10, and 23 deal with the regional exchanges.

recognition was now necessary, it is possible to plot the municipal system's expansion through this recognition process. SCRA recognition came in two phases – the first in the years immediately after the 1956 Act when seven exchanges were recognized, followed by a second phase in the 1980s when 13 exchanges were recognized. Much of the growth spurt in regionals came during this second phase, as the government – caught in the municipal mindset created by Section 13 – encouraged the growth of new exchanges. As a result, between 1980 and the late 1990s, the number of exchanges in India rose from 9 to 25, and this growth in exchanges is a record that will, in all probability, never be surpassed. For many years, the large universe of listed companies was also due to listings on these regional exchanges; on 31 March 2001, for example, there were 9,985 stocks listed, with many listings on the regional exchanges.

Regional listings were driven by the compliance requirement that a company had to be listed on two exchanges, which usually meant the BSE and one of the regionals. For some years, regionals also benefited from a 1985 requirement that existing listed companies had to list in the region where the registered office or main factory/asset of the company was located.[64] Ostensibly done to bring business to the regionals and to ensure that exchange activity moved to rural areas, the provision also ensured that company listing fees became a key source of income for regional exchanges. Nevertheless, the modern era's first burst of market activity in the mid-1980s and the Harshad Mehta bull move that followed bypassed the regionals, and most trading volumes were confined to the badla exchanges of ABCDM (Ahmedabad, Bombay, Calcutta, Delhi, and Madras). The absence of a forward/badla product hampered the regionals, and despite the 1985 rule, most had problems generating trading volumes for the companies listed on them.

Despite their marginal presence, the regionals figured prominently in early debates, and that seems surprising today. Oddly enough, and

[64] Ministry of Finance, Stock Exchange Division, 'Circular F14 (2)/SE/85,' 23 September 1985.

despite the regionals' patchy record, the 1991 Pherwani committee's terms of reference dealt almost exclusively with the formation of further exchanges – Gwalior, New Bombay, Shimla, Nagpur, and Chandigarh were to be the new regionals that would add to an already fragmented market. So, despite the fragmented municipalization that the SCRA had wrought, the mindset at the start of the reform effort called for computer linkages between existing national exchanges, and a further linkage with the regionals through a National Stock Market System, or NSMS, that would have been similar to the US ITS (Intermarket Trading System). Consequently, the regionals might well have been around today, except that one of the new exchanges – the New Bombay setup that became the NSE – would change everything.

With the NSE's arrival in the mid-1990s, any rationale for regional exchanges went away. With its online trading system NEAT, the NSE effectively cleaned up the market outside Mumbai; the BSE scrambled to respond and launched its own online system (BOLT) two years later. From about 2004 onwards, close to 99 per cent of the equity market was handled by the NSE and BSE among themselves. The growth of the national BSE and NSE networks, together with the clearing and settlement changes that reduced opportunities for inter-exchange arbitrage, put paid to any further growth by the regionals. From now on, network effects were simply too strong. Traders congregate at the largest liquidity pools, and the national character of the NSE and BSE networks made the regional exchanges redundant. Most regional brokers then switched to either, or both, of the two national exchanges. Crucially, the NSE's founding also reduced the income stream from listing fees that had been available to the regionals; till the early 1990s, the two-exchange listing requirement had meant the BSE and a regional exchange, but after the NSE's founding, that second exchange was always the NSE, which ended the income stream from listing fees.

Nevertheless, still strong was the conception of the market as a linked set of national and regional exchanges. As late as 1997, with both NEAT and BOLT firmly established, the Dave committee was still recommending an NSMS to connect the regionals.[65] By now, there was less need for the 1985 requirement that forced companies to list in the region where the registered office or main factory was located, and that requirement was abolished in 2003; companies did not have to meet this requirement, provided they were listed on two national exchanges, which now meant the BSE and NSE.[66]

Besides the NSMS, multiple attempts were made to revive the regionals, and these included an alphabet soup of names such as OTCEI, BSE IndoNext, and ISE. None really worked out. The OTCEI took its inspiration from NASDAQ; it should have been the next NSE, for it had a computerized limit order book before the NSE, it had depository facilities before the NSDL, and it had facilities for market-making the BSE floor lacked. But a flaw in market design put excessive onus on NASDAQ-style market-makers, which, together with the absence of a leveraged product, made the exchange a non-starter.[67] The regionals then tried to list their small companies on BSE's IndoNext platform, but small companies have a lousy track record at becoming big in India, and a specialized exchange that only focused on high-risk minnows was an unviable proposition. Finally, 14 of the regionals attempted to pool liquidity through an Inter-connected Stock Exchange of India (ISE); the ISE was set up to link the regionals in a national market and benefited from the indefatigable M.R. Mayya as chairman, but with the national networks of the majors, there was no need for the ISE, and it soon faded away.[68] The Municipal Era of India's stock market now came to an end, and the passing is momentous, for it finally put paid to the idea of a national market system that had dominated early

[65] Association of Merchant Bankers of India (AMBI), *Infrastructure for the Capital Markets: The Dave Committee Report*, Mumbai: AMBI, 1997, 16–17.

[66] SEBI, (Delisting of Securities) Guidelines, 2003, 'Circular SMD/Policy/Cir-7/2003,' 17 February 2003.

[67] The original rationale for the OTCEI is outlined in Nipun Mehta, *OTC Exchange of India: The Stock Exchange for You and Me*, Bombay: Jaico, 1992, 27–31.

[68] The original ISE proposal is outlined in Joseph Massey, 'The Inter-connected Stock Exchange of India,' *The Future of India's Stock Markets*, ed. Tushar Waghmare, New Delhi: Tata McGraw-Hill, 1998, 49–54.

thinking. By now, most of the regionals were reporting zero turnovers and were unable to meet SEBI's trading and net worth norms; as a result, they began exiting the exchange space, and most left between 2013 and 2016.[69]

Calcutta – the city's name has changed to Kolkata but the exchange still retains the old name – is the sole regional exchange still left. Calcutta has always seen itself as a national exchange, and at one time, it had listings and volumes that came close to rivalling Bombay. The exchange would take advantage of differing settlement cycles and did considerable business by rolling over the book between itself and Bombay; uniform settlement cycles have now eliminated that possibility. As of 2023, it was directed to stop its activity, but it has chosen the litigation route and its status continues in abeyance.[70]

If the NSMS had worked out, the regionals could have become important spokes in a hub and spoke market, and it is possible to conceive of Calcutta and Bangalore as similar to the Boston, Chicago, or Philadelphia exchanges in the USA. But the real issue was the quality of regional listings, though this was rarely articulated in the discussions; many companies listed on the regional exchanges had little business being in the listed space. Besides, exchanges are subject to those strong network effects, with the largest exchange getting inherently larger as traders congregate at the biggest liquidity pools. That the regionals defied poor listings and network effects and survived for years is a wonder. The real reason behind their survival is favourable regulation, or to use a favourite term of many participants – 'regulatory forbearance'. But this can work both ways, and the regionals also offered a lesson in the severe regulatory risk and reform risk that market participants face in India. In a few years, the regionals went from being essential to the market's microstructure to being a regulatory burden, following which they were

[69] This still left some companies that were only listed on regionals. Shareholders of such companies were provided exit facilities through a dissemination board on one of the national exchanges. The companies themselves had the option of delisting (or listing if eligible on the two national exchanges).

[70] Aniek Paul, 'A Requiem for the Calcutta Stock Exchange,' *Mint*, 23 May 2014; PTI, 'Calcutta Stock Exchange Stares at Uncertain Future on Samvat 2076,' 26 October 2019.

effectively abolished. Most finance literature concentrated on market risk but neglected the regulatory risk intermediaries and microstructure components endured in an environment where faceless bureaucrats made decisions amidst howls for reform.

The Indian stock market at its bicentennial demonstrates its own contradictions in a country of contradictions. It is a market with a first-world microstructure in a third-world milieu, demonstrating the same incongruity an astute observer might note while viewing the snazzy digital payment solutions that proliferate in a still underdeveloped country. After a certain point in their evolution, stock markets are only as good or as bad as the companies that trade on them, and by now, India's market had reached that point. Many of the microstructure-related issues have been resolved, and so our focus shifts from the stock market to the methods involved in trading the stocks listed on it.

PART TWO

APPROACHES AND METHODS

7

THE TEMPLE OF BRAHMA

The RBI in All This

The trinity of Brahma, Vishnu, and Shiva symbolize, in that order, the primordial process of creation, preservation, and destruction – the fate that underlies all matter. In a country of numerous temples and assorted other places of worship, Vishnu and Shiva have thousands of temples erected in their honour, but there is only one noted shrine dedicated to Brahma the Creator. This is the Temple of Brahma in Pushkar. In financial markets too, there is only one noted shrine to the creator. This singular 'Temple of Brahma', the Reserve Bank of India, creates something that the stock market lives on – money. It also sets the interest rate; everything has a cost expressed in terms of money, and the cost of money itself is the interest rate.

The RBI has no de jure independence as per the RBI Act of 1934, though it has some de facto independence. This de facto independence from the government arises from the simple fact that the political class is happy to let the RBI do its job on inflation control, particularly around election time; after all, elections in India are often won or lost over the prices of *aloo kanda* (potatoes and onions). But the RBI's ambiguous position often results in observers gingerly dancing around it, trying to decide how independent the central bank really is. In fact, the central bank's independence is one reform move that has never been seriously discussed, in a country otherwise given to vociferously debating all other aspects of reform;[1] perhaps the subject is simply too esoteric. Other than an occasional flare-up in public discourse, the RBI itself has remained strangely immune to any discussions on its independence, and this situation has prevailed since the start of the reform era.

Much of the discussion on connections between monetary policy and the stock market is – like the discussion on market structure – of recent origin. As an instrument in the macroeconomic policy mix, monetary policy has itself come into its own very recently. Historically, fiscal dominance and financial repression ensured that the RBI's prime role was monetizing and accommodating the government's large and perennial fiscal deficits within a system of administered interest rates. What monetary policy there was took place through quantitative measures and credit planning; blunt direct instruments such as the cash reserve ratio (CRR) and the statutory liquidity ratio (SLR) were the default choice of policy. It took two generations after Independence for a review of the system to come about, and the first attempts at change were made by a committee under Sukhamoy Chakravarty.[2] Successive reforms in the late 1980s and early 1990s then ended the RBI's default role in monetizing deficits, and the central bank moved from direct instruments to indirect market-based instruments; much of the administered interest rate structure was also done away with.[3] In 1999, a liquidity adjustment facility was introduced, which, from 2004, operated through overnight fixed rate and reverse rate repos. It was only as recently as 2011 that India got a formal policy interest rate and the repo rate was made the single policy rate; an overnight call money rate was then made the explicit operating target of monetary policy. A flurry

[1] Former RBI economist Anand Chandavarkar outlines the verbal contortions (of the political class and RBI governors) over the central bank's independence in 'Towards an Independent Federal Reserve Bank of India: A Political Economy Agenda for Reconstitution,' *Economic and Political Weekly*, Vol. 40, No. 35 (27 August–2 September 2005), 3837, 3839–45.

[2] Sukhamoy Chakravarty was an Indian economist, and a key architect of India's Five-Year plans.

[3] For an account by a former RBI governor, see C. Rangarajan, 'Some Critical Issues in Monetary Policy,' *Economic and Political Weekly*, Vol. 36, No. 24 (16–22 June 2001), 2139–41.

of reforms and the creation of a monetary policy committee then sought to reduce ambiguity regarding the central bank's independence. In 2016, the country moved to a 'flexible inflation targeting' framework, and the RBI Act was amended to formalize the statutory basis for this policy; the amended Act provided for an inflation target (presently at 4 per cent with a 2 per cent tolerance level on either side) to be set every 5 years by the government in consultation with the RBI.[4]

Whatever you do, don't be held responsible for a market crash. This unwritten rule at the RBI reveals one aspect of the central bank's uneasy relationship with the stock markets. The central bank began operations in 1935, a full century after the stock market came into existence. Both institutions are located diametrically opposite one another at Horniman Circle where the story started, each housed in skyscrapers that face off in silent surmise of the other. Historically, the RBI's attitude towards the stock market has been tinged with circumspection and a desire to isolate the banking system from the market's shenanigans;[5] it has done this with varying success over the years. The central bank does not regulate the stock market; that's SEBI's job. Figuring out the RBI's next move on the price of money – the interest rate – is the stock market's job.

Interest rates act like gravity on financial assets. Just as gravity pulls all down, rising interest rates – 'r' in the finance books – should bring

[4] Targeting inflation, rather than monetary aggregates or short-term rates, is challenging because of the central bank's indirect (and lagged) influence over nominal GDP and prices. To date, there has also been little work on the stability of the money demand function in the midst of the digital payments revolution that India claims to be undergoing; it remains unclear whether such changes pose challenges to an inflation-targeting regime.

[5] The RBI's regulatory and supervisory roles have occasionally come under the scanner, and one such instance was during the 2002 parliamentary hearings on the Ketan Parekh episode. See Joint Parliamentary Committee (JPC), *Report of the Joint Committee on Stock Market Scam and Matters Relating Thereto* (Thirteenth Lok Sabha), Volume I Report, New Delhi: Lok Sabha Secretariat, 2002, 222–51. For an account of the RBI's role in the Harshad Mehta case, see Debashis Basu and Sucheta Dalal, *The Scam: Who Won, Who Lost, Who Got Away*, New Delhi: UBS Publishers' Distributors Ltd., 1993, 241–55.

down the price of financial assets, including stocks. The price of financial assets like stocks is estimated through 'discounting', a process that is the reverse of the more familiar 'compounding'. In compounding, interest is calculated and compounded to arrive at the future value of an amount. In discounting, the reverse takes place and future values – such as a stock's dividend stream – are discounted at some interest rate (usually the appropriate risk-adjusted cost of capital) to arrive at a present value. Rising interest rates reduce the net present value of a stock's dividend stream, which in some valuation models is the price of the stock itself; as interest rates rise, that little 'r' in the right-hand side (RHS) of stock pricing equations goes up, and because it's in the denominator, it pulls down the left-hand side (LHS), which is the present value of the asset in all those fancy equations. These are first-order effects. Irving Fisher in *The Rate of Interest* discovered the net present value rule that John Burr Williams applied to good effect in the basic treatise of stock valuation, *The Theory of Investment Value*.

Second-order effects of interest rates are as pervasive as first-order effects, and calling them second-order effects is a misnomer. Rising interest rates slow down all economic activity in the economy as the RBI raises its policy rate – the repo – or reduces liquidity, usually in response to an inflation problem.[6] Corporate borrowing costs rise, increasing interest expenses on existing borrowing while also lowering profits. Future borrowing for new investment gets expensive, which lowers corporate investment, and if the notoriously volatile investment multiplier works, investment falls, and considerably. Working capital financing gets expensive – inventories and receivables cost more to finance, and hence reduce. Households spend less, borrowing to spend costs more, and consumption and disposable income fall. Entire consumption-driven sectors which produce durables such as autos and white goods – which households purchase by borrowing at higher rates – will see their demand fall off. The government finds its interest costs going up, which further increases its deficits, prompting reduced

[6] Open market operations and reserve requirements are other instruments used by the central bank.

government spending, perhaps on investments, which in turn also has multiplier effects on the economy. The rupee should strengthen, as portfolios – attracted by the higher yield on assets denominated in the home currency – rebalance in favour of those assets; but this impact is temporary as the rupee has to deal with other factors that contribute to its secular decline. Because of the above effects, economic activity and aggregate demand fall, and with them, corporate profits.

Crucially, because much of this plays out in the future, the price-earnings multiple that the market pays for future profits will also contract. Since the stock market is priced off corporate profits (or earnings) through the price-to-earnings (PE) multiple, the markets sell off in response to rising interest rates, leading to the familiar inverse relationship between interest rates and stock market levels.[7] Finally, as interest rates rise, competing fixed-income products such as post office deposits and small savings schemes offer better returns, raising the opportunity cost of equity investing and causing capital flows out of the stock market; in India, the government has distorted the fixed-income market to the point where these kinks become important, and doubly so nowadays because of the public's presence in both equities and the myriad small savings schemes.

One big wrinkle in all this is expectations – unanticipated shocks to rates will exacerbate the above effects depending on how credibly participants view the central bank's policy reaction function. In fact, since the stock market, by definition, adjusts to new information much faster than the real economy, unanticipated shocks to expectations will play out faster in the markets.

The above is a working description of the *interest rate channel* through which monetary policy as set by the RBI transmits through the economy and to the stock market. The RBI's role – the central bank's dharma if you will – is to be the spoiler at the party, raising interest rates and taking

[7] Empirical work on monetary transmission and the stock market falls into 3 categories: vector autoregression studies (VAR), event studies, and identification through heteroscedasticity methods (IH). Most such studies undertaken in developed economies confirm the inverse relationship, with unanticipated changes in monetary policy generating more significant changes in market levels.

away the *daaru* (alcohol) when the party of economic expansion is really under way. It does this to ensure inflation doesn't become a problem, but as seen, such rises have knock-on effects on corporate profits and consequently on the market.

Thus, though corporate profits are the first pillar of a bull market, it is no surprise that interest rates are the second pillar. Yet in India, the connection between policy rates and market bull–bear cycles is not clear-cut. There have been bull markets with policy rates at 12 per cent or higher, and the bear has come visiting when interest rates have been as low as 6 per cent.[8] The latter may seem high compared to some Western economies (where rates till recently have been at their lower bound of close to zero), but this is par for the course in an inflation-prone economy like India.

Nothing exceptional in all this, some would say. After all, monetary policy often takes effect with a lag.[9] Ideally, once the RBI changes its policy rate – the repo rate – the change transmits through the term structure of interest rates and onwards, to other interest rates throughout the economy;[10] only in later stages does this process of monetary transmission affect output and economy-wide prices. Rather like the creaky old plumbing in an old house – you turn on the hot water tap in the shower, and it takes a short while for hot water to come through. But something else is going on here, and it's not just the lagged effects of monetary policy.

The casual observer could be forgiven for not getting this tenuous connection between policy interest rates and the stock market. In fact, to the average observer and market participant, central bank policy on *vyaj* (interest) seems to be of paramount importance to the markets. At every RBI policy meet, the media circus reaches fever pitch. There's the

[8] Interest rates were well into double digits during the Mehta Bull and in single digits during the Rate cycle's downturn.

[9] Milton Friedman, 'The Role of Monetary Policy,' *American Economic Review*, Vol. 58, No. 1, 1968, 15–16.

[10] Monetary transmission outside developed economies is outlined in Prachi Mishra, Peter J. Montiel, and Antonio Spilimbergo, 'Monetary Transmission in Low-Income Countries: Effectiveness and Policy Implications,' *IMF Economic Review*, Vol. 60, No. 2 (2012), 270–302.

anchor with her impeccable bob and dainty hands chopping away at the air, as she makes a point in her sing-song accent. And there's the other anchor, usually of graver demeanour, but now getting beside himself and chattering away on the latest nuance of monetary policy. In fact, rather than the stock market, bank treasury rooms are where the action is on policy announcement days. Still, the stock market laps it all up, hanging on to every word and waiting for a market response that seldom happens.[11] After the announcement, there's a collective yawn, and it's on to the next item. The rate sensitives – banks, infrastructure plays, and real estate – jiggle around a little and the Sensex also squiggles on policy day, but it's all soon forgotten and participants move on to the next market-moving event. So, despite the media's Sturm und Drang, there is not much of an inverse relationship between the *vyaj* and stock market in India. Even if there was, the market's multiple causalities and massive lags in the pass-through imply that – for the market at least – rate forecasting and all the other brouhaha about rates is basically pointless.

The reason for this funny state of affairs lies in two unwieldy phrases: uncertain monetary transmission and segmented credit markets. In addition, the nature of the stock index itself plays a big role in the market's tardy response to rate policy.

Monetary transmission – the process through which RBI monetary policy affects the real and financial sectors in general and the price level in particular – is a contentious subject in India. Transmission issues have assumed added importance as policy has moved from blunt direct instruments such as the CRR and quantitative credit controls, to indirect market-based instruments such as the repo rate. Conventionally, transmission takes place through four channels: the

[11] Using event studies, Sasidharan finds no systematic market response on days before or after the policy announcement – irrespective of whether the policy move was contractionary or expansionary. Anand Sasidharan, 'Stock Market's Reaction to Monetary Policy Announcements in India,' *Munich Personal RePEc Archive*, June 2009, 13–14, http://mpra.ub.uni-muenchen.de/24190.html.

interest rate channel, the credit channel, the asset price channel, and the exchange rate channel. Transmission through these four channels should influence output and prices as targeted by the central bank and finally impact corporate bottom lines and the stock market. In India, the first two channels – interest rate and credit – dominate transmission.[12] This usually happens in the early stages of a monetary system's development; in more advanced stages of development and openness, asset price and exchange rate channels also influence aggregate demand.

The interest rate channel (as outlined earlier) is usually regarded as the major avenue for transmission and accounts for as much as half of all transmission effects on output and, inferentially, on company bottom lines.[13] The importance of the interest rate channel (sometimes called the money channel) has increased in the post-reform period.[14] As always, the catch here is lags – monetary policy and repo rates typically operate on output and bottom lines with a lag of about two to three quarters and sometimes even longer if the target is inflation.

The *credit channel* has quantitative effects that work on credit supply, as opposed to the interest rate channel, which impacts the demand for credit through the interest rate. When policy rates rise during a tightening phase, banks tend to cut back on their credit lines as the present value of collateral pledged with them falls; also, open market operations drain reserves – and hence deposits – from the banking

[12] Jeevan Kumar Khundrakpam and Rajeev Jain, 'Monetary Policy Transmission in India: A Peep Inside the Black Box,' Working Paper Series, Reserve Bank of India, Department of Economic and Policy Research, Mumbai, WPS (DEPR):11/ 2012, 16–20; Deepak Mohanty, 'Evidence on the Interest Rate Channel of Monetary Policy Transmission in India,' Working Paper Series, Reserve Bank of India, Department of Economic and Policy Research, Mumbai, WPS (DEPR): 6/ 2012, 10; Kanhaiya Singh and Kaliappa Kalirajan, 'Monetary Transmission in Postreform India: An Evaluation,' *Journal of the Asia Pacific Economy*, Vol. 12, 2007, 158–87; Abdul Aleem, 'Transmission Mechanism of Monetary Policy in India,' *Journal of Asian Economics*, Vol. 21, 2010, 193.

[13] Jeevan Kumar Khundrakpam and Rajeev Jain, 'Monetary Policy Transmission in India,' 26.

[14] In recent years, monetary policy has deemphasized the use of volume-based aggregative instruments like reserve ratios. Rates, the alternative, by definition have to be passed on (transmitted) through the financial and real sectors to be effective. Rakesh Mohan, 'Monetary Policy Transmission in India,' *Transmission Mechanisms for Monetary Policy in Emerging Market Economies*, Basel: Bank for International Settlements, BIS Papers No. 35, January 2008, 270.

system, reducing bank access to loanable funds. So, during a tightening phase, banks reduce the supply of credit, particularly impacting those firms that are heavily dependent on bank borrowings, which, in turn, makes such firms reduce their activities. In India, this effect is more pronounced in small banks than large ones; large banks with bigger resource bases and spreads are less likely to curtail credit supply to companies during a tightening phase.[15] Much of the credit channel's importance also derives from formal banking linkages; the more the number of borrowers dependent on formal banking, the greater is the channel's importance (this also accounts for its alternate name, the bank lending channel). All companies listed on the exchanges are from the organized sector with linkages to formal banking, so the credit channel's importance to the stock market is self-evident. In the broader economy, however, directed and priority sector lending targets lessen the efficacy of the credit channel.[16]

The two remaining channels for transmission – the *asset price channel* and the *exchange rate channel* – are not important in India, particularly for the stock market.[17] The asset price channel assumes that just as monetary policy influences the real economy and stock market,

[15] B.L. Pandit, Ajit Mittal, Mohua Roy, and Saibal Ghosh, 'Transmission of Monetary Policy and the Bank Lending Channel: Analysis and Evidence for India,' Reserve Bank of India, Department of Economic Analysis and Policy, Study No. 25, January 2006, 70, 75–83.

[16] Pandit and Vashisht (followed by Khundrakpam) found a credit channel, but subject to lags. B.L. Pandit and Pankaj Vashisht, 'Monetary Policy and Credit Demand in India and Some EMEs,' Working Paper No. 256, ICRIER, New Delhi, May 2011; Jeevan Kumar Khundrakpam, 'Credit Channel of Monetary Transmission in India: How Effective and Long Is the Lag?,' Working Paper Series, Reserve Bank of India, Department of Economic and Policy Research, Mumbai, WPS (DEPR): 20/2011.

[17] In the exchange rate channel, a monetary contraction or rate hike causes an appreciation in exchange rates, which reduces net exports and hence, the aggregate demand. In India's case, the small size of net exports (the external sector) in the domestic economy, lack of capital account convertibility and financial integration, and frequent downward intervention by the RBI while managing the dirty float, all reduce the effectiveness of the exchange rate channel as a transmission mechanism. Abdul Aleem, 'Transmission Mechanism,' 195; Rakesh Mohan, 'Monetary Policy Transmission in India,' 275–77; Prachi Mishra, Peter Montiel, and Rajeswari Sengupta, 'Monetary Transmission in Developing Countries: Evidence from India,' *IMF Working Paper* WP/16/167, August 2016, 39–40, 50. Some evidence of exchange rate pass-throughs comes from Rudrani Bhattacharya, Ila Patnaik, and Ajay Shah, 'Monetary Policy Transmission in an Emerging Market Setting,' *IMF Working Paper* No. 11/5, 2011, 5, 21.

so too will the stock market have feedback effects on the real economy. The main avenue is through wealth effects on households. For instance, if expansionary monetary policy and rate reductions lead to a stock market boom that increases household wealth, this, in turn, will create wealth effects as households consume more, thereby stimulating real economic activity. This wealth effect is especially strong with durables: if Nimeshbhai's portfolio goes from ₹5 lakhs to ₹20 lakhs during a bull run, he might feel a little wealthier and go out and buy his son Chotu his first motorcycle. The key point is that even if Nimeshbhai doesn't liquidate his portfolio to buy the motorcycle, he'd still be more inclined – because of the wealth effect – to finance the purchase from his present disposable income. In India, however, the percentage of household assets in equities is very low and equity markets don't have the same reach as in developed countries. Thus, there is little chance of wealth effects leading to an asset price channel;[18] some wealth effects are observable in Mumbai, which has the country's highest concentration of traders and investors, but these effects are anecdotal.

An asset price channel can also work through real estate; in a rate-induced real estate boom in developed countries, home equity can be monetized as people borrow against what is usually their biggest asset – their homes – to finance consumption and stimulate the real economy. In many cases, households can even borrow against just the paid-off portion of their home loans. But securitization and home mortgage markets are still in the early stages of development in India and are not sophisticated enough to allow households to borrow against accumulated home equity. Using real estate equity to finance consumption is therefore problematic.

So, the asset price channel is not very relevant in India, which reduces the stock market's influence in providing feedback effects to monetary

[18] By some estimates, even a 10 per cent increase in stock wealth leads only to a 0.3 per cent increase in consumption, with negligible consequences for aggregate demand. See Bhupal Singh, 'How Important Is the Stock Market Wealth Effect on Consumption in India?,' *Empirical Economics*, Vol. 42, No. 3, 2012, 915–27.

policy.[19] By contrast, in the US, market levels carry some weight in the setting of monetary policy, and some have called for policy and rates to be set with an eye to correcting misalignments in stock prices, which can reduce the possibility of asset bubbles forming. Against this is the argument that bubbles are impossible to identify ex ante (before the event); even if identifiable, they would require extraordinary levels of intervention – through rate increases – to deflate, thereby exposing the economy to the risks of recession. This sort of debate does not happen in India, primarily because of the marginal wealth effects from the asset price channel. Micro-prudential measures such as raising margin requirements on the loans against shares (LAS) product are sometimes used by the RBI to deal with market exuberance, but even this is only occasionally.[20] Nobody would suggest the RBI make policy with an eye to Nifty levels. The market's reaction is not a constraint on the central bank's ability to raise rates and end the party.[21]

The big issue is that monetary transmission in the Indian economy – and inferentially to company earnings and the stock market – has to deal with the Indian banking system's pass-through of policy rates.[22] Both the

[19] Much of this discussion focuses on whether the stock market responds to monetary policy as set by the central bank. Assessing the reverse response – whether the central bank responds to stock market levels – runs into methodological problems of endogeneity and simultaneity; stock prices can simultaneously react to interest rates, making it difficult to judge the effect of interest rates on stock prices. Correcting for this bias, Rigobon and Sack found a significant Fed policy response, with a 5 per cent rise (or fall) in the S&P 500 index increasing the likelihood of a 25-basis point tightening (or easing) by about a half. Roberto Rigobon and Brian Sack, 'Measuring the Reaction of Monetary Policy to the Stock Market,' *Quarterly Journal of Economics*, Vol. 118, No. 2, May 2003, 641–43.

[20] D.M. Nachane, 'Some Reflections on Monetary Policy in the "Leaden Age",' *Economic and Political Weekly*, Vol. 40, No. 28, (9–15 July 2005), 2992.

[21] Ibid.

[22] In 1988, H.T. Parekh had this to say about the banking system's disconnect on monetary transmission: 'Economists and policy-makers on the one hand and businessmen on the other seem to be functioning on different wavelengths. Inter-bank and inter-company rates as well as rates in the unorganised market fluctuate, but banks' lending and borrowing rates remain unaltered for years.' H.T. Parekh, 'Interest Rates and Development,' *Economic and Political Weekly*, Vol. 23, No. 35 (9 July 1988), 1420.

interest rate channel and the credit channel are subject to considerable asymmetry in transmission, primarily due to industry structure, customer stickiness, and government ownership of a chunk of the banking system. Banks are quick to raise rates during the tightening phase when the RBI raises rates, but are wary of lowering them when monetary policy eases. When the RBI raises policy rates in the contraction phase, banks increase their net interest margins by raising their lending rates faster than their deposit rates, but when the RBI lowers policy rates in the easing phase, banks tend to protect what net interest margins they have, by not lowering deposit and lending rates.[23] This means that as banks raise lending rates, the rise in interest costs reduces nonbank corporate bottom lines with ambiguous effects on the aggregate corporate profits that the stock market is concerned with. It also means that bank bottom lines can surge in the early phases of monetary contraction as policy rates rise and banks raise lending rates faster than deposit rates. But when policy rates fall with monetary easing, nothing much changes; bank lending and deposit rates stay about the same, as do bank and nonbank bottom lines. This considerable asymmetry in the financial system caused by implicit collusion between banks implies that contractionary monetary policy – rate hikes – transmit faster in the system, while expansionary monetary policy – rate reductions – transmit slower, if at all.

The reasons for this state of affairs have been extensively analysed and perhaps even rationalized. First, the distortions and kinks in the fixed-income market lead to competition between bank deposits and savings schemes from the likes of the post office or public provident fund. Such schemes set an informal floor below which the banking system cannot reduce deposit rates, lest it lose deposits to these other schemes.[24] Consequently, banks find it difficult to lower deposit rates even when the RBI lowers policy rates, and so, the lending rates to

[23] Downward stickiness of interest rates in India had been a phenomenon for some time. 'We seem ready to raise interest rates more readily but are not flexible enough when it comes to lowering them, though this counts a great deal in stimulating the economy.' Ibid.

[24] EPW Research Foundation, 'Downward Sticky Lending Rates,' *Economic and Political Weekly*, Vol. 44, No. 25 (20–26 June 2009), 25–31.

companies also don't change much. Second, the statutory liquidity ratio (SLR), through which banks have to (presently) invest 18 per cent of their deposits in government securities and fund the government's fiscal deficit, also constrains their ability to react to monetary policy. Third, government ownership of almost three-quarters of the banking system weakens the market signals and incentives that banks have to respond to. Fourth, priority sector lending – a big chunk of bank lending – is directed at certain parts of the economy and is also not very responsive to market signals.[25] Finally, in recent years, a long-simmering banking crisis and bad loan problem have increased banks' tendencies to resist rate reductions – the bad loan problem is making transmission difficult, as net interest margins have to be protected at all costs to raise internal resources to write off bad debts.

Faced with this uncertain monetary transmission, the government and RBI sometimes resort to 'jaw-jaw' during an easing phase and try to talk banks into reducing rates. Much of this moral suasion is ignored.

All this implies not much happens because of monetary easing/rate reductions, while some action does happen due to monetary contraction/rate increases. But the effect of such contraction/rate increases is also ambiguous and so this asymmetric response of the banking system also has a paradoxical effect on the stock market. As monetary contraction is more detrimental to the stock market than easing is beneficial, monetary transmission, in and as much as it does matter, should be net bearish for the market. But here too there is a twist, because the considerable increase in bank net interest margins (and profits) during a contracting phase has disproportionate bullish effects on a market index where banks make up over a third of index composition. The bearish effects on corporate bottom lines brought about by rate increases are offset by the increases that asymmetric transmission delivers to bank bottom lines, an increase that is attenuated by the banking sector's weightage in the indexes.

---

[25] Rakesh Mohan, 'Monetary Policy Transmission in India,' 282.

Besides erratic transmission, segmented credit markets are another reason for the doubtful influence of monetary policy on many of the stock market's listed industries. Credit market segmentation – the process by which lenders segregate borrowers into groups based on criteria such as credit scores, repayment records, or income – has pronounced effects in India. Because of this, borrowing industries carry very different risk perceptions and face wide-ranging interest rates; as a result, the elasticity, or rate of response, of their interest rates to RBI policy changes is very low. Industries such as real estate perennially borrow at rates as high as 20 to 25 per cent. Consumer credit and small and medium enterprise (SME) credit are equally impervious to policy rate changes across substantial ranges, with SMEs usually facing rates between 14 and 18 per cent.

Much of this credit segmentation is led by the banks themselves. Historically, Indian banks have done a lousy job of pricing credit risk, and the widely held perception is that credit to the corporate sector is systematically underpriced, while credit to informal sectors such as agriculture and small industries is systematically overpriced. This is because the informal sector and small companies generate information asymmetries compared to larger industries, which works against the banks lending to them; banks simply have to charge such enterprises higher rates to compensate for the risk of not knowing enough about them. Inferentially, in such a scenario, any RBI change to a policy rate such as the repo – itself many percentage points below the effective rates such sectors face – is just tinkering. At the margin, an industry borrowing at 13 per cent is not going to see much of a reduction in its cost of capital when the repo falls from, say, 6.5 to 6.25 per cent. Broadly then, credit market segmentation means policy rate changes have negligible effect at the ground level. Corporates with highly rated paper show some responsiveness to rate changes, but for the rest, severe credit segmentation results in sporadic pass-throughs of rate changes to bottom lines.

Finally, a narrower reason for the market's casual response to monetary policy is the composition of the index itself. The basic issue with India's stock indexes – their divorce from the real side of the economy – was outlined earlier. Here we see a related concern – their composition also renders them impervious to rate changes. The three sectors that make up a big chunk of the index – pharmaceuticals, consumer goods, and information technology – are not rate sensitive. In fact, one could argue that they are among the least sensitive to rate changes. Most people who get diseases, from common cold to cancer, and who buy the pharma industry's products, will do so irrespective of interest rates, as would the masses that buy soap and shampoo from the consumer goods industry; as for information technology, its dynamics are driven by international labour arbitrage and the exchange rate more than anything else. So, policy rate changes have negligible effect on stock indexes that are, in large part, made up of these rate-neutral sectors. From 2000 onwards, the financial sector's dominance of the indexes began to be felt and financials now account for about a third of the market. One would expect that financials, the most rate sensitive of sectors, would increase index sensitivity to rate changes, but paradoxically that is not the case. Banks load up on the Union of India's paper (government securities), which fluctuates in response to rates and results in treasury gains or losses, but the main lending businesses are marginally impacted by rate changes – and again the culprit is erratic monetary transmission.

Yet stocks react to international – particularly US – monetary policy and for the market it often seems that overseas monetary events matter more than domestic ones.[26] In recent years, rather than domestic rate policy, it has been global liquidity driven by foreign central banks that influences market movement. This was most apparent through monetary events originating at the US Fed – the Large Scale Asset Purchases (LSAPs) in 2008 and Operation Twist in 2011. Later described as quantitative easing, these large bond buying programs caused surges in global flows that went in search of yield in emerging markets, including

[26] Ammer et al. (in a study that includes India) found strong response of international stock prices to US monetary policy, particularly for cyclicals, firms with high turnovers outside their home countries, firms with high external finance dependence, and in countries with pegged exchange rates. See John Ammer, Clara Vega, and Jon Wongswan, 'International Transmission of U.S. Monetary Policy Shocks: Evidence from Stock Prices,' *Journal of Money, Credit and Banking*, Vol. 42, No. 1, September 2010, 179–98.

India, which led to large upward moves. Conversely, concerns about the programs' end caused turbulence to the downside in 2013 – the 'taper tantrums'.[27] This cycle would repeat between 2020 and 2022. In 2020, with the onset of the coronavirus pandemic, a monetary event similar to LSAP led to improved liquidity and caused major upward moves across emerging markets; in 2022, a sudden burst of inflationary pressure would end this last round of easing, and the resulting turbulence proved yet again that it was not domestic as much as US monetary policy that was now impacting the market.

In conclusion, because of tentative transmission, segmented credit markets, and the nature of the stock indexes themselves, RBI policy has uncertain effects on bottom lines and the stock market. Normal lags in the economy's response to monetary policy get exacerbated by peculiarities of the country's financial system. Most studies point to monetary policy's insignificant impact on the stock market.[28] Unexpected shocks to rates can impact equities, but the absence of a market similar to an overnight federal funds futures market[29] – needed to extract the stock market's response to the surprise element in monetary policy – makes it difficult to estimate how such surprises affect markets. Nevertheless, studies that use other proxies find that even unanticipated changes in monetary policy have only mildly significant impacts on stock indexes.[30] It is only when the cycle lasts a long time and goes to extremes that at the margin monetary policy has some effect on stock prices.[31] For

[27] Michael Debabrata Patra, Sitikantha Pattanaik, Joice John, and Harendra Kumar Behera, 'Global Spillovers and Monetary Policy Transmission in India,' Working Paper Series, Reserve Bank of India, Department of Economic and Policy Research, Mumbai, WPS (DEPR): 03/2016, 9–11.

[28] Edwin A. Prabu, Indranil Bhattacharyya, and Partha Ray, 'Is the Stock Market Impervious to Monetary Policy Announcements: Evidence from Emerging India,' *International Review of Economics and Finance*, Vol. 46, 2016, 166–79; Anand Sasidharan, 'Stock Market's Reaction to Monetary Policy,' 13–14; Partha Ray and Edwin Prabu, 'Financial Development and Monetary Policy Transmission across Financial Markets: What Do Daily Data Tell for India?,' Working Paper Series, Reserve Bank of India, Department of Economic and Policy Research, Mumbai, WPS (DEPR): 04/2013, 33, 43, 49.

[29] These reflect expectations about future changes in the Fed Funds rate.

[30] Edwin A. Prabu et al., 'Is the Stock Market Impervious,' 173.

[31] Chakradhara Panda, 'Do Interest Rates Matter for Stock Markets?,' *Economic and Political Weekly*, Vol. 43, No. 17 (26 April–2 May 2008), 107–17.

example, the significant easing cycle of almost 900 basis points between 1996 and 2003 clearly provided the displacement to the Rate Bull that began in 2003. But for most of the time it is business as usual for the stock market, through the twists and turns from Mint Street. Stock markets in developed countries have dedicated mavens who closely watch the central bank for clues on monetary policy and the future path of interest rates, but the Indian market has few such RBI watchers. In fact, here it is possible to read entire books about 'stock market gurus' and 'market masters' without coming across a single reference to the RBI, monetary policy, or interest rates.

So, what does all this have to do with the price of onions – what does it mean for the market participant? Do investors or portfolio managers allocate capital, pick stocks, or time markets in response to past or anticipated monetary policy? Most professionals would at least keep rate policy in mind, but due to the reasons outlined above, the RBI and rate policy are second-order causes in the game; as seen, monetary events as triggered by the US Fed can have larger effects on the market than domestic events. Attempts at rebalancing folios to position them better at various stages of the cycle do take place; cyclicals and capital-intensive stocks react more to rate changes, and rebalancing in their favour is sometimes done just when the rate cycle turns down for a substantial period. Similarly, firms that combine poor credit ratings, low free cash flows, high price-earnings ratios, and high debt levels should get disproportionately impacted by unanticipated rate increases, but there are few acknowledgements along such lines from participants. Industries such as autos or consumer durables, whose demand is impacted by household access to finance through car or durables loans, will also be impacted by rate shocks.

Another causal factor is firm size. Rate increases seem to affect small firms more than large firms, primarily because small firms have reduced access to domestic or international capital markets and less collateral to offer in a collateral-based lending system. Consequently, their stock prices tend to fall more than those of large firms in response to unfavourable shocks to rates and, *ceteris paribus*, will rise more when there are favourable shocks. But further research is required to confirm these observations.[32] So, while monetary policy has ambiguous effects at the aggregate market level, stock pickers dealing in small stocks with the above characteristics may have to keep monetary policy in mind.

The RBI has objectives and functions that are much wider than buoyant equity markets. Within the ambit of monetary policy, both controlling inflation and providing adequate credit to foster growth are equally important.[33] This apart, the central bank acts as a banking regulator (for deposit-taking institutions), public debt manager, government debt market regulator, currency issuer, payment system regulator, and exchange regime manager. With such a wide range of responsibilities, the stock market is way down the RBI's list of priorities; none would suggest that monetary policy is set with an eye to market levels, and there is little to no debate on whether the RBI should respond to asset price levels at all. Nevertheless, the RBI takes a keen interest in the market, and this is despite the market's cavalier response to the central bank's moves.

The RBI's concern with the market stems from its role in managing India's dirty float exchange regime. The biggest concern – managing those tidal waves of liquidity that enter and leave the market because of unconventional Western monetary policy – has been noted earlier. On a more tactical plane, market levels and FII flows also play a role in

[32] For early examples of research on the effects of monetary policy at the firm level, see Michael Ehrmann and Marcel Fratzscher, 'Taking Stock: Monetary Policy Transmission to Equity Markets,' *Journal of Money, Credit and Banking*, Vol. 36, No. 4, August 2004, 727–34; Mark Gertler and Simon Gilchrist, 'Monetary Policy, Business Cycles, and the Behavior of Small Manufacturing Firms,' *Quarterly Journal of Economics*, Vol. 109, 1994, 309–40; Lawrence J. Christiano, Martin Eichenbaum, and Charles Evans, 'The Effects of Monetary Policy Shocks: Evidence from the Flow of Funds,' *Review of Economics and Statistics*, Vol. 78, 1996, 16–34.

[33] A flexible inflation targeting framework has been in place at least since 2016, from when the central bank was mandated by the government to maintain price stability as its main objective while being cognizant of growth.

determining India's exchange rate through volatility spillovers between stock markets and currency markets.[34] For example, after FIIs sell stock in equity markets, they convert the rupees they get into dollars and then repatriate the proceeds; in turn, selling rupees and buying dollars puts pressure on the rupee-dollar pair, causing the rupee to sell off. Sometimes the rupee slides even before a market sell-off has begun to gather momentum, perhaps because key players among the FIIs have sold rupees ahead of the rupee weakness anticipated by their own selling. Currency dealers observing FII order flow then draw their own conclusions and also sell the rupee, further contributing to its depreciation; in this sense, sudden unexplained rupee sell-offs sometimes signal future moves to the downside in stocks. These volatility spillovers – most of which come from the equity rather than the marginal debt markets – have attendant consequences on the RBI's exchange management functions. If volatility spillovers are intense and prolonged, decisions will have to be made on intervention, which comes with its own costs.[35] So occasionally, the stock market does intrude on the Temple of Brahma's deliberations.

The RBI also controls the stock market's access to the banking system as a source of financing, and here casual observers often find the central bank's position tinged by hidebound conservatism. But there are historical reasons for this institutional instinct, reasons that stem from the Pied Pipers's attempts to access the banking system for funds – Premchand Roychand, Harshad Mehta, and Ketan Parekh had helped themselves to the banking system to keep their bull moves going, with disastrous consequences. The RBI's role is to make sure that sort of thing doesn't happen in future, and even if it does happen, to ensure that the systemic consequences are manageable. The efforts have been successful, but only by so much – in recent years, rather than market participants, it

[34] Evidence on volatility spillovers from the stock markets to the currency markets – but less so the other way round – comes from Manish Kumar, 'Returns and Volatility Spillover between Stock Prices and Exchange Rates: Empirical Evidence from IBSA Countries,' *International Journal of Emerging Markets*, Vol. 8, No. 2 (2013), 120–21.

[35] Mentioned by N.R. Prabhala, Professor of Finance at Johns Hopkins University's Carey Business School, in an interview with the author, Mumbai, 2017.

has been politically connected strong-arm promoters who have helped themselves to the banking system.

Controlling market access to the banking system often involves changing micro-prudential norms to regulate the system's exposure to the stock market. This happens most often as a bull move progresses, and is done through various measures like, say, capping bank exposure to the stock market at 5 per cent of a bank's total advances.[36] When leaning against the wind, the RBI's micro-prudential norms can be as significant as more conventional measures such as moving rates and, in fact, are used more often. For example, during the big 2003–07 Rate Bull, the central bank changed prudential norms twice: in October 2005, it restricted bank exposure to the capital market as a percentage of net worth, while in April 2006, it further increased provisioning requirements on loans and advances qualifying as capital market exposures. Though this sort of regulation brings forth negative reactions from market participants – the usual grumble about the loans against shares (LAS) product, for instance, is that the leverage is too conservative – the market's excessive volatility makes the RBI's position look prudent. Nevertheless, market grumbling about RBI positions on matters like arbitrage seems justified. RBI policy would prohibit banks from engaging in, or funding, arbitrage trades.[37] This was quite inexplicable, when one considers the risk-free nature of the arbitrage process. More technically, bank funding of arbitrageurs would reduce their cost of capital and carrying costs, which would, in turn, reduce the spread between cash and derivatives segments and improve market efficiency.

The Temple of Brahma's final role is in integrating the banking system with the market's system for clearing and settlement – that vital back office function where cash and shares change hands. The banking

[36] This figure includes direct investments, loans against shares (LAS), loans to stockbroking firms, and bank guarantees to broking firms.

[37] Interactions between the stock market, the banking system, and RBI policy that influenced the market in the reform years are discussed in Ajay Shah and Susan Thomas, 'Policy Issues in Indian Securities Markets,' in *Reforming India's External, Financial and Fiscal Policies*, eds. Anne Krueger and Sajjid Chinoy, Stanford Studies in International Economics and Development, Stanford University Press, 2003, 129–47.

system integrates with the stock market at two levels: first, between the customer and the broker, and later, between the broker and the exchange's clearing house. The market's clearing and settlement reforms of the 1990s were actually way ahead of the banking system's capacity to keep up at either level.[38] By the early years of the new millennium, the market was ready for real-time settlement but was held up by the banking system's constraints on fund transfers. The transition to a five-day settlement cycle (T+5) had taken place, but moving to the international standard of (T+2) proved to be a problem. A small group of 10 banks that pioneered the technology for high-speed funds transfer ended up dominating the business – but the rest of the system lagged. It was only after the RBI introduced the Real Time Gross Settlement (RTGS) in 2004, together with its derivative, the National Electronic Funds Transfer (NEFT), that the rest of the banking system caught up with the stock market.[39]

And yet, when all is said and done, the microstructure of equity markets contrasts with the opaqueness and lack of transparency that continues in debt markets, both sovereign and corporate.[40] Debt markets in India – regulated in large part by the RBI – have continued to face severe issues that impede their development.[41] Successive scams often

[38] The T+2 settlement was criticized by market participants mainly because fund transfers through the banking system lagged stock clearing systems. When introduced, it was a step ahead of other developed markets. See R.H. Patil, 'Interest Rates and Equity Markets,' *Economic and Political Weekly*, Vol. 38, No. 12/13 (22 March–4 April 2003), 1104–06.

[39] Initially, the RTGS netted transactions of ₹2 lakhs and above, individually and in real time. NEFT netted transactions in hourly settlement batches between 8 a.m. and 7 p.m. on weekdays and less frequently on weekends.

[40] Ajay Shah, Susan Thomas, and Michael Gorman, *India's Financial Markets: An Insider's Guide to How the Markets Work*, Noida: Elsevier, 2008, 191–92, 212. Even NSE founder R.H. Patil couldn't replicate the NSE's success in the debt markets. See Shaji Vikraman and M.C. Govardhana Rangan, 'Founder of National Stock Exchange RH Patil Is No More,' *Economic Times*, 13 April 2012.

[41] These include: high transaction costs, negligible secondary market trading, presence of the 'statutory liquidity ratio' (SLR) in the pension and insurance sector, disintermediation of trading platforms by members, absence of counterparties for corporate debt trading, market participants with the biggest bond portfolios such as pension funds and insurance companies who preferred to hold rather than trade them, kinks in the benchmark yield curve for the government securities, a limited FII presence leading to few catalyst effects, and no real junk bond market. See Susan Thomas, 'How the Financial Sector in India Was Reformed,' *Documenting Reforms: Case Studies from India*, ed. S. Narayan,

acted as a spur to the development of equity markets but rarely led to corresponding changes in debt markets. Perhaps this is because the private-sector character of equity participants allowed them to respond faster to reform initiatives, while the predominantly public-sector character of debt market participants – mainly government-owned banks – led to tardier responses. Perhaps this is also because the scams led SEBI into successive bouts of reformist zeal, but the RBI, especially in the early years of the reform effort, constructed a narrative that minimized its own regulatory shortcomings while playing to popular mistrust of the broking community.[42] For example, the Harshad Mehta episode involved both debt and equity markets, but in later years the brokers would repeatedly say that it was not seen as such, and there were loud complaints of brokers as fall guys while the RBI gently glided away.[43]

So, the Temple of Brahma is also a player in the Indian equity market, but with a presence that's not as overwhelming as other central banks enjoy in their countries. Many savvy participants advise the perplexed to simply ignore the coverage on monetary policy and focus only on their stock picks. To see why this is so requires a segue into topics as diverse as monkeys and market efficiency.

New Delhi: Macmillan India, 2006, 189–93; Former Finance Minister P. Chidambaram, Remarks at the 20th Anniversary Celebrations of the National Stock Exchange, Mumbai, 14 December 2013.

[42] Some of these issues are mentioned in John Echiverri-Gent, 'Why Do Some Financial Markets Develop and Others Do Not? Politics of India's Capital Market Reform,' Paper presented at The Workshop on States, Development, and Global Governance, University of Wisconsin Law School, Madison, Wis., March 2010, 20–22.

[43] Sameer Kochhar, *BSE: Journey of an Aspiring Nation*, New Delhi: Skoch Media, 2015, 91–93.

8

BEATING THE MONKEYS

Efficient Markets

Market efficiency is the central idea of modern finance that begins the formal study of the stock market. It deals with the interaction between information and a stock's price – especially the idea that varying amounts of information are incorporated in a stock's price.[1] Controversy gets generated over how much information is actually incorporated, and how fast. This academic field of study is called the Efficient Market Hypothesis (EMH).[2] In theoretical finance, it is captured by the idea that you cannot always beat the market. It posits that stock picking – looking for Lakshmi's diamonds in Golconda – is difficult because all information releases get priced immediately into a stock or the market. No telegrams to Bombay to inform traders of events in faraway America that took place a month ago; nowadays, it is just the instantaneous dissemination of information and immediate adjustment of the stock price.

The idea's origins go back to French mathematician Louis Bachelier's work at the turn of the nineteenth century, but it gained ground in academia in the 1960s with the publication of Paul A. Samuelson's

[1] Efficiency in a financial market is informational efficiency, as opposed to popular notions that may relate efficiency to issues such as paperless trading or reduced clearing and settlement time.

[2] The term was first coined by Harry Roberts in 1967.

article 'Proof that Properly Anticipated Prices Fluctuate Randomly'.[3] Samuelson, in turn, was followed by the person most associated with the idea and its doughtiest defender – Eugene F. Fama of the University of Chicago. Fama's early career coincided with the computer's entry into American campuses in the 1960s. Computers allowed for analysis of massive volumes of numerical data that financial markets generate. With James Lorie and Lawrence Fisher, Fama founded the Center for Research in Security Prices (CRSP; pronounced 'crisp') at the University of Chicago. Here, Fama and his academic collaborators spent many an engrossing day designing the early event studies that evaluated market efficiency.[4] Always the great empiricist, he took vast amounts of data, crunched it to test theory, and then thought about what his results revealed about the world. Though not known primarily as a theorist, Fama's findings contributed to that most enduring of theories – the efficient market hypothesis.[5]

The EMH evolved through a set of empirical observations about markets that went in search of a theory, and much of that evolution is traced through Fama's work. In a landmark 1970 survey article titled 'Efficient Capital Markets: A Review of Theory and Empirical Work', Fama evidenced something people had observed for some time – that the effective impounding of securities information into price was becoming a reasonable first-order approximation of reality in developed financial markets. Two more review papers would follow a generation later, to drive home the point that security prices reflect all available information.[6]

[3] Paul A. Samuelson, 'Proof That Properly Anticipated Prices Fluctuate Randomly,' *Industrial Management Review*, Spring, No. 6, 1965, 41–49. The evolution of market efficiency as the dominant paradigm in financial markets – till recently at least – is traced in Elroy Dimson and Massoud Mussavian, 'A Brief History of Market Efficiency,' *European Financial Management*, Vol. 4, No. 1, March 1998, 1–9.

[4] Besides his work on the efficient market hypothesis, Fama's enduring contribution to finance may well be the establishment of CRSP as a world centre for empirical financial research.

[5] The published version of Fama's doctoral thesis used serial correlation tests to show that prices follow a random walk. See Eugene F. Fama, 'The Behavior of Stock-Market Prices,' *The Journal of Business*, Vol. 38, No. 1, January 1965, 34–105. Earlier tests that produced similar results were conducted by Maurice Kendall (1953) and Paul Cootner (1962).

[6] The three survey articles are Eugene F. Fama, 'Efficient Capital Markets: A Review of Theory and Empirical Work,' *Journal of Finance*, May 1970; Eugene F. Fama, 'Efficient Capital Markets II,'

The basic insight of the EMH is best illustrated by a well-known joke about a professor and a student who are walking down a street. The student sees a hundred-dollar bill and stoops to pick it up. The professor stops him and says, '*Don't do that. It's not really there. If it was, someone would have picked it up by now.*'

The critical point is that in efficient financial markets, competition grinds fine. There are no easy pickings, because there are lots of people looking to do the same thing – buy undervalued securities. When everybody's looking to do the same thing, such securities will always get bid up and traded at their fair value; if the pickings were really there, someone would have taken them by buying up the stock and raising the price till it traded at its intrinsic value. So, with most stocks at most points in time, prices fully reflect all available information. As a result, technical trading systems or stock picking by professional money managers does not work. In fact, monkeys throwing darts at the stock-listing pages of a financial newspaper – as Burton Malkiel's original anecdote went – could produce the same results as an ace fund manager. Like many exaggerations, this has a grain of truth associated with it, though reality is more complex.

The principal driver of all this is information, especially the interplay of information and market price. Following Fama, the EMH has three forms that deal with the types of information – past/present or public/insider – that are incorporated in a stock's price. For analytical convenience, these three forms get categorized as weak, semi-strong, and strong form efficiency. Weak-form efficiency hypothesizes that all past information is in the price; semi-strong-form postulates that all public (including all past/present) information is in the price; and the strong-form assumes that all public and private/insider information is

Journal of Finance, December 1991; and Eugene F. Fama, 'Market Efficiency, Long-term Returns, and Behavioral Finance,' *Journal of Financial Economics*, 49, 1998.

in the price.[7] Think of the forms as a series of concentric circles around a common centre, starting with weak-form efficiency as the first and smallest circle, semi-strong as the middle circle, and strong-form efficiency as the outermost circle. Besides having its own characteristics, each larger circle incorporates the characteristics of the smaller circle it encompasses.

Strong-form efficiency is for EMH fanatics and does not exist in the real world; if it did, it would imply that even insiders don't have an edge in the market, and most participants would tell you that is simply not true. But even if semi-strong form efficiency held and all public information was in the price, stock picking and market judgment based on public information would also be essentially useless – hence the original comment about simians popping darts at stock pages. This observation is also rejected out of hand by most participants, particularly in emerging markets like India; the debate in emerging markets is usually over whether markets are even weak-form efficient.

Much of the early work on efficient markets concerned 'event studies' – a sort of controlled experiment in a financial market that isolated the effect of firm-specific information release on a stock's price during an event window; the event window was typically a defined period of a few weeks preceding an event, such as an earnings announcement. The idea was to estimate the abnormal return on a stock that could be attributed only to the information release on the day of the event, after stripping out the market's behaviour during the event window and then removing the stock's 'typical' movement with the market's behaviour. Many of the early event studies dealt with how quickly information was incorporated in a security's price. In the US, Fama and those who followed him proved that the incorporation takes place almost immediately. These are competitive financial markets, perhaps the broadest, deepest, and most efficient in the world.

[7] This classification builds on the distinction between weak- and strong-form tests that was first suggested by Harry Roberts. Fama has since suggested that these categories change (respectively) into: groupings for return predictability, event studies, and tests for private information.

In emerging markets like India – well, there's room for those hundred-rupee bills. India's market may not even be weak-form efficient, as much recent work suggests.[8] The extensive presence in Indian markets, for instance, of successful technical analysts who use past prices to predict future prices, indicates as much, as does evidence on seasonal anomalies such as December effects. The Indian stock market – as old-timers will tell you – just 'tends' to go up in November and December, possibly because massive spending on year-end religious festivals like Dussehra and Diwali kicks in, which leads to a pickup in economic activity that feeds into the stock market.[9] If the EMH holds, this should not be the case. Someone would just buy in October to take advantage of this effect; hey, maybe there is a hundred-rupee bill there. Except that if everyone bought in October to take advantage, the market would go up in October; outguessing the October traders would result in September buying, and so on. This sort of inverted reasoning explains why markets go on a random walk all over the place – the December effect now happens in September, so to speak. So, properly anticipated security prices, as the title of Samuelson's early paper pointedly states, will fluctuate randomly. It is future news – inherently unanticipated,

[8] For early work that found evidence of weak-form efficiency, see Samir K. Barua, V. Raghunathan, and J.R. Varma, 'Research on the Indian Capital Market: A Review,' *Vikalpa*, Vol. 19, No. 1, 1994, 21–22. Later work was done with higher frequency daily data (in contrast to earlier studies that often used weekly/monthly data) and reflected improvements in statistical and econometric methodology. Subsequent surveys of the empirical work found substantial inefficiency, presence of serial autocorrelation, and some return predictability. Recent work using serial correlation and runs tests, together with variance ratio tests, also reached the conclusion that Indian markets are not even weak-form efficient. For studies done at 10-year intervals that reach this conclusion, see Ankita Mishra, Vinod Mishra, and Russell Smyth, 'The Random-walk Hypothesis on the Indian Stock Market,' *Emerging Markets Finance and Trade*, Vol. 51, No. 5, 2015, 879–92; A.C. Worthington and H. Higgs, 'Weak-Form Market Efficiency in Asian Emerging and Developed Equity Markets: Comparative Tests of Random Walk Behaviour,' Working Paper Series, University of Wollongong, School of Accounting and Finance, No. 05/03, 2005, 16–18; and Sunil Poshakwale, 'Evidence on Weak-form Efficiency and Day of the Week Effect in the Indian Stock Market,' *Finance India*, Vol. 10, No. 3, 1996, 605–16.

[9] This end-of-year effect has been documented both in the pre-reform era and in recent years. See Roger Ignatius, 'The Bombay Stock Exchange: Seasonality and Investment Opportunities,' Discussion Paper 29, Bond University School of Business, *Discussion Papers*, 1992, 7–9; Anokhi Parikh, 'The December Phenomenon: Month-of-the-year Effect in the Indian Stock Market,' January 2009, nseindia.com/content/press/NS_ jan2009_1.pdf.

unknowable, and therefore random – which is the only component that moves prices. Randomly.

Working against the EMH's conclusion that stock picking doesn't work most of the time, is an existing and active equity research industry that identifies and picks stocks – often at heavy expense of time and money. After all, if the market is efficient and stock picking doesn't work, it makes sense to just throw up your hands and not bother with the expense involved in equity research and picking stocks. Yet, the sizable and expensive equity research industry exists. Perhaps that's because if everyone threw up their hands, stopped doing equity research, and said, 'No point, market's efficient', the incorporation of information into price would not happen and the market would become inefficient. So, there has to be just the right amount of inefficiency to justify the presence of that expensive equity research industry.

This idea leads to the work of economists Joseph Stiglitz and Fischer Black who, with Samuelson and Fama, round out the theoretical core of the EMH.[10] Stiglitz, together with Sanford Grossman, proved the logical impossibility of perfectly efficient markets using the above example. If at any time prices fully reflect all available information, informed traders who pay a lot for their information would not earn a return on the amounts invested to obtain that information. If the EMH held and information was costly, competitive markets would break down. Every informed trader would simply stop investing in information because they would do as well as an uninformed trader, so there would be no need to invest in gathering information. Yet, in the real world that does not happen, as the existence of that vast equity research industry suggests. (In fact, managers running large folios find that even incremental returns from research translate into considerable amounts. Just a 0.5 per cent increase in return from quality equity research translates into $250 million on a $50 billion portfolio; at the margin, a fund manager would spend most of that $250 million on

[10] Andrew W. Lo, 'Introduction,' *Market Efficiency: Stock Market Behaviour in Theory and Practice Vol. I*, International Library of Critical Writings in Financial Economics, ed. Andrew W. Lo. Lyme, NH: Edward Elgar Publishing, Inc., 1997, xiii.

research, if the research could guarantee that increased return of 0.5 per cent.) Hence, the impossibility of perfectly efficient markets, and the reality that there must be just the right amount of inefficiency to compensate investors for investing in all that research.[11]

From Fischer Black came an intuitive concept to round out the EMH's theoretical side – noise. The idea of noise is both intuitive and satisfying, given the terrific cacophony so apparent in the Indian environment. To Black, noise is the idea that a large number of small events matter more than a small number of large events.[12] In a market that only has information and no noise traders, not much trading would take place, as one party must be wrong and would simply decline to trade, which would make markets illiquid. But in a market with both information and noise traders, the latter provide liquidity. Often, noise traders think they're trading information when in fact they're trading noise, and so, they lose out as a group to the information traders. In fact, noise traders supply the profits of the information traders, who are the Stiglitz-Grossman diligent types.

Applying the theory to the 'real world' of data and numbers requires a move from the theoretical to the empirical. The EMH reigned unquestioned as the dominant view on markets for over a generation and fit in well with the rational expectations revolution that dominated economics. But to some observers, by the late 1970s, it had turned into theology bordering on dogma, and the people who articulated it – mainly academics rather than participants – had become a priesthood. Multiple findings that contradicted the EMH's rational view on markets were emerging, and these prompted other lines of inquiry. Wall Street's crash

[11] Sanford J. Grossman and Joseph E. Stiglitz, 'On the Impossibility of Informationally Efficient Markets,' *American Economic Review*, Vol. 70, No. 3, 1980, 403–05.

[12] Fischer Black, 'Noise,' *Market Efficiency Vol. I*, 3–15. The B in the BSM (Black–Scholes–Merton) option pricing models, Black died shortly before the other two received the Nobel Prize for their work on option pricing. For an account of the personalities behind advances in theoretical finance, see Peter Bernstein, *Against the Gods: The Remarkable Story of Risk* (New York: John Wiley, 1996).

of 1987 further extended the search for alternate explanations of stock market behaviour; 40 to 50 per cent drops in price over a few days were not seen as particularly rational or efficient. Almost a generation later, the 2008 sell-offs that preceded the Great Recession further accelerated the skepticism on efficient markets. Behavioural explanations for the above phenomena were advanced, and people spoke about a shift in the basic paradigm. The emphasis of much of the empirical work now moved to refutations – many behavioural based – of efficient markets, rather than their proof.

Andrew Lo of MIT identified three streams that run through this vast literature on the EMH. These streams – actually groupings of empirical tests of the EMH – include variance bounds tests, anomalies, and studies of overreaction/underreaction.[13]

Variance bounds tests deal with the insight that stock prices vary too much compared to the dividends that stocks pay. Technically, in an efficient market, a stock's price should approximate the present value of its future dividend stream discounted at an appropriate risk-adjusted cost of capital. But what if that price varies much more than a stock's dividend stream?

Variance tests of the EMH owe much of their origin to Robert Shiller of Yale. Freshly minted as an economist in the 1970s, Shiller made his name by living dangerously and defying the priesthood, which can be a hazardous proposition for a young professor. In a landmark paper published while he was still making his way in the world as an academic, Shiller asked two fundamental questions.[14] The first dealt with whether stock prices equalled the discounted flows of firm profits, and the second asked if changes in stock prices reflected changes in those profit flows and the discount factor. The answer to both questions was a guarded 'No'. Shiller showed that stock prices fluctuate much more than can be explained by changes in either dividends or discounting. Measures of stock price volatility were simply too high to be attributed

[13] Andew W. Lo, *Market Efficiency Vol. I*, xi.

[14] Robert J. Shiller, 'Do Stock Prices Move Too Much to be Justified by Subsequent Changes in Dividends?,' *American Economic Review*, Vol. 71, No. 3, 1981, 421–36.

to new information about future real dividends.[15] He also showed that underlying changes in the earnings stream were simply too low to justify the movement of stock prices.

Naturally, all this provoked a severe reaction, and attempts were made to explain away the disconcerting findings.[16] Yet, for practical traders and investors, Shiller's insights ring true, more so in a market at India's level of informational inefficiency. In India, stocks routinely treble and then halve over a calendar year, which is simply too much if you believe in the dividend discount model as a valuation model for stocks. Besides, dividend payout ratios hardly fluctuate and dividend policy is rarely used as a corporate finance tool by Indian managers.[17] So, the argument holds on both sides – prices fluctuate too much and dividends too little – making Shiller's finding relevant to Indian markets. Though extensive variance bounds tests have not been done in the country, they would, in all likelihood, simply prove that levels of market inefficiency are so extreme that dividend discount models of stock valuation have to be treated with scepticism.

Anomalies, in a peculiar naming twist, actually deal with regularities – regularities in stock prices that can be profitably exploited in a manner anomalous to the EMH. If they did exist, anomalies could lead to the generation of profitable trading rules that generate excess returns. One complication is the vigorish (vig) or transaction costs, and a second complication is the risk involved.[18] Finding an anomaly that generated

[15] Robert J. Shiller, 'From Efficient Markets Theory to Behavioral Finance,' *Journal of Economic Perspectives*, Vol. 17, No. 1, Winter, 2003, 85–86.

[16] Explanations involve questions of statistical inference (the sample sizes were too small and the variance bounds violated due to sampling variation) or risk aversion. Andrew W. Lo, *Market Efficiency, Vol. I*, xiv.

[17] Payout ratios have increased in recent years as corporate taxes and growth opportunities have reduced.

[18] In assessing anomalies, the first complication is transaction costs such as: the familiar brokerage commission, taxes, the impact cost of moving the price with a large order, and bid-ask bounce. The second and more serious complication is adjusting for risk preferences, which involves: selecting an asset pricing model; specifying the parameters of that model; using the model to predict expected returns; and comparing those expected returns with real returns to arrive at 'abnormal' returns. This second complication runs into the joint hypothesis problem: tests of market efficiency are also tests of the asset

excess returns after adjusting for the vig and risk would be like discovering a money machine that generated perpetual profits. If the EMH holds, this should not be the case. Nevertheless, because of their potential as money machines, a lot of time and effort goes into finding and exploiting anomalies. In the US, extensive research on the EMH documents such anomalies that should not exist but are nevertheless present, which, in turn, prompts the need to explain them away if the efficiency hypothesis has to hold. There are calendar effects such as 'day of the week' and 'January' effects, under which the market exhibits excess returns during certain time periods; there are size effects, whereby small firms outperform large firms even after adjusting for risk; and there are price-to-book effects, in which a simply calculated and easily available heuristic like the ratio of a firm's market price to its book value predicts excess returns.[19] Finally, there are value effects such as the famous 'Value Line Enigma' where buying the 'best buy' recommendation in the widely available Value Line Investment Survey resulted in abnormal returns.[20] Proving or disproving such anomalies keeps empirical academic finance humming with activity.

On calendar effects, for example, part of the corpus on anomalies documents January effects, particularly for small firms, in US markets. Small stocks tend to offer higher returns in January according to some studies. These January effects are often attributed to tax loss-based selling, as investors sell stocks in December (the close of the financial year) on which they have accumulated losses and buy the same back in January. The December selling captures losses that can be set off against other profits/income, thereby lowering taxes; the January buyback maintains investors' positions in the counters and causes the market to tick upwards, leading to the anomaly. Benefits accrue if the tax saved

---

pricing model used, and abnormal returns may reflect market inefficiency, *or* an inaccurate asset pricing model that is not capturing some element of risk for which investors are being compensated, *or both*.

[19] Eugene F. Fama and Kenneth R. French, 'The Cross Section of Expected Stock Returns,' *Journal of Finance*, 47, 1992, 427–65.

[20] Thomas E. Copeland and David Mayers, 'The Value Line Enigma (1965–1978): A Case Study of Performance Evaluation Issues,' *Journal of Financial Economics*, Vol. 10, No. (3), November 1982, 289–321.

exceeds the transaction costs and bid-ask bounce involved in getting in and out of the position.

In fact, anomalies are more likely to occur in inefficient markets like India. Consider a railway stock anomaly that was noticed for years by market participants but not the academic community. The railway budget was traditionally presented a day before the Union budget in the last week of February, and was considered 'market moving' for listed companies that dealt with the railways. The uncanny tendency of these stocks to go up in the buildup to the railway budget is noteworthy of itself and was exploited for years by certain market participants. The anomaly was well known, but only just enough for it to be profitably traded by a select few. Whether the excess return was simply compensation for the risk taken and whether the anomaly was exploitable on a large scale after transaction costs, still begs the question that the effect existed for years. Presently, the reason for the anomaly has been removed as the railway budget is subsumed within the government's Union budget.

On calendar effects based on tax loss selling: in India the financial year ends in March, which would imply a corresponding April effect, and there is some evidence documenting a stronger April compared to other months in the year.[21] Other calendar effects include end-of-month abnormal returns due to increased institutional turnover.[22] Excess returns on Mondays have also been detailed.[23] This is because the earlier 14-day badla settlement that ended on alternate Fridays (or the subsequent seven-day settlement that ended every Friday) caused a bump upward on Monday openings as traders rolled over their long positions – an effect that would be particularly strong during bull markets (it is unlikely, however, that this anomaly would have survived badla's end and the market's move to a T+2 settlement period). Finally,

[21] Some evidence of excess April returns comes from Mahendra Raj and Damini Kumari, 'Day-of-the-week and Other Market Anomalies in the Indian Stock Market,' *International Journal of Emerging Markets*, Vol. 1, No. 3, 2006, 243.

[22] Daniela Maher and Anokhi Parikh, 'The Turn of the Month Effect in India: A Case of Large Institutional Trading Pattern as a Source of Higher Liquidity,' *International Review of Financial Analysis*, Vol. 28, 2013, 57–69.

[23] Mahendra Raj and Damini Kumari, 'Day-of-the-week and Other Market Anomalies,' 241–42.

buying stocks based on simple and widely available heuristics such as low PE ratios (or low price-to-book ratios) is such a widely followed practice in India that even viewing it as an anomaly appears eccentric.

A related issue is the tendency of anomalies to disappear as soon as they become known.[24] The anomaly gets arbitraged away by participants some time after the anomaly presents itself – as seen earlier, a properly anticipated November Diwali effect can happen in September, so to speak. (In fact, the US small stock January effect also seems to have been arbitraged away since its discovery and publicity.) This is taken by EMH adherents as proof of market efficiency.[25] However, in India, the academic community's engagement with the market is less vigorous, and so, anomalies are not discovered regularly. Besides, market participants who discover profitable anomalies would be busy making money off them and would keep the news private to retain their advantage. So, similar to other emerging markets, chances are that anomalies in India continue in exploitable fashion for periods of time with resulting increases in inefficiency. Against this must be balanced the fact that anomalies can sometimes be difficult to exploit on a large scale in India's thinly traded markets, where volumes and liquidity outside the index stocks are always an issue.

Investor underreaction or overreaction is the third stream in EMH literature, and it was among the first phenomena to be examined through event studies. It concerns reactions to breaking information and applies especially to earnings announcements. The puzzle was 'post-earnings announcement drift' – the tendency of prices to not impound positive (or negative) earnings news immediately but to drift upwards (or downwards) after the announcement of such news.[26]

[24] G. William Schwert, 'Anomalies and Market Efficiency,' *Handbook of the Economics of Finance Vol. 1, Part B,* eds. G.M. Constantinides, M. Harris, and R. Stulz. Amsterdam: Elsevier B.V., 2003, 939–74.

[25] The synthesis that developed markets are efficient most of the time – and that anomalies, while identifiable, are often difficult to exploit – comes from Burton G. Malkiel, 'The Efficient Market Hypothesis and Its Critics,' *Journal of Economic Perspectives*, Vol. 17, No. 1 (Winter, 2003), 60, 80.

[26] Some event studies on Indian stocks indicate post-earnings announcement drift, which should not happen if weak-form efficiency holds. For drift after monetary policy announcements, see Gaurav Agarwal, 'Monetary Policy Announcements and Stock Price Behavior: Empirical Evidence from CNX Nifty,' *Decision*, Vol. 34, No. 2, 2007, 133–53.

As markets have become more efficient in the West, investor underreaction has vanished. Subsequent event studies have found prices adjusting immediately to breaking news and announcements; cumulative abnormal returns for stocks show marked jumps on announcement days, indicating that markets immediately impound breaking news. But in India, insider trading and news leakages to market participants result in upward price drifts before the announcement date on (say) positive news. Often, insiders load up, following which the information leaks via a steady process of osmosis to a magic circle of participants who are 'in touch' with company managements. More than the insider trading, it is this osmotic news leakage to the magic circle, and later to the media, that causes a run on the price. Technical traders then pick up the price action on their charts and buy in, exaggerating the up move. As a result, there is no jump in prices on announcement day as the impounding of news into price has already happened. In fact, stocks often sell off on announcement days as market participants in the magic circle unload to an unsuspecting public.[27] 'Buy the rumour, sell the news' is one of those oft-bandied chestnuts repeatedly acted on in Indian markets.

Trading overreaction, on the other hand, deals with buying stocks that have had recent gains and selling/short selling stocks that have had recent losses. Overreactions of this sort – first studied by Richard Thaler of the University of Chicago and Werner De Bondt of DePaul – will drive prices beyond fair value on both sides and undermine the EMH.[28] This is similar to studying momentum and contrarianism, as prices overreact and show momentum in the short term, followed by mean reversion over the long term, which allows both momentum and contrarian investors to put on trades. More technically, serial correlation is positive in the short term and negative in the long term,

[27] Some empirical evidence of this comes from John M. Griffin, Patrick J. Kelly, and Federico Nardari, 'Do Market Efficiency Measures Yield Correct Inferences? A Comparison of Developed and Emerging Markets,' *Review of Financial Studies*, Vol. 23, No. 8, 2010, 3241.

[28] W.F.M. De Bondt and Richard Thaler, 'Does the Stock Market Overreact?' *Journal of Finance*, Vol. 40, No. 3, 1985, 793–805. De Bondt and Thaler found that buying stocks that performed poorly over a three-to-five-year horizon while selling stocks that performed well over the same horizon yielded abnormal returns.

allowing traders to profitably trade momentum in the short term and be contrarian in the long term.[29] Whether these momentum effects – first explored by Narasimhan Jegadeesh of Emory and Sheridan Titman of the University of Texas, Austin – are due to market inefficiency or just a correction of risk premia is a tricky question, and reams of complex statistics argue for and against both explanations. In India, momentum effects are pronounced, with some empirical evidence now coming out to confirm that observation; much of this is because the short side ban since badla's 2001 abolition allows for long momentum to easily build up. In fact, buying small-cap stocks that are cheap on value parameters and that are showing momentum is an article of faith among professional market participants.[30]

The EMH has become something of a philosophical ideal in finance, like the idea of a frictionless plane in physics or Adam Smith's familiar lodestar of the invisible hand. Like many ideals in the social sciences, it is an extreme version of reality, but studying the ideal allows the contrast with a messy reality to stand out a little more and generates its own insights. This is why its formal treatment is important for the participant. When professional market participants in India and around the world evaluate a stock, or react to breaking news, there is one usual query – '*Is it in the price*?' Here the '*it*' is information, and the question is acknowledging the core of the efficiency hypothesis – the reaction of price to information. Rather like Jourdain in the Moliere play *The Middle Class Gentleman*, who eagerly went around seeking the meaning of the word 'prose', till someone reminded him that 'prose' was what he was using to speak, market participants in India explicitly use the EMH, often without consciously knowing that they are doing so. In

[29] Jegadeesh and Titman (discussed in the following sentence) emphasize momentum aspects of this phenomenon over short and intermediate horizons of 3 to 12 months. See Narasimhan Jegadeesh and Sheridan Titman, 'Returns to Buying Winners and Selling Losers: Implications for Stock Market Efficiency,' *Journal of Finance*, Vol. 48, 1993, 65–91.

[30] Academic studies also document this effect. In a study of emerging markets, Nusret Cakici et al. found strong momentum effects for the Indian market, particularly for small stocks. See Nusret Cakici, Frank J. Fabozzi, and Sinan Tan, 'Size, Value, and Momentum in Emerging Market Stock Returns,' *Emerging Markets Review*, Vol. 16, 2013, 46–65.

fact, the real value of the vast – and daunting – empirical research on the EMH to the average participant lies less in the multiple anomalies that they believe can be profitably exploited and more in a mental approach and discipline that forces a pause before rushing in, an approach which cautions the participant that the 100 rupee note – if really there – should have been picked up by now. Perhaps the notes can be found, but only after insight and resources have been deployed in finding them and, more critically, after suitable amounts of risk have been taken while picking them up.

All this is important stuff with real-world implications. The Efficient Market Hypothesis is doubly relevant in emerging markets like India because stock picking is the dominant approach among the public and the pros. But looking for Golconda's diamonds presupposes that they are lying around, waiting to be picked. Stock picking makes the key assumption that the market in its inefficiency has overlooked the Kohinoor or the Wittelsbach that's just waiting there. This is possible only if the market is weak-form efficient, or perhaps even less than that. So, asking whether stock picking is the best approach to the market is the same as asking how efficient the market really is. If the market is semi-strong efficient (with all public information in the price), it would be difficult to use the stock picking approach, but the approach selects itself if the market is only weak-form efficient or less. Further, selecting the area of activity within such a broad market makes a difference to the end result. In all likelihood, stock picking is easier among the over 5,000 non-index counters where there is greater inefficiency;[31] non-index stocks also have sketchy analyst coverage, which makes it easier for amateurs and pros to find pickings among them.

[31] Gourishankar S. Hiremath and B. Kamaiah, 'Variance Ratios, Structural Breaks and Non-Random Walk Behaviour in the Indian Stock Returns,' *Journal of Business & Economic Studies*, Vol. 18, No. (2), Fall 2012, 67–68. Many professionals believe that there are only 200 to 300 stocks in this large universe that are actually of investible quality; only about half the universe trades on a daily basis.

A participant's view on efficiency also conditions his view on technical and fundamental analysis. Even if weak-form efficiency holds, past information such as past prices should have no predictive effect on future prices, in which case technical analysis – using charts of past prices to predict future prices – should have little predictive value. Yet, in India, there is a thriving technical analysis industry with a considerable following, implying that the Indian market is less than weak-form efficient and also signifying that technical analysis is passing a considerable 'market test' among a sizable trading community. This is confirmed by research on technical trading strategies such as the 50 day moving average (DMA) and relative strength index, which have shown results that outperform simple 'buy and hold' strategies in India's market.[32] Conveniently enough, most of these studies tend to ignore transaction costs, and it remains unclear if the results will hold after including the heavy transaction costs that come with the technical approach.

In fact, if semi-strong-form efficiency holds – and all public information available for a stock is always impounded in its price – then even fundamental analysis is essentially useless.

This is a rather dismal conclusion that would be rejected out of hand by many market participants in India. In fact, some research points to successful stock picking on the basis of simple and easily available fundamental heuristics such as PE ratios or price-to-book ratios.[33] Here even basic forms of fundamental analysis work, indicating that semi-strong-form efficiency does not hold. So, the presence of a thriving technical analysis community, together with extensive – and successful – use of fundamental analysis by professionals, all point to considerable market inefficiency in India.

[32] For evidence that technical trading rules based on the 50 day moving average (DMA), relative strength index (RSI), and moving average convergence divergence (MACD) beat simple 'buy and hold' strategies in India, see Terence Tai-Leung Chong, Sam Ho-Sum Cheng, and Elfreda Nga-Yee Wong, 'A Comparison of Stock Market Efficiency of the BRIC Countries,' *Technology and Investment*, Vol. 1, 2010, 237. Note, however, that the study did not include transaction costs.

[33] For empirical evidence of return predictability based on dividend yield and price-earnings ratios, see Paresh Kumar Narayan and Deepa Bannigidadmath, 'Are Indian Stock Returns Predictable?' *Journal of Banking & Finance*, Vol. 58, 2015, 507.

Paradoxically, one of the earliest studies that examined Indian market efficiency in 1977 actually confirmed the random movement of stock prices and found the markets to be broadly efficient and conforming to a random walk.[34] This is surprising as the sine qua non for efficient markets – an equity research industry needed to identify and bid up undervalued stocks – itself came into existence only after the early 1990s. Further, this implies markets were more efficient in the pre-reform era and this is a counter-intuitive conclusion. One explanation is that information flow in the 1970s was effectively zero; with no information flow, stock price movements (as seen through the prism of that flow) would be random by definition, and studies that tried to isolate the effect of information on price would be pointless. Another explanation is that the old badla system – by effectively creating, through the naked short play, the same unlimited supply of stock for the short side as it did for the long side – also generated the most basic of conditions for an efficient market and allowed for randomness when compared to modern times.

One reason for present inefficiency is the competitive structure of the securities and mutual fund industry. Recall that a bedrock belief of the EMH is a sizable and far-reaching brokerage industry and buy side that's always vacuuming up those hundred-rupee bills. Contrast here the size of Wall Street with the small size and reach of India's brokerage industry and nascent buy side. The situation has improved since the late 1990s, but brokerages and fund management in India continue to be on the small side. Further, that small size stands in sharp contrast to the country's large universe of stocks. Consequently, the EMH's basic assumption – that extensive competition among firms in a large brokerage/buy-side complex leads to the instantaneous incorporation of information into price – is something of a stretch in emerging markets such as India. Finally, widely dispersed share ownership tends to be associated with more analyst coverage. But in India, the preponderance of public-sector firms together with large promoter holdings leads

[34] See J.L. Sharma and R.E. Kennedy, 'A Comparative Analysis of Stock Price Behaviour on the Bombay, London and New York Stock Exchanges,' *Journal of Financial and Quantitative Analysis*, Vol. 12, 1977, 391–413.

to ownership concentration that also works against wider analyst coverage.[35]

Market microstructure also impinges on and lowers market efficiency. A core belief of the EMH is that there exists a 'smart money' class that drives prices back to intrinsic value.[36] But what if microstructure constraints prevent such a class from arbitraging differences between price and value? As seen earlier, since the millennium's turn, the short side has been virtually eliminated in India. So, even when knowledgeable about values, a 'smart money' class cannot arbitrage away deviations to the upside, as short selling in the cash market is next to impossible. The only thing the smart money can do is sell their current holdings, but when even those sales get absorbed by the public and the momentum traders – as often happens during long upside moves – what then? Deviations from fundamentals can be considerable, as the most optimistic traders at the margin set prices. In fact, even when short selling is allowed but constrained, as in some markets, short interest is negligible, and the smart money faces limits to arbitrage.[37] In India, short selling is not just constrained but near impossible, which contributes to market inefficiency.

The dichotomy between academics and professionals that is palpably present in the West does not exist in India, and this is striking. Technical trader claims of predictable prices and mutual fund claims of continued outperformance are irresistible to Western academics, who enjoy stomping on these cherished shibboleths of the trading and investing fraternity. The EMH – its proof or its refutation – is fertile ground for the empiricism and number crunching that typifies much of the academic approach to the markets. The vast data that markets generate, together with the expansion and relative cheapness of computing power, have doubly facilitated this academic empiricism; in turn, these factors

[35] James J. Chang, Tarun Khanna, and Krishna Palepu, 'Analyst Activity Around the World,' Working Paper No. 01-061, Strategy Working Paper Series, Harvard Business School, Cambridge, MA, January 2000, 12.

[36] Robert J. Shiller, 'From Efficient Markets Theory,' 96–97.

[37] Ibid., 97–99. Also see Andrei Shleifer and Robert W. Vishny, 'The Limits of Arbitrage,' *Journal of Finance,* 52, No. 1, March 1997, 35–54.

meet the 'publish or perish' atmosphere of the academy and result in reams of studies probing market efficiency or its violations. In the West at least, this approach leads to participants and academics occupying different worlds, but in India there are no glaring differences between the conclusions of the academic community and market belief. The few studies that exist all agree on considerable market inefficiency, which is anyway the buy side's belief structure. In turn, the buy side is content to have its job made easier by the rampant inefficiency in India's markets, and it is also happy to credit its own skill – rather than abstractions like efficiency – for this state of affairs. Farsighted fund managers are now looking for academic studies on when this happy state of affairs will end (as it must at some point), but so far at least, there is not much work from academia on that phenomenon.

Finally, all this has implications for active fund management. If the strong-form EMH held, active fund management would yield uncertain results. Most US studies of efficiency make the point that mutual funds, together with other institutional investors as a class, cannot outperform the market;[38] this simply points to higher levels of market efficiency. Besides efficiency, another reason actively managed US funds don't do well is because as a group they *are* the market; for example, institutional investors make up as much as 80 per cent of the US market, and outperforming yourself is regarded as an oxymoron.[39] In India, by contrast, some evidence points to mutual funds as a group outperforming the market, indicating significant inefficiency. Also, and unlike the US, in India the professional buy side consisting of mutual funds and LIC holds just about 15 per cent of all publicly held equity. So, mutual funds are just one component in a fine balance and a small component at that. There is always someone to trade against in India's

[38] Burton G. Malkiel, 'Reflections on the Efficient Market Hypothesis: 30 Years Later,' *Financial Review*, 40 (1), February 2005, 1–9. Malkiel's conclusion echoes research that dates from Michael Jensen's influential 1968 article on mutual fund underperformance.

[39] On Wall Street, the absence of promoter families as a coherent group, insignificant government shareholdings, and negligible (direct) public presence account for the dominance of institutional investors, particularly of mutual funds.

markets, and this accounts for mutual fund outperformance; so, despite the proposition that no group can consistently beat the market over time, in India there is evidence that mutual funds as a group do so, and some studies find outperformance.[40] The caveat here is that studies which measure fund outperformance rarely control for survivorship bias or risk. If they did, then any remaining outperformance can only be explained away by appealing to the combination of market inefficiency and superior stock-picking skill.

This brings us to the other side of the coin – passive fund management or indexing. In the US, Fama's conclusion that markets are broadly efficient means that stock picking does not always work and implies that active fund management is not effective at beating the market. Ex ante, some markets and some managers will do better over certain lengths of time, but that is not forecastable. Far better therefore to hold the market itself and capture that long-term upswing. This conclusion led to index funds – funds that don't bother picking stocks, but just hold all the stocks that make up an index, such as the S&P 500. Popular perception has Fama as the progenitor of index funds and the Nobel announcement mentions it as such.[41] But credit for the discovery also goes to John Bogle, who reached the same conclusion on the ineffectiveness of active funds a generation before Fama did.[42] He approached the idea from the transaction-cost side, as opposed to the efficiency angle that had been Fama's preoccupation. Till 1975, the gentlemen at that cozy club called the New York Stock Exchange – while exercising their monopoly rights for eons under something called the Buttonwood Agreement – had an 'arrangement' to hold brokerage at high levels. This increased the cost of trading and investing substantially, and Bogle found this ate away at returns of active mutual funds, further reducing their chances of beating

[40] For one recent study, see Surbhi Khanna, '52% equity mutual funds outperform against their benchmarks in 3 years,' *ET Online*, 5 May, 2025.

[41] 'Press Release,' *Nobel Prize*, 14 October 2013, Web, 7 March 2025, https://www.nobelprize.org/nobel_prizes/economic-sciences/laureates/2013/press.html.

[42] John C. Bogle, 'The Economic Role of the Investment Company,' Thesis, Princeton University, 1950.

the market. Many years later, Bogle developed his idea of the index fund, which simply bought a broad market index such as the S&P 500 and held it forever. This effectively solved the stock picking problem, while reducing transaction costs like brokerage and fund management fees. The result was Vanguard, founded in 1976 and presently one of the largest mutual funds in the world. Trillions of dollars are now managed this way worldwide, and indexing now accounts for between a quarter and a third of the US mutual fund industry.

Indexing's legitimacy was reinforced by advice from experts such as Burton Malkiel, whose book *A Random Walk Down Wall Street* popularized the idea of efficient markets by surveying, and endorsing, the considerable academic research on the subject. First published in 1973, the book did much to spread the word on indexing. Malkiel's basic advice – that indexing was the investing public's solution to the problem of stock picking and transaction costs in efficient markets – did not change right through the book's eleven editions.[43] If anything, the relentless progress towards market efficiency further reinforced the basic truth of the approach.

In India though, indexing is less popular, and repeated attempts – especially by the NSE – to popularize it have yielded less than spectacular results. This is surprising, since, as shown earlier, the index committees have packed the indexes with blue chips that don't represent much of the economy but play to India's domestic consumption story and the country's international comparative advantage in areas such as IT services. So, buying the index would be trebly advantageous. Besides solving the stock picking problem and reducing transaction costs, it would mean buying into a basket of blue chips where high-performing sectors of the economy are disproportionately represented. Yet, the idea has not taken off.

Indexing has to deal with the professional biases of managers on the buy side, a *jaati* (community) that fancy their careers as stock pickers above all else; besides, compared to passive indexing, active management – in

[43] Burton G. Malkiel, *A Random Walk Down Wall Street*, 11th ed., New York: W.W. Norton, 2015, 393.

the absence of newfangled techniques such as statistical arbitrage or computational finance – can also charge a lot more in fees. Indexing also has to deal with the issue of narrowly defined indexes; the main indexes – the Sensex and Nifty – contain 30 and 50 stocks respectively, and some managers may be reluctant to index their entire portfolios to such a narrow benchmark of stocks.[44] So, India is still a stock picker's market, due to those pockets of inefficiency and an active fund industry that sometimes manages to beat the market. In the US, efficiency ensures that superior judgment and insight are marginally rewarded, but in India's inefficient markets, marginal judgment and insight yield superior results. Market efficiency is increasingly being felt in front-line index stocks, but the presence of over 5,000 scrips besides the big boys implies large areas of market inefficiency in India. Perhaps among the many stocks that are listed, there are hundred-rupee notes waiting to be picked up. Who knows, perhaps there's even a really big sparkler like a Kohinoor – or a Unitech.

[44] Broader indexes used for benchmarking and fund management are not widely followed by the public.

9

AND FINALLY, A MULTI-BAGGER

The Unitech Saga

It is one of the most staggering moves in the history of India's markets. In fact, the performance of Unitech – a real estate developer – over a seven-year period that ended in early 2008 must also rank among the largest moves in the history of world markets. From its April 2001 low of ₹30, the stock rose to ₹70,980 in early 2008, which made it a 2,366 bagger or a stock that went up 2,366 times;[1] in percentage terms that's a move of 2,36,500 per cent over seven years.

A lakh ($2,100) invested in Unitech in 2001 would have grown to almost ₹24 crores ($6.15 million) by January 2008, and there were a lot of people who had that lakh to invest in 2001 (dollar returns are higher because of exchange rate effects during this period). Now, as diamonds go, that's a Princie or a Kohinoor or a Wittelsbach; and suddenly, that army looking for Lakshmi in Golconda makes a lot of sense.

This would have been a once-in-a-lifetime bet if it had worked out in its entirety – meaning if someone had bought at (or near) the

[1] Unitech's price point of ₹30 was repeatedly observed between 12 April and 30 April 2001. After adjustments for stock splits and stock dividends (bonuses), the price touched ₹546.8 on 2 January 2008. Dividends are not included in holding period returns computed for this exercise. National Stock Exchange, Security-wise Archives (Equities), https://www.nseindia.com/report-detail/eq_security.

bottom and exited close to or at the top. No one catches exact highs and lows, but so considerable was the Unitech move that even catching a portion of it would have been very profitable. After profiting from it, there would have been little need to have anything more to do with the stock market; after it, a participant could look forward to a comfortable retirement bathed in that happy, warm, fuzzy belief that it was skill that had made it all possible. Retirement would have been a good idea, as any subsequent investing would have seemed disappointing. In fact, every future bet was doomed to feel frustrating and wrong, as compared to Unitech going right.

Yet, in India, Unitech's example has not got the attention it deserves. It is a commonplace that classical Indian civilization produced noted mathematicians and astronomers but never a noted historian. Is Unitech's case, together with the inattention to its lessons, another instance of that lacuna? Was there no instinct to compare events to either international yardsticks or to the past?

In fact, the Unitech case has not caught the attention of the world either. Unitech's rise over this seven-year period was many times more than the rise of Radio Corporation of America (RCA) during Wall Street's Roaring Twenties. Radio's rise from $1.63 to $490 over an eight-year period that ended in September 1929 became one of the most storied and written about stock moves in American financial history.[2] Unlike Unitech, Radio also had the advantage of starting as a penny stock that traded on the kerb, which allowed its subsequent rise to appear exaggerated. Despite this advantage, Radio was up a mere 306 times as compared to Unitech's 2,300 times up move over a comparable period. Unitech's move was also larger than moves in the 'tronics' stocks of Wall Street's Go-Go 1960s, and even larger than the moves of most dot-coms during the internet mania. Many of those rises seem small in comparison to what Unitech did, and yet no one bothered to make these comparisons or notice their significance. People just shrugged

[2] Alex Planes, 'Why Did the Greatest Bull Market in History Last So Long?,' *The Motley Fool*, 3 September 2013, Web, 20 March 2018, https://www.fool.com/investing/general/2013/09/03/why-did-the-greatest-bull-market-in-history-last-s.aspx.

their shoulders and moved on – participants in an oral tradition that left recording and research to the mercy of chance.

The rise was matched by the fall. The stock would subsequently lose all its value, and the equity by 2022 had been effectively wiped out. Rising from almost nothing, Unitech would build up to a valuation of close to ₹90,000 crores ($22 billion) in 2008, before falling again to nothing.

But this price behaviour was not very different from that of many other stocks. Blue chips in India often lost 70 to 80 per cent of their value during a bear market, behaving like blue chips in the Great Depression after 1929. But Unitech's case had something much more to it. Why hasn't anyone said anything about it? And what was going on?

Besides the sheer scale of the Unitech move and the apathy towards history's lessons, several other things about this case stand out.

First, Unitech's performance was unusual for a publicly listed stock. Such returns are regarded as more appropriate in a private equity transaction; even then, this sort of return would become the subject of myth – but it would not be unheard of. Private equity thrives on a scattershot approach to investing, where 19 out of 20 investments could be *dabba*s (worthless), but that doesn't matter as the 20th investment goes into a Unitech equivalent, like a still-private Google or Tencent. Consider Naspers's $32 million investment in Tencent in 2001, that grew to $175 billion by early 2018 – which makes it a 5,500 bagger over almost two decades.[3] This is one of the most storied investments of all time, but note that the deal started out as a private equity transaction that was open only to a select few.

In Unitech's case, the stock was publicly traded and available long before the move began. In fact, the company was founded in 1971 and went public in 1986, but the shares meandered in a trading range –

[3] Loni Prinsloo, 'Tencent's 60,000% Runup Leads to One of the Biggest VC Payoffs Ever,' *Bloomberg*, 22 March 2018.

for the better part of a generation – from the listing all the way till the real move's start in 2001.[4] The company's returns did not accrue to clubby venture capitalists who cut a deal which got them onto a private elevator at basement level that no one else could ride on. In Unitech's case, anybody and everybody could have joined in the move and many did; this availability of the deal matters when it comes to judging moves of this magnitude. The sheer access to the opportunity adds to its rarity.

Second, consider the staggering number of stock distributions engineered through splits and stock dividends. At almost ₹71,000 – the price it touched on 2 January 2008 – Unitech actually quoted just ₹546. To people who are not seasoned participants, this is puzzling, but to market mavens, it's all in a day's work. As Unitech went higher, the promoters split and then 'bonussed' the stock down; the stock split from a face value of ₹10 to ₹2, following which stock dividends – which in India are called 'bonus' shares – were issued to the nth degree. This accounting device (utilized if there are enough general reserves available) makes the stock seem cheaper than it actually is, which is an incredible statement to make if you believe in market efficiency.[5]

How can a stock be 'made' to seem less expensive than it is by simply changing a numeraire? A firm's equity capital is like a pizza pie cut into, say, 100 slices or shares. If the firm announces a 1:1 bonus, the pizza pie gets cut into 200 slices, and every share a person holds is sliced into two, giving them two shares. The day the stock goes 'ex-bonus',[6] its price falls in half, so there's no net gain. The size of the pie stays the same, and yet someone holding 8 slices before the announcement might feel happy because they've now got 16 slices, though they are each half the previous size.

[4] Unitech Limited, *Annual Report*, 2009–10, 1–2, Web, 2 March 2018, http://www.unitechgroup.com/pdfs/unitech-limited-annual-report-2009-10.pdf.

[5] For stock dividends (bonus shares), a book entry transfers an amount from the reserves account to the share capital account. This debit of general reserves/securities premium reduces them, and the credit to the share capital account increases share capital and the number of shares outstanding. Net worth (the sum of the share capital and the reserves accounts) remains unchanged.

[6] 'Ex-bonus' stocks are no longer eligible to receive a bonus, as they trade after the date (the ex-date) stocks are eligible to receive that bonus.

Unitech's capital history between 2001 and 2008 (the period examined here) reveals multiple such stock splits and stock dividends that finally resulted in the ₹546 price on 2 January 2008. The stock split from ₹10 to ₹2 paid up, leaving each shareholder with 5 shares for every 1 held. This was followed by a 12 to 1 bonus issue, leaving each shareholder with 13 shares for every 1 held. Finally, this was followed again by a 1 to 1 bonus issue, leaving each shareholder with 2 shares for every 1 held.[7] Cumulatively, a person holding 1 share in 2001 was left with 130 shares (5 × 13 × 2) in 2008. Since the price at the top was ₹546, the unadjusted price *before* adjusting for splits and stock dividends was 546 × 130, or ₹70,980. The only valid reason for the entire elaborate exercise was to make the stock seem more 'affordable' to retail investors. To put this into perspective: as a matter of principle, Warren Buffett does not split or bonus stocks of his company Berkshire Hathaway down. As a result, Berkshire Class A common traded at over $300,000 in early 2018 – or almost ₹2 crores for a single share.

Third, the extent to which the public gets conned by stock splits or stock dividends is surprising. Perusing message boards on sites such as moneycontrol.com shows the extent to which the public gets deluded. Many members of the public actually believe stock distributions like bonus shares are good for them, and it is common to see traders trying to bull a stock by spreading rumours about impending bonus issues on the message boards. Don't they get that the price falls by half on the day the share goes 'ex-bonus' if the announcement is 1:1?

It's all a giant rope trick and the promoters are responsible. Till 1999, Indian capital market provisions prohibited any face value other than ₹100 or ₹10, so the only splits that took place reduced par from 100 to 10. Since 1999, any face value is allowed, provided post-split par values are not a fraction of ₹1. Since then, the frequency of stock distributions has increased. As a stock soars higher, promoters split and bonus it down

[7] Unitech's capital history in the period under discussion – between 2001 and 2008 – shows that it split from ₹10 (face value) to ₹2 (face value) in June 2006, followed by bonus issues in June 2006 (12:1) and August 2007 (1:1). Unitech Limited, *Annual Report*, 2008–09, 13, Web, 2 March 2018, https://economictimes.indiatimes.com/unitech-ltd/infocompanysplits/companyid-12874.cms.

to make sure it stays 'affordable' to the retail investor, and the frequency of these stock distributions is another sure sign of a bull run. The idea is to keep the stock in a trading range, which in turn might attract more retail investors and improve liquidity.[8] In fact, a 2010 survey indicated that as many as 90 per cent of Indian managers preferred a price below ₹400 (about $9 at that time) as the trading range for their stocks.[9] But though the trading range hypothesis sounds innocuous, the real reason may be to camouflage and obscure a vertiginous rise. In Unitech's case, ₹546 just 'seems' a saner price compared to ₹70,000 for the same stock.

Another reason for stock distributions is to signal better times ahead, but management announcements – or, better still, raising dividend payouts – would have the same signalling effects.[10] Stock distributions might also widen the shareholder base, as small retail shareholders are less deterred by a lower price post the split or 'bonus'.[11] Nevertheless, small investors in India tend to be more speculative in their market activities, and so such moves encourage a more speculative and easily frightened shareholder base. Many companies don't seem to mind this. An ephemeral (and as yet unexamined) advantage of such distributions might be that the minimum 5 paise uptick is a greater percentage move of a 'bonussed' stock than of an 'unbonussed' one, which in turn allows the 'bonussed' stock to double over fewer upticks than the 'unbonussed' one. Good for you if you're a quibbling trader, but eventually, this effect is trivial.

So, are companies deliberately misleading the public? No, it's all perfectly legal and commonplace, though the frequency with which Indian companies use the technique is unusual. Also strange is the public's gullibility and its preternatural tendency to get conned by all

[8] Early evidence of companies using stock distributions such as splits or dividends to keep stocks in a trading range – the trading range hypothesis – comes from Josef Lakonishok and Baruch Lev, 'Stock Splits and Stock Dividends: Why, Who, and When,' *Journal of Finance*, Vol. 42, No. 4, 1987, 913–32.

[9] Chhavi Mehta, Surendra S. Yadav, and P.K. Jain, 'Managerial Motives for Stock Splits: Survey-based Evidence from India,' *Journal of Applied Finance*, Vol. 21, No. 1, 2011, 115.

[10] Kent H. Baker and Sujata Kapoor, 'Why Indian Firms Issue Stock Distributions,' *Managerial Finance*, Vol. 41, No. 7, 2015, 669. Chhavi Mehta et al., 'Managerial Motives for Stock Splits,' also found that managers prefer liquidity and trading range objectives to signalling.

[11] Chhavi Mehta et al., 'Managerial Motives for Stock Splits,' 110–11.

this, which is the reason why promoters use the technique so often.[12] Consider, for example, the following exchange in 2009 as reproduced verbatim from an internet message board for the Unitech stock:

Boarder 1: anybody knows about ever high of unitech?
Boarder 2: the management of this co is a little different as i found. the keep on changing things not needed. the split was as v saw in ABAN and L & T last year. ABAN got 1/20 lnt 1/2. unitech i dont remember exact but it split twice or thrice.
Boarder 2: all merge and split took place in last two yrar.. the level v see on sites are averaged levels.. bt i think those 35000 doesn't matter at all.... but 545 is important to keep in minds.
Boarder 1: but how it raised from 35 to 35000
Boarder 2: yes it started at 35 and rised to 35000 because they first merged it and then again splitted
Boarder 3: yes but at 14148 unitech declared a bonus of 12 shares for every 1 share held and then a stock split but this same stock was 40 Rs once upon a time near about 2000
Boarder 2: but the averaged ie the high according to this rate 89 is 546 last year
Boarder 2: yes u r . it was launched on high as 35000. then divided many times
Boarder 1: its all time high is 14148 made on 1june 2006. am i right?
Boarder 4: 500+ i have seen last year, but i don't know ever high of unitech[13]

You can protect the sheep from the wolves, but who will protect the sheep from themselves?

What happened here? The fundamentals that resulted in the stock's up move were good and still in place, and these fundamentals led to

[12] For one early study that found excess returns around the split's announcement date, see Jijo Lukose P.J. and S. Narayan Rao, 'Market Reaction to Stock Splits: An Empirical Study,' *ICFAI Journal of Applied Finance*, Vol. 8, No. 2, 2002, 26–40.

[13] 'Unitech,' *Mudraa*, Web, 1 March 2018, http://www.mudraa.com/trading/7416/0/unitech.html.

the continued advance on the split and 'bonussed' shares. Nevertheless, after sustained stock distributions, the public – and occasionally even the pros – lose track of the capital structure and valuation and get taken in by the advance. In fact, even the publicly available charting services sometimes produced nonsensical results with the Unitech price charts. That the public would get taken in by all this is understandable, but in Unitech's case, the analysts were no better than the public. Right through that massive advance, many had been advising caution and had sell calls out. But the price rise continued for years and by the time the final surge took place, analysts had been crushed into submission by the sheer extent of the rise, and most were simply on for the ride.

Fourth, the lack of sponsorship or operator activity was noteworthy. Unitech's move was legitimate and did not have that funny smell of an operator-driven favourite. Some of the most well-known brokerages in the world sized it up and initiated research coverage, and the FIIs bought heavily into the counter. As a final – and decisive – mark of respectability, the stock even entered the major indexes, becoming the first real estate company to enter the NSE's Nifty index, on 5 October 2007[14] (the inclusion would come just three months before the stock reached its peak). Unitech passed the smell test, and at its peak was one of India's largest companies, with the aura and respectability that come with size.

Fifth, despite the name, Unitech was not hi-tech. The name Unitech itself was an acronym for United Technical Consultants Pvt. Ltd., which was the company's name when it started out as a soil-testing consultancy. Most up moves on this scale are associated with technology companies, particularly product companies such as Facebook or Google that can promise and deliver on dazzling visions about a brave new world. But Unitech was a real estate developer, which is about as old economy as it gets.

[14] Unitech Limited, *Annual Report*, 2007–08, 12. DLF, the other real estate major, had already been included in the Sensex; see Devangshu Dutta, 'Nifty, Sensex: Different Strokes,' *Rediff.com*, 26 November 2011.

Sixth, even the insiders got it wrong. As the stock was scaling its final peak in early 2008, the promoters attempted a capital-raising exercise through an equity sale.[15] The deal was carried out through a 'qualified institutional placement', where the buyers are institutions; this required fewer regulatory clearances, which led to quicker deals with lower issue costs. But the issue fell through, predictably enough, over valuation. The amount offered by the buyers was simply not enough, and in the promoter's opinion, it 'undervalued' the company. This, despite the fact that a price point on valuation – itself the end result of thousands of transactions in an open market – was continuously observable. The problem was that the price point was running away to the upside every day. At the negotiations – subsequently called off when the 2008 bear gathered momentum – consider the spectacle of potential buyers for the Unitech stock, themselves seasoned professionals, desperate and dying to lose money and yet being saved by an accident of karma. For buyers, the escape was providential. The seller's greed and the 2008 sell-off saved their skin.

Finally, the scale of the collapse was sobering. Unitech subsequently lost over 99 per cent of its value in a one-way descent, and today, the equity is gone. The stock traded at ₹1 in 2021, but just the minimum brokerage of ₹1 on each side of a round trip led to ₹2 in transaction costs, implying that the equity had been all but wiped out. Equally sobering was how little the fundamentals would have helped in assessing the situation. Looking at Unitech's 2007–08 annual report is a good illustration of how markets can diverge from financial statements; an excellent balance sheet covering the glorious year that ended on 31 March 2008 came out that August, and yet by October the stock was down almost 90 per cent from its January 2008 high. Looking at the stock's long-term chart today shows a perfectly inverted V, with long flat tails on both sides and little break in the downside pattern to even hint at a bear market rally. Value investors waited for the stock to fall 90 per cent from its high of 546 to 54 and bought, and then it fell to

[15] Surajeet Das Gupta, 'I Am Not Even Thinking of Monetising Telecom,' *Business Standard*, 20 January 2013.

5 – a fall of another 90 per cent.[16] A purchase at 5 led to a price of 0.45, another 90 per cent fall. The public (and even some pros) don't get the math of falling share prices, but this is a good enough illustration. To use a common market term, this was not catching a falling knife. This was catching a guillotine with a little finger.

Analyst confidence would get destroyed by the downside. Throughout that long descent from 546 to nothing, prestigious brokerages – local and foreign – would repeatedly come out with reports that were basically rationalizations for the latest stock price. The typical report would carry reams of complex calculations valuing the company, which meant the land bank and projects, on a net asset value (NAV) basis, i.e., after knocking off the debt. The usual result was a price target that was typically 15 to 20 per cent higher than the market price prevailing at the report's preparation. The market price acted as a terrible and heavy anchor, and the reports essentially rationalized the extant price. But the stock kept falling until it reached single digits, way below all the NAV calculations. So, in the final stages of the descent, the desperate brokerages randomly applied massive discounts of up to 50 or 60 per cent to the calculated NAV figures and arrived at price targets that were a little above the extant price. But the stock still did its own thing and kept heading towards zero.

And the many stories all along that upswing and subsequent collapse! The lucky fool buying at 60 and exiting at 120, who found it too expensive to re-enter at 200 and simply could not summon up the courage to buy as the stock roared higher after that, only to live in regret for the rest of his life as it went to 70,000 – but at least he kept his capital with a profit. The unlucky fools, the '90 on 90' traders outlined earlier, who thought they were buying value when the stock was 90 per cent down, only to lose another 90 per cent of capital as the stock fell to single digits – their mistake was believing the research from the swanky

[16] On the way down, price points between ₹3 and ₹4 were repeatedly observed in February and May 2016 on large volumes. See National Stock Exchange, Security-wise Archives (Equities). In 2009 and 2010, convertible warrants were allotted to the promoter group and later exercised in small amounts. This led to some increase in the equity base, whose effect is ignored in the calculations. Including them would not change any of the conclusions reached. Unitech Limited, *Annual Report*, 2009–10, 48, 85.

wire houses. The mid-cap mutual fund that became the industry's star performer for years only because it had Unitech as the largest holding. And somewhere out there, the luckiest of them all – the small-time investor with a few forgotten physical share certificates locked up in the drawer, who woke up one day to collect all his bonus shares at one shot and was forced to sell near the top to buy the apartment across the corridor that was suddenly on the market. Typically, only the winners told the stories and embellished them with the telling, while the losers shuffled away, sulked over their demat statements, and lived in regret for the rest of their lives.

There is a possibility that except for the promoters, none really caught the complete move from bottom to top. The promoters never caught the move as it is, but they simply went through a roller-coaster ride of exhilaration and despair as they watched notional paper wealth soar to unimaginable levels and then melt away.

Unitech represents an unusual and extreme move on both sides which, together with the historic precedents it would set in the stock market and elsewhere, is why it was chosen as an example for this account. This sort of example is surprisingly common in India, and the wire houses even have a comfortable euphemism to describe the phenomenon – the 'transitory multi-bagger'. Thankfully – for the cardiac health of participants at least – most stocks do not do a Unitech even if they have everything going for (or against) them.

Unitech was a stock in one volatile asset class – equities – with its underlying business – real estate – in another volatile asset class. Both asset classes are sensitive to interest rate changes, and the displacement caused by the near 900-basis point reduction in policy interest rates between 1996 and 2004 worked its magic on both classes.[17] The

[17] Between September 1996 and September 2003, G-Sec yields fell from 14.3 per cent to 5.08 per cent. Available at 'India 10-Year Government Bond Yield,' Trading Economics, Web, 10 January 2018, https://tradingeconomics.com/india/government-bond-yield.

displacement had led to the Rate Bull, and Unitech was the star of that move. This accounts for its singular rise, but what accounts for the fall?

Real estate as an asset class represented all the promise and peril of India. A population of over 1.3 billion was urbanizing rapidly, driven in large part by migration from rural areas; by some measures, one out of every six people getting urbanized globally would be from India, which amounted to 11 to 12 million annually. As a result, urban population was projected to increase from about 365 million in 2008 to over 800 million by 2050.[18] Further, India accounted for about 17 per cent of the world's population, but less than 3 per cent of its land area, which led to population density of a different order. It was clear that entire new cities were needed to accommodate the shift, but not a single city had been founded. At most, there were a few extensions of existing cities – Gurgaon, Navi Mumbai, and Rajarhat had come up as extensions of Delhi, Mumbai, and Kolkata respectively. Societal shifts from a joint-family system to nuclear-type arrangements where families lived separately also contributed to the increased demand in urban areas. Finally, increasing credit availability and the growth of a nascent housing finance industry made it easier for people to buy homes on credit and added to the attractiveness of real estate as an asset class.

As a result of all this, population pressure on existing urban land resulted in stunning price increases for Indian real estate. Annual price increases between 12 and 15 per cent were seen as normal in these years and touted as such by the real estate industry and assorted other investment advisors. The advisors would not have been guilty of hype – the RBI's all-India House Price Index (HPI) indicated annual growth rates of 14 per cent between its inception in 2010 and 2017.[19] By comparison, S&P's Case–Shiller Home Price Indices indicated annual price increases of almost 13 per cent during the absolute peak of the US housing bubble in early 2006. Ergo, price rises identified as bubbles

[18] United Nations, Department of Economic and Social Affairs, *World Urbanization Prospects: The 2014 Revision, Highlights*, New York: United Nations, 2014, 1, 12.

[19] In nominal terms, the central bank's All-India House Price Index (HPI) grew from 100 (in its 2010 base year) to 251 in 2017. 'Database on Indian Economy,' *Reserve Bank of India*, https://dbie.rbi.org.in/DBIE/dbie. rbi?site=statistics.

in mature markets were viewed as normal in India and were confirmed as such by official data over extended periods of time. Against this backdrop, prospects for urban real estate were seen as limitless, and Unitech's stock reflected this promising scenario. In fact, the dazzling projections from 'top down' statistics were confirmed by the stock's rise over many years, and this combination was guaranteed to reinforce a participant's confidence in their stock picking ability.

Yet against all this promise was the peril of doing business in India, and real estate – behind the computer generated razzmatazz of project launches that filled the newspapers – was a good illustration of that. Urban land parcels with clear ownership histories were few and far between, and developers had to bid insane amounts to get the little serviceable land that was available for development. Infrastructure was often sparse and had to be created at significant cost by the developers themselves. Interest and financing charges bore little relation to policy rates; to account for risk, capital was obtained at massive premia to policy rates – coupons from 14 to 17 per cent on well-known developers' debt were routinely reported in the business media – and this was another example of the extreme credit market segmentation discussed earlier.[20] Rent-seeking behaviour and corruption were present, as the industry interfaced for permits and clearances with city and local governments, which were seen as the most corrupt of all government levels. Clearances were a hit-or-miss affair, with low-level bureaucrats capable of withholding clearances and holding up projects worth billions, which in turn increased costs. All this resulted in a wonderful euphemism – something called 'affordability'. Projects came up at such high rates that most people couldn't afford them, and developers often asked themselves existential questions like whether they had priced themselves out of the market. High prices also meant that rental yields on residential real estate were typically less than 2 per cent, among the lowest in the world.[21] The government would recognize all this by

[20] See Henry Foy, 'Soaring Realty Ambitions Belie Rocky Foundations,' Reuters, 27 October 2011. For smaller developers with riskier capital structures, borrowing rates would have been much higher.

[21] Sachin Dave, 'Property rental yields decline,' *Hindustan Times*, 25 August, 2011.

launching a major initiative aimed at encouraging 'affordable housing' – but the choice of name itself suggested that the situation before the initiative was 'unaffordable housing'.[22]

Even after clearances were obtained and the project pre-sold, the shaky status of the developer sometimes meant delays of many years. In later years, developers would run headlong into consumer activism generated by apartment buyers angered at being taken in by their promises. Buyer anger was understandable, as in many cases buyers occupying rental premises had taken home loans to pay sizable advances on apartments that were delayed indefinitely. In such cases, the project delays resulted in EMI payments on the home loan and concurrent rental payments on present accommodation.[23] Of all sectors in India, real estate was not for the faint-hearted. Itself an asset class, real estate could be perennially subject to bubble-like conditions and yet have companies in its listed space whose share prices went south to Australia.[24]

Unitech was quite literally in the middle of all this – most of its activity was in the National Capital Region around Delhi, which after Tokyo is the second largest urban agglomeration in the world.[25] The company started out in the early 70s as a soil testing consultancy, morphed into a turnkey construction major, and finally moved into real estate development by the mid-80s. Nothing much happened for over a decade, following which the real up move began, led in large part by the interest rate cycle's downturn and the market's subsequent discovery of listed real estate.

Why didn't valuation parameters send out red signals during Unitech's massive rise between 2001 and 2007? There was little question of normal valuation parameters rising by the same magnitude as stock

[22] The Pradhan Mantri Awas Yojana, the Smart Cities Initiative, and AMRUT were among a host of initiatives aimed at affordable housing and urban transformation.

[23] Pooja Thakur, Upmanyu Trivedi, and Dhwani Pandya, 'Phantom Flats Have Homebuyers Fleeing a Once-hot Property Market,' *Bloomberg*, 31 January 2018.

[24] Over a 10-year period between January 2008 and February 2018, the NSE's Nifty Realty Index had gone from 1878 to 330 – a fall of 82 per cent. See National Stock Exchange, Equities, Indices, Historical Index Data (Nifty Realty Index).

[25] United Nations, Department of Economic and Social Affairs, *World Urbanization Prospects*, 1.

prices, so they should have flashed red as the stock soared. But that did not happen because the parameters were themselves changed during the stock's rise. Just as the dot-com boom had resulted in valuations based on 'eyeballs', valuations based on land banks for real estate companies became the norm. In turn, most developers took to heart Mark Twain's dictum – 'Buy land, they're not making it anymore' – and competed to outdo one another in expanding their land banks. By the move's final stage, Unitech's land bank had grown from 8,000 acres in 2006 to 14,000 acres in 2008.[26]

Later, allegations would surface that many companies were padding land banks with dubious barren land rather than serviceable land, followed by the claim that analysts tracking the companies simply did not know the difference. Further, much of the land was agricultural land acquired from individual marginal farmers, which had to be 'consolidated' under a single title, and then 'converted' from agricultural to commercial use before actual development could start. This process – particularly the final 'conversion' stage – was usually done through bureaucratic fiat, subject to multiple caveats, and riven by corruption. All this took place on a pan-India basis and large land banks were acquired across the country by many players.

In some cases, as much as 75 per cent of the land bank was accumulated before 'conversion' could take place. Given the uncertain outcomes of the conversion process, this accumulation carried considerable risk. But the stock market didn't really care, for once the land bank was acquired, the stock market's inclination to value the company on its land bank could be exploited. The completion of each stage in the 'conversion' process would send land prices higher, and they sometimes reached levels that were 20 times higher than the initial price.[27] The stock market then played along, assigning higher valuations to the land bank and bidding developer stocks even higher. As a result of all this, Unitech's price would soar to that dazzling peak of January 2008.

[26] Surajeet Das Gupta, 'The Land That Unitech Built,' *Business Standard*, 3 June 2006; Unitech Limited, *Annual Report*, 2007–08, 8.

[27] John Samuel Raja D. and Kausik Datta, 'What's Wrong with the Real Estate Sector in India,' *Economic Times*, 9 June 2011.

Encouraged to accumulate land banks by the stock market's higher valuations, companies such as Unitech financed them almost entirely through debt. As a result of the land bank binge, debt rose to considerable levels.[28] With the onset of the 2008 Lehman crisis and Great Recession, the property market essentially died on Unitech and other developers, and this debt-fuelled land binge was exposed as unsustainable. Much of the debt was short term but the commitment to property and development was longer term, resulting in asset-liability mismatches. Short-term debt isn't inherently bad as long as it can keep getting rolled over, but with the onset of the 2008 crisis, the market for rolling over this short-term debt basically evaporated, despite which activity had to continue and projects completed.

Further, monetary aggregates had yo-yoed in these years and the rate cycle also turned violently upward in 2009 and 2010. Interest rates rose 12 times in succession, as the RBI, already behind on the curve, tightened monetary policy. The cost of capital rose, which raised rates at which banks advanced housing loans to customers, and put pressure on housing demand. Nevertheless, at the company level, the effects of higher rates were more manageable as developers anyway borrowed at much higher rates than policy rates. Many developers then turned to private equity, but private equity in India operated on a grotesque hybrid model. When things went well, they were content to term their investments as equity and get the upside at an IPO, but when things didn't work out, their investments magically became debt, and they wanted their money back at rates – internal rates of return – as high as 20 to 25 per cent.[29]

To its credit, Unitech undertook vigorous steps to come out of the situation. Land bank monetization, faster project delivery, deleveraging, and asset sales all followed. The company embarked on attempts to

[28] Unitech's debt touched a peak of almost ₹11,000 crores by 2009. Long-term debt would not appear inordinately high, but note that buyer advances against projects were accounted for separately. Source: Unitech Annual Reports.

[29] Mezzanine financing, involving subordinated debt with embedded warrants, might have suited Unitech but would have been catastrophic for lenders as the equity got wiped out.

monetize its land bank through focused execution and then made the move to affordable and mid-income housing; by 2010, the land bank was down to 7,500 acres.[30] Operational improvements were made in project delivery that reduced costs and completion time, while new projects were aggressively launched and sold. Equity was raised and debt drawn down; coming off the bottom in 2009, the company concluded two successful equity placements with institutions before the market closed on it.[31] Pan-India expansions were seen as a mistake and were subsequently unwound through asset sales. Finally, a demerger of its infrastructure business into another entity was attempted, but never really completed.

Unitech's efforts were initially successful, but the 2G allocation scam from 2010 onwards would dominate the company's destiny. A company subsidiary had obtained a valuable pan-India telecom license and 2G spectrum under a controversial 'first come, first serve' policy rather than through open auction. Within months of getting the license and spectrum, Unitech flipped the subsidiary where the license was parked – a subsidiary which had no significant assets or business record of any sort – to a Norwegian telecom company, at five times what it had paid for the license.[32] The resulting uproar and investigation with the company and others at its centre became known as the 2G corruption scandal. The court cases against the promoters and others went on for years, only to result in acquittals and pending appeals against acquittals. While all this was unfolding, the share price had begun its long, slow descent into single digits.

The margin call played a big role in the stock's descent. In India, promoters took considerable risk with their own stock because of the liquidity of listed holdings, the large weightage of those listed holdings in their net worth, the intimate knowledge they thought they had of their enterprise valuations, and the anchoring effects and reality of extant price.

[30] Unitech Annual Report, 2010.

[31] Unitech Limited, *Annual Report*, 2009–10, 26.

[32] For a summary of the issues Unitech faced in this period, see Nivedita Mookerji, 'From Real Estate Kings to 2G Scam, the Rise and Fall of Unitech's Chandras,' *Business Standard*, 11 April 2017.

Unitech was no exception to this, and its promoters repeatedly pledged their holdings to raise funds from lenders. But as the price headed lower, the promoters couldn't meet margin calls, and lenders typically sold the stock to recover the pledged amount, causing it to crash further. Between 2011 and 2017, a promoter group that had once held close to half of equity now found itself losing control of the company. In early 2011, Unitech promoters held about 48 per cent of equity, with two-thirds of the holding pledged, but by December 2017, promoters held 15 per cent, of which almost three-quarters was pledged.[33] The reduced holding led to principal–agent problems and raised questions about the promoter group's motivation and commitment. Promoter families losing control through excessive stock pledging would become a routine feature in corporate India.[34] The stock market was performing its usual role as a market for corporate control, but in an indirect fashion. The hubris and misjudgement of some among the promoter class ensured that the market's role as an arbiter of corporate control was fulfilled – not through the highfalutin manoeuvring of mergers and acquisitions but through the humble margin call.

Unitech's practice of conducting significant business through subsidiaries did not help its evaluation. The company's 2009–10 annual report listed 303 subsidiaries incorporated in India, 32 subsidiaries incorporated outside India, and 30 joint ventures or associates.[35] Subsidiaries multiplied endlessly the 'related party transactions' between the main company, the promoter family, and the subsidiaries. In Unitech's case, the possible combinations of transactions between these parties could run into tens of thousands. This combinatorial explosion of possible 'related-party transactions' made it hard for analysts to effectively track and value the stock. Further, accounting policies such as the percentage of completion method left much to the discretion of the

[33] Somasroy Chakraborty and Raghavendra Kamath, 'Margin Calls on Pledged Shares Add to Unitech's Troubles,' *Business Standard*, 20 January 2013; Press Trust of India, 'HDFC Sells, Invokes Pledged Shares of Unitech,' *Mint*, 14 December 2017.

[34] Anjana Raju and Kanak Sapra, 'Convenience to Curse: Pledging of Promoter Shareholding in India under Scanner,' *Journal of Wealth Management*, Vol. 12, No. 4, 2010, 78–100.

[35] Unitech Limited, *Annual Report*, 2009–10, 49–52.

company.[36] All this made it difficult to arrive at a correct picture, and the stock distributions through splits and bonuses only added to the haze.

Unitech's obsession with building its land bank flowed from its outlook on historical time. According to this outlook, in a country where population pressure on land was significant and where land prices kept rising rapidly every year,[37] the earlier the land bank was acquired, the better. That early acquisition was seen as a key determinant of profitability. Naturally this pressured the company to take advantage of what it saw as a one-time opportunity before it closed, and this urgency is a recurring theme in its annual reports.[38] But in India, the problem was less with the absolute amount of land – which was vast – and more with policies which released that land, i.e., land supply. This perspective was inadequately considered by the company. Part of the urgency also came from the spike in land prices caused by the 900 basis point rate displacement at the millennium's turn, but there is little indication that the company saw the displacement as the one-time move that it was. So, faced with soaring land prices caused by the rate displacement and the stock market's fashion for valuing developers on the basis of land banks, the company attempted to borrow and augment its own land bank. Nevertheless, taking on large amounts of high-cost debt to create assets that simply lay around was not a viable business model. The assets still had to be monetized quickly enough to service that debt, but the company could not do this.

[36] This is a revenue recognition method where revenues and gross profits are recognized for each period based upon the progress of the construction, which is the percentage of completion. Inaccurate estimates (common in an industry prone to weather delays, equipment breakdowns, and material shortages) can lead to significant cost overruns as a project progresses. John Samuel Raja D. and Kausik Datta, 'Real Estate: Experts Doubt "Percentage Completion" Method of Revenue Calculation by Builders,' *Economic Times*, 23 June 2011.

[37] 'We will look at housing as a manufacturing business. Land is one of our key raw materials. Construction is second. One of the key things in our business is "when" you bought land – it determines profitability – and the second, "what" was the product, and "how" you would make that product,' Sanjay Chandra, Unitech Promoter, Interview with Raghavendra Kamath. Raghavendra Kamath, 'How Unitech Managed During the Crisis,' *Rediff*, 15 January 2010.

[38] Unitech Limited, *Annual Report*, 2010–11, 2, 19, 20. Unitech Limited, *Annual Report*, 2011–12, 3, 9, 10. The 2013–14 annual report is the last to mention the term 'land bank'. From the 2014–15 annual report onwards, there is no mention of its land bank.

Another drawback of a land bank strategy as opposed to, say, a lease-based strategy is that the land bank gets used up with outright development and sale, putting pressure on the company to keep acquiring land and adding to the bank. A lease model would have been more stable, but neither would it have allowed for land bank accretion, nor (more critically) would it have appealed to the stock market's infatuation with valuing those land banks.

Unitech's portfolio was also heavily skewed towards residential projects; typically, up to 50 per cent of residential construction was funded through buyer advances, which became another source of financing. Building a land bank was easier when partly financed through buyer advances, and in some cases buyers' advances were applied to the land bank and not the projects for which the advance was made. This hidden leverage – buyers' advances were also a source of company borrowing – further exacerbated the crisis when it came. The company's focus on residential projects – at one point, almost 80 per cent of the company's projects were residential – would also have serious consequences.[39] When deliveries slowed, the buyers turned to consumer and political activism. Between 16,000 and 19,000 home buyers were left dangling when Unitech's projects started grinding to a halt. As the mess unfolded, the watching buyers' fear and resignation gradually turned to anger. Slowly and surely, they gathered together for mutual protection and then coalesced into a political force through activism.[40] As mentioned, many were simultaneously incurring mortgage and rental payments. But many were also speculators, who took on execution risk by buying allotments at the pre-launch stage, following which the allotments were flipped closer to project completion (strangely enough, the industry described such speculators as 'investors' and contrasted them with end-user buyers who actually invested in homes to live in).

Unitech's location in the National Capital Region and the geographic proximity to the Supreme Court also meant that much buyer activism and legal wrangling could easily go all the way to the apex court. By now, the

[39] Unitech Limited, *Annual Report*, 2009–10, 10.

[40] Ashwini Kumar Sharma, 'A Real Estate Lesson from the Unitech Case,' *Mint*, 11 April 2017.

company had also defaulted on fixed deposits taken from retail investors, and the end result of all this was the arrest, release, and re-arrest of its promoters. The government then attempted to take over the company but was rebuffed by the Supreme Court, which proceeded – in another historic precedent – to interfere directly in operational decisions that impacted the buyers and the company.[41] This dynamic between a dodgy business class and a civil society that set multiple precedents by fighting back through a creaky judicial system would dominate India's political and business atmosphere in later years. Debt levels fell substantially, but servicing even the reduced amount using operating cash flows proved difficult. Besides, there was the hidden leverage taken as advances from apartment buyers, against which project delivery had ground to a halt.[42]

Ironically, it was the buyer activism that initially protected the company from insolvency and liquidation. Outright liquidation – and the company had met flow-based insolvency criteria for some time – could have happened, but that would have left the apartment buyers high and dry. Home buyers ranked low in the settlement order under the new insolvency code (just ahead of preferred and common stockholders), and it was only much later that subsequent changes would rank them on par with financial creditors.[43] The insolvency code was just being tested through precedents in the law courts, so it was far better to let the company limp along and hope the situation would resolve itself

[41] Press Trust of India, 'Bail to Unitech Bosses Possible Only After Data Is Collated: Supreme Court,' *Times of India*, 15 September 2017; Samanwaya Rautray, 'Supreme Court Stalls Government's Move to Take over Unitech,' *Economic Times*, 13 December 2017; Sanu Sandilya, 'SC Asks Unitech to Deposit Rs 1,000 Crore for Considering Chandra's Bail Plea,' *Economic Times*, 23 October 2017; A. Vaidyanathan, 'Supreme Court Likely to Auction Unitech Properties: "You Cheated Buyers",' *NDTV Business*, 12 March 2018.

[42] As submitted by a Supreme Court *amicus curiae*, (by some reckonings) in December 2017 the company still owed over ₹7,800 crores to more than 16,300 homebuyers in its 61 projects. Samanwaya Rautray, 'Supreme Court Stalls Government's Move.'

[43] Under Section 53(1)(f) of the Insolvency and Bankruptcy Code (IBC), home buyers ranked at the end of the settlement list and just ahead of preferred and common shareholders. Vatsala Kamat, 'Are Housing Companies Such as Unitech too Big to Fail?,' *Mint*, 11 December 2017. Subsequent reviews would recommend that home buyers be treated as financial creditors by treating damages – for breach of contract – as financial debt, and modifications were subsequently enacted that ranked them on par with financial creditors.

down the road. In another paradox, the insolvency code should have been facilitating company exit but in this case was doing the opposite.

The Unitech case also resulted in a move to regulate real estate through The Real Estate (Regulation and Development) Act, 2016 (RERA).[44] RERA mandated the opening of escrow accounts for projects and checked fund diversion somewhat. It also mandated that developers use at least 70 per cent of pre-sale proceeds to complete residential projects, effectively reducing the free financing to build land banks that had caused much of the Unitech crisis.

Similar to real estate, there are many stories among sectors that make up that listed universe of over 5,000 stocks. Take telecom, airlines, power, automobiles, digital payments, infrastructure, media, e-commerce, hotels, or retailing and notice that the promise and peril of India go hand in hand through these sectors. Around each sector swirls the siren song of market potential, the Great Indian Middle Class, and the consumption story; 'The sky's the limit' was the IPO tag line of a prominent airline that later went bust. Market potential – industry numbers touted by a consulting firm or brokerage – is a big part of the promise. The numbers are always staggering and even the most hardened businessman could fall for their promises. The peril comes when you go down a level of analysis to the company. Here, the siren song sometimes turns into a screech. So, in a country teeming with paradoxes, consider another – that of an India with great potential, where companies dealing in that great potential often had stock prices that dropped down to single digits.

It is tempting to see the Unitech saga as a morality play – that typically Indian combination of hubris, incompetence, corruption, self-interested dealing, and bad karma on a grand scale which defines horror

[44] Karan Choudhury, 'Experts Say RERA Rules Would Prevent Unitech-like Situations,' *Business Standard*, 4 April 2017.

stories when they do happen. Yet, the concern here is not Unitech the Allegory but Unitech the Stock.

What to make of all this? What to make of an old economy stock that did nothing for almost a generation, then rose over 2,30,000 per cent in a one-way up move over a few years, and then gave it all up in a one-way down move over the next few years? What to make of a market that never saw through this rise and fall, that never even managed to calculate its exact dimensions? How to distinguish between the transitory multi-bagger and something more permanent, between the ephemeral and the real, between the speculative and the investment grade? Clearly, what was once seen as an investment – and a superlative one at that – was not so and was later revealed to be more speculative. Yet, deciding between the speculative grade and the investment grade is not everything. Distinguishing between the activities of speculation and investment is also imperative.

10

STORMING LAKSHMI OR LAYING SIEGE

Speculation and Investment

Does one storm Lakshmi or carefully lay siege to her? This question is important and gets to the heart of any approach to the stock market. Storming Lakshmi and attempting to capture her head-on implies taking more risk and perhaps indulging in speculation (*satta*). Patiently laying siege to Lakshmi and hoping she falls to you as time and compounding together work their magic implies a more investment-oriented approach to the market.

Notice there is no mention of the word 'trading' in the chapter headline. This is deliberate. A case can be made that there is nothing called trading, as 'trading' is just a comfortable word the brokerage community uses for speculation. It's far better in life – and especially in this business – to call a thing by its name.

Speculation and investment. Most of the stories in the Indian stock market – and there are many – spring from an inability to understand the exact difference between these two terms. Many investors in India are trapped speculators. They are speculators who bought for a price turn that never worked out. They trade and buy a stock for price action, and it falls, and so they stay 'invested' till they get their price back. Sometimes, that never happens. And when it does, and they do get their price back after the sell-off, they're often so unnerved by the experience that they're quite happy to get out with a 10 per cent upside, only to see the stock go up another 10,000 per cent. The extreme volatility in the Indian market environment makes this rollercoaster quite routine, but it also rewards those who appreciate the distinction between these two activities.

Organized gaming markets have been around in India for a long time, much before investment policy and Graham and Dodd.[1] The annual coming of the monsoon to the subcontinent brings its own timeless rhythm to the structure of commercial life and provides regular openings to profit from changes in the price of commodities. But the monsoon also brought opportunities to earn more directly from its progress, and among these chances was rain gambling or *Barsaat ka Satta*. From the early nineteenth century onwards, the bazaars of Calcutta had regular markets in rain gambling, with much activity concentrated around the Tulapatti of Burrabazar.[2] In Bombay, rain gambling took place in areas such as Pydhonie and Khetwadi and usually through the Calcutta '*mori*' form of betting, a wager on how much rainwater would filter through a standardized sandbox; gambling also took place through *Lakdi Satta*, which was a bet on whether rainfall within a certain period would cause a receptacle to overflow.[3] Wagering on New York Cotton Exchange closing prices, which were conveyed via teleprinter to the Bombay Cotton Exchange, was also a common practice that later evolved into *matka*, a form of gambling based on lots drawn. The colonial government's usual reaction was to ban most forms of

[1] Benjamin Graham and David Dodd were professors at Columbia Business School when they collaborated on *Security Analysis*; first published in 1934, the book is still regarded as the foundational text of value investing.

[2] Aditi Roy Ghatak, *Down Lyons Range*, Kolkata: P K Ray for the Calcutta Stock Exchange Association, 2008, 37–39.

[3] Jehangir Ruttonji Screwvala, 'Rain Gambling,' in *Federal Observer*, Stock Exchange Special Number, Vol. 1, Nos. 42 and 43, 30 March 1941, 11.

gambling,[4] but this proved ineffectual and either led to the activity going *dabba* (informal) or moved speculative capital into other markets. This sequence of unintended consequences would foreshadow a century of future interaction between the state and the market.

Markets in commodity derivatives then came into existence. Shekawati Marwaris dominated activities in *fatka* (futures) markets for cotton and jute, perhaps because of their sophisticated information networks between cultivation areas in the interior and the market centres of Calcutta and Bombay.[5] Local Calcutta firms used the price signals generated by these *fatka* markets to offer quotes on upcountry jute and occasionally to hedge; European firms usually did neither and so were at a disadvantage.[6] This would set a pattern of local firms dominating commodity businesses till the product was docked, following which European and expat firms used their global networks to ship into international geographies. The move from commodity *fatka* markets into markets like stocks followed, and the earlier speculative temperament came with it; badla, the unmargined naked forward, was similar to commodity *fatka* contracts, and the stock market's obsession with leverage was another holdover from early commodity trading.

During the Century of Marking Time, the speculative nature of market action was noted by observers such as Atlay, Morison, and Thomas. The Morison report of 1937 estimated speculative activity – or 'gambling in differences', as it politely called trading in the marked to market portion of naked forward contracts – at between 80 and 90 per cent of daily volumes.[7] In the early 90s and towards the end of the badla

[4] Banning rain gambling while allowing activities such as horse racing – seen as more upmarket and elitist – led to charges of hypocrisy against the colonial administration and stirred Marwari public identity. For a detailed account see Anne Hardgrove, 'Marwaris and Moral Economies: From Rain to Ghee,' *Community and Public Culture: The Marwaris in Calcutta, c. 1897–1997*, New York: Columbia University Press, 2004, 116–66.

[5] Ibid.

[6] B.R. Tomlinson, 'Colonial Firms and the Decline of Colonialism in Eastern India 1914–1947,' *Power, Profit and Politics: Essays on Imperialism, Nationalism and Change in Twentieth-Century India*, ed. Christopher Baker, Gordon Johnson, and Anil Seal, Cambridge: Cambridge University Press, 1981, 469–70.

[7] Walter B. Morison, *Report of the Stock Exchange Enquiry Committee*, Bombay: Government Central Press, 1937, 3.

era, one study on market volumes estimated that about 65 per cent was squared up on the last day of settlement, about 25 per cent was carried forward to the next settlement, while only about 10 per cent was actual delivery-based buying.[8] The extreme concentration of volumes in the forward badla list, the low ratios of delivered volumes to total volumes, and the high velocity of turnover to market capitalization all pointed to the speculative markets of badla's heyday.[9]

Many of these characteristics continue today, and the derivatives markets in particular have ensured that the speculative orientation continues into the modern era. India's derivatives markets are dominated by individuals and proprietary traders,[10] who have fewer hedging needs than institutions. Hedging is therefore negligible, but all (non-arbitrage) derivatives activity that is not hedging is speculation – and so, it is a fair conclusion that most derivatives activity is also speculative in nature.

But though speculation is pervasive in India's equity markets, its precise extent is hidden behind the reams of statistics that the exchanges churn out, and ignoring its presence is one of those unrecognized hypocrisies India abounds in. To judge its extent, consider that the average daily turnover (ADTO) of the cash and derivatives segments of Indian equity markets for FY 2020 came in at a staggering ₹14,39,000 crores ($197 billion). ADTO in the cash market came in at ₹39,000 crores ($5.5 billion) for both exchanges, while ADTO in the derivatives market came in at ₹14,00,000 crores ($191 billion).[11] Cash thus accounted for

[8] L.C. Gupta, 'The Volume and Nature of Speculation on Indian Stock Exchanges: Regulatory Implications,' *Expert Study of Trading in Shares in Stock Exchanges*, Volume 2, Appendices – Working Paper/Note 1, New Delhi: The Society for Capital Market Research and Development, 1991, 20.

[9] For one early study on these effects, see L.M. Bhole, 'The Indian Capital Market at Crossroads,' *Vikalpa*, Volume 20, No. 2, April–June 1995, 33.

[10] Securities and Exchange Board of India (SEBI), 'Discussion Paper on Growth and Development of Equity Derivative Market in India,' 12 July 2017 at https://www.sebi.gov.in/reports/reports /jul-2017/discussion-paper-on-growth-and-development-of-equity-derivative-market-in-india_35295.html .

[11] ICRA Ltd, 'Indian Brokerage Industry on a Roll Despite Challenges; Expected Revenue Growth in FY2021 at 10-12%,' *ICRA Press Release*, 23 September 2020. Following an aborted attempt at buying its way into the derivatives segment by offering heavy discounts, the BSE, in 2020, did not have a presence in derivatives. So, cash numbers are from both exchanges, while derivatives numbers are from the NSE. Later the BSE would gain a foothold in the derivatives segment.

less than 3 per cent of the daily turnover, while derivatives – where activity is mostly speculative – accounted for the balance 97 per cent.[12]

Notice also that the daily cash figure of ₹39,000 crores consists of shares bought for delivery as well as non-delivered shares. Non-delivered shares are a consequence of activities such as day trading or scalping, where shares are bought and sold the same day without delivery; this is also outright speculation (though some might go further and classify it as gambling). Note that in FY 2020, the ADTO for delivered shares, or actual shares bought for delivery beyond a *single* trading session, averaged 21 per cent of that total daily cash figure of ₹39,000 crores.[13] This comes to about ₹8,190 crores ($1.2 billion), and this amount represents the outer limit of investment-grade buying. But this is only about 0.57 per cent of the total ADTO figure of ₹14,39,000 crores, and when seen from this perspective, 99.43 per cent of Indian market action in FY 2020 was speculative in nature.

In fact, the estimate for investment-grade buying may be even lower. The ₹8,190 crore figure itself consists of shares bought for delivery beyond a *single* trading session, but the entire amount so bought and delivered to buyers' demat accounts is not investment-grade buying. These buyers include India's vast universe of technical traders as well as scalpers and those among the public who also buy for turns of a few days or weeks – all of which are also inherently speculative activities. So, actual investment-grade buying should be even lower than that 0.57 per cent of daily volumes, though the exact value cannot be estimated.

The culprit – in part, but only in part – is the way derivatives turnover is calculated. This low proportion of 0.57 per cent is also because the large ₹14.39 lakh crore ($197 billion) base is itself distorted. Over 80 per cent of derivatives turnover comes from options rather than futures, and a quirk in how options turnover is calculated exaggerates the figure.

[12] Hedging is negligible in Indian derivatives markets because of extremely short contract tenors. Most contracts have tenors of 1 month or less, making them unsuitable as hedging instruments. Consequently, most derivatives trading is speculative.

[13] 'Monthly Statistics,' NSE, https://www.nseindia.com/report-detail/monthly-settlement-statistics. A corollary is that more than three-quarters of the daily cash figure of ₹39,000 crores comes from non-delivery turnover through day trading and scalping, which are wholly speculative activities.

For example, a deep 'out of the money' ₹8,00,000 call option contract might need as little as a ₹3 premium to purchase, but that ₹14,00,000 crore ADTO figure will include the trade at ₹8,00,000 and not at the ₹3 premium. More technically, deep 'out of the money' options that the public trades heavily are accounted for at notional face value in the turnover calculations, but the actual premia needed to trade them is negligible. As the market moves closer to monthly expiry, the ₹8,00,000 call option mentioned above will see its ₹3 premium fall to nothing, which makes it more attractive to speculators as a trading instrument. The resulting volume increases further exaggerate the effect of derivatives trading on market volumes.

One conservative solution is to only take into account the futures turnover and option premium when calculating the derivatives daily turnover, which leads to a derivatives ADTO figure of ₹92,843 crores in FY 2020.[14] After adding in the ₹39,000 crore cash ADTO figure, we get a total of ₹131,843 crores as the average daily market turnover across cash and derivatives segments. This would make the figure of ₹8,190 crores – which is actual delivery-based buying beyond a *single* trading session – just 6 per cent of the ADTO figure of ₹131,843 crores computed above. Finally, we can safely assume that technical traders, scalpers, and price action traders who buy and take delivery beyond a *single* session will square up in the near future after that – which is also speculation. If such parties take up half the ₹8,190 crore figure, then the daily investment grade buying drops to about ₹4,000 crores, which is about 3 per cent of the daily market turnover of ₹131,843 crores.

In turn, this implies that up to 97 per cent of daily market action would amount to speculation. This proportion is larger than the 80 to 90 per cent badla share in daily volumes that Morison had estimated in the 1930s. In a supreme historical irony, the reform era's introduction of derivatives to combat the market's speculative orientation has only served to increase it.

[14] Full-year derivatives turnover in FY 2020 (in ₹ crores): index futures 67,01,072; stock futures 1,49,19,551; index option premium 10,82,514; stock options premium 2,29,034. Figures are summed up and averaged over the 247 trading days of FY 2020. See https://www1.nseindia.com/products/content/derivatives/equities/historical_fo_bussinessgrowth.htm.

Evidently, going just by the numbers, speculation plays a vital role in the market's drama. This is partly because of the liquidity it provides to the order book. After all, if everybody bought and kept their shares locked away in their demat accounts, there would be no market. It is the constant buying and selling that makes for a continuous intertemporal market in securities which results in that most precious of outcomes – price discovery across time. Speculation allows fundies and other buy-side players to exist, and this it does by providing a certain thickness to the order book that allows them to accumulate or dispose of big stakes. Speculation's role in providing liquidity has been appreciated since the early days, and in fact, this role was seen by K.R.P. Shroff and M.R. Mayya as the sine qua non for badla's existence. Its role in the market has only increased over time, and its importance has doubled in today's market, built as that market is around an electronic limit order book (ELOB) with no specialists or market makers. In an order-driven market without specialists or market makers, the ELOB simply collects and aggregates orders, and it is speculation that allows for the thick order books needed in a functioning market.

So, one can avoid it or embrace it, but one must know about it because of its pervasive presence in the markets. Think of the activity as part of a spectrum of market possibilities. On the extreme left of the spectrum, write down the word 'speculation'. Here would be included: short-term trading for price action, focusing on small or popcorn stocks, anything to do with derivatives, putting all your capital in six or fewer stocks, trading for the fall (short selling), and borrowing to buy stocks (leveraging). On the extreme right of the spectrum, write down the word 'investment'. Here would be included: long-term buy and hold investing, emphasizing seasoned blue chips, running away at the sound of the word 'derivatives', holding a well-diversified folio of about 15 to 20 stocks (institutions hold many more), not trading for the fall (short selling), and never borrowing to buy stocks (leveraging).

Notice, however, that these are extremes, though many would say that in this case it pays to be a right-wing extremist and be on the spectrum's extreme right. Nonetheless, somewhere in the middle is a fascinating area on that spectrum of possibilities. Here takes place what, for want of a better term, we could call 'speculative investment'.[15] Though this is an unwieldy oxymoron and lacking in analytical precision or meaning, it will be used till its use is explained. Many of the dervishes of Dalal Street – the big independent traders – have made their fortunes in the spectrum's middle, which makes it interesting. That middle is also where the market's siren song is at its most seductive, and in fact, much of the activity that passes for investment in India's financial markets belongs to the spectrum's centre.

On the spectrum, notice also how there's no mention of an activity that carries symbolic import in Indian cultural imagination – gambling. Many Indians may not be good gamblers – confusing, as they often do, karma with the odds – but whether bazaar *satta* or another form of it, they have always loved to gamble, and it has been a social activity since ancient times. Excavations at the Harappan civilization sites dating from about 2000 BCE have yielded various types of dice.[16] From the later Vedic Age, around 1300 BCE, we come across the 'Gambler's Lament', one of the few non-religious hymns in the Rig Veda. This hymn on the psychology of the gambler is among the world's oldest literary pieces on games of chance, and the piece is remarkable because it stands out as a profane work in a sea of sacral verse, a testimony perhaps to the importance of the social pastime it described. Traders, especially those dealing in India's colossal derivatives markets, will be familiar with the sentiments of this passage:

> The gamester seeks the gambling-house, and wonders, his body all afire, Shall I be lucky?
>
> Still do the dice extend his eager longing, staking his gains against his adversary. (…)
>
> Downward they roll, and then spring quickly upward, and, handless, force the man with hands to serve them.

[15] 'Speculative investment' as an approach can also be identified with Gerald M. Loeb and his book *The Battle for Investment Survival*, Wiley Investment Classics, Hoboken, NJ: John Wiley and Sons, Inc., 2007; first published 1935. Loeb himself never used the term in his book.

[16] A.L. Basham, *The Wonder That Was India*, New York: The Macmillan Co., 1954, 37.

> Cast on the board, like lumps of magic charcoal, though cold
> themselves they burn the heart to ashes.[17]

Better known is the narrative in the Mahabharata epic which pivots around a game of dice. The good king Yudhisthira is felled by his indulgence in it, gambling all till he has nothing left to gamble away, almost like a futures trader in his death spiral who is borrowing to meet a margin call.

Gambling is an uncomfortable word. Yet, it is important to define precisely: it is a monetary wager on a game of chance and uncertain outcome, undertaken for pleasure and subject to the laws of probability. Gambling's what you would be doing if you went to Mahalaxmi, took on risk for the enjoyment of risk-taking, checked the tote, and bet on Mr Poonawalla's horses. On the spectrum, it lies even further left of 'speculation' and is not treated here.

Yet it was on this fault line between gambling and speculation that much of the state's early interactions with the market took place. In the colonial era, that interaction would alternate between paternalistic concern aimed at protecting the public from the evils of gambling and recognizing legitimate (but speculative) local market practices. Academic Ritu Birla, in her extensive work on the evolution of the state's attitude towards speculative markets in the colonial era, notes two distinct periods. In the first period, between 1880 and 1925, there was the criminalization and policing of bazaar trading. But the second period, between 1925 and 1947, was marked by recognition of the activity, followed by an attempt (via establishing contract law precedent) to co-opt it into established commercial procedures like risk mitigation and hedging.[18]

Much of the latter attitude would carry into the post-Independence era. But, as always, the flashpoint was over delivery of the underlying, whether stocks or a quintal of wheat or suchlike. Delivery or the

[17] *The Rig Veda*, trans. Ralph T.H. Griffith, 10.34.

[18] Ritu Birla, 'Speculation Illicit and Complicit: Contract, Uncertainty, and Governmentality,' *Comparative Studies of South Asia, Africa and the Middle East*, 35, (3), December 2015, 398–401.

intention to deliver, together with execution on a recognized exchange, legitimized the transaction as speculation; in their absence, the activity was a wager, or gambling.[19] The 'intention to deliver' was itself a legal fiction, necessary to legitimize the vast quantity of speculative badla trading that took place on the exchanges. The BSE's entire system of badla trading – essentially naked forward contracts where traders had the option to deliver – needed this 'intention to deliver' legal fiction to get classified legally as speculation rather than gambling.[20] Much Indian common law precedent would concern itself with these distinctions, but these were legal fine points that did not easily translate into public attitudes. As a result, the idea that the market is a gamble is still entrenched in the Indian public's imagination and unconscious mind, and much of that attitude was informed by the state's attitude to the fault line between gambling and speculation.

Now onto the left of that spectrum and its troubling nature. Depending on how much of an etymologist you are, the word speculation can carry different meanings. In its non-financial sense, it implies 'intelligent contemplation, consideration; an act of looking' from the French *speculation*; there is also the sense of 'close observation, rapt attention' which comes directly from the Latin *speculationem*. A related meaning is the 'pursuit of the truth by means of thinking', as in a philosopher's speculations. In Indian markets, it is often used to emphasize that the matter under discussion is conjecture or rumour, as when a company loudly proclaims that it does not comment on market speculation. As if there was any other type of conjecture in financial markets.

The word speculation, however, has a specialized meaning in the world of financial markets. *Speculation is decision-making exclusively*

[19] Influential case law from *Thacker v. Hardy* (1878) 4 QBD 685 would establish this view. Ibid., 397–98, 404.

[20] *Madhubhai Amathalal Gandhi v. The Union of India*, 1961 AIR 21; also 1961 SCR (1) 191, as summarized in Ritu Birla, 'Speculation Illicit and Complicit,' 404.

on the basis of price action, not dividend receipts or valuation, and using what you know to predict and act on a single future state of nature – the behaviour of price. The Phoenicians, the great traders of antiquity, kept a man with keen eyesight on the crow's nest of a fishing boat to see dark shoals of fish that stood out against the clear blue of the Aegean. The sophisticated speculator in financial markets tries to do something like that, spying the future with a keen eye and taking a position before that future arrives. Unlike horse racing bets, where risk is taken on for the pleasure of risk taking, speculation – at least among professionals who think about such matters – is willingly taking on risk assuming both a positive risk-return trade-off and a risk premium that justifies the risk taken.

The masters themselves defined the activity in a negative sense, which probably reflected their distaste of the process. In their definitive text *Security Analysis*, Graham and Dodd first defined investment and then negated that to define speculation. To them an investment operation was '… one which, upon thorough analysis, promises safety of principal and a satisfactory return. Operations not meeting these requirements are speculative'.[21] This and *not this* – therefore *that*. The approach is sometimes used in Indian spirituality, as in the works of Nisargadatta Maharaj. The continued negation 'not this, not this' or '*neti, neti*' might lead finally, when there is nothing left to negate, to *that* – an ultimate reality called Brahman.

From a business and real economy standpoint, all business activity has a speculative element to it, but the uncertainty of the activity, its speculative element, gets hidden behind the tangibles that go into setting up a business. To speculate in the real economy is to bring together people, materials, machines, and money in pursuit of a venture. So, it is also to see what no one can see and try to go where no one has gone. TISCO's beginnings in 1907 and that of Infosys in 1981 are famous examples in which the subsequent success of the companies as blue-

[21] Benjamin Graham and David Dodd, *Security Analysis*, 6th ed., New Delhi: Tata McGraw Hill, 106.

chip investments hid the essentially speculative nature of the venture. But do the many others like them – Indian Iron and Steel Company (IISCO), Silverline, and many more – who also set out in the storm and faltered and got left behind, count as speculations or investments?

From a market standpoint, speculation (or trading) is acting on future price action with no thought to valuations or dividend income. Its first and most crucial feature – particularly in retail-driven Indian markets – is the time frame. Anything bought for a turn, to be sold in a few days or weeks, is speculation; in some cases, the time frame compresses to a few hours, as in the popular pastime of day trading, but it is proper to exclude day trading as a gambling pastime that does not belong on the spectrum. A second feature of speculation concerns the instruments used, of which the two most common ones are: leverage (buying in excess of the capital on hand, usually through margin trading or taking on debt by borrowing to purchase stock) and derivatives (futures and options). Any trade that involves leverage or derivatives is properly speculation. A third feature is short selling or trading for the fall, which is also inherently speculative. A fourth (and underappreciated) feature is concentration – ignoring the benefits of diversification and concentrating folios in large positions is also highly speculative, but easily disguised. A fifth (and equally underappreciated) feature is quality – buying small-cap stocks in the obsession to find the next multi-bagger is also speculative, and in India, there is a large universe of over 2,000 stocks to indulge that obsession. Finally, it is not the precise definition of the act as much as the motivation behind it that matters; it is the unreasoned buying for the price turn without recognizing its consequences, the rush of blood to the head, that causes all the problems.

All combinations of the above features are easily facilitated in India's market, and this accounts for speculation's pervasiveness. Consider that leveraging folios (through the loans against shares product) and using the capital so raised to take positions in momentum-driven small stocks in the derivatives markets using one-month tenor contracts is surprisingly common in India's markets, and helpful intermediaries are always at hand to assist the participant who embarks on such a course (taking the short side in this combination brings into play all five speculative features mentioned above). Naturally, the stress involved rules out pleasure as a motive, so among large sections of the public in a poor and capital-scarce country like India, the dominant motive is not pleasure as much as the need to build up capital by taking on little understood risk.

In fact, among India's trading communities, speculation has often been seen as a necessary first step in the accumulation of capital.[22] Many of the great industrial houses have been built on capital generated from its successful practice, though many of those same houses are careful to airbrush it out of their histories. G.D. Birla, to take a noted example, accumulated considerable profits trading in jute during the First World War boom.[23] The sandbags that lined the trenches of the Western Front were made of jute that Dundee, Scotland, could not supply in large amounts; Calcutta stepped in, which precipitated a boom in jute prices that G.D. Birla traded in to make profits. Ramkrishna Dalmia reportedly enjoyed similar success in bullion.[24] But from an earlier generation, a young J.N. Tata was not so lucky, and he was almost wiped out by the undertow of the 1865 Cotton and Share Mania.[25]

More generally, much of the capital Marwaris utilized to take over British enterprises in later years came from trading in commodities during the First World War and its aftermath. Calcutta's European agency houses needed capital in the slump that followed the war's end, and many were financed through – and later taken over by – Marwari speculative profits; these arrangements, together with information networks in jute-growing areas, later facilitated the community's entry

[22] Ritu Birla, *Stages of Capital: Law, Culture, and Market Governance in Late Colonial India*, Durham, N.C.: Duke University Press, 2009, 152–54; Gijsbert Oonk, 'The Emergence of Indigenous Industrialists in Calcutta, Bombay, and Ahmedabad, 1850–1947,' *The Business History Review*, 88, (1), March 2014, 43–71; B.R. Tomlinson, 'Colonial Firms and the Decline of Colonialism,' 461–63.

[23] Medha Kudaisya, *The Life and Times of GD Birla*, New Delhi: Oxford University Press, 2003, 45; Aditi Roy Ghatak, *Down Lyons Range*, 49.

[24] Gurcharan Das, 'Introduction,' in Thomas A. Timberg, *The Marwaris: From Jagat Seth to the Birlas*, New Delhi: Penguin Books, 2014.

[25] F.R. Harris, *Jamsetji Nusserwanji Tata: A Chronicle of His Life*, London: Oxford University Press, 1925, 5–11.

into jute and other industries.[26] In other cases, the earlier trading outlook continued even after the move into industry.[27] Remarkably, even after making the transition to industry, many of Bombay's cotton industrialists continued to trade in raw cotton and persisted in using their mills as entities for both speculation and production.[28] As industrialists, they should have been content hedging cotton as an input to their production, but their trading origins saw them speculating in cotton as a commodity.

Speculation and trading can be a lot of fun, but they can also be dangerous to financial health. As the old adage goes: if you were to write biographies of Wall Streeters who speculated and made a fortune, they would fill a bookshelf, but if you were to write biographies of those who speculated, made and then lost a fortune, they would fill a library. Speculation must be attempted, if at all, only by professionals.

Yet most people in India's markets do it, and based on the above accounts, some would say that they have illustrious predecessors. Many do it without even knowing they're doing it. Most participants who buy for a turn don't even know they're speculating, because in their eyes, they're 'taking delivery' and holding for their 'price targets'. The simple fact that you can be taking delivery of the underlying shares and still be speculating – because of a variety of other inherent features such as the time frame, using the LAS product, or the unreasoned buying for the turn – is lost on many participants. Again, the earlier flashpoint between state and market on delivery may be responsible for this attitude – because not taking delivery in the old badla system was inherently speculative, taking delivery was somehow investment. For large sections of the public, there is considerable temptation to punt their way to a fortune using these easily available methods; with more people entering the markets every year through the demographic dividend, those sections must only be growing. Fee-based brokerage revenue streams are driven by getting the public to trade, which incentivizes the wire houses to

[26] Gijsbert Oonk, 'The Emergence of Indigenous Industrialists,' 46–51.

[27] For the argument that some houses found it difficult to overcome the mentality of the bazaar, see Harish Damodaran, 'The Marwari Business Model – I and II,' *The Hindu*, 7–8 April, 2013.

[28] Gijsbert Oonk, 'The Emergence of Indigenous Industrialists,' 56–59.

market speculation under the comfortable euphemism of 'trading'. Also, technical analysis (charting) has a vast following in Indian markets and that approach is inherently speculative. Finally, the NSE's derivatives segment is one of the world's biggest casinos, where most activity is speculative.

And yet, successful speculation places almost impossible demands on an individual's personal attributes – 'capital, courage, and judgment' were Philip Carret's three required qualities.[29] 'Self-reliance, judgment, courage, prudence, and pliability' were on Dickson Watts's list.[30] For Watts, having most of those qualities did not help as the qualities were required in toto – the absence of a single virtue was enough to cancel out the presence of the remaining qualities. Finally, remember all this is separate from the vast technical knowledge of the stock market and its listed companies that's also required to pull it off.

For those who still choose to do it, and in India that is a large section of the public, speculation is subject to certain clearly defined but little understood laws. Some of these laws were notably articulated by Watts in his book, *Speculation as a Fine Art and Thoughts on Life*. First, never leverage or buy in excess of the capital at hand. Second, accumulate your line on the way up but never on the way down – always average up and never average down. Third, never 'double up', meaning never reverse from buying to short selling if the original buy decision was wrong; demoralization and collapse can quickly follow if a streak of doubling up goes wrong. Fourth, cut your losses and let your profits run.[31] Finally, losses per trade should never exceed 2 to 3 per cent of the capital at risk; conservative traders will have even lower thresholds.

Of these, the fourth axiom – on cutting losses and letting those profits run – seems to be the most important. Taking a small loss is

[29] Philip Carret, *The Art of Speculation* Wiley Investment Classics, Hoboken, NJ: John Wiley and Sons, Inc., 1997, Preface. Philip Carret was an investor and founder (in 1928) of the Pioneer Fund.

[30] Dickson G. Watts, *Speculation as a Fine Art and Thoughts on Life*, Vermont: Fraser Publishing Company Edition, 1979, 8–9. Watts was a president of the New York Cotton Exchange in the late 19th century.

[31] Ibid., 10–11.

like putting a Band-Aid on a finger, but letting the loss grow would later mean wholesale amputation without anaesthetic. If losses are not cut, the combination of the above techniques together with the leverage guarantees a later amputation. The definition of a good trader is simply one who can cut his losses.

For experienced participants, one money management rule is to allot a small portion of the corpus to speculating with a 'funny money' account. From this, they can periodically skim away profits but *not* add capital to the account in case of losses; account drawdowns are then made whole again only through the trader's skill and future lucky streaks. For the rest, the following advice might come in handy: 'If you are ready to give up everything else – to study the whole history and background of the market and all the principal companies whose stocks are on the board as carefully as a medical student studies anatomy – if you can do all that, and, in addition, you have the cool nerves of a great gambler, the sixth sense of a kind of clairvoyant, and the courage of a lion, you have a ghost of a chance.'[32] That much-quoted counsel is from Bernard Baruch, one of Wall Street's great financiers and one of the few who made a fortune through speculation – and kept it.

The basic predicament is that financial markets in general open you up to the problem of induction. Deductive logic argues from the general to the particular and relies on syllogisms like: 'All people must die. X is a person. So, X must die.' The premises – major and minor – being definitive and a priori, the conclusion is cogent and true and follows by demonstration. By contrast, inductive logic argues from the particular to the general, with statements like: 'X sees a thousand swans. All thousand swans are white. So, all swans are white.' John Stuart Mill noted that for centuries humankind used inductive logic to argue that all swans were white – till in 1697 Willem de Vlamingh discovered in Australia, lo and behold, a black swan, and the logic was refuted. This leads to the problem of induction, most closely associated with David Hume.

[32] As quoted in Paul A. Samuelson and William D. Nordhaus, *Economics*, 13th ed., Singapore: McGraw Hill, 1989, 255.

Paraphrasing Hume, John Stuart Mill observed that: 'No amount of observations of white swans can allow the inference that all swans are white, but the observation of a single black swan is sufficient to refute that conclusion.' When we argue – and infer – from the particular to the general, the conclusion can go awry even though the premises are true. So, we can never be totally sure.

Notice also the similarity between Hume's swan statement and the following statement on stocks: 'X sees a hundred stocks. All hundred stocks go up on expectations of good results. So, X's stock, TCS, goes up on expectation of good results.' With this in mind, the participant puts on the trade and buys TCS for the rise on result expectations, and lo and behold something happens, and TCS falls instead of going up. In a small and everyday sort of way, through the exercise of custom and habit, the generalization from experience has got him. Nassim Taleb extends this idea to the analysis of extreme outlier events, and the human tendency to rationalize *ex post*, the causes behind such outliers.[33]

Speculation and trading are vulnerable to Hume's problem of induction. In some human activities – and the activity under discussion is surely one of them – a certain inductive skepticism is necessary. Yet every day, most traders face Hume's induction problem without even seeing it that way.

The middle of the spectrum has an area marked out as 'speculative investment'. For the highly skilled, it is here that the siren song of the Indian market is at its most seductive. In their salad days, many of the dervishes of Dalal Street made their fortunes by adapting some of the

[33] Taleb's concern with extreme events was apparent many years before he wrote his 2007 book, *The Black Swan: The Impact of the Highly Improbable*. See, for example, this comment on value at risk statistical techniques from his November 1996 interview with *Derivatives Strategy*: 'To me, VAR (value at risk) is charlatanism because it tries to estimate something it is not scientifically possible to estimate, namely the risk of rare events.' Joe Kolman, 'The World According to Nassim Taleb,' *Derivatives Strategy*, December/January 1997, 36–38.

principles of speculation to their investing activities. Today with age and size, a certain aura of respectability surrounds the dervishes, but many were big *satodia*s (speculators) in their younger days. The risk-taking was necessary to build up capital and their preferred method usually lay in fine – and lucky – judgments on the market cycle, rather than the business cycle. Early in their careers many had repeatedly caught the basic cycle by buying when there was panic and selling into mania. Their stock picking was also marked by the uncanny ability to pick fundamentally sound small stocks, following which concentrated positions were taken in them before the displacement became widely known. This activity was easier in the early days of the modern Indian stock market, when there was less efficiency. Finally, they used the leverage badla afforded to take concentrated positions in a few stocks. This sort of risk-taking through 'speculative investment' seems to have come naturally to the dervishes, and once settled on as an approach, it was remarkably easy to execute in the badla margin trading era that ended with the millennium.[34] Given the infamous volatility in the Indian environment, pulling it off could lead to substantial fortunes.

In today's times, fund managers who take sector or thematic bets ahead of the crowd – typically on changes in the business cycle, industry conditions, or government policy – are also practicing 'speculative investment' and operating in the middle of this spectrum. Sector rotation, for instance, refers to identifying and getting into promising sectors just before the market crowd enters and drives prices up; it is pervasive among diversified mutual funds as a bull move progresses. Other examples include buying a basket of housing finance companies in anticipation of government policies that favour affordable housing or lightening up on airline stocks because of unanticipated changes in oil prices.

Among seasoned participants, 'speculative investment' also manifests as the long pull trade with a holding period of a few months, though ideally for a little over 12 months to avoid the short-term capital gains

[34] Badla's easy margining, rollovers, and uncomplicated shorting requirements allowed for the implementation of speculative investment as an approach.

tax.[35] Many managers also give themselves the flexibility of timing the market by going into debt in large amounts, and this qualifies as part of the approach. Speculative investment is also pervasive in India's portfolio management services (PMS) industry, which thrives on the inability of clients to judge where they are on the spectrum between speculation and investment. The PMS industry is a fragmented part of the buy side where we see the most common manifestation of disguised speculative investment – concentrated small-stock portfolios that pay little heed to diversification. Factors that distinguish the activity from outright speculation include: the time frame, absence of leverage, and taking delivery. Critical also is casting a reasoned gaze into the immediate future in a chaotic and noisy environment, and in this sense, its essence is discriminating between reasoned fact and noise. Noise trading is a common technique in markets, but this is noise investing. In a highly inefficient market, it is best if participants think of themselves as part of a limited pool of trading capital that drives stocks up to fair value by incorporating information into price.

The approach is also heavily dependent on finding a suitable exit, and it helps if the participant, in keeping with efficient market theory, knows that fair value where it's all 'in the price'. This is a subjective call in a chaotic environment, and it explains the common complaint of many participants that they don't know when to sell.[36] The problem lies more with the approach of 'speculative investment' than with their selling skills, and the ubiquity of the complaint is due to the pervasiveness of the approach rather than any inherent lack of selling ability. Because speculative investment repeatedly forces participants to sell in the face of the market's long-term up swing, participants often see stocks rising after they have exited. Many participants thus live in regret, at least when they're not navel-gazing over their lack of selling skills.

Yet the approach of 'speculative investment' is not new. Its noted practitioner was the most distinguished economist of his age and

[35] The reimposition of a long-term capital gains tax has changed time frames.

[36] See interviews with Sanjoy Bhattacharyya and B.N. Manjunath in Saurabh Mukherjea, *Gurus of Chaos*, New Delhi: Bloomsbury Publishing India, 2015, 24, 156.

subsequent history would remember him as an economist who was also successful as a participant. But John Maynard Keynes was lots of things besides being an economist: Renaissance man, member of the Bloomsbury group, director of an insurance company, and a cofounder (with Harry Dexter White) of the Bretton Woods system that was to dominate global finance in the period after the Second World War. Keynes was also a notoriously good practitioner of 'speculative investment' and used his analogy of the beauty contest to make trades. As bursar at King's College in the University of Cambridge, Keynes accumulated a minor fortune for himself and his college, an achievement all the more remarkable as the Great Depression of the 1930s coincided with his investing lifetime. Early in his trading career, one mistake almost ruined him and led to a bailout by a wealthy admirer. But that blooper was on a currency trade.[37] His judgment on stocks was surer, and all he needed (or so the story went) were the morning newspapers and corporate annual reports. Following a close perusal of them, often read in bed with his tea, Keynes placed his orders with his brokers.[38] And that was that.

In a typical beauty contest only participants get a prize, but in a Keynesian beauty contest even the judges on the panel can get a prize, and that prize goes to the judge whose opinion most closely matches the winning opinion of the panel as a whole.[39] In the Keynesian contest, personal criteria of beauty are not important, and you don't select the face that you like, but instead guess at the face other people are most likely to fancy. In fact, this is what stock picking in trading and 'speculative investment' is all about. You don't pick the stocks that you fancy but choose instead what everybody else will finally fancy – because it is their buying that will drive prices higher. The problem arises when everybody thinks the same way. Then the game degenerates into guessing what the

[37] Robert Skidelsky, *Keynes: The Return of the Master*, New York: Public Affairs, 2010, 61–63.

[38] Charles Henry Hession, *John Maynard Keynes: A Personal Biography of the Man Who Revolutionized Capitalism and the Way We Live*, New York: Macmillan, 1984, 175.

[39] John Maynard Keynes, *The General Theory of Employment, Interest and Money*, London: Macmillan, 1936, 156–57.

average opinion of the average opinion is going to be. There are multiple equilibria in this unstable game.

Yet the Keynesian beauty contest remains an idea that is particularly applicable to Indian equity markets. It forces the participant to ask: 'Will someone buy this stock after me in sufficient quantity to ensure that it goes up?' For sophisticated participants, it is this instinctive tendency to keep an eye on the market crowd and what it will do next that distinguishes speculative investment from investing.[40] There is the recognition that it is only the follow-up buying – when the displacement occurs and the market crowd recognizes the displacement and takes the stock or sector higher – that makes the trade possible. The array of touts who appear on India's business channels to hustle their stock picks are in essence trying to generate that follow-up buying and bring about the displacement. The beauty contest is also relevant because liquidity is a perennial issue in Indian markets – recall the attempts of Roychand, Mehta, and Parekh to access the banking system capital to keep their moves going. Consider also the sheer range of the 5,000 stocks, about half of which are actively traded; available liquidity has to be spread over that large universe. All this in a country where large amounts of trading capital are sucked out by the colossal derivatives markets, and where a buy side is only now coming into its own.

In recent years, the liquidity distortions caused by Western quantitative easing have somewhat reduced the concerns on follow-up buying, but they will return. So, using the Keynesian beauty contest as an analogy forces the participant to ponder the special features of the selected counter from among those available. Has the participant picked one out of that large universe that will catch the fancy of others? Will the liquidity displacement in the counter be enough to take it up? Of course, the fundamentals matter, but who will buy even with the good fundamentals?

[40] 'At any point in time, an investor needs to understand what the market is focusing on. If you are focused on a specific idea or theme and the market is not willing to buy that theme, you will get the stock call completely wrong. The important thing is to know what the market is thinking.' Alroy Lobo of the Kotak Mahindra brokerage, as quoted in Saurabh Mukherjea, *Gurus of Chaos*, 68.

Now on to the right of that spectrum of market possibilities. That is investment, and it stands in contrast to the previous activity of speculation and its hybrids. In this chapter, we're concerned with investing as a process, particularly investment policy (the focus here is only on the marketable claims of equity and debt, but investment policy can include wider asset classes such as real estate, bullion, currencies, derivatives, international equities, or commodities). If formally practiced, investment policy usually involves some definitional clarity on risk, followed by the pursuit of a risk-return trade-off through three activities: asset allocation, security selection, and market timing. Other approaches to investment policy (not covered here) adapt the basic process outlined above by adjusting for individual needs, clientele effects, taxes, regulatory constraints, liquidity requests, and time horizons for exits. Finally, one option is not to have an investment policy by investing in an index fund that tracks a broad market index; but less than 5 per cent of buy side assets get managed this way in India, in contrast to, say, the US where as much as a third of industry assets is managed through passive indexing strategies. Active investing through a formal or informal investment policy is therefore the dominant approach in India, primarily because of substantial market inefficiency.

Specifically, investment policy builds on the following themes:

- Risk and Diversification: The idea that a diversified list of stocks protects investors from individual stock risk and leaves them free to decide how much actual systematic (or market) risk to take.
- Asset Allocation: The idea that a portfolio combining some proportion of risky assets (say stocks) and risk-free assets (say fixed deposits) on an efficient frontier is optimal and is the single biggest determinant of the returns an individual obtains. Factors such as life cycle, absolute wealth levels, and personal proclivity then combine to make an individual decide how much risk to take, which in turn

determines an optimal asset allocation between risky and risk-free securities.

- Security Selection: The idea that India's market, despite what the Efficient Market Hypothesis says, misprices stocks, implying that a portfolio manager can add value by identifying and picking such mispriced securities.
- Market Timing: The idea that the market (or a stock) goes through bull/bear phases, implying that a portfolio manager can exploit these phases by timing asset allocation or security selection.

Investment policy is a new field in an old market. Its basic insights, developed from what is known as Modern Portfolio Theory (MPT), were late in coming to the country and have been applied only since the turn of the millennium. Before that, the BSE's intransigence and UTI's monopoly in the fund space meant that even the generation of managers who trained in investment management at India's better business schools had little opportunity to apply its tenets in markets that hadn't changed much since the nineteenth century. The UTI's approach to investment policy in the early years is difficult to decipher from its statements and documents. Long viewed as the Finance Ministry's handmaiden, investment policy often boiled down to acting on that ministry's instructions to keep the markets propped up when required. Risk itself was not properly understood, and the UTI repeatedly paid the price for that. The other major player was LIC, but not much was (or is) publicly known about its investment policy, other than its contrarian bias.[41] The private sector's absence from asset management till the mid-1990s also contributed to the absence of formal approaches to investing. So, there was little attempt at investment policy by the Indian buy side until recently, and this is still the first generation of fund managers that has systematically thought about the subject.[42]

[41] 'Our total focus is on long-term investments... and we are contrarian investors traditionally,' then–LIC chairman V.K. Sharma, in 'LIC Books Rs19,000 Crore Profit from Market in FY17,' *Indian Express*, 17 May 2017.

[42] Saurabh Mukherjea, *Gurus of Chaos*, 160.

But first, that most important of four-letter words in buy side finance – risk. MPT's idea of risk dates to Harry Markowitz. We will later see why some noted practitioners such as Warren Buffett – following the precepts of his teacher Benjamin Graham – look at MPT's conception of risk with a certain agnosticism. Some of that doubt is justified, particularly in the Indian context, but we will also see why the formal treatment of risk as outlined in portfolio theory can generate insights for a market participant.

The basic idea of buy-side finance, the risk-return trade-off, develops through the work of Harry Markowitz, James Tobin, and William Sharpe. The idea on risk dates to Markowitz's 1952 doctoral thesis at the University of Chicago. Risk to Markowitz is the standard deviation of a stock price over time, or how much it moves around its average. Standard deviation is simply a measure of dispersion – it just shows how volatile a stock price is around its average, or mean.[43] Risk here is the chance that the expected return of a security will not happen, especially to the downside. The chances of disappointment to the downside increase the greater the volatility, and the volatility which causes that increased chance of disappointment is risk. Diversification is one way of dealing with this risk, and Markowitz proved it as such (other ways of dealing with risk are hedging and insurance).

One noted example concerns the stocks of a candy manufacturer and sugar plantation.[44] The candy manufacturer uses sugar as a basic raw material input and is highly exposed to sugar prices. An upward shift in sugar prices hurts the candy manufacturer, but it benefits a sugar plantation company for which sugar is the output. Combining risky assets such as these two stocks into a single portfolio led to an astonishing result that Markowitz showed mathematically – portfolio returns are the weighted average of individual stock expected returns, but

[43] Standard deviation is the square root of the sum of squared deviations from a mean.

[44] Through many editions, *Investments* by Zvi Bodie, Alex Kane, and Alan J. Marcus used the candy manufacturer/sugar plantation two-stock portfolio as the first example in its exposition of portfolio theory.

portfolio risk is *less* than the weighted average of individual stock risk.[45] In the above example, the returns on this two-stock portfolio are the average of the expected returns on the two stocks, but the portfolio's risk is less than the average risk of these two stocks. This is because portfolio risk is a function of the risk of the portfolio's constituent assets *and* the extent to which those risks vary in relation to one another (covariance). In this example, the candy manufacturer and sugar plantation carry extreme negative covariance with each other, which is beneficial when they combine as a portfolio. Finding and combining stocks that carry negative covariance (or negative correlation coefficients) with each other reduces the portfolio's risk without affecting its return, and this risk reduction through diversification is one of the few free lunches in finance.

In fact, stocks don't even need to have negative correlations for diversification to work; as long as correlations are less than perfectly positive, diversification will carry benefits and reduce risk. The risk associated with individual stocks cancels out in a portfolio, so an efficient portfolio of, say, 50 securities, should eliminate individual stock risk and leave the holder with the highest return per unit of risk taken.[46] Much of Markowitz's efforts focused on the mathematics of proving all this through a technique called mean variance optimization (MVO), which resulted in an efficient frontier of portfolios with optimum returns per unit of risk taken (the Markowitz bullet).[47] In India, this formal process of optimization is not done, so for practical purposes, a well-diversified all-equity fund can be taken as an efficient portfolio. For centuries, people have understood risk to mean aphorisms like, 'Don't put all your eggs in one basket'; Markowitz provided a formal proof.

James Tobin at Yale developed the idea further, and his seminal breakthrough introduced the idea of a risk-free asset that Markowitz

[45] Harry M. Markowitz, 'Portfolio Selection,' *Journal of Finance*, 7 (1), March 1952, 77–91, together with related work published in 1959 and 1970.

[46] Some studies show that individual investors obtain adequate diversification benefits from as few as 15 stocks. Institutional investors – facing compliance issues on concentrating portfolios or liquidity constraints on entering and exiting counters – will hold many more stocks in their portfolios.

[47] Portfolio efficiency is different from the concept of market efficiency discussed earlier.

had ignored.[48] In fact, in India's financial markets and the advisory business, much of the practical day-to-day application of portfolio theory comes – in the main – from Tobin's contribution to the field. Introducing the risk-free asset (for simplicity, taken here to mean a bank fixed deposit) to the Markowitz mix of only risky assets (such as stocks) produced interesting effects and resulted in the separation theorem, one of a series of such separation theorems in finance. Assuming a universe of risky and risk-free assets similar to what most people face, optimal portfolio choice depended on some allocation between a risky (but efficient) portfolio of assets and the risk-free asset. The ratio of risky assets to one another was irrelevant if the risky portfolio itself was efficiently constructed. So, changing an individual's risk exposure involved changing the proportion of risky assets (stocks) relative to risk-free assets (fixed deposits), rather than changing the proportions of risky assets (stocks) relative to one another; what matters in determining risk is the ratio between the risky and risk-free assets.

So, now we get the idea that the investment process or investment policy can be separated into two distinct steps: First, the construction of an efficient portfolio as described by Markowitz, which technically is a mathematical outcome of mean variance optimization that is irrelevant to risk preference; and second, the decision to combine that efficient portfolio with a risk-free asset, such as a bank deposit. The optimal allocation between the efficient portfolio and the risk-free asset depends on investor preference towards risk, and it is this and only this allocation that decides the risk an individual bears.[49] As Tobin saw it: 'You would choose the same portfolio of non-safe assets regardless of how risk-averse you were. Even if you wanted to change the amount of risk in the

[48] James Tobin, 'Liquidity Preference as Behavior Towards Risk,' *Review of Economic Studies*, Vol. 25, No. 2, February 1958, 65–86.

[49] More technically, the graphical solution to all this is the point of tangency between a capital allocation line depicting all risk–return combinations available to investors, and a hyperbolic investment opportunity set that is mean variance efficient. This optimal portfolio is then combined with the risk-free asset, and the combinations depend on an individual's degree of risk aversion. If all investors are mean variance optimizers with homogenous expectations, this optimal portfolio is the market portfolio itself. *Investments* by Zvi Bodie, Alex Kane, and Alan J. Marcus provides a detailed treatment.

portfolio, you'd do it by changing the amount of the safe assets, relative to the nonsafe assets but *not* by changing the different proportions in which you held the nonsafe assets relative to each other.'[50]

Tobin's great result – discovered incidentally when he was trying to estimate a demand function for money based as much on portfolio choice as on money's transactional importance – also provided the conceptual reason behind a mutual fund's existence, and a variant of the separation result is also called the mutual fund theorem. Before Tobin's insight, the alternative would be to tailor individual portfolios for each client based on the client's attitude towards risk or liquidity preference, which is tedious and near impossible for a mutual fund with thousands of clients. But now it was possible for fund managers to devote all their energy only to the technical task of putting together and managing an efficient portfolio like a well-diversified equity fund. Fund managers could construct such efficient portfolios and once they did so, their task was pretty much done, leaving the individual client to decide their optimum risk level. After that, depending on an individual's risk preference and liquidity needs, combining that efficient portfolio of stocks (the risky asset) with, say, a bank deposit (the risk-free asset), led to the actual risk an individual would take. The risk-averse might take 50:50 as the ratio of stocks to fixed deposits, while the more venturesome who could take more risk would choose, say, 75:25 as the ratio of stocks to fixed deposits and so on.[51]

Extreme risk-taking individuals such as the dervishes of Dalal Street – the big professional traders – might have 100:0 as the ratio of stocks to fixed deposits, and in fact, most dervishes' portfolios had proportions that came close to that ratio. If that hazard was not extreme enough, leveraging or borrowing to buy stocks on margin was also possible, and with this activity, we approach the extreme end of the risk-taking

[50] David Fettig, 'Interview with James Tobin,' *The Region*, Federal Reserve Bank of Minneapolis, 1 December 1996.

[51] More technically, modelling risk with a standard risk utility function and a coefficient of risk aversion can lead to more precise allocations, but this is never done and some sort of estimated allocation suffices for most people.

spectrum. But is it possible to imagine risk-taking even beyond buying stocks on margin? In fact, for many years the BSE badla system – where participants traded for the marked to market difference in unmargined naked forwards that had embedded options – operated even beyond the extreme end of the risk-taking spectrum. Later, margins were introduced but that only somewhat reduced the high levels of risk.[52] So many of the dervishes of Dalal Street – who went beyond even the riskiness of all-stock portfolios when making their fortunes on the badla trading system – were essentially the survivors of a high-risk game where luck and skill combined in equal measure. Because badla deliberately operated at the extreme end of the risk-taking spectrum, entire generations of the Indian public saw the market as a dangerous and risky place. Yet, as portfolio theory would tell you, the market was not inherently dangerous or risky; it was the proportion of your exposure to the market through an efficient portfolio that really mattered, and it was this proportion, rather than the types of stocks in the efficient portfolio, that determined risk. The earlier aphorism had been, 'Don't put all your eggs in one basket'; but after Tobin's work a better dictum would be: 'Regardless of your degree of risk aversion and caution, you will only need two baskets for all your eggs.'[53]

So, Tobin's result is also the conceptual source of the basic allocation decision between the baskets of equity (the risky asset) and high-quality debt or its equivalents (the risk-free asset), which dominates the day-to-day decision-making of financial advisors. (Technically, cash also belongs in the mix, but for most individuals, having about three to four months' living expenses as cash suffices, leaving the rest to be allocated.) His ideas – as seen in that commonly advised 75:25 equity to debt mix – have become the equivalent of sliced bread to the mutual fund and financial advisory industry. Just as everyone uses sliced bread daily without knowing who invented it, financial advisors and

[52] Badla's unmargined naked forward contracts required negligible capital to initiate and offered leverage whose risk was routinely underestimated by the average trader.

[53] Willem H. Buiter, 'James Tobin: An Appreciation of His Contribution to Economics,' *NBER Working Paper* No. 9753, June 2003, 3, at http://www.nber.org/papers/w9753.

managers routinely use Tobin's ideas without acknowledging him as their source.

The above example can be developed further if you go into the bells and whistles of financial advisory work. The 75 risky asset allocation can be broken down further into, say, 3 equal allocations of 25 each to domestic large-cap stocks, small-cap stocks, and gold, while retaining the original 25 that went into the fixed deposit (the risk-free asset). Then you're getting into the nitty-gritty of fund management and advisory work, which involves asset allocation to new classes such as real estate, bullion, currencies, derivatives, international equities, or commodities. In such cases, what matters are the relationships (or covariances) among asset classes, rather than the relationships (or covariances) among individual stocks.

In some countries, private markets such as hedge funds, private equity, and natural resources (like timber forests or oil fields) also get categorized as asset classes, and it is in these alternative asset classes where market inefficiencies, networking, and the ability to pick savvy managers can yield substantial results. Many of these private markets are highly illiquid, but for some investors – and especially those with long horizons who reject the earlier approach as formulaic – that illiquidity can become an underpriced virtue. Among such investors, David F. Swensen of Yale's Investment Office was a pioneer in generating superior returns through this emphasis on alternative private markets, and now there are other institutions with similar approaches.[54] Sometimes even paintings, stamps, racehorses, wine, and vintage cars get touted as asset classes, almost always entering the asset mix after they have had a substantial run-up in price. These are investments with high non-pecuniary value and heterogenous (or non-homogenous) expectations;[55] in such cases, collector and connoisseur interest combines with the desire for financial gain, but the latter is always kept politely in the background.

[54] David F. Swensen, *Pioneering Portfolio Management: An Unconventional Approach to Institutional Investment,* Fully Revised and Updated, Florence, MA: Free Press, 2009.

[55] In MPT, homogeneous expectations implies that investors are rational actors and that all investors have the same expectations, preferences, and decision-making criteria. Alternate asset classes, like racehorses or stamps, bring out heterogenous (different) investor expectations and preferences.

The generalization of the Markowitz–Tobin results to the demand side of an asset pricing model happened through Stanford's William Sharpe and others. Sharpe, together with John Lintner, Jan Mossin, and Jack Treynor, built on the earlier work to develop the Capital Asset Pricing Model (CAPM), a cornerstone of modern finance for the pricing of financial assets in equilibrium.[56] Our focus here is on the model's insights for investment policy, but it has wider applications in areas such as corporate finance, where it is used to determine the cost of capital or hurdle rates for investment, among other applications. Yet this move to the CAPM is a big leap in emerging markets, and its central ideas are not really practiced in India, especially with regard to our concern – investment policy. Nevertheless, generalizing to the CAPM leads to one standard classification of risk into 'systematic' and 'unsystematic' risk, which generates insights for the participant.

Markowitz and Tobin had mainly focused on risk inherent to a stock (or unsystematic risk) and how that risk (defined as variance or volatility) could be eliminated. If a portfolio manager does the job right and combines stocks in an efficient portfolio, this unsystematic risk gets diversified away. What remains then is systematic risk (or market risk), and this is the risk of being in the market in the first place; this risk cannot be diversified away and has to be assumed by an individual. After unsystematic risk has been diversified away in an efficient portfolio, it leaves the participant free to decide how much systematic risk to really

[56] The single-factor CAPM is developed in William F. Sharpe, 'Capital Asset Prices: A Theory of Market Equilibrium under Conditions of Risk,' *Journal of Finance*, 19 (3), 1964, 425–42; John Lintner, 'The Valuation of Risk Assets and the Selection of Risky Investments in Stock Portfolios and Capital Budgets,' *Review of Economics and Statistics*, 47 (1), 1965, 13–37; Jan Mossin, 'Equilibrium in a Capital Asset Market,' *Econometrica*, 34 (4), 1966, 768–83; and Jack Treynor, 'Toward a Theory of Market Value of Risky Assets,' Unpublished Manuscript, Fall 1962. Subsequent extensions – in the wide-ranging literature of asset pricing – include multifactor approaches which seek to find other factors (besides the market) that can act as proxies for systematic risk. Among these are the three-factor models of Eugene Fama and Kenneth French, where besides the market, size and value are also introduced as factors. Mark Carhart adds to the Fama–French model by introducing momentum as a fourth factor. Arbitrage Pricing Theory, as developed by Stephen A. Ross, introduces arbitrage-based arguments – as opposed to the CAPM, which uses dominance arguments – and generalizes to multiple factors, including unanticipated changes to macroeconomic variables like inflation and interest rates.

take. So, the market, as the CAPM points out, rewards you for taking on this systematic risk.

What matters then is the insight that you simply need to take on more of that systematic risk to earn a higher return, which leads us to one version of the risk-return trade-off. One measure of systematic risk is beta, the standardized covariance of a stock with the market. Stocks with a beta of 1 will rise 8 per cent with an 8 per cent rise in the market. Stocks with, say, a beta of 1.5 will rise 12 per cent for the same market rise. Since such stocks are riskier than a market portfolio, they command a higher expected return, and so, the CAPM posits a linear relationship between a stock's beta and its expected return. Beta, technically a measure of how much a stock contributes to a portfolio's risk, is sometimes recklessly used in India's speculative markets as a trading tool; financial advisors occasionally suggest buying high-beta stocks coming out of a market downswing, in the hope that they will move more than the market when that market itself moves to the upside.

Though investment policy is practiced by the buy side in India, the lessons are internalized through heuristics or thumb rules, rather than through the formal process of optimization suggested by Modern Portfolio Theory. If followed by institutions, that formal optimization would entail: a) specifying return parameters of all securities, including their expected returns, variances, and covariances, and b) using an optimizer software package such as Morningstar® EnCorr®, which minimizes the tedious computations necessary to arrive at an efficient portfolio of stocks. Finally, at the individual (or client) level, the third step would involve: c) allocating some fraction based on risk preference between the risky efficient portfolio arrived at in the first two steps and a risk-free asset like a fixed deposit.

At a practical level, extensive paraphernalia is needed to make it all work. That apparatus would include input lists of estimates (ideally forward-looking rather than historical) for parameters such as expected returns, covariances, and correlation coefficients – calculated for all exchange-listed stocks – which would then run on computer-driven optimizers to produce lists of efficient portfolios. Much of this input list does not exist in the Indian market, so there is little question of formal mean variance optimization (MVO).[57]

The technical part of portfolio theory is not implemented because of the lack of inputs, but its lessons on efficient diversification are still applied through a combination of heuristics like Talmudic (or naïve) diversification and judgment. Talmudic diversification refers to the Talmud's exhortation to divide assets in thirds between the available choices of land, one's own business, and the liquidity need of keeping some amount ready at hand.[58] Essentially Talmudic diversification is a choice heuristic, where a menu of 'N' choices leads to 1/N asset allocation. This does not make sense when confronted with a 5,000-stock universe and would result in a highly fragmented portfolio with 1/5,000 in each stock. But recall that from these 5,000 stocks (of which about half are traded at any given point in time), the actual investible universe that compliance regulations and liquidity constraints allow fund managers to enter is seen as much smaller – perhaps as few as 200 to 300 stocks. Experience and further security analysis might reduce this to about 60 or 70 stocks, following which building a portfolio of N = 70 stocks should lead to about 1/70 in each and is not such a stretch. In practice, Talmudic diversification combines with judgment, which is then used to increase allocations to sectors (or themes) based on belief systems of fund managers.[59] Stock picking then follows and stocks with higher expected returns (ergo with better valuations) in promising sectors or themes get slightly larger weightings. The focus is only on expected returns; risk – and inferentially any trade-off between risk and return –

[57] Even if parameters existed, the model's output is sensitive to errors in parameter estimates, and particularly on expected returns. Other multifactor models, such as those of Fama and French or Carhart, don't use constrained optimization techniques while making their predictions.

[58] The Talmud is a central text of Rabbinic Judaism that deals with secular and religious law, together with commentaries.

[59] For an array of fund manager interviews confirming the above, see 'BFSI and Financial Advisors Interviews,' *Advisorkhoj*, accessed 15 May 2018, https://www.advisorkhoj.com/interviews?pageid=1.

is never explicitly addressed. The implicit assumption is that with adequate stocks in the portfolio, unsystematic stock-specific risk gets diversified away, but whether that diversification is efficient is never overtly addressed in India.

Talmudic diversification is practiced especially at the financial advisory level, and you can have financial advisors practicing it who'll hand over money to portfolio managers, who also in turn practice it. So, the overall impression is that the technical part of Modern Portfolio Theory is not followed, but its lessons on diversification are disseminating and getting into the market's DNA.

Even if the apparatus to make MPT work had existed in India, market inefficiency and the buy side's tradition of stock picking would render superfluous some of its ideas. Even if done right, the mathematical computation of efficient portfolios using standardized inputs would become a formulaic exercise across the mutual fund industry, and the realization that it is only stock picking which generates alpha (or excess return) would remain. Estimation errors on the complex input list might also produce swings in portfolio weights that would render optimization unreliable, even when compared to the simple naïve diversification rule. So, among the buy side, the overwhelming impression is of stock pickers who see alpha generation through security selection and timing as the only source of their value as fund managers.[60] More technically, after practicing naïve diversification, the Indian mutual fund industry ends up hoping it's on the Pareto optimal efficient frontier – the Markowitz bullet – and not inside it. Diversification might be suboptimal with this approach, and there may be portfolios out there that offer similar returns with lower risk (variability). Alternately, there may be portfolios out there that offer higher returns with similar risk levels, but nobody's gone actively looking for either type.

The reason behind this indifference is to be found in the definition and treatment of risk. Risk to Markowitz is volatility, or how much a stock moves around an average, and this treatment later segues into the standard

[60] Saurabh Mukherjea, *Gurus of Chaos*, 67–70.

distinction between systematic (market) risk and non-systematic (stock-specific) risk. Some participants might turn around and say: '*What's the big deal in all this*?' What about the most important risk of all – the risk of overpaying? Valuation risk, the price risk of overpaying for value, is what comes through again and again in discussions with the buy side in India and is the origin of the well-known stock market saying '*Bhav Bhagwan Che*' or 'Price is God'. Risk sometimes gets broken down into other components like business risk or promoter risk, but it is valuation (or price) risk that dominates discussions.[61] This is a corollary of looking for value through stock picking in an inefficient market. If finding value through stock picking is the basis for investment policy – and indeed for all investment decision-making – then overpaying for value must be the basis for all risk. This is the risk of Graham and not the risk of Markowitz, but more on that later.

Discussions with fund managers confirm the same. Publicly available interviews are dominated by discussions of the market cycle and its stages, entry or exit based on valuations, sector or theme rotation, where the market crowd is headed next, where fund flows will come from, and so on.[62] Cyclical approaches to the market – still used worldwide – are doubly emphasized in India, and this is not surprising. Indian civilization's approach to history is itself cyclical rather than linear, based on a world view that sees time as a series of 'endless cycles of creation and reabsorption into the divine, a picture of the cosmos that predicated a cyclic and not a linear history'.[63] In the Hindu view of time, cycles of *yugas* (an age of time) were contained within cycles of *mahayugas*, which in turn were within larger cycles of *manvantaras*, many of which were within a *kalpa*, which was a day of Brahma that extended a mere 4.3 billion earthly years. Yet that was only a half, as there was a night of Brahma of the same 4.3-billion-year duration. 360 such cycles of days and nights made up a year of Brahma, and Brahma went on for a hundred years.

[61] Ibid., 155.

[62] 'BFSI and Financial Advisors Interviews,' *Advisorkhoj*.

[63] J.M. Roberts and Odd Arne Westad, *The Penguin History of the World*, 6th ed., London: Penguin Books, 2013, 310.

Emphasizing cyclical approaches to the market would be a natural corollary of this vast and all-encompassing world view. It is common for veterans to advise novices that the latter need to live through a few market cycles to build understanding and rare is the fund manager interview that does not use the word 'cycle' many times. Typically, leading economic indicators (LEIs) and interest rates are key inputs used by an investor in assessing a market cycle, but in India, the absence of LEIs and the second-order effects of interest rates from uncertain monetary transmission make such an assessment difficult. Even if the data were available, it would imply successfully analysing both a business cycle and a market cycle, which is subjective and prone to chance. Consequently, the cycle is usually interpreted through the familiar expansion and contraction of the Sensex or Nifty's PE ratio. But noise intrudes on the analysis, and interviews with fund managers, who seek their assessment on the above issues, revolve in large part around discussions of macroeconomic or sectoral noise.[64]

Notice also that the market in India is first and foremost a crowd, and yet there is little mention of the crowd in portfolio theory's precise discussion of standard deviations and optimizations. So, the singular feature of the crowd – the howling madness at the heart of it all – is missing in Modern Portfolio Theory. Portfolio theory is all mathematical and logical and different from the experience of most participants of being contrarian and '*chipkaoing*' (sticking) it to the public at the great market tops or loading up at market lows and so on. The effort put into anticipating what themes the crowd will get into – effort that takes up so much of participants' energy and that is indicative of 'speculative investment' as an approach – is also missing in portfolio theory's discussion of investment policy. In fact, it is the crowd's absence in portfolio theory's framework that has led to the reaction from behavioural finance, an alternate paradigm of recent years.

Accordingly, in India, there are few decisions based on an expected return/variance process, at least as defined in portfolio theory. One

[64] 'BFSI and Financial Advisors Interviews,' *Advisorkhoj*.

obvious temptation then is to sex up the portfolio by concentrating it excessively in a few sectors or stocks, thereby taking on more risk;[65] the resulting outperformance then seems due to superior stock-picking skill, but in reality, it is just compensation for the greater risk taken.[66] Lacking the insights and inputs to construct efficient portfolios, much of the portfolio management services segment runs around trying to figure out the precise number of stocks that offer the optimum trade-off between risk and return. Funds that invest in small or mid-caps and the PMS segment are especially prone to being selected for absolute returns rather than on a risk-return trade-off. In fact, one could argue that the entire Indian buy side is an absolute return equity shop with no concept of risk-adjusted returns and little analytical apparatus to adjust for risk. Consequently, style and theme drift – as, for example, when a diversified equity fund starts morphing into a mid-cap fund – was a common trend, till recent changes in mutual fund regulations attempted to put an end to it.[67]

Market timing is explicitly frowned upon but often tried. Mutual funds typically give themselves the option of going heavily into the risk-free asset, in effect retaining the flexibility to time the market.[68] Many fund prospectuses allow for 'dynamic' asset allocation even in all-equity funds that are supposed to be fully invested; in such cases, market timing is done by going to debt levels that can be as high as 35 per cent.[69] These attempts at timing – like those at concentration – are an upshot of the cohabitation of investing and speculative temperaments, and may be seen as efforts to replicate the 'speculative investment' that

[65] Saurabh Mukherjea, *Gurus of Chaos*, 69–70.

[66] Tracking error studies that might pick up such activity are rarely done for the buy side.

[67] SEBI circulars SEBI/HO/IMD/DF3/CIR/P/2017/114 and 126 of 2017 categorized schemes into equity, debt, hybrid, solution-oriented, and other schemes. Many of the equity-related changes were concerned with anchoring at least 65 per cent of the scheme's assets in the category for which the scheme was marketed.

[68] Saurabh Mukherjea, *Gurus of Chaos*, 106.

[69] Mutual fund investment policy was also driven by regulatory changes. For example, in 2018 SEBI introduced new rules that forced mutual funds to reclassify their schemes as per 36 categories that SEBI had laid out. Kayezad E. Adajania, 'What Should You Do If Your Fund Gets a New Name and Strategy,' *Mint*, 1 May 2018.

made the dervishes' fortunes. Nevertheless, these timing attempts raise issues for investment policy at the client level which have not been thought through. Worldwide, mutual funds do a lousy job of timing the market, and Indian funds are no exception, so some might view such timing attempts as questionable.[70] A 70:30 asset allocation to stocks at the client level will not make much sense if the 70 allocation goes into an all-equity mutual fund that gives its fund manager discretion to exit a big chunk of the portfolio. Such moves leave the client at the mercy of the fund manager's timing ability and confuse – in fact, render irrelevant – the client's own asset allocation. In riposte, mutual funds might argue that asset allocation is better done at their level, rather than at the level of an emerging advisory profession that is yet to find its feet.

International diversification – MPT's big contribution to risk reduction – is also ignored in India, and domestic bias is pervasive.[71] Consider, for example, that shifts in the international terms of trade have widely divergent effects on stock markets worldwide. Sudden oil price rises – a negative terms of trade shock – adversely impact India, which imports almost 85 per cent of its oil, but would benefit oil exporters like Russia, Saudi Arabia, or Indonesia; a portfolio of Indian stocks that also included those countries' equities should convey considerable diversification benefits, effectively eliminating exposure to oil as a risk factor, and this is just one obvious example. Consider also that Indian companies have a much smaller percentage of their turnovers and profits coming from international operations. American shareholders in Apple or German shareholders in Siemens indirectly obtain the benefits of global diversification from the large profits these companies derive from their international operations. By contrast, Indian shareholders don't get much of this indirect exposure as global operations account

[70] Most studies find little evidence of market timing skills. For one recent example that uses monthly data for 80 mutual funds between 2000 and 2012, see Joyjit Dhar and Kumarjit Mandal, 'Market Timing Abilities of Indian Mutual Fund Managers: An Empirical Analysis,' *Decision*, 41 (3), September 2014, 299–311.

[71] Burton Malkiel, *A Random Walk down Wall Street*, 11th ed., New York: WW Norton, 2015, 201–08.

for a much lower share of Indian companies' turnover or profits; so, to local shareholders, the benefits of international diversification would be greater. Finally, the secular long-term depreciation in the rupee-dollar pair would work in favour of domestic investors; giving up, say, ₹45 in 2010 to buy a dollar of stock in international markets, would have led to receiving ₹80 in 2022 for every dollar of the same stock sold, and this is before any price appreciation on the foreign stock.[72]

Yet capital market segmentation that cut the country off from international markets was both de jure and de facto from Independence till the liberalization program in 1991. With liberalization, de jure autarky and segmentation have reduced but continue in muddled form, while there is still de facto segmentation with domestic bias in investment policy. In fact, as the Rate Bull account pointed out, domestic bias is so pervasive that even viewing it as bias seems eccentric. The complete absence of global diversification in most portfolios is almost bizarre and yet understandable. Global diversification has benefits, but hazy regulatory and tax compliance issues, a cultural predisposition towards the home market, fund managers with no competence or experience in international investing, and a narrow, inward-looking *kupamanduka* mindset condemn the Indian buy side to the local market. Constraints on foreign investing are not numerical as much as cultural, for by 2020, RBI rules allowed up to $250,000 to be invested annually outside India.[73] With globalization, correlation coefficients among markets have risen, somewhat reducing the benefits of diversification, but they are still significant. Further, overseas investing – if widely practiced by India's now sizable investing population – would also lessen the need for the RBI to intervene and sterilize foreign inflows. So, the stock market,

[72] Pegged at about ₹4.77 to the dollar for much of the Bretton Woods system of fixed rates, the rupee has been on a managed float regime since the end of the Bretton Woods system in 1971. The rupee was trading at ₹80 in 2022.

[73] Under the RBI's Liberalised Remittance Scheme (LRS), individuals (including minors) can invest up to $250,000 per fiscal year (or $1 million for a 4-person family) in current or capital account transactions. As usual, the relaxation was subject to a limitation – in this case, limits of $300 million per fund house (subsequently doubled) and $7 billion for the domestic mutual fund industry.

in its studied ignorance of portfolio theory, was also ignoring one of its biggest lessons. India's $2.5 trillion market was less than 3 per cent of world equity capitalization, but almost 100 per cent of all portfolios were invested in the country's equity markets.[74] Global investing, just a logical corollary in the next step of capital market development, is often seen as vaguely disreputable, and the little that takes place is usually through modifying allocations of existing diversified funds rather than through introducing specific fund offerings. Perhaps – and in line with efficiency arguments – pointing out this situation might lead to its correction in future, but for the present, the overwhelming tendency is to think in terms of domestic stocks rather than global asset classes.

Finally, work is required on some issues that get raised from such concepts. For example, few studies exist on the percentage of portfolio returns that can be attributed to asset allocation. Studies in the West have found that as much as 90 per cent of a folio's returns can be attributed to asset allocation, but such studies have not been conducted here.[75] Similarly, research also suggests that naïve diversification (as widely practiced here) may not be all that naïve, implying that there isn't much difference in risk levels between folios constructed through such naïve diversification and folios constructed through Markowitz-style mean variance optimization, but research is yet to be conducted on this central aspect of Indian fund management.[76]

Hence, in India, the basic lessons on diversification and portfolio theory have been internalized but without the formal optimization

[74] In January 2020, India's $2.14 trillion market capitalization accounted for about 2.4 per cent of world equity capitalization of $85 trillion.

[75] For one early study that established the primacy of asset allocation in portfolio performance, see Gary P. Brinson, L. Randolph Hood, and Gilbert L. Beebower, 'Determinants of Portfolio Performance,' *Financial Analysts Journal*, July–August 1986, 39–44.

[76] Victor DeMiguel, Lorenzo Garlappi, and Raman Uppal, 'Optimal versus Naive Diversification: How Inefficient Is the 1/N Portfolio Strategy?' *Review of Financial Studies* 22 (5), 2007, 1915–53. In fact, Harry Markowitz himself practiced naïve diversification for his personal investing by equally dividing his investments between the risky and risk-free buckets with occasional rebalancing and leaving it at that. 'I visualized my grief if the stock market went way up and I wasn't in it – or if it went way down and I was completely in it. So I split my contributions 50/50 between stocks and bonds,' Harry Markowitz (as quoted by Jason Zweig) in Jason Zweig, 'Investing Experts Urge "Do as I Say, Not as I Do",' *Wall Street Journal*, 3 January 2009.

process that can lead to greater efficiency. These lessons also get adapted – as they must – to the mores of a speculative market, resulting in a hybrid approach to investment policy. And yet, every year it seems that the market gets more investment-oriented in its approach. The spread of the mutual fund product through the SIP and the recent creation of a pension fund industry have also contributed to the popularity of investment as an approach. Against this must be balanced that tradition of two centuries in financial trading and speculation, itself a minor span of time compared to the millennia reaching back to the Rig Veda and its *Gambler's Lament*. Consider also the steady stream of fresh faces entering the markets every year through the demographic dividend, gamesters seeking the markets with their bodies 'all afire' and their minds saying 'Shall I be lucky?', a new generation waiting to learn the lessons of the old, a new breed of traders trying to trade their way to a fortune. With each cycle, the market learns a little more and changes a little less.

11

TRADE SELECTION

Technicals and Fundamentals

The dominant approaches of speculation and investment lead on to two types of trade selection, namely technical and fundamental analysis. All other things equal, technical analysis is more speculative, while fundamental analysis should lead to a more investment-oriented approach to the markets.

Technical analysis is the study of past price and volume action – as depicted in a chart – for clues on future price action. *Fundamental analysis* uses relative valuation approaches through the price-earnings (PE) ratio or absolute valuation approaches through discounted cash flows to arrive at the value of a stock. Of these, the *PE ratio*, a heuristic that values stocks based on a ratio of current market price to earnings (or profits) per share, is an approach that most participants tend to use in India. The second model based on *discounted cash flows* is analytically rigorous and places heavy demands on the analyst; it can produce such imprecise results for publicly traded equities, despite the formidable calculations involved, that it has to be used with care. Fundamental analysis also refers to stock picking – the combination of some sort of fundamental analysis together with detailed probing of a company's prospects, including (but not restricted to) its industry, promoter quality, and the firm's ability to hold competitive advantage for long periods.

A peculiarity of the Indian stock market is how the market alternates between being in the grip of the technical or the fundamental camp. When in the technical camp, the talking heads will comment on how the market is 'moving on technicals', while 'valuations are cheap' talk rises when the market is in the fundamental camp.

The technical approach to the stock market – whatever its pitfalls and the scorn heaped on it by purists in the fundamental camp – has a vast following in India. In fact, the following is large enough to make the market behave in a technical fashion. Because the technical approach is speculative, it also contributes to the inherently speculative nature of Indian markets.

This also presents the purist with a dilemma: how to reconcile the stuff in the textbooks with the actual situation on the ground? Sure, the academic mafia and many in the fundamental camp say technicals don't work and fundamentals are the only things that matter. But in a bull move that continues over years, the Sensex nicely retraces to its 200 day moving average (DMA)[1] line – a technical indicator – before continuing on its up move. Or the Sensex bounces off and takes support at the DMA and does so with the regularity of clockwork, sometimes for weeks on end. Alternately, the market wildly thrashes around the 200 DMA, plunging below the line and then soaring back above it. The talking heads then exaggerate the effects of normal news flow on the market as they search for causal explanations for this bizarre movement. What does all this mean, and what is going on here? Is technical analysis all smoke and mirrors (as many in the fundamental crowd believe) or is there something to it?

Technical analysis (TA) is the study of past price and volume action as depicted in a chart, for clues on future price action. It holds that prices

[1] The day moving average (DMA) is a technical analysis tool that smooths out price data by averaging the closing prices of an asset over a specific number of past days.

move in trends, and those trends are predictable because past price action gives us the secret to, and therefore allows us to predict, future price action. As a result, 'The trend is your friend till it ends,' and this nifty observation further decomposes into 'What goes high, goes higher and what goes low, goes lower.' The grandfather of all technical analysis is the Dow Theory, named after Charles Dow, founder of the *Wall Street Journal*.[2] Its aim is to identify situations leading to those 'higher tops and higher bottoms' that establish a primary or long-term trend; if that primary trend is 'up', the market (or stock) is bought into. Besides the primary trend, there are intermediate and minor trends, which are short- or very short-term deviations (pullbacks) from the primary trend; based on the inclinations and time horizon of the trader, these can be ignored or acted on.

Technical traders believe the market has a memory and that the market crowd clusters around supports and resistances. If a stock keeps bouncing off a certain level on the way down, that level is a support, while a price advance that repeatedly stalls at a certain point faces a resistance at that point. Techies tend to 'buy the support' and 'sell the resistance'.

Technical analysis assumes that a chart of price-volume action includes all information about earnings, dividends, and future prospects that any analyst can possibly hope to know. True chartists don't care about a company, an industry, prospects, profits, the level of interest rates, or the overall economy. In fact, most of them believe it's extremely dangerous to think in such terms![3] After all, that line on the chart represents the opinion of millions of people who are already thinking on those terms. It's all there on that line.

The study of these price patterns can go to elaborate levels. The standard work on technicals is Robert Edwards and John Magee's *Technical Analysis of Stock Trends*. This tome – revered by technical analysts – explores hundreds of patterns that provide true believers

[2] Richard Russell, *The Dow Theory Today*, Vermont: Fraser Publishing Company, 1997, 3–29.

[3] To eliminate any extraneous influence on his charting activity, John Magee, the pioneering chartist, reportedly boarded up the window of his office and only read two-week-old copies of the *Wall Street Journal*.

with knowledge about the behaviour of stock prices. Notable patterns mentioned here include 'double tops', 'double bottoms', and the most famous of all, a 'head and shoulders'. There's a thriving publishing segment that supplies books adapting the patterns of Edwards and Magee to Indian stocks. Such material basically keeps the original's insights while looking around for Indian chart patterns that conform to those insights, but this is not a difficult undertaking, given the millions of patterns that over 2,000 traded stocks exhibit at various times; just fiddling with the X axis – the time dimension – produces scores of patterns for a single stock. The advent of the computer allowed for computerized charting, which with automatic updating of price databases through the internet has made technicals easy to execute for the average trader. The numbers and charting are all very impressive and bring an air of sophistication to the activity. Technical analysts and chartists also have regular time slots allotted to them during broadcast media's daily coverage of the markets, which contributes to the approach's popularity; in turn, the channels fill extensive programming time at little cost through such reportage.

Technicals may work when trends persist for long periods, either because of mass psychology or because – as the efficiency hypothesis tells us – in an inefficient market like India, it takes time for a stock price to adjust to fundamental information. In fact, weak-form efficiency would imply that all past information (including information on past patterns) is incorporated into price, but stocks in India take their own time adjusting to information releases, which is in keeping with a market that may not even be weak-form efficient. During that time, the stock trends higher or lower, and this allows a trend follower to put on a trade.[4] So despite what the purists say, technical analysis has a place in trade selection – and mainly because of the known inefficiency of the Indian markets against information.[5] Again, this may be especially true of the thousands of counters that are not in the Sensex or the Nifty.

[4] For an analysis of post earnings announcement drift after monetary announcements, see Gaurav Agarwal, 'Monetary Policy Announcements and Stock Price Behavior: Empirical Evidence from CNX Nifty,' *Decision*, 34(2), 2007, 133–53.

[5] Gunasekarage and Power conclude that technical trading rules have some predictive power in South Asian markets, including Mumbai, Colombo, Dhaka, and Karachi. Abeyratna Gunasekarage

Technical analysis also has a place because of the considerable news leakage that takes place in Indian markets;[6] a country that has little sense of privacy finds it natural to extend that attitude to its financial markets. Often, when insiders and a magic circle of participants get into a stock based on privileged information, it sets the stock on a pronounced uptrend that gets noticed in the charts of the technical crowd, who then join the party and exaggerate the up move.[7] Nowadays, even inside information isn't necessary. Competent analysis of prospects based on news leakage leads to participants loading up on a sector; this starts an uptrend that the techies notice on their charts and their buying then brings the sector further into play. Finally, some of technical analysis's basic tenets – among them, that the market is constantly under various stages of accumulation or distribution – are widely held and part of market lore and vocabulary.

Nevertheless, technical analysis has significant conceptual shortcomings associated with it. If stock prices follow a short-term random walk, there is no serial correlation between day-to-day prices, and what look like patterns are nothing more than the streaks of heads (Hs) or tails (Ts) that come from repeated coin tosses. Consider the analogy of a fair coin toss. After a sequence of coin tosses – HHTHTTHHHHH – the next likely outcome might seem an H, if one has a technical mindset. But though a run of heads ends the tossing sequence, there is equal probability of heads or tails with a fair coin on the next toss. A similar logic applies in technical trading. After 6 up (UUUUUU) days, technical analysis would predict an uptrend and foretell a seventh up day instead of a down day. This is incorrect – assuming short-term prices follow a random walk[8] similar to the coin

---

and David Power, 'The Profitability of Moving Average Trading Rules in South Asian Stock Markets,' *Emerging Markets Review*, 2(1), March 2001, 17–33.

[6] Manish Agarwal and Harminder Singh, 'Merger Announcements and Insider Trading Activity in India: An Empirical Investigation,' *NSE Research Initiative*, Paper No. 8, 29–31.

[7] For evidence of this phenomenon in merger announcements, see Pawan Jain and Mark A. Sunderman, 'Stock Price Movement Around Merger Announcements: Insider Trading or Market Anticipation?,' *Managerial Finance*, 40, No. 8, 2014, 821–43.

[8] Gambler's fallacy, where one believes the probability of an event is lowered the more that event has occurred in the recent past, would lead to a bet on the other outcome of a down day in the above example.

toss example – and the seventh outcome has an equal probability of an up or down day. Most traders forget they're trading on the right edge of the chart, where the present falls off into an unknown future. Statistics teachers sometimes get an introductory class to guess and replicate the sequences of a coin toss by writing down capital Hs or Ts on blank paper. One student then actually tosses a fair coin and notes down the sequence, but the teacher doesn't know who that student is. When the teacher has to guess the identity of the coin-tossing student from the responses, the guess is usually right. The reason: oblivious to randomness, the class has neatly interspersed Hs and Ts, while the fair coin toss shows large streaks of Hs or Ts in the response, allowing the teacher to guess correctly at a glance.[9]

Technical analysis's unspoken assumption about the short-run demand schedule for stocks is also problematic. Consider the following example: if an entry-level Maruti car is priced at ₹4 lakhs, lots of people would demand it; if the same car is priced at ₹9 lakhs, fewer people would demand it; and priced at ₹20 lakhs, only a complete madman would demand it. The demand curve based on this schedule slopes downward, from left to right. This is normal. But when Bajaj Hindustan is 40, nobody wants it; when the stock goes to 80 a few weeks later, a huge crowd demands it; and when it keeps trending higher and crosses 200 a few more weeks later, the whole world and their grandfathers demand it. This is technical analysis. The above actually played out with the Bajaj Hindustan stock in mid-2009, and the scenario routinely recurs in Indian markets. But it's the same stock at each of those prices, with the same levels of cash flows or profits behind the stock at each of those prices, and no information release over a few weeks that could take its price up almost 400 per cent; in other words, it's the same Maruti.[10]

[9] The example is from Larry Swedroe's *Rational Investing in Irrational Times*, as quoted in Burton Malkiel, *A Random Walk Down Wall Street*, 11th ed., New York: W.W. Norton, 2015, 235–36.

[10] Most finance theory assumes near-horizontal demand curves for stocks. Some event studies that examine stock inclusions in indexes conclude that demand curves for stocks slope downward, based on the observation that price increases follow index inclusion.

The main reason technical analysis should not work is that chart patterns tend to destroy themselves when enough people follow them. As seen earlier, if enough people believe the market will go up in December and the pattern is widely known, the market will go up in November as each person tries to outdo the other, and get in early. The pattern has destroyed itself. This is an unstable game, a random walk.

In India's markets, technical traders play an important role at turning points, and this is because of the even balance between them and the fundamental crowd. At market tops, trend-following technical traders buying into a significant up trend are usually on the long side and will constitute the buyers. Fundamental traders – at least those who believe markets are overvalued – will be selling into the market counterweight the techies helpfully provide. So, at market tops, techies make the market for the fundamental types; this effect also applies to individual stocks, and in fact, it is more likely in single stock moves. The situation is less clear at market lows. Towards market bottoms, techies backing a trend should be short selling but cannot do so because short selling doesn't really take place in the cash market, and so, markets drift downwards and form bottoms gradually; at the margin, tired buyers lose hope and sell out, leading to that listless down move to the low. So, when the fundamental crowd comes to buy because value is available, there is no short selling counterweight, and as a result, markets tend to flare up from bottoms.

Technical analysis is good for summarizing the past at a glance, but future prediction is controversial and a big leap; in India, stocks have a way of smashing through supports and resistances. Many pros use both technical and fundamental approaches; if nothing else, the price-volume layout of technical analysis charts allows them to size up at a glance what the crowd is doing. Technical analysis tends to perform better in bull rather than bear markets, with the usual caveat that it's difficult to know *ex ante* whether one is in a bull or bear, as significant time passes before either is 'confirmed'.[11] Assuming some serial correlation,

[11] Eui Jung Chang, Eduardo José Araújo Lima, and Benjamin Miranda Tabak, 'Testing for Predictability in Emerging Equity Markets,' *Emerging Markets Review* 5 (3), 2004, 295–316. This study

technicals work best in the middle of a trend that has been in motion for some time, but many chartists get in and out too late because their 'signals' get triggered too late. Some of this is because of interpretation; like two people will find different patterns looking at the same ink blots of a Rorschach test, two techies looking at the same chart can give you contradictory opinions.

But technicals may be important on occasion, like when price clusters around the 200 DMA line. For example, buying a stock when it surges above its 200 DMA on massive volumes is a common technical strategy in India. Similarly, when moving averages of shorter duration such as the 50 DMA cross above the longer duration 200 DMA – a situation dramatically called the Golden Cross – a buy signal gets triggered which could be profitable. There are several examples of such trades, and yet the key issue here is transaction costs; the frequent trading of technical analysis generates high transaction costs that eat away at returns.[12] Studies that certify the approach's efficacy often conveniently ignore these transaction costs. In turn, brokerages are more than happy to generate account statements that carefully conceal the high cost of technical analysis trading. Individual contract notes are mandated by law to include commission costs, but quarterly or yearly account statements don't carry that obligation and technical traders frenziedly executing scores of trades simply don't calculate their total trading costs over those longer periods.

Costs are so important to the technical approach that it is appropriate to discuss them separately under the rubric of the vigorish. In the gaming industry, the vigorish (known variously as the juice/take/house edge/vig) is what a bookmaker charges to accept a wager. In the stock market, the vigorish broadly refers to that combination of brokerage, taxes, impact costs, and bid-ask spreads that the market (the house) takes away from a trader on a round-trip transaction. Brokerage and taxes are

---

also finds some predictability for technical rules even after taking into account transaction costs, but not enough to be statistically significant, 313.

[12] Subrata Kumar Mitra, 'How Rewarding Is Technical Analysis in the Indian Stock Market?,' *Quantitative Finance,* 11, (2), 2011, 287–97.

cash-based and easily observable from contract notes; competition has reduced brokerage substantially, but taxes are considerable and include the Securities Transaction Tax, state stamp duties, service taxes, and SEBI taxes (India is one of the few countries in the world where the regulator levies its own private taxes). Nevertheless, it is the unobservable components of the vigorish, such as impact costs and bid-ask spreads, that impose the real costs. Impact cost, where the trader moves the price higher on himself while executing, say, the buy trade, is considerable for large traders; this is doubly so in India, an order-driven market that lacks specialists who could moderate the impact of large orders hitting the market by meeting such orders through their inventory. The bid-ask spread has to be constantly negotiated through buying high and selling low when reaching for market price; it applies especially to impatient traders who are anyway the bulk of the trading population. Neither impact costs nor the bid-ask spread is observable in the contract note, and yet these hidden effects are the real cost of the vigorish and can mount with the technical approach.

So why do so many brokers encourage it? Technical analysis results in high-frequency trading that benefits brokers through increased commissions. Other beneficiaries include those who publish technical analysis newsletters and the organizers of conferences where people pay a fee to attend and grasp these Eleusinian mysteries.[13] Given India's vast numbers, equipping the traders who are running behind Lakshmi is often more profitable than doing the running yourself, which had been Cobden's advice during the 1865 Cotton and Share Mania. In recent times, stock market simulation has become a vast business, and this is essentially the old technical practice of paper trading in a modern app-based avatar; googling 'stock market simulation india' pulls up many pages of entries, which make tall claims about turning participants into technical trading geniuses.

And why do so many people follow it? Technical analysis's tendency to encourage magical thinking synchronizes well with the Indian

[13] At the array of technical trading conferences, audiences are typically male and between the ages of 25 and 40.

temperament, and enough people believe in it, just as enough people in India believe in astrology and palmistry. Public reports suggest that launch countdowns in India's space program are timed to avoid *rahukaalam*, an inauspicious time slot in astrology, so for the rocket scientists, both astronomy and astrology are stocks in trade.[14] Similarly, using TA to trade stocks seems as natural as using an astrological horoscope to select a spouse in marriage – another common Indian practice. Horoscope matching – the supernatural validation of a choice of mate – remains a widely followed practice in twenty-first-century India, and just as multitudes use a horoscope as one criterion in spousal selection, so also do large crowds use technical analysis as one approach to stock trading; after the fundamental decision on purchase has been made, it is common to see fund managers and successful investors keep an eye on technicals to time their entry. So, technical analysis is a matter of faith for many participants, and one early 1989 discussion at the BSE Training Institute even likened technical analysis to the practice of religion, while emphasizing the role of faith in both pursuits.[15]

The ahistoricity of the culture also accounts for the extensive prevalence of technicals in India's markets. Till that line on a chart drops off into an unknown future, it is in the past with the events of that past acting on it, but to the average trader the line and its squiggles depend less on historical forces acting on it – and certainly not on the mathematics of random Brownian motion – but more on the magical thinking of 'a trend'. This makes vast sections of the public inclined towards technical analysis for trade selection. In fact, there are a fair number of successful technical analysts in India, in contrast to Wall Street, where a condescending observation is that techies tend to be the ones with holes in their shoes.[16] Finally, the extreme volatility at

[14] Indo-Asian News Service, 'Isro Scientists Superstitious, Follow Rahu Kaalam, Unlucky 13 Before Rocket Launch: Former Official,' *India Today*, 21 July 2019.

[15] Bombay Stock Exchange, *The Stock Exchange Review: November 1989*, Bombay: BSE, 1989, 21.

[16] For evidence that in India technical trading rules based on the 50 day moving average (DMA), relative strength indexes (RSI), and moving average convergence divergence (MACD) beat simple 'buy and hold' strategies, see Terence Tai-Leung Chong, Sam Ho-Sum Cheng, and Elfreda Nga-Yee Wong, 'A Comparison of Stock Market Efficiency of the BRIC Countries,' *Technology and Investment*,

the company level makes technical analysis – with its certainties and its reliance on charts – a comfortable alternative to deciphering and evaluating the numerous fundamental factors that affect a stock's price.

So, multitudes among the trading public (together with many pros) believe in technical analysis and use it for trade selection. This leads to the great paradox of India's market – it has just the right number of technical traders to make its prophecies self-fulfilling. Consider that if enough people believe a stock will take support at its 200 DMA, they will hold off buying as the stock moves closer to the DMA line. The line then sucks the stock towards it, and the stock drops to the DMA. If enough traders believe the stock will take support, they buy at that level and the stock comes roaring back from the DMA. If the stock breaks the line, they all exit at the same time and the stock 'breaks support' and collapses below the DMA. Either way, the prophecy has come true. This sort of reasoning accounts for the tendency of stocks (or the market) to wobble and tussle around their DMAs. The crowd is trying to make up its mind on the right technical signal to read from the tea leaves.

That leaves us with the fundamentals, or fundamental analysis, an approach that is instinctively treated with a certain reverence. After all, this is the dominant approach to the stock market and almost all professionals will follow some sort of fundamental method while evaluating stocks and deciding whether they are cheap or expensive. The end purpose of all fundamental analysis yields a calculated value, V. If the observed price P is less than the calculated value V, the stock is bought at P because it is cheap, and either sold for a profit when it goes up to its fair value V, or held because of an upward reassessment of V itself. It sounds simple, but as companies have perpetual succession, the

1, 2010, 237; Camillo Lento, 'Tests of Technical Trading Rules in the Asian-Pacific Equity Markets: A Bootstrap Approach,' *Academy of Financial and Accounting Studies Journal* 11 (2), 2006. The study by Chong et al. does not include transaction costs, but Lento finds profitable technical trading on the BSE after transaction costs.

equity contract is a perpetuity that lasts forever, and valuing something that lasts forever is as much an art as a science. The process is not known to produce accurate results.[17]

Despite that, fundamental analysis is the basic idea behind stock valuation. Unlike speculation or speculative investment, both of which are concerned with foreseeing changes in price or valuation ahead of the public, the investment approach emphasizes superior forecasts of earnings and dividends, together with wider judgments on risk and interest rates. If the forecasts and the valuation based on those forecasts are accurate, the market recognizes the opportunity (hopefully after the investor) and bids up the price P, which results in the price trending towards fair value V. At least, that's the fond hope. Practically, repeated upward reassessments of V are used to rationalize a long-term position, and this is properly the investment approach.

Three families of models are employed in fundamental analysis, each with varying degrees of application in Indian markets. First, there are relative valuation approaches based on PE ratios. Second, there are absolute valuation approaches based on discounted cash flow (DCF) analysis or dividend discount models. Finally, there are miscellaneous approaches, including price-to-book ratios, Tobin's *q*, or liquidation values. None of the above approaches yield consistent results and participants should know enough about the pitfalls and limitations of all approaches; if nothing else, it aids the investor in interpreting results and helps in triangulating between different models. The internet and the democratization of research have made these calculations widely available, so it is not the mechanical computations but their interpretation that has some value.

Fundamental analysis uses two dominant models – PE ratios or discounted cash flows – to arrive at the value of a stock based on its earnings power. Of these, the PE ratio, a heuristic that values a company's share price as a ratio to its profits (earnings) per share, is the dominant approach. In India, it is the combination of the price

[17] Note what Burton Malkiel has to say: 'God Almighty does not know the proper price-earnings multiple for a common stock,' in Burton Malkiel, *A Random Walk Down Wall Street*, 127.

earnings heuristic together with elaborate stock picking that defines the dominant approach of fund managers and dervishes. This merges with the willing assumption of risk, but whether successful performance is just compensation for the risk taken or actual stock-picking skill is not analysed, and the buy side gets a free run in this regard. After surveying the basic types of fundamental analysis that provide the starting point, we move to the other details of stock picking in the next chapter.

Relative Valuation Approaches through the Price-Earnings (PE) Ratio

The price-earnings (PE) ratio is a relative valuation approach, as opposed to DCF analysis, which arrives at an absolute valuation for the stock. In relative valuations, what matters is a stock's price relative to another variable, like its underlying earnings or the earnings of comparables.[18] If stock X – priced at ₹840 with profits (earnings) per share of ₹70 – consequently trades at a PE multiple of 12 (840/70), it implies that the market is valuing the stock at 12 *times* company X's profits (per common share) of ₹70. The temptation here is to see a lower multiple as cheaper, and therefore better, than a higher multiple. By itself, however, the PE ratio (or capitalization factor as it is sometimes called) of 12 doesn't mean much; here it simply says an investor is giving up ₹12 for every ₹1 of company profits.

Still, the comparison relative to a benchmark can yield some insight. If X is in software and other stocks in that sector trade at an average of 20 times earnings, then X at 12 times earnings is *ceteris paribus* cheaper relative to those others; a start has now been made, following which the picker can move to other aspects of stock selection, especially those dealing with future growth. Those other aspects might lead the picker to reason that the stock *should* trade a little closer to the sector benchmark of 20, perhaps at 17 times earnings or ₹1,190 (17 times ₹70). This

[18] Relative valuation approaches were used extensively by the father of value investing – Benjamin Graham. See Benjamin Graham, *The Intelligent Investor*, New York: HarperCollins, Revised Edition, 2006. His *Security Analysis* (written with David Dodd) outlines the approach in detail.

suggested value V of ₹1,190 is 42 per cent higher than the observed price P of ₹840, leading perhaps to a Buy recommendation.

Sometimes a stock may appear cheaper relative to the market itself. If X at 12 times trades at a lower multiple than the benchmark Nifty, which trades at (say) 26 times the earnings of its constituent companies, it leads to another starting point that may, after further analysis, lead to the picker assigning a higher multiple to the stock's earnings.

The key issue here is the Latin phrase *ceteris paribus* – other things being equal. But other things are never equal and idiosyncrasies keep popping up even at the starting point. Extraordinary or nonrecurring items in the profit and loss statements produce strange results and must be adjusted for. Stocks making losses or turnaround plays coming out of a loss-making period cannot be compared under this method, and produce the familiar NA (Not Applicable) listing in tables. Cyclical stocks in a range of sectors, from steel to sugar, can also produce absurd results, mainly because of the artificially low multiples caused by the surge in cyclical earnings; experienced pickers often buy at 30 times and sell at 8 times to take advantage of the cycle.[19] Asset plays – companies where the picker feels unrecognized assets are not in the stock price – also do not figure in calculations which have only earnings in the denominator. Finally, debt-laden sectors or companies with high debt levels will need metrics besides the PE ratio – like the ratio of enterprise value to its operating profits (EV/EBITDA) – for proper appraisal.[20]

But the main issue is the benchmark itself, the bogey, relative to which the evaluated stock is deemed cheap or expensive. The previous

[19] Investing in cyclicals – and especially when it revolves around commodity cycles – can turn relative valuation on its head. Experienced participants sometimes advise buying when multiples are very high and selling when they are very low. The cycle depresses earnings and raises multiples artificially, but the market doesn't see through this adequately, so when it is time to buy at the low point in the cycle, earnings are low and multiples artificially high. The effect is amplified by high operating and financial leverage. See also Parag Parikh, *Value Investing and Behavioral Finance*, New Delhi: Tata McGraw-Hill, 2009, 116–33.

[20] The numerator of economic value (EV) takes the market value of both stock and debt, adds back preferred stock, and deducts cash; the denominator of EBITDA is operating profits. The measure is not impacted by choice of capital structure, allowing for comparison across companies with different capital profiles.

statement, '*Software stock X with its low PE of 12 is ceteris paribus cheaper than Stock Y in the same space or cheaper than the average PE of the software space (and hence a good buy)*,' is problematic when the software space is itself downgraded or sells off; this happens during 'sector rotation' in a bull market, as entire sectors come into play, both to the upside and the downside. Similarly, the statement '*Software stock X with its low PE of 12 is ceteris paribus cheaper than the market (and hence a good buy)*' is problematic when the entire market sells off due to the systematic risk discussed in the previous chapter. This is a problem with all relative valuation benchmarks.

Assuming the above idiosyncrasies have been addressed, the real reason behind different PE multiples is growth and its incorporation. Incorporating growth into the analysis is complex and involves subjective judgments. Other things being equal, the market will pay a higher multiple for a stock offering more rather than less growth, and a still higher multiple for extended periods of that higher growth. This explains the obsession – in recent years and among certain participants – with 'moat' investing; with a unique source of competitive advantage around a business like a moat around a castle, the duration of that high growth period can be projected a little longer into the future, which allows for the higher multiple.[21] This is earnings visibility or the visibility of earning power. If a chunk of that growth gets paid out in dividends all the better, though Indian markets tend to be lax in evaluating this as a criterion and prefer earnings to compound in a business as retained earnings rather than get paid out as dividends; so aggregate dividend yields tend to be low, usually in the region of 1 to 2 per cent for the market.

In a sense, the above analysis is static and backward-looking, and the real rewards go to those who can guess whether the market itself has

[21] Warren Buffett, to whom we owe much of the concept's popularity, had this to say about it: 'I want a business with a moat around it. I want a very valuable castle in the middle. And then I want… the Duke who's in charge of that castle to be honest and hard-working and able. And then I want a big moat around the castle, and that moat can be various things.' 'Warren Buffett MBA Talk - Part 3 [Video],' *BITZ FILMS*, 2007, Retrieved 1 August 2018, https://www.youtube.com/watch?v=r7m7ifUz7r0.

correctly estimated growth rates and the forward multiples that should go with them. Sometimes, the market will underestimate a stock's earnings growth rate, which later leads to the holy grail of stock picking – soaring earnings capitalized at a higher multiple. Earnings rise higher than expected, the market belatedly recognizes this, and then awards the higher earnings a higher PE multiple. In company X's example, two years of unexpected doubling of earnings would take them from ₹70 to ₹140 and then to ₹280, and the market – extrapolating into the future – might price the stock at 100 times earnings, or ₹28,000. The stock price has moved from ₹840 to ₹28,000 and this leads to a 33-bagger; this happened to software stocks during the dot-com bubble and later to real estate stocks during the Rate Bull. So, this double whammy to the upside results in the 'multi-bagger', an increasingly rare species as Indian markets progressively move towards stronger forms of efficiency.[22] But to a retail clientele, ₹28,000 sounds alarmingly 'high' for a stock, and so – as in the Unitech example – the stock is often 'bonussed' and split down to disguise the extent of the price rise.

Of course, not many sane people would buy a stock at 100 times earnings, and so analysts extrapolate the recent doubling of earnings into the near future. Projecting a doubling of earnings over the next 12 months – from ₹280 to ₹560 in our stylized example – results in the stock trading at 50 times forward earnings (₹28,000/560). Suddenly the stock looks sweet and reasonable at projected or forward earnings. Sometimes the projected forward earnings don't occur, resulting in that most dangerous of situations – the 'official' growth stock whose earnings don't materialize – leading to the double whammy to the downside, as both earnings and the multiple get marked down.

This also happened when the dot-com and real estate bubbles burst. Stocks in India routinely lose as much as 80 to 90 per cent of their values when this happens. Behind all the numbers and quantification and glossy reports, much of day-to-day equity research essentially wrestles with the above issues, but in less exaggerated form.

[22] Peter Lynch coined the term 'multibagger' in his 1988 book *One Up on Wall Street*. The term is extensively used in India as compared to other countries.

So, unlike technical analysis, fundamental analysis can escape into the future and use that future as an excuse. As a result, one key issue is the use of trailing earnings from the previous 12 months versus projected (or forward) earnings over the next 12 months. Since the future is the only thing that matters, conceptually at least what counts are forward earnings. Financial statements can only be understood backward, and yet investing life must be lived forward, and this imposes a terrible contradiction on the process. Unfortunately, forward earnings are often the figment of an overheated analyst's (or equity strategist's) imagination. Even if imaginations remain sober and collected, there remains the well-known inability of analysts to look into the future and forecast correctly.[23] Inevitably, forecasts get influenced by the market itself, and when liquidity drives the market higher, weak-minded analysts use the forward earnings fantasy to justify any valuation. In fact, it is usually the combination of heated imaginations, forecasting incompetence, and liquidity that is at work in computations of forward earnings during a bull run's final stages.

So, to Graham and Dodd, it was usually trailing earnings 'normalized' or averaged out over a time period of around three years that figured in the calculations. Many value investors and brokerages pay ritual obeisance to Graham and Dodd's precepts, but somehow this key advice of the Masters slips their minds. This happens especially in the final stages of a bull move, when the normal tendency to cheerlead the market gets heightened by severe conflicts of interest.

For example, consider that PE ratios are a widely used thumb rule for forecasting the market itself. Historically – before the distortions caused by global bond-buying programs – the Indian market has traded between 15 and 17 times trailing twelve-month earnings. The multiple ranges from 9 to 11 at bear market lows, to between 25 and 30 at bull market highs.[24]

[23] Malkiel has a detailed analysis on Wall Street's inability to forecast correctly for various reasons, including: creative accounting by companies, the influence of random events or 'unknown unknowns', conflicts of interest, and the basic incompetence of analysts themselves. Burton Malkiel, *A Random Walk Down Wall Street*, 160–74; see also Benjamin Graham, *The Intelligent Investor*, 517.

[24] These figures are published on exchange websites and are based on the trailing 12-month earnings for the index's components, adjusted for their free floats.

In March 2018, the Nifty at 10,000 traded at 25 times trailing 12-month earnings. During this period, however, it was common to hear brokerages say the market traded at 18 times forward earnings. Triangulating between these two multiples would show the market's earnings for the trailing 12 months at ₹400 (10,000/25) and for the forward 12-month period at ₹556 (10,000/18). The implied growth rate between these two earnings figures of ₹400 and ₹556 is 39 per cent over the coming 12 months. This was absurdly high by any standard, especially when one considers that earnings growth had been in anemic single digits in the quarters immediately before this period (there wasn't a low base effect either). This sort of hot air routinely bubbles up from the brokerages, and especially when they are rationalizing the final stages of bull market up moves; in fact, it is exactly the sort of hot air the Masters warned against when they insisted on using normalized trailing earnings as an antidote to the tendency. Examples like the above became particularly relevant during the coronavirus pullback of 2020 and 2021, when the gap between a liquidity-driven market and a real economy caught in the grip of repeated virus waves made such forward calculations tricky.

Most attempts at forecasting exploit the public's gullibility about this distinction between trailing and forward earnings. Wild-eyed projections can produce any stock (or market) valuation if earnings are projected into the future, and such projections are rarely challenged, despite the fact that the numbers to challenge them are widely available from newspapers or websites. But it's far better to triangulate from the past and use it as a jumping-off point. Using research to discover that a stock (or the market) is trading cheap relative to past growth and then making adjustments for profit growth into an immediate future is inherently more reasonable than looking wild-eyed only at the future.

Despite these drawbacks, the relative approach has certain key advantages, and these apply more to individual stocks than the market.[25] If used well, it puts the focus squarely on the gap between

[25] Empirical evidence on the efficacy of fundamental analysis based on dividend yield and price-earnings ratios also comes from Paresh Kumar Narayan and Deepa Bannigidadmath, 'Are Indian Stock Returns Predictable?,' *Journal of Banking & Finance*, 58 (2015), 507.

the picker's opinion (and information) and the market's opinion of the stock; experienced participants will usually work in that gap. Well-known sectors such as chemicals, consumer goods, or steel have a wide range of well-researched firms, and averaging across these reduces the idiosyncratic variations that manifest when discussing individual stocks. So, averaging across five mid-cap specialty chemical stocks gives a fair idea of the comparable multiple the market pays for similar firms and allows for a comparison with the evaluated firm, which can then be used as a starting point for the further detailed probing that goes into stock picking. Many pickers find it difficult to translate a jumbled mass of accumulated information into a decision on a stock's value, but this approach takes into account the market's collective judgment to help arrive at a decision. Historically, the Indian market has traded at about 15 to 17 times trailing earnings, with aggregate earnings growth between 10 and 13 per cent, so buying stocks with multiples lower than the market's long-term average, that after adjusting for idiosyncrasies show growth rates higher than the market's long-term average, is usually reasonable.

Absolute Valuation Approaches through Discounted Cash Flow (DCF) Analysis

Discounted cash flow (DCF) analysis is an absolute valuation approach, and it is, in fact, the only definite way to value stocks. Unlike relative valuation, which cannot arrive at a definite judgment on a stock's value, DCF analysis leads to a precise value for a stock. Nevertheless, though theoretically sound, the method faces substantial issues in practical implementation, which renders its results as suspect as the relative approach.

Three key factors in the DCF exercise are: a) projected earnings and their growth rate, b) risk levels, and c) market interest rates. More technically, the DCF process involves projecting free cash flows available to a company's debt and equity holders into an infinite future; bringing back (discounting) those future flows to the present moment at the risk-adjusted weighted average cost of capital (adjusted for the tax shield); knocking off the value of the debt; arriving at an aggregate equity value for the company; and dividing that (after suitable adjustments for special items such as warrants or preferred stock) by the number of shares outstanding to arrive at an equity value per share. It is beyond the analytical capacity of most individual investors, but that shouldn't matter as it will be institutional research which produces the result, and the individual investor's task is simply to use that end result. The emphasis here is on drawing investors' attention to pitfalls that arise when they evaluate and use that research for a stock purchase.

DCF analysis for traded equities in India faces significant issues, and the extreme quantification gives the analysis an air of accuracy and sophistication which it does not deserve. The most common issue arises at the first stage itself – because the equity contract is a perpetuity, cash flows have to be projected far into a volatile future. Practically, after an arbitrary cut-off period of (say) 5 to 7 years, formulae have to be used to calculate values from the end of the cut-off period into the indefinite future. These terminal values end up forming a big chunk of the stock's value V. More technically, they also render the calculation highly sensitive to changes in estimates for the cost of equity capital, which is anyway not accurately calculated in India.

As a result, most analysts fiddle with DCF models while keeping an anxious eye on the stock's current price P. The current price P acts as a heavy anchor, and from there it is a short step to manipulating the above parameters to arrive at a target value V that – depending on whether the outlook is bullish or bearish – is a little higher or lower than the extant price P. Most brokerage forecasts are for periods ranging from three months to a year, and at the end of these periods new research is brought out that further rationalizes the stock price P prevailing at that time; as a result, analyst timidity and anchoring render most of the calculations futile.

Shortcuts such as divided discount models are sometimes used to get around the complexity of DCF methodology, and one such shortcut is the three-stage Gordon dividend discount model. But these models come with their own pitfalls. More technically, the interest rate has to be greater than the dividend growth rate for such models to work; when the growth rate tends towards the interest rate – as often happens in high-growth markets such as India – the forecast price tends to infinity, and the results are meaningless.[26] Also, growth stocks may not pay dividends for a long time, which makes it difficult to use such models (unless one makes the unrealistic assumption that a one-time liquidating dividend will be paid).

Most analysts get lost in these calculations and don't appreciate the terrible power of Time – usually corrosive, but in this case accretive – which is behind all this. Even if there was no real progress or growth, stock markets would only go higher over time, and more so in an inflation-prone country like India. This is because sales and earnings are priced nominally before inflation and will rise with it, assuming some pricing power among companies (which is not unreasonable). The stock market simply prices this nominal growth through the PE multiple, so even if that ratio was a constant, nominal earnings growth before inflation would rise and send markets higher.

Miscellaneous Approaches: Price-to-Book Ratios, Tobin's *q*, and Liquidation Values

The price-to-book ratio – the ratio of a company's stock price to its book value per share (the summation of share capital and reserves) – is another common metric. This is an accounting-based valuation device and therefore subject to the distortions that accrual accounting can introduce into calculations of book value. Though it could act as a floor to a stock price, it rarely does so in real life, as there is little conceptual reason for it to act as a floor. Book values tend to be more important for sectors such as banking, where a common market practice is to adjust book values for unprovisioned bad loans and apply that

[26] D/r-g is the basic generalization of the perpetuity formula to perpetuities (in this case, dividends) that grow at a constant rate. It is highly sensitive to changes in both r (the interest rate or required rate of return on a stock) and g (its expected growth rate), but less sensitive to changes in D (the dividend forecasts).

as a valuation metric. In India, however, the widespread presence of chartered accountants among market pros – and their training, which instinctively makes them focus on book values from statements – ensures that price-to-book ratios have an importance here that are not enjoyed elsewhere; it is common for participants to check if the ratio falls below some measure, say 2, to see if a stock is cheap. Price-to-book ratios for the aggregate market are also computed daily by exchanges and vary from about 2 at market lows, to between 4 and 6 at tops; in 2000 and 2008, the ratio reached highs of 4.5 and 6, respectively.[27]

Tobin's *q*, or valuation based on replacement cost, is another way to assess the stock market. As noted earlier, it figures in a famous episode of Indian stock market history – when Harshad Mehta used it in hazy fashion and without proper attribution as a rationale for his bull run. But it is rarely applied and is mentioned here only for the sake of completeness. Tobin's *q* is the ratio of the market value of a firm's debt and equity to the replacement cost of its assets less liabilities.[28] If that ratio were much greater than 1, competitive firms would find it worthwhile to enter the industry and replicate – or replace – the firm, thereby driving down the value of a firm's marketable claims (the numerator), which brings the ratio closer to 1 again. Mehta's snake oil involved claiming that the ratio was much below 1; this he did by exaggerating replacement costs (in the ratio's denominator) to the point where the marketable equity claims (the numerator) appeared cheap, which in turn allowed him to drive their prices higher. Since accurate replacement costs are difficult to compute (which allowed Mehta to exaggerate them in the first place), book values are often used as a substitute, and then Tobin's *q* becomes the ratio of the market value of equity and debt to the book value of its equity and debt. In contestable industries, the ratio should therefore tend towards 1, but in practice it can deviate over unity for large periods of time.

[27] Googling 'NSE archives' brings up the time series data.

[28] James Tobin, 'A General Equilibrium Approach to Monetary Theory,' *Journal of Money, Credit and Banking* 1 (1), 1969, 15–29.

Liquidation values arise when a company is liquidated and has its assets (excluding intangibles) sold and used to pay off debt, following which the residual liquidation value is distributed to shareholders through liquidation dividends. Technically a stock should be a buy if the price falls much below the company's liquidation value as derived from the above calculations. It is an alternate method of triangulation that can set a floor to a stock's price, but it relies heavily on arbitrage-based arguments. It usually needs an arbitrageur, or someone who buys in public markets – after recognizing (just as the investor has recognized) the discrepancy between market price and liquidation value – and then undertakes the steps that realize liquidation value. Nevertheless, it depends heavily on the market for corporate control, but that is not very active in India (the absence of a market for corporate control also means that investing based on 'special situations' such as merger arbitrage is infrequent).

More practically, the approach needs someone who recognizes the discrepancy (hopefully just after the investor) and launches a takeover or a related type of transaction to capture value. This rarely happens in India because most companies are owned by promoters who treat their firms as family jewels and who consequently do not take kindly to corporate raiders. In this, they are helped along by a slumbering buy side; key buy side institutions such as LIC and the mutual funds are usually content to sleepwalk through the promoter's decisions. Besides, government-owned LIC often has questions asked about its own corporate governance practices, while the mutual funds – themselves often owned by promoter families – are naturally reluctant to raise issues about other promoter-owned companies.[29] So, breaking up and wrecking a company – 'because it's wreckable, all right!' as that memorable line from the film *Wall Street* goes – does not really happen. As a result, the gap between price and liquidation value can persist for years, which frustrates a public shareholder's attempt to realize the same.

[29] For further evidence on the passivity of institutional investors at all levels of equity ownership, see Jayati Sarkar and Subrata Sarkar, 'Large shareholder activism in corporate governance in developing countries: Evidence from India,' *International Review of Finance*, 1, No. 3, 2000, 161-194.

Nevertheless, with the passage of the Insolvency and Bankruptcy Code in recent years, such calculations might begin to assume importance in the future.

So where does the above discussion leave us? Unfortunately, no one really knows what the intrinsic value V of a stock should be – behind the precision and glossy research, everyone is guessing. Not knowing what something is worth in a business dedicated only to knowing what those things are worth seems like a severe and intractable problem. But there is one famous answer to this predicament, and it comes from Benjamin Graham and David Dodd. Think of it as trying to guess the weight of a fat man. When a fat man approaches, you don't need to know his exact weight to know he's fat; you look at him and the observation suggests itself. Similarly, with a stock or the market itself, sometimes you don't need to know its exact value to know it's competitively priced. As long as you are certain about getting it cheap enough and at the right discount from its fair value, you know it's inexpensive, and sometimes – and only sometimes – the market gives you that chance.

The secret to the great and enduring relevance of Graham and Dodd lies in their solution to the valuation dilemma through this fat man approach. Their solution was to buy a rupee worth of stock for a price P of 50 or 60 paisa. As long as an investor is reasonably sure he is buying at P for that large discount, what does it matter if the intrinsic value V of the stock is actually a rupee, or 80 paisa, or ₹1.45? This leads to the idea of value investing the Graham and Dodd way, and to its central concept – the margin of safety. Price is what you pay, value is what you get.[30] The difference between market price P and intrinsic value V is the margin of safety; the lower that market price is compared to

[30] 'Long ago, Ben Graham taught me that "Price is what you pay; value is what you get." Whether we're talking about socks or stocks, I like buying quality merchandise when it is marked down.' Berkshire Hathaway, *Annual Report* 2008, Accessed on 9 January 2018, 5,http://www.berkshirehathaway.com/letters/2008ltr.pdf.

intrinsic value, the better, and that is the gap in which Graham and Dodd operated. (A practical short cut to the approach would entail acting on research that uses the most conservative assumptions to arrive at a stock's projected value. If that is 30 to 40 per cent more than its market price, then the difference is the margin of safety.)[31] So, risk to Graham is the risk of overpaying for a stock and not the risk of how volatile a stock is around its mean. By contrast, in portfolio theory, risk to Markowitz is the standard deviation (or variability) of a stock price over time, or how much it moves around its average; in later avatars and within the framework of portfolio theory, risk is the stock's contribution to portfolio risk.

Graham had three measures for his margin of safety, all applied with extensive diversification.[32] The three measures (calculated after checking for a conservative debt-to-equity ratio) were:

a. the *net current assets rule*: buying a stock at 2/3 or less of its net current assets value, i.e., taking current assets, deducting all liabilities (short and long term) in full, while ignoring all fixed assets and claims ahead of the common (like preferred stock);[33]
b. the *earnings yield rule*: buying a stock only when its earnings yield was twice the yield on government securities (G-Secs);[34] and
c. the *dividend yield rule*: buying a stock only when its dividend yield was not less than 2/3 the yield on government securities (G-Secs).

Criterion (a) was essentially a liquidation value approach that was lucrative in the years following the 1930s Great Depression, which coincidentally was when the first edition of Graham and Dodd's book *Security Analysis* popularized the rule; nevertheless, in keeping with the

[31] Warren Buffett's recounting of the track records of some of the school's disciples is in Warren Buffett, '*The Super Investors of Graham-and-Doddsville,*' in Benjamin Graham, *The Intelligent Investor*, 537–48. The 'margin of safety' approach is outlined in the same, 512–24.

[32] Benjamin Graham, *The Intelligent Investor*, 518–19.

[33] Ibid., 390–93.

[34] Ibid., 350, 514–15.

tenets of market efficiency, the approach became progressively more difficult to implement as it became more popular. On criterion (b), a 6 per cent yield (say) on G-Secs would imply picking a stock with an earnings yield of 12 per cent; in turn, the earnings yield is the reciprocal of the PE ratio, so this would imply buying stocks with a PE ratio of 8, or thereabouts (the reciprocal 1/8 would result in an earnings yield of roughly 12 per cent). Criterion (c) would imply buying stocks that offer dividend yields of about 4 per cent, or about 2/3 the 6 per cent G-Sec yield in the example (government securities are used in this example because of the absence of a robust market in blue-chip corporate bonds). Upward shifts in the term structure of interest rates would lower multiples across the board in these calculations, which simply illustrates the earlier assertion of rates acting like gravity on financial assets.

Finding stocks that met these measures used to be possible in the early days of the Indian market's modern era, but such finds are rare nowadays. Stocks in India rarely meet Graham's strict criteria because the market is perennially priced for growth rather than value, and it is only at bear market lows such as those of 2003 or 2009 that some stocks meet these norms. Nevertheless, the approach's value lies in its discipline and the way it relates equity valuation to the overall level of market interest rates. This is a pawn shop approach to investing, and it is an ideal that some disciplined investors aspire to. Near the great tops, few stocks will meet Graham's criteria when screens are run and this itself acts as a warning to the conservative investor.

As a concept, the margin of safety is regularly applied by professional investors in India, but less rigidly than in its strict Grahamian avatar. In fact, market inefficiency and the extreme noise and volatility of the Indian environment allow for its application a lot more here than in the West. There are simply a lot more downside events taking place in India's volatile and noisy environment, allowing for prices to dip below intrinsic value by a wide margin – frequently.

Towards the highs, the approach can also be adapted by bringing into play the effect of market-wide interest rates. For example, in January 2008 the market (Nifty) traded at 28 times earnings when government securities were yielding 8 per cent. The earnings yield on the market (the risky asset) was at 3.6 per cent (1/28 expressed as a percentage), and yet rates on G-Secs (the risk-free asset) were at 8 per cent. If rational investors were risk averse and demanded a risk premium, why would they buy the stock market (a risky asset) that yielded just 3.6 per cent when they could make 8 per cent risk free? For the market to become attractive on Graham's criteria, either earnings yields had to rise (meaning PE multiples had to fall as markets sold off) or G-Sec yields had to fall. In this case, it so happens that subsequently both took place – the market sold off and G-Sec yields also fell as the government eased monetary policy in response to the Lehman crisis. In early 2022, a similar situation presented itself on the above parameters, but this time was different.

12

SEARCHING FOR THE KOHINOOR

Stock Picking

The initial screening of fundamental heuristics such as price-earnings ratios is further developed through security analysis or stock picking, and the focus then moves to businesses and promoters. Stock picking's prevalence is primarily due to market inefficiency and the studied ignorance of portfolio theory. Market inefficiency, more than anything else, is what drives the stock-picking approach. Even semi-strong efficiency would imply that all publicly available information is incorporated in a stock's price, rendering any sort of stock picking futile, and yet the activity is pervasive in India; so, stock picking's prevalence and successful use (especially by professionals) suggest that semi-strong efficiency also does not hold, but this is simply in keeping with the efficiency schematic. The studied ignorance of portfolio theory also leads to a cavalier attitude to risk, which further encourages the stock-picking approach, as higher returns are often seen as the reward for stock-picking skill rather than as compensation for taking on risk.

The first thing that strikes the observer about stock picking in India is the diversity of approaches and results. Because of the large universe of stocks, every picker's list seems to differ widely from every other picker's list. This is not a bad thing. Differences of opinion are what make horse races and the stock market work. Figuring by strong consensus on the lists of all and sundry indicates that a stock has been anointed a market favourite, which in turn usually means that its best days are over. Yet this observation is also tempered by striking exceptions. For years, HDFC Bank under the able leadership of Deepak Parekh and Aditya Puri enjoyed the strongest consensus as a Buy and was on everyone's list – often at valuations approaching six times price to book value – and yet the stock consistently outperformed the market.

Event-based displacement approaches and company-specific non-displacement approaches are the two broad categories of stock picking in India. The displacement approach is event- or news-driven, and participants talk of 'triggers' that bring about the displacement. Examples of the approach include buying public-sector bank stocks displaced by a pending government recapitalization or buying airline stocks as oil prices fall. The sector's displacement acts as the framework within which stock picking takes place, so in the displacement approach, sector picking and stock picking often go hand in hand and close attention is paid to sector selection at a practical level. Sector selection matters because of the crowd's tendency to think in terms of sectors as much as stocks, and much Indian equity strategy consists of anticipating displaced sectors where the market crowd will get in next.[1] Cyclical stocks, dependent either on their peculiar industrial cycle or the overall business cycle, are also included in this displacement approach and here the displacement is the industry's dynamics (typically on inventories or capacities) as it moves through the cycle. Given the pervasive influence of government on much economic activity, sectors often flare up on reform initiatives taken by the government, following which stock selection within those sectors takes place. Rather than stock picking, it is pertinent to view such approaches as noise investing through the long-pull trade. These event-based displacement approaches are news dependent, not open to generalization on precepts, and reliant on speculative investment as a technique.[2] Critical to the approach is recognizing the distinction

[1] Basant Maheshwari, interview, Basant Maheshwari's Investment Mantra [Video],' *NDTV*, 2015, Retrieved 10 August 2018, http://ndtv.com/video/basant-maheshwari-s-investment-mantra-360959.

[2] For another view on 'speculative investment', consider this statement of a fund manager: 'At any point in time, an investor needs to understand what the market is focusing on. If you are focused on

between it and the more conventional company picking, because recognizing the displacement's importance (to the trade) also alerts the picker to its impending end.

This chapter, however, focuses on the company-specific non-displacement approach. Almost all non-displacement stock picking in India clusters around three poles – business, promoter, and valuation – and their interplay will drive the final decision. The art may lie in the picker's ability to emphasize the right pole at the moment of decision. Besides the three poles, miscellaneous criteria such as the long corner and regulatory interface also intrude on the decision. A formal treatment follows, but the extent to which market practice adheres to this prescription will vary.

The Business and Its Industry: Strength of Franchise and Its Duration

A stock picker's interest in a company revolves in large part around the company's franchise strength – something a company does particularly well compared to others. Ideally, as a stock picker, you want this franchise strength to continue for as long as possible before the natural process of competition erodes it. Franchise strength and its duration then decide the PE multiple that the market awards to a stock, with prolonged periods of high growth being the single-most important factor behind higher valuations. Franchise strength keeps competition at bay and creates a 'moat' around the business, akin to a moat around a castle. The resulting intangible is competitive advantage, and it can be formally evaluated using various frameworks

---

a specific idea or theme and the market is not willing to buy that theme, you will get the stock call completely wrong. The important thing is to know what the market is thinking,' Alroy Lobo of the Kotak Mahindra brokerage, as quoted in Saurabh Mukherjea, *Gurus of Chaos: Modern India's Money Masters*, New Delhi: Bloomsbury India, 2014, 68.

drawn from fields such as industrial organization or competitive strategy.[3]

Here, professionals will use different frameworks. One publicly available example comes from fund manager Saurabh Mukherjea, who in his book *Gurus of Chaos* takes the themes of brands, networks, and innovation, and applies them as a framework for understanding 'moats' in the Indian context. He uses an *Economic Times* Brand Equity survey to show how powerful brand builders like Colgate, Unilever, Nestle, and Glaxo also beat the stock index comfortably.[4] Networks, that complex combination of formal and informal contracts that bind employees, customers, and suppliers, can also produce advantage; good companies, for example, have systems and processes that allow for informal networks of employee information sharing on problem solving. Innovation is another source of franchise strength, but it has to be relentless and continuous, because innovation comes together with its handmaiden, imitation by competitors, which erodes the innovator's edge; the management consultancy profession even has terms for organized imitation – 'benchmarking' or 'best practice transfer'.

But the above factors are the soft sources of a moat; harder sources include strategic assets such as licenses and patents, natural resources accessed on preferential terms, economies of scale that lead to cost advantages, intellectual property, unregulated natural monopolies, and political contacts.[5] Distribution networks that are difficult to replicate are also a critical cause of advantage in a country of India's size and complexity, but their potential as a source of competitive advantage has been curiously neglected by participants; some companies, including HUL, Marico, and Dabur, have distribution networks established over generations, and these act as formidable barriers to entry for a newcomer. It also helps if the company under consideration has little competition from the unorganized sector, as that sector has certain advantages, particularly on issues like compliance and taxes.

[3] Among these are the Porter 5 Forces framework, together with its progenitor, the structure-conduct-performance paradigm of industrial organization.

[4] Saurabh Mukherjea, *Gurus of Chaos*, 31–33.

[5] Ibid., 36–37.

Ideally, soft and hard sources of the moat should lead to cost leadership, which is seen as important (particularly for commodity industries, but also more generally), because it allows companies to follow strategies that appeal to a price-conscious, value-driven customer – and in India that is the vast majority. Most fail to appreciate that between the generic strategies of cost leadership and product differentiation, it is usually cost leadership that really matters.

Choosing a business has the same consequences as selecting its industry, and the industry's dynamics will also work on the optimality of the stock choice. Again, techniques vary. Top-down approaches to selection will emphasize sector/industry selection over stock selection, though this approach belongs more to the areas of investment policy and speculative investment, as discussed earlier. Bottom-up approaches will do the reverse, emphasizing the stock pick over the sector/industry. Both approaches command an equal following in India. The professional buy side is inclined towards a top-down approach because of the large amounts of money being handled. Individual pickers, with smaller portfolios and fewer compliance restrictions, often follow a more bottom-up approach.

In turn, all this translates into the picker's obsession with scalability. Scalability is the company's capacity to ramp up into a sunrise sector with a clearly addressable market opportunity, which in turn translates into considerable growth over many years. Successful small enterprises in highly scalable businesses can grow into the multi-bagger, and the search for the multi-bagger is what stock picking is all about. Often, overall portfolio performance comes from a large number of mediocre picks that are more than compensated by the one multi-bagger that is present. So, finding a small cap or mid cap with scalability is vital.[6]

[6] By definition, most scalable opportunities were in the smaller companies. For evidence of market inefficiency that helps the search for small-caps, see Vinod Mishra and Russell Smyth, 'The Random Walk Hypotheses on the Small and Medium Capitalized Segment of the Indian Stock Exchange,' *Information Efficiency and Anomalies in Asian Equity Markets: Theories and Evidence*, eds. Qaiser Munir and Sook Ching Kok, Routledge Studies in the Modern World Economy, Vol. 162, Abingdon and New York: Routledge, 2017, 34–48.

Historically, most multi-baggers have existed in two broad areas of activity, that play either to India's comparative advantage in international markets or to its large, consumption-driven domestic market. International comparative advantage usually comes through labour arbitrage in industries like software or business services, and much of it is driven by the favourable tailwinds of a secularly depreciating currency. But the larger opportunity is in the country's consumption-driven domestic market, which means industries such as two-wheelers, retail banking, or consumer goods. Here the emphasis is always on volumes. Successful big business in India has usually been about very small values spread over very large volumes, and much of this is a function of the country's demographic profile – a huge population base that is essentially still poor to lower-middle class. Both these spaces have become overcrowded and overvalued over the years, and the trade has gotten a little long in the tooth, but the addressable opportunities are large with many quality companies available, and so, most portfolios are overweighted in them.

However, great danger lies in selecting the transitory multi-bagger, a comfortable euphemism for a stock that rises, say, a 1,000 times and then gives up the increase. Much of the hazard comes from the inability to distinguish between the event-based displacement approach and the longer-lasting company-specific approach; there is the inability to gauge the ephemeral nature of the displacement, as a result of which a pick is seen as something more enduring and company specific. The interest rate displacement of the Rate Bull years resulted in some of the great multi-baggers of market history, but many gave up all their gains; Unitech was a prime example of such a passing phenomenon, rising over 2,300 times before moving to nothing.

The Promoter: Competence and Integrity

Promoter competence and integrity are important because promoters and their managements matter more in India than in other countries. Stock picking also implies picking company managements, and while this is true in all countries, it matters a little more in India, as majority ownership usually rests with promoter families whose interests may differ from those of outside shareholders. As noted earlier, India is removed from a Berle and Means world. In *The Modern Corporation and Private Property*, Adolf Berle Jr. and Gardiner Means proposed the separation of ownership and control, as diffuse shareholder ownership of modern corporations led to company boards dominated by managements, who were expected to act more in their own interests than those of shareholders. Realigning principal/shareholder interests with those of the agent/management to get the agent to act in the principal's interests, rather than in the agent's own interests, results in a class of problems called corporate governance, and in India it is still a work in progress.[7]

In India, promoter families provide concentrated ownership, and some academic surveys indicate average promoter holdings of about 50 per cent of outstanding equity.[8] Promoters often actively run companies they have promoted – while professional management is appointed, promoters still call the shots. This is understandable, as owning up to half of equity naturally gives promoters the biggest stakes in decisions. But as a result of this, stock picking in India also implies picking a promoter, together with picking that promoter's ability to either find sound management or provide sound management from within the promoter family. This double selection comes with its own complications.

The emphasis on promoters also results in differences between Indian and Western notions of corporate governance. In India, the market's view is opposed to the Berle and Means world of diffused shareholder

[7] Seminal works from the vast literature on the principal–agent problem as applied to corporate governance, include: Adolf Berle and Gardiner Means, *The Modern Corporation and Private Property*, New Brunswick and London: Transaction Publishers, 1991; Michael C. Jensen and William H. Meckling, 'Theory of the Firm: Managerial Behavior, Agency Costs, and Ownership Structure,' *Journal of Financial Economics* 3 (1976): 305–60; Eugene F. Fama and Michael C. Jensen, 'Separation of Ownership and Control,' *Journal of Law and Economics* 26 (1983): 301–25; and Stephen A. Ross, 'The Economic Theory of Agency: The Principal's Problem,' *American Economic Review*, 63 (2), May 1973, 134–39.

[8] Melvin Jameson, Andrew Prevost, and John Puthenpurackal, 'Controlling Shareholders, Board Structure, and Firm Performance: Evidence from India,' *Journal of Corporate Finance*, 27, 2014, 1–20. In a sample size of 1796 firms, close to two-thirds had promoter families with an average shareholding of about 50 per cent.

ownership in widely held companies. Here the market favourably views companies that are not widely held and that have large promoter holdings, under the assumption that such companies are run by promoters with more 'skin in the game'. In fact, so focused are markets on promoter 'skin in the game', that they neglect to distinguish between price rises that are the result of promoters maximizing the value of their holdings and price rises that are simply due to the long corner that comes from excessive skin in the game. Markets tend to reward companies where promoters have fewer interests or financial stakes outside their listed holdings; keeping track of promoter dealings between the listed entity and the outside sphere becomes easier when there are fewer outside interests.[9] Markets also obsess over how promoters allocate capital among diverse opportunities, but such 'capital allocation' is properly shorthand for business strategy in a volatile environment.[10] Often the next generation from the promoter family is also closely watched for its induction into the business.

But in a conservative and status quo value system, the key factor is longevity and track record – promoters who have been around long enough and who deliver over the longest periods of time, tend to be trusted more than others. This can result in bloopers, however, with the most common one being mechanically buying into affiliates of old and established business houses that diversify into the wrong industry.[11] Stock pickers then learn the hard way Warren Buffett's insight, that when a management with a reputation for excellence tackles an industry with a reputation for poor economics, it is usually the reputation of the industry that remains intact.[12]

[9] Saurabh Mukherjea, *Gurus of Chaos*, 54.

[10] Ibid., 89.

[11] For empirical evidence that Indian firms affiliated with most business groups – especially the small to mid-sized groups – underperform unaffiliated firms, see Tarun Khanna and Krishna Palepu, 'Is Group Affiliation Profitable in Emerging Markets? An Analysis of Diversified Indian Business Groups,' *Journal of Finance*, Vol. 55, No. 2, April 2000, 867–91. By contrast, very large business groups internally replicate various markets for product, labour, and capital – markets that are anyway flawed and imperfect in most emerging markets – companies affiliated with such large groups might have advantages that stock pickers need to reckon with.

[12] 'Thoughts on the Business of Life,' *Forbes Quotes*, https://www.forbes.com/quotes/9638/.

Promoters, in turn, deal with a level of analysis problem. Typically, as experts in the single company that is under their watch, they don't realize that the market – a weighing machine for thousands of companies in aggregate – doesn't really care about that single company. This leads to the commonplace that promoters usually know a lot about their companies and industries, but little about the market. A promoter's default mentality is that the market is undervaluing the company which is at the centre of their universe. Completely focused on their company and with most of their substantial net worth tied up in the market's valuation of their stake in that company, they get unnerved by the market's freedom to exit at the push of a button and view that freedom as somehow inherently wrong and 'speculative'. Not knowing much about the stock market, most actively shun any discussion on it and choose to focus on running their companies; and yet, this is vastly preferable to the alternative – too savvy by half promoters, who connive with operators to ramp stock before, say, preferential allotments or rights issues.

Promoter integrity is particularly important in state-dominated sectors such as infrastructure or real estate. Such is the operating environment in these sectors that a grim and unspoken first-order assumption is that promoters in such sectors are crooks, unless proven otherwise.[13] In recent years, the market has lost some of its infatuation for the politically connected 'strong arm' promoters of the Rate Bull years, and political proximity is now seen as bad rather than good. This puts promoters of such sectors in a bind that many haven't fully appreciated. The political proximity is essential to 'get the job done', but on the other hand, that same proximity devalues promoters' prime source of wealth – the market's valuation of their holdings in listed companies. Brokerages are also discreet about raising issues of promoter integrity, mainly because they don't want to jeopardize ongoing investment banking relationships, but also because laws that criminalize defamation can be used as instruments of harassment by unscrupulous promoters. This acts as a deterrent to anyone but the hardiest truth teller. So, it is common

[13] Saurabh Mukherjea, *Gurus of Chaos*, 53–54.

to see experienced stock pickers dismiss what look like excellent stock picks on 'concerns over promoters', and it is equally common to wonder whether it is rumour mongering or 'concerns' that are the issue. Nevertheless, committees from Cadbury to Irani to Kotak might fret and worry and come out with all sorts of corporate governance mechanisms, but stock markets have their own simple way of enforcing corporate governance – pressing the Sell button.

In recent years, there has been some murmuring about the above arrangements, and yet, when the system worked, it worked well, and the vast majority of the non-MNC success stories in India's corporate sector were promoter-driven companies. Large ownership stakes and diligent successor generations among the promoter class usually addressed the principal-agent problem in Indian corporate governance. Driven by the zeitgeist, some sniping of the promoter class had also set in, and the market took professional management as a sort of cure-all for promoter-run companies, without realizing the huge advantages of a well-groomed successor generation that had learnt the business at the breakfast table.

The Valuation: Firm-level Financial Analysis and the Quality of Statements

The previous chapter emphasized relative valuation approaches through the PE ratio.[14] After establishing that the stock under consideration has a 'reasonable' PE ratio, the focus moves to financial analysis and other valuation factors that impinge on the fundamentals. The professionals are at an advantage here, but other participants having a go at it will realize that required calculations are available through the internet; so, it is not the mechanical computations but their interpretation and use that has some value; that is the focus of this section.[15] The key point is

[14] Some evidence that buying low PE Sensex stocks is better than buying high PE Sensex stocks comes from Parag Parikh, *Value Investing and Behavioral Finance*, New Delhi: Tata McGraw-Hill, 2009, 68–74. The period selected is from 1995 to 2006.

[15] Various books, including Benjamin Graham's *The Interpretation of Financial Statements*, deal with financial statement analysis.

that the statements and analysis deal only with the past up to the present moment, but successful stock picking is also a kind of futurology which implies looking into an unknown future with a discerning eye. It is this peep into the future that really counts, and here an amateur with the right imagination can hope to narrow the gap with the professional.

Besides a low to moderate PE ratio, key factors in the valuation exercise are: a high return on equity (ROE) or high return on capital employed (ROCE), growth at a reasonable price (GARP), earnings visibility into a near future that reflect in cash flows, and financial strength through moderate leverage and low debt-to-equity ratios. Finally, of importance is the quality of statements and dealing with the accounting red flags unique to the Indian environment; here too the pros are at an advantage, but it is for other participants to at least be aware of the issues.

Return on Equity (ROE) and Return on Capital Employed (ROCE)

The starting point for the analysis is a ratio that summarizes the firm's overall performance vis-à-vis both the firm's own past and the financial position of other firms in an industry. This is usually the firm's return on equity (ROE) or its return on capital employed (ROCE).[16] Since equity is the instrument under discussion, the ROE – the ratio of the firm's profits to its equity book value (share capital plus reserves) – is paramount. The ROE is then compared to a firm's cost of equity capital and should exceed it for the firm to create value. Calculating a firm's cost of equity is a complex matter and technically requires an asset pricing model; it will also rise as the firm takes on additional debt, thereby making the capital structure riskier for existing equity holders. The calculation is not covered here but the cost of equity capital is rarely below 12 or 13 per cent in the scheme of things (assuming moderate leverage through debt-equity ratios that are in a target range). So, finding ROEs that meet or exceed 12 to 13 per cent for substantial periods is a

[16] The third ratio is the Return on Sales, and the ROS, ROE, and ROCE (or its related avatar, the ROIC) make up the basic ratios for inter-firm comparison. The Return on Invested Capital (ROIC) measure is similar to the ROCE but makes adjustments for (and deducts) cash balances.

first-order approximation in successful stock picking. For smaller firms, the greater risk and therefore the higher cost of equity mean upward adjustments will have to be made for required ROEs.

For further insight, the ROE can be decomposed and broken down into a subset of ratios: net profit/sales × sales/assets × assets/equity produces the ROE figure of net profit/equity. In this calculation, shareholder returns are respectively a function of operating margins, asset turnover, and financial leverage, and this decomposition allows the picker to further examine the sources of high ROEs and whether they are sustainable in the future.[17]

The ROE's drawback is that it does not adequately account for debt in the capital structure, and as a result, it works best only when comparing firms with similar capital structures. Companies with very high debt might show high ROEs because the measure's denominator of equity is low to begin with; this effect is pronounced when the firm is coming out of a downturn in economic activity. As a result, some professionals in recent years have voiced a preference for the return on capital employed (ROCE).[18] The ROCE is earnings before interest and taxes divided by total assets net of current liabilities.[19] The numerator measures returns to both equity and debt holders and the denominator measures capital employed, which includes fixed assets plus the day-to-day working capital requirement; the measure is therefore sensitive to debt in the firm's financing and penalizes firms with excessive leverage (however, it does produce artificially high numbers for older firms with heavily depreciated fixed assets).

Finally, the ROCE is usually compared to the cost of generating it – the firm's weighted average cost of capital (WACC).

The basic idea is that the returns a firm makes on its invested resources (ROCE) should exceed the cost of funds – both equity and

[17] This is well known as DuPont analysis.

[18] Saurabh Mukherjea, *The Unusual Billionaires*, Gurgaon: Penguin Random House India, 2016, 10–13, 333, 343–44.

[19] Measured from the claims side, the denominator would have equity capital and reserves, together with long-term debt.

debt – that financed those resources (WACC); it is only then that value creation takes place or that economic profits get generated. The WACC will vary based on the riskiness of a business, i.e., the level of operating and financial leverage the firm is exposed to. The higher the operating leverage – the ratio of fixed to variable costs in the firm's cost structure – the higher the risk as the firm goes through the business cycle; the higher the financial leverage – the ratio of fixed claims (debt) to variable claims (equity) in the firm's capital structure – the higher the risk to residual variable claimants such as equity holders. The WACC will be a little lower than the cost of equity discussed earlier – assuming the firm is not all equity financed and that the tax code allows for a tax shield on debt – but it is rarely below 11 to 12 per cent in India. So, finding ROCEs that exceed 11 to 12 per cent for substantial periods is another first-order approximation of successful picking, with upward adjustments for required ROCEs in firms that are smaller or riskier.

Growth at a Reasonable Price (GARP)

A second theme is buying growth at a 'reasonable' price, or GARP investing. This hybrid of the growth and value approaches involves buying stocks with moderately high retrospective earnings and earnings parameters only slightly less than, say, an industry average. Finding good companies at reasonable prices can be as sound a strategy as Graham and Dodd's cigarette-butt method – and is in fact a more realistic approach – but it also means paying more through higher multiples. The caution here is that even high PE multiples can be justified if growing earnings get projected far enough into the future. So those who can guess at a reasonable price in an inherently unreasonable business are at an advantage here. The Price-Earnings-to-Growth (PEG) ratio is one shortcut for incorporating growth into the analysis, and it is widely practiced in India.[20] The PEG ratio is the ratio of a ratio to a rate – the

[20] 'Prashant Jain on his stock picking strategy [Video],' *NDTV*, 2016, Retrieved 10 August 2018, https://www.youtube.com/watch?v=Vz79lgveutE. This is part of a series of interviews with various market professionals titled 'Value Investing Decoded'.

price-earnings ratio is divided by the earnings growth rate expressed as an absolute number. If X from our example in the previous chapter, which had a PE ratio of 12, was growing at 18 per cent annually compounded over the past three years, the resulting PEG ratio would be 12/18 or 0.66. PEG ratios below 1.5 are seen as reasonable, while those above 1.5 less so, and by definition, the lower the ratio the better. This example deals with trailing numbers from the past and is therefore subject to the usual distortions that come from cyclicity or earnings surges. Larger rewards go to those who can guess at future growth rates that go into the denominator of the PEG ratio; this is where moats become important, as the sounder the picker's judgment on the moat, the more accurate the estimate of future growth rates. Since the Indian market is perennially priced for growth rather than value, much effort is spent on divining whether the price paid for that growth is reasonable. GARP is the compromise between the market's obsession with growth and the conservative Graham-like streak of trading communities who influence that market.

Earnings: Their Translation into Cash Flow and Final Deployment

Another key theme is cash generation. Most pros will talk about the importance of cash flow, which basically means the ability of earnings to translate into that cash flow.[21] At the end of the day, the business and promoter analysis must ideally translate into selecting a cash-generating business. Once this happens, succeeding activities move the cash: into the business through reinvestment (or plowback); into other diversifications, either related or not; into successful deployment in mergers and acquisitions; and when none of the above is possible, back to shareholders. Now the market for corporate control in India is sketchy, with few successful mergers and acquisitions, and most Indian companies are reluctant to return cash to shareholders. Consequently, by a process of elimination, the emphasis is usually on the first two options of successful reinvestment back into the business or other

[21] Saurabh Mukherjea, *Gurus of Chaos*, 64–65.

diversification.[22] The market refers to this as 'capital allocation', but it is just business policy at work (more technically, future growth is also a function of high ROE and successful reinvestment through a high plowback ratio; hence the emphasis on reinvestment/diversification in a growth-obsessed environment).

Also, shenanigans are usually discovered by finding gaps between reported profits and cash flows, so it is good practice to focus on cash flow statements as much as the income statement. One key ratio is the cash conversion ratio, or the ratio of operating cash flow to EBITDA, which brings out working capital issues in the company.

Leverage

All these characteristics are futile unless they apply to a firm with a sound financial position – one that has moderate to controllable borrowings, together with the capacity to refinance those borrowings. Usually this means keeping an eye on debt-equity ratios and current ratios. Here industry practice will vary widely, but debt-equity ratios above 2 and current ratios (current assets to current liabilities) below 1.5 to 2 usually call for further investigation.

The Quality of Statements and Accounting Red Flags

It is not just the quantity of disclosure but also its quality that matters. Anything for the steadily increasing earnings that reflect an ongoing business, deviate little from trend, and are discernible from clear financial statements. And better still if those earnings are easily distributable as cash dividends. The quantity of disclosures has increased in recent years, but this must be balanced against earnings management by companies, anyway a habit magnified by the well-known Indian tendency to complicate things that don't need to be complicated. International studies that include India in their surveys find that local firms have high

[22] Stock pickers' emphasis on capital allocation is brought out in Saurabh Mukherjea, *The Unusual Billionaires*, 342–45.

disclosure requirements on criteria such as ownership structure, business operations, and corporate governance, but the studies also find that those high disclosure requirements are matched by correspondingly high levels of earnings management.[23] In recent years, voluminous disclosure has made the picker's life easier but earnings management by companies has made the picker's life harder – and in this clash is competence tested. This usually means that 'non-recurring' items in the statements are OK, but recurring 'non-recurring' items may not be OK. Generally, in India, red flags crop up more on the expense side than the revenue side; for instance, capitalizing operating costs and converting them to assets, rather than simply treating them as costs that should be expensed, will artificially raise earnings. Fiddling with depreciation schedules, i.e., moving from accelerated depreciation to straight-line depreciation, raises earnings, but it also raises the tax outgo. In a high inflation environment like India, the choice of inventory valuation – FIFO (first in, first out) or LIFO (last in, first out) – becomes important; with high inflation, switching to LIFO will reduce the tax outgo but may not be adopted because it raises the cost of goods sold and reduces earnings. Further, switching between the methods will make a difference to the bottom line.

Two perennial red flags are 'related-party transactions' and bloodbath accounting. Related-party transactions usually occur between three sets of entities: listed company, promoter group, and other private entities controlled by the promoter group. As seen in the Unitech case, the combinatorial explosion of related-party transactions between these three entities can, in theory at least, reach dizzying levels and make even the most competent and determined analysts simply throw up their hands. At that point, such arrangements will have served their purpose. So, markets tend to reward companies that have fewer related-party transactions and give such companies better valuations. Bloodbath accounting has also become a recent phenomenon and is prominent in some sectors (like banks) whose accounting policies give managements much leeway. It usually involves bunching up and

[23] See Rajesh Chakrabarti and Sankar De, 'Introduction,' *Capital Markets in India*, eds. Rajesh Chakrabarti and Sankar De, New Delhi: Sage Publications, 2010, 26.

disclosing all the bad news at one go, which sends the stock down but also leaves the market free to price in upside potential later. Incoming bank CEOs – and especially those public-sector bank CEOs who have tenures of limited duration – are prone to it, as they can take credit for the later upside that coincides with their tenures. Nevertheless, these manoeuvres complicate the market's discounting function and make a mess of analyst projections.

Red flags in three important areas – research and development costs, options, and pension plans – don't occur in India with the same frequency as they do in other markets. Whether R&D costs are expensed or treated as an asset (and later amortized) can make a big difference to earnings, but the category is not large in absolute terms, as Indian companies have among the lowest R and D spends in the world. Stock options with potentially dilutive properties (which reduce the proportional ownership of shareholders) that go unrecognized are relatively unused (either as incentives or corporate governance tools), mainly because the promoter class that majority owns and manages most Indian companies has less need for using options as a motivational device; in the West, by contrast, stock options whose value derives from short-term earnings give managers powerful incentives to manage those earnings, but here managerial compensation is less likely to be influenced by stock options, which, in turn, lowers the likelihood of earnings manipulation. Finally, underfunded pension plans can raise red flags elsewhere, but in India's low-wage economy, low labour costs and the resultant low future pension costs are not a major item in most cost structures.

Concern over the quality of earnings is appropriate in the Indian operating environment.[24] An inefficient market is less likely to look

[24] Other accounting red flags from the income statement include: extraordinary one-time income items that don't relate to ongoing business, sudden and severe reductions in discretionary costs such as advertising and R&D, payroll denials, and reducing gross margin percentages. Accounting red flags from the balance sheet include: disproportionate increases in receivables, longer accounts payable turns, decreasing inventory turns, significant 'hole plugging' enlargements in intangible assets such as brand values and goodwill, large increases in short-term borrowings, large net working capital reductions that flow from supplier funding, and large swings in deferred tax or reserve accounts. One usually unacknowledged 'blue' flag is a tax loss carry forward/carry back that can make the evaluated company an attractive takeover candidate to highly profitable firms.

through and find manipulation, which gives added reason for pickers to be diligent in their efforts – the rewards for that diligence are correspondingly much greater. Relying on the crowd and assorted pooh-bahs on corporate boards can only take you so far. Satyam won something called the Golden Peacock Global Award for Excellence in Corporate Governance just four months before its promoter confessed to massive fraud on national television.[25] A Harvard Business School professor with expertise in accounting, control, and corporate governance sat on its board for many years before that disclosure (the award itself was subsequently retracted).

Other Criteria: Free Floats and the Long Corner

Free floats – the actual percentage of stock available to the public for purchase – vary widely in India, and a low free float can be a key criterion in stock picking. For years, the minimum offering at IPOs was just 10 per cent, and it was not unusual to see promoters retain holdings as high as 90 per cent in companies. Attempts have been made in recent years to increase the minimum public offering, but in most cases, it still remains at 25 per cent, which allows promoter holdings as high as 75 per cent and reduces the free float considerably. So, the long corner becomes a possibility and, as previous sections showed, substantial buying on a low free float can drive a stock's price to spectacular levels. Sometimes the long corner calculation can include entities regarded as part of the promoter group or friendly fundies who sit on big holdings for long periods. As much as 80 to 90 per cent of a company's shares can be locked up in this fashion, leaving a low free float to be bid up. Experienced pickers try to get the long corner to work in their favour, but rarely articulate it as such, and in fact this book is likely the first to use the phrase.

For an amazing example of the long corner, consider MMTC, the public-sector commodity trading company. In November 2007, the

[25] Press Trust of India (PTI), 'Satyam Stripped off Golden Peacock Global Award,' *Economic Times*, 8 January 2009.

stock traded at over ₹42,500 with ₹25 in earnings, which meant a PE multiple of 1,700! At that time, over 99.33 per cent of its equity was held by the government, leading to a free float of only 5,456 shares held between 808 shareholders.[26] MMTC is an unusual case, but less extreme situations with promoter group holdings of between 70 and 80 per cent are surprisingly common in India, and the resulting long corner can distort price discovery to the point where valuation becomes a second-order effect.

Another sterling example of the long corner in action comes from a noted stock operator who entered the retailing business; after all, who better than an operator to understand the long corner and its advantages. This worthy accumulated a fortune in stock operations, invested a chunk of that fortune in real estate, tacked a middling retailing business onto the real estate, and used his ownership of both to rent out the real estate at lower rates to the retailing operations, effectively subsidizing the retailing operation through lower rentals. Rentals are the major cost item in retailing, so the subsidy benefited the retail operations and they showed considerable profits and potential. He then took the subsidized retail business public, retained over 80 per cent for himself and the promoter group, and sold close to 20 per cent in a public offering; the offer included large chunks allotted to friendly participants and fundies with the implicit understanding that they would not flip their stakes at the offering, or for some time later (the allotments were based on relationships built up over a lifetime of market operations). This reduced the free float even further – from the official 20 per cent to perhaps as low as 7 to 9 per cent. Naturally, the stock rocketed higher from the IPO and kept going up. Along the way, our man kept selling small amounts to bring his holding down to the mandated 75 per cent, a requirement that had to be met within three years of the IPO.

Our man got his price all right, for all this manipulation resulted in multiples that went beyond 100 and stayed there. Consider that during

[26] Nimish Shukla, 'MMTC Dearest Share at Rs 42, 483,' *Times of India*, 3 November 2007. The importance of free floats is also brought out in Parag Parikh, *Value Investing and Behavioral Finance*, 141.

this period, Walmart, one of the world's noted retailing operations, traded at between 9- and 14-times earnings. Further, even as revenue and bottom lines collapsed during the coronavirus pandemic, the multiple crossed 200 and the stock chugged higher. Along the way, the public approvingly noted the worthy's astuteness and sagacity as exhibited in his cross-subsidized retailing business, and participants showed a touching faith that one of their own would deliver the goods. Both kept buying in.

By now, the Street had begun to sense what was going on but did a poor job of articulating it; perhaps there was some awkwardness over telling on one of their own, or perhaps the extant stock price acted as its own reality to weak-minded analysts who could not see through all this. Nevertheless, the few who had substantial stakes were watching the promoter's holding closely. Critically, the biggest variable in the valuation and the whole shebang was our man's moves on the 75 per cent holding, together with the intentions of those friendly fundies. If our man sold a chunk of his holdings to capture the bizarre valuations, it would mean going through an awfully small exit; daily traded volumes were much, much smaller than his large holdings, and the selling would have collapsed the price. Effectively, the stratospheric valuation rested on negligible daily volumes. By now the exercise was like pedalling a bicycle; stopping suddenly would risk falling off. One way out of all this was to use the bizarrely overvalued stock as currency to buy into stock that had more sober claims over assets and cash flows; merger and acquisition activity duly began, where the overvalued stock was exchanged for undervalued stock in other companies. The overvalued stock was also used as currency to get into real estate and a portfolio of projects and real estate was duly accumulated.

The entire operation – a mediocre retailing business being distributed at multiples of between 100 and 200 – ranks as one of the world's great exercises in stock distribution and worthy of a James Keene. In fact, our man is James Keene *ka baap*. Presumably, this distribution will continue into the future and the worthy will keep selling those small packets along the way, hopefully till the point where the free float is sizable and valuation is no longer a second-order effect. All this is perfectly legal (at least presently), but the morality and ethics of distributing stock at a 150 multiple is not the same as doing it at a 20 multiple. Despite questions about the bizarre valuation, the price cannot adjust downward as the free float is locked up and the promoter, a noted operator himself, is standing by to support the stock during the distribution. If the price cannot adjust downward, volumes will simply dry up, but note that our man, as a former operator, is an expert at manipulating volumes anyway. The situation is interestingly poised; brokerage reports are cautiously bullish while justifying those 150 multiples, and the debate will get heated only when the party ends. Till that point our man benefits from using the bizarrely overvalued stock as currency, and everyone else is simply on for the ride.

Other Criteria: Regulatory Interface

Finally, choosing companies with little government involvement or regulatory interface is a key principle of many stock pickers. Historically, the government in India reminded one of actor David Niven's comment on his good friend Errol Flynn: '*You can count on Errol Flynn. He'll always let you down.*'[27] Some might take the view as cynical, but is it a coincidence that the best-performing sectors in the market, including IT services, two-wheelers, and fast-moving consumer goods, have negligible government interaction and little rent-seeking behaviour? The problem is further complicated by the uncertain quality of regulation in India. The instinctive tendency in the political economy of Indian regulation is to side with the *aam aadmi* or common man, often at the cost of the shareholder/owner. Consequently, sectors with little government involvement or regulatory interface are viewed favourably by the market.

---

[27] 'Philip French's screen legends,' *Guardian*, https://www.theguardian.com/film/2009/dec/06/errol-flynn-screen-legends.

Analysing stock picking in detail reveals as many success factors in play as there are stocks, and the energetic participant finds that noise investing is just as likely as noise trading. Generalizing, other than on the above lines, is difficult. Besides the obvious *valuation* plays discussed earlier, one hears of *throughput plays*, where the upcoming removal of a production bottleneck will send output soaring, with absorption guaranteed by the product's market. There are *turnaround plays* everywhere, and here turnarounds caused by changes in management/promoter groups are better regarded than turnarounds caused by changes in industry conditions or the policy environment. *Conscience plays* combine business sense with ethical dimensions like corporate governance or environmental redressal, and here the fond hope is that the market creates positive externalities by rewarding good behaviour and driving up the valuation of such companies. Seeming paradoxes arise with *cyclical plays,* where stocks are bought at multiples of 30 and sold at multiples of 5; the industry contraction causes the high multiple, following which the massive cyclical up move and resulting earnings expansion in the denominator causes the PE multiple to appear low when the stock is fully priced. Among the most difficult to judge are *asset plays*, and it is common to hear promoters complain that the stock's price does not reflect hidden assets; it is equally common to hear of stock pickers, who – after initiating a position in such asset plays – have the same complaint.

So what would the perfect stock pick look like? The perfect stock pick – let's call it Tiddlywinks – that summarized the above criteria and became a 1,000 bagger would have: a strong moat around the business, scalable growth over many years, a small to middling market capitalization, presence in an area playing either to India's international comparative advantage or with exposure to the consumption side of its large domestic market, negligible unorganized sector competition, sound management with integrity, a low to moderate PE ratio, a high ROE or ROCE, a low ratio of PE to growth, earnings visibility that reflects in cash flows together with the deployment of those cash flows in successful reinvestment or dividend payout, moderate leverage, no accounting red flags, a high promoter shareholding, a low free float, and little government or regulatory interaction.

Has such a stock ever existed? One canonized stock – a real Tiddlywinks that ticked most of the above boxes – was Page Industries. The South Asian licensee of one of the world's leading innerwear brands – Jockey – Page went public in early 2007, after over a decade of successful operation in the country. The stock became a 95-bagger as it went from its 2007 issue price of ₹360 to over ₹34,000 by 2018. Surprisingly, Page continued to outperform for years after its selection as a market favourite, itself testimony to how strong a pick it was.

Consider here the Tiddlywinks criteria as applied to Page Industries. The moat was the Jockey brand and access to its international innovations, together with a carefully built network of individual distributors; scalable growth over many years was evident in the compounded 35 per cent growth in sales, with comparable profit growth; the stock was a small cap at its 2007 listing with a trifling capitalization of ₹400 crores; the company played to the domestic consumption story, as the small unit cost of innerwear went together with large volumes generated by the country's huge population; there was severe unorganized sector competition, and this worked against the pick; it was publicly reported that management quality was not a concern as most of the founding team was still around, and capital allocation had to pass strict hurdle rates; the PE ratio was sweet and reasonable in the early years but almost touched 100 by 2018, as the after-effects of being a market favourite kicked in; ROE and ROCE were usually over 50 per cent during the up move;[28] the PEG ratio also stayed reasonable during most of the up move, though it deteriorated in later years as the stock's price moved ahead of earnings growth; earnings fully reflected in cash flows as the industry's working capital cycle was favourable and cash rich to its players, which also meant dividend payouts as high as 60 per cent of earnings; leverage was always moderate as the industry was not capital intensive and had little need to borrow and take on debt; there were no publicly reported red flags; the promoter holding was almost 50

[28] Saurabh Mukherjea, *The Unusual Billionaires*, 155.

per cent; four other institutions held another 23 per cent, which meant that the long corner was firmly in place as the promoters and these four institutions owned almost three-quarters of equity, leaving a low free float available for the public;[29] and finally, the innerwear industry had little government interaction or regulatory interface which meant that rent-seeking was minimal. As a result of all this, by 2016, books were being written about the stock and others like it.[30]

A less elaborate framework that builds on some of the above criteria comes from Motilal Oswal, a retail-oriented brokerage; it is mentioned here not as an endorsement, but only to illustrate how professionals formalize the stock-picking approach. In this framework, stocks pass through a QGLP filter – Quality (of management), Growth (in earnings and return on equity), Longevity (of competitive advantage), and Price (paying a fair price for a good business).[31] Sometimes a Size filter is also added. Just from simple correspondence, it can be seen that Quality corresponds to the promoter criterion, Growth and Price correspond to valuation criteria, while Longevity corresponds to the moat's endurance in the business criterion. So, behind the acronyms, this is basically GARP investing with the Size filter ensuring a small- to mid-cap bias.

There remains the final act of going about all this and looking for stocks.

In decreasing order of systematization, the main tools involve screens, scuttlebutt, or simply looking around. Screens are a top-down approach and formally filter the stock universe based on quantifiable valuation criteria, which still leaves the picker to do the vital assessments of businesses and promoters. Scuttlebutt is a bottom-up approach

[29] The calculation was done for June 2018.

[30] Saurabh Mukherjea, *The Unusual Billionaires*, 143–78.

[31] As of 2018, the framework's formal measures include: a) stocks with a market capitalization of less than ₹3,000 crores, b) price-to-earnings multiples of not more than 25 times trailing earnings, c) return on equity (ROE) of 15 per cent or more, and d) businesses which offer a play on value migration or niche opportunities. Source: https://www.motilaloswalmf.com/about-us/chairman-speak/6. A detailed description of the methodology is available at Motilal Oswal, *QGLP: Our Mantra for Wealth Creation* at https://www.motilaloswal mf.com/Campaigns/QGLP Contest/images/QGLP-Booklet.pdf. Both accessed on 1 August 2018.

and involves checking out a firm by questioning an array of parties, including the firm's customers, competitors, and suppliers; one shortcut to scuttlebutt is staying in touch with the magic circle of professional participants, though some would say this is a dubious exercise and no substitute for the actual work of selection. Finally, simply looking around implies observing companies that enter the investor's personal space and fulfil the investor's needs and wants; it can also mean scanning India's array of personal finance and investment advisory magazines for stock ideas that match the above criteria.[32] Patient and astute participants will do all of the above to obtain a list of stocks and then wait for the fat man to approach.

Just like the fat man whose weight we don't have to guess at to know he's fat, so too with the market whose value we don't have to guess at to know it's cheap. The fat man approach is possible only because of Graham's famous parable of Mr Market.[33] In this parable, every person who owns stocks is in an imaginary 50:50 partnership with a moody and mentally unstable manic depressive named Mr Market. Every day between 9.15 a.m. and 3.30 p.m., Mr Market gets up and tries to buy out the participant's stake in the partnership; simultaneously, Mr Market offers to sell his own stake to the participant. Whether the participant likes it or not, every day, day after day, Mr Market gets up and hammers away at the participant and makes his quotes. The problem is Mr Market's mental imbalance. Sometimes he bids to buy out the participant's stake in the partnership at an absurdly large amount, and sometimes he bids next to nothing. The reverse is also true on the sell side; sometimes Mr Market offers to sell out his stake in the partnership to the participant for some absurdly large amount, and sometimes he offers next to nothing.

The solution to this bizarre problem is to focus on Mr Market's purse and not his moods. When Mr Market is all gung-ho and happy

[32] The array of magazines offering advice on stock picking includes: *Capital Market, MoneyLife, Dalal Times, Investor's India, Outlook Money, Dalal Street, Wealth Insight, and Finapolis.*

[33] Chapter 8 of Benjamin Graham's *The Intelligent Investor*, titled 'The Investor and Market Fluctuations', contains the parable.

and cheerful and volunteers to buy out the participant at an absurd amount, the participant should happily accept and *sell* his half share in the partnership to Mr Market. Similarly, when Mr Market is in a funk and depressed and offers to sell his share in the partnership to the participant for next to nothing, the participant should happily accept and *buy* Mr Market's half share in the partnership from him. With increasing market efficiency these situations don't present themselves very often, and usually there is no fat man approaching, and everyone around is nice and sleek and just so, as the efficiency school says they should be. But sometimes Mr Market gets into one of his moods, and the fat man approaches, and when that happens, the participant should load up on the list of stocks he has picked based on the above criteria. Over the 40-year span of a typical investing lifetime, these situations present themselves only occasionally, so identifying them when they do occur and loading up (or selling out) becomes important.

For most investors, stock picking isn't even recommended. The volatility of the Indian environment, together with the mass of factors that go into the exercise, make the activity simply too risky for the average investor, and most would be better off in a mutual fund, ideally through a systematic plan. Yet there remains the thrill of the chase, that soaring indefinable feeling that comes from being proven right. Further, large areas of market inefficiency – particularly in the swathes of stocks outside the major indexes – ease the way for the amateur picker and make the task a little easier. The important thing is to keep the exercise small and systematic, at least till the investor finds he has a flair for picking. Keeping the bulk of the investor's corpus in professionally managed mutual funds and a small remaining amount to be systematically run along the above lines is a workable compromise.

13

OTHER PRACTICAL APPROACHES

Contrarianism, Growth, and Momentum

There are many approaches to the markets, but what works for one person might not work for another. Above all, the adage *gnothi seauton*, or know thyself, applies. Self-awareness makes it easier to find an approach that works and is preferable to the alternative – going through the agony of letting the market point out, through a process of elimination, the other approaches that don't suit the participant. Most of these other approaches find followers in India, and among them are contrarianism, growth, and momentum.

Contrarianism

It is axiomatic that all great investors are contrarians or at least need a contrarian streak, but like many aspects of the market, what is axiomatic is a short step from becoming a cliché. Contrarianism is a famous yet dangerous market approach that when done well becomes the stuff of market lore. At a basic level, it means buying from the crowd what the crowd hates and selling to the crowd what it loves – effectively, this amounts to dealing with the market at its extremes.

There are two formal criteria to doing contrarianism well. First, there must be a strong consensus on future price movement, and that consensus must be unanimous and near total. Only then can one draw the conclusion that crowd psychology has been taken to its extreme.[1] Second, that strong consensus must be supported by 'weak' reasons. A weak reason in contrarianism is not necessarily an error in logic or reasoning that undermines the earlier consensus, but rather a belief that is widely known, so much so that it can be safely presumed to be 'discounted' or 'in the price'.[2] In the stock market, what everyone knows is not worth knowing.

So, when the sun is out and shining and the beer is nice and cold and everything is just perfect – then there is unanimous consensus that it's all perfect, and the reasons for that consensus like, say, sector prospects or the displacement, are known to one and all, down to the shoeshine boy. When that happens, the last buyer has come in; there is no one left to buy and so the deluge; by this time, the contrarian has made their move and exited at a market top. With the advantage of hindsight, the behaviour of software stocks in 2000 or infrastructure counters in 2007 clearly met the above criteria; sometimes the entire market can be seen conforming to the above criteria. But this is all in hindsight, and at those times, everything looked eminently reasonable to a vast range of people. The main point is that the reason behind the move is widely known, which leaves the market open to the element of surprise. When everything good is known, the slightest bad news has a large impact on price; the hot sector is over-owned in all probability, and the combination of over-ownership and bad news causes a sell-off. The reverse applies to good news in a beaten-down sector; the beaten-down sector is under-owned in all probability, and the combination of under-ownership and good news causes prices to flare to the up side as new buying comes in. Alternately, in the case of a beaten-down sector, prices fall so low that valuation considerations start to prevail.

In the main, contrarianism in India is always – and safely – practised by buying on the downside rather than short selling on the upside. Buying

[1] Richard J. Teweles and Frank J. Jones, *The Futures Game: Who Wins, Who Loses, & Why*, New York: McGraw Hill Professional, 1998, 277–304, 325–31. Futures trading is inherently contrarian as each contract has a counterparty on the other side of a trade with a contrarian view on price.

[2] Ibid.

from the crowd (or Mr Market, as Graham would have it) what it hates and later selling to the crowd what it loves implies taking advantage of Mr Market only when he moves excessively to the downside and stocks get exaggeratedly cheap. So, the first leg of the contrarian trade is usually buying low followed by selling high. The reverse – when stocks get expensive, the first leg of the transaction is short selling high followed by the square up of buying low – should theoretically be possible with the same ease; in recent years, the gush of liquidity from quantitative easing (QE) has led to extensive overvaluation, and yet this reverse trade almost never happens because there isn't an adequate short selling mechanism. In earlier days, the badla system's exact duality made the reverse trade equally possible through the naked short play, but with badla's removal and the continued absence of an adequate short selling product, the bias to the long side manifested itself, and the short trade moved from being built into the microstructure to effectively banned.

In fact, nowadays the market's systemic bias to the long side makes the short contrarian trade suicidal, but few have noticed this. And yet, and despite being very dangerous, the reverse trade happens – and frequently at that – through the derivatives market. The single stock futures (SSF) segment of India's colossal derivatives market allows for easy short exposure, especially in the larger and more liquid stocks which anyway make up the bulk of volumes; the index futures and options also allow for short exposure to the entire market, if so required. The high volumes and low transaction costs of the derivatives market allow for tempting and easy short-side exposure; rather than go through the bother of borrowing and selling short Wipro shares, it is a small matter to short sell a Wipro futures contract. Nevertheless, there is extreme risk in taking short side derivatives exposure, when the entire cash market from which those derivatives derive their value is biased long, because of the absence of a short-selling product there. But the masses that crowd the derivatives market rarely see things this way and happily trade the short side as contrarians with the odds stacked heavily against them.

Experts and the smart money will occasionally put on their contrarian caps and trade the derivatives short side by using the above situation to their advantage; because there is no short side in the cash market, one-way long moves result in vast numbers of long-side stop-loss sell orders bunched up below present price. So, money comes much faster to the derivatives short side – as the market collapses through the cash market's stop-loss honeycomb – than it does to the long side.

A certain amount of contrarianism also appears in stories of the dervishes of Dalal Street, the big professional traders. Contrarianism was especially apparent at early stages of their investing careers, and many made their fortunes by catching the market cycle's turns in the previous century's closing decades. LIC is the other major participant that publicly acknowledges a contrarian bias.[3] LIC does not face redemption pressures, so contrarian strategies are easier to implement, but not much else is publicly known about its investment policy or strategy, and the annual reports don't provide any details.

Yet, contrarianism must be used very carefully. Many people in India's stock market are superficially contrarian, especially on the sell side, and it is common to see participants sell a stock just because it has gone up and an artificially set price target has been met. An inherently speculative mindset makes this all the more likely. In fact, in India, superficial contrarianism might be a bigger problem than the conformity that produces herding and other crowd behaviour discussed in Western studies of market extremes. As a result, it is common to hear stories of people exiting early. As shown, selling Unitech after it had flared up 900 per cent from 60 to 600 would have led to missing the move to 70,000, and this routinely happens in Indian markets. Of course, superficial contrarianism – genuinely applied – would imply short selling Unitech in the derivatives markets, which is a suicidal move by any standard.

It is also common to hear of contrarian disasters on entry. Till recently, companies didn't go bankrupt but got 'sick' instead; the 2016 bankruptcy code is beginning to change this, but conventional triggers for bankruptcy are still not widely known or calculated. Buying a stock

[3] 'Our total focus is on long-term investments… and we are contrarian investors traditionally,' LIC chairman VK Sharma, as quoted in 'LIC Books Rs19,000 Crore Profit from Market in FY17,' *Indian Express*, 17 May 2017.

that trades in low double digits on expectations of a turnaround might result in buying a company that is bankrupt, but this fact is not widely known, and so the stock takes its own time drifting to zero. The problem is exacerbated by the presence of those short constraints in the cash market; because of them, the move to zero as the equity gets wiped out takes place very slowly and over long periods. Not realizing this, the crowd often gets lured into buying these low-priced stocks as contrarian plays, and this trade can manifest for extended periods.[4]

Used excessively as a mental outlook, contrarianism can also breed a certain kind of arrogance. Presumably crowds also have some type of wisdom behind them. Extremes of crowd psychology are also few and far between, which implies that the big contrarian trades are put on rarely. But in the extended time between such trades, the contrarian mindset's temptation is to see every market wiggle and squiggle as suitable for putting on a trade, and this is accentuated by the speculative character of the market.

In all this, the main issue is the disconnect between the contrarian's thinking and the market's thinking, and that space is key. The wider that space (after diligent analysis), the higher the possibility of the trade working out, and it is in that disconnect where the contrarian mulls a position. In fact, fundies and dervishes – when trying to get a handle on the disconnect – will actively seek out contrary opinion of the bearish kind and listen carefully to the arguments made, as a sort of counterweight to their own bullishness.[5] Nevertheless, because of domestic bias and lack of global diversification, this happens only at the stock level and never at the country level. Value investors will also have a contrarian streak and ponder their investments in this disconnect between their thinking and that of the market. In fact, by definition value

[4] With the firm itself as the underlying, it is tempting to see these stocks as trading at their call option values with an exercise price equivalent to the present value of the firm's debt, but it is unlikely that participants would undertake the complex calculations necessary to establish such option values. More probably, public shareholders as call option holders on the bankrupt firm have chosen not to exercise their options, punted the firm to the bondholders and simply walked away, but short constraints and the public's penny stock obsession allow prices to linger on their way to zero.

[5] Saurabh Mukherjea, *Gurus of Chaos*, New Delhi: Bloomsbury Publishing India, 2015, 123–24.

investors will have to be contrarians, and this also goes back to market efficiency.[6] Value investing is widespread and possible only because the Indian market is inefficient. In more efficient markets, like the US for example, many participants would see value investing as an anomaly.

Contrarianism is also getting complicated by the inherently contrarian positions the Indian public itself is taking. With the onset of quantitative easing since 2008, the contrarian 'buy on dips' trade has always worked, and so, the public's psychological conditioning into this 'buy on dips' trade has been complete and total. Soon an entire generation of traders will have been conditioned into this trade. Bear market durations have progressively reduced – in the new millennium, the last time a bear market of any significant duration took place was between 2000 and 2003 – which also strengthens this psychological conditioning of the public. It is common to see advisors and experts offer contrarian guidance, and '*Wait for a correction to enter*' is standard cocktail party advice, given without the realization that there simply won't be a correction if everybody thinks the same way. The moment a correction happens, the most optimistic buyer at the margin in '*Wait for a correction*' mode enters, the correction gets corrected, and the market advance resumes to the upside. The psychological conditioning of the successful 'buy on dips' trade over this generation of traders exaggerates this effect. So, when the public is contrarian, there doesn't seem to be anyone to be contrarian against. In that case, perhaps the contrarian's position is to become a trend follower. Market mavens are familiar with this sort of inverted reasoning.

And yet there remains one party – the foreign institutional investor (FII) – against whom the entire market can put on a contrarian trade. As seen earlier, the frequency with which domestic institutional investors cross FIIs almost on a daily basis is almost uncanny. So FII flows wax and wane in response to unconventional Western monetary policy, and the domestic buy side, instead of diversifying internationally, takes on a

[6] From a value investor's perspective, the essence of contrarianism is outlined in David Dremen, *Contrarian Investment Strategies: The Next Generation*, New York: Simon & Schuster, 1998, 7–8, 137–92, 405–10.

contrarian role and defends its home turf against those flows, pointing to systemic and market-wide contrarian positions against FII flows.

Growth

This is a popular approach, and market obsession with growth is considerable. GDP growth envy (similar to the Cold War's missile envy) is common among policymakers and chattering classes nowadays, and it is usually accompanied by dire predictions about the social unrest that will follow if high growth rates are not met. The word 'growth' has considerable incantatory significance in India, and this is not surprising in a country that invented the *mantra*, that most basis of incantations. Just as 'Om' is the primordial sound that underlies all Creation, 'Growth' is the elemental chant that underlies all wealth creation in the stock market. Those with a fine ear also notice that just as the first sound gets drawn out into auuummmm, so too does the second get drawn out into grooowwthhh. Participants obsess over growth more than India's policymakers or chattering classes do, which is itself quite an achievement; it is hard to find a brokerage strategy report that does not mention the word several times. Philip Fisher was the most noted theorist of the approach and one of its early practitioners. Blessed to be located at Silicon Valley before it even acquired that nomenclature, Fisher spent many a weekend packing a sandwich and driving around the Valley, looking for growth titans – mainly from the technology space – that would shape America's future after the Second World War.[7] Ever since Fisher, in the West at least, the central theme has been a long view of technology, scientific, and engineering stocks.

But in a growth-obsessed economy like India, the growth stock approach has a wider application and most of it is tied to demographics. As the demographic dividend makes its way through the economy, the way a meal bulge goes through a python, growth manifests itself here in ways that are different from mature Western markets. A well-

[7] Fisher's approach is outlined in Philip A. Fisher, *Common Stocks and Uncommon Profits*, New York: John Wiley, *Wiley Investment Classics*, 2003, 3–4, 18–60.

defined population cohort causes explosions in product categories that it demands at various stages of its life cycle – the same 200-million cohort of young people demand online education services, then move on to marriage-related services, followed by home buying and furnishing, and so on. Alternative growth scenarios come from transitions and graduations: hence the two-wheeler industry which captured the transition as millions graduated from bicycles, or the consumer goods industry which benefited as more people chose toothpaste over the neem leaf (or its powder). In fact, rather than the complex quantitative calculations of a brokerage report, it is often qualitative insights along the above lines that can yield results.

The main idea is that growth in long-run cash flows over many years, from (among other things) proprietary technology or fast-growing markets, will compensate for the high 40 to 50 times multiples one pays for the stock.[8] In India, it is not technology as much as the rate of change in market growth that is relevant, and here the key factors are competition and industry saturation. At some point, competitive entry – attracted by the high growth rates – will drive industry returns down to the cost of capital. The remedy for this is the 'moat', or something a company does well enough to create a barrier that can keep out the competition and hold off, for a while at least, this tendency of competitive markets to drive returns down to equilibrium. These moats come in various forms and can include innovation, brands, closely held licences or patents, and networks that are difficult to replicate; broadly, they may also include favourable long-term contracts with a range of stakeholders, including employees or vendors or distribution channels built over generations.

As for saturation – industries in India tend to mature and saturate a lot faster than most people realize. In fact, often even the analysts covering such industries don't realize how fast they saturate, and here it might be the stock market's obsession with growth that is responsible for its blindness to saturation.

[8] Ibid.

But if assumptions about competitive pressure and industry saturation on the evaluated stock are reasonable, growth investing can be rewarding. Practically, much growth investing in India boils down to GARP investing – or buying Growth at a Reasonable Price. As mentioned earlier, key to all this is deciding on a 'reasonable' price in an inherently unreasonable business. The Indian market's obsession with growth meets its conservative Graham-like streak through the GARP concept. India's trading communities – inherently conservative and obsessed with bargaining their way to the best price – dominate the market's activities, and to most of them '*Bhav Bhagwan Che*' – Price is God. So, there is little question of paying extravagant multiples for growth, and the resulting GARP compromise dominates the thinking of many professional investors.[9] The emphasis on GARP investing becomes increasingly strident as the market goes higher. After all, mutual funds with a mandate to stay fully invested have little choice other than to insist that they're practising GARP investing when they're fully invested in a market that trades at 35 times earnings with little earnings visibility. More generally, fundies' market babble moves from value to GARP as the market heads higher. As seen earlier, one metric used in all this is the PEG ratio, or the ratio of price-earnings to the growth rate, with PEGs below 1.5 usually seen as reasonable. The PE ratio in the numerator is always known in absolute terms, so the PEG ratio's application depends on the time frame over which the earnings growth in the denominator can be reliably projected.

Graham would have turned away from much of this, but Fisher was a natural at it and discovered the likes of Texas Instruments, Motorola, and Dow Chemical. In India, most of the dervishes and fundies try hard to be growth investors because that's where the money is. Yet, the approach comes with the usual caveats with which investing abounds. Despite the conservative Graham-like streak the market claims to have, overpaying for growth is a common problem in India; but this is inherent in the approach itself, especially in a country so obsessed

[9] See for example the views of Prashant Jain. 'Prashant Jain on his stock picking strategy [Video],' *NDTV*, 2016, retrieved 10 August, 2018, https://www.youtube.com/watch?v=Vz79lgveutE.

with the growth phenomenon. Exaggerating the resilience of the moat will also justify many a valuation. Further, investors are prone to first selecting high-growth sectors and then buying smaller companies in those sectors' listed spaces, trying to find the next Infosys, so to speak. The search for the multi-bagger and the obsession with scalability are responsible for this, but that obsession can result in ignoring subtle company-specific factors that go into stock selection;[10] trying to find the next Infosys, many end up with the next DSQ.[11] 'Official' growth stocks that are anointed as such by the market also have very high PE ratios. Finally, growth extrapolation into the indefinite future in a manner that ignores market saturation is a big issue, and telecom is the best recent example of that.

So sometimes that meal bulge going through the python gets stuck, and the python develops indigestion. In the earlier example, the transition from bicycles to two-wheelers did take place, and two-wheeler demand exploded as the market hit an inflection point. But the next logical transition from two-wheelers to automobiles has not taken place, and the automobile industry is, to use a comfortable euphemism, in 'a challenging environment'. In fact, the Indian automobile industry is a poster boy for what can go wrong with this approach and illustrates how growth investing must be triangulated carefully with facts on the ground to make sure it's not a castle in the air.

For years an official growth industry, the automobile industry must now deal with government policy that disincentivizes high-margin large cars through taxes and duties that are deliberately lower for small sub-4-meter cars. Rampant congestion means fewer parking spaces, which together with affordability issues signifies robust demand for small cars – but these are low margin. Also, setting up a dealer network in urban areas requires large showrooms that come with high rentals. Industry structure has been a case of Snow White and the Seven Dwarves, with

[10] See Parag Parikh, *Value Investing and Behavioral Finance*, New Delhi: Tata McGraw-Hill, 2009, 161–65. Smaller brokerages tend to do this more than the large wire houses.

[11] During the IT Bull, DSQ was among the notorious K-10 stocks, which were reportedly trading favourites of operator Ketan Parekh. The stock lost most of its value in the bust that followed.

Maruti in the lead role; the early entrant Maruti captured more than half the market, leaving the rest (barring Hyundai) with market shares that were perennially in the low single digits. For generations, the government subsidized diesel fuel, and so consumers favoured diesel engine cars that were cheaper to run; industry capacity went along with the market and moved into diesel engines, following which the long-time diesel subsidy got removed and the market moved back to petrol engines, leaving industry capacity stranded in diesel. In recent years, encouraging electric cars has become official policy, which means the industry now faces huge upfront capital expenditure and bets on creaky roadside infrastructure, but still has to deal with uncertain outcomes on product acceptability; an industry already traumatized by a wrong bet on diesel is now being asked to make a right bet on electric. To all this, add government-engineered increases in the cost of car ownership, brought about by increased safety and emission norms, together with enhanced insurance and driving licence requirements.

The Chindia portmanteau developed by the international media and Indian policy elites reflexively clubs China and India, but on many real indicators it is usually 90 to 10 in favour of China, and automobiles was another case in point.[12] Many focused on that date in the future when India would become the fourth (or third) largest car market in the world by volumes, but most did not notice that the cities had run out of roads for those cars. Ultimately, India probably needs about 40 to 50 new cities to accommodate rural to urban migration, but it does not have a single new city, resulting in unbearable pressures on existing urban infrastructure. So rapid and unbridled urbanization has brought with it disastrous consequences and bred policy responses that seek to encourage public transport and disincentivize car ownership by raising its overall cost. This disincentivization is a good thing, but against it is pitted the aspirational value of car ownership for the Great Indian Middle Class together with industry belief in India as the next big thing, and the automobile industry has been caught and crushed in this conflicting dialectic.

[12] An extreme example of this comes from Mercedes-Benz, which had 2018 car sales of about 650,000 in China and 15,500 in India, or 98:2 in favour of China.

So, the top line trap is as great a danger in growth investing as in business strategy. The siren song of industry and top line growth is so powerful that it blinds analysts to the simple fact that in the stock market you buy bottom line rather than top line growth. Apart from automobiles and telecom, a vast swathe of industries, including airlines, power, real estate, infrastructure, media, e-commerce, and hotels, are subject to the top line trap.

Widely recognized 'official' growth stories also become expensive very quickly. Consider by way of example, the 'consumption story' that is a reflection of the demographic dividend. As hundreds of millions have transitioned to using toothpaste, consumption by the category should explode.[13] This benefits companies such as Colgate that have cast-iron brands, negligible capital expenditure needs, and strong distribution networks built up over generations. Colgate and others such as Hindustan Unilever are the dividend zamindars (revenue collectors) of the stock market, throwing off lots of cash from stable high-growth businesses.[14] Alas, everybody's thinking the same way, and so, as 'official' growth stocks they carry very high price-earnings ratios – in most years, the average industry multiple for Indian consumer goods rarely move below 40 to 45.[15] Other businesses, namely online retailing, payment solutions, and e-commerce, are also 'official' growth industries, but in such nascent stages of industry structure that the action is still with the private equity types who are running around outdoing one another on valuation rounds that are 'up round' or 'down round'. Presumably, there will be an IPO some day for such stocks, by which time most of the upside would have been priced out of the offering by the smart money.

Historically, growth investing in India was easier to practise because of the absence of a venture capital/private equity industry. Infosys is cited as a textbook example of successful growth investing, but its 1993 public

[13] Even after the transition, there is the marketing challenge of getting per capita consumption to rival that of other countries. This also ensures high growth rates well into the future.

[14] Zamindars were a quasi-aristocratic land-owning rentier class who were responsible for collecting and remitting land revenues.

[15] 'Indices and Ratios,' BSE, https://www.bseindia.com/markets/keystatics/Keystat_index.aspx.

issue took place when there was no real private equity industry. With private equity funding, the company would have felt little need to tap public markets at such an early stage in its life cycle, and consequently, public shareholders would have been unable to buy into a piece of the action that early. Heavily funded by overseas limited partners, the private equity industry finances firms at early stages of their life cycle and takes away the gains from growth investing previously accessed by that earlier generation of the Indian public who bought in at IPOs. The venture capital/private equity industry now gets onto the elevator on the ground floor, and they don't send it back for the crowd till the IPO. But this may not be a bad thing. In recent years, the private equity industry has been all dressed up with nowhere to go; outside the complex of software, consumer goods, and pharma/life sciences, there are few quality companies available for the Indian private equity space to invest in. So, the private equity firms run around and elbow one another out of the way, while bidding valuations higher for the few good ideas that are available. Compared to the public, they are in a better position to judge high-risk, high-return payoffs, so in this sense there is a better equilibrium in corporate financing compared to the previous era.

Momentum

Using value arguments to buy mid-cap stocks that are showing momentum is one of those articles of faith in the markets. Typically initiated with a glance at a chart followed by a discussion with the technical analyst in the house,[16] the approach is not even seen as momentum-based, and no aura of disrepute attaches to the method. Some might even view it as respectable and investment-oriented, which is simply in keeping with the importance of speculative investment as an approach to the markets.

In the Indian context, it is best to think of momentum as a hybrid of fundamental and technical styles. If buying for the rise, it involves

[16] Momentum and timing approaches are outlined in Ashwath Damodaran, *Investment Fables*, New York: FT Prentice Hall, 2004, 391–426, 475–515.

buying stocks for the myriad fundamental reasons listed earlier but usually when those stocks are showing relative strength or meeting other momentum measures. If trading for the fall, it means short selling overvalued underperformers, though this runs into the short constraint.

Speculative investment underlies momentum as an approach, and it is common to find fund managers or individuals with core holdings that rarely change, who attempt to build a little alpha (or excess return) through momentum-based speculative investment.[17] Favourable news or government policy acts as a 'trigger' for sector valuations and prompts the herd to veer into that area, which builds upward momentum. As the short constraint makes contrarian positions difficult at this stage, the one-sided nature of the buying leads to a flare-up in price. Low free floats accentuate this effect. As stocks break their resistances, it shows up on the charts, and India's vast technical crowd gets into the act. At this point, fundamental and technical participants are both on the same side of the trade, and an inflection point in the momentum is soon reached. The initial momentum then develops into a full-blown trend – ideally the 6-to-18 month long-pull trade. In effect, the market's momentum has selected the next sector to be in, and for most participants (including value players), this is enough. In this sense, momentum-based approaches avoid liquidity traps and indicate the stocks the market crowd is headed into next.

It helps if there is a major bull move behind this, and it is possible during such a run to see the minor waves and eddies of such momentum

[17] Academic studies also document this effect. In a study of emerging markets that includes India, Nusret Cakici *et al.* find strong momentum effects, and particularly for small stocks. See Nusret Cakici, Frank J. Fabozzi, and Sinan Tan, 'Size, Value, and Momentum in Emerging Market Stock Returns,' *Emerging Markets Review*, 16, (2013), 46–65. Studies replicating Jegadeesh and Titman's early work on momentum by Raj S. Dhankar and Supriya Maheshwari, and others, also document pronounced momentum effects in Indian stock markets. See for example, Ashish Kumar Garg and Pankaj Varshney, 'Momentum Effect in Indian Stock Market: A Sectoral Study,' *Global Business Review*, 16, No. 3, 2015, 494–510. Evidence that Indian investors who achieve high overall returns favour large, growth, and high momentum stocks comes from John Y. Campbell, Tarun Ramadorai, and Benjamin Ranish, 'Getting Better or Feeling Better? How Equity Investors Respond to Investor Experience,' *NBER Working Paper* No. w20000. They find that both novices and highly experienced investors favour momentum a little more than investors with more middling experience.

in various parts of the market. But a bull run is neither necessary nor sufficient for a momentum approach, and it is the natural desire of the public to be long that suffices. More technically, all this requires positive serial correlation intertemporally or across substantial time periods.

Momentum to the downside is trickier to call, especially since the badla system was abolished. Because badla allowed for an unlimited supply of short stock through the naked short play, it allowed for severe downside momentum. With badla's abolition, the short side was effectively done away with; powerful political constituencies like mutual funds and the SIP-investing public now take constantly rising markets as a birthright. This has made downside momentum impossible to generate through market action. So, nowadays (as seen in the chapter on the Rate Bull) momentum to the downside usually comes from activation of the stop-loss honeycomb – those thousands of sell orders below the market price that successful momentum traders have put in place to capture profits. By constantly raising their 'stop-loss' orders behind an advancing price, the buy-side momentum traders create the coiled conditions that other traders can exploit when the market goes into a reaction. As the market crashes through this honeycomb of sell orders, terrific downside momentum gets generated. The fundamental and technical crowd may then exit the momentum trade together, so the effects can be pronounced over short periods as traders exit all at the same time.

But anticipating all this and getting the selling point right is practically impossible on momentum trades, which accounts for the common complaint among participants that they don't know when to sell with momentum-based speculative investment. Selling implies knowing fair value V to sell at, so what they're effectively saying is that they cannot estimate fair value V; in turn, this implies participants are being rewarded not for their knowledge of values, but for their assumption of risk. Because momentum participants cannot estimate fair value V, the best they can do is set a 'stop loss' behind present price P. So, for all practical purposes, in momentum trades it is the 'stop-loss' discipline rather than knowledge of selling point V that really matters.

But when everyone thinks that way and follows the stop-loss discipline, the honeycomb gets generated and then triggered, following which the momentum trade collapses in a spectacular fashion. Then the momentum crowd looks for reassurance among an array of technical razzmatazz such as Relative Strength Indexes (RSIs), TRINs, and oscillators, but usually to little avail. Historically, FIIs and the public were major sources of downside momentum, but with the advent of the SIP and home turf defence by domestic institutions, countervailing forces are now in play.

PART THREE

PLAYERS

14

THAT SAVIOUR OF THE PROFESSIONAL

The Public

All money in the stock market thinks it is smart money. If it thought of itself as dumb money, it wouldn't be there, and if it was dumb money, it wouldn't be there for long. Yet, only recently has the public begun to realize this.

The public is the oldest player in the market, though it now figures towards the end of a list of participants ranked by holdings. By 2022, promoters held about 45 per cent of all listed equity.[1] The foreign buy side held 20 per cent, while the domestic buy side (consisting mainly of mutual funds, insurance companies, and banks) held about 12 per cent. The public held about 10 per cent through direct holdings, while the government owned about 5 per cent through the President of India holdings in listed public-sector enterprises. The balance 8 per cent was held by 'others', including non-promoter corporates.

Historically, too, the public's presence – particularly in the colonial era – was marginal in India's equity markets, and it usually registered

[1] All figures are from NSE, *India Ownership Tracker*, 11 April 2022, Vol 3, Issue 3, Mumbai: NSE, 2022, 1.

only at the top of a market wave. In fact, there were only five occasions in the colonial period when the public's presence was large enough to even find mention in the record. The first was when the public entered the story with a bang during the Cotton and Share Mania of the 1860s. It receded into the background thereafter, perhaps because of the excesses from that episode, and for an ensuing half century, the record was silent on public presence in the markets. The second occasion with a significant presence occurred between 1916 and 1920, around the time of the First World War and its aftermath. A third instance from the late 1920s coincided with Wall Street's Roaring Twenties, followed by a fourth episode during the worldwide steel boom of the mid-1930s. The fifth and final occasion was between 1943 and 1946, during and after the Second World War.

All booms ended in excesses, with the public led to the shearing shed, following which there would be an outcry that led to the appointment of various commissions. It is no historical coincidence that the commission reports of Atlay (1924), Morison (1937), and Thomas (1948) closely followed these boom-bust cycles. In his dissenting note to the Atlay Committee's deliberations, noted lawyer and committee member Bhulabhai Desai was the first to observe that the howling mob of public opinion acted as a spur to authorities, who had to show they were doing something in response.[2] But the commissions of that era would be, in the main, unsympathetic to the public, and they took the stand that protecting the sheep from the wolves was not their job. Getting the wolves to change should have been their job, but that was attempted only in part. Nevertheless, what we know of markets in that epoch we owe to the public; the commission reports that resulted from the ensuing uproar contained valuable first-hand observations by participants and other members of the public who were invited to depose before the committees.

It is generally understood that the public in the pre-Independence era consisted of groups of wealthy individuals clustered around the

[2] Sir Wilfrid Atlay, *Report of the Bombay Stock Exchange Enquiry Committee*, Bombay: Government Central Press, 1924, 21–22.

main trading markets of Bombay, Calcutta, and Ahmedabad, with some representation from rural areas of what later became the states of Maharashtra, West Bengal, and Gujarat. The market remained confined to physical trading rings in these cities, which – together with the presence of trading communities in such areas – led to these urban clusters. The public would often throng the trading halls of the exchanges, but unauthorized transactions resulted in a ban from the arenas, and visitors' galleries were then set up, which allowed people to observe the physical ring.[3] The wealthy background of most participants also explains the hands-off attitude of the commissions; the presumption was that these participants knew what they were doing and, like hedge fund investors of present times, did not merit significant attention in the name of a wider public interest. Yet the first attempt to recognize the public as a player in the market's drama came from the Atlay Committee.[4] Before that, in Bombay at least, Article XV of the Native's founding charter – 'to support and protect the character, status, and interests of brokers dealing in shares, stock, and other like securities in Bombay…' – was both letter and spirit.[5]

The public's marginal presence in the pre-Independence era is not surprising. Poor market infrastructure and practices acted as a severe deterrent to anyone other than the hardiest trader. The traditional regard for asset classes such as land or gold put equity at a disadvantage. Finally, corporate governance as a concept was non-existent, which left the outside trader at a disadvantage compared to the promoter/insider. Yet, one contemporary reason for marginal public presence – the high opportunity cost of equity investing resulting from competing debt instruments which offered better returns – was less of an issue in the colonial era. In the colonial era, debt instruments offered low returns of between 3 and 4 per cent, which barely kept up with dormant inflation,

[3] Walter B. Morison, *Report of the Stock Exchange Enquiry Committee*, Bombay: Government Central Press, 1937, 33.

[4] Sir Wilfred Atlay, *Report of the Bombay Stock Exchange*, 4. The Atlay Committee also reached out to various market participants during its inquiry, and many appeared as witnesses before it.

[5] Ibid., 34.

and this lowered the opportunity cost of equity investing. It was only in the post-Independence era after 1947 that reasonable risk-free returns from small savings schemes and other debt instruments raised the opportunity cost of equity investing and made the equity risk-return trade-off daunting and unnecessary for the average household. In fact, debt returns usually did not beat the high inflation of later years, but this did not matter in an unsophisticated financial environment, concerned in the main with nominal returns.

The first signs of a real public presence in the markets became visible around Independence. The end of the Second World War and the tumult of Partition saw a mushrooming of new exchanges, together with colossal surges in kerb market activity. Much of this was recorded in the 1948 report of P.J. Thomas, the country's first chief economic advisor (the 'chief' part of the title would come later). The first report issued after Independence, it was also the first report to explicitly assert a public interest in the market's drama.[6] Assessing the public's presence as the colonial era ended, Thomas found it still confined to wealthy individuals, with some representation from the professional and middle classes.[7] Many of the latter were company employees of the large listed companies or drawn from the urban middle class.

Like most other participants, the public traded rather than invested in the markets, and this was typically done through the badla forward system. As seen earlier, by simply not asking for capital as an entry requirement, badla's forward trading was geared towards tempting the public to enter and trade in the markets. In fact, even the commissions – despite consisting of members who were financially sophisticated for that time – struggled hard to find meaningful differences between legitimate speculation (which was seen as a necessary activity in stock markets) and trading in 'mark to market' differences in forward contracts, which was often seen as gambling.[8] Consequently, their suggestions would

[6] P.J. Thomas, *Report on the Regulation of the Stock Market in India*, New Delhi: Ministry of Finance, 1948, 103–05.

[7] Ibid., 36–39.

[8] Walter B. Morison, *Report of the Stock Exchange*, 1–2, 21–22.

alternate between making it difficult for the public to enter and trying to ensure that there was something of a level playing field (this attitude finds echoes in the modern era, as SEBI oscillates between making it easier or more difficult for the public to trade in derivatives – by fiddling with contract sizes and margins). In sharp contrast to the attitude of these commissions, the broker-dominated exchange authorities had a clear agenda – making it simple for the public to enter and trade, which, in turn, generated the brokerage the industry depended on.

Badla was designed to suck the public into the market, but at least it was formal, in contrast to the unofficial kerb market on the streets outside the exchanges. Kerb markets acted as a check on the formalization of exchange activity, and whenever the exchanges enforced rules viewed as onerous, the public – in an early example of regulatory arbitrage – would simply flock to the street exchanges on the kerb where compliance and transaction costs were negligible.

The problem was acute in Calcutta, and its *katni* market on the street outside Lyons Range usually had volumes far larger – by some estimates as much as 10 times larger – than the formal market in the building inside.[9] There were no cash transactions or delivery, and the public simply paid up or received the difference in quotations. All this implied that the *katni* market was essentially a colossal bucket shop with gambling in differences. Even price continuity between the kerb and the official market was maintained; first thing the next morning, kerb trades were entered on the official market through synchronized 1-2-3 transactions, where brokers on the count of three entered the closing kerb trade in the official system.[10] Because of restricted trading hours on the official exchanges, kerb trading often had an exchange member on the other side of a trade, despite the SCRA's prohibition on members dealing with anyone other than fellow members.

So, kerb markets, aided in large part by their physical proximity to the regular market's facilities, competed with those regular markets in a sort

[9] P.J. Thomas, *Report on the Regulation of the Stock Market*, 75–77.

[10] Ibid., 11–12, 30; Aditi Roy Ghatak, *Down Lyons Range*, Kolkata: P.K. Ray for the Calcutta Stock Exchange Association, 2008, 113.

of regulatory arbitrage; unfortunately, they also lowered commercial morality. This regulatory arbitrage, in which tedious regulation drove commercial activity underground where it thrived on informal caste or community-based contract enforcement, was a recurring feature of financial market development in the post-Independence years.

In the post-Independence era, the first formal attempt at evaluating the public's presence in Indian markets took place towards the end of the Second Five Year Plan (1956–61). A 1961 shareholder survey by the National Council of Applied Economic Research (NCAER) was one of the earliest such surveys done in an emerging market, and it systematically recorded, for the first time, the presence of independent businessmen, company executives, and urban professionals.[11] This group of participants was sharply different from the wealthy individuals who had viewed the market as a sort of plaything, not very different from a racetrack. It was a difference that K.R.P. Shroff, who as BSE chairman saw the game at close quarters for almost half a century, was also to comment on in his account. Here in Shroff's 1962 account, we also find for the first time, the perennial claim of the brokerage fraternity that the Indian public was turning away from its obsession with land and gold and moving into equities.[12] A latent middle class – drawn from salary-earning, managerial, and executive classes rather than capitalist ranks – was stirring and entering the markets for the first time.

Shroff estimated public participants at about a million in 1960.[13] The number was arrived at by totalling shareholder registers for listed BSE companies across industry categories. The figure was subject to double

[11] K.R.P. Shroff, *History and Present Position of the Stock Market in India*, Bombay: BSE, 1962, 49–50.

[12] 'People in general were turning away from landed estates and bullion – the traditional modes of investment – and were more inclined to invest in equities, especially during the period covered by the Second Five Year Plan.' Ibid., 49.

[13] Ibid., 63.

counting – as some shareholders with stakes in multiple companies were counted more than once – and consequently overstated the shareholding public. But it was calculated only for the Bombay exchange, so it excluded shareholders at Calcutta and other regional exchanges. This exclusion would understate the entity, and assuming both effects cancel out, Shroff's 1960 estimate of a million is the first approximation of the shareholding public in India. As the public could not enter through mutual funds – the fund industry was created later with UTI's 1964 founding – the one million number is also an absolute estimate of the shareholding public in the markets.

As much as 90 per cent of these shareholders had shareholdings of less than ₹10,000, indicating broad-based public holdings.[14] Metals and cotton milling had the largest numbers of shareholders, mainly because of the large shareholder bases of the Tata Iron and Steel Company (TISCO) and various small textile firms; banks and cement companies also led the distribution of shareholders by industry.[15] Paradoxically, the low promoter holdings of that time and the absence of a mutual fund industry resulted in widely held companies, and a larger percentage of company share capital was held by the public as compared to today; in TISCO's case, an astonishing 70 per cent of its 1960 outstanding equity was held by the public.[16] By contrast, today, high promoter holdings – usually in excess of 25 per cent to ensure promoters have powers to block special resolutions – are the norm, and this together with an expanding mutual fund industry reduces equity that is directly held by the public.

Here too, discerned for the first time, was the tendency to use stock distributions to reduce face values and bring stocks into an 'acceptable' trading range for the public. Stock splits were the preferred instrument, in contrast to later years when stock dividends (bonuses) would become common. Between Independence and the early 1960s, the number of companies remained about the same but their outstanding shares increased threefold, mainly because many companies were abandoning

[14] Ibid.

[15] Ibid., 67–68.

[16] Ibid., 62–63.

the dominant ₹100 face value denominations of earlier times and splitting stocks down to ₹10.[17] By 1961, three-quarters of shares issued (by number) had face values of ₹10 or below, signifying that the preference of previous generations of promoters for high face value shares was reducing.[18] This tendency to reduce face values continues into the present era;[19] CNBC's ticker carries face values on the upper left hand corner of the share symbol, and even a casual perusal reveals many scrips with face values of ₹1, 2, and 5.

This preference for low-denomination shares was another reason – besides low promoter holdings (caused in large part by the managing agency system) and the buy side's absence – for that brief period in the 1960s and early 1970s when company ownership was broader based than at present. Evidence of this is empirically difficult to establish, as most companies did not publish shareholder distributions by number of shares held. Nevertheless, many large companies in the Tata group published such distributions, and these showed that by 1960, individuals held 70 per cent of the shares of TISCO and about two-thirds of the group's electricity complex, which included Andhra Valley, Tata Hydro, and Tata Power.[20] In absolute numbers, TISCO was the most widely held company in 1960 with about 70,000 shareholders, followed by ACC (44,000) and Scindia Steam Navigation (39,000).[21] The public was also heavily present in the primary market; a dipstick survey of the primary market between 1958 and 1961 showed that as many as 90 per cent of applications were from the public, and their subscriptions accounted for almost 40 per cent of issue size.[22]

[17] Ibid., 60–61.

[18] Ibid., 62.

[19] In certain jurisdictions, high face value stocks can sometimes lead to contingent liabilities if sold below par value, i.e., at a discount. Original purchasers of stocks issued below par are contingently liable to creditors (but not to the corporation itself) upon dissolution or liquidation; the contingent liability is the discount at which they purchased the stock. In such jurisdictions, this has led to a move away from high face values, but there is little evidence that this effect led to the move away from high face values in India.

[20] Ibid., 62–63.

[21] Ibid., 67.

[22] Ibid., 49.

In 1970, one of the earliest BSE reports to summarize stock market activity estimated the public at about two million shareholders, which is a decadal doubling over Shroff's 1960 estimate.[23] About 44 per cent of company equity was estimated to be held directly by the investing public.[24] In those years, nascent institutional ownership was passive and dormant in its approach, which meant that the public was an important provider of liquidity to the market. In fact, much of the literature from this period deals with liquidity-based justifications for the badla system and mentions the public's role in providing that liquidity.[25]

By the 1990s, the first surveys of the public's presence in the markets were being done, and two such studies published by L.C. Gupta in 1991 and 1994 are of historical interest.[26] The 1991 survey estimated about 9 million shareholders spread over 3.8 million households, representing an annual growth rate of about 7.6 per cent over the three decades since Shroff's 1960 estimate.[27] Multiple shareholders in the same household – either for tax planning or legacy reasons – were common, and the average household had 2.3 shareholders. Shroff's observation that the shareholding class was widening was confirmed here, and the move away from the wealthy gamblers featured in the Morison and Thomas reports was now apparent. The demographic churn that characterizes today's markets is seen for the first time, and the survey found that two-thirds of respondents had entered in the 10 years prior to the survey.[28] Gupta's 1991 work was also the last survey done in the pre-reform era and, understandably, the public's dominant concerns were over bad

[23] Bombay Stock Exchange, *Profile of Stock Exchange Activity in India*, Bombay: BSE, 1970, ii, 36–37.

[24] Ibid., vi, 30–31.

[25] Ibid., vii.

[26] The Society for Capital Market Research and Development (SCMRD), New Delhi, conducted five surveys between 1991 and 2008. Besides 1991 and 1994, surveys were published in 2001, 2005, and 2008, but the latter were overtaken by the SEBI/NCAER and SEBI/Nielsen surveys that had larger sample sizes. Investor issues of the 80s were also laid out by L.C. Gupta, *Stock Exchange Trading in India: Agenda for Reform*, New Delhi: Society for Capital Market Research and Development, 1992, 19–27.

[27] L.C. Gupta, *Indian Shareowners: A Survey*, New Delhi: Society for Capital Market Research and Development, 1991, xxiv–xxv.

[28] Ibid., xxiii.

deliveries, eccentric clearing and settlement, and delayed payments; in some cases, for example, it took two months for an investor to get cash for shares that had been sold[29] (once these concerns were removed by the reform effort, new worries over 'price volatility' and corporate mismanagement would emerge in later surveys).[30]

The majority reported unsatisfactory experiences based on the markets of the 1980s but part of that was self-inflicted – due to negligible knowledge of portfolio theory, diversification was insignificant, and slightly more than half of participants had fewer than five stocks in their portfolio;[31] most respondents were taking on unnecessary levels of unsystematic risk without being compensated for it. Diversifying adequately – holding, say, 10 to 15 stocks across a range of industries – would have given them the same returns with lower risk, but this realization was still in the future. Larger shareholders reported better experiences than smaller ones, perhaps because of the greater skill and better luck that allowed them to become large in the first place.[32] Finally, a majority had entered equities through the new issue rather than the secondary market, perhaps because they had taken part in the first post-Independence IPO wave of the mid- and late-1980s; in later years, the situation would reverse, and most would enter through the secondary markets.

The subsequent 1994 survey under L.C. Gupta focused on geographic distribution and found the shareholding public mainly urban and concentrated in the west and south of the country.[33] Despite

[29] Ajay Shah and Susan Thomas, 'David and Goliath: Displacing a Primary Market,' *Journal of Global Financial Markets*, Vol. 1, No. 1, Spring, 2000, 18.

[30] Society for Capital Market Research and Development, *Indian Householders' Investment Survey: 2004*, New Delhi: SCMRD, 2005, 33–39.

[31] L.C. Gupta, *Indian Shareowners*, xxiv. Gupta's follow-up studies also found inadequate diversification across income and age. See SCMRD, *Indian Householders' Investment Survey*, 95–116.

[32] Ibid., xxv.

[33] Gupta's estimates of the shareholding public are at 2.4, 6, 9, and 12 million respectively in 1980, 1985, 1990, and 1992. L.C. Gupta, Naveen Jain, and Yash Kulshreshtha, *Shareholders' Geographic Distribution, City-wise, Urban-rural, and State-wise*, New Delhi: Society for Capital Market Research and Development, 1994, 3–6.

increases in overall numbers, the percentage share of cities stayed about the same across time, indicating shareholder growth in the same cities rather than through further geographic spread. The four metros and Ahmedabad accounted for about half the shareholding population, and semi-urban and rural India was not really represented[34] (Gujarat was the exception). Also observed here for the first time were 'local hero' effects – the public located in a particular city/state tended to buy into the 'local hero' company headquartered in that city/state; company registers were dominated by residents of the cities where companies were headquartered.[35] The study estimated the shareholding public at about 16 million in 1994, with much of the increase due to the second post-Independence IPO wave of the early 1990s and the Mehta Bull market.

From 1993 onwards, SEBI's annual reports have tracked the public's presence through the growth of total beneficiary (or demat) accounts with the two depositaries, NSDL and CDSL.[36] According to SEBI, demat accounts were at 41 million in March 2020.[37] This is the last full year before the distortions caused by the COVID-19 pandemic with its 'work from home' lifestyle changes and liquidity-induced price surges. Gupta had reckoned the investing public at about 9 million in 1990, so the 41 million SEBI number represented an annual growth rate of 5.1 per cent in the three decades since his estimate. It is worth noting that those thirty years encompassed the entire reform era and were a time of significant market activity. It was the era that witnessed four great bull tops – Mehta, IT, Rate, and the SIP top of early 2020 – each of which brought the public into the market in waves. Despite that, this 5.1 per cent growth rate showed no significant historical break and, in fact, was

[34] Ibid., 4.

[35] Ibid., 8.

[36] Typically, accounts were evenly split among depositories; in 2018, there were 17 million and 15 million beneficiary demat accounts at the two depositories, the NSDL and the CDSL, respectively. Securities and Exchange Board of India, *Annual Report for the Fiscal Year 2017–2018*, Mumbai: SEBI, 2018, 56.

[37] Nasrin Sultana and Ashwin Ramarathinam, 'Demat Accounts Gain Currency in FY2020 as Retail Investors Took to Equities,' *Mint*, 2 May 2020.

lower than the 7.6 per cent growth rate between Shroff's 1960 estimate and Gupta's 1990 figure. One explanation (besides the obvious effect of the low 1960 base) is that much of the public's activity in recent years has been through mutual funds and SIPs, neither of which require a demat account. Moreover, the 5.1 per cent growth rate is still more than five times an annual population growth of less than 1 per cent. Much of India's population is below 40, which is the cohort most active traders come from, and this demographic profile also accounts for the surge in beneficiary accounts.

In the modern era, the public's presence and behaviour also get charted through SEBI's periodic investor surveys, the first of which was conducted with the NCAER in 1999. An unusual finding in the 2015 investor survey was the relatively unseasoned nature of the public.[38] In this, the survey echoed the 1990 Gupta report but without making any explicit comparison with those results. Gupta had found that two-thirds of the public had entered markets for the first time in the 10 years prior to his survey.[39] The 2015 survey found that nearly 75 per cent of the public had entered for the first time in the previous five years, a finding rendered all the more remarkable as there was no market top or IPO wave to bring in the public around the 2015 survey period.

The survey was indicative of an accelerating demographic churn in the markets.[40] India's demographic dividend was working its way through the markets as a large bulge of youthful first-time participants. The vast majority of traders entered after 2010, ignorant of the market's story prior to that date, and in all likelihood, unaware of market movements beyond the immediate ken of their short trading lives. Primary markets and IPO waves had been the entry point for an earlier generation, but that too was changing, and now the secondary market was the source of entry. Rapid urbanization together with changing socioeconomic profiles were seen as the main drivers behind increases in the public's numbers.[41]

[38] Nielsen's 2015 survey covered 2,00,000 urban and rural households at the listing stage and 50,000 at survey stage.

[39] L.C. Gupta, *Indian Shareowners*, xxiv.

[40] Securities and Exchange Board of India, *SEBI Investor Survey 2015*, Mumbai: SEBI, 2016, 81–83.

[41] Ibid., 16–17.

The 2015 survey also elicited the following ordinal ranking among financial instruments: bank fixed deposits, post office saving schemes, insurance schemes, pension schemes, and finally, equity.[42] This had been the usual result since surveying started, indicating little change from earlier years. In marked contrast to the Gupta surveys, mutual funds were preferred over direct investing, and more than half who voiced this preference had used rupee cost averaging products like the SIP, indicating that massive public education programs were getting their message across.[43] Education and occupation too continued as better predictors of equity market participation as compared to age or income status. Among active traders, over three-quarters still preferred the phone to call in their trades with their brokers, which may indicate significant technological aversion but could also imply the absence of broadband infrastructure needed for widespread net-based trading.[44]

Controversially, the 2015 study found that trading frequency was reducing, which flew in the face of what the wire houses were saying; if true, this was a positive development, given that trading frequency is tied to the increased likelihood of losses. Finally, the survey continued to reveal the pronounced urban bias in the shareholding public. Attempts to sample rural investors in an earlier 2011 survey had resulted in such low responses that the effort was abandoned and case studies were undertaken instead;[45] the 2015 survey went ahead with rural sampling, which revealed 32 investors out of 13,697 survey respondents, or about 0.2 per cent.[46] Marketing of stocks (and IPOs) to a rural public was hampered by the arbitrage generated from the tax-free status of agricultural income. Most wealthy rural investors simply found the tax disadvantage of investing in equities considerable.

[42] Unsurprisingly – given the moribund state of India's bond markets – awareness of corporate bonds was very low, usually ranking with equity/commodity derivatives.

[43] Ibid., 73–75.

[44] Ibid., 87–88.

[45] National Council for Applied Economic Research, *How Households Save and Invest: Evidence from NCAER Household Survey 2011*, New Delhi: NCAER, 2011, 2–3.

[46] Securities and Exchange Board of India, *SEBI Investor Survey 2015*, 53–56.

The 2020 coronavirus pandemic and lockdown brought a jolt to public participation in the markets. The 'stay at home' lockdowns and the successive market highs led to another surge in account openings; many found their thoughts turn idly to the market, and by May 2021, there were over 60 million demat accounts in the country. In fact, most account opening records were broken between 2020 and 2022, and these years marked an inflection point for the market. By 2022, another great milestone was reached, and the number of demat accounts touched 100 million.[47]

Like previously, the public came into the market in waves, but these digital surges lacked the drama of earlier episodes. Though a large number of participants came from the tech-savvy high earners of India's software and digital space, the numbers were also driven by surges in small-town and rural India. By now, small-town India was trading derivatives on mobile phones, and it was becoming clear that digitization aided speculation rather than investment.[48] In 2021, reports started surfacing of something called contracts for difference (CFDs); openly advertised and targeted mainly at a Hindi-speaking populace, they sounded uncannily similar to the early badla trade and the Roychand time bargain.[49] These digital *dabba*s were the equivalent of early bucket shops, and some reportedly offered leverage of up to 1000 to 1.

Nothing had changed.

Despite the market's high profile, equity trading and investing is just coming out of the marginal exercise it used to be in an earlier era. There are those 100 million beneficiary (demat) accounts recorded with the two depositaries, the NSDL and the CDSL. Since all shares have to

[47] 'Demat Accounts Cross 100 Million for First Time, Steep Rise in Last Four Months,' *Economic Times*, 6 September 2022.

[48] Ashish Rukaiyar, 'How Stock Trading on Apps Seized Bharat,' *Mint*, 19 May 2021.

[49] Debashis Basu, 'Boom in Digital Dabba Trading,' *Business Standard*, 19 July 2021.

be recorded in demat accounts to trade and since shares in physical form cannot be sold unless 'dematted', the 100 million demat number is an estimate of the absolute number of direct participants in the stock market. While a large number in absolute terms, it's just about 7 per cent of the country's population. At the household level, the 2015 SEBI investor survey estimated that about 19 million households (or about 8 per cent of the country's 250 million households) invested in equities.[50] By comparison, a little over half of all American households have equity exposure. Yet India's 8 per cent figure compares favourably with the 10 per cent of German households that own equities (Germany has fewer issuers, as corporate financing is dominated by internal generation and bank financing from external sources, which, together with financial conservatism among investors, produces the low figure).

Measuring the public's participation through demat accounts is confounded by forces working in favour of underestimation and overestimation. The demat number underestimates the population exposed to equities because you don't need a demat account to buy mutual funds or start an SIP, and so, there are large groups investing through these instruments who don't get captured by the demat figure. Similarly, the demat number underestimates public exposure at a systemic level because it does not capture indirect public investing through LIC, which collects policy premia to invest in equity markets. In fact, the 2015 SEBI survey found that insurance was the public's second-most popular financial product after bank deposits, and LIC is India's largest equity investor, so this indirect exposure must be considerable.

Likewise, figures arrived at through demat accounts may overestimate exposure to equities, because many participants have multiple demat accounts, either for tax-planning purposes or because of legacy issues. Also working towards overestimation are demat accounts that invest only in debt instruments like non-convertible debentures, which in recent years have required demat accounts for subscription.

Fortunately, measuring the active trading public at any point in time has become easier. This can be done by estimating the number of

[50] Securities and Exchange Board of India, *SEBI Investor Survey 2015*, 6, 9.

demat account IDs where a transaction has occurred in the previous 12 months.[51] Since the public rarely transacts in debt markets, the assumption is that all such transactions are in equity. As an indication of how public interest mounts during a bull market, consider the following data points in the SIP bull move between 2010 and 2018. In 2010, there were 1.25 million active IDs on a demat base of about 17.7 million, implying that 7 per cent of the public actively traded in that year;[52] by 2018, there were 8.28 million active IDs on a demat base of about 32 million, implying that 26 per cent of the public actively traded.[53] The rise in the proportion of active IDs from 7 to 26 per cent is significant, and yet it contradicts the results of that 2015 SEBI survey, which showed preferences for mutual funds and a reduction in trading frequency. One explanation is simply that new participants are investing in mutual funds and trading actively.

So, the demat base grows in absolute terms, and this is mainly a function of India's vaunted demographic dividend. The dividend simply bypassed the market in an earlier era, but is now finding its way there. This is unsurprising as equities are a business of risk-taking, and young people – based on a lifecycle model of investing – simply take more risk. As a result, a population getting younger by the day should continuously find its way into the stock market. Because of all that risk-taking, in percentage terms active client IDs are now rising faster than the demat base. Though this rise is driven by the demographic dividend, a host of other factors, including the rise of discount brokers, falling transaction costs, and the sheer ease of online trading, have contributed. Long-running bull markets have also helped, with the SIP Bull sucking in a large number of young traders who were actively speculating.

Paradoxically, the heavy volume of active trading has made little difference to the public's direct holding in the market. At the millennium's

[51] The NSE's Form 1C provides data on active client IDs during the year. Because corresponding figures for the BSE have not been used, this figure is an underestimate but not by much, as the NSE is the dominant exchange. See https://www.nseindia.com/invest/content/ arbitration_status.htm.

[52] https://www.nseindia.com/invest/content/arbitration_reports/report_1c_2009_10.htm.

[53] https://www.nseindia.com/invest/content/arbitration_reports/report_1c_2017_18.htm.

turn in 2000, the public directly held about 20 per cent of all equity. So, the decline in the public's direct holding to the present level of about 10 per cent is despite all this active trading, indicating rises in trading velocity and turnover. Promoter and government holdings rarely change, so it is the foreign and domestic buy sides that have gained at the expense of the public. Intriguingly, the number of individual demat accounts rose from 2.5 million to 100 million between the millennium and 2022, so this decline in direct public holding has been despite the colossal surge in demat accounts – further indicating the public's speculative orientation and excessive presence in the derivatives segment.

The public's geographic concentration is also significant, and Mumbai accounts for about 60 per cent of all trading volumes.[54] The fund management industry that collects capital nationwide to invest in markets tends to be headquartered in Mumbai, and it is this concentration of the trading desks in Mumbai, rather than any penchant for equities among the city's residents, which accounts for the city's dominance. Other major centres are Delhi, Kolkata, Chennai, Bangalore, Hyderabad, Ahmedabad, Vadodara, and Rajkot; together with Mumbai, they account for about 90 per cent of the game. So, the public is urban and concentrated mainly in the west and south of the country.[55] Early shareholder surveys from the 1990s also showed the same results, indicating that the public's geographic location stubbornly refuses to change.[56]

Rural India is still not significant in this setup, despite years of trying to promote a shareholding class there. This situation has now begun to change, and attempts to incentivize distributors in smaller towns have had considerable success in recent years. The SIP's growth also means that small town and rural India is beginning to get some exposure to equities. The active trading public still come mainly from the above cities, but by 2021, this observation was tempered by significant increases in trading activity from Tier 2 or Tier 3 towns. Women were also participating in

[54] SEBI, *Annual Report for the Fiscal Year 2017–2018*, 50–51.

[55] Ibid.

[56] L.C. Gupta, *Indian Shareholders*, xxiii–xxviii; L.C. Gupta et al., *Shareholders' Geographic Distribution*, 1–9.

record numbers, and by 2021, some estimates indicated that as much as a fifth of all new signups were women, and mainly from Tier 2 and Tier 3 towns. The SIP Bull was now slowly and inexorably sucking in diverse publics.[57]

Lore has often emphasized a communal basis to the market. Communities such as Gujaratis and Marwaris have a significant presence, which is not surprising as they pride themselves on being trading communities. Myth has it that Gujaratis tend to be perennially bullish while Marwaris tend to be bearish and trade for the fall, but in today's times, these observations have to be tempered.[58] Lore also has it that Haribhais are likely to treat stocks like stable marriages, while the Maddus enter and exit with the swiftness and ardour of a Casanova pursuing and dumping a pretty woman. In an early 1991 study, L.C. Gupta even attempted to categorize by background the public who traded at that time: he identified exchange members and their authorized assistants as the main group, followed by a motley crowd that included wealthy individuals, professionals, property dealers, bullion dealers, retirees, company insiders, and, oddly enough, teachers.[59]

The market's demographic churn of recent years has rendered irrelevant many of these traditional distinctions, and new entrants come from all backgrounds. Nevertheless, one clearly defined sub-group that did not exist in Gupta's time but is now making its presence felt is the many from among the million engineers and 300,000 MBAs who graduate every year and drift into the markets.

Gauges that measure public participation include the Non-member Short Sales Ratio, but these do not exist in India. This ratio measures the short sales of parties who are not brokers/members of stock exchanges and has the comfortably smug presumption that the public is always

[57] Namrata Singh and Partha Sinha, 'Women Turn Investment Hobbies into Habit,' *Times of India*, 25 September 2021.

[58] From the author's interview with long-time participant, K.R. Choksey.

[59] L.C. Gupta, *Expert Study of Trading in Shares in Stock Exchanges*, Volume 2, Appendices, Working Paper/Note 1, 'The Volume and Nature of Speculation on Indian Stock Exchanges: Regulatory Implications,' New Delhi: The Society for Capital Market Research and Development, 1991, 19.

wrong. Since the public is wrong and so excessively short at a market bottom, a higher ratio – indicating a large public presence on the short side – also points to the market being oversold and due for a rapid pullback; in turn, this provides food for thought to a contrarian. Such ratios are not calculated, and gauging the public's presence in India is a hit-or-miss affair. Consequently, the search for the public is done anecdotally, and depending on the proclivity of the opinion holder, any conclusion can (and will) be blithely drawn on national television. Mass media plays a big role in all this, because the public's main objective is to make a killing without being killed, and the public wants to be told how to do it. Mass media obliges, and the resulting coverage gives the stock market a prominence that it does not deserve.

Historically, deficient microstructure and poor market practices were critical reasons behind the public's wariness of the stock market, but the NSE's formation and the 90s reform effort did away with these traditional explanations for the public's caution. The reforms – especially those involving clearing and settlement – solved many of the microstructure issues and made it easy to trade stocks with low transaction costs. Further improvements in digitization and net access accelerated this process. Nevertheless, those reforms and subsequent improvements did little to change the public's basic attitude towards the markets – an attitude that hinged in large part on unrealistic approaches to risk. Because of that unrealistic approach, everybody knew someone who knew someone who'd lost their shirt or made a sudden fortune in the markets. So, despite the changes to the microstructure, the Indian public's outlook towards the markets would still oscillate between perennial mistrust and a longing to give in to the market's temptations for a quick buck – temptations made stronger, ironically enough, by the improvement the reforms and digitization had wrought. This made for an unstable relationship between the public and the stock market.

The public is the crowd. Or so the fund managers and pros fondly believe, without realizing they're part of the crowd too. Market belief has it that the crowd behaves normally and so it always loses – the public enters at the top and gets screwed over as a result. These days, however, that notion is getting a little stretched. It appears that the public is catching on to the game. The public – if it chooses to play the game – has one advantage over the pros; unlike the buy side, it is not bound by compliance restrictions or the mandate to stay fully invested. Perhaps the fund managers are the dinosaurs because of their mandate to stay fully invested, and maybe they are the *bakra*s (fall guys) in all this.

Nowadays, it appears that the public exercises a fair amount of common sense in its investing. The public's become contrarian, it seems, and buys when markets start to fall, so if you're a fund manager and a contrarian at that, there's no one to be contrarian against. Presently, the only difference between the public and the pros is that the public starts buying a little earlier. The public's caught on – but only by so much; it's buying on the way down and losing confidence a little earlier towards bear market lows. Unnerved by a bear market's steady erosion of values, the public's happy to get out as soon as it gets its capital back with a small return, and this is done by selling out early, just as the next bull market begins its upswing.

The public is an elusive beast, almost like the Yeti or the Abominable Snowman of the Himalayas. Sightings of the public in Indian markets are as rare as Yeti sightings, and rarer still are public sightings among the fund managers and dervishes. Even at market tops with the public abundantly present, the fundies with their soothing voices will insist that the public is not in the market as yet, and that a 'left out feeling' is abroad in the land because so few have participated in the up move. The dervishes of Dalal Street, the big professional traders, sweetly reasonable or robustly blunt depending on their personality types, make similar points about growth stories and the public's lack of exposure to said stories. It's almost as though they're trying to entice the public into the market with all their seductive talk.[60]

[60] Exhortations to enter the market also come from the political class. 'My fourth concern is increasing retail participation.' Finance Minister P. Chidambaram, Remarks at the 20th Anniversary Celebrations of the National Stock Exchange of India, Mumbai, 14 December 2013.

Perhaps the public's job is to be the saviour of the professionals, coming in at the top to take expensive stock off the pros. In fact, the idea that the market tops out only when the public is in it, and the related idea that the public buys at the top as the pros *thoko* (hit) it to them, is as firmly ingrained in the market's unconscious mind as the idea that good promoters are essential to good companies. In the market's unconscious, the public has to be present at a market top, but for a fundie who is always fully invested and cannot exit, there can be no market top – at most, the top is only a blip in that infinite upward march of the market – and so, for a fundie, the public is never present but is always arriving shortly. Consequently, even when the public is heavily present in the market, the fundies, the one group with the experience and astuteness to note the public's presence, are incentivized only to proclaim its absence.

The idea of a psychological crowd with a mental unity congregating around a central image at key market moments is an important element of mythos among the dervishes, but it is never stated as such, and in fact, they are careful never to articulate it, except among themselves. The idea itself has a long history in the analysis of stock markets and goes back to observers such as Charles Mackay and Gustave Le Bon.[61]

The crowd doesn't reason; it just thinks it reasons. As Jesse Livermore the plunger noted, it is warm and comforting to be part of a crowd rather than wander the lonely wolf-infested prairies of contrary opinion, and the Indian mindset seems encouraging of this attitude. The crowd, as le Bon points out, is moved by two main forces – suggestibility and contagion. Suggestibility is easy because of the crowd's tendency to think in terms of images – whether India Shining or the Dancing Elephant or the India Growth Story or a Modi Wave – that translate into mantras that are ceaselessly chanted into the market's unconscious; sometimes the government encourages matters by contributing its own mantras like Make in India or *Atmanirbhar* (Self Reliance).

[61] Charles Mackay, *Extraordinary Popular Delusions and the Madness of Crowds* and Joseph de la Vega, *Confusión de Confusiones*, Wiley Investment Classics, Hoboken, NJ: John Wiley and Sons, Inc., 1995. Gustave Le Bon, *The Crowd: A Study of the Popular Mind*, Mumbai: Sterling Book House, 2002.

The other force that moves a crowd – contagion among participants – happens after a period of steadily rising prices, as in the final stages of a bull market. Contagion is helped along by rumour mongering, that pervasive and bedrock practice of Indian markets, but the real contagion comes simply from following price action and talking about it.[62] The tape tells its own story, everybody shamelessly talks about the successful part of their books, the media acts as a vector, and Hema the Housewife just has to get into the market after hearing Mrs S talk about that killing she just made in Godrej Consumer Products.[63]

The public loves a tip and gets taken in by the *khabar* (news), preferably of the inside kind. The peculiar problem with tips is they're not much use, even on the rare occasion when they get you into a stock at the right time. Acting on a tip does not instil the same confidence that comes from doing your own homework and then buying, and as a result, traders buying on tips have a marked tendency to sell early; alternately, often the tipster has long exited the stock but neglected to tell the punter, who is still holding when the stock sells off. The public often uses the word *tehlokho* (Gujarati for 'they'), and '*Tehlokho upar lehse*' (They'll take it up) is a common refrain among traders on Dalal Street. The 'they' in this context is the mysterious and unfathomable 'other'. To an earlier generation 'they' meant the dervishes, but nowadays, in the public's unconscious, the term refers to a mix of FIIs, fundies, or LIC, and 'they' becomes shorthand and code for those with a lot more capital and competence at their disposal.

The public is also susceptible to 'bonus share' issuance and other gimmicks. As favourable conditions lead to a bull market in a stock, promoters issue stock dividends and bonus it down to keep the stock in an acceptable price range for the public. The public does not distinguish between favourable fundamentals acting on the stock and the wealth effect of getting 'free' shares. As the Unitech example showed, the

[62] Friends and television were the main sources of market information in the pre-internet era, and they continued as the main sources well into the internet age. SEBI, *SEBI Investor Survey 2015,* 78, 105–06.

[63] Feedback effects in the stock markets date from the time of Tulipmania but are rarely included in conventional finance books. See Robert J. Shiller, 'From Efficient Markets Theory to Behavioral Finance,' *Journal of Economic Perspectives*, Vol. 17, No. 1, Winter, 2003, 91–96.

fundamentals keep taking the stock higher, but the repeated bonuses disguise the extent of the stock's rise.

There is also a fatal attraction for penny stocks, or stocks trading at single-digit prices. When even the basics of share valuation are not internalized, penny stocks trading at ₹2 or ₹4 are seen as cheap.[64] The minimum price move (share tick) of 5 paisa, or ₹0.05, is a larger percentage of a penny stock's price than that of the ₹800 blue chip, which allows a penny stock to double over fewer upticks than the blue chip, and so, the trading public buys the penny stock, in the hope of doubling its money sooner. In turn, the brokerages with their minimum brokerage charges lie in wait for the penny stock crowd. A ₹1 minimum brokerage is a whopping 25 per cent of a ₹4 share price, a far higher brokerage rate than the 0.1 per cent usually charged. In fact, it's 250 times – or 24,900 per cent – higher than the 0.1 per cent brokerage usually charged, and that's just on one side of the trade.[65]

The absence of a bankruptcy regime (till recently at least) means that penny stocks are often stocks of bankrupt companies whose share prices linger and drift down on their move to zero. The severe constraints on short selling also contribute to the stock's tendency to gradually move to nothing; initiating short positions would immediately drive the price down and the equity would get wiped out at once, but the short constraints mean that the equity takes a while to go to nothing. This gradual wipeout makes penny stocks deceptively attractive to the public for long periods of time. Since the public buys on the way down, companies on their way out will also have shareholder registers that show significant increases in the proportion of capital held by small retail investors.[66] Penny stocks are an attractive business not just because of the high margins, but also because there is a large universe of penny stocks that are survivors of the first two IPO waves in the post-Independence era; by one recent reckoning, there were over 400 stocks

[64] Samie Modak, 'Small Shareholders Left Holding Dud Stocks,' *Business Standard,* 27 May 2015.

[65] Martin Scorsese's film *The Wolf of Wall Street* uses this insight, among others, to show how boiler rooms flog penny stocks to an unsuspecting public.

[66] Samie Modak, 'Small Shareholders Left Holding Dud Stocks.'

with prices below ₹1 and over 1,400 stocks priced between ₹1 and ₹10 that were listed on the BSE.[67]

Other documented biases of the Indian trading public – in line with findings worldwide – include: inadequate diversification, the tendency to get more aggressive when on a roll, and the disposition effect, i.e., selling winners early and holding on to losers for too long.[68]

In recent years, the SIP has begun to change – and perhaps momentously so – the public's relationship with the stock market. Through the SIP, the public also started getting over its traditional obsession with real estate and gold. The reasons for that obsession were not difficult to see. Real estate prices – particularly in big Indian cities where most of the shareholding population comes from – were compounding at 12 to 15 per cent on an annualized basis;[69] population migration from rural areas and the lack of new cities to accommodate that shift ensured those stunning price increases. Many, especially those priced out of the market, spoke about a bubble but came to accept the reality of property prices doubling every five or six years. Gold, that other object of obsession, had always exercised a hold on the Indian psyche due to its traditional uses for ornamentation, daughters' inheritances, or small business collateral. As a result, both property and gold dominated household folios, and this is despite their obvious disadvantages; real estate's capital threshold for participant entry was high, while gold offered only price appreciation and no dividends (both were also opaque markets as compared to equity, which by the new millennium was among the most transparent of asset classes). As a result, the public's fetish for land and gold usually had the unfortunate consequence of reducing the residual capital available to invest in equities.

[67] Stocks sorted by price were available on various websites. For one listing, see 'Companies in Similar Price Band,' *Rediff*, https://money.rediff.com/companies/price-sorted.

[68] See John Y. Campbell, Tarun Ramadorai, and Benjamin Ranish, 'Getting Better or Feeling Better? How Equity Investors Respond to Investment Experience,' Working Paper No. 20000, National Bureau of Economic Research, Cambridge, MA, March 2014.

[69] Consider that the RBI's All-India House Price Index (HPI) indicated annual growth rates of 14 per cent between its inception in 2010 and 2017; the index grew in nominal terms from 100 in its base year of 2010 to 251 in 2017. At 'Database on Indian Economy,' *RBI*, https://dbie.rbi.org.in/DBIE/dbie.rbi?site=statistics.

All this changed with the SIP, and equities now started competing somewhat with land and gold for the public's attention. By the millennium's turn, household savings, at least at the margin, have started moving back into equities. Much of that shift is through the SIP, which allows the public to invest small, fixed amounts at any periodicity – weekly, monthly, or quarterly. This regularity takes away the temptation to time the market. Doing it continuously gets the investor in at market highs and lows, which average out over time, and this rupee cost averaging allows the public to capture the market's long-term upswing. At least, that's the theory.

The SIP is an instrument that can increase the public's exposure to equities. By curbing the Indian public's well-known appetite for chasing outperforming asset classes and losing in the process, it may even be merciful in its effect. The extent to which the SIP is flogged depends largely on incentive schemes offered to the advisors and distributors who do the flogging. SEBI's incentive schemes have successfully got the public into rupee cost averaging, which in turn has allowed the domestic buy side access to a steady stream of sticky capital that acts as a counterweight to the FIIs. The public also benefits from financial literacy programs aimed at increasing its residual allocation to equities, and much of the SIP's success in recent years has also been due to the efficacy of these literacy programs.[70]

So, the public is still present in the markets, but that presence is now moderated through a vast industry of financial advisors, distributors, media personalities working in personal finance, and slick public relations departments at the mutual funds. The financial advisors and their related *jaati* sweet-talk the public with the mantra of long-term wealth creation, and they do so with the same cute reasonableness that Premchand Roychand had exhibited over a century ago. Their designated role is to handhold the beast when the beast gets jittery, and they are quite frank about it. The advisory *jaati* is at its persuasive best when the market wobbles and moves to the downside. After all, those

[70] Securities and Exchange Board of India, *SEBI Investor Survey 2015*, 78, 103–10.

SIP flows have to keep coming in from the public; else it's back to the nightmare of those dramatic collapses during the bad old days when foreign investors sold with no counterbalance to them. '*Keep SIPping*' is the wonderful mantra that the advisors circulate among the public nowadays, its breeziness getting a little shrill during a down move. The advisors' emotional investment in the SIP can be felt on social media or Twitter, and further explications of the '*Keep SIPping*' mantra are outlined in reams of newspaper columns that the community has appropriated for itself.

That the SIP has not been tested as yet by the time correction of a prolonged bear, that the momentum of years of market up move has bred a certain complacency, that the high opportunity cost of Indian equity investing shows itself even when the market goes into a trading range, and that dollar cost averaging is widely prevalent in other markets but did not prevent noted bears in those markets, are basic lessons that will be learnt the hard way. But that's all in the future.

15

'SIDDHU BORIVALI THI CHURCHGATE'

Why and How People Trade?

One of the Indian market's great mysteries is why the public trades at all. This is a game where information – meaning access to that information *and* its interpretation in the quickest possible time – is the only thing that matters. Insiders will always have an advantage, followed by institutions, which have in-house research capability and those expensive Bloomberg boxes. By definition, the public is the last to access information or its interpretation, and it doesn't have institutional resources. Yet despite the odds, the public is heavily present in the market. Their motivations are the same as that of the pros: everybody's in the game to make money and come out ahead. In Mumbai at least, there seems to be a strong connection to real estate, and many Mumbaikars trade to generate surpluses they can use to buy apartments. As a result, real estate prices tend to surge at the end of a market boom, as the lucky ones cash out and buy that apartment. In recent years, the unreal move in Mumbai real estate has brought even this time-tested relationship into question, and Mumbai real estate prices – irrespective of market levels – continue to move on a one-way ticket to the moon. Despite that, for many traders the idea is to make a killing that allows them to move *siddhu* (straight) from Borivali at the suburban north end of the train line to the upmarket south end at Churchgate. Now that would be something.

The strong public presence in Indian markets allows for some noted market archetypes to be identified and developed. Examine here the motivations and actions of Hema the Housewife, Paresh the Professional, Cursetjee the Crab, Saurabh the Student, Ekta the Executive, Hetal the HNI, and Jimbo the Operator.

Hema the Housewife

Hema the Housewife has a rather surreptitious affair with the stock market, brought about in large part by her standing in society. People think she is upper middle class, but secretly she knows in her heart of hearts, that she is lower upper middle class. But she aspires to the middle upper middle class – everybody in India is aspiring anyway – and the stock market is going to help her get there. She got hooked on the market when at a party she overheard Mrs Puri tell Mrs Gupta how she made a killing in Bajaj Finance, which allowed her family to go to Thailand on vacation. Who knows, Mrs P mused, maybe next time she'd buy a Santro with her winnings.

All this was too much for Hema, and she decided to take the plunge. Entering the stock market was easy. She knew so much about it anyway, after watching those guys on CNBC yammer on about stocks. The children were packed off to school by 7, which left her free to track stocks and place orders with her broker. So, she persuaded her indulgent husband to loan her some money and bought in, following which she picked up on the market by diligently watching CNBC and learning technicals. Soon she was swinging a small line – 100 Sun Pharma here and 200 Wipro there – but that line got bigger as she reinvested her profits. Trading was usually a man's game in India but more and more women are now turning to it, Hema among them. Soon Hema finds she is getting better at trading by the day.

The same Hema who goes up and down Big Bazaar, comparing prices and looking for a good deal on a small *bartan* (utensil), will, with abandon, buy hundreds of shares of an unknown company after a phone conversation with a relative stranger – her broker Bimalbhai. Hema loves to call Bimalbhai up and chat about her stocks and the market. She simply needs to be in the market, to be a part of what's going on. The profits seem ancillary to that indefinable feeling that comes when she buys a stock and sees it go up, that soaring feeling that comes from having her judgment confirmed. She believes a stock should go up after she's bought it, and in fact, she often believes the stock should go up because she's bought it.

Hema is favourably predisposed to Bimalbhai's advice and often goes strictly by it. So, if a stock falls after she buys it, she simply holds on because Bimalbhai said, '*Paachu aose upar*' ('It will go up again'). As a result, when a bear market ends, Hema's portfolio is filled with stocks that are down 80 per cent, stocks that stubbornly refuse to behave like Bimalbhai says they should.

Sometimes the market makes Hema go through quiet paroxysms of anxiety that she is careful to hide from her husband and family. These convulsions are as intense as the fits she got when Chhotu got only 95 per cent in his maths exam or when her elder son, Aakash, did not get into the IIT. She is currently in the middle of these market-induced convulsions. You see, there is the matter of Sosoft Software and its aftermath that she is coming to terms with. On Bimalbhai's advice, she bought a small amount of Sosoft at 14, and it soared to 143. She should have been ecstatic and overjoyed as the trade developed into a 10-bagger in short order, but instead, she was consumed with regret as she had bought only a small amount. As the stock soared, she actually begged and pleaded for the stock to fall, so she could buy more – such trades were so difficult to come by anyway – after which it would go up again, and she'd make a killing.

She went into a mild depression and even began to neglect her housework and the *phulka*s got burnt a little and her husband got angry. But through all this, the stock didn't listen to her and did its own thing, and so, Hema made a small absolute amount on the trade, though she was totally right. Bitterly, she learnt and swallowed her lesson.

And next time, she put her entire capital on a stock we shall call Maharashtra Mushrooms at 27 – 'another sure thing' according to Bimalbhai – and it promptly went to 3.

And there went the Santro.

Paresh the Professional

Paresh the Pro belongs to a hardy breed of small-time traders and scalpers who eke out a living from the stock market. Every day, you can see Pareshbhai clutching his briefcase and a little *potla* (bag) of food as he makes his way to a broker's office. The back-office boys spread newspapers out in the corridors outside the office, face the wall, and eat their packed lunch. But Pareshbhai has office-eating privileges and consumes the *potla* quickly between 1.30 and 2 p.m. while staring at his screen, and this is why India's market volumes fall a little during that period.

With much trading on the internet nowadays, Paresh could stay at home and carry out his business, but he likes the drama of dressing up and coming to Dalal Street every day, even if it means commuting all the way from Mulund. Shortly after the market closes, you can see him on Dalal Street, chatting with his cronies over chai and *sing chana* (peanut lentil mix) outside the Allahabad Bank building. Often, he's joined by Yogeshbhai, a kindly broker with a penchant for talking about the old days. From a roadside vendor called Jay Snacks, Paresh will sometimes order a Tomato Paneer Omelette Masala Dosa, which is a powerful concoction of cottage cheese, assorted vegetables, sauces, and masalas, all pressed down and pish-pashed into the dosa. Like a bear market collapse, this is something that only he can stomach.

The BSE's rabbit warren of offices, similar to the sub-broker and franchise offices around the country, are packed with Pareshbhais. Like many others of his breed, he is either a Gujju or a Maddu. Surprisingly, Paresh does not use technicals or fundamentals for his trade selection; he is what the trade would call a pure scalper. All day, he just looks at that big BOLT screen which lists the BSE's stock universe. All up moves are in blue and down moves are in red, and Paresh's eye moves naturally to the blue upticks, following which his fingers move with lightning speed on the terminal as he scalps 20 shares here and 50 shares there. Most trades are then exited a few points higher during the same session. To him, stock market profits are like the morning fog in Kodaikanal – you reached out to grab it, only to see it slip between your fingers.

Paresh tends to be a momentum man. He buys stocks when they are going up; the only reason being that they are going up and the BOLT screen is showing it. This is a technical philosophy, but Paresh was educated in a Gujarati-medium school and does not read or understand the technical newsletters as they are mostly in English. Then again, he doesn't need the newsletters, and the *Gujarat Samachar* is enough for him. After 30 years scalping stocks from the BOLT screen, Paresh has developed a feel, an intuition, for the game. He has also learnt from long experience to cut his losses if things don't work out, and that is quite often. More than the intuition, it is this loss-cutting discipline that sees him through, and because of the combination, he does quite well for himself and supports a family by scalping stocks.

Occasionally, his wife, Manibehn, will throw a pan in his direction if he says he lost too much, but by and large, he comes out ahead and she stays with him. When on a roll, Paresh notices that he uses Amazon's 'Price: High to Low' sort feature a lot more, but he's afraid to tell his wife about the lucky streak as her browsing habits might also change in the same direction.

So no computers, no high-frequency trading, no algos or such like. Note also that Paresh isn't even a tape reader. Classical tape reading is about the interaction of price and volume and insights gleaned therefrom, but it's nothing like that for Paresh – here it's just 'Buy' if Hindalco shows a blue 2 per cent on the screen with some order buildup or momentum intuited from the ELOB's bid side. Over the years, Paresh has got so good at it that he could even scalp to the upside during a pronounced bear move. He is aided in his exertions by the absence of an uptick rule for day trading, which allows for those occasional (but terrific) intraday up moves during which he makes his money.

There are over 2,000 traded stocks on the BSE, and Paresh remembers the six-digit BOLT code (required for placing an order) of at least a 1,000 among them. This is a remarkable feat of memory that deserves to be in some sort of record book. Like most others of his breed, Paresh doesn't scalp the short side and trade for the fall, though he started his career in the old badla system when such trades were frequent. If he makes a mistake while buying, he can take delivery the next day, but that is not as easy with a short sale; as a result, shares are usually scalped for a pop to the upside, which adds to the market's upside momentum.

Paresh's cousin Raju is a diligent technical trader and occasionally gives Paresh a tip, but our man is strangely reluctant to follow Raju's advice. Long experience has taught him to be wary of tips, even when they come from cousin Raju – and besides, listening to Raju's tips is not as satisfying as exercising his own judgment. Somehow, acting on tips is against Paresh's professional code and the way he sees himself as a professional trader, albeit a small one. Paresh is the backbone of many small brokers on Dalal Street or around the country, and their offices are full of people like him; the sub-broker offices of the big boys are also full of Pareshbhais. Paresh even has a small network of clients who trade through him, and he splits the brokerage with the office he frequents. All informal and trust-based, of course. No need for those cumbersome power of attorney documents with all their stamp duty charges and paperwork, if it's done this way.

Of late, Paresh has been complaining that his sub-brokerage from the client network that trades through him is often larger than his market pickings. Also, the free chai at the broker's office used to be unlimited, but it's now down to a morning and evening cuppa. But the broker says that the chaiwala's charges have gone from ₹5 to ₹15 a cup in the past two years, and the broker saves ₹10,000 a month by rationing the tea.

Cursetjee the Crab

There are only occasional sightings of Cursetjee the Crab. When markets collapse you can see him scurrying like a crab into the offices on Dalal

Street and placing his buy orders. He walks with a cane because he is 80 years old. Not impressed by modern India, he spends his days crawling out of it in the congenial environment of the Ripon Club, and it was there that he once upended a bowl of *dhansak* (a lentil and mutton dish) on the head of an irritating lawyer.

Among the trading crowd, Cursetjee is an unusual man, for he buys stocks by the hundredweight only at certain times; in his long life, he must have bought stocks only about six or seven times. It was as though he had a BEST bus ticket in his head that could get punched only on those occasions, and otherwise, he went along with his life as though nothing had happened. He approaches the stock market the way a farmer approaches the seasons, believing that there is a time to sow and a time to reap. But unlike the farmer, Cursetjee has never reaped. When the pink papers scream bloody murder and the end of the world is nigh, Cursetjee moves around sideways and crab-like to his broker's office and buys indiscriminately. Then he keeps the stocks and reinvests the dividends, which he doesn't need anyway. The dividends are usually reinvested only in the same stocks that generated those dividends, a useful discipline that over the long run ensures that his holdings increase in profitable high-dividend-paying companies. And that is that.

He has seen it all, has old Cursetjee. His father, Burjorjee, had known the solicitor F.E. Dinshaw, at about the time when Dinshaw was forging a group of cement factories into the giant called ACC. Over lunch at the Willingdon, Burjorjee had picked up a small stake in ACC through the trusts Dinshaw had set up to control the company. That was how corporate finance was done in the old days. The stake stayed in the family and grew over the years through the magic of compounding, and as was his habit, Cursetjee reinvested the dividends received back into ACC. With him, it was 'ACC as Religion'. He had applied the same approach to stalwarts of the time such as Indore Malwa, Azam Jahi, Howrah Jute, and Indian Iron and Steel, but over the years they all went to 0, and it was ACC that rescued his portfolio.

The ACC stake was never sold, and in fact, whatever entered the Cursetjee household was not sold, just kept. However, in 1992, this iron rule was almost violated. You see, Harshad Mehta took the stock from 200 to 10,000, based on some snake oil called replacement cost valuation. This led Cursetjee to consult with ACC's then chairman, the late Nani Palkhivala, who shook his head and said he was clueless about the stock price of the very company where he was chairman. Palkhivala advised Cursetjee to sell into the madness and get out. Cursetjee mulled over this deeply and for a long time; after all, it was Palkhivala the advice was coming from. Despite that, Cursetjee did not sell. ACC collapsed, and everyone around cursed him for not listening to the advice, but he just went on with his life as though nothing had happened. Many years later, the stock came back and went beyond the peak attained during the Mehta bull run. And Cursetjee still went on with his life as though nothing had happened.

Then in 1999, Cursetjee's son suggested diversifying out of ACC as the stake was now a big chunk of the family's portfolio. We are not diversified enough, his son Maneckjee argued, drawing on his training as a chartered accountant in England. The son had seen India's future, and it was in software and tech and all the other sunrise industries. Infosys and Wipro were suddenly too expensive, Maneckjee said, but the smaller tech stocks like Silverline, Global Tele, and DSQ also represented that future very well, and they were still cheap. Maneckjee strongly recommended selling most of the ACC which was 'so yesterday' and buying into the likes of Global Tele, DSQ, and Silverline.

Cursetjee swore at his son and told him to keep quiet. *'Chokroh kai samaj toh nathi,'* he later grumbled to his cronies at the Ripon. Later, when Silverline and DSQ went to 0, he never even bothered saying, 'I told you so' to his son, but just went on with his life as though nothing had happened. With Cursetjee there was always *santosham*, that wonderful Tamil word which means a certain easy-going, satisfied, contented happiness. As gruntled as a Googler, he can still be found at the Ripon Club, taking an afternoon catnap while lolling around in those big chairs whose arms open out.

And the ACC is still there in his portfolio.

Saurabh the Student

Saurabh the Student is a new entrant in the markets. The wire houses babble on about demographic dividends, but Saurabh represents the real demographic dividend the markets benefit from. Thousands of Saurabhs enter the Indian stock market every year, a new generation waiting to learn the lessons of the previous one. The country produces over 1 million engineers and 300,000 MBAs every year, and there are few jobs available. But entry into the equity markets is free and entry barriers are negligible, usually a simple matter of opening a 3-in-1 account online. Consequently, many drift into the markets after graduation, and this ensures a steady stream of fresh-faced young traders entering every year.

But in Saurabh we have an enthusiast who is trying his hand even before he completes his education. Saurabh is a student at a Mumbai management institute that we shall call P.S. Jana. Part of a considerable process of social change unfolding across the country, he comes from a small town, and back-office India is his escape from the dreariness of that milieu. Like the rest of the crowd he belongs to, he is an engineer of some sort from a college somewhere down south. Following graduation, Saurabh completed a two-year seasoning in the canyons of Gurugram or Bengaluru with one of the Big Four firms. At the end of all this, his resume was full of acronyms that only the cognoscenti could understand; after perusing the resumes of all the other Saurabhs that got posted on LinkedIn, India's obsession with credentials became quite apparent. Done with his 'work ex', Saurabh then cracked a standardized test where he correctly answered 20 questions every 20 minutes, and this, together with some extracurricular activities, got him into business school. About 8 of every 10 entering students at P.S. Jana are from the same cookie cutter as Saurabh, and it's 9 out of every 10 at some of the IIMs.

India's business schools are not business schools as much as finishing schools for engineers. Most business schools are not confident about their 'value add' to an incoming student and prefer to rely on the admittees' undergraduate degrees and work experience to ensure they obtain jobs after graduation. This attitude leads the schools to admit students with an engineering degree and some IT experience – as that raises chances of employability in the country's burgeoning IT services or back-office space. In effect, most students enter from the vast tech services and back-office space, and most return there after business school. The business schools had discovered their nice little niche in recycling India's tech services and back-office crowd back to the tech services and back-office industry.

With Saurabh – the well-trained mechanical engineer – the idea of the universe as clockwork prevails. If that clockwork breaks down, it is but a matter of taking it apart, examining its inner contents, finding and solving the problem, and putting it all back together again into the whole. So, it is natural and altogether fitting that he brings this world view to the markets. To Saurabh, the market is that malfunctioning clockwork that can be opened up to yield its secrets through this reductionistic process. There is a formula somewhere – there is always a formula somewhere – and it can be applied to a problem to generate a solution. That Saurabh is applying his mind to the wrong problem, or worse, that there is no solution because there is no problem, is unthinkable. There are vast multitudes who share Saurabh's world view, and this is why microstructure – the study of the market's plumbing – carries much resonance in India.

Saurabh is trying to apply what he learns to the markets, which he does by setting up a 3-in-1 account and trading stocks from his hostel room. This turns out to be a crapshoot, but our Saurabh is getting his experience early in life and that is a good thing. As Lefévre noted, the game will teach him the game, and it will not spare the *danda* (rod) while teaching. Losses are the *gurudakshina* (offering to a guru) you pay the market for the lessons it teaches you, but unlike real-life gurus – who may be more forgiving if they don't receive their *gurudakshina*s – the market is a stern and ruthless guru who will take its *gurudakshina* from you, whether you give it or not. But Saurabh does not see things this way, and so has a marked tendency to talk more about profits than losses on his trades.

Saurabh is smart, in fact he's very smart. The product of an education system that was in the main a funnelling system, he's one of only 200 who made it into P.S. Jana from an applicant pool of almost 20,000. Still, the basic issue is what Saurabh is learning at business school. His textbook, *Investments* by Bodie, Kane, and Marcus, is a venerable tome with math-packed pages most participants would run a mile from, but for Saurabh with his engineering background, it's all child's play. Propounding that state of nature called efficient markets, the book introduces students to that workhorse of asset pricing models – the Capital Asset Pricing Model (CAPM). Filled with complex math, the CAPM (pronounced 'Cap Em') and its variants hold considerable appeal to Saurabh and his classmates. Saurabh doesn't know what Ben Graham, the dean of Wall Street, once said:

> In 44 years of Wall Street experience and study, I have never seen dependable calculations made about common stock values, or related investment policies, that went beyond simple arithmetic or the most elementary algebra. Whenever calculus is brought in, or higher algebra, you could take it as a warning signal that the operator was trying to substitute theory for experience.[1]

But Sulu Laljani, with his dyed black bouffant and edgy style and Rajesh Khanna mannerisms, has taught them only about the CAPM in investments class. And in the security analysis class, that earnest professor – the accountant trying so hard to be an economist – has only taught them about financial statements. The faculty has lifted the syllabus from a typical US business school without any attempt at adapting it to Indian conditions, and Saurabh, coming from the world of Laplace transforms and heat transfer equations, has lapped it all up. This is what finance was all about. This is his entry into the game. Besides, Saurabh himself is a formula in search of a problem; give him a problem and he'll search for the right formula and apply it perfectly. Much of his educational background and training has hammered this approach into him, and as

[1] Benjamin Graham, *The Intelligent Investor*, New York: HarperCollins, Revised Edition 2006, 570.

a result, this is how his mind works. Unfortunately, in real life, markets rarely behave in the fashion that most Saurabhs want them to. In fact, it's almost guaranteed that they never behave in a formulaic fashion.

And the contradictions of the market! God, the contradictions! How to deal with the technical boys screaming 'Sell' and the fundamental crowd screaming 'Buy' at the same time? After all, at the age of 15, in keeping with the requirements of India's 10+2 school system, Saurabh had stopped studying subjects other than applied natural sciences. As a result, there was little of the leavening and well-rounded effect that came from exposure to the social sciences or humanities. In the main, India's education system produced the plumbers of tech but never its poets, always the C++ or C-- types but never a Steve Jobs, and this also explained the predominance of service rather than product companies in the IT space. That ability of the broadly trained mind to hold two contradictory propositions in it at the same time and still function without getting paralysed does not come easily to Saurabh. Perhaps the ability will come with market experience and wider reading, but that is still in the future. Till then, Saurabh tries and tries, and often finds solace in the complexities of technical analysis. Ah, technical analysis. Even the name is reassuring – '*Technical* Analysis'. With its intricate charts, its certainties, and its occasional formulae, it is comfortably familiar, and to this he naturally turns after mastering the mathematics of mean variance optimization and the CAPM.

So, Saurabh buys a nicely trending stock that we shall call GKCRL, which is an infrastructure company that was a client of the Big Four firm he worked at before coming to business school. The stock doubles in short order, raising visions of the multi-bagger. But then something happens and the stock moves to single digits. *How could it?* He had even produced a research report on it for his security analysis class. Such is his conviction that he keeps buying more and averaging on the way down. As the stock goes to single digits, he obsessively keeps track of it by pecking away on his smartphone. As poor Saurabh gets cleaned out, all he can do is think about the stock, and as a result, he almost flunks his exams.

Perhaps Saurabh will treat this the way it should be treated, as just another part of his learning experience. Perhaps he may figure out that his engineering background makes him suited for the quantitative debt/fixed income side, and less so for the equity side, where insight into people, materials, machines, and money and how they interact is required. Perhaps he might even realize that capital markets are never in equilibrium in India, that the assumptions of the CAPM are often violated even in the broadest and deepest capital market in the world, the United States, that most masters of the Indian market think the Cap Em is a kind of cap, and that India is a stock picker's rather than an optimizer's market. But that's all in the future, and right now, Saurabh doesn't even know what he doesn't know.

Ekta the Executive

Like Saurabh, Ekta the Executive represents a new breed of trader in the markets. Perhaps she's a Saurabh in his second or third job, and like Saurabh, she uses the freedom of the 3-in-1 account to trade stocks from anywhere. Ekta's advantage over Saurabh is that she's earning for herself. She's drawing a larger salary than her husband, there are no children as yet, and there's surplus to invest; what better time to trade stocks than in your late twenties, when there are few encumbrances and risk appetites are high. Also, there's the minor issue of buying an apartment in a city where they are always a little beyond reach. A killing on Sosoft together with a home loan from HDFC might do the trick. Why give hard-earned capital to those fuddy-duddy fundies who underperform the market anyway? Trading stocks on your own is so exciting.

Perhaps Ekta works in corporate finance for a big securities firm. Here, there will be compliance issues that restrict her trading, but these can be difficult to enforce in a fragmented brokerage industry with hundreds of brokers. Ekta's married name differs from her maiden name, so who's to know if she opens an account in her parent's name at one of those firms and trades a little on the side? Now this is interesting. There's all this inside information lying around, especially on the open offer side. There may be SEBI investigations, but so far no one's been caught in the clubby world of corporate finance. Unlike assault or battery, insider trading is often seen as a victimless crime in India, but don't tell that to the poor fellows who're short-selling futures on a stock that's going up on inside information. You'll get an earful from them as they feel battered, all right.

So, a big MNC makes an open offer to buy out local shareholders at a premium to the current market price, and insiders like Ekta (who is on the investment banking team) get in on the act. Because of insider buying, the price rises too much before the offer date, and this wipes out the surprise element necessary for the offer's success. As insiders bid the market price close to the open offer rate, the MNC and its bankers agree informally to a cooling-off period, and the offer is put on hold for the moment. This happens twice, and on each occasion, the stock sells off and pulls back. But the open offer is finally announced, and the stock lurches upward to the offer price. The stock never reaches the exact offer price because of tax liability issues, arbitrage considerations, and uncertainty on the offer's response rate.

Nevertheless, Ekta makes a killing. Through the wild roller-coaster ride, she has been buying heavily but not in cash; instead, she's using India's single stock futures (SSF) market to get the leverage it provides. Ekta's been using the certain payoff from inside information to undertake that most risky of trades – she's pyramiding into the up move and using the profits from early contracts as capital to buy new contracts. The pullbacks on the roller coaster almost wipe her out – showing how risky even 'sure shot' inside information can be – but she manages to come through. Naturally, the combination of inside information, risk-taking, and leverage amplifies returns so much that every 100 put up is now 900 in four months. And she makes the move from Andheri to Worli, where the new apartment awaits a housewarming to which she will invite the MNC executives who were responsible for her killing.

Ekta's cousin Bhavna tries to do the same but without the certain payoff that inside information represents. Bhavna works for a company we call Sodunk and can access its results; she uses that information to buy when she gets *khabar* (news) of good results. Here things get a little peculiar and fuzzy. Sometimes Sodunk goes up on good results, and equally often, Sodunk goes down on good results. This puzzles and shocks cousin Bhavna – she's losing money on insider trading, and that simply should not happen. The Bhavna types know a lot about their industry, but do they know a little about the market? Bhavna can't figure out that the stock has already run up and 'discounted' some of Sodunk's good results, and hence the sell-off. Compared to Bhavna, the market professional is at least aware of the 'discounting' but less certain on how much has actually been discounted.

A related type is Ekta the Ex-Executive. This is the executive who drifts into the markets after moving out of corporate life. This avatar of Ekta can be seen trading quite fervently – and depending on how she's doing – finding it a lot more fun than selling widgets or writing code.

Hetal the HNI

Hetal the High-net-worth Individual (HNI) is the Big Swinging Dick in the game (but that's Wall Street nomenclature, and Dalal Street is coy and modest about such things). Hetal can swing a big line of stock for his own account, and hence the nomenclature; LIC's a lot bigger than Hetal, but it has those bureaucrats and their darn committees. By contrast, Hetal is his own man and can make his own decisions – and quickly at that – which makes him a bigger player than those LIC bureaucrats with their acres of required approvals. Hetal swings a big line, so he's a BSD. QED.

Hetal the HNI is prominent on the primary side, where entire schemes are devised to keep him happy and part of the game. He is the patron saint of the IPO market, which is a necessary anointment given the public's distaste for new issues and the number of times they've got burnt in them. Special buckets in the IPO allotment process are assigned to him and his *jaati* and financing schemes are arranged – often at annualized rates between 20 and 30 per cent – that allow him to take part in the issuance. As a stag, his designated role is to use the leverage provided by the financing schemes to pick up the shares allotted to him in the buckets. Often, Hetal and his ilk signal demand for the IPO by subscribing heavily on issue opening day, and this stagging then creates an information cascade, in turn reassuring the other investors who are waiting on the fence and trying to make up their minds about the issue's viability. When the issue lists, Hetal flips his allotted shares to the public. Depending on the public's response at listing and the financing terms, Hetal can make a killing.

Or he can get killed. Much also depends on the overall market, the activation of greenshoe options by the underwriters, and, critically, his judgment of the issue's pricing.[2] If all factors are in his favour – and especially if the pricing is reasonable – the stock lists on opening day at a premium to its issue price. Because of the leverage inherent in many financing schemes, Hetal can make a healthy return on his initial investment, but if he's wrong, he loses the equivalent amount.

In the wider scheme of things, Hetal's designated role is the assumption of risk; he can simply take more risk – and with more shares – than anyone else. Hetal is also suited to the game by temperament, and this, more than the capital he commands, makes him a player in the game. Not all HNIs are in the game, but those in the game, are Hetals.

Together with his fellow stag and cousin Sanju Bhambi, Hetal demands a certain respect for his participation, and accordingly, suitable deference is given to them. The big banks and brokerages have divisions with fancy names that cater exclusively to people like Hetal and Sanju; words like Royal, Premium, Gold, or Club usually figure as part of the division's nomenclature. The big brokerages wine and dine Hetal and claim to have a special relationship with him. For the brokerages, this jealously guarded relationship is important, as HNIs like Hetal often rescue IPOs that might otherwise devolve. But his role in the

[2] Greenshoe options give an underwriter the option to purchase additional shares at the IPO price to cover over-allotment; effectively, a short cover of a deliberately oversold IPO.

secondary market is less clear, for there he is at a disadvantage compared to the fundies or the dervishes of Dalal Street, the big professional traders. Hetal might be in the diamond or wholesale business, and not necessarily in the stock market, so his competence is questionable and, by definition, less than that of the pros. So, Hetal courts the pros as a matter of abundant caution and a careful dance ensues between them; the HNIs try to be on the same side as the dervishes and fundies and are always anxious to know what the latter are doing.

India's IPO market has been moribund for some time, and so Hetal's a little *thanda* (cold) nowadays. Besides, he and his *jaati* have been displaced in recent years by the private equity crowd.[3] Private equity now gets onto the elevator at ground level as they fund companies in the early stages. But India's private equity *namuna*s (specimens) have a conception quite different from General Georges Doriot, who founded the industry. To the General, it was staying with the companies after listing that yielded outsized rewards, but the private equity crowd here looks for listing day exits. So, a delicate question remains: is the private equity crowd competing with the Hetals to sell on listing day? An equally delicate question is why the public would buy at all on listing day, when the smart money is selling and exiting.[4] But that doesn't seem to have occurred to the private equity crowd.

Jimbo the Operator

Jimbo is a stock operator and conman. He has five offices in the maze of old buildings around the Fort area and moves among them whenever the heat gets too much. A lanky fellow with a face that looks like a withered walnut, Jimbo dyes his thinning hair jet black but sometimes leaves it white. He is part of the Palmoni group, a shady business headed

[3] For an early overview of the private equity industry, see Afra Afsharipour, 'The Indian Private Equity Model,' NSE Working Paper, WP/8/2013, July 2013.

[4] India's private equity industry reportedly invested $32 billion (₹1,30,000 crores) in the three-year run up to the end of 2008 and had spent the years since then figuring out how to get it back. See Rasmeet Kohli, 'Venture Capital and Private Equity Financing in India,' Unpublished paper, National Stock Exchange of India, Mumbai, 2009.

by a small-town industrialist with a moustache named Paya Sukit. Jimbo operates in the shadowy underbelly of the stock market, with the occasional foray into real estate and assets of distressed companies. As a white-collar criminal, he finds the murkiness of such activities to his liking.

There is a vast conspiracy of silence around white-collar crime in India. Comfortable words and euphemisms like bogus or *hera pheri* (hanky-panky) or *golmaal* (bungling) are used to describe activities that would land people in jail in most other countries. Not like murder or battery that is committed by 'people like them', white-collar crime is committed by 'people like us' who are usually English-speaking, professional, and educated. White-collar criminals caught doing fraud are compelled to use the judicial system to their advantage – if they do not appeal, the fraud is accepted, but if they go through the appeals process, they can say the matter is 'under appeal' for the next 20 years. Naturally, with this trade-off they choose to use the black hole of India's legal system to their advantage, which leaves their 'learned friends' quite rich, even if that comes at a cost to their reputations.

Once the matter reaches court, crooked lawyers with silver tongues are always available to keep white-collar criminals like Jimbo out of jail; this they do by throwing a cloud of legality around Jimbo's fraudulent transactions and going on about technicalities such as jurisdiction and limitation. The lawyers say *choo-manta*r (abracadabra) and everything just disappears poof-like in that cloud of legality. Much of Jimbo's criminal activity takes place in the law courts through such lawyers, and he benefits from the cloak of respectability these activities invoke. This, together with a professional background and knowledge of corporate law and procedure, makes it easy for him to get away with it all. So, he roams around freely, relying on a battery of bent lawyers to stay out of jail.

But Jimbo is also a stock manipulator, one of a select group of operators who exercise their talents across India's wide universe of over 2,000 stocks. He is an old-fashioned 'pump-and-dump' man, and this he does with the promoters of two-rupee companies that no one has heard of.

Take the case of a stock we shall call Datatel, a wonderful counter that Jimbo and his associates took from 3 to 100 in a little over two years. That's a 33-bagger for a stock which is a piece of paper with not much behind it in terms of business, assets, or cash flows. Never mind that the stock went back to its starting price before heading to 0 and a delisting. Datatel had a bull market behind it, but the key thing to remember about the Indian 'pump and dump' is that it doesn't need a bull market behind it. The Datatel move can take place in any sort of market because of the confined and specialized nature of the operation, the natural desire of the public to be long, and the effective ban on the short side.

Like much of Indian market practice, the 'pump and dump' has never been written up, and knowledge of the practice is passed on only through word of mouth. Successful execution remains confined to a select group, and others who try their hand have often bungled. In reality, the 'pump and dump' is a most elaborate operation. First, a big chunk of the promoter's holding is locked up with suitable safeguards (the unlocked balance will be used for the operation). This is vital as most Indian companies have large promoter holdings that present both an opportunity and a threat to the operation. Locked-up promoter holdings straight away remove a large chunk of stock (often over half the float) from the market, but an incompetently done lock-up runs the risk of the pumpers two-timing and dumping on one another. After all, if Jimbo is pumping a stock in collusion with the promoters, he has to be sure the promoters are not dumping on him. These are crooks who cannot even rely on honour among thieves to safeguard their arrangements.

Second, the stock is accumulated by the operators themselves. Usually volumes are low, so the first step is to build volumes, and this is done by discreet circular trading among various cards and terminals, all controlled by Jimbo and the pool. Heavy buying takes the stock up on large volumes, following which the stock is actually sold to drive out the technical traders and chartists who get attracted to rising price-volume action. It's too early to allow them to pile on. This gradual process of buying and selling – with a little more buying than selling on each round – builds volumes, but with negligible price action to the upside. This is an ideal situation to build a position, and the stock is duly accumulated.

The locked-up promoter holding and dear Jimbo's exertions on the accumulation have now reduced the free float – the stock which is actually available to the public in the market – even further. It may even be cornered. Now complex calculations are made to find out exactly how much stock has been accumulated and deposited in various demat accounts.

Once the position is accumulated, the propaganda has to start, and this is usually through the initiation of analyst coverage. Respectable brokerages such as Golden Socks or Murugan Srini (as the pink papers informally refer to certain entities) will not initiate coverage on Datatel, so it is usually the smaller brokerages that oblige Jimbo. In return, perhaps a part of the accumulation is given to the *sethiya* (business leader) who owns the small brokerage or perhaps he is part of the action all along. The analyst at the small brokerage is barely competent and under strict orders to think up a 'story'. Everything is the 'story', and this tale is usually a 'turnaround story', because those are the most plausible and therefore the easiest to sell. The 'story' is never outright fiction or fabrication, but more in the nature of scraps and titbits of positive news interwoven with embellishments. Perhaps the company has undiscovered land in Uttar Pradesh that's not in the stock price, or there are sales orders that are coming through; perhaps it's a beneficiary of impending regulatory or policy action by the government, or there are merger announcements in the offing. Best of all, perhaps it's a combination of the above, and so, the 'story' is duly spun using this fundamental news. With the internet and message boards, the propaganda is easy to spread around.

Then it's time to let her rip, and massive buying by Jimbo and the pool takes place. By now, the free float has been reduced drastically through the locked-up promoter holding and Jimbo's exertions. This heavy buying on a low free float drives the stock up, which attracts the technical traders, the scalpers, and the scores of people in Indian markets who buy price action. Now the public starts getting the bit between its teeth and bids the stock even higher. To them, all the equity research and propaganda in the world are no substitute for the price action on the tape. The stock is simply going up! Nothing else matters. Along the way, even the pros and the buy side may take a peek and like what's going on. The crucial point is that the fundamental titbits in the story, like the incoming sales orders or the UP land, combine with the technical price action on the tape. Even to sophisticated participants, it looks like speculative investment – after all, this is the Keynesian beauty contest in action – and the stock gets bulled up.

Periodic selling by Jimbo and the pool keeps the move from running away from itself. At the top, the public's in the move, especially the hardcore trading public. But now, it is time for Jimbo and the promoters to exit. In the old days, UTI or some such public sector undertaking in the mutual fund space could be relied on to take the stock off Jimbo's hands, but now that avenue is a little restricted, and so, the stock has to be sold on the market. Almost always, this selling – or distribution – takes place on the way down and never on the way up. Once the stock peaks and begins its downtrend, it has periodic up moves. These up moves – routinely mistaken by the technical crowd as a resumption of the uptrend and labelled as 'false breakouts' by them when they realize their error – are sold into by Jimbo and the pool. There's just a little more selling than buying on the distribution, and that is how it takes place. Finally, as the stock heads even lower, there's the fatal attraction retail traders have for penny stocks, which creates a considerable market for the stock at very low levels.

16

THE DERVISHES OF DALAL STREET

The Big Professional Traders

They are a small group nowadays, these dervishes of Dalal Street, the big professional traders who answer to none but themselves. To Ayn Rand, the trader was the embodiment of a self-reliant individual, and in *Atlas Shrugged,* she gets John Galt to say in that rambling speech, 'A trader is a man who earns what he gets and does not give or take the undeserved. A trader does not ask to be paid for his failures, nor does he ask to be loved for his flaws.'[1] The dervishes remind one of that observation, and in this *roman à clef*, consider three of them, all so diametrically opposed to one another as to invite caricature – Rocky Juju, Chintan Pathak, and Doma Ramani.

Rocky Juju

Rocky Juju is the only noted character the Indian stock market has thrown up in recent years. Volatile, blunt, unprepossessing,

[1] 'The symbol of all relationships among [rational] men, the moral symbol of respect for human beings, is the trader. We, who live by values, not by loot, are traders, both in matter and in spirit. A trader is a man who earns what he gets and does not give or take the undeserved. A trader does not ask to be paid for his failures, nor does he ask to be loved for his flaws.' Ayn Rand, *Atlas Shrugged*, New York: New American Library, reprint, 1999, 1022.

rambunctious, coarse, fat, and utterly without pretension, he is almost Shakespearian in scale. In fact, the physical parallel with Falstaff in *Henry IV, Parts 1* and *2* is remarkable. There is the same portliness, the same expansive girth, and a face whose dominating feature is a pair of huge jowls that go all the way down to his neck. He could have been Ralph Richardson essaying the role, but he is Rocky Juju, larding the lean stock counters among which he walks.

There are echoes of the old-style Dalal Street operator about him, except that the word 'operator' is a misnomer nowadays. Besides, there are not many of his ilk around, and the business has become too professional for all that. So, now Rocky calls himself a trader and investor.

He made his money the old-fashioned way, by buying low and selling high. To this day, he sees himself as an intuitive trader, but behind the intuition is a lot of experience, both real and vicarious; it may take him only 40 minutes to put on a large position, but behind the decision lies almost 40 years of that experience. In the early days he must have taken insane amounts of risk to build his fortune, but that is a closely guarded secret. 'When I was young, people called me a gambler. As the scale of my operations increased, I became known as a speculator. Now I am called a banker. But I have been doing the same thing all the time,' Sir Ernest Cassel, the financier, had reportedly said.[2] And so it is with Rocky. With considerable wealth has come respectability, and the days of *sattabaazi* (speculation) are now behind him.

There is a hint of dissipation to him, but just a hint. Unlike the other dervishes of Dalal Street, who started off as – and remained – good middle-class boys with that dominant Gujarati Marwari trading ethic and its decent respect for the hypocrisies of humankind, Rocky Juju is unabashedly flamboyant, direct, and colourful. Like Falstaff, it is rumoured that he loves his sack, and there was a time – or so the stories go – when he frequented the Marine Plaza bar on his way home

[2] As quoted in Bernard M. Baruch, *Baruch: My Own Story*, New York: Henry Holt and Company, 1957, 247.

and polished off a half bottle of single malt. His office used to be in a perennial cloud of cigarette smoke brought about by a multipack-a-day habit. Blessed from birth with a portly and robust constitution, he has spent the rest of his life abusing it, but with age saner times have come, and he has now reluctantly given up the excesses of youth.

Rocky has his office overlooking the Arabian Sea, in the South Mumbai office district of Nariman Point. The obligatory Bloomberg screens perch on a large wall-facing desk, their flickering orange prices in silent communion with him. He and the screens are all of a piece, and during meetings his eyes often stray to them. An unusual feature of the cabin is a small but distinguished collection of books on the stock market, perhaps the finest in all of India. Each hardcover is diligently wrapped in an archival-quality jacket, and the entire collection is housed in a teak bookcase. Indicative of the wide range of fields the stock market encompasses, the collection includes works on psychology and sociology, financial history, accounting and finance methodology, investment policy, market microstructure, and open economy macroeconomics. The breadth of subjects reminds one of noted businessman Charlie Munger's remark that to be a successful investor one must carry around a mental latticework of models.[3] And yet the range is surprising, given his background. For, like many market participants, Rocky had a narrowly technical education as an accountant (or a chartered accountant, as the profession is known in India).

Despite the inherent mystery of his proprietary companies, Juju maintains a high-profile media presence that is itself excellent cover for the secrecy considered essential to his operations. Much of that media presence conforms to a tightly scripted format that is designed to give nothing away. Thrown at him, either by an anchor or market participant, are the usual anxious questions about the state of the economy and market levels. Juju's ripostes – usually a blend of candidly bullish assertions and wild surmise on the India Growth Story – reveal him in

[3] The idea is developed in Robert G. Hagstorm, *Investing: The Last Liberal Art,* 2nd ed., New York: Columbia University Press, 2013, 1–12.

his element. Yet that optimism is tempered by a certain native Marwari horse sense, and this quality has ensured that he always bought into functional but undervalued businesses with strong profits or cash flows. Concept stories or 'new economy' plays are antithetical to Rocky Juju, and he looks with pronounced petulance and distaste at entire sectors such as e-commerce or online retailing.

But the singular feature of his personality is that robust congenital bullishness, often bluntly expressed. His life story reinforced the essential truth of that approach. The accumulated fortune confirmed it and so that trait got pronounced and defined with age. Equities, by definition, are a business of the future, and an unquestioning belief in that future always helps. This conviction contrasts with the fashionable pessimism of many of Juju's countrymen, and it is this conviction that is responsible for the contrast between his market experience and that of his compatriots. In recent years, and especially after the spread of the coronavirus pandemic, the pessimism of those compatriots has ceased to be fashionable and become alarmingly prescient about the real side of the economy. But Rocky operates on the financial side where the distortions caused by Western quantitative easing, the long corner, the gushing capital from rupee cost averaging products, and the absence of a short side all continued to confirm his sunny-side-up optimism. The only intrusion on this most charmed of existences is his odd and pervasive fear of nuclear adventurism by India's neighbours.

At the time of this writing, he is in the process of winding down a long and eventful life. Realization has dawned that in contrast to industry (where people leave behind wealth that commemorates them in concrete form), wealth accumulation in the market manifests only as a collection of demat statements with large amounts next to the entries. What follows is a desire for something more tangible and a subsequent interest in philanthropy. This concern for the common weal is, in itself, a notable departure from his fellow dervishes. Despite this stated change in life goals, his natural interests and avocation lead to a keen and continued interest in the markets.

Chintan Pathak

Chintan Pathak is another noted personality among the dervishes. From one of Dalal Street's dominant communities – the Gujaratis – he is what Vikram Seth would call a suitable boy.

With regular features and a quiet, reserved manner, he reminds one of a successful MNC executive, the sort who would sell soap for Unilever. Unlike Rocky Juju, Chintan comes from a pedigreed background. Rocky made his own money but Chintan inherited wealth that he had the good sense and luck to build on, which in turn brought the capital necessary for independent operations. Ivy League-educated and the owner of a website, Chintan is academically inclined and a visiting faculty member at a business school. He gives frequent interviews during which he refers to the likes of Aristotle, Zeno of Citium, and someone called Sextus Empericus. The self-conscious intellectualism is wearisome and sounds a little trite, coming as it does from someone with little training or exposure to philosophy.

Damn Empericus, tell us about the markets.

Along the way, and notwithstanding the copious references to the Stoics and Seneca, he acquired a reputation as one of India's value investors and was part of the residents of Graham and Doddsville. He is lucid and clever while discussing his investment philosophy, but it was the Sextus stuff and the windbag intellectualizing that was his downfall. After a while, one wished for Juju's robust and intuitive approach.

Chintan is painfully earnest, a lot less colourful than Rocky, and has made a religion out of being conservative. Chintan should have been free of *chinta* (worry), but he is full of it, and he goes around with a perennially concerned look on his face, like the world is going to fall on his head. But at least he takes time to think and write, which is beyond the inclinations and capabilities of the other dervishes. Wisdom literature is a big thing with Chintan. Rocky is happy calling it like it is, but with Chintan, everything has to be earnestly analysed. Premchand Roychand's hard-earned motto had been '*Wisdom above Riches*', and with Chintan, that is a way of life. Rocky's interviews are always blunt and direct, and the interviewer has to deal with his innate crabbiness and petulance, but Chintan's interviews are a soothing mélange of philosophical rambling, often only tangentially linked with markets and stocks. Perhaps this is not by design. In India, the public's subliminal urge to find a living guru is matched by the equally strong desire of many people to play one.

Juju was boundlessly optimistic and gung-ho, but with Chintan, there is a sense of profound realism that bordered on the fatalistic. In contrast to Juju, Pathak actually has a coherent philosophy of investing, and his interviews – at least when he isn't philosophizing – are sprinkled with terse saws that outline his method. Pathak is a value investor with a special situation bias. Not enamoured with growth, Pathak assesses value through the usual Graham metrics, which also set him apart from Rocky. There is the acknowledgement that discounted cash flow analysis, while analytically rigorous, could produce nonsensical results. Unlike most of the other dervishes, Pathak understands the macros but disdains them in line with the teachings of his guru, Graham. Also, leverage is never used in his folios; from the early days, he has been well capitalized, and there is little need to borrow to build capital.

All very safe and orderly and respectable, just like Graham had said: 'Investing is most intelligent when it is most businesslike.'[4] Nevertheless, diversification is a key area where Pathak's approach differs from that of his guru. Graham had been seared and all but wiped out by the appalling experience of Wall Street's crash of 1929 and the Great Depression that followed. The experience left an indelible mark on Graham, and in later years, he always diversified heavily. But for Pathak (and the other dervishes) the march of history had been kinder, and he often took concentrated positions in a few stocks after doing his research. With Pathak, as with the other dervishes, performance comes from concentration married to turnover, and this shortcut to juiced-up performance is not even seen as a shortcut.

[4] Benjamin Graham, *The Intelligent Investor*, New York: HarperCollins, Revised Edition 2006, 523.

Doma Ramani

And finally, Doma Ramani, the most amiable and easy-going of the dervishes, with a geniality that comes from great wealth easily acquired. Short, dark, and dressed often in white, he has a quick and cautious air about him that reminds one of a snow-covered ferret. Famous (like Rocky) as both a speculator and an investor, he made his fortune by taking large bets in the inefficient and undervalued markets of the 1990s. Now attracted to other sunrise industries, he has less time for the market but simply cannot leave it alone.

The inheritor of a family business, Ramani happened into the stock market as that inheritance included a broking card. He entered the market in his mid-thirties, which was late compared to the other dervishes, but like them, he started off as a speculator and took on more risk to build his capital. A keenness to learn came with the temperament of a born listener, and here the contrast with a talker like Juju is striking. Also, unlike Rocky, Ramani is an obsessively private person and almost reclusive; not particularly articulate, he has hardly ever given an interview during his long career in the markets.

With Ramani, the astuteness of the thinking could sometimes be hidden behind almost childlike observations. He will say something like: 'Buy Gillette because as development progresses and more people get wealthy, they'll switch from Malhotra's *sada* (plain) blades to Gillette.' These subjective insights on growth dawned when the inefficient Indian market severely undervalued that growth which, together with those leveraged positions, led to a substantial pile. Unlike Juju and Pathak, who are highly qualified, Ramani has little by way of formal education, but there is the autodidact's desire to learn together with those listening skills.

Known to give one and all a patient hearing, he is equally known for ignoring what is said and making his own decisions. Renowned for his patience in letting his winners run, he is not afraid to get in or out in one fell swoop; this is again the marriage of speculative and investing temperaments and a holdover from those trading days. He is also famous – and foremost among the dervishes – for his ability to take his losses and get out, perhaps another remnant of his early experience as a speculator.

A final leftover from the early days is his unjust reputation as a big bear. Nowadays, substantial fortunes cannot ensure to the bear side in India because of the secular uptrend of the market and the long bias caused by the absence of a short-selling product. But when Ramani started out, the badla system was at its height, and the market was more balanced between long and short sides, which would have made it easier to trade for the fall. Perhaps because of that, Ramani has a reputation for playing the short side, though this is undeserved in the eyes of many who know him. It is just that the short calls from the early years took place under dramatic circumstances and got a lot more attention than the long positions did. In truth, working both sides of the market comes easily to him, and this is simply another characteristic of the born speculator.[5]

This facility for working both sides resulted in ruinously narrow escapes in 1992 and 2000. Incapable (like most participants) of recognizing the historic nature of the Mehta Bull run as it happened, Ramani built massive short positions while betting against the rise. When the market kept moving to the upside, he redoubled his losing short positions in the runaway market by averaging against the trend. This was a near-fatal violation of the rules of speculation and led to 'ruin risk' for a while. Market participants readily acknowledge that a few more weeks of the Mehta Bull would have led to him wiping out, meeting the fate of many speculators. But the G-Sec scandal came in the nick of time, the market sold off, and he made a fortune. Insane levels of risk-taking had coupled with strong nerves and a healthy dose of luck. One might have thought Doma Ramani would have learnt his lesson, but the situation repeated itself during the IT bull run in 2000, and again there was a narrow escape, though not as dramatic as 1992. The Dark Lady was at it again.

[5] Many of the older dervishes were adept at short selling, mainly because of the short side's prominence in the badla era.

In keeping with the informal practices of that era, he could have a considerate side. Small investors trapped in his stock manoeuvring were often helped along and offered exits at negotiated prices. Conversely, if delivery was an issue, Ramani, as a member in good standing of the club, would sometimes arrange that delivery.

There is a rough egalitarianism to these big boys, the dervishes of Dalal Street. They are all self-made men in Mumbai, and Mumbai embraces them just like she has embraced other adventurers before. There is a raffish quality to many of the dervishes, particularly the older lot. This is not a business where pedigree is important; perhaps in corporate finance and banking a pedigree counted, but not in the stock market.

In corporate India, it is possible for corporate politicians and mediocrities to rise to the top, but in the market it is different. In the stock market, it is not politics or mediocrity, but skill and luck and luck and skill, that go about their relentless and continuous weeding out, never giving a chance to the more calculating qualities that come into play in the corporate world. As a result, here a certain equality prevailed – at least till you made your fortune. After that, the deference started. When a man has money in his pocket, he is very handsome, and he is very clever, and he *sings* very well, goes an old Jewish proverb.

Books and articles often extol the dervishes as 'money masters' and 'movers and shakers'.[6] Most are interviews or anecdotal accounts that document how the dervishes have accumulated their fortunes.[7] These accounts attempt to distil lessons from the dervishes' experiences in the hope that others will find those lessons useful, but they hardly ever use survivorship bias as an explanation for the dervishes' stories.[8] Survivorship

[6] See, for example, Chetan Parikh, Navin Agarwal, and Utpal Seth, *India's Money Monarchs: Conversations with Leading Investors*, Mumbai: Cerebrum Online Pvt. Ltd, 2005.

[7] For a series of magazine interviews, see 'India's Best Market Minds,' *Outlook Profit, 18* March 2010.

[8] Also relevant is survivorship bias in the Sensex itself – the index's tendency to reflect only the survivors, and not the stocks that have been removed from it. Similarly, most studies of mutual fund

bias – the tendency of performance studies to skew to the upside as they document only winners (who are survivors), while excluding the losers who fall by the wayside and are left out of the databases – is a big issue in India.[9] These dervishes, who whirl and twirl and whose activities the pink papers breathlessly report on, are essentially the survivors from among many who set out on the same journey, but who faltered and got swept away by the market's storm. The proper way to study the matter is to go back in time, pick a random sample of traders, and track them as they dervish-ed through the years, thus eliminating the natural bias to the upside that results from survivorship. But such data is simply not available – and would be inconvenient for the hagiographers, even if it were.

Survivorship bias also applied (and more so) to the companies the dervishes and their predecessors had invested in. 10 of the top 25 companies on the BSE's 1969 Cleared List of the largest and most liquid companies did not exist – and those 10 (40 per cent of that top quartile) included blue chip titans of the era such as Metal Box, Calico, Indian Iron and Steel, and Union Carbide.[10] Survivorship bias grew starker and more apparent as one went down that list of large companies. 15 of the 20 companies ranked from 81 to 100 in the list of largest companies by number of shareholders did not exist – and those 15 (75 per cent of the last pentile) included Indore Malwa, Elphinstone, Polson, and Cochin Malabar.[11]

When two people worth 100 and 200 respectively are arguing with each other in the stock market, listeners will unconsciously value the latter's opinion twice as much as that of the former. It is an absurd

---

performance in India simply do not correct for survivorship bias that occurs as poor performers exit or are merged into other funds. For an example of a US study that gauges positive bias on mutual fund performance, see M.M. Carhart, J.N. Carpenter, A.W. Lynch, and D.K. Musto, 'Mutual Fund Survivorship,' *Review of Financial Studies,* Vol. 15, No. 5, 2002, 1439–63.

[9] On the complexities of judging survivorship bias using statistical T-tests, see Larry Harris, *Trading and Exchanges: Market Microstructure for Practitioners,* New York: Oxford University Press, 2003, 452–66.

[10] Bombay Stock Exchange, *Profile of Stock Exchange Activity in India,* Bombay: BSE, 1970, 23.

[11] Ibid., 29. Survival rates would increase in the modern era.

situation, because what does relative net worth have to do with the present facts under discussion? Yet this is just how things are.

In the Indian tradition, knowledge that is complex or esoteric – and most stock market knowledge qualifies as such – transmits best from a guru to a disciple. Powerful subconscious cultural customs like *guru shishya parampara* (the tradition of a lineage, or succession of teacher-pupil relationships) shape this transmission of knowledge. In keeping with that custom, each of the dervishes has, at some point in their careers, sought out and found a living guru.[12] So Rocky Juju's own guru was Doma Ramani, while a big fund manager we shall call Momo Kania regarded Rocky as his guru. The incentives to do this are considerable; since this is the stock market and not spiritual enlightenment that is being discussed, the monetary benefits of the encounter with the guru could prove substantial. Submission to that guru once he is found is an equally important part of the tradition, and taken together, the incentives and the submission perhaps explain 'eminent guru syndrome' – the fawning deference lesser participants exhibit as they angle to get a dervish as their own guru.

The dervishes have made their fortunes and do not need to trade or invest anymore. By now, the money is just a way of keeping score, and if not stocks, they'd trade marbles or something like that. They differ in temperament from the fundies. The dervishes can do as they wish, but the fundies are bound by compliance issues and informal versions of the 'prudent man' tenet.[13] It is an iron rule with most of the dervishes never to take anyone else's money to trade or invest, and this is sensible given the risks involved in India's volatile markets. But the fundies only take other people's money, and hence the difference in character and temperament.

[12] The importance of finding a guru is also highlighted in Saurabh Mukherjea, *Gurus of Chaos: Modern India's Money Masters*, New Delhi: Bloomsbury India, 2014, 9–10. The word 'guru' is used twice in the opening paragraph of his other book, *The Unusual Billionaires*.

[13] The 'prudent man rule' directs fiduciaries 'to observe how men of prudence, discretion and intelligence manage their own affairs, not in regard to speculation, but in regard to the permanent disposition of their funds, considering the probable income, as well as the probable safety of the capital to be invested.' *Harvard College v. Amory*, 26 Mass (9 Pick), 446 (1830).

Asset allocation between debt and equity is rarely done and would be unthinkable for most of the dervishes. Right from the start of their investing careers, they have invested most of their capital in equities – it was the only thing they knew and understood – and this added to their outperformance over the years. They take the risk of such a one-sided allocation lightly, and in fact, most of them never even see it as risky. To them, risk is overpaying for a stock and not under-diversifying on a portfolio; it was the risk of Graham and not the risk of Markowitz. This indifference to asset allocation is also because the march of history has been kind to them over the short span of their investing lifetimes. Events such as the Great Depression or the OPEC oil shocks that could ruin a lifetime of investing performance had never been experienced, were not part of any institutional memory, and were therefore beyond their ken. They lack the long view of events, and their experiences are confined to the Indian market since 1991; the sesquicentennial of market movement before the reform era has never been documented (till this book at least) and is therefore irrelevant. In fact, so clueless was the Indian market about its own past that even intellectually inclined dervishes could give elaborate presentations – that used financial bubbles and manias from other countries as instructive examples – without mention of similar episodes that were drawn from India's market. Likewise, the extensive reading lists compiled by the academically inclined among them rarely mentioned a tome on the local stock market.

And yet it remains a great irony that the dervishes made their fortunes by ignoring the lessons of history, rather than heeding them. Long-term investing was not practised during the Century of Marking Time, and this is in keeping with the companies and markets of that period. If there was a lesson professionals gleaned from the badla era, it was to 'book the profit' or take money off the table when trades were profitable. Yet so fragmented is the historical record that no study (empirical or otherwise) exists that could document or prove this 'book the profit' lesson; it is also unlikely that the dervishes privately made any systematic study of the market that could yield this lesson. As a result, many of the dervishes remained blissfully ignorant of the 'book the profit' lesson, and that ignorance allowed them to commit to its opposite with relative ease. In fact, even if they had been knowledgeable about that lesson, it would still have been a dubious one, as the market, coming out of the Century of Marking Time, began rewarding patience and long-term investing. So, to the dervishes, history was bunk, and rightly so – but perhaps only this time.

The dervishes use some of the stock-picking criteria listed in an earlier section. Screens are often run to identify those counters from among the listed universe of over 2,000 stocks that meet their criteria. They are also at the centre of networks of other participants and promoters, which often brings ideas. The financial analysis then follows, with an emphasis on scalability, i.e., how far the business can scale up operations and size.[14] For the smaller companies, the company visit to kick the tyres and size up promoters is also important. If it all works out, the position gets taken.

Most of their investment picks were based on some combination of the Tiddlywinks criteria outlined earlier. But the trading picks were usually event-based, relying on their signature approach of speculative investment; here, the displacement – or 'trigger' as some called it – was important. Trading positions were also initiated based on views of government action, and some even tried to get an edge by maintaining contacts among Delhi's babudom; many areas of the market came under this approach because of the state's pervasive role in economic activity. For all such trades, the key feature was getting in before the public found out about the displacement and took the stock higher.

Scuttlebutt – the informal, yet structured, exchange of information about stocks – was also a source of stock-picking ideas. Regular scuttlebutt was a practice long known in markets and typically involved checking out a firm through its competitors, suppliers, or customers; unlike your friendly neighbourhood broker or fundie, these parties were not inclined

[14] For issues that go into stock picking at this level, there are a series of interviews between 1999 and 2004 on capitalideasonline.com. See 'Investment Ideas from Money Masters,' *CapitalIdeasOnline*, https://www.capitalideasonline.com/wordpress/category/interviews/investment-ideas-from-money-masters/.

to shouting a company's virtues from the rooftops. In his *Common Stocks and Uncommon Profits*, Philip Fisher had first popularized the technique and elevated it to an art form.[15] The dervishes used scuttlebutt a lot, first while checking out a company and later when they shared the results amongst themselves. Scuttlebutt with fellow dervishes took place after the position was initiated and completely taken, rarely before; quite natural after loading up on 1,00,000 Sofine Software to let others know about the stock's charms.

Needless to say, scuttlebutt was always stronger when it came to initiating a position, and less clear when it came to exit. But in the local context, scuttlebutt's biggest drawback was its severe contamination by rumour mongering, that bedrock practice of India's stock market.

The dervishes are storehouses of the kind of knowledge that comes only from long experience in trading stocks. Many know the backgrounds and calibre of company promoters and often dismiss apparently good companies on concerns over promoters – this sort of knowledge simply never comes from analyst reports. In their salad days, they made their money in the middle of that spectrum of possibilities between speculation and investment, which usually involved judgments on the business cycle and (more typically) on the market cycle. Some caught the market's tides perfectly, taking concentrated positions using leverage when there was blood on the streets and then selling into euphoria. Clearly in the Indian tradition of stock pickers, some are among the best around.

They are also totally clued into India's complex and volatile business environment, and to a person, all their experience comes from the local market. In fact, by global standards, India is a small pond – the country represents between 2 and 3 per cent of world equity market capitalization – and yet the dervishes have virtually their entire portfolios invested in the country. In this, they are no different from other participants. Pervasive domestic bias in the Indian market resulted from hazy regulatory and compliance issues on global investing, together with

[15] Fisher's original explication is in Philip A. Fisher, *Common Stocks and Uncommon Profits*, New Jersey: John Wiley and Sons, 1996, 44–47.

that narrow *kupamanduka* (frog at the bottom of a well) mindset. So, like other participants, the dervishes were also quite naïve – indeed incompetent – at international investing. For a dervish, being a big fish in a small pond is the obvious advantage, but note that it does not matter even if you are a small fish in a small pond, as long as the rest of the pond's fish are smaller than you. In investing and trading, it is relative rather than absolute competence that matters. Statistically, in the markets, all that's needed is a small edge over the next person to take that person's capital away from him, and that edge comes to the dervishes only in India. Never macro people, they did well when the market rewarded stock-picking behaviour, as it had since 2010. But when there was a collapse in the general list – like in 1992, 2001, or 2008 – presumably they lost as much as everybody else.

The public closely watches the dervishes, keeping track of their holdings in various companies, often buying the same stocks the dervishes invest in. The public is helped along in dervish watching by media coverage in magazines and pink papers. Magazines often carry interviews with the dervishes (and other buy side players) that are filled with the latest nostrums, and the pink papers faithfully report market rumours on the dervishes as they whirl and twirl.[16] Dedicated sites on the internet also keep track of dervish holdings.[17] The pink papers give the dervishes fanciful names such as Old Fox, Pink Panther, and Rareing Bull – nomenclature that leaves little doubt about the real identity of the concerned dervish.[18] After the public buys the dervishes' holdings, it realizes that sometimes the magic works and sometimes it does not. Most participants do not comprehend that the dervishes are also a hit-or-miss bunch on stock picking, and often dervish stocks that the public buys do badly. The dervishes have large portfolios held through multiple

[16] For nostrums from a new crop of money masters, gurus, and wizards, see Pravin Palande, 'Wealth Wizards: Follow the "Keep It Simple" Policy for Investments,' *Forbes*, 6 July 2015.

[17] Besides the guesswork and rumour mongering on the internet boards, entire sites are dedicated to checking out the dervishes and their positions. See, for example, http://equityfriend.com.

[18] 'Grapevine has it that the Rare(i)ng Bull and the "Old Fox" are still accumulating the stock, though some believe this is unlikely because valuations are no longer cheap.' Harish Rao and Nishanth Vasudevan, 'Heard on the Street,' *Economic Times*, 5 November 2010.

anonymous entities, and often their success came from a few outsized holdings in those folios; many of the remaining holdings are *dabbas* that the public ends up with. When mimicking the holdings, the public does not realize that many of the dervishes' outsized holdings were accumulated during a sweet spot in the market's evolution. Besides, though the public knows about the holding, it cannot usually tell the price at which that holding was accumulated; also, participants never know when the dervishes sell, as that information comes out only when the exchanges publish it at the quarter's end. What the public should do is replicate the entire portfolio of the concerned dervish, but that is not public knowledge.

The dervishes were part of a blessed generation. Now in their sixties and seventies, they have benefited from the Sensex's massive surge from 100 to beyond 60,000 over a 40-year period.[19] This period – most of it is in the post-1991 reform era – coincided with their investing lifetimes, and so they profited from that single accident of history. They had bought just after George Fernandes issued his FERA dilution rules, and they had bought when FIIs entered and drove the market up. Critically, they started their investing careers just when the Indian stock market was moving out of its Century of Marking Time, and so, they benefited from three transitions. The first transition was the market's move from complete inefficiency to something more efficient; the second transition was the market's one-time re-rating from low single-digit multiples to multiples that rarely went below 20; and the third transition was the economy's move to a higher growth path (at least till the second decade of the new millennium). The dervishes did not know it, but they had taken on colossal and haphazard exposure to systematic market risk in an era when the valuation cushion was considerable and no one wanted stocks. In fact, no amount of dervish-ing or stock picking would have worked if their investing lifetimes had coincided with the Century of Marking Time. Consider that there were no dervishes in the century that passed since the heyday of the first dervish, Premchand Roychand;

[19] The Sensex dates from 1986, but with 1978–79 as the base year from a starting value of 100.

note also that most of the literature on 'market gurus' and 'money masters' and assorted others who made it in the markets, dates from the post-reform period that started in the 1990s.

So, there remains an interesting question. Are the diamonds of Golconda, that lay around during the dervishes' lifetime waiting to get picked, still there? Or does the market's move to something more efficient than rampant inefficiency mean that the ease of their generation's success will be difficult, if not impossible, to replicate?

Many of the dervishes don't see it that way. Lacking the long view of events, they are flush with massive success in a milieu indifferent to time, and as a result, many see the skill element predominating in their sagas. And yet some did get it. When one of them says, 'Whatever I have, *sab uparwala neh diya hai*,' perhaps it is an acknowledgement that he belongs to that blessed generation.[20]

[20] 'Whatever I have, has been given by the One above.'

17

ATITHI DEVO BHAVA

The Foreign Institutional Investor

Call him Asa M, and he is a familiar figure on Indian business TV, what with his plummy accent, impeccably cut suit, and steel grey hair. He covers the emerging markets universe for a big bank, which entails flying in and out of about 30 countries and diligently pontificating on their stock markets. The factors that intrude on forecasting a market are unfathomable to begin with – more so in a country of India's complexity – but Asa M is unfazed by it all. Assuming he divides his time equally between the countries in his coverage mandate, he gets a grand total of about 100 minutes a week to spend on India, which presumably is enough time to unveil the mysteries of the stock market and its listed companies. Because of the time constraint, he needs to make mental shortcuts while analysing the market and finds it safe to reduce the jumble to just two variables – interest rates and corporate profits – which is followed by an occasional reference to government action (or the lamentable lack of it) on the reform front. He goes on and on in clipped and confident tones on the above lines, expressing comfortable and anodyne views on the market that are earnest and very much in the mainstream. He flies in like a bird, leaves stuff lying around, and then flies out to the next country. The locals – having regard for the Sanskrit saying *Atithi Devo Bhava* or 'A Guest is like a God' – listen carefully to his talk, following which they clean up the stuff left behind and get on with their trading.

Asa M and others like him are foreign institutional investors or FIIs.[1] Before foreigners invested in the rupee-denominated capital of Indian companies, they invested in sterling-denominated capital of British companies with operations in India. These sterling companies of the colonial era had boards and shareholder registers located in the UK (usually London) and dividends were declared there, while India-domiciled boards managed country operations subject to final control by the London board. People assume that market booms occur only in India, but these London-listed sterling companies often had booms based on their Indian operations. The strangest of these occurred in 1880 and 1881 when gold reef discoveries near Wayanad in Kerala briefly triggered a mania in mining companies that were set up to exploit the discovery. 41 companies raised over £5 million in short order, and so great was the investor demand that companies cancelled allotments reserved for Indian shareholders and preferred to meet subscriptions only from the UK. This was unwise, as the mania ended shortly thereafter when one of the companies received a telegram from India that corrected a mistake in yields – an earlier telegram that helped trigger the mania had mentioned a yield of 2 oz per ton, but this should have read 2 oz per 19 tons.[2]

Other than these curiosities, FII interest in the colonial era was confined to the occasional Calcutta managing agency, but even that ceased in the era of autarky after Independence. Yet it is a common misconception that FIIs entered the market with autarky's end and the onset of the reform era in the 1990s. Before FIIs came to India, India

[1] In 2014, the nomenclature was changed to foreign portfolio investors (FPIs).

[2] Radhe Shyam Rungta, *The Rise of Business Corporations in India 1851–1900*, London: Cambridge University Press, 1970, 136–48.

went to them. In 1986 and 1988, UTI (with Merrill Lynch) launched its India Fund and India Growth Fund with listings in Mumbai and London, and foreign investors were allowed to buy local equities through them.[3] These were the first vehicles to give foreigners exposure to the country, and the UTI India Fund of 1986 remains the oldest extant offshore fund still investing into Indian markets.

A press note of 14 September 1992 marks the date when the Narasimha Rao–Manmohan Singh duo decided to do away with the East India Company mentality and allow foreign investors to enter the market.[4] A little over a year later, this entry led to the double top of the Mehta bull, and since then, FIIs have been a fixture in the markets.[5] FIIs were a dominant presence in equities for a generation after their entry in the early 90s. By the late 1990s itself, they were seen as a major influence on markets and had acquired a fair amount of floating stock, as M.G. Damani, the BSE's president, noted in 1998.[6] So influential were FIIs in the early years that many participants obsessively tracked their positions and often bought into companies that disclosed substantial FII holdings. From now on, watching the daily figures on FII volumes was an anxious pastime for many a participant. Sometimes participants would not wait for public disclosures and tried to front-run FIIs, just as many from an earlier generation had tried to front-run UTI.[7] Direct market access came only in 2008, and in its absence, FIIs had no choice but to trade through the broking community, which made the front-running possible.

Like all newcomers to the market, FIIs also had to go through their learning curve in the school of hard knocks. In the first flush of

[3] The UTI India Fund of 1986 was set up as a closed-end Guernsey-based unit trust and restructured in 1993 as an open-ended fund incorporated in Mauritius. SBI and Canara Bank also launched country funds in 1989 and 1990.

[4] Ministry of Finance, Press Note, 14 September 1992.

[5] The SEBI (Foreign Institutional Investors) Regulations were finally drafted and notified only in 1995. Following a further rationalization of categories, updated regulations were notified in 2014.

[6] M.G. Damani, 'Revival of Capital Market', *The Stock Exchange Review: July 1998*, (Bombay: BSE, 1989), 5–6.

[7] In later years, SEBI's surveillance system would pick up cases of such front-running.

liberalization, they saw up ahead in the distance a shimmering light – the light of India Shining. Heads giddy, eyes starry, they took the market to that double top of the Mehta Bull. No one felt this giddiness more than investors in the Morgan Stanley Growth Fund that raised funds only to enter the market at that double top. It would be many years before the fund's NAV crossed its initial value.

Despite the immediacy of FII entry to our time, it is reasonable to divide their presence into two phases, with 2010 serving as a convenient marker. The period from the early 1990s till about 2010 was one of continuous and considerable FII influence on India's markets, as the entry and egress of their capital led to pronounced rises and falls. Nevertheless, in the main, this was an age of inflows, with 1998–99 and 2008–09 as the only years that logged significant outflows.[8]

This led to incessant FII accumulation of Indian equity, and the share of foreign ownership in the market continued to rise, till it varied between a fifth and a quarter of market capitalization. The narrowness of the market indexes increases FII impact on the market; because of the liquidity and compliance requirements in their investment mandates, most FIIs bought only big blue chips, and since the indexes mainly consisted of such stocks, their influence on the narrow indexes was exaggerated. Over time, it became apparent that FIIs had accumulated large chunks of stock, particularly in the few blue chips that had no discernible promoter group; for such companies, it was common to find as much as half or more of outstanding equity held by FIIs.

By 2010 or thereabouts, about a fifth of the country's market capitalization was held by FIIs.[9] This 20 per cent holding has stayed about the same since then – in 2020, FIIs held about ₹30 lakh crores ($400 billion) of about ₹150 lakh crores ($2 trillion) in market capitalization. The sum, while large in absolute terms – and larger than the corresponding LIC or mutual fund holdings of about ₹10 lakh crores

[8] National Securities Depository Limited, 'FPI Net Investment Details (Financial Year),' *NSDL*, accessed on 18 October 2020, https://www.fpi.nsdl.co.in/web/Reports/Yearwise.aspx?RptType=5.

[9] Ami Shah, 'FII Flows to Indian Stocks Hit Record in 2019, Analysts Gung Ho about 2020 Too,' *Economic Times*, 31 December 2019.

and ₹12 lakh crores respectively – in fact, understates their influence. Removing promoter holdings and the government's stake held through President of India holdings in public-sector companies, both of which rarely change and are effectively denied to other participants, leaves you with the free float, the stock that's actually available for participants to buy. Doing this shows that FIIs held as much as 40 per cent of the 'free float' in 2020.

For many years after their entry, FIIs were the biggest game in town – perhaps the only game in town. As a result, for many years the market obsessed over what would happen if FIIs exited in one go. If that happened, someone would be needed to buy from them and take paper off their hands; in the absence of such countervailing buying power, there could be a huge market sell-off.

This concern was not academic; such sell-offs had happened before – in 1998, 2002, and 2008 – when the counterweight was not sufficient. The counterweight was usually the DII, which for all practical purposes meant LIC and the mutual funds. But for many years both had issues of scale. LIC, in the years before 2000, was believed to have bought between ₹20,000 and ₹40,000 crores annually, which was not a large sum compared to the aggregate FII holding of that time. Mutual funds were subject to redemption pressures; besides, money usually came in towards a market top, which intensified the pressure on fund managers to deploy money when valuations were at their most unfavourable. That left the public, which also had a tendency to come in at the tops; it remained a cliché among the pros that the market never topped out till the public was heavily in it. So, there were always concerns in markets and policy circles about whether money would come in to counter FII exits.

Nevertheless, from about 2010 onwards, we enter a second phase in the FII story – when their influence over markets should have increased, but did not. In the main, this is because of the rise of domestic players and their averaging products. FII influence over the market should have increased during the periods of unconventional monetary policy, as bond buying by Western central banks caused liquidity surges in global financial markets that went in search of yield; the first surge began in 2008 as a policy response to the Great Recession, while the second came after the 2020 coronavirus pandemic. On both occasions, this quantitative easing through bond-buying programs sent great tides of liquidity surging through global markets, with FII portfolio inflows as the channel into the Indian market.

Because of the liquidity surges, the earlier concern about counterweights should have increased during this period. But here, an extraordinary thing happened. Despite the liquidity surges, FII influence over the market was balanced by DIIs using capital accessed through rupee cost averaging products like the SIP. FII buying was offset by DII selling – and vice versa.

This has been a significant change. Those bouts of international liquidity don't have the dominant effects they once did. The influence of foreign investors in the Indian market continues to be felt, but now there is an effective offset. Rather than participating in an international capital market like everyone else, DIIs use SIP flows to explicitly defend their home turf, and the frequency with which local and foreign flows cross each other – sometimes even on a daily basis – is almost unsettling.

One is struck by the resilience of the FII belief in India, and in fact, but for four years, there have been net inflows between their entry and 2021–22.[10] The resilience is surprising as they have a penchant for buying at the top and selling at the bottom. This is a difficult statement to prove as FII performance figures are never disclosed, but consider by way of proxy the long-term performance of the market they are investing in. The Nifty in February 2020 – just before the distortions caused by the coronavirus collapse and liquidity-induced pullback – was still below its early 2008 level, a level set 12 years prior. The domestic bias of India's participants makes this observation come as a shocker to many, but in

[10] Annual outflows took place in 1998–99, 2008–09, 2015–16, 2018–19, and 2021–22. National Securities Depository Limited, 'FPI Net Investment Details (Financial Year).'

dollar terms it's true.[11] FIIs face a dollar-denominated index rather than a rupee-denominated one, and the dollar Nifty (or Defty as it used to be called) is in a long-term bear market. The rupee–dollar pair was at 39 in January 2008 and at 72 in February 2020, so whatever market gains accrued in rupee terms disappeared in dollar terms; even a rough conversion shows a dollar Nifty of 164 in January 2008 (6,400/39) and a dollar Nifty of 160 in February 2020 (11,600/72). Dividends add to returns over the long run, but the Indian market is perennially priced for growth rather than value and so dividend yields are low; including dividends will improve holding period returns, but only by so much.

So, at best, FIIs are flirting with a long-term bear market in India, ergo their performance as a *jaati* of long-term investors in such a market should also be below par. But a conspiracy of silence in the market hides this simple fact.

FIIs are fighting a secularly depreciating currency, which accounts for their underperformance. After Independence, the dollar gradually displaced sterling as the vehicle currency of Indian markets, and rupee–dollar became the dominant currency pair. Consider that the rupee was at ₹3.30 to the dollar at Independence in 1947 and was then pegged for much of the Bretton Woods system of fixed exchange rates at about ₹4.77.[12] This went on till 1966. Chronically high inflation differentials caused in large part by war-related government expenditure, current account deficits, and enduring dependence on oil and gold imports resulted in the first of a series of devaluations in 1966, followed by an abandonment of the fixed peg and the gradual adoption of a dirty float exchange regime. Since the 1971 collapse of the Bretton Woods system, the rupee has been in secular decline, with its brief appreciation in the period between 2002 and 2007 as the only substantial exception to this trend. Support from invisibles such as software exports, inward remittances from the world's largest diaspora, and direct investment

[11] Investing.com provides historical data on the dollar Nifty. See 'NIFTY 50 USD (NSED),' *Investing.com*, https://in.investing.com/indices/s-p-cnx-defty-historical-data.

[12] Reserve Bank of India, 'Exchange Rate 1945–71,' *RBI*, accessed 18 October 2020, https://www.rbi.org.in/commonperson/english/scripts/FAQs.aspx?Id=1877.

inflows, simply cannot overcome chronically high trade deficits, high inflation/interest rate differentials, and MNC dividend outflows. Portfolio money then sloshes into and out of the stock market – occasionally hiding the above fundamentals while doing so – and this remains the basic dynamic working on the Indian balance of payments. The result is a chronically weak currency.

Though the official exchange policy is that there is no policy and the rupee is allowed to find its own level, in reality the RBI intervenes occasionally, which results in a managed or dirty float regime. It sometimes appears that the central bank is nudging the rupee along this part of secular depreciation, in the hope that it will lead to export-led growth. This it does through repeated intervention and sterilization – intervening by selling rupees and buying dollars weakens the rupee, but increases foreign exchange reserves and enhances the monetary base, so sterilizing by selling bonds and mopping up rupees offsets the inflationary impacts of the monetary base increase. More generally, inflows are encouraged but outflows go through a wringer of obstacles, both procedural and cultural, that bring about a peculiar form of capital market segmentation.

In recent years, capital inflows from Western quantitative easing are handled through sporadic intervention and sterilization (though the dirty float makes this less of a necessity). Capital inflows that appreciate the currency are met with sterilized intervention, while outflows and trade balance factors that depreciate the currency don't merit intervention. This asymmetric approach to exchange management has led to long-term depreciation with some reserve build-up, but the capital market segmentation and interest rate differentials lead to a permanently high cost of capital, with consequences for private investment.

Behind all this is the assumption that the exchange rate – rather than infrastructure or factor productivity – is the biggest determinant of export-led growth. If low-wage manufacturing exports gained it would be one thing – and the benefits of large-scale job creation in a nation of over 1.3 billion could be substantial – but much of the benefit of a depreciating currency goes to a tiny cosseted bunch of about 3 to

4 million in the country's IT services and back-office space.[13] Dollar reserves have increased considerably with these manoeuvres, though the source of these reserves is sterilized inflows rather than a current account surplus. But in recent years so pronounced was this trend of currency intervention that India has been in danger of being branded a currency manipulator.[14] As a result of all this, the rupee–dollar pair was closing in on ₹80 by 2022.

So, for FIIs, on average, between 3 and 4 per cent of annual folio returns disappear in currency conversion from rupees to dollars on exit. Hedging could reduce this currency risk but in the absence of deep currency futures markets, overseas forward markets are the only alternative, which makes long-term hedging against the rupee quite expensive.

Ergo, exchange is the dominant factor in FII performance but not the only one. After the exchange rate remain all the other issues that everyone else deals with. There are the occasional macroeconomic imbalances, parlous factor markets for land and labour, a tottering financial sector, barely coherent monetary transmission, the creaky

[13] The extent to which India's IT service companies benefit from the interplay between the country's exchange regime and its demographics has not been fully appreciated. In fact, entry-level dollar-denominated real wages had collapsed in India's IT industry because of the exchange rate and the infinite supply of cheap labour from the demographic dividend. The monthly salary of a fresh coder in the IT/back-office space was in the ₹30–35,000 range in 2008, and it stayed at that level through 2022, despite significant rises in the price level. But the rupee–dollar pair had fallen from 40 to 80 over this period, and so, the $800 nominal monthly wage of 2008 was now $400 in 2022; given this unprecedented decline in nominal dollar wages, the decline in real dollar wages was also substantial.

IT service companies (competitive to begin with) saw their global competitiveness rise even further because of these favourable fundamentals on exchange and demographics. Faced with higher global prices relative to the cost of their biggest input – labour – India's IT service companies massively expanded hiring and output, and their profits soared. Some firms had close to half a million workers toiling away at the grunge of entry-level coding and systems maintenance (multinationals, through their global capability centres or GCCs, had also begun to realize this and much action was now in this GCC space). Salary differentials between these multitudes and their supervisors also remained among the highest in the world. It was not uncommon for IT CEOs to make 1,500 times (or more) of these entry-level salaries; at the other extreme, Scandinavian CEOs rarely made more than 40 to 50 times the remuneration of their entry-level hires.

[14] India was added to the US Treasury's Monitoring List of currency manipulators in 2018 and removed in 2019. United States Department of the Treasury, *Macroeconomic and Foreign Exchange Policies of Major Trading Partners of the United States*, April 2018 and May 2019.

judicial system, the absence of commonsense regulatory economics, predatory tax authorities, stretched urban infrastructure, questionable economic data, majoritarian social turmoil and its reaction, the steady decline in the country's international standing, the drip-drip of scams, and the slowdown in growth, accentuated in recent years by the coronavirus pandemic.

Despite all this, FIIs stay on, and for the moment at least, flows seem immune to those violent turns the country's political climate or economic cycle is prone to. In fact, in recent years, FII flows depend less on country performance or market valuation and more on the exigencies of unconventional monetary policy as practised by Western central banks. Nevertheless, whether the end of quantitative easing will bring into sharper focus the downward shifts in the country's political status and economic growth rate remains a critical and unanswered question. When really large tides go out, even countries can be found swimming naked.

So, despite exchange and all the other issues listed above, FIIs believe and stay on, and in fact, they believe more than the locals do. This FII patience is saintly and commendable, as one would have thought that, at some point, patience is a finite commodity even for a saint. One reason for all this patience on the part of FIIs is the remarkable belief system at work here – a belief in the 'India Growth Story'. Earnest reporters from the media are often heard chirpily asking hardened businessmen and seasoned portfolio managers: 'Sir, do you believe in the India Growth Story?' To which the answer usually was a resounding 'Yes', but nowadays it's a more guarded 'Yes'. It's actually like someone being asked if they believe in God. The stock answer of the respondent should be that it's a private affair – so get lost. But the above-mentioned businessmen and fund managers don't have that luxury on national television, so they grit their teeth and play along and say, '*Yes, I believe.*'

The need to believe in India is as imperative and as urgent as the need to believe in God, and it almost seems like the 'India Growth Story' has a religious dimension to it. The use of the word 'believe' is key here, presupposing as it does that doing business in India is an act of faith, instead of an act of reason. The FIIs must be reminded of what Russian poet Fyodor Tyutchev once said about his country: 'Russia cannot be known by the mind ... Russia can only be believed in.'[15] For the FIIs too, one cannot understand India with the mind – one can only hope to believe in her.

This FII belief in the India Growth Story still holds solid despite mounting evidence to the contrary. As seen earlier, after a period of soaring growth brought about largely by an interest rate displacement between 2003 and 2007, the growth rate and corporate profits have fallen off, and this happened even before the collapse brought about by the coronavirus pandemic. This being India, there is no dearth of quibbling over the extent of this decadal fall. But after 2020 – and despite the pandemic – reductions in corporate taxes, fiscal over stimulus, and economic formalization (brought about by indirect tax reform) led to another surge in blue chip profits, which incidentally are the only FII concern. So, the extreme volatility in the Indian environment allows for much clever opinion on both sides.

But if you think all this is a subject only for clever and opinionated economists – of which there is no short supply in India – consider for a moment the case of Ford and General Motors on the foreign direct investment (FDI) side. These are the companies that invented assembly line manufacturing, and both are considered models of excellence in automotive engineering and marketing, with operations that span the globe. Till recently, Ford and General Motors appeared to be following a 1-2-3 business model in India – after 1 generation in the country, they each had a 2 per cent market share, and about ₹3,000 crores in accumulated losses. Of late, even the 1-2-3 model was out of date, and the accumulated losses had gone way beyond the earlier figures. In fact, old Henry Ford must have been turning in his grave at the suicidal and stubborn belief behind these numbers. Both companies have now wound down their country operations.[16] MNCs then discover that exit

[15] 'Fyodor Tyutchev,' *RuVerses*, https://ruverses.com/fyodor-tyutchev/russia-cannot-be-known-by-the-mind/424/.

[16] See Trefis Team, 'Why GM Is Pulling out of India,' *Forbes*, 27 May 2017; Parvatha Vardhini C., 'Why Is Ford Motors Exiting India,' *Hindu BusinessLine*, 1 October 2019.

is itself problematic, and many feel like they are in a *chakravyuh* – a mythological, labyrinth-like battle formation, where the other side's forces, after entering, get lost and disoriented to the point where they find it difficult to exit.

The GM–Ford scenario is being repeated across a wide range of sectors. In fact, other than a few complexes of excellence in the economy – including healthcare/pharmaceuticals/hospitals, fast-moving consumer goods, the IT services/back-office space, and some private banks – this scenario is the norm. But it is swept under the carpet, in a country where appearances have to be maintained above all else. Outside these complexes, it appears that the rest of the country is a banana republic. The index committees responsible for maintaining the Sensex and Nifty think the same way, which is why they've gone and loaded the indexes with these complexes of excellence.

The India Growth Story then gets married to that most dangerous of convictions – belief in the long run. As the truism from Keynes goes, 'In the long run we're all dead' and yet many investment rationalizations carry this belief. Various reasons are given for this belief in the long run – the Great Indian Middle Class, the demographic dividend, the large domestic market, and so on. For these reasons, the future is always on that distant horizon, a horizon that keeps receding as we advance. The present may be a mess, but the future on that horizon is always glorious. If only we could reach it.

India will *always* be a country with a promising future. Now try getting someone to accept the irony behind that statement.

The practical business problem is that both interest rates and the cost of doing business are high, so high that that belief in the future quickly starts getting expensive. The interest rate is also the opportunity cost of capital, and it's what you would make elsewhere, say in a bank, if you never made the investment. 100 invested by Ford at 10 per cent would have been up almost 12 times over the 20 years of a generational presence. Instead, most of it has been written off, and even amounts taken out of the country have to deal with that depreciating rupee. At a 10 per cent cost of capital, the opportunity cost of believing in the future is very high. In fact, the de facto cost of equity capital in India is usually taken at 13 to 14 per cent and is much higher for smaller enterprises; capital market segmentation and incoherent monetary transmission give a semi-permanent cast to such estimates. With these numbers, that horizon needs to be reached very quickly.

Actually, a case can be made that there is no future on that horizon. There is no real future, and the future comes in a series of present moments. Counting 1-2-3-4 and onwards to reach the future at 10 needs a unit of 1 for the counting. That unit of 1 is the present, and thinking about the future without regard to that present is like trying to count without that unit of 1. It is this realization – an insight from Ramana Maharshi's *Forty Verses on Reality* – that is yet to strike many people, including the FIIs.

But belief in the India Growth Story and waiting for that distant horizon cannot be the full account. There is something else going on here. Investment strategies and patterns also explain the FII presence in India and its continued influence. The saintly patience of FIIs towards the country's situation may have a simple explanation – perhaps they don't care about performance on the economy's real side. It seems India is programmed to receive capital, and they are programmed to send it, and to see this counterintuitive result requires some knowledge of portfolio strategies.[17]

The fact is that most FIIs are asset allocators looking for the benefits of international diversification. Usually based in countries with absolute capital account convertibility and a strong tradition of global investing, FIIs invest everywhere. The world is their oyster. They are generally not stock pickers or market timers, and investment for most of them is primarily an asset allocation problem.

[17] Some of this material appeared in the author's 2015 piece on Firstpost. Adil Rustomjee, 'The Dilemma of Being an FII in India: Only Entry, No Exits,' *Firstpost*, accessed 18 October 2020. https://www.firstpost.com/business/economy/decoding-the-remarkable-belief-of-fiis-in-india-1206073.html.

Since India accounts for only 2 to 3 per cent of world capitalization, allocation decisions usually imply whether to put similar amounts in Indian markets. The actual percentages may vary, as does the rationale behind the strategy, but the allocative nature of the process does not change. As numbers, these percentages are not large, but they apply to actual amounts of capital that run into hundreds of billions of dollars. At the margin therefore, the move from 2 to 3 – or its reverse – for every 100 is considerable, and that money flows into a small market whose recent capitalization has moved between $2 and $3 trillion.

The main sources of FII money also give primacy to asset allocation as a strategy. Consider these four main sources: global equity funds (GEFs), global emerging market equity funds (GEMs), Brazil/Russia/India/China/South Africa funds (BRICS), and India dedicated exchange-traded funds (ETFs). The global nature of the fund families decreases as we move from left to right along this spectrum of acronyms. Global equity funds (GEFs) might allocate just 2 or 3 per cent to India in keeping with the country's share of world markets; at the other end of the spectrum, India-dedicated ETFs will invest their entire corpus in the country's market. Notice also that the first three fund families tend to be asset allocators across countries, and it is only the last that are India dedicated, and therefore pickers or timers. Consequently, most money entering India is asset allocation money, driven by professional imperatives arising from diversification benefits, yield differentials, and opportunities.

In contrast, and as noted in earlier sections, domestic participants have little global diversification in their folios, and domestic bias is pervasive and total. Partly, this is because Indians don't enjoy the benefits of full capital account convertibility. Over the years, the RBI has imposed – and then fiddled with – a series of monetary limits on how much investors can move abroad; these outflow controls that keep domestic savings at home to lower borrowing costs remain a key instrument of financial repression. Besides convertibility, the high vigorish (costs) of global investing is also an issue. But these restrictions are easing, so nowadays it is that odd cultural predisposition, together with the absence of a global mindset, that biases participants to the home market.

Recent BJP sloganeering on *Atmanirbhar Bharat* (self-reliant India) has also contributed to this predisposition, and investing only in the local market is seen not as domestic bias but rather as contributing to that self-reliance. The belief in the India Growth Story is so entrenched that it makes any sort of normal global diversification seem vaguely disreputable and a forbidden treat at best, or downright heretical at worst. Besides, the many years in autarky and recent fund diversions abroad have ensured that there is a hush-hush quality to overseas transactions, and as a result, capital market segmentation that was once officially sanctioned is now unofficially or socially sanctioned. So, most Indians have little international diversification in their portfolios and are typically 100 per cent invested in India.

More technically, FIIs reduce portfolio betas (risk) by diversifying globally. DIIs and the public choose not to (or cannot) diversify globally; instead, they reduce risk by going to cash and selling to FIIs. Domestic investors, obsessed as they are with Indian market levels, find the absence of a corresponding FII obsession – together with the FII ability to pour money in at any market level – a little puzzling. But that reduces when one remembers that FIIs are more interested in achieving the benefits of global diversification; there's always a bull market somewhere in the world that will reflect in their performance, if they're reasonably diversified.

In the first phase of FII flows before 2010, flows were considered vital to the point where participants obsessed over them. At that time, it seemed as though the FIIs could enter but could not leave. They faced the classic dilemma of the small-time speculator who takes a large position in a thinly traded small-cap stock. The speculator's very buying takes the stock up, and his exit will take it down – on himself. The FIIs faced the same predicament, and in 1998, 2002, and 2008, their selling took the market down on themselves. Despite this, FIIs rarely saw this as a concern because India was a very small proportion of their overall portfolios.

FII exit was also the elephant in the room during the government's policy discussions, and much policy was made with an anxious eye on how they would react. Participants were quick to point out consequences of government action – on, say, taxation or the 'Mauritius route'[18] – that may have had deleterious effects on FIIs, and to accommodate such concerns, the government often bent over backwards without seeming to bend over backwards. In fact, it had not dawned on the government that FIIs were doubly influential because of their influence on India's narrowly constructed indexes. As asset allocators, the usual FII policy was to buy index stocks of the allocated country; their compliance compulsions also called for investments in the bigger, well-capitalized, and transparent companies with large free floats, and such criteria were usually met only among index stocks. So, most FII flows went into the 30 or 50 stocks that made up the Sensex or Nifty, ignoring in large part the over 2,000 other traded stocks. This exaggerated their influence over that widely watched index that most people thought of as 'The Market'.

In the second phase of FII flows after 2010, the surges and ebbs of global liquidity should have exaggerated FII influence over the markets – but did not. In response to the Great Recession and the coronavirus pandemic, unconventional monetary policy through bond buying programs led to massive capital infusions in two waves, starting 2008 and 2020. Markets began moving in response, and much of the story in recent years has been the reaction of asset markets to these liquidity surges. Some of this liquidity ended up chasing yield in riskier asset classes like emerging markets, which effectively meant allocations to the four fund families outlined earlier. Since most of these funds are asset allocators, the liquidity surges caused larger amounts to be allocated to the Indian market. The sheer size of quantitative easing should have exaggerated the already critical importance of FIIs to the market.

Further, the easing had not been attempted before on this scale, implying that neither had its end – the taper – been attempted. Once US (and global) conditions improved or once goods and labour

[18] FIIs often invest in India through Mauritius, benefitting from the tax treaty between the two countries.

markets tightened to the point where inflation became a concern, the unconventional period would end. There was much concern about the market's reaction to this taper, as the liquidity ebb would cause the tide to reverse at the margin, leading to the asset allocation process outlined earlier also going into reverse. When that happened, flows into the fund families would fall, and since most were asset allocators, the allocation to emerging markets such as India would also fall. As FII flows turned negative, markets would sell off, and there was concern about the countervailing power available to deal with such a reversal.

These concerns were justified, as even a small absolute reduction in FII holdings ($400 billion in 2020) would be much larger than the ₹40,000 to ₹60,000 crores ($6 to $8 billion) a year that LIC invested; it was also thought that other sources of liquidity like the public or the mutual funds were simply not large enough to absorb FII outflows.[19] Yet markets wobbled briefly in 2013 – due to what became known as the taper tantrums – but there was no real sell-off and domestic flows stayed strong, aided by hopes generated from the BJP's 2014 electoral victory. A second wobble took place in 2022, but the market was still holding up despite FII selling touching an all-time high.

So, the surges and ebbs should have exaggerated FII influence over the markets, but did not. None of the above concerns have materialized so far. For this fortuitous situation, thank the rise of rupee cost averaging products. The rise in averaging products like the systematic investment plan (SIP) commences from about 2010, around the same time as quantitative easing and its liquidity waves crash into the market. This is a lucky coincidence that not many have noticed. This gave the DIIs much-needed ammunition to bolster the market, changed the basic inflow dynamic into equity funds, and ended much of the concern on FII sales.

Nevertheless, these SIP inflows into the market continued right through a steady deterioration in growth rates and fundamentals

[19] ENS Economic Bureau, 'LIC Books Rs19,000 Crore Profit from Market in FY17,' *Indian Express*, 17 May 2017.

that raised PE ratios and valuations. Without any attempt at global diversification, DIIs kept socking SIP flows into the domestic market, though they were careful to do so only when the FIIs sold. Whenever FIIs bought, the DIIs sold to them and vice versa. This pattern of DII activity always offsetting the ebb and flow of Western quantitative easing is pervasive during the second phase since 2010. The pattern is not insignificant. As DIIs propped up the market with SIP money and unofficially enforced capital market segmentation, it led to a baffling situation which continues into the present – a market that rises irrespective of fundamentals. As FII buying and selling is almost exactly offset by DII activity, the confounding effect further disconnects the market from the real economy. More generally, the period of unconventional monetary policy after 2010 and the confounding effects of DII responses distorted India's equity markets to the point where valuations and the real side did not matter. With the onset of the coronavirus pandemic, this disconnect between a soaring market and the real economy reached surreal proportions.

Then again, as often happens in markets, there is just enough rationality to justify irrationality. As seen, most FII money went into index stocks. Courtesy the index committees responsible for their construction, almost half of those narrow indexes consist of stocks from those four complexes of excellence mentioned earlier – health care, consumer goods, software/business services, and private banks. Companies in these sectors are doing very well for themselves, either due to comparative advantage from a favourable exchange rate or because the domestic market for their products is considerable. Such companies are growing with healthy bottom lines, and their valuations – anyway derived mainly from the PE multiple expansions caused by this liquidity flow – are thus easier to rationalize. Justifying any valuation based on their performance becomes a little easier, and in turn, their performance provides some rationality to this otherwise peculiar situation. As most FIIs simply buy heavily into the Sensex or Nifty, index stocks enjoy higher valuations than non-index stocks, and this is to everyone's benefit when flows are high but will have a disproportionate effect on the market when flows reverse and the SIP ammo runs out.

This situation begins immediately after the Great Recession's 2008 sell-off, continues into the QE-dominated decade, and persists right through the 2020s coronavirus sell-off and pullback. All this leads to that dangerous cat-and-mouse game between DIIs and FIIs. There are offsetting foreign and domestic flows over extended time periods, and the way the flows counteract one another, sometimes even on a daily basis, is uncanny. The pattern is even more noticeable on a monthly basis.[20]

The resulting clash between a sizable FII presence driven by quantitative easing that ebbs and flows into an Indian market whose domestic participants unofficially enforce capital market segmentation leads to a peculiar type of stock market dynamic. In this dynamic, domestic investors act as turf defenders of their own market and take it as their bounden duty to counter foreign flows, in the process almost making a market for FIIs when they buy and sell. Rather than diversifying internationally and taking part freely in a market for global equities, DIIs simply choose to use the SIP flows to defend their own domestic market. Since about 2010, DIIs have been using the SIP inflows to prop up the local market and in doing so give FIIs the free option to sell and exit. This is the SIP put, and foreign investors are quite happy to be given the right (but not the obligation) to sell and for free. But while investing in and defending their domestic market, DIIs may be ignoring their role as fiduciaries who use global diversification for the benefit of their unit holders. Crucially, DII outflows as part of a program of international diversification would also reduce the valuation pressure that mounts as FII and SIP money steadily bids up the limited supply of quality paper that is available in the domestic

[20] For example, over a 36-month period from October 2015 to September 2018, there were only 6 months when FIIs and DIIs were on the same side of the market; for the remaining 30 months, they were on opposite sides, often with FII selling almost exactly offset by DII buying and vice versa. The phenomenon can be observed at Moneycontrol.com, 'FII & DII Trading Activity,' *Moneycontrol*, https://www.moneycontrol.com/stocks/marketstats/fii_dii_activity/index.php.

market. This would reduce the pressure to bid up domestic valuations and might even reduce the RBI's problems in managing one-way capital flows.[21]

Nevertheless, things could get awkward if FIIs run out of patience with the India Growth Story at the same time that DIIs discover the joys of international diversification; similarly, if retail patience is tested by prolonged market declines (or even by range-bound markets), the retail-sourced SIP could see its flows dry up, leading to more awkwardness. As the countervailing flows ebb, outflows will then dominate, and the market could sell off. Presumably, the bureaucrats at SEBI and RBI will then start their panicky fiddling with percentages to address the balance. Such scenarios are barely indicated presently, though in future they might come into play.

The ebb and flow of capital and investment strategies as outlined above must not detract from the historic role FIIs played in the market's evolution. They entered at a crucial time in the early 1990s, and much of the market's one-time rerating to higher multiples is because of their sustained buying and accumulation over a generation. They also brought much-needed best practice transfer with them. FII standards on transparency and disclosure raised overall market standards and spurred a fledgling regulator to also work in that direction. Direct also was their influence on various market participants, and the buy and sell sides benefited from their presence.[22] FIIs selectively changed market practice and raised standards in fund management, equity research, and broking, besides providing regulatory inputs on issues such as rolling settlements and dematerialization. Thematic equity research also owes much to their presence. Critical too was a view of events that was a little longer than what prevailed in the market, which began a change from the speculative orientation towards something more investment-like.

[21] The extremely small sizes – usually less than $50 and often less than $20 – of most SIPs make them unlikely to clear the threshold of the vigorish in international investing, but the aggregator function of mutual funds would lower this cost threshold considerably.

[22] M.R. Mayya, *Glimpses of Indian Stock Markets*, Mumbai: Indian Institute of Capital Markets, 2010, 168.

Looking back in time, most participants agree with the above assessment.[23] But whether FIIs raised corporate governance standards overall remains an open question. By taking big positions in large, well-run companies, they gave those companies and their promoters an edge with the prestige of their association, but little else. More generally, they were, and remain to this day, portfolio investors rather than activist investors, willing to exit by pushing the Sell button, rather than actively intervening with promoters over strategy or governance.[24] Perhaps that's also because they operate under political, cultural, and linguistic constraints that prevent them from being little more than bystanders as promoters go about their job of running companies.

[23] C.H. Rajeshwer, 'FIIs: A New Force of Support and Discipline,' *Equity Markets: A New Paradigm*, ed. G Kumara Swamy Naidu, Hyderabad: ICFAI Press, 2002, 25–26.

[24] For an early statement of this position, see Jairus Banaji, 'Investor Capitalism and the Reshaping of Business in India,' Working Paper Series, No. 54, Queen Elizabeth House, Oxford Department of International Development, University of Oxford, September 2000.

18

THE BUY SIDE

LIC and the Mutual Funds

After FIIs, the buy side's big players are domestic institutional investors (DIIs), particularly LIC and the mutual funds. Historically, LIC's operations have been more prominent, and it is only in recent years that mutual funds have started to vie with the life insurer for importance. Lesser players on the buy side include portfolio management schemes, pension funds, and family offices. Portfolio management schemes are aimed at retail investors with larger portfolios and are seen as attractive (despite their considerable fees) because of their higher risk-return profiles and lower levels of regulatory supervision. Pension funds for long have been restricted by overtly conservative regulation that ignored the evidence in favour of long-term equity investing by them, and it is only recently that the situation has begun to change; they have also had to deal with opposition from the Left, besides the traditional mistrust of equity investing among the public.[1] Finally, the rise of family offices has

[1] Stand-alone retirement funds and provident funds are allowed to invest between 5 and 15 per cent of their corpus in equities. From 2015, the state-run Employees' Provident Fund Organisation (EPFO) was allowed to invest up to 5 per cent of its incremental corpus in equities (this limit was raised to 15 per cent in 2017). The National Pension Scheme (NPS) now allows its entrants to invest up to 75 per cent of their funds in equities.

led to a new class of players on the institutional side.[2] Now numbering over 30, these are set up by promoters to manage their surplus wealth; while technically retail, their large size makes them almost institutional in nature, and it is not uncommon to find family offices that are larger than a small mutual fund.

An insurance company is an unusually good vehicle for investing in equity markets. The nature of the claims business makes an insurance company suitable for equity investing; insurance companies charge premia against a risk that eventuates in the future, in the process generating large amounts of cash that lie about waiting to be deployed. Since the premia come in at the present and steadily but the payouts happen in the distant future (and often lumpily), insurance companies generate large sums called available reserves that, after paying out underwriting claims and losses, must be put to good use. These available reserves – or floats – should ideally be invested in liquid assets that can be readily realized to pay future claims, and markets for stocks and bonds are the prime markets for such liquid assets. Insurance companies capitalize on this and use the float to invest in stock markets, thereby capturing their long-term uptrend. In fact, insurance companies are better adapted for long-term investing than even the mutual fund business; an insurance company, unlike a mutual fund, is not subject to short-term redemption pressures from a fickle public.

Consider Warren Buffett's Berkshire Hathaway as an example of an insurance company's suitability for equity investing. Berkshire started life as a New England textile firm before morphing into an insurance company. Now so diversified that it is close to losing its original character, Berkshire still counts insurance among its main lines of business. Berkshire's float is now over $100 billion. Here, disciplined

[2] Shivani Shinde Nadhe, 'Family Office Concept Takes a Foothold in India,' *Business Standard*, 8 May 2014.

underwriting leads to an underwriting profit, meaning in fact that people are paying the company to take their money, but this is unusual and due mainly to Berkshire's superb skills in assessing risk probabilities. More commonly, and given the competitive nature of the insurance business, premia taken in over time are less than claims paid out (and business expenses), leading to an underwriting loss which is in fact just the cost of getting the float, almost like paying interest to get a bank loan. Investment income from stocks and bonds into which the float has been deployed then ensures that the insurance company turns a profit.

So, it is not surprising that in India too, insurance companies like LIC enjoy a certain prominence, further enhanced by the negligible presence of competitors like pension funds. LIC is India's largest player, and by late 2020, it had an equity portfolio of over ₹6,50,000 crores ($90 billion),[3] with an annual net deployment into stock markets of about ₹50,000 crores ($7 billion) and rising. Because it is almost fully owned by the government, LIC effectively answers to the dictates of the finance ministry and no one else. This also means that LIC is the government's buyer of last resort, standing ready to pick up any shares that remain unsold when the government sells its PSU shareholdings to finance the fiscal deficit. In times of market stress, a big chunk of such an issue may remain unsold (or devolve), only to be picked up by LIC.[4] In 2015, for instance, LIC picked up 86 per cent of the ₹9,400 crore offering in Indian Oil Corporation.[5] Since LIC is itself almost fully state-owned, the government is simply shifting the incidence of the fiscal deficit from one pocket to the other.

There is little available in the public domain on LIC equity operations. Its activities remain something of a black box, and the annual reports are strangely devoid of any commentary on its equity investments. LIC

[3] Towards the latter half of the SIP Bull, LIC's equity portfolios through its linked and non-linked businesses were ₹5,62,511 crores and ₹39,611 crores respectively. Life Insurance Corporation of India (LIC), *Annual Report* 2017–2018, Mumbai: LIC, 2018, 253.

[4] Prominent PSU offers rescued by LIC just between 2012 and 2016 included: Coal India, ONGC, IOC, and SAIL, among others.

[5] Swaraj Singh Dhanjal, Ankit Doshi, and Asit Ranjan Mishra, 'Institutional Investors Lap up NTPC's Offer for Sale,' *Mint*, 24 February 2016.

managers move markets but have no public profile; the quality of people managing its portfolio is virtually unknown, and none appear in the media. This opacity comes naturally to LIC's investment side, as they believe they answer to no one but the government. But they also answer to millions of policyholders who entrust their hard-earned life savings to them. Except that portfolio losses or gains get distributed among LIC's family of products, and if a policyholder gets a small haircut on his annual bonus declaration, none's the wiser. LIC's opacity is also enhanced by the large number of small brokers who are empanelled with it. LIC often trades through this small army of brokers – breaking up order flow among them hides its operations from the market and prevents front running – and many marginal brokers subsist on the organization's order flow to them.

Listing LIC would take its operations into the public domain and subject them to market oversight, which would make these shenanigans public and give the government less leeway to use the insurer as a handmaiden. Consequently, the debate to list LIC or not is usually resolved in favour of it remaining fully government-owned. Still, with the onset of fiscal pressures from the coronavirus pandemic, there was a renewed push to sell a small percentage of LIC's equity, and this was duly completed in 2022.[6] But many of LIC's operations continue to remain exempt from SEBI provisions, which in turn allows for its continued use as a handmaiden.[7]

But acting as a handmaiden and rescuer of last resort can have its benefits, and some unwanted issues rescued by LIC have done quite well later. In 2012, LIC picked up over 80 per cent of an ONGC issue that devolved and later sold parts of that issue for a profit of ₹7,000 crores.[8] LIC gets roundly blamed by the chattering classes when it rides

[6] Presently, LIC is about 97 per cent government-owned.

[7] A range of non-life insurance businesses were nationalized in 1972, consolidated into the General Insurance Corporation (GIC), and then reconsolidated into four subsidiaries. Presently, GIC only provides reinsurance to the domestic market, while the four subsidiaries don't have the dominant presence that LIC enjoys.

[8] Dheeraj Tiwari, 'Waiting for Divestment: LIC May Raise Holding in Public Sector Companies,' *Economic Times*, 29 October 2014.

to the rescue and somehow it seems inherently wrong.[9] But shouldn't LIC be congratulated for turning a profit after picking up paper no one else wanted? So, the healthy profits it makes after doing something that earns it censure are a sort of poetic justice.

Traditionally seen as a countervailing source of funds in the market, LIC's approach is thus heavily contrarian. There is an institutional bias to this approach that has been publicly acknowledged by various LIC chairmen.[10] SEBI's daily release of fund flows from DIIs does not distinguish between LIC and the mutual funds, but it is common knowledge that a chunk of offsetting buying comes from LIC when foreign funds are selling. This contrarian approach has worked well. LIC's booked profits on equities have been soaring in recent years and trebled between 2013 and 2022, rising from ₹14,000 to ₹42,000 crores.[11] No other single entity takes as much money out of India's equity markets. With the rise of mutual funds, a part of LIC's contrarian role has now been taken up by the fundies. Nevertheless, LIC's contrarian role still looms large, and this is not surprising given that it has the largest portfolio with the lightest redemption pressure.

In the early years, LIC went through an accumulation phase when it was more a buyer than a seller.[12] LIC has been investing in stock markets since a little after its 1956 founding and, like the dervishes, it has benefited considerably from the inefficient markets of that era; it acquired large holdings at throwaway prices, and these legacy holdings

[9] In 2013 (which was a typical year for the divestment program), LIC bought almost a fourth of the ₹47,000 crores raised by the government. 'LIC Is the Government's ATM,' *equitymaster.com*, accessed 10 November 2015.

[10] 'Our total focus is on long-term investments… and we are contrarian investors traditionally,' LIC chairman V.K. Sharma, as quoted in 'LIC Books Rs19,000 Crore Profit from Market in FY17,' *Indian Express,* 17 May 2017.

[11] Booked profits in fiscal years 2013, 2014, and 2015 came in at ₹14,000, ₹21,000, and ₹24,000 crores, respectively. LIC Annual Reports and Press Trust of India, 'LIC Net Profit up 15 pct from Equity Play at Rs 24,373 cr in FY15,' *PTI,* 3 August 2015. ENS, 'LIC Made Rs 42,000 Crore in FY22 from Equity Market,' *Indian Express*, 1 June 2022.

[12] Norman S. Poser and David Silver, *Regulation of the Indian Securities Markets: A Preliminary Survey,* United States Securities and Exchange Commission (SEC), Washington, D.C.: January 1965, 9–10. Other development finance institutions such as ICICI and IDBI also had substantial legacy portfolios from the early years.

are one reason behind the large profits. When multinationals were forced to dilute and sell their equity at confiscatory prices in the 1970s, LIC and Unit Trust of India (UTI) perforce picked up big portions of the offerings because there was no mutual fund industry at that time; as a result, both organizations were among the biggest beneficiaries of these FERA dilutions. LIC's oversized influence on the primary side is another legacy from the early years that continues into the present day. LIC's massive presence in equity markets also means that the Indian public's exposure to equity as an asset class is not as low as it seems. All the life insurance premia LIC collects from the public and invests in equity markets form part of that public's exposure to equities, and the bonuses the public receives on LIC policies are also due (in part) to the profits LIC makes in stock markets.

Large shareholders like LIC also help create the market for corporate control, but here LIC's role is underwhelming. As seen earlier, stock markets exist to raise capital, manage risk, and measure and store value, but a fourth and vital function is the market for corporate control. In theory at least, public equity markets should help align shareholder (principal) interests better with management (agent) and address the principal-agent problem. It should be possible for managements to be ousted via a hostile takeover through the markets if they don't deliver, and that scenario gets set in motion through activist large shareholders like LIC; alternately, LIC's voting power can also be used to leverage good corporate policies and punish bad policies. Neither happens often. Deference and respect towards the original founding family of promoters is an ingrained part of the value system in the country, and activist large shareholders are a rarity. So, company managements in India don't need Delaware registrations or 'poison pill' defences in their articles of association to buttress their existences.[13] LIC is happy to give them a free ride.[14]

[13] The US state of Delaware remains the standard for company-friendly incorporation, mainly due to tax breaks, privacy for directors, and the absence of residency requirements for incorporation. Poison pill defences (such as shareholder rights plans) provide incumbent managements with defences against activist investors/acquirers who are trying to launch a hostile takeover.

[14] For empirical evidence on the passivity of institutional investors at all levels of equity ownership, see Jayati Sarkar and Subrata Sarkar, 'Large Shareholder Activism in Corporate Governance in

---

Mutual funds – that part of the buy side which should have mattered but didn't for many years – are now beginning to come into their own. Unlike brokerages, which date back to the early nineteenth century, the mutual fund industry is a product of Nehruvian India and reflects both the strengths and foibles of that era. Mutual funds (or investment trusts) were first mentioned by the Indian Central Banking Enquiry Committee in 1931 and then by A.D. Shroff's Committee on Finance for the Private Sector in 1954. Most such committees recognized the need to mobilize public savings to invest in financial markets but also noted that implementation was hampered by microstructure issues and the public's preference for land and gold.

The founding of the UTI in 1963 through the passage of the eponymous act marked the beginning of India's buy side. The founder of India's mutual fund industry is T.T. Krishnamachari in his capacity as Nehru's Economic and Defence Coordination Minister. TTK (as he was often called) made for an unlikely founding father of a market institution – his first stint as finance minister in the 1950s had been cut short by a stock market scam, the Mundhra affair. Building on conceptual work done earlier at the central bank, Krishnamachari, during his second spell as a union minister from 1962 to 1966, raised the issue of UTI's founding in a memo to Nehru; as noted earlier, TTK had seen press coverage of Pakistan's development of an investment trust, and this sharpened the spur of his intent. The matter was passed on to Finance Minister Morarji Desai but nothing much came of it. Desai's resignation as finance minister and TTK's second stint in that post allowed for the necessary impetus, and it was the pursuit of a minister's pet idea that led to the foundation of India's mutual fund industry.[15]

Developing Countries: Evidence from India,' *International Review of Finance*, 1, no. 3, 2000, 161–94. The big mutual funds – often themselves owned by promoter families – are naturally reluctant to raise issues about other promoter-owned companies.

[15] This account is from the memoirs of the first executive trustee of UTI. See V.G. Pendharkar, *Unit Trust of India: Retrospect and Prospect*, New Delhi: UBS Publishers and Distributors, 2002. A former

Since then, the mutual fund industry has gone through three phases, with 1993 and 2010 as convenient dividers. The industry's first phase between 1963 and 1993 was characterized by a wholly public-sector presence, with UTI dominating events for most of the period. Set up by an act of Parliament in 1963, UTI was regulated by the central bank in its early years, but it practically functioned in a regulatory vacuum till SEBI's creation a generation later. Founded in the heyday of public-sector dominance of financial markets, it had RBI, LIC, and SBI as its original shareholders till, in 1978, the RBI stake was taken up by IDBI.[16]

FIIs and private mutual funds were still in the future, and so UTI dominated proceedings – its 1988 corpus amounted to about 20 per cent of the Indian market's capitalization. It was a dominance no other entity would ever attain; even today, LIC's massive portfolio, India's largest, is barely over 2 per cent of market capitalization, and that is because the market has grown so much. UTI's early years were fraught with the missteps that could be expected of a buy side pioneer finding its feet in a volatile and speculative market. Both the government and the brokerage community used it as a handmaiden – the former in its attempt to prop up markets and the latter when it needed a buyer of last resort. But it was TTK's original vision of UTI as 'an adventure in small savings' that proved an issue as the fund wrestled with the problem of offering its customers fixed returns on a variable return investment. For decades, UTI offered the public fixed dividends and guaranteed redemption prices on its units – this, despite investing the public's capital in equities, an instrument that offered no guarantees on either dividends or prices. This glaring contradiction was not apparent to the sponsors, and as a result, the fund went through repeated collapses followed by government bailouts.

Launched in UTI's first year of operation was its founding scheme – the checkered Unit Scheme (US)-64. Its maiden dividend of 6.1 per

---

RBI staffer, Pendharkar was also part of the RBI team that worked on the concept papers that led to the UTI Act.

[16] 'History of Mutual Funds in India,' *AMFI*, accessed 5 August 2018, https://www.amfiindia.com/research-information/mf-history.

cent was deliberately set to exceed the 4 to 6 per cent offered on bank deposit rates of the time. Favourable tax treatment also contributed to the scheme's attractiveness, and as a result, US-64 remained UTI's most popular plan for many years. The guaranteed returns popularized the mutual fund product among a latent investing class; but an untoward side effect was the public's addiction to 'guaranteed' high returns on equity products, an addiction that would be overcome the hard way in later years.

Towards this phase's end, other public-sector entities such as government-owned banks were allowed into the mutual fund industry. They were led by SBI's 1987 foray through its Magnum schemes. Industry assets under management (debt and equity) grew from the low base of ₹25 crores raised by UTI in 1965 to ₹47,700 crores by 1993, a compounded annual rate of about 31 per cent.[17]

The industry's second phase, from 1993 to about 2010, started with the reform push of the early 1990s and was characterized by the entry of private players, legislative initiatives that laid the basis for regulation, industry consolidation, and tax incentives that improved the attractiveness of the mutual fund product. Significant boom–bust cycles – Mehta, IT, and the Rate Bull – would mark this as a coming-of-age period whose defining feature remains private sector entry. Though Mumbai would later house the industry, the first private mutual fund, Kothari Pioneer, was founded in Madras by Bhadrashyam Kothari in July 1993; it was later acquired by Franklin Templeton, but its Bluechip and Prima funds continued, and they remain the oldest extant private fund schemes in India.[18] Regulation of the nascent industry also passed to SEBI, effectively ending the earlier ad hoc regulation from the RBI. A first draft of regulations came out in 1993, followed by a comprehensive 1996 version which still serves as the basis for industry regulation.[19]

[17] 'Research and Information: Mutual Fund History,' *AMFI*, accessed 5 August 2018, https://www.amfiindia.com/research-information/mf-history.

[18] Kayezad E. Adajania, 'History of Private Mutual Funds in India, as Told by Pioneers,' *Mint*, 4 September 2018.

[19] The regulatory framework's early years are discussed in Subrata Sarkar, 'Mutual Funds in India: Structure and Regulatory Framework,' in *Institutions Governing Financial Markets*, ed. Shubhashish Gangopadhyay, Mumbai: Allied Publishers, 1997, 130–64.

Various foreign and domestic players entered but many also exited, not enthused by the high cost of acquiring equity retail assets in that era; tie-ups with foreign firms to obtain their back-office processing expertise were also common. Tax incentives such as exempting amounts invested annually from income tax, exempting investments in mutual funds from long-term capital gains, and exempting dividends distributed by funds from taxes, also led to significant tax arbitrage in the industry's favour; such incentives had been missing in the buy side's early years.[20] As a result, industry assets under management (debt and equity) grew from ₹47,700 crores in 1993 to ₹6,13,000 crores in 2010, at a compounded annual rate of 16 per cent.[21]

This second phase was also noteworthy for the UTI crisis that effectively ended the public sector's dominance of the fund industry. For many years, US-64 did not declare a net asset value (NAV) – the actual portfolio value per unit – and only purchase and redemption prices of its units were announced. This was ostensibly done to protect small investors from panicking during periods of volatility, but the practice had the unfortunate side effect of making investors believe the fund was immune to that volatility. The problem compounded as UTI increased equity allocation after the early 1980s – allocations that were usually below 30 per cent increased to as much as 70 per cent during the Harshad Mehta bull market of the early 1990s. The fund's volatility increased, and it morphed from an income fund (the original purpose) to an equity fund, just at a time when the market was entering its most violent boom-bust phase. US-64's portfolio fell substantially in the aftermath of the Mehta sell-off during the mid- and late-1990s, followed by further drawdowns led by falls in PSU stocks that UTI had obligingly purchased from the government during the latter's divestment program.

But the announced redemption prices continued to be high, leading to a severe disconnect between them and the actual portfolio value per

[20] Some of these incentives were gradually withdrawn, and in later years, long-term capital gains were taxed at 10 per cent, with the first ₹1 lakh being exempt.

[21] 'Research and Information,' *AMFI.*

unit. By 1998, this fact became widely known in the media and sparked a redemption crisis that became known as the 'US-64 controversy'.[22] A committee was duly appointed to get UTI out of the mess, further capital infusions to bridge the disconnect took place, and the PSU stocks were spun off to another scheme that the government, obligingly enough, bought back from UTI at prices that compensated it for the declines. After this, the government learnt its lesson, and LIC became the designated handmaiden for rescuing the government's divestment programs.

There was a widespread feeling that management problems at UTI were also responsible, and so, various management changes were suggested and new trustees appointed. These new worthies promptly increased asset allocations to hot software stocks in late 1999 – right at the top of the tech bubble – and the collapse that followed caused another steep decline in the fund's NAV. By now, private mutual funds had established themselves, and UTI was no longer central to the market's well-being, but this simple fact took a while to sink in. The fund's wild roller-coaster ride of the 1990s would mark the last occasion when it featured prominently in the market's story. The organization was bifurcated into two – one part (consisting essentially of legacy assets) continued to be exempt from fund regulation and was run by the government, while the other part was brought under SEBI regulation.[23]

The mutual fund industry's third phase from 2010 onwards features accelerated growth in assets under management, led by further acceptability of the mutual fund product among households, all set against the backdrop of a constantly rising market. Its defining feature has been the acceptance and growth of rupee cost averaging products such as the systematic investment plan (SIP), and 2010 marks the start of this trend. In a historic change, the buy side's steady and regular access to household savings through the SIP has reduced the Indian

[22] For an outline of the US-64 controversy, see 'The US 64 Controversy,' in *Case Studies in Finance, Volume II*, Hyderabad: ICFAI Center for Management Research, 2004, 133–39.

[23] In 2002, the UTI Act was repealed and further structural changes made to US-64, but UTI's centrality to the market would continue to diminish in later years.

market's reliance on foreign investors. In the two decades from the IT bust year of 2002 all the way to 2021, there has been only one significant down year in 2008, and this is because of the SIP. Asset growth in this phase has been robust, except for a hiatus between 2008 and 2012 in the aftermath of the Great Recession.[24] Assets under management (debt and equity) grew from ₹6,13,000 crores in 2010 to ₹53,00,000 crores in 2024, at a compounded annual rate of 16.7 per cent, and much of this growth was through the SIP, though a near trebling of market levels also contributed.[25]

But the SIP's success has not been tested by a prolonged period of falling prices, and the product has benefited from – or perhaps even resulted in – a steadily rising market. So, it is still unclear whether this is a structural move or just another cyclical household rotation into equities, brought about by a quiet period in real assets like land or gold. In fact, in 2017, the percentage of household financial assets in equities was still lower than in the Mehta Bull's aftermath of 1993 and 1994. Nevertheless, the impression is of an industry benefiting from two significant transitions – first, a household move from real assets to financial assets and second, a move from other financial assets into equities. The second transition is of immediate significance. Traditionally, about two-thirds of household financial assets went into bank deposits or corporate deposits, while equity allocations were usually in low single digits, but the success of averaging products and a steadily rising market has seen these allocations rise to almost 10 per cent.[26]

From about 2015, SIP inflows have also allowed mutual funds to act as a counterweight to foreign flows. Historically, Indian markets mirrored the movement of fund flows from FIIs, with these being the major sources of volatility. As seen, correlations between FII flows and

[24] CRISIL, an analytics company, has come up with an omnibus listing of factors driving mutual fund growth, including: economic growth, low mutual fund penetration, rising disposable income, increased financial savings, rising retail participation through rupee cost averaging products, expanding geographic reach, higher digitization, and supportive government policies.

[25] 'Research and Information,' *AMFI.* AMFI and Crisil Intelligence, The *Sahi* Journey, AMFI-Crisil Factbook, 2024, 10.

[26] AMFI and Crisil Intelligence, The *Sahi* Journey, 7.

market movements were straightforward – markets sold off when FII outflows peaked. Led by LIC and the mutual funds, domestic investors then tried to act as counterweights to FIIs, but in the early years, they lacked the capital to be effective balancers, and markets sold off heavily. Now, however, SIP household allocation to equities – the product accounts for almost 40 per cent of DII inflows into the market – allows domestic investors to act as a countervailing force to FII selling. Now the monthly DII and FII figures would regularly offset one another, as DIIs bought what the FIIs sold and vice versa. SIPs are doubly valuable as a counterweight because they are sticky and inclined towards inertia by philosophy and design; once started, they tend to go on and on. For the first time, the little guy is coming to the market's rescue.

Historically, mutual fund assets under management (AUM) in India came in at about 10 per cent of GDP, lower than the 40 to 60 per cent for BRICS peers like South Africa or Brazil, and much lower than the 100 per cent of GDP for a mature market like the US. Between 2000 and 2018, and depending on the market cycle, AUM fluctuated between 4 and 10 per cent of GDP. Around the time of the coronavirus pandemic, an inflection appears to have taken place, and by 2024, AUM came to over 18 per cent of GDP.[27]

Overall, the buy side accounts for about 11 per cent of the market's capitalization and this is well into the post-2009 SIP-led boom. In the 1990s, observers thought India's high savings rate, the increasing sophistication of financial markets, and private sector entry would result in take-off for mutual funds, but for many years, performance belied the hopes of liberalization. High returns from alternate opportunities such as debt, real estate, or gold provided competition and significantly raised the opportunity cost of equity investing. To this must be added chronic distrust of equities as an asset class, and as a result, the fund industry

[27] Ibid., 8.

faced a perennial challenge in marketing its products, which lasted till it discovered the wonders of the SIP.

Unlike banking or insurance, where entrenched public-sector players have managed to hold on to market share, the mutual fund space has seen the private sector take over after it was allowed in. There were 44 active mutual funds in India in 2020 – with 35 from the private sector and 9 (including UTI) from the public sector; almost four-fifths of industry assets were organized under private-sector funds. The top ten players accounted for about 80 per cent of assets, leaving the remaining 34 funds with about 20 per cent.[28] Till about 2015, the profits of the top ten were larger than the profits of the entire industry, indicating that the smaller funds had been losing money for years. These numbers had prompted Fidelity, one of the largest and most well-known fund houses in the world, to exit India in 2012; more foreign funds would follow, unable to crack issues such as distribution and high costs.

Mutual funds were subject to the same complex Indian mix of promise and peril that manifested in companies the funds invested in. Similarly, industry grandees noted the demographic dividend as a factor behind the growth of companies they invested in, without mentioning that their own industry should also have been a beneficiary of that dividend. A large growing population that is getting younger – and facing a lower dependency ratio – can take on more risk. Equities, as a business of risk-taking, should have benefited from that dividend. But in the early years, the industry did not gain from this phenomenon, and it is only recently that assets have grown significantly in absolute terms.[29]

Growth rates in AUM during the second and third phases are over 15 per cent, despite the asset base getting progressively larger. Much of that growth has been due to soaring markets and rising net inflows (new fund offers could have contributed, but they are negligible). *Ceteris paribus* – even if inflows and redemptions balance out, leading to net

[28] The largest players included: SBI Mutual Fund, ICICI Prudential, HDFC, Nippon India, Kotak Mahindra, Aditya Birla Sun Life, UTI, Axis, Mirae Asset, and DSP.

[29] Association of Mutual Funds of India (AMFI), Assets under Management data, *AMFI Quarterly*, January–March 2018 and onwards.

inflows of zero – a doubling in market levels will anyway lead to a doubling in AUM. Yet the stock market has compounded at about 13 per cent annually, and industry assets have grown at a slightly higher rate, so growth has also been due to rising net inflows.

With these growth rates, mutual funds should, at some point, start competing with banks for the household savings pool, just as they do in mature markets like the US. After all, funds operate in markets less regulated than commercial banking, and the regulatory arbitrage that results can work in their favour. Surprisingly there has been little concern voiced by banks on this, perhaps due to the absence of money market checking accounts and other mutual fund products that have savings account features. So, banks still don't see mutual funds as competition for household savings, though that may change if these industry growth rates continue. Besides, many banks are themselves fund sponsors and have their own mutual funds, so if the above situation comes to pass, cannibalization could become as much a concern as competition.

Equity funds get classified on structure as open or closed,[30] on style as active or passive,[31] and on objective as growth or income oriented.[32] Most equity funds in India are open-ended (over 90 per cent of equity assets) and active (for over 95 per cent of equity assets), but evenly balanced between the investment objectives of growth and income.[33] A

[30] Investors in open-end funds buy into the value of the fund's holdings on that date, net of any expenses or liabilities – its net asset value, or NAV. Closed-end funds issue shares to raise resources which are then used to invest in equities; these closed-end fund shares themselves trade on an exchange, usually at or close to the value of their underlying equities. Sometimes they trade at a big discount, which is a source of mystery to financial economists who believe in efficient markets.

[31] Active funds use asset allocation, security selection, or market timing to generate returns, while passive funds simply hold an index.

[32] Growth funds try mainly for capital appreciation, while income funds provide monthly income to their clients.

[33] There were 41 funds in 2018. Securities and Exchange Board of India (SEBI), *Annual Report for the Fiscal Year 2017–2018*, Mumbai: SEBI, 2018, 108. The numbers fluctuated based on market conditions, with 32 funds in 2000 and 28 in 2004.

mutual fund in India comprises four separate entities – sponsor, trust, asset management company, and custodian. Farsighted but historically unacknowledged early decisions have led to this robust framework. Also unique to India is the presence of promoter families and industrial houses among mutual fund sponsors; these families typically operate well-diversified conglomerates that comprise several other firms operating in a wide range of industries. Unlike banks, funds don't deal with a regulator that discourages ownership by promoter families, so many funds have an association with a business family and piggyback on the promoter's longevity, reputation for trust, or brand name.[34] Banks (public and private) also figure prominently as fund sponsors, and consequently, promoter families and banks together account for a little over half of all mutual funds.

Historically, physical assets like land and gold constituted over half of all household wealth, while insurance and bank deposits took up about a quarter, which left mutual funds only with the balance to grow their business. From an asset gatherer's standpoint, the retail segment typically accounted for about two-thirds of equity assets and corporates made up the rest; the proportions were reversed for debt, and corporates accounted for two-thirds of debt investment, mainly due to the dictates of treasury and working capital management.

Asset gathering meant distribution, which was a key challenge in the early years; the industry remained largely confined to the big cities, till various schemes incentivized mutual funds to look beyond them. The absence of regular allocation to equity markets through individual retirement accounts (IRAs) or pension plans also increased the system's reliance on distribution. The retail bias, household preferences for real assets such as land and gold, and the absence of pension allocations made asset gathering for equity investing very expensive in India. Third-party distributors – commission-driven and expensive – dominated the marketing channels, and about two-thirds of mutual funds were

[34] Pulak Ghosh, Jayant R. Kale, and Venkatesh Panchapagesan, 'Do Indian Business Group Owned Mutual Funds Maximize Value for Their Investors?,' National Stock Exchange, NSE–NYU Stern School of Business, Initiative for the Study of Indian Capital Markets, January 2014, 1–10.

sold through a combination of independent financial advisors (IFAs), national-level distributors, and banks.[35] Of these, the IFAs became increasingly important, as the relationship-oriented nature of Indian society allowed for personal relationships between the public and IFAs, and it was the latter who drove distribution, particularly of the SIP.

Because of these challenges, alliances and partnerships in distribution were crucial, but expensive.[36] Friction across the distribution channel was also common and frequently reported as such.[37] It was always 'pull' from the industry rather than 'push' from the public that dominated channel dynamics, and the only exception to this rule occurred at the great bull highs when the public pushed capital naturally into the industry.[38] This heightened the pressure on managers to deploy funds, and because of the mandate to be fully invested, money coming in at tops (and deployed at that time) had corresponding effects on performance. As a result of all this, sales and distribution departments led staffing at most mutual funds.[39] Again, the SIP and its success reduced somewhat the lumpy nature of equity flows and lessened the distribution problem. Distribution was also aided by substantial investor awareness that was funded by the 2 basis points (0.02 per cent) of fees that funds had to annually set aside for initiatives on investor education. Of these initiatives, the most

[35] At HDFC (one of the largest mutual funds), independent financial advisors, national distributors, and banks respectively generated 40 per cent, 25 per cent, and 20 per cent of their equity-oriented AUM, while the remaining 15 per cent was invested through direct plans (as of 31 December 2017). See HDFC Asset Management Company Ltd, Draft Red Herring Prospectus, filed 14 March 2018, from the SEBI website, accessed 15 October 2018, 22. This channel mix varied widely among mutual funds.

[36] KPMG India, 'Indian Mutual Fund Industry: Distribution Continuum Key to Success,' Mumbai: KPMG India, 2014, 2–11.

[37] Joydeep Ghosh, 'Tussles in Mutual Fund Industry as Distributors, Big Fund Houses Lock Horns,' *Business Standard,* 27 March 2015. Wrangling over service tax incidence and capping of upfront commissions were other key distribution issues. Also see Chandan Kishore Kant, 'MF Distributors Continue to be a Worried Lot,' *Economic Times*, 7 May 2015.

[38] 'In India, mutual funds are sold, not bought.' Alroy Lobo, as quoted in Saurabh Mukherjea, *Gurus of Chaos: Modern India's Money Masters*, New Delhi: Bloomsbury India, 2014, 67.

[39] Tetsuya Kamiyama, 'India's Mutual Fund Industry,' *Nomura Capital Market Review*, 10, (4), Winter 2007, 68–69.

prominent was the campaign run by the Association of Mutual Funds of India (AMFI) with the '*Mutual funds sahi hai*' tagline.[40]

Like almost every variable that defined the industry's economics, distribution costs were also impacted by regulatory issues. Historically, the industry had exhibited an urban bias right from its founding in Calcutta and Bombay. Typically, three-quarters of mutual fund assets came from the top five cities, and a little over 80 per cent of all assets came from the 15 largest cities.[41] Like the game itself, the industry was largely an urban phenomenon till regulatory changes from about 2009 sought to broad base the industry and remove this urban focus.[42] Funds were incentivized and allowed to charge a higher management fee for assets raised from smaller towns. They were also made to set aside a portion of fees for distribution incentives and allowed to incentivize distributors in cities beyond the 15 largest (the so-called B15) by offering them larger commissions.[43] In 2018, this scheme was widened, and the industry was allowed to incentivize distributors in the B30, i.e., cities beyond the largest 30.[44] With the onset of the coronavirus pandemic, action did shift to smaller towns, but digitization ensured that activities such as stock trading on smartphones benefited more than asset gathering. This micromanagement of an industry's structure and incentives is a distinctive feature of Indian regulation, and mutual funds simply fall into that pattern. Larger houses tended to reward distributors more for raising expensive equity, so these measures have disproportionate effects on the small and mid-sized funds that have not attained scale.

[40] Loosely translated as 'Mutual funds are right'. AMFI, the industry lobbying group, would also play a key role in investor education.

[41] As of early 2018, the top 15 ('T15') cities accounted for the majority of mutual fund assets with a share of 81 per cent. 'B15' cities were behind the top 15, and usually with populations less than theirs.

[42] The spread to rural areas is noted in AMFI and Crisil Intelligence, The *Sahi* Journey, 16.

[43] In 2012, SEBI allowed fund houses to incentivize sales from 'B15' towns by offering distributors in these towns extra commissions of 0.30 per cent. In recent years, growth rates for assets raised from these 'B15' towns had picked up, indicating that the incentive campaigns were working but also showing how the SIP bull market was sucking in the mofussil public.

[44] In 2018, SEBI again changed the definition of a small town from 'B15' to 'B30'. Now small towns were those behind the top 30 cities.

Like distribution costs, the fee structure of mutual funds was perennially in regulatory play and subject to levels of dirigiste fiddling by SEBI so high that, to an industry outsider, it became difficult to keep track of the changes over time. Direct fees, including the entry load, were abolished by 2009, leaving a 1 per cent exit load as the only direct fee.[45] Indirect fees, such as the annual expense ratio, were more relevant, and the maximum expense ratio (first kept at 2.5 per cent in 1996) was also determined by the regulator with funds free to charge lower amounts if they wished. Later this was reduced and a sliding scale introduced, where the expense ratio fell the more the AUM grew.

With increases in AUM, the industry's top line and profit margins also increased rapidly. By 2017 and in the middle of the SIP Bull, soaring AUM led to a fee pool of about ₹11,000 crores, which was considerable but still lower than the ₹20,000 crore pool the brokerage industry had enjoyed in its heyday. Despite the freedom to charge less, most funds applied the highest expense ratio allowed to the swelling assets they managed, something any profit-maximizing entity subject to economies of scale would do. Industry dynamics should have lowered fees as funds competed to attract business but that did not happen, and as a result, some leading mutual funds became very profitable; HDFC Asset Management Company, a prominent mutual fund, reported an average return on equity (ROE) of 39 per cent in the three years prior to its 2018 IPO.[46]

Now mutual funds could reap further scale economies if allowed to do so, but the political economy of Indian regulation never allowed them to realize those benefits. After the abolition of entry loads in 2009, further restrictions on the expense ratio were introduced in 2018. The 2018 changes introduced restrictions on total expense ratios, restricting the largest funds to a maximum of 1.05 per cent and allowing smaller

[45] Entry load abolition should have reduced amounts entering the industry, but that was not the case. See Santosh Anagol, Vijaya Marisetty, Renuka Sane, and Buvaneshwaran Venugopal, 'On the Impact of Regulating Commissions: Evidence from the Indian Mutual Funds Market,' *World Bank Economic Review*, 31 (1), 2017, 241–70.

[46] HDFC Asset Management Company Ltd, Draft Red Herring Prospectus, 114.

funds to charge more on a progressive scale; the smaller the fund, the more it was allowed to charge, with the smallest fund allowed to charge up to twice as much as the largest fund fee of 1.05 per cent. This brought down fund management costs but also penalized the larger funds and disincentivized scale economies that the industry thrived on.

The fee issue illustrated how mutual funds operated under the long shadow of government regulation, always a hit or miss affair because of Indian regulation's tendency to lapse into dirigisme, or directive state control of economic activity. One study documented – with nonchalance and without the slightest hint of condemnation – four 'regulatory regimes' on fees just between the initiation of regulation in the early 1990s and 2010.[47] Mutual funds did not figure prominently in the reforms of the 1990s, so unlike microstructure and clearing, which went through 'big bang' one-time reform measures, mutual funds were subjected to a continuous 'drip drip' of reforms that continue in never-ending progression to the present day. As the discussion on expense ratios showed, much of this was in the nature of tinkering – or 'tweaking', as the media was fond of putting it. '*SEBI tweaks norms for...*' was a common start to a headline and as likely to elicit groans as cheers.[48] There were few sources of regulatory talent outside the government, and many regulators were retired government bureaucrats either from the ministries, the central bank, or the myriad organizations that had regulatory components. Their attitude mirrored their backgrounds, and regulation revealed a marked tendency to micromanagement as the years went by.[49] The level and detail of regulatory pronouncements would keep rising, substantially raising compliance costs for the industry and going so far as to include detailed guidelines on the sort (and size) of graphics the industry had to carry in its advertising.

[47] For an early discussion of regulation's effect on the fee structure, see Ekta Selarka and Susan Thomas, 'The Mutual Fund Industry in India: Growing with Regulatory Reform,' *Finance Research Group Technical Note*, IGIDR Mumbai, November 2010, 1–12. Observations that documented changing attitudes over large swathes of time were a rarity in the markets.

[48] Googling 'SEBI tweaks' produces many pages of story headlines.

[49] The industry had been lightly regulated in the early years till a scandal involving a mutual fund, the Arihant Mangal Growth Scheme, that was run by the CRB group of companies.

More pertinently (as the discussion on fees suggests), regulation had the capacity to impact industry structure and profitability in a manner that was rare in other countries, and much of that capacity was driven by regulation's pronounced *aam aadmi* bias. Customers of mutual funds who were coming into their own would now reach for political influence, and the shorthand for any such public grouping that mobilized in its own interest was the *aam aadmi*, loosely translated as the 'common man'. In the political economy of regulation, taking regulatory decisions carried political overtones in industries where the customer base had a strong *aam aadmi* component, and regulators carefully thought through decisions that were perceived to antagonize them. In such situations, regulators instinctively sided with the *aam aadmi* and not the industry's shareholders, which led to any conflict between shareholders and the *aam aadmi* being decided in favour of the latter.

Mutual funds would provide another example of that bias. The higher fee funds earned when their AUM bases swelled infuriated the investing populace and the chattering classes. To them, those fees were a cost, and so, the howling mob of public opinion would be mobilized against the industry. Many among the public had bought into the story of long-term investing in steadily rising markets, and complicated studies that showed savings through reduced fees over many years were produced, following which columnists uniformly came out in favour of regulatory action to drive down fees and industry top lines. 2018 was a landmark year for mutual funds, as it marks the first time this *aam aadmi* effect affected the industry through those regulations on the total expense ratio. Typically, regulatory capture happened when agencies ended up doing the bidding of the very industries they were tasked with regulating, but in India, capture came from the *aam aadmi* end users of an industry rather than the industry itself. Because of this *aam aadmi* bias, industry growth brought forth regulatory action that appropriated profits which accrued from economies of scale and distributed it back to customers in their *aam aadmi* avatar.

As a consequence, mutual funds had gone the way of airlines and telecom, also industries where large and articulate publics bought into the industry's output at cheap and uneconomic prices – buy-ins that were egged on by a biased regulator and cheerled through the media. In all this, little thought was given to consequences on the fund industry's dynamics. It was better and less risky to be a shareholder in a mutual fund's investments through its NAV, rather than a shareholder of a mutual fund's own shares.

Nevertheless, in recent years, mutual funds were cosseted behind the soaring markets wrought by the wall of quantitative easing and SIP liquidity. Heavy compliance costs were now – for the big boys at least – spread over the large AUM surges of recent years.

Yet as a result of all this, expense ratios had started approaching levels usually seen in mature markets. The asset-weighted expense ratio of actively managed US equity mutual funds in 2017 was 0.78 per cent but achieved through the dynamics of competition.[50] In India, after the 2018 changes, the average expense ratio for the largest actively managed equity funds was now a little over 1 per cent but achieved through heavy-handed regulation.

Naturally, all this regulation brought arbitrage in its wake, as the industry bought into low-regulation jurisdictions while reducing its presence in high-regulation jurisdictions. Unlike mutual funds, portfolio management schemes had regulatory leeway both on fees chargeable and fund management strategies, which aided their growth. The effect on hedge funds was the opposite, and tax and regulatory incentives favoured the mutual fund product so much that hedge funds had a hard time taking off in India. More complicated arbitrages arose from differences in asset management (or product) guidelines between the mutual fund, insurance, and pension fund industries, each of which had its own regulatory silo. These industries were mainly (or incidentally) in the business of asset management, but their guidelines depended on the extent to which the concerned regulator saw its role as 'developmental' to that industry.[51] Gaming the guidelines then became the goal of regulatory arbitrage.

[50] Investor Company Institute (ICI), *2018 Investment Company Fact Book: A Review of Trends and Activities in the Investment Company Industry*, from ICI website, accessed 15 October 2018, 120, 126.

[51] Remarks by K.N. Vaidyanathan, in Jayant R. Kale and Venkatesh Panchapagesan, 'The Indian Mutual Fund Industry: Opportunities and Challenges,' *IIMB Management Review*, 24, (4), 2012, 255–56.

After the fee pool is divvied up between the fundies and distributors, the capital that comes in has to be invested, which raises issues of performance and its measurement. India tends to be an absolute return equity shop, with the public implicitly comparing fund returns with the interest rates they get on fixed income instruments; as a result, relative return measures like beating a benchmark are less pertinent. Intuitions on risk-adjusted returns work even less, and in fact, they are practically non-existent outside a select professional circle. Further, competition from tax-free small savings products – usually launched by the government – makes stocks daunting for the investing public, and they simply want the former. Never a favoured investing vehicle, mutual funds have had a tough time convincing the public about the worth of equities.

Generating alpha – an excess return over the market's return – that's enough to justify the fees of active management is a tough task, and this is a worldwide problem.[52] Alpha generation in India is also difficult because the market is a narrowly defined index of 30 (or 50) stocks, disproportionately loaded in favour of high-performing sectors such as technology, pharmaceuticals, consumer goods, and private-sector banking. A narrow and loaded 50-stock bogey such as the Nifty jumps around a lot more (and especially to the upside) as compared to a well-diversified 100-stock mutual fund, and it is also more difficult to beat; in turn, a well-diversified mutual fund should provide a little more downside protection when compared to a narrow index, but telling people their portfolios have lost a little less than the market rarely works in an absolute return equity shop.

[52] The observation that mutual funds as a group underperform the market and have negligible timing skills is backed by a vast literature and substantial international evidence. For early studies, see William F. Sharpe, 'Mutual Fund Performance,' *Journal of Business*, 39, No. 1, January 1966, 119–38; Michael C. Jensen, 'The Performance of Mutual Funds in the Period 1945–1964,' *Journal of Finance*, 23, 1968; and Jack L. Treynor, 'How to Rate Management of Investment Funds,' *Harvard Business Review*, 43, 1, January–February, 1965, 63–75.

As a result, some empirical work indicates that Indian mutual funds underperform the market.[53] The underperformance is despite the fact that performance data simply does not correct for survivorship bias. With survivorship bias, funds that are poor performers exit or are merged into other funds, but the time series data do not correct for that; over time, the data only reflect the high-performing survivors, which results in positive upward biases to aggregate measurements of fund returns.[54] Yet despite this inherent upward bias to fund numbers, studies using such uncorrected time series data find underperformance.[55]

Beating the index was easier prior to 2018. Before that date, fund returns included price performance and dividends, while the index obviously moved only on price performance. Further regulations later called for comparisons with a 'total return index' that included dividends in the index calculation, which have made it tougher to beat the enhanced bogey; dividend yields for the index are usually between 1 and 1.5 per cent per annum, so moving to this framework meant funds have to generate that additional amount to beat the index in its total return format.

A 1970 BSE study found that most mutual funds of that era were dormant and passive investors.[56] Later, in the trading range markets of the 1980s and 1990s, there was a marked bias towards trading and churning of portfolios. Styles would again shift as markets started

[53] For a recent study on mutual fund underperformance, see Prateek Sharma and Samit Paul, 'Testing the Skill of Mutual Fund Managers: Evidence from India,' *Managerial Finance*, 41 (8), 2015, 806–24. The study also found no evidence of persistence in relative performance of mutual funds. For an early study that found traces of persistence, see Soumya Guha Deb, Ashok Banerjee, and B.B. Chakrabarti, 'Persistence in Performance of Indian Equity Mutual Funds: An Empirical Investigation,' *IIMB Management Review*, 20, (2), 2008, 172–87.

[54] Backtesting fund performance would mean including all funds that have exited or merged with other funds over the study period. For some of the issues involved, see M.M. Carhart, J.N. Carpenter, A.W. Lynch, and D.K. Musto, 'Mutual Fund Survivorship,' *Review of Financial Studies*, 15, (5), 2002, 1439–63. In India, most time series data did not correct for survivorship bias.

[55] Measuring fund performance in India is also confounded by issues like a high noise-to-signal ratio and the short duration of time series data. See Ajay Shah, Susan Thomas, and Michael Gorman, *India's Financial Markets: An Insider's Guide to How the Markets Work*, Noida: Elsevier, 2008, 189–90.

[56] Bombay Stock Exchange, *Profile of Stock Exchange Activity in India*, Bombay: BSE, 1970, ii, 36–37.

trending nicely in the first decades of the new millennium, and composite styles that emphasized a core portfolio holding together with a trading component would come into play. In the golden age between 2002 and early 2008, most stocks rose in the broad-based Rate Bull, and this was an ideal situation for the diversified folios most funds held; the mantra of long-term investing really worked in this advance. This was rudely interrupted by the Great Recession sell-off, though from 2010 onwards the situation repeated itself (albeit through a less broad-based advance) in the SIP Bull.

The fact is that the market keeps swinging around from time to time to oblige the funds in their dominant style of being fully invested and well-diversified. Since the turn of the millennium, the style has stayed about the same while the market has repeatedly swung around and rewarded it. When the market is in a steady uptrend that is broad-based – as it was during the Rate and SIP Bulls – it behaves in a way that syncs with the dominant style of being fully invested and well-diversified; 'sector rotation' then sets in as the fundies, better informed than other traders, exit sectors that flare up and reach peak valuations, following which they enter other sectors.[57] Core holdings usually remain unchanged, but the trading component gets churned through the 'sector rotation'.

Sometimes the world changes and the markets move in a trading range for prolonged periods, or the advance becomes less broad based; nothing really happens to overall market levels or the broader market, but the fundies are chanting the same mantra, and then they begin to look like dinosaurs. The public starts to leave and redemption pressures pile up (this happened last in the 1990s, but the market has lost its memory of that period). When the market goes up, the fundies congratulate themselves on their ability, and when the market goes down, they blame the market. Nevertheless, since they're always long

[57] Sector rotation requires persistent momentum across stocks in a sector. For evidence from US markets, see Mark M. Carhart, 'On Persistence in Mutual Fund Performance,' *Journal of Finance*, 52, 1997, 57–82. Carhart shows that momentum in a fund's underlying stocks drives persistence in mutual fund performance, with returns falling when momentum reduces in the underlying. Consequently, identifying high-performing managers on the basis of past returns is difficult.

they capture the market's upward trend over extended periods, and this remains the basic rationale for their existence.[58]

Mutual funds cannot leverage or short sell, which makes generating alpha a tricky proposition. Nevertheless, prohibiting funds from such activities – both inherently speculative in nature – is a good thing as they are investing the public's hard-earned life savings. A more relevant issue is their inability to use India's vast derivatives markets for hedging, despite being allowed to do so at least since 1999. The short tenor of derivative instruments is responsible for this; most contracts have month-long tenors, and using them implies taking a short market view. As mutual funds are always long, hedging usually means insuring against the downside through buying protective put options or short selling index futures. Since the contracts have monthly tenors, using them to hedge implies taking a view on how the market will behave over the next 22 trading sessions. This is an impossible task. One solution is to maintain the hedge by rolling over the contracts every month. But monthly rollovers (possible only with index futures anyway) benefit the brokerage industry rather than the mutual funds, for whom rollovers are a cost.

Increasing the tenor of the entire options and futures chain from 1 to 3 months would help, but the brokerage industry starts yelping if such a move is proposed; the 3-month tenors would reduce their annual commissions from 12 rollovers in a year to just 4. Faced with this two-thirds reduction in commissions on the lucrative rollover trade, the brokerage industry's time-honoured manoeuvre is to play the volume card and claim that the measure (in this case, increasing contract tenors) will lead to a decline in volumes traded. In fact, this was the same argument used when badla was repeatedly banned in the pre-reform era. (Presently, longer-dated tenors coexist with the one-month contracts, but that has not diminished the popularity of the monthly instruments. Even weekly derivatives contracts have been introduced to feed the public's speculative instincts.)

[58] Burton Malkiel, 'Reflections on the Efficient Market Hypothesis: 30 Years Later,' *Financial Review*, 40 (1), February 2005, 1–9.

So, all this means that most alpha has to come from stock picking. If funds pick well, there is no issue on how much to buy, as regulations allow up to 10 per cent of a fund's assets to be invested in a single company – twice as much as usually permitted in mature markets. This allows for concentrated folios spread over fewer stocks, and the industry has a pronounced bias towards them. Concentration allows for higher returns with corresponding risk increases, but since the market is an absolute return equity shop, there is no matching rise in risk perceptions among the public or the advisors. Further, deciding whether the enhanced performance was due to stock-picking skill – or just sexing up the portfolio by concentrating it in fewer stocks and taking on more risk – calls for a level of analytical expertise that is not exercised here, and so, the buy side gets away with it all.

Reducing folio concentrations would lead to well-diversified performance with less risk; after all, there are over 5,000 stocks to choose from, of which about half are traded daily. But the actual investible universe is always seen by the fundies as much smaller – usually between 200 and 300 stocks – and so, the ability to concentrate is important, as practically there are few stocks to choose from. Even so, two factors working against concentrated folios are market microstructure and small company size. In India's market, the absence of specialists in the microstructure makes it difficult to build the large positions with low-impact cost that are essential for running concentrated portfolios; small company size is also a binding constraint for the larger funds. Despite that, for many of the fundies, performance comes from concentration married to turnover.

And what of the fundies themselves? Many are engineer-MBAs, which is unsurprising as close to 90 per cent of students entering Indian business schools come from an engineering background.[59] A degree

[59] Sreeradha D. Basu and Devina Sengupta, 'Engineers Comprise 90% of Students at IIMs, 36% at Harvard and Wharton,' *Economic Times*, 10 September 2013.

from the Indian Institute of Technology (IIT) followed by management training at an Indian Institute of Management (IIM) is a preferred combination, though massive expansions of both franchises in recent years make the older institutes among them more sought after. Their basic training is usually tough and rigorous, but it is in the technology-intensive field of applied natural sciences like engineering, with little of the leavening effect that comes from broad exposure to the social sciences and humanities. A hodgepodge transition to one part of the social sciences – business studies – is then made in business school. They bring a certain technical approach to the markets. As a result, broader judgment about people, materials, machines, and money needed for success in the equity markets comes from experience and subsequent reading, rather than formal academic training. Many gravitate naturally towards the firm-level intricacies of stock picking, approaching it in the structured way a horologer might open up a clock and peer at what's inside to find out how all the movements work together.

The other type represented is the chartered accountant, with his nattering knowledge of rules and regulations; though the accountant's background is not highly regarded for fund management in most parts of the world, in India it is deemed appropriate because of the hideous complexity and dirigiste orientation of the regulatory environment. One would be hard pressed to find a fundie who did not share either of these two backgrounds. Among them it would be difficult to find someone with the background of a Templeton with his formal training in history and religion, or a Soros, the self-described 'failed philosopher'. Notable also was the contrast between them and the man they strove to emulate – Graham, *bon vivant* and student of the classics.

Many start out doing equity research before making the leap to fund management; worldwide, this is a traditional career path and India is no exception to this. The grounding in research is a sort of boot camp that enables them to grasp the technicalities of valuation and company-level analysis. More critically, if there are bloopers – and this is a business of gaffes and bloopers – the consequences are limited to producing a wrong report. As analysts, there are no buy-sell decisions –

that all-important pulling of the trigger – which is the only thing that matters.

Analysts know a lot about one thing – their particular industry of chemicals or pharma or airlines – but the fund manager has to know a little about many things. The distinction is similar to what Sir Isaiah Berlin brought out in his essay *The Hedgehog and the Fox*. Some minds – the hedgehogs – tend to know a lot about one big thing and see much of the world through that single idea; other minds – the foxes – are more pluralistic and know a little about many things. The analyst has to be a hedgehog who knows a lot about his industry, and the better ones graduate to being fund managers – or foxes – who know a little about lots of industries and promoters. This is a big leap. The analysts are like the cymbalist or violinist in an ensemble, but the fund managers have to be Zubin Mehta and know how the components of an orchestra – or portfolio – can play together and produce a good result.

The ability to strategize about the economy and markets, to internalize the dynamics of sectors and their peculiarities (or cycles), and to know about an array of companies and their promoters, together with the flair to select stocks after analysis and valuation, distinguishes those who make the leap from analysts to fund managers. All that combines with intellectual curiosity about how things work, and to this must be added emotional discipline and the ability to let go, to 'operate without anxiety', as Adam Smith put it in *The Money Game*.

Fundies tend to be the regular upper middle-class types those scheming aunties in Vikram Seth's *A Suitable Boy* went looking for when they wanted to get their daughters married off.[60] Innately conservative by nature, they are also bound by the 'prudent man' rule, and speculation or trading is not for the prudent man. None of them are gunslingers, and one would be hard pressed to find a Gerry Tsai among them.[61] Fundies are like cricketers because they work in a field which is highly

[60] 'But perhaps because the country is so prone to major upheavals – both social and economic – those who achieve long-lasting success in India are often those who are unflashy, introverted, determined and intelligently tenacious.' This low-profile self-image is from Saurabh Mukherjea, *Gurus of Chaos* 286–87.

[61] Gerald Tsai Jr. was an early pioneer of momentum investing.

measurable. Being evaluated all the time does have some advantages as it allows them to tom-tom successful performance, which happens naturally when markets are up. The constant evaluation also has downsides, as most prefer to err and make mistakes as a group – far better for worldly reputation, as Keynes once said, to fail conventionally than to succeed unconventionally. Except that the true test of handling money is always the record of achievement and not the opinion of the respectable.[62] Like cricketers, they find it difficult to have a good time in public, for if they did have a good time followed by a bad patch, the howling mob would say the later bad patch was because of the previous good time that was had. This was a society where the many have-nots never lost the chance to scoff at the slip-ups of the few haves.

Most fundies buy stocks after some sort of fundamental analysis has shown they are cheap, and as seen, buying growth at a reasonable price is a pervasive approach. The purists among them condemn technical analysis, while the wise ones keep it in mind as another factor in their decision set. Most are not timers as the product does not allow them that luxury; even if they did try to time the market, the record, in keeping with their peers worldwide, would be uneven.[63] As they operate within a limited universe of about 300 stocks, they often buy the same stocks but usually in different proportions. As a result, they either tend to cluster around the same performance levels or deviate randomly from those performance levels based on the differing proportions or chance. In turn, the public wants to buy funds that have gone up the most in the

[62] 'We recognize the risks of unconventional investing, but the true test of performance in the handling of money is the record of achievement, not the opinion of the respectable.' The Ford Foundation, *Annual Report 1966*, 7, from The Ford Foundation website, accessed 15 October 2018. In that era, trustees of American university endowments saw themselves as bound by the 'prudent man' rule that applied to personal trustees, and simply did not allocate capital to equities. McGeorge Bundy's urging in his President's Review was aimed at getting endowment managers to escape these self-imposed restrictions and allocate more to stocks. The exhortation was sound but the timing unfortunate, coming as it did well into Wall Street's 'Go Go' market of the 60s. The comment is sometimes used to emphasize that in money management, conventional approaches often produce conventional results, or alternately, to point out the dangers of herding.

[63] Joyjit Dhar and Kumarjit Mandal, 'Market Timing Abilities of Indian Mutual Fund Managers: An Empirical Analysis,' *Decision* 41(3), 2014, 299–311.

recent past, though if you believe in mean reversion that is the opposite of what you should be doing.[64] Many investors and their advisors also search for consistency in fund performance, despite the inherent contradiction between that search and the mandatory statement in all fund advertising that 'Past performance is no indicator of future returns'.

Successful fundies reportedly have the ability to mingle with those holding a contrary opinion on a stock, which allows them to extract views that can be balanced against the fundies' own bullishness.[65] Masters of the detailed firm-level analysis required for valuation and stock picking, most fundies are less certain when it comes to macroeconomics, perhaps because many completed their professional training at a time when India was a closed economy. Yet given the tenuous connection between macros and the market, this is not a bad thing. Further, most have no international experience, which also does not matter because the industry's structure and incentives ensure that negligible sums are deployed globally. But the lack of international experience accounts for their wild comments on the global side. A default view is that there are few countries which offer India's prospects and that every entity *has* to be in India, because 'that's where the growth' is.

And yet for a fundie with the skills and some luck, India is the place to be for active fund management. The country has just the right amount of market inefficiency, confounding noise, technical traders, and market breadth, all of which act as catalysts for the dominant approach of stock picking.

[64] 'Immediate past performance is critical, as it controls how much comes into a fund for the next 1 or 2 years.' Alroy Lobo, interview in Saurabh Mukherjea, *Gurus of Chaos*, 68. Like a rubber band that snaps back, mean reversion assumes that financial assets return to long-term averages after diverging substantially from them.

[65] Ibid., 124.

19

THINGS ARE NOT WHAT THEY WERE

The Brokerage Industry and the Primary Side

Before the mutual funds and FIIs and before the exchanges themselves, there were the brokers. Starting from about the 1830s, the brokers had gathered on the Bombay Green in front of Town Hall, following which they moved around in the Fort area before finally settling down on Dalal (or Broker's) Street. In 1875, they organized themselves as the Native Share and Stock Brokers' Association, and from that date they ran the stock market. With the passage of the Constitution in 1950, stock markets were put on the Union (as opposed to the State or Concurrent) list, which formally ended broker control of the market and brought the central government into the picture.

This change, while far-reaching in theory, had little practical effect, and the finance ministries of Nehruvian India were happy to leave undisturbed an activity they little understood. Nevertheless, by the 1990s, the brokers' inability to manage their own affairs – together with the contradictions and agency problems inherent in running a market while being a market intermediary – led to periodic clashes with the government over the market's microstructure, which, in turn, afforded the NSE a one-time opportunity to intervene and change the stock market in doing so. When this happened, the brokers' centrality to the market's story was ended, and in that sense, an era had passed.

Yet the historic heart of the stock market, '*share bajhar*' as it is still known, remains the Fort area around the BSE building of Phiroze Jeejeebhoy Towers, and many intermediaries still retain busy establishments there. The building itself is a rabbit warren of offices, many with an average size of less than 350 square feet or thereabouts; occasionally, an enterprising denizen has bought the coop next door and joined two offices to make a slightly larger place. In the main building, the offices are laid out in circles surrounding a central stairwell, while an adjacent rotunda houses what was once the physical trading floor. The BSE building – unlike the NSE's – is shared by the exchange's management and its brokers, a legacy of the days before demutualization and the separation of brokers from management. The brokers occupy their cubby holes on the lower floors, while the management takes up the higher floors, almost signifying ascendancy to the top of the greasy pole. The ring where the brokers gathered and did their trading through open outcry is now a vast amphitheatre that is rented out for important functions that often feature world leaders. The harbour view from the top floors is spectacular, but the overall impression is of a maze of cramped offices overflowing with people, paper, and computers, an overflow that is a metaphor for the state of the brokerage industry.

Traditionally, the brokerage industry was fragmented, over-brokered, undercapitalized, and dominated by small family-owned firms from communities that had a long presence in the markets. Broker numbers had increased over the market's first century, but since this was the Municipal Era, numbers have to be collated at the local level. K.R.P. Shroff records the Bombay brokers at 333 in 1896 and at 478 in 1920.[1]

[1] K.R.P. Shroff, *History and Present Position of the Stock Market in India*, Bombay: The Stock Exchange, Bombay, 1962, 6.

By 1960, Bombay had 504 brokers while Calcutta and Ahmedabad had 620 and 461 brokers each, leading to over 1,500 brokers on an all-India level at the major exchanges.[2] For much of the Century of Marking Time, institutional entry was opposed by the exchange as a matter of policy. As a result, most brokerages were sole proprietorships or partnerships, but the resulting unlimited liability that should have provided a useful discipline to risk-taking was often diluted by the practice of petitioning exchange authorities for 'relief'. It was only from July 1987 that corporates were allowed as members – with the proviso that a majority of their directors had to be members in their individual capacity. Naturally, this did not change things much, till in November 1992 an amendment removed that proviso and corporates were allowed as members without any such conditionality.

The spread of regional exchanges and the NSE's foundation led to a significant increase in the number of brokers. Thirteen regionals had been established in the decade prior to 1991, and the resulting increase in broker numbers was captured by SEBI's all-India figures for the first time. The NSE's foundation increased industry capacity, but this event that changed so much else in the equity markets had little effect on industry structure in the early years. Perhaps this is because the NSE's initial strategy was predicated on getting the same lot to trade on its platform, and it was only in later years that new firms entered the industry, which effectively ended the BSE's monopoly on broking and raised competitive intensity.

The entry of foreign brokers from the early 1990s also had an impact on the institutional side; foreign brokers usually refused to deal with retail segments and preferred to focus on the high-volume institutional business, which allowed domestic brokers to keep their retail clientele. As a result of all this, in 2013, there were over 10,000 brokers, a number that had remained stable for some years.[3] Yet by 2018, the number of

[2] Ibid., 8, 10.

[3] Brokers in the cash market peaked at 10,128 in 2013, while the low for the 10-year period prior to that date was 8,652 brokers in 2009. The number is arrived at by simply totalling the broker membership at relevant exchanges, and so, it includes the same intermediaries who may be members of multiple

brokers had fallen drastically to about 3,000.[4] This extraordinary drop of almost 70 per cent was far more than the normal industry winnowing that took place after bear markets, and in fact, the drop had taken place during a prolonged upswing.

The demise of regional exchanges offers one explanation for this state of affairs, as the 10,000-figure had been inflated by brokers who traded on the regionals. By 2015, many of the regionals had been wound up for not meeting SEBI's net worth and turnover criteria. Regionals such as Magadh, Pune, Madras, and Hyderabad ceased business in this period. With the regionals' end, inter-exchange arbitrage and the book rollover between exchanges also came to an end, which further reduced broker presence.

Nevertheless, besides the regionals, other factors were responsible for the industry shakeout, and chief among these was a dip in the commission pool. The annual commission pool – the industry's top line or its total sales – had risen steadily during the reform era to a high of about ₹14,000 crores in 2007, before falling to about ₹8,000 crores in 2013. During this period at least, all the talk of India Shining that the brokerage industry put out in its reports wasn't coming through in its own numbers.[5]

---

exchanges; actual numbers are therefore lower. Most derivatives segment brokers would also have cash market registrations. All data are for fiscal year endings, i.e., as of 31 March of the corresponding year. 'Handbook of Statistics of Indian Security Market 2013,' *SEBI*, https://www.sebi.gov.in/reports/handbook-of-statistics/jul-2014/handbook-of-statistics-on-indian-securities-market-2013_27253.html.

[4] BSE brokers 1,354; NSE brokers 1,318; and MSEI brokers at 429. Securities and Exchange Board of India (SEBI), *Annual Report for the Fiscal Year 2017–2018*, Mumbai: SEBI, 2018, 102. A third national-level exchange, the Metropolitan Stock Exchange of India (MSEI) is a recent initiative of public and private sector banks, together with domestic institutional investors.

[5] The shakeout also impacted the sub-broker network that many wire houses had built up and maintained. See Nitin Shrivastava, '13,000 Sub-brokers Have Shut Shop in Last Six Months,' *DNA India*, 1 November 2013. Sub-brokers had risen from 13,684 in 2005 to 83,952 in 2011, before falling to 25,642 in 2017. Sub-brokers were an important link for many retail investors, especially those who were not tech-savvy. Since only a principal broker could issue a contract note, sub-brokers issued *katcha* (informal) receipts which had no legal validity and sometimes led to malpractices. For an early account of sub-brokers, see Securities and Exchange Board of India (SEBI), *Report on the Working Group on Recognition and Regulation of Sub Brokers*, Mumbai: SEBI, 1989. By 2018, SEBI would ban them as market intermediaries and make them change status to 'authorized persons' or trading members.

But the brokerage commission pool's 2007 Rate Bull high of ₹14,000 crores was reached again in 2017 and exceeded by 2020, when it crossed ₹20,000 crores. Much of this was driven by massive volume increases from the cyclical upsurge of the SIP Bull market.[6] In fact, these volume increases were quite staggering. The average daily turnover of India's stock markets was approaching ₹7,00,000 crores ($110 billion) in FY 2018, led in large part by a highly active derivatives segment.[7] By 2020, this daily turnover number had doubled again to over ₹14 lakh crores ($197 billion), and as a result of this cyclical up move, the commission pool surpassed its previous high.[8] Both cyclical and structural forces were at work behind these numbers. The violently cyclical nature of the industry – it simply did better in bull markets than in bear markets because of the natural desire of the public to be long – continued to hide deep structural changes.

This intermingling of structural and cyclical change, against the backdrop of technical transformation caused by online trading and back-office digitization, is the brokerage industry's dominant theme in the modern era. The changes would have mixed effects on the industry's top line and its cost structure.

On the revenue side, chief among these structural changes was the public's shift to the derivatives market in futures and options. Cash market trading, which gave high yields to brokerages, faced severe competition for volumes from the very low-yield derivatives market. Most of the active public had given up any pretence at trading or investing

[6] ICRA Research Services, 'Indian Brokerage Industry, Mumbai: ICRA, September 2017, 4–5.

[7] In FY 2018, the average daily turnover (ADTO) of the derivatives segment, by now dominated by the NSE, was ₹6,71,000 crores. The ADTO of the cash segment was ₹33,000 crores, leading to a combined ADTO of ₹7,04,753 crores. SEBI, *Annual Report 2017–2018*, 58.

[8] In FY 2020, the ADTO of the derivatives segment was ₹14,00,000 crores. The ADTO of the cash segment was ₹39,000 crores, leading to a combined ADTO of ₹14,39,000 crores ($197 billion). ICRA Ltd, 'Indian Brokerage Industry on a Roll Despite Challenges; Expected Revenue Growth in FY2021 at 10–12%,' *ICRA Press Release*, 23 September 2020.

in the high-yielding cash markets and were enamoured of one-month derivatives, i.e., futures and options on stocks or indexes. As a result, as much as 95 per cent of the Indian market's average daily turnover (ADTO) figures came from the NSE-dominated derivatives segment (a quirk in options volume computation exaggerates the impact of derivatives on daily volumes, but the effect is still substantial).[9] Because of this structural shift, net yields – or the brokerage top line derived from orders on cash and derivatives markets – had fallen from 50 basis points (half a percentage point) to as low as 10 basis points in recent years.[10] Industry talk was that this could fall even further to five basis points.

The impact of a violently fluctuating top line was further enhanced by its narrow distribution – the top 100 brokers accounted for over 80 per cent of volumes.[11] Some reports indicated that the top 25 brokers accounted for about half of market turnover, of which a major portion was from proprietary trading; in all probability, much of that proprietary book was itself from high-frequency algorithmic volumes. This narrow distribution of the commission pool left little for the myriad smaller players in the industry.

Structural changes were also taking place on the cost side – particularly with salaries, rentals, technology, and compliance – which, in turn, influenced the industry's bottom-line profits. Salaries had gone up with inflation (often as much as 8 to 10 per cent annually), though in recent years this was allayed by digitization. Much of the industry was concentrated in Mumbai, which had the most expensive real estate in the country, and this raised rental costs; many of the big players who enjoyed the prestige of a South Mumbai address had moved to the

[9] Over 80 per cent of derivatives volumes came from options, rather than futures. More technically, deep out-of-the-money options that the public traded heavily were accounted for at face value in the volume calculations, but the actual premium needed to trade them was negligible. For example, with the Nifty index at 10,500, a deep out-of-the-money Nifty call option with a strike price of 11,000 and a lot size of 75 would count as ₹8,25,000 (11,000 times 75) in the volume figure, but the actual money (or premium) needed to trade it could be as low as ₹4 or 5; the effect got exaggerated as the market moved closer to expiry on the last Thursday of every month.

[10] Pravin Palande, 'Why Indian Brokerages are Looking Elsewhere,' *Forbes*, 9 May 2013.

[11] SEBI, *Annual Report 2017–2018*, 54.

suburbs as the industry's economics simply did not allow leeway on rentals. Technology was another component of the cost structure that had risen in recent years; technology never sits still in the markets, and the move to online trading, digitization, and the investments required for algorithmic trading (among the more ambitious, at least) all involved outlays.[12] Technology and systems costs were an issue for the larger established firms rather than the smaller family-owned ones.

But a significant increase in the cost structure came from compliance, though its pinch would be hidden in the SIP Bull's later years by huge surges in the commission pool. A consequence of a regulatory authority running amok and the natural Indian tendency to complicate things that did not need to be complicated, compliance costs, by some reckonings, had doubled in recent years and accounted for a fifth or more of the cost structure, with a disproportionate burden on the smaller firms.[13] At one time, it took almost 75 signatures to open a 3-in-1 account with a power of attorney that allowed a broker to handle a discretionary account, and some regulations even dealt with the number of centres required for receiving IPO applications.[14] There were over 100 million demat accounts in India, so if SEBI decreed that a certain document was mandatory, efforts had to be made to secure that document for those 100 million accounts; despite the digital initiatives, that often meant large amounts of additional paper in the system. Every requirement casually put in place by a clueless bureaucrat meant that considerable effort went into meeting the requirement.[15]

[12] There was less pressure to invest in high-frequency trading (HFT) because SEBI tended to frown on the activity. See Palak Shah, 'SEBI Wants Bourses to Provide a Level Playing Field for HFT Traders,' *Economic Times,* 11 April 2014. As a result, HFT accounted for a smaller share of market activity in India. See Biswajit Baruah, 'High Frequency Trades Form Just One-third of Total Volumes in India,' *Economic Times,* 11 April 2014.

[13] Sneha Padiyath, 'Retail Broker Count Shrinks Further,' *Business Standard,* 2 June 2015.

[14] See G. Sabarinathan, 'SEBI's Regulation of the Indian Securities Market: A Critical Review of the Major Developments,' *Vikalpa,* 35, 4, October–December 2010, 15.

[15] Taxes and Transaction Costs, together with Exchange Regulations and Competition, were listed as the biggest reasons for business declines. Securities and Exchange Board of India, *SEBI Investor Survey 2015,* Mumbai: SEBI, 2016, 128–29. This is the first survey to include intermediaries among respondents.

Basically, India's entire digital ecosystem leaked like a sieve, providing multiple opportunities to fraudsters and other criminals. In response, regulators kept fiddling with regulations to ensure banks and brokerages stayed a step ahead of the criminals, which only added to the compliance burden for all and resulted in 'death by compliance'. A small army of clerks and back-office people was required to handle the work generated by compliance or Know Your Customer (KYC) norms, and that army's crucial job was keeping 'death by compliance' at bay.[16] In later years, an entire new industry would spring up to accommodate and electronically handle compliance paperwork; these were the eKYC firms, and they would later be thrown into a tizzy when Supreme Court judgments pronounced on what could or couldn't be used for KYC norms.[17] Attempts to centralize the KYC norms in a central registry – a bureaucratic response to a bureaucratic stimulus – were ongoing.[18] India remains one of the few countries in the world where these KYC registries actually figure in a list of the microstructure's components, sharing space with traditional intermediaries such as stock exchanges and depositaries.[19]

This interplay between digitization and 'death by compliance' would come to define brokerage back offices and lead to a peculiar dynamic where digitization helped but also hurt – some measures such as Aadhaar-driven onboarding mitigated the compliance burden, while other measures increased it. At one recent conference, a well-meaning question raised the possibility of terrorist funds entering the stock market. There was little need to be alarmed, for the average terrorist would have been terrorized by the compliance norms of the Indian stock market.

[16] For an early listing of a typical brokerage's compliance requirements, see Bandi Ram Prasad, 'The Securities Industry,' *Capital Markets in India*, ed. Rajesh Chakrabarti and Sankar De, New Delhi: Sage Publications, 2010, 328–30.

[17] A 2018 Supreme Court judgment would uphold the constitutional validity of Aadhar – a unique ID number – but ban private entities from using it for eKYC norms. This would later change.

[18] Devendra Raghav, 'Is the Central KYC Registry a Boon for the Finance Sector,' *Economic Times*, 17 February 2016.

[19] SEBI, *Annual Report 2017–2018*, 85.

Traditionally, for the big wire houses at least, the front office's job was to buy low and sell high, while the back office's job was to collect early and pay late.[20] The front office did its job through its main arms of business development, equity research, and trade execution. Business development got the customer into the door, equity research supplied the customer with trading ideas, and these were executed by the trading desks for the all-important brokerage. But the real action was in the back office, regarded as less glamorous than the customer-facing front office but nevertheless important. The back office ensured that the firm collected early from the customer and paid late to the exchange's clearing house. This became a crucial task over the years because of the high cost of capital and the market's move to progressively tighter settlement norms – the leisurely settlement norms of a previous era had got compressed to T+2 settlements by 2003, and the full impact of meeting this tight settlement cycle through a ponderous and unwieldy banking system fell on the back office. The back office's main areas were operations, risk management, and compliance. Operations saw to it that the whole gamut of clearing and settlement obligations between customer, broker, and clearing house was met, risk management made sure everybody stayed within margin requirements and didn't blow up, and compliance ensured that the whole shebang met SEBI's ever-shifting and often incoherent guidelines.[21]

The big wire houses such as Motilal Oswal or Sharekhan had a better time of it than the smaller firms, as scale economies allowed

[20] A list of the larger domestic wire houses would include: Angel Broking, Bonanza Portfolio, Edelweiss Financial Services, Emkay Global Financial Services, Geojit BNP Paribas, Groww, HDFC Securities, ICICI Securities, Indiabulls Securities, India Infoline, JM Financial, Karvy Stock Broking, Kotak Securities, Motilal Oswal Financial Services, Religare, Sharekhan Securities, and Zerodha. In recent years, this list kept changing as firms entered or dropped out. Foreign brokerages active in India include Credit Suisse, Macquarie Securities, Morgan Stanley, and CLSA.

[21] For a detailed outline of clearing and settlement procedures through a 3-in-1 account at the broker level, see ICICI Securities, 'Frequently Asked Questions,' *ICICI Direct*, accessed 1 November 2018, https://www.icicidirect.com/indexfaq.asp.

them to hire large departments staffed with experts in areas such as information technology and compliance.[22] For the larger firms, extensive distribution networks usually built up as franchise models also gave them the opportunity to cross-sell financial products.[23] The large firms also had to compete with the foreign brokerages for the lucrative FII business. Most FIIs preferred dealing with foreign brokerages, either because of technology access or alignments with global relationships; covering counterparty risk was also easier for foreign brokerages with their global networks. As a result, the foreign brokerages had taken over a big portion of the institutional market, while domestic brokers tended to focus on the retail segment.[24]

The small family-owned brokers simply made do with less overhead; most never had a website and kept costs down by hiring low-skilled labour instead of the more expensive MBA types who worked for the big firms. The small firms also did little business development or equity research, but they had the dividend cushion of the *sethiya*'s (owner's) portfolio to fall back on when times got tough. There was also the option of being empanelled with LIC and subsisting on that behemoth's order flow; LIC was happy to split its orders among myriad small firms to keep the market guessing about its moves. Over the years, some of the smaller brokers had spread their wings and escaped from the rabbit warren, but most lacked ambition or capital to do anything other than what they had been doing all along.

Small brokerages rarely made a distinction between the firm's and the *sethiya*'s personal expenses; as a form of tax planning, all the owner's personal expenses were put on the firm's books to reduce taxes. If there were profits during a bull phase, losses were 'bought' from the market

[22] Large brokers, now called Qualified Stock Brokers, were recently subjected to ever more elaborate compliance requirements. This prompted some to avoid the QSB classification altogether simply to reduce further compliance; rather than deal with the additional compliance, some chose to cap their ambitions and deliberately stay out of the big league.

[23] Motilal Oswal Financial Services Ltd. (MOFSL), *Annual Report* 2008–2009, Mumbai: MOFSL, 2009, 13, 45. Cross-selling is a recurrent theme in the annual reports of some brokerages.

[24] Ashley Coutinho, 'Can Foreign Brokerages Crack the Retail Code?' *Business Standard*, 18 August 2015.

to cover up those profits and lower taxes even further. Systematically doing the above for years violated accounting's 'business entity' concept and distorted the firm's financial statements to the point where they did not make much sense. As a result, it was difficult to ascertain the exact profits many small brokerages made, but that didn't matter, as much of the firm's income came from dividends on the *sethiya*'s portfolio. No bank would accept such distorted statements for credit appraisal on a loan, but that also never mattered, as any borrowing was collateralized through stocks pledged from the *sethiya*'s portfolio. None of this meant much to the customer either, though it was in the customer's interest to deal with a financially stable broker; the exchange's trade guarantee fund and the clearing house's practice of novation made broker stability less of an issue in the modern era. For small brokers, risk management did not exist and was not even seen as necessary, as most clients came with personal relationships behind them.

Escaping the rabbit warren was also difficult because of principal–agent problems in the brokerage industry. The problem deals with how a customer (the principal) can get a broker (the agent) to act in the customer's interest, rather than in the broker's own interest. Also called 'conflict of interest issues' in India, they were rampant in the country and particularly among smaller brokers. A common manifestation was front running – the broker's tendency to buy ahead of the customer who was accumulating a position, which raised the price on the customer; front running has reduced with direct market access and better surveillance, but it is still prevalent among smaller players. Principal–agent problems also arose when a broker fell in love with his own picks and loaded up on them before recommending them to a client; perhaps there were many better stocks out there in India's large universe, but the consideration set had already been narrowed to the *sethiya*'s choice.

Finally, brokers themselves could be both principals *and* agents. Many small brokers made no distinction between proprietary trading (as principals for themselves) and their brokerage business (as agents for clients), and this had been an issue from Premchand Roychand's era. Proprietary trading imposed the biggest agency costs on brokers.

Trading proprietary books was a strenuous task in the volatile Indian environment that, once embarked on, distracted brokers from their agency functions; consequently, most of their energy went into trading their own portfolios, rather than working for their clients. Many small brokers concentrated on their principal proprietary books while neglecting their agency functions, and as a result, most stayed small and in the rabbit warren.[25]

Brokers never got rewarded when they made a good recommendation and never got punished when they made a bad recommendation. The broker made a commission irrespective of whether the client turned a profit, and commissions were directly tied to how actively clients traded; as a result, the broker's real motivation was to keep the client's inventory of stocks moving. Consequently, folio churning was the usual strategy brokers recommended to their clients.

The volatile top line and cost structure changes from salaries, rentals, technology, and compliance had led to fluctuating bottom lines for many in the industry. The listed wire houses had seen their stock prices fall as much as 80 per cent between 2007 and 2014, before recovering in the SIP-led bull market of recent years. Many had diversified and morphed into NBFCs (non-banking financial companies) with a focus on mid-market finance, and typically only half (or less) of their top line now came from their core business of brokerage.[26] The wire houses had found new avatars for themselves in other businesses including financial distribution, housing finance, wealth management, or margin-based lending, and much of the recovery in their share prices in recent years was due to successful diversification into these areas. Most of these businesses had annuity-based income streams that were stable, as compared to fee-based income streams such as brokerage commissions that depended on market conditions. Many of these businesses also received a welcome boost from the government's quixotic move to

[25] Shailesh Menon, 'Why Brokerages Prefer Proprietary Trading over Winning New Clients,' *Economic Times*, 28 May 2015.

[26] Pravin Palande, 'Why Indian Brokerages are Looking Elsewhere.'

demonetize most currency notes in 2016; this moved capital into formal channels and benefited some of the mid-market businesses the brokerages had diversified into. A further boost came from the 2020 coronavirus pandemic, which decimated the wider economy but helped the brokerage industry – locked down at home, large swathes of the public found their thoughts turn lightly to a market surging on liquidity infusions from Western quantitative easing (QE), and retail volumes took off.

All this was on the secondary side of the business – the trading in seasoned issues that dominates media coverage and that comes to mind when people think about a stock market. Yet a basic function of a stock market – conducted through the sell-side brokerages under their moniker as investment bankers – is raising risk capital by selling stock of newly listed enterprises through initial public offerings (IPOs) in the primary market.[27]

Primary markets have a long history in India and go back to the early nineteenth century, with much activity in Calcutta and Bombay. India's primary market started in Calcutta, and a burst of joint-stock company formation took place in early nineteenth-century Bengal, just prior to the advent of a British managing agency system that came with its own bias towards extractive industries that shipped commodities to England. In this era, social and commercial intercourse between Europeans and Indians took place on terms more familiar than would be possible in later years, and shareholder meetings from the 1830s and 1840s bear witness to that. Some of these early meetings – filled as they are with the warp and weft of some Western shareholder events such as

[27] Presently, IPO issuance is regulated substantially through the SEBI (Issue of Capital and Disclosure Requirements) Regulations of 2009, with other requirements in the Securities Contracts (Regulation) Act of 1956 and the Companies Act of 2013. Further regulations on disclosures are outlined in the SEBI (Listing Obligations and Disclosure Requirements) Regulations of 2015.

proxy fights, hostile bids, and shareholder revolts – make today's annual general meetings seem like tame affairs.[28]

As seen earlier, the foundational event of India's primary market was the Union Bank issue of 1829, floated by Dwarkanath Tagore and other merchants for ₹50 lakhs, issued as 2,000 shares of ₹2,500 each. The bank was started to provide factoring, bill discounting, and working capital finance for the indigo trade in Bengal.[29] Other enterprises Tagore financed through equity issuance included Calcutta Steam Tug Association, Bengal Salt Company, Steam Ferry Bridge Company, Bengal Tea Association, and the India General Steam Navigation Company.[30] Much of this activity took place despite the absence of the key enabling provision that allowed for company formation – limited liability.[31]

Other than this occasional issuance focused on Bombay and Calcutta, there was no organized IPO market in the colonial era. IPO listings in the early years did not even need the exchange's permission, and it was only from 5 November 1915, at Jamnadas Morarjee's suggestion, that the Bombay exchange's permission was required for a new issue listing.[32] In fact, the founding documents and by-laws of the Bombay exchange dealt exclusively with secondary operations, and as a result, the various commissions that looked into the stock market also chose to focus only on secondary activity. Some issuance took place through the managing agency system, but there were no procedures or regulations for primary activity; procedures that did exist applied only to seasoned companies – listed companies that were issuing follow-on equity or executing rights

[28] For records of an early shareholding meeting that raised subscriptions, see 'Calcutta Courier, 17 January 1837,' *Calcutta Monthly Journal-Asiatic News* Vol. XXVI January 1837, 37.

[29] Blair B. Kling, *Partner in Empire: Dwarkanath Tagore and the Age of Enterprise in Eastern India*, Berkeley: University of California Press, 1976, 198–229.

[30] Ibid., 122–55.

[31] For the consequences of unlimited liability on the Union Bank IPO, see Blair B. Kling, *Partner in Empire,* 219–24.

[32] Seth Jamnadas Morarjee J.P., 'The Native Share and Stock Brokers' Association: Origin and Growth of the Bombay Stock Exchange,' *Federal Observer*, Stock Exchange Special Number, Vol. 1, Nos. 36 and 37, 10 November 1940, 13.

issues. Listing requirements were used as prerequisites for admission to the exchange, but here too, it was only the Bombay exchange that had formal listing guidelines. These listing guidelines indirectly influenced primary procedures, but there was no real jurisdiction over the primary market, which existed in an informal fashion.[33]

Consequently, brokers informally doubled as investment bankers to carry out stock issuance and were the main agents who raised risk capital in an age without a private equity industry. Even the Thomas report of 1948 – which was otherwise critical of secondary market practices – noted this important role played by brokers as the only sources of risk capital in the informal primary markets of that time.[34] This situation would continue into the Independence era, and the Controller of Capital Issues (CCI) would formalize the primary market in 1947 but only to control it. So, till the mid-1980s, the overall impression was of occasional new issue activity confined mainly to Bombay and Calcutta.

Besides this occasional activity in the two cities, it is the waves of new issuance that are of historical interest. The IPO market has gone through five waves since the markets were founded in the early nineteenth century, with two waves recorded in the pre-Independence era and three distinct waves of new issue activity since 1947.[35] In the pre-Independence era, the primary market went through two notable waves during the World Wars and their immediate aftermath.

The first IPO wave lasted from about 1915 to 1920, and the second IPO wave occurred between 1943 and 1946;[36] as late as the mid-1970s, H.T. Parekh, HDFC founder and a seasoned market observer, would claim that he had still not seen the same mania as exhibited in the second wave that coincided with the Second World War.[37] In

[33] P.J. Thomas, *Report on the Regulation of the Stock Market in India*, New Delhi: Ministry of Finance, 1948, 40.

[34] Ibid., 75.

[35] The secondary markets that made the first two IPO waves possible are discussed in a later chapter on Highs and Lows. Secondary markets during the remaining waves are covered in Part One.

[36] K.R.P. Shroff, *History and Present Position*, 13, 26–27.

[37] H.T. Parekh, 'Indian Capital Market-Past, Present and Future,' *A.D. Shroff Memorial Lecture*, Bombay: AD Shroff Memorial Trust, 1975, 10.

both cases, initial uncertainty caused by the outbreak of hostilities gave way to boom conditions as local manufacturers took up the slack that followed disrupted imports.[38] Wartime price controls on essential commodities also diverted speculative capital from those markets into the stock market, and the violent up moves that resulted led to frenzied new issue activity in the final stages. There is little record of significant activity outside these boom phases, which is in keeping with lore that talks of primary issuance happening in distinct waves.[39] In India, it was always market conditions through these distinct waves – and not a firm's stage in its life cycle – that dictated the firm's capital-raising efforts, and this tendency manifested from the early years. Like most other activity in that era, companies legitimate and less than legitimate raised capital; the latter were described as 'mushroom companies' that sprouted up like mushrooms, realized the subscription, and 'upped and awayed'.

Here too are recorded, for the first time, patterns of activity that would dominate the primary market for generations and that continue into the present day. Noted figures would be appointed to corporate boards to reassure the public, following which there was self-allotment of watered stock to promoters and their family or friends. Then, supply of stock offered at the IPO was deliberately restricted to whet the public's appetite for the issue. All this was a prelude to the most crucial step of all: the creation and stimulation of the kerb (or street) market. As the name suggested, the kerb market was the informal market that sprang up on the street outside the exchange; for years, it functioned in a sort of vacuum, tolerated because it was just how things were done in that era.[40] Kerb market stimulation generated a substantial premium over the issue price, and this brought the public in droves into the issue itself. The small issue size and restricted paper supply, together with the kerb premium, led the public to apply for large amounts of stock in anticipation of small percentage allotments. In fact, for some among

[38] Sir Wilfrid Atlay, *Report of the Bombay Stock Exchange Enquiry Committee*, Bombay: Government Central Press, 1924, 21.

[39] K.R.P. Shroff, *History and Present Position*, 11–14, 23–27.

[40] P.J. Thomas, *Report on the Regulation*, 6–8, 75–77, 136.

the public, the mental accounting of the large amount applied for times the premium on the kerb was the notional profit, and the lure of these notional profits proved fatally irresistible.[41] Sections of the promoter group (and some initial allottees) would then sell into the kerb market and collapse the premium, while simultaneously making allotments to the public, who were now effectively locked in and waiting expectantly during the long period – usually two to three months – that lapsed between allotments and actual listing.

The public would then try to flip the allotted stock at the actual listing, but after all this manipulation, the post-listing performances were often dismal, as most of the fireworks had already taken place on the kerb. Stags among the public who bought into IPOs, hoping to flip at the listing, were at a disadvantage compared to insiders.

The kerb market would lose its prominence in later years and then disappear, though rumours of kerb markets – or 'grey markets' as they were later called – for issues such as Reliance Power would persist.[42] In fact, internet searches suggest that the IPO grey market is the one component of the kerb that has survived well into the modern era, and the extent to which the above practices continue in today's grey market remains an interesting question.

Much of this primary activity was handled by what P.J. Thomas called independent firms, and they were the precursors to investment banks.[43] Independent firms were usually located in Bombay and Calcutta, and the second IPO wave saw a surge in their activities, particularly in Calcutta. They existed in that nebulous area between the kerb and the regular market and were managing agencies, NBFCs, brokers, arbitrageurs, and OTC market makers all rolled into one. Independents also played key roles in the primary market, and on occasion, their services were utilized by exchange members who wanted to disguise stock cornering and

[41] K.R.P. Shroff, *History and Present Position of the Stock Market*, 43.

[42] Contrary to popular belief, IPO 'grey market' contracts were not illegal but void under exchange bylaws and IPO regulations. M.R. Mayya, *Glimpses of Indian Stock Markets*, Mumbai: Indian Institute of Capital Markets, 2010, 236.

[43] P.J. Thomas, *Report on the Regulation*, 8–12, 75–80.

manipulation. Such was their range of operations that it is possible to see Calcutta's independent firms, rather than Grindlays or State Bank of India, as the first investment banks.

The second IPO wave and the 'mushroom company' phenomenon between 1943 and 1946 prompted the passage of the Capital Issues (Control) Act of 1947 and the formation of the Controller of Capital Issues (CCI).[44] So, after Independence, the primary market was controlled by the CCI and that office magisterially decided the all-important price at which paper was issued. By now, the license raj had begun, and strange as it may sound today, government licensing policy was a major driver of the IPO market in the four decades that followed Independence – after all, it was only after obtaining the necessary licenses that a firm could approach the primary market. Deliberate under-pricing by the CCI was a norm, and so, oversubscriptions of up to 100 times were common in that era.[45] The under-pricing also acted as a deterrent to promoters' issuing equity in the first place, but the CCI's existence and the licensing requirement curbed the 'mushroom companies' to some extent.

Despite the pernicious influence of the CCI, two milestones were to define the primary markets in the post-Independence era, and both took place in the mid-1970s. Reliance's first public issue in 1977 and the forced dilution of multinational equity through the Foreign Exchange Regulation Act (FERA) essentially jumpstarted the primary market.

A third IPO wave in the mid-1980s then followed, triggered by these milestones and Rajiv Gandhi's initial reform efforts. This was the first post-Independence IPO boom and led in large part by leasing companies, with mini cement and mini steel plants also widely represented.[46] This

[44] As noted earlier, the Defence of India Act of 1939 (together with an extended set of 1943 rules) was enacted to curb rampant speculation in commodities during the Second World War. These controls were extended into the post-Independence era through the Capital Issues (Control) Act of 1947.

[45] K.R.P. Shroff, *History and Present Position*, 39, 42. Companies also found rights issues more convenient.

[46] H.T. Parekh, 'The Changing Pattern of the Indian Capital Market,' *Seminar on Capital Markets: Problems and Prospects*, 4 February 1988, Bombay: BSE, 1988, 11.

third wave has been overshadowed by one that followed in the early 1990s, but it is nevertheless important because it marks the first break from the sedate issuance of the past. From Independence all the way to the mid-1970s, annual issuances had averaged between ₹50 and ₹70 crores but now that rose to about ₹4,200 crores in 1986–87.[47] The wave also resulted in the shareholder base rising to about 10 million by the late 1980s; M.R. Mayya estimated this number as the third largest shareholding population, just behind the US (50 million) and Japan (22 million).[48]

For the first time, the government discovered that PSUs could raise resources by piggybacking on an IPO boom rather than through budgetary support. It is also from about the time of this third IPO wave and onwards that an investment banking industry – whose genesis lay in those independent firms – started formalizing itself and coming into its own. Grindlays had entered with investment banking (merchant banking) activities in the late 1960s, but it was only from the 1980s that industry formation accelerated.[49] These early investment bankers handled the issuer, while the brokers handled the investor, who was typically retail and part of the broker client base. So, brokers played a key role in issue marketing till the 1990s, and they doubled as underwriters and marketing agents for issues well into the reform era.[50] In later years, investment bankers would develop their own placing power through client mailing lists and the institutional buy side would take off, which further reduced the role of retail-oriented brokers in primary markets.

[47] M.R. Mayya, 'Recent Developments in Stock Exchanges,' *Seminar on Capital Markets: Problems and Prospects*, 4 February 1988, Bombay: BSE, 1988, 7–10.

[48] Ibid.

[49] H.T. Parekh, 'The Changing Pattern of the Indian Capital Market,' 11. National Grindlays, Citibank, and State Bank of India were among the first entrants into investment banking and established divisions in 1967, 1970, and 1972, respectively. This pattern of commercial banks establishing investment banking divisions was to continue after 1972. In 1986, SBI Capital Markets was to break this trend and got established as a subsidiary, rather than as a division.

[50] Nimesh N. Kampani, 'Marketing of Corporate Capital Issues-Role of Merchant Bankers as Intermediaries between Companies and Brokers,' *Primary Capital Market-Seminar July 9, 1988*, Calcutta: Calcutta Stock Exchange Association Ltd, 1988, 35–38.

A fourth IPO wave between 1992 and 1996 was triggered by the CCI's abolition, and from now, the primary market starts assuming its present form. The CCI's closure in May 1992 and the resulting freedom to price paper led to this euphoric fourth wave, which was also the second post-Independence issue boom. Book building procedures came much later, and in the hiatus between the CCI's abolition and their introduction, IPOs of the fourth wave came to market at prices that were a figment of a feverish entrepreneur's imagination.[51] The absence of a private equity industry at that time meant that high-risk projects could only be funded by the public markets, and this also led to a flood of companies tapping the markets. Promoters and pirates issued shares at will in a mania that ended with the MS Shoes scam. So maniacal was the new issue market that this remains the only historical period when buoyant primary conditions that 'drained away' capital were cited as a bear factor in secondary market operations.

The fourth IPO wave in particular explains the much-bandied observation that India's listed universe is among the world's largest. 4005 companies listed between 1 April 1993 (the start of the first financial year after the CCI was abolished) and 31 March 1997, and even today, much of the mandatory advertising of quarterly results that fills the pink papers comes from companies that went public in this period.[52] Aquaculture, floriculture, plantations, granite, and NBFCs were heavily represented in the mania. Intriguing especially were the floriculture and plantation companies that literally tried to convince investors that money grew on trees, and that with the right agricultural inputs, cash crops like strawberries, mushrooms, or teak could be grown profitably.

In the final stages, listings took place at the rate of 100 companies a month – an unheard-of rate that has never been replicated since.[53]

[51] Book building is the standard price discovery mechanism used by companies that are issuing shares to the public for the first time.

[52] 'Handbook of Statistics of Indian Security Market 2005,' *SEBI*, 19.

[53] In this wave, Ajay Shah documents high IPO issuance, together with under-pricing (especially for smaller issues) and listing delays. Ajay Shah, 'The Indian IPO Market: Empirical Facts,' Centre for Monitoring Indian Economy, Mumbai, June 1995, mimeographed.

There was a colossal increase in intermediaries, and investment bankers registered with SEBI rose from 74 to 1163 between 1993 and 1997, before falling back to 186 by 2000. The mania also led to the first boom in financial services advertising. Without blue sky laws, IPO advertising and prospectus disclosures were plagued not as much by untrue facts as by vague claims like 'latest and proven technology', 'assured markets', 'low breakeven point', and 'guaranteed dividend'.[54] For large sections of the public, these IPOs were their first real introduction to the markets, and the wave resulted in spikes in account openings. Most of these account openings were in urban areas, and in the early years, IPO marketing was always an urban phenomenon. Rural marketing was hampered by the tax-free status of agricultural income; with agricultural income being tax free, a wealthy rural clientele felt little need to deal with instruments such as shares that had taxable features.[55]

Together, the third and fourth IPO waves led to the number of listed companies crossing 6,000 in a few years. Much of India's listed universe originated in the fourth wave, and as many as 2,500 companies were brought to market between fiscal years 1994 and 1996 alone.[56] Nevertheless, many of these companies were undercapitalized and under-owned with no financial performance to speak of; trading and market making in their shares would not resolve any of their outstanding issues, as most had no business being listed in the first place.[57] On aggregate, they would weigh down the BSE's standing as an exchange, and the reformers of the 1990s would use the post-listing

[54] M.R. Mayya, 'Regulatory Framework for Stock Markets: The Indian Experience,' *Symposium on Capital Market Development and Privatisation*, Mumbai: Commonwealth Secretariat, 1990, 185. Blue sky laws try to safeguard investors from securities fraud and worthless speculative offerings.

[55] Nimesh N. Kampani, 'Marketing of Corporate Capital Issues,' 35–38.

[56] 'Handbook of Statistics of Indian Security Market 2005,' *SEBI*, 3. Data are for fiscal year endings, 31 March of the corresponding year.

[57] The quality and size of listed companies was an issue even before the fourth IPO wave of the 1990s. As late as 1989, about 72 per cent of listed companies on the BSE had paid-up capital of less than ₹3 crores; 73 per cent of companies had less than 10,000 shareholders. Arthur Andersen & Associates, *Review of International Experience of National Stock Market Systems*, Mumbai: Arthur Andersen, 1992, 34.

performance of such companies to make their case for taking on the BSE. So, corporate governance continued to be a hit-or-miss affair, and the 'mushroom companies' of an earlier era were now referred to as 'disappearing companies'.

Sixteen thousand crores were raised at the top of the fourth wave in 1994–95, following which the primary market entered a moribund phase that would not be surpassed till 2007.[58] Issuance would then rise in 2007–08 to a record ₹42,000 crores, in line with the worldwide bull market that peaked about that time.[59]

A fifth IPO wave marks itself from about 2010 onwards, not because of wave-like conditions but because the primary market shifted to regularly raising amounts that were significantly larger than the earlier era. 2017–18 was a record year for issuance, at ₹83,000 crores, helped along in large part by issuers rushing to market to beat an impending increase in the long-term capital gains tax.[60] The capital raised increased significantly, but the number of companies did not reach the euphoric levels of previous years, indicating that only larger companies were approaching the markets; despite being a record year, 2018 had only 199 issuances.[61]

The primary market has hollowed out in recent years with big-ticket issues from established public-sector entities (that have the government's implicit backing) or insurance/capital markets businesses that are embedded subsidiaries of large banks.[62] By 2020, four of the five largest IPOs were listings of public-sector behemoths.[63] But in 2021, at the

[58] 'Handbook of Statistics of Indian Security Market 2005,' *SEBI*, 19. Actual amounts may be slightly lower because of devolved issues or withdrawn issues. Data are for fiscal year endings, 31 March of the corresponding year.

[59] 'Handbook of Statistics of Indian Security Market 2010,' *SEBI*, 16.

[60] https://www.sebi.gov.in/reports/sebi-bulletin/jun-2018/sebi-bulletin-april-2018_39228.html. Actual amounts may be slightly lower because of devolved issues or withdrawn issues.

[61] Brokerages active in issuance and syndication include: ICICI Securities, Axis Capital, Edelweiss Broking, Kotak Securities and JM Financial. League tables are compiled by the Prime Database. See *The Prime Database*, New Delhi: Praxis Consulting and Information Services Pvt. Ltd., 2017. Prithvi Haldea of PRIME Database is a pioneer in aggregating data on the IPO market.

[62] In recent years, rights issues (from existing shareholder bases) had raised more than IPOs.

[63] These included: Coal India (2010) ₹15,400 crores; General Insurance (2017) ₹11,100 crores; SBI Cards (2020) ₹10,300 crores; and New India Assurance (2017) ₹9,600 crores. The only private-sector entity on this list was Reliance Power (2008) at ₹11,700 crores.

height of the global liquidity surge from Western quantitative easing, the food delivery platform Zomato would raise ₹9,700 crores; this was followed by Paytm, a payment solutions firm that raised ₹18,300 crores ($2.5 billion), making it India's largest IPO and putting it at the head of the list.[64] Zomato and Paytm briefly triggered an IPO frenzy in digital companies that ended the public sector's dominance at the big-ticket end and led to ₹111,000 crores being raised in 2021–22, the highest sum ever. At the other end, small and marginal firms still approached the markets, which left a missing middle of mid-sized companies.[65]

Outside these distinct waves, primary activity remains a quiet business, and it is tempting to say that the poor soil for entrepreneurship has led to this state of affairs. But that observation is too general, and three specific reasons for a quiet primary side include: pricing, the pressures on the private equity industry, and the mechanics of issuance itself.

First, on pricing, the tendency of Indian businessmen to squeeze blood from a stone and price issues to perfection means little money left on the table for retail investors.[66] The pendulum has oscillated from the rampant under-pricing of CCI days to the other extreme. In contrast to the Indian experience, primary issues worldwide are underpriced to leave money on the table for investors, and this, together with efforts by the investment bankers to reduce information asymmetries between issuers and investors, allows the issue to go through.[67] But in India, IPOs

[64] After listing, the Paytm stock lost almost three-quarters of its value in the secondary market. Digital payments were regarded as a game changer by many, but a leader in that segment lost most of its value after listing. Like in Unitech's case, the siren song had turned into a screech.

[65] In 2019–20 for example, 68 of 79 issuances raised less than ₹500 crores ($70 million). Securities and Exchange Board of India (SEBI), *Annual Report for the Fiscal Year 2020–2021*, Mumbai: SEBI, 2021, 32.

[66] See Swaraj Singh Dhanjal, 'Valuation tussle delaying IPO plans,' *Mint*, 20 November 2015.

[67] An extensive literature documents IPO under-pricing in world markets. For surveys, see Alexander Ljungqvist, 'IPO Underpricing,' *Handbook of Corporate Finance: Empirical Corporate Finance Volume 1*, ed. B. Espen Eckbo, Amsterdam, Oxford: North - Holland, 2007, 375–422; Jay Ritter and Ivo Welch, 'A Review of IPO Activity, Pricing, and Allocations,' *Journal of Finance*, 57, 2002, 1795–1828.

are usually priced so aggressively that they invariably fall off after listing and go below their issue prices, which reduces the public's appetite for future issues.

Traditionally, reputation effects prevent investment banks from pricing shares too aggressively; after all, if that keeps happening and shares keep slipping below their issue prices, the market would simply avoid issues from such investment banks, and the resulting reputation effects would lower the success of their future issues. Even so, reputation effects tend to be negligible and Indian investment banks remain strangely immune to them.[68] Or perhaps it is the reverse. Conceivably, reputation effects after years of aggressive pricing and post-issue pricing collapses are so pervasive that the entire investment banking fraternity has been tarred with the same brush, and there is little to distinguish one from the other on reputation.

Academic work has found some evidence of IPO under-pricing but the research (in line with standard practice) usually takes the issue price and compares it with the listing day's closing price to gauge the degree of under-pricing and, to that extent, finds some of it.[69] But flipping on listing day is rampant as the retail crowd buys in through a host of short-term financing programs provided by underwriters and then sells (or flips) on listing day. Once this flipping is absorbed, the absence of intertemporal short selling in Indian markets allows for a routine pop on listing day that turns into a temporary surge; listing day manipulation is easy because of short constraints that make the short trade difficult (if not impossible), and so, issues often have extreme price volatility to the upside on listing day.[70] Most studies only take listing day closing prices

[68] One recent survey found that most regular IPO investors still relied on brokerages for recommendations on subscriptions. Securities and Exchange Board of India, *SEBI Investor Survey 2015*, Mumbai: SEBI, 2016, 66–67.

[69] For a survey of recent academic research, see Rajesh Chakrabarti, 'IPOs in a Major Emerging Market Economy: India,' *The Oxford Handbook of IPOs*, eds. Douglas Cumming and Sofia Johan, New York: Oxford University Press, 2019.

[70] Some research found that the public's unmet demand played a big role in listing day outperformance, with voluntary under-pricing coming in as a second-order effect. See Jonathan Clarke, Arif Khurshed, Alok Pande, and Ajai K. Singh, 'Sentiment Traders & IPO Initial Returns: The Indian Evidence,' *Journal of Corporate Finance*, Elsevier, 37(C), 2016, 24–37.

into account, and so, IPOs appear underpriced compared to their listing day price surges. Consequently, impressions of IPO under-pricing that are in line with international evidence are created, but this flies in the face of the majority of participants' experiences.

Actually, most IPOs simply fell off a cliff in the months following their listing and much coverage highlighted that observation.[71] In fact, the wave-like conditions of IPO issuance almost guaranteed high short-term performance with long-run underperformance. Heavy oversubscription and buoyant secondary conditions have not been able to overcome aggressive pricing and the expiry of anchor investor lock-ins.[72] In 2021, a news item mentioned that one Paras Defence & Space Technologies was oversubscribed 304 times, making it one of the most heavily oversubscribed IPOs in capital market history. The article obligingly mentioned another 8 IPOs with record oversubscriptions ranging from 165 to 273 times but neglected to point out that 5 of these 8 were trading below their issue prices. All the listings with record oversubscriptions had taken place between 2017 and 2021 – in the middle of a roaring bull market – and yet the majority could not sustain post-listing performance.[73]

Most IPOs that list at a premium have to deal with two important levels during their seasoning. The first is the IPO price itself, while the second – and more crucial level – is the listing day's closing price. Long traders riding momentum bunch their stop-loss orders under the listing day's closing price; faced with a strong listing, flippers who are allotted

[71] See for example, Ami Shah, Ravindra Sonavane, and Ashwin Ramarathinam, 'Most IPOs in Last Six Years Trading Below Issue Price,' *Mint*, 5 January 2015; Sameer Bhardwaj, '7 of 10 biggest IPOs of 2018 in Losses,' *Economic Times*, 1 October 2018. For empirical evidence of negative long-run performance at 12-, 24-, and 36-month intervals based on a large sample of 2,713 IPOs between 1990 and 2004, see Vijaya B. Narisetty and Marti Subrahmanyam, 'Group Affiliation and the Performance of Initial Public Offerings in the Indian Stock Market,' *Journal of Financial Markets*, 13, 2010, 196–223. Interestingly, promoter group affiliation made little difference to long-run survival.

[72] Anchor investor lock-ins prevent promoters or major investors from selling their shares for a designated period. Their expiry can lead to a large proportion of the issue coming up for sale at the same time.

[73] Times News Network, 'Paras Def Most Bought IPO at 304 x,' *Times of India*, 24 September 2021.

IPO stock might also decide not to exit on listing day and choose instead to ride the trade with sell orders under the listing day's close. Because of massive volumes on listing day, these stop-loss (sell) orders are colossal in number, and so share prices of newly listed IPOs fall dramatically as they go through their listing day's close; in recent years, many hot IPOs such as Nykaa and Zomato collapsed through their listing day closes. That still leaves the IPO price itself, and offers that slip below their issue prices also have a problem coming back above them, mainly due to the supply overhang of anxious retail subscribers waiting to sell at the issue price to get their capital back.

So, new issues got seasoned through a pervasive pattern that has gone unrecognized to date: aggressive pricing with the issue price somehow maintained on listing day through manipulation and the short constraint, followed by a slide in the months after listing driven in large part by the expiry of anchor investor lock-ins, followed again by dramatic collapses through the listing day's close, and IPO price (in that order), with pullbacks constrained by the supply overhang at the IPO price. More technically, greenshoe options might have helped and had been around since 2003 but were rarely used by investment bankers.[74]

A second factor contributing to low issuance is the pressure on private equity, which makes that industry's valuation demands less reasonable than even those of the promoters. This matter has come to the fore in recent years, as many IPO candidates have taken private equity funding on their way to a listing.[75] So, the private equity crowd were looking for

[74] A greenshoe overallotment provision allowed an issuer/investment banking syndicate to oversell an issue by as much as, say, 15 per cent. Effectively the 15 per cent became a short sale; if the issue price fell on listing day, the syndicate's short cover buying acted as a price support. But if the price did the opposite and rose on listing day, the issue size was expanded by 15 per cent to prevent the syndicate from covering at a loss. It was first used by the Green Shoe Manufacturing Company (later the Stride Rite Corporation, and now part of Wolverine World Wide Inc.). Profits on after-market stabilization – if the transaction takes place – are supposed to go to an Investor Protection and Education Fund and not the bankers/issuers, which may account for their lack of popularity.

[75] Early private equity activity in India is covered in Rasmeet Kohli, 'Venture Capital and Private Equity Financing in India,' National Stock Exchange, Mumbai, 2009, unpublished. Private equity also contributes to public markets through a remarkable oxymoron called PIPE (private investments in public equity), and in some years, considerable private equity flows enter public markets through the PIPE route.

'exits' at the IPO but had to deal with their own concerns, typically on currency. Since most of the funds India's venture capitalists invest come from limited partners in the US, the secular decline in the rupee–dollar pair over the years has effectively eroded their investments in dollar terms. For example, every dollar invested in early 2008 meant getting ₹40 in unlisted equity of funded firms, but just to get that dollar back in late 2018 meant giving up ₹72 in IPO-listed stock after those funded firms went public. In this example, private equity needed returns way over 50 per cent just to get their dollar-denominated capital back, and any actual returns came after that. As a result, IPO pricing demands by private equity firms to recover their capital with a healthy return are, if anything, even more aggressive than promoter demands, which contributes to the pricing pressures.[76] The tendency of private equity to see IPOs as 'exit' opportunities does not help, for if the smart money is exiting, why would the public enter?[77]

Finally, the mechanics of the IPO process contribute to the low issuance.[78] The listing process takes a long time, and it is the compliance and legal formalities, rather than the actual book building or road shows, that increases lead times.[79] There is limited provision for shelf issuance, i.e., completing IPO formalities and keeping the issue 'on the shelf' with actual issuance taking place when market conditions are favourable.[80] SEBI's founding and impressionable early years coincided with the

[76] Swaraj Singh Dhanjal, 'Valuation Tussle Delaying IPO plans'.

[77] Ajay Shah, Susan Thomas, and Michael Gorham, 'Private Equity and the IPO Market,' *India's Financial Markets: An Insider's Guide to How the Markets Work*, Amsterdam: Elsevier, 2008, 45–54.

[78] The key legislation behind IPOs is the Securities and Exchange Board of India (Issue of Capital and Disclosure Requirements) Regulations, 2018 (the ICDR Regulations), together with an earlier 2009 version.

[79] The book building process is a form of Walrasian *tâtonnement* (or auction) where a price band is announced, and (after road shows are held) a demand schedule constructed based on aggregation of the buy side's bids; this, in turn, is placed against the shares on offer to determine a market clearing or 'cut-off' price. In practice, and because of the aggressive pricing by issuers, most bids come in at the low end of the price band. In contrast to other jurisdictions, underwriters in India have negligible discretion on allocation, which happens based on complex regulatory requirements; also, in contrast to some other jurisdictions, the book building process is public and reported on exchange websites.

[80] Shelf registration for non-convertible bonds is allowed for certain entities such as banks, financial institutions, and public sector firms.

aftermath of the fourth IPO wave of the mid-1990s, and the wreckage of that aftermath led the organization into a futile search for the perfect IPO norms – only profit-making companies could be listed, following which only dividend-paying companies could be listed, and so on, and this tradition of fiddling with IPO rules continues into the present day.

So, unlike the secondary market reforms, SEBI's attempts at reforming the primary market – including attempts at anchor investors, IPO grading, and disclosure of investment banker track records – have yielded mixed results, and the underlying structural issues remain.[81] SEBI cannot be faulted for want of trying – one analysis found that the regulations which governed IPO issuance were modified 30 times just between 2011 and 2015, resulting in a regulatory environment of bizarre and unmatched complexity.[82] Protecting the sheep from the wolves had morphed into protecting the sheep from themselves, but the latter was a task rooted in human nature that no regulator could legislate into being. Even so, SEBI often attempted just that.

This is most evident in regulations that deal with offer size and investor buckets. The minimum amount offered for public subscription has varied over the years, but the dense tangle of pronouncements makes this difficult to see. Immediately after Independence, over half the issue had to be offered, but that requirement kept falling over the years, to as low as 10 per cent. In effect, this made it easy for the promoter class to retain control while getting the valuation benefits of a public listing backed by the long corner, but it also simplified the investment banker's job because there was less paper that had to be flogged. In recent years, the pendulum has swung yet again, and the minimum amount to be offered has risen to 25 per cent (here too there are the usual caveats and exceptions). The promoter's interest calls for control, the investment

[81] For a review of regulatory work in the early years, see G. Sabarinathan, 'SEBI's Regulation of the Indian Securities Market,' 13–26. For the consequences of taking away discretionary allocation powers from underwriters, see Amit Bubna and Nagpurnanand R. Prabhala, 'IPOs with and without Allocation Discretion: Empirical Evidence,' *Journal of Financial Intermediation*, 20, no. 4, October 2011, 530–61.

[82] Jayshree P. Upadhyay, 'Much Change in Fund Raising Norms,' *Business Standard*, 7 December 2015.

banker's interest calls for marketing lower issue sizes, and public policy calls for a company's shareholding to be reasonably wide. All these have to be balanced by the IPO regulations, but there is no attempt to consciously distil these conflicting interests in the above manner, and so, the regulations degenerated into complex manipulations of percentages across company size and investor buckets. Reform to the typical politician-bureaucrat usually meant fiddling with percentages, and primary market variations allowed for this in full measure.

Because of the above factors, brokerages under their investment banker monikers make little in corporate finance or issuance fees, and among the listed brokerages (for whom such figures are available) it was usually less than 10 per cent of revenues.[83] More generally, Indians have a problem paying for advice and this applied to financial advice as well. The government is a key source of business because of the large government holdings that are periodically offered to reduce budget deficits, but the government does not help matters by asking intermediaries to work virtually for free.[84] In turn, brokerages and investment banks often work for nominal amounts to maintain their standings in the league tables.

Finally, there are concerns about the behaviour of issuers and intermediaries. When the smaller promoters go shopping for an investment bank, a typical practice at the beauty parade is to promise the promoters a high issue price to 'bring 'em in and lock 'em down'. The banks then work on the promoter and reduce price expectations. The lengthy IPO process ensures that the promoter will find it difficult to go elsewhere, and besides, it might send a bad signal at a crucial time if the promoter shops around for another investment bank; perhaps there is something wrong with the financials or the firm itself that due diligence by the investment bank has brought out. In another common practice, the investment banker commissions (presumably for a fat fee)

[83] 'ICICI Securities Ltd,' *SEBI*, Draft Red Herring Prospectus, filed 15 December 2017, accessed 15 November 2018.

[84] Low IPO fees were always a concern and in the early years often resulted in negligible marketing efforts by brokers. Hemendra M. Kothari, 'Expansion of the Primary Capital Market,' *Primary Capital Market*, Calcutta: The Calcutta Stock Exchange Association Ltd, 33.

a well-known ratings or research house to come up with a report on the issuer's industry, the contents of which are prominently featured in the prospectus; naturally, the fees ensure that the research house will say good and glowing things about the issuer's industry.

Getting seasoned companies to meet listing norms is also difficult, and many just limp along because an exit regime is still being put in place. The number of listed companies has stayed roughly the same since the reform effort's early years, as the few additions from the IPO process have been offset – either by delistings through open offers or the exchanges' efforts to weed out moribund listings. As a result, by March 2021 and well into the SIP Bull, the total number of listed firms on the BSE and NSE stood at 5,477 and 1,968 respectively, with the larger BSE number mainly due to legacy companies from the fourth IPO wave.[85]

Customarily, the sell side brokerages spend on equity research, which they pass on to the buy side mutual funds, who then buy through the brokerages, which generates the commission pool on the institutional side. In India, this model still works because the buy side is dominated by active fund managers rather than passive indexers. By contrast, passive index funds (a big component of the buy side in other countries) charge very low asset management fees and so have less money to pay out in brokerage commissions; besides, as indexers who buy every stock in a predefined index, they anyway have little need for research that the brokerages generate.

So, the Indian market's obsession with stock picking incentivizes good research, and yet its quality is all over the place. There are a number of reasons for this.[86] Most of the big wire houses have compliance rules

[85] SEBI, *Annual Report for the Fiscal Year 2017–2018*, 48.

[86] Equity research's evolution is outlined in Alroy Lobo's interview in Saurabh Mukherjea, *Gurus of Chaos: Modern India's Money Masters*, New Delhi: Bloomsbury India, 2014, 55–71.

that restrict analyst trading, so the latter do not develop that feel for valuations that comes from trading stocks – a feel considered doubly important in a trading-oriented market. There is also a remarkable tendency to rationalize away any market valuation – and make either a bull or bear case – by excluding or including sectors. For example, if oil companies suddenly have lower profits because of fluctuations in the price of that commodity, index valuations will be computed 'ex oil and gas', i.e., excluding the oil and gas companies. Including oil and gas companies would lower Sensex earnings and increase the PE ratio, making the market look expensive and reinforcing a bear case. Excluding the oil and gas companies does the opposite – 'ex oil and gas' raised Sensex earnings, lowered the price-to-earnings ratio, made the market look cheaper and reinforced a bull case. Similar exercises are conducted with other sectors – and depending on whether a bull or bear case was to be made – a typical table would have index valuations that are 'ex oil and gas', 'ex financials', 'ex PSUs', and so on, resulting in more ex's than a list of Elizabeth Taylor's ex-husbands.

Rationalizing valuations is easier because of anchoring, a pervasive market practice. Analysts anchor their targets to the current price, and reports are typically elaborate, fact-filled validations for an extant price. Timidity in forecasting is pervasive and usually takes the form of short-term forecasts over horizons of three months to a year, which effectively reinforces speculative investment as the dominant approach to the market. Few are willing to stick their necks out and make the long-range forecasts essential for long-term investing. Since the purpose of all equity research is a calculated value, most equity research during bull markets simply means repeated upward reassessments of value over short time periods. So, it is possible for a stock that has gone up 20 times over a few years to have had reports brought out every three months during the up move that essentially justify a prevailing market price by setting a value that is 5 to 10 per cent above that prevailing price. This allows the analyst to tom-tom the accuracy of the price forecast, but for the customer, acting on such research might have meant selling the stock early on one of the many occasions when the target was met. Rare is the report that can make an accurate long-term prediction over an entire move.

Commission pool reductions have made many wire houses cut back on research coverage that was the industry's bedrock, and this has also delayed the market's move to more efficient states. There is little back-checking of analyst reports, and short shelf lives ensure that reports disappear within weeks of being issued. Also, Indian academia conducts little research *ex post* to determine how successful the reports were in their predictions, though this is not a bad thing as the results might be embarrassing for the brokerages. The basic issue is the impossibility of stock price forecasting in the volatile Indian environment. Equity research analysts – the hedgehogs who knew lots about one thing – usually had excellent industry knowledge, but translating that into stock predictions happened with the usual variability in results.

The business of buying and selling stocks has become commoditized in an over-brokered market, and there is little to distinguish one player from the next. The cyclical nature of the business makes brokerages wary about adding staff – and overhead – when times are good, because of complications in cutting back when the cycle turns down. Further, the internet is disintermediating the broker, and online trading is now a large part of retail volumes. Historically, the broker existed as the intermediary customers approached when they wanted to access the market. Later, in the early reform era, this raison d'être changed to providing information and research.[87] Now both functions can be done with negligible cost through the internet, and the end result is an ongoing industry shakeout that is periodically moderated by the market's violent up moves.

The shakeout is helped along by two prominent trends – the rise of banker brokers and the entry of discount brokers.[88] Banker brokers are

[87] Virendra Verma, 'The Face of Stock Broking Has Changed: Interview with Motilal Oswal,' *The Hindu*, 27 April 2004.

[88] In 2019 – of the top brokers by active clients – one was a discount broker (Zerodha), four were private banks (HDFC Bank, ICICI Bank, Axis, and Kotak), while the remaining four were full-service wire houses (Sharekhan, Angel, Motilal Oswal, and Karvy).

subsidiaries of banks like ICICI Bank, Kotak Mahindra, and HDFC Bank who offer broking services through 3-in-1 accounts that accelerate the disintermediation of the industry.[89] A demat account linked to a bank account with access to an internet trading platform allows customers seamless access to the market's electronic limit order book (ELOB). Banker brokers also have a number of advantages in arranging payments and clearing and settlement through their own back offices. Besides, the bankers get the float. Customers who choose not to buy stock and stay in cash for extended periods generate floats similar to low-cost savings deposits, and it is easy for banks with their sophisticated treasury operations to capture this float; customers usually receive token interest on their unused cash balances, but banks can earn higher returns on the unused balances through their treasuries. Strong parent balance sheets and access to cheap technology, together with inherent advantages in settling trades and capturing float, are leading to this new class of banker brokers taking market share from traditional brokers.[90] By contrast, pure play brokers lacked the infrastructure to capture such floats and found it less profitable to manage them. In recent years, however, complex and ever-shifting regulatory and compliance requirements appear to have reduced the float advantage to banker brokers.[91]

Finally, the rise of discount brokers is also gaining momentum. Discount brokers such as Zerodha and Groww violate an ancient principle of broking whereby brokerage is charged – after the usual negotiation – as a percentage of order size. Discount platforms charge a flat fee, irrespective of order size.[92] After all, for most retail trades at least, the broker's marginal effort on trade execution through the electronic limit order book (ELOB) is the same. Moreover, most new

[89] Rajesh Mascarenhas and Anita Bhoir, 'Brokerages Shutting Down Retail Business, While Banks Reap Profits,' *Economic Times*, 20 November 2013.

[90] By 2018, the two largest brokers by active clientele – HDFC Securities and ICICI Securities – were both connected with India's largest private sector banks. Their positions would be taken over by discount brokers a short while later.

[91] Drawn from the author's conversation with Nikunj Modi. 29 March 2024.

[92] Santanu Chakraborty, 'Free Indian Stock Trades in Sight as Top Brokerage IIFL Reduces Fees,' *Mint*, 7 November 2014.

customers come from the young, tech-savvy demographic dividend that is surging into markets, and this new breed is comfortable punching their own orders. More generally, order-driven markets with ELOBs place fewer demands – as compared to, say, dealer-driven or open outcry markets – on the trading skills required to fill orders, and this rule applies especially to the small orders most retail investors place in the system.

But in all this, clients are on their own and without the research or backend support that a full-service brokerage can provide. The brokerage saves on the staffing and real estate outlays necessary to maintain an army of customers' people, but the client misses out on the comfort of a research-backed voice at the other end of the line. Flat-fee discount platforms are the final step in the commoditization of broking, their existence driven by the possibilities of the internet and digitization.[93] Digitization has commoditized broking and driven down brokerage revenues, and yet that same digitization presents other income streams at the touch of a button; consider that shaving off ₹8 (9 cents) a month from those 100 million demat accounts could lead to easy money of almost ₹1,000 crores ($125 million) a year for the industry.

[93] For early coverage of the discount broker phenomenon, see Rajesh Mascarenhas, 'Stock Broking Industry to See an Intense Price War,' *Economic Times*, 21 October 2014.

PART FOUR

MISCELLANY

20

'DID YOU UNDERSTAND THAT?'

Derivatives

> 'The best way to make a lakh in derivatives markets is to start with 10 lakhs.'

This version of the Wall Street joke would be familiar, through hard experience if nothing else, to the many retail traders who dominate India's derivatives markets. Starting with the larger amount will – through a trader's hard work and diligent efforts – often result in closing account equity nearer the small amount.

Derivatives have been around a long time. One early reference from Aristotle's *Politics* concerns the philosopher Thales of Miletus who, based on his knowledge of astronomy and the elements, discerned in winter that there would be an abundant olive crop the following summer. Thales bought the right – but not the obligation – to use the presses of Miletus and Chios to turn the olives into oil. When the abundant crop came in and the presses were overburdened, Thales sold his option to use the presses to others who needed to use them, presumably for valuable consideration. Philosophers, Aristotle concluded, could also make money on occasion if they chose to, but he hastens to add that it was not something they cared much about.[1]

[1] Aristotle, *Politics*, translated by H. Rackham, Loeb Classical Library, Cambridge, MA: Harvard University Press, 1932, Book I, Chapter 11, 1259a, 1.

In India, too, the two basic types of derivatives – futures and options – have been around since the markets themselves. Trading usually started in the commodity markets before adoption by the stock market, and this is a historical pattern. Early Bombay traders dealt in cotton futures, and Roychand's time bargains from the Cotton and Share Mania of 1865 were unmargined naked forward contracts on stocks. By the late nineteenth century, Marwari traders were using *fatka*s (futures) on jute in Burrabazar and the other markets of Calcutta.[2] Local Calcutta firms used the price signals generated by the *fatka* futures market to offer quotes on upcountry jute and occasionally to hedge; expatriate British firms usually did neither and were at a disadvantage.[3] Options were also pioneered in the commodity markets and trading in the grain markets had option-like characteristics;[4] trading for the rise was through indigenous options like the *teji* (call) and trading for the fall was through the *mandi* (put), with the option premium known as the *nazrana*, and to this day, jargon for a market in a bull or bear phase is *teji* or *mandi*, respectively.[5] Derivatives practice in early twentieth-century Bombay included trading on daily closing prices of New York

[2] A lively account of rain gambling and related pastimes among traders in nineteenth-century Calcutta comes from Aditi Roy Ghatak, *Down Lyons Range*, Kolkata: P.K. Ray for the Calcutta Stock Exchange Association, 2008, 37–39.

[3] B.R. Tomlinson, 'Colonial Firms and the Decline of Colonialism in Eastern India 1914–1947,' *Power, Profit and Politics: Essays on Imperialism, Nationalism and Change in Twentieth-Century India*, ed. Christopher Baker, Gordon Johnson, and Anil Seal, Cambridge: Cambridge University Press, 1981, 469–70.

[4] Ritu Birla, *Stages of Capital: Law, Culture, and Market Governance in Late Colonial India*, Durham, NC: Duke University Press, 2009, 153.

[5] Early derivatives trading (including *kaccha khandi* transactions) is outlined in *Emperor vs. Thavarmal Rupchand*, ILR1929, 53, Bom 367. *Kaccha khandis* were the Mahajan Association's weekly non-deliverable forward contracts on Broach cotton that undercut the fortnightly settlements and higher lot sizes of the East India Cotton Association's contracts. Evidently, fiddling with settlement periods and lot sizes to attract the speculative crowd – and gain market share from rival exchanges – was an established practice. Also see, C.A. Bayly, *Rulers, Townsmen and Bazaars: North Indian Society in the Age of British Expansion: 1770–1870*, Cambridge: Cambridge University Press, 1988, 412, 418–20. For the Calcutta exchange, Aditi Roy Ghatak records alternate terminology of Jota Phatak, where Jota was the right to buy (the call option) and Phatak was the right to sell (the put option). See Aditi Roy Ghatak, *Down Lyons Range*, 93.

cotton futures; today's options traders are familiar with American and European options, but these contracts were called American futures.[6]

Because of its speculative nature and the absence of delivery, derivatives trading generated predictable complaints from the authorities. Established agency houses claimed *fatka*s had been invented by traders who had been deprived of the pleasures of rain gambling, to satisfy 'their craving for the gains of chance in a system of contracts purporting to evidence the purchase and sale of jute … but we believe in no single instance has jute ever been delivered under them.'[7] In later years, SEBI would occasionally rumble about the large size of India's derivatives markets and then fiddle with lot sizes or eligibility requirements, but this is not new and it has all happened before.

Yet, unlike stock markets, commodities markets had formal derivatives activity. Derivatives markets in agri-commodities had the advantage of sound founding legislation through the Forward Contracts (Regulation) Act of 1952.[8] But these markets had to deal with a government that was struggling to feed a growing population through lower agri-commodity prices; such a government was always psychologically short a price trend, and it readily banned derivatives markets when they inconveniently went up instead of down. Commodity derivatives periodically went through such existential crises, disappearing from time to time after normative issues resulted in government bans.[9] In effect, substantial price surges usually resulted in bans that were subsequently revoked and markets reinstated.[10]

[6] *Emperor vs. Thavarmal Rupchand.*

[7] This is from a 1911 Indian Jute Mills Association report to the Bengal Chamber of Commerce, as quoted in Ritu Birla, 'Speculation Illicit and Complicit: Contract, Uncertainty, and Governmentality,' *Comparative Studies of South Asia, Africa and the Middle East*, 35, (3), December 2015, 392.

[8] The Forward Contract (Regulation) Act of 1952 was drafted on the basis of the A.D. Shroff committee's recommendations.

[9] T.V. Somanathan, *Derivatives*, New Delhi: Tata McGraw-Hill, 1998, 229–33.

[10] Commodity markets were reviewed in a series of reports from committees headed by A.D. Shroff (1952), M.L. Dantwala (1966), A.M. Khusro (1980), and K.N. Kabra (1994). See Ministry of Civil Supplies, *Report of the Committee on Forward Markets*, New Delhi: Ministry of Civil Supplies, 1994, 3–5.

Nevertheless, some of this derivatives trading resulted in speculative profits that were ploughed back into industry. Industrialists G.D. Birla and Ramkrishna Dalmia both generated substantial surpluses trading jute and silver derivatives respectively during the commodity surges of the First World War, surpluses that were later used as foundation capital for industry.[11]

The Nehruvian era made its attitude towards derivatives clear right from the beginning and the Securities Contracts (Regulation) Act (SCRA) of 1956 banned options in its preamble itself. Despite that, for decades, one Babu Phatak ran an options bucket shop at the entrance to the BSE, and organized an informal options market at the door of the country's premium exchange.[12]

Despite the government's attitude, it was on the equity side that the influence of derivatives was really felt. As seen earlier, the BSEs badla system on a 'specified list' of the largest companies was an extension of the Roychand time bargain, and most of the Indian stock market at that time consisted of unmargined naked forwards with fortnightly tenors and embedded options, that kept getting rolled over on alternate Fridays. The bureaucrats had banned options under the SCRA but could not recognize that the entire badla system ran on forward contracts with embedded hidden options. Like the commodity markets, the stock market's badla system was periodically offered, banned when payment crises arose, and reinstated when the trading community's clamour for a leveraged product grew really loud. As seen earlier, notable bans took place in 1933, 1943, 1962, 1969, 1987, and 1993, followed by a

[11] Medha Kudaisya, *The Life and Times of G.D. Birla*, New Delhi: Oxford University Press, 2003, 45; Gurcharan Das, 'Introduction,' *The Marwaris: From Jagat Seth to the Birlas*, Thomas A. Timberg, New Delhi: Penguin Books, 2014; B.R. Tomlinson, 'Colonial Firms and the Decline of Colonialism,' 461–63.

[12] 'Allow Weekly Contracts in Stock Futures' in M.R. Mayya, *Glimpses of Indian Stock Markets*, Mumbai: Indian Institute of Capital Markets, 2010, 341.

final proscription in 2001; except for the last episode, all bans were followed by reinstatements, and the historical pattern of banning and reinstatement is as marked as in the commodity markets. Given the influence of badla trading on the market – the badla 'specified list' often accounted for as much as 90 per cent of volumes – it can be argued that for generations the Indian market's superstructure was dominated by some form of derivatives trading.

With the dawn of the reform era, the first steps were taken towards the development of modern derivatives markets, and the 1991–2003 period is significant in this regard. But new markets to trade futures and options (the basic derivative contracts) would have to compete with an existing market that had embedded derivative features, and this situation led to extensive politicking over the market's microstructure.[13] Badla was a complex combination of a cash market, a derivatives market in forwards/options on forwards, and a settlement system, and it was this concatenation that had caused repeated crises in the system. Separating the cash market from the forward market while simultaneously doing away with the derivative-like features of badla was one way out of the tangle, and much early thinking went along those lines. But this separation – together with the market's perennial need for a leveraged trading product – called for introduction of a derivatives segment and was the main reason behind its creation. Note that a cash margining system could have been another outcome, but there appears to have been little discussion on the same. Finally, decisions on badla were complicated as it was both a carry forward product and a settlement system, so decisions on it – in an example of the sequencing problem in economic reform – went together with decisions on the settlement system.

Understandably, there was resistance from the incumbent to change. Badla's derivative-like features were a defining part of the BSE system

[13] John Echeverri-Gent, 'Politics of Market Micro-Structure: Towards a New Political Economy of India's Equity Market Reform,' *India's Economic Transition: The Politics of Reforms*, ed. Rahul Mukherji, New Delhi: Oxford University Press, 2007, 328–58.

and responsible both for its popularity among the trading public and the heavy volumes that resulted. The strictures on bank lending into the stock market had led to an era when trading capital was scarce. So, both the liquidity pool and the resulting price continuity that were vital essentials of a financial market depended on allowing participants to trade with negligible capital. This the badla system excelled at. The resulting large volumes were also critical to the BSE's existence and market leadership. Besides, the BSE management itself now came from the badla brokers of that era; Manu Manek had passed on, but his successors were also dependent on the system and derived much of their power from the size of the liquidity pool and the financing opportunities that badla provided. Given the stakes, much of the debate revolved around the effect these new markets would have on the BSE's badla product.[14]

Much of this also took place against a volatile political backdrop with three elections in as many years in the late 1990s; the market environment was equally volatile, bracketed as it was between the Mehta and Parekh scams. Derivatives introduction gives one the impression of a chaotic series of events and actions set against a milieu of remarkable turbulence that somehow worked out in the end. For the market, it is an important period as many of its present features can be traced back to events of that era.

One starting point is the 1992 Harshad Mehta scam that, predictably enough, led to a badla ban the following year. The resulting collapse in volumes led to a 1995 G.S. Patel committee report that recommended a Revised Carry Forward System; this was later implemented by the BSE and amounted to a reintroduction of badla.[15] The report is

[14] In 1992, former RBI governor M. Narasimhan made one of the earliest references to derivatives trading as an alternative to badla. M. Narasimhan, *Financial Sector Reform and the Capital Markets*, Fourth Phiroze Jeejeebhoy Memorial Lecture, Bombay: BSE, 1992, 19.

[15] Securities and Exchange Board of India, *Report of the Committee on the Review of the Present System of Carry Forward Transactions*, G.S. Patel Report, Mumbai: SEBI, February 1995. The committee was headed by G.S. Patel, a former UTI chairman, and other members were Deepak Parekh and M.R. Mayya. Paragraph 149 of the committee's report constituted the core recommendations and they included: confining the forward list to widely held companies, ensuring that regional exchanges

significant because it considered – but flatly rejected – the introduction of derivatives markets. In turn, this was followed by a 1997 J.R. Varma committee report that undertook further changes to the carry forward system and resulted in a 'modified badla' system.[16] By now, the National Stock Exchange (NSE) had commenced cash market operations and had even overtaken the BSE on volumes, an extraordinary achievement as it did not even have a carry forward product at that time. In December 1995, the NSE threw its hat into the ring and put forward a request to start a derivatives segment. This effectively started policy debates on the trade-offs between a new derivatives segment and the continuation of an existing market with embedded derivative features.

There would be a five-year hiatus between the NSE's 1995 proposal and the commencement of derivatives trading in 2000 – a hiatus caused in equal part by the clashes between an incumbent dependent on badla, a fledgling regulator who could not imagine a market without badla, a disruptor that wanted to coexist with badla, and other players intent on reforming badla.

During this interval, derivatives became a flash point for much of the politics and debates behind the market's microstructure and following these arguments is important for an understanding of the segment's

outside the 4 metros and Ahmedabad needed special clearances, restricting the carry forward system to exchanges that had (or intended to have) screen-based trading, segregating the delivery from the carry forward transactions with special trading sessions for carry forward transactions, 15 per cent margins on all shares with weekly mark to market, ensuring that badla rollovers by the same person beyond 90 days were certified by an external auditor, ensuring that institutions (rather than just wealthy individuals) could lend into the *vyaj badla* market to finance the system, and standardizing settlement periods across exchanges. Most of the proposals were accepted by SEBI and subsequently implemented by the BSE. SEBI's own counter proposal – increasing margins, as and when the 90-day limit for rollovers was reached – had to be dropped due to market resistance.132–53.

[16] The committee was headed by J.R. Varma, and other members were M.G. Damani, R.C. Gupta, K. Kannan, M.M. Kapoor, and R.H. Patil. Its recommendations resulted in a Modified Carry Forward System or 'modified badla'. The committee did away with the 90-day limit for carry forward transactions (which was being subverted anyway by rollovers between exchanges or into subsequent periods) and suggested a 10 per cent margining system with daily mark to market on both delivery and carry forward trades. The Patel committee recommendations on segregating cash and forward markets were also seen as irrelevant with daily margin collections, and were done away with. Most recommendations were accepted by SEBI, but the limit imposed for carry forward transactions was reduced to 75 days.

later evolution. Those in favour of introducing derivatives pointed to the experience of international markets, the improvement in risk management practices that hedging with derivatives could bring about, and the gains in trading volume and market capitalization that usually followed their introduction. Those against their introduction produced 'but not as yet' arguments that emphasized: the negligible size of cash markets, inadequate infrastructure, the risk to retail traders, a nascent and still immature buy side, and the dangers of excessive speculation.[17] In an argumentative and opinionated country, the debates were often heated, and multiple conferences were held where these views were aired. At times, it seemed that derivatives markets would just remain an idea.[18]

Nevertheless, come into existence they did. Two committees – headed by L.C. Gupta and J.R. Varma – played an important role in outlining the derivatives segment's basic features. In its March 1998 report, the L.C. Gupta committee recommended badla's abolition and the introduction of derivatives markets, and SEBI's subsequent acceptance of that report would prove crucial to further development work on the markets.[19] The L.C. Gupta committee emphasized the benefits of derivatives' hedging function and repeatedly mentioned hedging as the main reason for the segment's introduction. The report even used surveys that tried to measure market demand for hedging

[17] For a summary of these debates in case study format, see ICFAI Center for Management Research, 'Derivatives Trading in India,' *Case Studies in Finance, Volume II*, Hyderabad: ICFAI Center for Management Research, 2004, 17–19.

[18] Technical assistance on regulatory aspects of markets came from the United States Agency for International Development (USAID) through its Financial Institutions Reform and Expansion-Regulatory (FIRE-R) project and some of the early conferences were organized under their auspices. It was a long 13-year association between 1994 and 2007, with contract administration by Price Waterhouse. The conference materials are important sources for the early discussions on market microstructure. The BSE was not included as a first-tier agency on the FIRE-R project for reasons that remain unclear. See W. Dennis Grubb, 'Foreword' *The Future of India's Stock Markets*, ed. Tushar Waghmare, New Delhi: Tata McGraw-Hill, 1998, vii–viii.

[19] Securities and Exchange Board of India, *Report of the Committee on Derivatives*, L.C. Gupta Report of 1998, Mumbai: SEBI, March 1998, iv. The committee was headed by L.C. Gupta and had 24 members.

activity.[20] The surveys found extensive interest in the hedging benefits of derivatives, though – in what was a closed autarkic economy with little knowledge of international best practice – it is unclear how participants could have identified derivatives' hedging features even before they were introduced.

Surprisingly, the Gupta report did not consider alternatives like a straightforward margining system in the cash market, perhaps because of the similarity between such a margining system and the BSE's badla product. More crucially, a new segment offered a chance to start with a clean slate and bypass the messiness of adapting an existing system, but this is also not explicitly mentioned in the report.

The Gupta report also recommended that derivatives be treated as 'securities', as defined in the SCRA, effectively bringing them under the ambit of the existing regulatory framework. This was a crucial change that removed the ambiguous status derivatives had endured for decades. It led to the creation of these new markets and allowed regulation to catch up with existing market practice. Inexplicably, given the BSE's record at self-regulation in those years, the Gupta report also recommended a two-tier regulatory structure with the regulator on one tier and the exchange on the other. The emphasis would be on regulation at the exchange level; the exchanges would be 'self-regulating organizations' with overall regulation under SEBI's auspices, but this was in effect a glittering generality that would have little bearing on final outcomes.[21] Predictably, the BSE's president of the time wrote a strong dissenting note in which he noted the effects the new markets would have on the BSE's own badla system.[22]

Despite that dissenting note, there was complacency on the BSE's part when it came to judging the effects of a derivatives segment on its

[20] The BSE noted the poor response rate to the Gupta survey – 112 responses out of 300 sent out – in a report that questioned the speedy introduction of derivatives markets. See Ramesh Gupta, 'Derivatives Committee Report: Four Queries,' *The Stock Exchange Review: June 1998*, Mumbai: BSE, 1998, 5–10.

[21] SEBI, *Report of the Committee on Derivatives*, iv–v.

[22] Ibid., MG Damani, '*Comments on the Report of the Committee on Derivatives*,' December 2, 1997.

badla product. Since badla was offered only on individual stocks and not indexes, it was not the derivatives market as much as the single stock futures (SSF) segment of a derivatives market that posed a threat to the BSE. In turn, SSFs had little international respectability at that time and only a few countries had introduced them. For a while, this led to the view that India would also not introduce SSFs, and as a result, the BSE underestimated the threat that derivatives would pose to its dominant carry forward SSF product.

Most of the Gupta report only made a case for creating the derivatives segment without discussing the technical nitty gritty of margining, risk management, surveillance, and compliance that would go into creating the market's microstructure. These critical issues were addressed by a second committee, headed again by J.R. Varma of the Indian Institute of Management, Ahmedabad.[23] The October 1998 Varma report worked out the operational minutiae of the margining system, a Value at Risk (VAR) methodology for charging initial margins, broker net worth and deposit requirements, real-time monitoring arrangements, and the myriad other details that went into creating the microstructure. Crucially, both committees focused only on exchange-traded instruments and not over-the-counter (OTC) instruments that were customizable or privately arranged between parties.

There followed a transition period filled with massive chaos and uncertainty when badla, the old settlement cycle, and derivatives markets were all in play. In this period, both exchanges competed in launching carry forward products. Important preparatory work was initiated on rolling settlements, progressive reductions in the settlement cycle took place, and a T+5 rolling settlement cycle was introduced for the first time in January 1998. It would be the first in a series of reductions in the settlement cycle that could have reduced the efficacy of badla by reducing the option value of the system's embedded options,

[23] Securities and Exchange Board of India, *Report of the J.R. Varma Group on Risk Containment Measures in the Indian Stock Index Futures Market*, J.R. Varma Report of 1998, Mumbai: SEBI, October 1998. The committee was headed by J.R. Varma, and other members were R.H. Patil, Ravi Narain, Janak Raj, Himanshu Kaji, Ajit Surana, Brian Brown, K.R. Bharat, Sarosh Irani, and O.P. Gahrotra.

but significantly, the reduction in cycles did not apply to the BSE's 'A' group badla stocks. In February 1999, the NSE launched its Automated Lending and Borrowing Mechanism (ALBM), which was essentially a mechanism to borrow and lend stocks under a forward system. The BSE then responded with further modifications to its 'modified badla' system.

In January 2000, another committee headed by J.R. Varma recommended a move to rolling settlements within the framework of this modified badla system.[24] A SEBI board meeting in January 2000 was critical of these modified badla proposals because of their similarity to derivatives markets and delayed their introduction; the majority view recommended the continuation of the badla system, but in a significant move, a dissenting note by J.R. Varma and R.H. Patil recommended the abolition of badla and the move to a derivatives market that included SSFs.[25] Though SEBI finally approved the modified badla system in June 2000, derivatives markets had anyway begun their rollout based on earlier approvals. Modified badla did not work as expected. and the BSE made another attempt to create a carry forward product, BLESS, that could compete with the NSE's ALBM.[26]

In March 2001, the Ketan Parekh crisis hit. By now, the recurrent settlement crises were beginning to change views on the badla system and its continuance. Badla was a controversial product, indigenously designed and tailored to local conditions, but undermined by occasional leveraged overtrading and the haphazard enforcement

[24] Securities and Exchange Board of India, *Report of the Committee on Carry Forward under Rolling Settlements*, J.R. Varma Report of 2000, Mumbai: SEBI, January 2000. The committee was headed by J.R. Varma, and other members were P.K. Bindlish, M.M. Kapoor, A.K. Narayanan, R.H. Patil, and Anand Rathi.

[25] 'The weekly carry forward system under rolling settlements is conceptually very close to a futures contract on individual stocks with five different futures contracts (with maturities of 1, 2, 3, 4, and 5 trading days) open for trading on any day. Moreover, the risk management of a proper futures contract is much better understood. As such, Dr. Patil and Prof. Varma recommend that the weekly carry forward product should swiftly migrate to a full fledged futures contract in individual stocks. When this is done, the product will cease to be regulated as a carry forward product and will be regulated exclusively as a derivatives contract.' Ibid., 5–6.

[26] BLESS stood for the Borrowing and Lending Security Scheme.

of a self-regulatory framework, particularly in the era after Shroff and Jeejeebhoy.[27] Critically, the system could not handle the volume scale-ups that happened with the onset of the reform era, FII entry, and the bull runs of that time. Ironically, the product allowed for the all-important trading floor volumes, but settlements and the back office proved to be its undoing; note also that floor volumes were all that mattered to the inveterate traders who ran the BSE, and as a result, back-office neglect became institutionalized to the point where it could not handle badla's pressing settlement issues. Finally, the ease with which badla allowed for a naked short side was now becoming a political liability in an age when the little guy was heavily in the market through the mutual funds.

A final J.R. Varma committee report of April 2001 was crucial in recommending the end of the century-old badla system and a migration to derivatives trading.[28] In the decisive period between March and December 2001, when the BJP's Yashwant Sinha was finance minister, both the ALBM and BLESS were banned, rolling settlements were extended to the BSE's badla shares, and SSFs were introduced to give the market access to a leveraged product. As a result, by December 2001, all stocks had moved to T+5 rolling settlements. Further reductions to T+3 and T+2 took place in 2002 and 2003 respectively.

As noted earlier, the badla ban was to have one historic consequence that is felt on a daily basis into the present moment. The naked short play disappeared and with it went the unlimited shorting capacity that was built into the system. Crucially, banning BLESS and the ALBM ended the mechanisms for borrowing and lending stocks that were required for short selling, which meant that borrowing stocks to short sell them could not be done in the cash market. ALBM products would be reintroduced later but never really took off, which implied that the 2001 decisions had effectively done away with the short side of the

[27] SEBI, *Review of the Present System of Carry Forward Transactions,* 10.

[28] Securities and Exchange Board of India, *Report of the Group on Deferral Products in Rolling Settlement*, J.R. Varma Report of 2001, Mumbai: SEBI, April 2001. The committee was headed by J.R. Varma, and other members were Pratip Kar, A.N. Joshi, Ravi Narain, C.B. Bhave, M.G. Damani, P.K. Singhal, and K. Kamala.

Indian market. In the chaos of transition, the market had gone from the extreme ease of badla's naked short selling to its complete abolition, and no one really noticed. Then again, those among the pros that did notice were quite happy to live among the 1,000 baggers that presented themselves in this rah-rah land of a long-only market. All this would bias the market to the long side and have repercussions on valuations and market movements in the coming years.

In retrospect, two phases can be discerned in the market's transition to its modern derivatives-dominated avatar. In the first phase, the idea of a derivatives segment moves from rejection to acceptance and then coexistence with a badla product (with its embedded derivatives features). This is followed by a second phase, when attempts at reforming badla give way to its abolition in favour of a derivatives segment.

The transition's first phase comes between the Patel (1995) and Gupta (1998) reports. G.S. Patel had flatly rejected derivatives while painting a frightening picture of the dangers of derivatives markets, and yet by 1998, L.C. Gupta's central recommendation called for their speedy introduction.[29] Clearly something had happened between these reports. The repeated crises on badla – the Harshad Mehta end game, MS Shoes, and Videocon/BPL/Sterlite – all fell between these two dates and played a role in this attitudinal shift from badla to the better risk containment that derivatives promised.

In the chaotic second phase between 1998 and 2001, repeated attempts at reforming badla gave way to its abolition, mainly because the immediate aftermath of these crises and the reform era's volume build-ups brought the system's viability into question. The recommendation on badla's abolition figures for the first time in the dissenting notes from Varma (2000), and the reasons cited include the similarity between badla's carry forward and a futures contract, together with better systemic risk management offered by futures markets. Here too, the aftermath of the IT stock sell-off and the pending arrival of an alternate

[29] SEBI, *Review of the Present System of Carry Forward Transactions*, 112–23; SEBI, *Report of the Committee on Derivatives*, iv.

leveraged product – SSFs – influenced the decision, and by 2001, the old system was gone.

Much of this had taken place during the tenure of D.R. Mehta, to date the longest serving SEBI chairman. Mehta was pilloried in his time, but his term between 1995 and 2002 is also the most significant among SEBI's heads.

So, the market in its derivatives-dominated modern avatar dates from about mid-2001, by which time the NSE had won its committee battles with the BSE, following which the BSE's badla product was banned, the cash and derivatives segments separated, and derivatives markets introduced. Participants whose interests are influenced by committee decisions should realize the importance of being represented on such committees; the BSE brokers – consumed as they were with trading their proprietary books – showed little inclination to influence committee events, and besides, by now the exchange's leadership and management were turning over frequently as per government diktat.

In all this, the five committees headed by J.R. Varma between 1997 and 2002 played a key role, and in this sense, J.R. Varma is the Father of India's Derivatives Markets.

Trading started with futures on indexes, followed by a progressive rollout of options on indexes, options on stocks, and futures on stocks, with the rollout completed by November 2001[30] (currency and interest rate derivatives were introduced in 2008 and 2009 respectively, but their volumes and profile would not match those of equity derivatives). The NSE then proceeded to monopolize the derivatives market with a near 100 per cent market share that was briefly, but unsuccessfully, challenged by the BSE.[31] The result of that monopoly is one of the world's biggest casinos, and this ensures that the historical importance of derivatives in the market's superstructure continues into the modern

[30] Trading in index options commenced in June 2001, while trading in stock options commenced in July 2001. Futures contracts on 22 individual stocks were launched in November 2001.

[31] In recent years, the pendulum has swung once again, and the BSE has begun using weekly options and futures contracts to gain back some market share in derivatives.

era.[32] By 2018, measured by number of contracts traded (or cleared), the NSE was the world's largest exchange for index options and the second largest for stock futures.[33] In 2019, the exchange would become the world's largest by number of contracts traded.[34] The casino also benefits from a vast conspiracy of silence between the regulator, the exchanges, and the brokers, with a usually raucous media reluctant to comment due to the complexities of the subject.

Derivatives, as the name implies, are financial contracts whose values are derived from an underlying financial instrument. There are a range of such underlying instruments – equity, debt, commodities, currencies, and even intangibles like an interest rate – but here the concern is equity derivatives where the underlying is a stock.[35] Derivatives divide into two major types – futures and options.[36] *Futures* have symmetrical pay-offs that move one-on-one with the underlying, which in the case of equity derivatives is the stock's price. *Options*, which further divide into calls and puts, have asymmetrical pay-offs that can be quite unusual. At advanced levels, it is possible to combine futures and options to create any sort of pay-off desired. In India, futures and options are offered on underlying indexes (mainly the NSE's Nifty) and on between 150

[32] For an overview of derivatives markets just after their creation, see Securities and Exchange Board of India, Advisory Committee on Derivatives, *Report on Development and Regulation of Derivative Markets in India*, Mumbai: SEBI, 2002; Susan Thomas and Jayanth Rama Varma, 'Derivatives Markets,' *Capital Markets in India*, eds. Rajesh Chakrabarti and Sankar De, New Delhi: Sage Publications, 2010, 178–203. The basic features, as outlined in these studies, remain the same to the present day.

[33] Securities and Exchange Board of India, *Annual Report for the Fiscal Year 2017–2018*, Mumbai: SEBI, 2018, 58.

[34] Staff Writer, 'NSE Is World's Largest Derivatives Exchange for 2nd Consecutive Year,' *Mint*, 21 January 2021.

[35] Currency derivative markets in India compete with active offshore markets for currency derivatives (typically non-delivered forwards) in Singapore, London, and New York; markets for interest rate derivatives are nascent and illiquid, in keeping with the condition of bond markets.

[36] Forwards and swaps are also derivatives but they are directly negotiated between parties, while the focus here is on exchange-traded derivatives.

to 200 individual stocks. In the early years of its latest NSE avatar, the derivatives market was dominated by futures trading, mainly because of the market's historical familiarity with the badla forward product that had extensive futures-like characteristics. Nevertheless, in recent years, options trading has gained traction and options volumes now exceed futures volumes, though the actual trading capital committed to the futures side (as margin money) may be larger.[37]

Futures are conceptually easier to understand.[38] A futures contract on stock X is a promise to receive or pay the future price of X at a future date (technically the settlement price prevailing at 3.30 p.m. on the last Thursday of the month). If the price on that future date is higher, contract buyers receive the difference and sellers pay out the identical difference; symmetrically, if the price on that future date is lower, contract buyers pay out the difference and the sellers receive it. The caveat is that rather than a single payment on that future date, the pay in or pay out happens at the end of every day through a mark to market system and is based on that day's closing price. In the absence of such a daily mark to market system, losses would grow to the point where they become large and unmanageable by settlement day, which raises default and counterparty risk in the system (in fact, this had been badla's problem, but daily pay in and pay out on badla was difficult in an era that had neither computers nor an efficient banking network). It isn't necessary to wait for that last Thursday to square up, and the contract can be unwound by an offsetting sale or purchase at any prevailing market price, which makes such contracts ideal instruments for trading and speculation.

So, if you were to trade in futures, instead of buying a single share of X at, say, ₹2,995 in the cash market, you would buy it in the derivatives market where it could be simultaneously quoting at, say, ₹3,000. Except

[37] Futures volumes divide about equally between index futures (mainly the Nifty and Bank Nifty) and SSFs. By contrast, options volumes are dominated by index options (mainly on the Nifty) with negligible volumes from single stock options. More technically, the option chain – the range of strike prices – is extensive, but despite that volumes are low and mainly in 'at the money' options.

[38] A wide range of books cover derivatives valuation and trading. A standard treatment is John Hull, *Options, Futures, and Other Derivatives*.

that in the derivatives market, a bundle of X shares has to be bought through a standard futures contract – in this case, you would have to buy a standard contract of, say, 125 shares (the contract multiplier or lot size) with 20 per cent put up as margin.[39] This allows you, the contract holder, to control ₹3,75,000 (₹3,000 times 125) worth of stock X with ₹75,000 (20 per cent of ₹3,75,000) in capital put up as margin.

This leverage – the leverage factor is 5 to 1 here, or 3,75,000 divided by 75,000 – amplifies the return on both sides. A 2 per cent increase in X's price, a daily – sometimes hourly – occurrence given volatility on the bourses, results in a profit of ₹7,500 (2 per cent of ₹3,75,000) on the contract. This is a 10 per cent return on the amount of ₹75,000 put up (transaction costs are ignored here); assuming the move happened over an hour, the trader has made in an hour more than what someone holding a fixed deposit would make in a year. This often leads to overtrading as traders routinely abuse leverage by buying the maximum amount their capital allows them, which then exposes them to the downside – a 2 per cent decline in X's price results in a 10 per cent loss on the capital of ₹75,000 put up and a sequence of such losses opens the trader up to ruin risk.

So, futures amplify the returns to trading on both sides – the leverage is simply amplifying the returns by the extent of the leverage factor, here 5 to 1. This amplification is risky to the downside and that risk has to be borne by the contract's holder. After all, the trader has bought the contract in an impersonal market from someone who has a diametrically opposite view on price. If the trader bets wrong, he pays the opposite party through the exchange's clearing house, and if he bets right, he receives the equivalent amount through the clearing house. The mathematical expectation of the speculator – as Louis Bachelier pointed out – is 0 and this is seen most plainly in the futures market.[40]

[39] Special equity events such as stock splits and stock dividends (bonuses) will change contract specifications. For example, a 1:1 bonus usually doubles the lot size as the stock price halves.

[40] A mathematical expectation is the mean of the possible values a random variable can take, weighted by the probability of those outcomes.

The expectation is actually less than 0 if you take the vigorish – the taxes and transaction costs – into account but that is too unnerving for the average trader to contemplate.

Brokerage commissions are often quoted on notional contract amounts and not the capital put up as margin, which makes the percentage amounts sound innocuously small, but those commissions can mount rapidly for the average trader abusing leverage.[41] As noted earlier, in India, big money can be made by shaving away tiny slivers from very large volumes, and fiddling with software settings in a fully computerized back office is an easy way to do just that. For example, derivatives traders and technical traders see the small commissions charged to them on individual contract notes but not on their quarterly or annual statements; if displayed, the aggregate amounts incurred at the end of a quarter or year would be considerable.

By definition, the X share in the derivatives segment must trade at *almost* the same price as it does in the underlying cash segment. After all, it's the same thing. The exact link is governed by the spot-futures parity theorems or what participants call the 'cost of carry' relationship. Under parity relations, futures usually – but not always – will trade at a slight premium to their underlying cash (or spot) price.[42] That premium or basis (₹5 in this example) is the cost of financing the futures position that must be borne by its holder; more technically, the cash price financed or 'carried' at a risk-free interest rate over the time to expiry should equal the futures price. Naturally, the basis reduces gradually over the life of the contract, which in India is a month. On settlement day, as the basis disappears because there is no time period left to finance, the

[41] A SSF contract with a 10 per cent margin might cost 0.01 per cent to trade. But that's on the contract's outstanding value of ₹5,00,000, and not on the margin of ₹50,000 required to trade it.

[42] Since futures don't earn dividends, futures prices will be lower than spot prices in months (typically July and August) when annual dividends are due. Commodity futures – because of storage, carrying charges, and insurance – usually trade at a premium to spot (contango); on occasion – and depending on tight spot conditions – they can trade at a discount (backwardation). More technically, single stock futures are usually in contango and (other than the dividend scenario) rarely in backwardation. So, compared to commodity markets, backwardation in stock futures is rare, but happens on occasion like in the collapses of 2008 and 2020.

futures price approaches or 'converges' to whatever cash price prevails at expiry. India is among the world's largest markets for SSFs – usually ranked with South Korea, Russia, and South Africa – and this is also a legacy of the market's familiarity with the badla product.[43]

The tenor (or duration) of contracts is typically a month with near, next, and far month contracts trading at any point in time. So, on 6 January, the near month contracts are the January contracts that expire on the last Thursday of January, while the next and far month contracts expire on the last Thursdays of February and March respectively. Practically, though, all the action is in the current month 'near' contract and volumes fall off drastically for the subsequent contracts. Longer duration contracts for futures and options exist but their volumes are negligible; recently introduced weekly contracts have better volumes because of the speculative nature of the market. There is no actual delivery of the underlying stock, though attempts are being made to change this, and most contracts are cash settled by squaring up before expiry.

The size of India's derivatives market – colossal to begin with – is also exaggerated by the way that size is calculated. To understand this, consider that ADTO for FY 2020 came in at ₹14,39,000 crores ($197 billion) for the cash and derivatives segments of equity markets. Of this, ADTO in the cash market came in at ₹39,000 crores, while the balance came from daily derivatives turnover amounting to a staggering ₹14,00,000 crores.[44]

A market trading ₹14 lakh crores a day sounds impressive and most would wish to know where all this capital is coming from. The answer is that it doesn't come at all. This large amount is the notional value of contracts traded daily. The actual capital entering the market is only a small fraction of this amount, and it enters as margins on futures (as

[43] NSE, Market Pulse Monthly Market Review April 2018, 14.

[44] Cash figures are from both exchanges and derivatives figures are from the NSE. See ICRA Ltd, 'Indian Brokerage Industry on a Roll Despite Challenges; Expected Revenue Growth in FY2021 at 10-12%,' *ICRA Press Release*, 23 September 2020.

in the ₹75,000 for stock X) and premia on options. More pertinently, over 80 per cent of derivatives volume comes from options rather than futures, and a technicality in how options turnover is calculated exaggerates the figure. With the market at a Nifty level of 9,900, a deep 'out of the money' call with a strike at (say) 10,600 and a contract multiplier of 75 would have a notional value of ₹7,95,000 (10,600 times 75) but the actual premium to trade it might be as low as, say, ₹5.[45] The public gets attracted to the low premia required to deal in deep 'out of the money' calls or puts and trades heavily in them. So, that huge ₹14,00,000 crore daily volume figure calculates the above trade at ₹7,95,000 but the capital to trade it is just ₹5, and this results in that exaggerated number.[46]

Despite this explanation, the staggering size of the derivatives market is noteworthy of itself. Worldwide, the ratio of derivatives to cash volume is between 1 and 2, but depending on how you look at the situation, it is many times more in India.[47] By some estimates, derivatives volumes are between 2.5 times (using option premium values) and 15 times (using option notional values) of cash market volumes.[48]

Derivatives have two main purposes – speculation or hedging. As the futures example showed, traders use the contract's leverage to enhance speculative returns. The demographic dividend, the growth of online

[45] The effect increases as the market moves closer to expiry, and premia on deep 'out of the money' options will fall to zero as options expire on settlement day (typically the last Thursday of every month).

[46] Options also benefit from favourable tax treatment. The Securities Transaction Tax (STT) is levied only on option premium, in contrast to futures where it is levied on the notional contract value.

[47] For an early observation on this, see Andreas A. Jobst, 'The Development of Equity Derivative Markets,' *International Journal of Emerging Markets,* 3 (2) 2008, 163–80.

[48] Securities and Exchange Board of India, 'Discussion Paper on Growth and Development of Equity Derivative Market in India,' 12 July, 2017, 15–16, https://www.sebi. gov .in/reports/reports/jul-2017/discussion-paper-on-growth-and-development-of-equity-derivative-market-in-india_35295. html. Taking just the futures results in a ratio of futures volume to cash volume that is usually between 4 or 5 to 1.

trading on mobile phones, the rise of discount brokers, and the resulting fall in transaction costs have all made speculative derivatives trading widespread. By contrast, hedging activity involves protecting against downside risk on existing portfolios – typically by short selling futures or buying protective puts. But hedging activity in India's derivatives markets is negligible, mainly because of the short duration of derivatives contracts. The next and far month contracts have little liquidity, and so only the near month contracts can be used. As the liquid-near contracts have a tenor of a month, fund managers short selling, say, futures to hedge portfolios incur significant costs as they have to roll over the contracts every month to maintain the hedge. In turn, short selling the 'near' contract implies taking a one-month view on the market and that's a mug's game; even a position taken on the very first day of a monthly settlement hedges only the next 22 days of market movement.

By contrast, in the US, the S&P futures contracts have three-month tenors with thick liquidity in the 'next' and 'far' months that allow fund managers to maintain their hedges at reasonable cost. Attempts to introduce longer-dated contracts in India have not worked out because brokers are happy with the current arrangements that yield commissions on 12 rollovers a year, as opposed to the four rollovers annually if the contracts had, say, a three-month tenor. As a result, hedging with derivatives is infrequent in India's equity markets, and even plain vanilla hedges such as selling futures or buying puts are used infrequently by the buy side.

Hedging's absence is ironical because the raison d'être behind introducing derivatives as a badla substitute was the hedging opportunities that the new instruments could offer participants.[49] L.C. Gupta – who produced that 1998 report recommending the introduction of derivatives – had in an earlier 1991 work also emphasized that hedging was a vital part of the market and that a derivatives market based only on trading and speculation would be a tenuous proposition. He went further and pointed out that a derivatives market with no

[49] SEBI, *Report of the Committee on Derivatives*, iv.

hedging activity that only allowed for trading and speculation would be downright unviable.[50] The conception itself is unexceptionable and typical of a derivatives market. Most experts would agree, and yet in India, derivatives markets have negligible hedging activity and are still extremely viable.

So, subsequent market development would negate Gupta's conclusion – and unlike the classical conception where a speculator often has a hedger on the other side of a trade, India's derivatives markets only have speculators (or arbitragers) on both sides of a trade. As a result, almost all derivatives volume is speculative or arbitrage-driven, and it is the public's appetite for speculation and the presence of larger players doing arbitrage that accounts for the world ranking in some segments such as SSFs. The philosophy at their introduction was sound and recognized the importance of both hedging and speculation to a healthy and well-functioning derivatives market, but something changed along the way and the derivatives market morphed into the casino it is today.[51]

Derivatives have a third use in arbitrage that is distinct from hedging and speculation. For example, futures are used as the derivatives leg in an arbitrage between the cash and derivatives markets. In the previous illustration, the futures price of stock X in the derivatives segment should trade within a certain range of its cash price in the cash segment; after all, it's the same stock. That range provides arbitrage bounds within which the futures price of X should trade compared to its cash price. Prices outside these arbitrage bounds result in a deviation from the Law of One Price and provide an arbitrage opportunity. If the X futures contract trades outside arbitrage bounds in the derivatives markets, arbitrageurs simply buy in cash and sell in futures to lock in the basis. On settlement day – as the futures price converges to the spot price – arbitrageurs reverse the trade and make a small profit on the basis. In the old days, entire rooms in the BSE were filled with traders doing

[50] L.C. Gupta, *Expert Study of Trading in Shares in Stock Exchanges*, New Delhi: The Society for Capital Market Research and Development, 1991, 27.

[51] SEBI, *Report of the Committee on Derivatives*, iv.

the above with physical keyboarding, but now programs and algorithms execute the technique.[52]

Doing this arbitrage continuously over the monthly settlement makes for derivatives' third use besides hedging and speculation. The increased volumes from the cash leg of arbitrage transactions also thicken and provide liquidity to the ELOB, and this is a vital, if underappreciated, advantage of having a huge derivatives segment. In this example, seeing X's order book in the cash segment ELOB will show blocks of 125 shares being frequently bought and sold. Because there is no NYSE type specialist system to guarantee liquidity, the volumes from this inter-market arbitrage provide the much-needed liquidity to the order book, and these arbitrage volumes are a major reason behind the NSE's growth and dominance. Many would credit the NSE's success to its dominance of the derivatives segment, but note that the ascendancy had started prior to the introduction of derivatives – driven in large part by the exchange's changes to the microstructure and its discovery of new trading communities outside Mumbai.

Because of the derivatives market's enormous size, its interaction with the cash market through the arbitrage engine is important in India. The arbitrage engine keeps the cash and derivatives markets in equilibrium. It hums along smoothly most of the time, but at market turning points, the engine takes on its own dynamic.[53] At turning points to the downside, like the 2008 Rate Bull crash and the 2020 coronavirus sell-off, the derivatives segment can become a big house of cards that comes crashing down. As seen earlier, participants who are overtrading and abusing the leverage inherent in derivatives contracts tend to be long at the top of a big up move. Overtrading is facilitated by pyramiding –

[52] In the early years, foreign investors were active in arbitrage, which picked up after a 2005 regulation that allowed them to use stocks (instead of cash) as collateral for arbitrage transactions. Most interexchange arbitrage is now handled by algorithms. See Deepak Shenoy, 'Algos Are Changing India's Stock Markets,' *Mint*, 13 January 2020.

[53] For an early treatment of arbitrage between cash and derivatives markets, see Ashok Jogani and Kshama Fernandes, 'Arbitrage in India: Past, Present and Future,' *Derivatives Markets in India*, ed. Susan Thomas, New Delhi: Tata McGraw-Hill, 2003.

using accumulated profits from existing positions as capital to finance new positions. The accumulated leverage from this technique together with the stop-loss honeycomb makes individual stocks – and the market – very unstable at tops and leads to those spectacular crashes. A sudden sell-off in the cash markets triggers margin calls in the derivatives markets, which forces traders to sell some of their holdings in the cash market to meet those calls, further exacerbating the collapse.[54]

Competition between the BSE and NSE for the huge derivatives market usually took the form of offering smaller contracts with reduced tenors that required lower margins. For example, the BSE introduced options with one-week tenors (a world first) and a mini-Sensex contract that prompted the NSE to introduce its own mini contracts. The BSE also offered various programs, such as the Liquidity Enhancement Incentive Program, where it drastically reduced bulk fees charged on options that traded on its platform.[55] BSE volumes picked up for a while till the inventive scheme was in place, but fell off after the scheme's withdrawal.[56] Because most derivatives trading in India is speculative, all this inter-exchange competition made it easier for the public to use derivatives for speculation, a public policy outcome of dubious significance; in fact, those weekly options contracts had crossed the line and were simply gambling instruments.

So, sometimes the arms race between the two exchanges came at the cost of good public policy. Many of the experts were at the exchanges rather than SEBI, and so, market developments of this sort continued for years unchecked by a regulator. Recently, the BSE has again made an attempt to claw its way back into the derivatives segment by offering smaller, weekly tenor contracts, whose expiries are expressly set to differ from NSE expiries; in turn, this allows for better margin use between exchanges. The effort has met with considerable success.[57]

[54] The chapter on market highs and lows has a more detailed treatment.

[55] For example, the BSE's 2012–13 Liquidity Enhancement Incentive Program charged just ₹50 (as compared to the NSEs ₹5,000) for option premium trades worth ₹1 crore. See Pravin Palande, 'How Ashish Chauhan Is Reviving the BSE,' *Forbes*, July 2013.

[56] SEBI, *Annual Report for the Fiscal Year 2017–2018*, 58.

[57] Drawn from the author's conversation with Nikunj Modi. 29 March 2024.

The regulator's view on the market has shifted as the market has grown. In the early years, the emphasis was on market development and making it easy for the public to trade derivatives, but as markets got bigger, this morphed into paternalistic concern over the public's preference for derivatives. These shifts in emphasis were usually implemented by manipulating contract multipliers or lot sizes. Low contract values made it easier for small and marginal players to trade derivatives and higher values did the opposite. In the early years, attempts were even made to keep contract sizes low, around ₹2,00,000, by adjusting the contract multiplier (the 125 in the X example); ₹2,00,000 (about $4,500) was a level far below contract sizes in developed or other Asian markets.[58] But contract sizes fluctuated with the market and the limit of ₹2,00,000 was itself made redundant in the huge bull markets that followed. As underlying stock prices exploded higher in bull markets, contract sizes naturally increased which led to repeated reductions of the multiplier to bring contract sizes down to the ₹2,00,000 level.

As derivatives markets grew substantially in later years, the trend would reverse and concern would now mount over the public's presence in derivatives markets. So, contract sizes would increase substantially as fewer attempts were made to reduce lot sizes;[59] SEBI also started fiddling with eligibility criteria and raised them to reduce the number of stocks that were eligible for the derivatives segment. In later years, SEBI annual reports would bang away on what a good thing derivatives markets were, but this official crowing would now alternate with the occasional attempt to control access to them.[60]

Quadruple witching hour takes place between 2.30 and 3.30 p.m. on the last Thursday of every month with attendant increases in volatility.

[58] A.A. Jobst, 'The Development of Equity Derivative Markets,' *International Journal of Emerging Markets*, 163–80. Pegging the contracts at about ₹2 lakhs had been a suggestion of Parliament's Standing Committee on Finance.

[59] Contract sizes are presently in the region of ₹5,00,000 ($6,000) with adjustments made at six-month intervals.

[60] Rajesh Mascarenhas and Reena Zachariah, 'SEBI Seeks to Cut Retail F&O Bets,' *Economic Times*, 12 March 2018.

Quadruple witching is the simultaneous expiry of all four classes of derivative instruments – futures and options on indexes, besides futures and options on stocks. As computer programs unwind the arbitrage transactions by executing the 'squaring up' leg, waves of buying and selling take place that move the market up and down. It is Turbulent Thursday, and the talking heads go on about 'settlement day volatility'. Arbitrage in SSFs that dominate India's markets is anyway easy to execute, and their unwinding further increases that volatility.

On expiry, the derivatives market rolls over into the next month. Long speculators sell the present month and buy into the next month to maintain their positions (the short side will do the opposite), while arbitrageurs lock in the first leg of arbitrage trades for the next month that are outside arbitrage bounds (such trades are easier to find amidst settlement day volatility). The waves of volatility roiling the markets then subside and everybody breathes a sigh of relief as the rollover 'is behind us'. The short tenor of derivatives contracts ensures that this *dramabaazi* (histrionics) takes place every month as opposed to every quarter on Wall Street, though the regularity of the phenomenon has reduced its novelty.

Who trades is a big mystery. The domestic buy side has compliance restrictions that limit its presence and FIIs, while active, also have a marginal presence.[61] Some of the dervishes are present in a big way, as are several brokerages, though both groups are careful not to earn a reputation for doing this; besides, they can only be present by so much. Consequently, a reasonable conclusion is that the public is heavily present, and in fact, some studies indicate that individuals and proprietary traders contribute over four-fifths, of traded volumes. A 2017

[61] The buy side has always had a marginal presence in India's derivatives markets. See Rajendra P. Chitale, 'Use of Derivatives by India's Institutional Investors: Issues and Impediments,' *Derivatives Markets in India,* ed. Susan Thomas.

SEBI study found that the domestic and foreign buy sides accounted for 0.4 per cent and 14 per cent of turnover respectively, while proprietary desks and a variety of non-institutional investors like individuals and partnerships made up the balance 85 per cent.[62]

The absence of the domestic buy side in derivatives markets is striking. In emerging markets with derivatives segments, a fair generalization is that the retail crowd provides the speculative activity and the institutions provide the hedging interest. The fundies and LIC should be natural hedgers, and in fact, they have been allowed to use derivatives markets for hedging since the early days.[63] But there is little of that in India. By and large, mutual funds account for less than 1 per cent of derivatives volume and insurance companies, pension funds, and banks also have a negligible presence. Contract tenors are one possible reason for the negligible presence. As seen earlier, hedging on large 'long-side only' portfolios involves short selling futures or buying protective puts, both of which are expensive undertakings when contracts have one-month tenors with no liquidity in the 'next' and 'far' months. Short selling futures in large quantities runs into the high transaction and impact costs of month-to-month rollovers; buying protective puts involves paying and losing put premium every month, which can get very expensive as the market keeps going higher in long-drawn-out bull markets. As the absence of a short side biases the market to those long-drawn-out up moves anyway, it's better to simply stay unhedged long and not repeatedly pay expensive low-duration term insurance. As a result, the institutional side which has hedging needs is largely absent.[64] Individual investors have few hedging needs anyway, all of which imply that most derivatives activity is speculative or arbitrage related.[65]

[62] SEBI, 'Discussion Paper on Growth,' 9–10.

[63] The L.C. Gupta report of March 1998 recommended that mutual funds be allowed to use derivatives for hedging and portfolio balancing. SEBI, *Report of the Committee on Derivatives*, v. The Mutual Fund Regulations were amended accordingly.

[64] The silo-like nature of Indian regulation – banks, insurance, mutual funds, and pension funds all have separate regulators – implies separate regulatory clearances for derivatives trading.

[65] The regulator has made attempts to improve fund participation in the derivatives segment through measures like call writing. Pavan Burugula, 'SEBI to Ease Norms for MF in Derivative Investment by

The typical derivatives trader from the public is a real Popat Popatlal. The average life of a derivatives trader has not been estimated but it cannot be very long, typically not more than a year or two; the leverage inherent to derivatives is a deadly drug that the average trader repeatedly abuses and most blow up in even less time. Yet the offices of derivatives brokers are chock full of clients, and market volumes keep soaring year after year as India's favourable demographics ensure a steady stream of traders entering.[66] There's that bandied about figure of 12 million people entering India's work force every year with few jobs available. If that number's too large and too vague, try the annual output of over 1.3 million engineers, or the over 2,00,000 who graduate from business schools every year[67] – many from both groups are skilled, math-literate, and capital-light, which ensures that they naturally gravitate to the derivatives side. Choosing any of these estimates as a starting point allows for large churn in the derivatives markets.

A regular flow of traders entering – and then blowing up – is a central part of the business model of derivatives brokers, but they are careful not to explicitly articulate the idea. On the derivatives side, more than anywhere else, complete ignorance is a blessing, but a little knowledge is a dangerous thing. The biggest fatalities occur in those with some knowledge. So, the Popats learn the wisdom of Bachelier's comment the hard way, if at all. After they blow up, the Popats slink out through the broker's back door, but only after a tantrum over hidden brokerage charges or incomprehensible account statements. The fresh-faced new entrants from the demographic dividend then come in through the front door, all smiling and beaming and cautiously optimistic about their chances. Nowadays, the flow is aided by the low-cost internet-based

---

Raising Cap on F&O,' *Business Standard*, 28 May 2018. With call writing, fund managers can sell calls to pocket the premium, but if they make a mistake the stock can get 'called away' from them. Call writing in a market without a short side can also be riskier than it usually is.

[66] The dominance of individual investors was apparent from the early years. Susan Thomas and Jayanth Rama Varma, 'Derivatives Markets,' 178–203.

[67] Deepto Banerjee, 'Pursuing engineering once a fad, now a dilemma: Only 10 percent of 15 lakh graduates likely to land jobs this year,' *TOI Education*, 29 October, 2024. Rica Bhattacharyya, 'Specialised skills are killing it! MBA seen losing edge', *ET Bureau*, 7 January, 2024.

infrastructure put in place by derivatives brokers; for some time now, South Korea and India are the Asian leaders in this.[68]

Many brokers with big derivatives businesses do no proprietary trading, and this is sensible given the risks involved. Nevertheless, without proprietary trading, the only way to increase brokerage revenues is by getting new customers or flogging the existing customer base. Getting new customers wasn't difficult, and growth came from the demographic dividend that poured into the markets, rather than from poaching other brokerages' customers; flogging the existing base usually meant getting the customer to over trade, but that wasn't even necessary, as most traders abused leverage anyway.

Because of the huge derivatives volumes, some discount brokers take the trading mindset to an extreme. In Zerodha's case, stock trading for holding periods of more than a day is free, and it is only derivatives trading and day trading in the cash market that generates commissions.[69] Close to three-quarters of Zerodha's volumes come from mobile phones where novice traders used five inches of screen real estate to play around with stocks or derivatives.[70] With all this, Zerodha is overtaking the bigger wire houses and is on its way to becoming India's largest broker.

Futures-dominated derivatives turnover in the early years after the 2001 introduction, and this is because of the market's familiarity with the badla product. Later, market activity and volumes moved to options which were trickier to value and trade. Options trading was actually like three-dimensional chess, but in India, only the premium traded and the public traded that premium for sport. Since the markets just traded the option premium and since all volume was speculative, it did not matter if there was the occasional mispricing. Presumably some entity arbitraged it away. More technically, put-call parity relationships were frequently violated in the early years, but later research showed fewer such violations, indicating that the market was beginning to price

[68] A.A. Jobst, 'The Development of Equity,' *International Journal of Emerging Markets,* 163–80.

[69] Rahul Satija, 'Burned-out Broker Got Rich Giving Free Trades to Millennials,' *Bloomberg*, 8 May 2019.

[70] Ibid.

options fairly.[71] Spot-futures parity relationships also held and most futures traded within arbitrage bounds.

Derivatives have one important use on the short side. Lending and borrowing mechanisms that allowed for short selling stock had been abolished with badla in 2001, and their subsequent reinstatement produced a tepid response that continues into the present day. As a result, getting short side exposure is problematic in the cash market because of the absence of a proper lending/borrowing mechanism for stock. But for the trader at least, this does not matter because the derivatives side allows short exposure at negligible cost; the range of SSFs – between 150 and 200 – and their huge volumes allow traders to short futures and thus get short exposure to the underlying stock. Nevertheless, short constraints in the cash market together with the ease of short selling in derivatives markets also presents a paradox. Despite attempts to reinstate a lending/borrowing mechanism and give it prominence in the cash market, the ease of short exposure in the derivatives markets through SSFs means that traders have little incentive to borrow and short stock in the cash market, which, in turn, sabotages attempts to reinstate the mechanism and improve price discovery. Finally, short selling in the derivatives market should be very risky because of the upward bias in the underlying cash market caused by short selling's absence there; yet extensive short selling happens in derivatives markets, perhaps because of a substantial retail presence.

So, what is the economic utility of all this? *Raising resources*, both spatially and across time, is one core function of a financial system, and yet nothing like that takes place in India's derivatives markets; there is no savings channelization from households or capital raising by firms, as both activities take place through IPOs and other cash markets offerings. *Price discovery* is another function, but derivatives derive their price from an underlying cash market; stocks are residual claims on a firm's real assets, and the valuation of those claims based on contrasting

[71] For early evidence on considerable inefficiency and options mispricing, see Ajay Shah, 'Market Efficiency on the Indian Equity Derivatives Market,' *Derivatives Markets in India,* ed. Susan Thomas, 99–119.

visions of the future takes place through buying and selling in the cash market.[72] Finally, *risk management* is a vital function in finance, but there is no risk management in India's derivatives market as hedging is simply too expensive for the buy side; because there is negligible hedging, there is also little inter-temporal transfer of risk from those who cannot bear risk to those who can. Against the above must be balanced improvements in cash market liquidity that result from arbitrage activity – particularly in SSFs – between both markets. Yet other than this improved liquidity, the bizarre fact is that there is little economic utility to what is seen as a crowning achievement of India's financial reforms.

So, there is a certain logic to winding up the derivatives segment, though prima facie, the idea sounds downright heretical, dangerous, and subversive. Yet that winding up would not hurt anyone except the NSE and its shareholders, the brokers, and the speculating public.

Consider each in turn. For the NSE, the segment is crucial as a big part of the exchange's perennially delayed IPO valuation comes from its derivatives monopoly; besides, at some point, the NSE's outside shareholders might tire of the discreet game of musical chairs that is the NSE's valuation exercise and decide to cash out at the IPO, which makes the valuation-boosting monopoly important. The brokers make vast sums from commissions generated by the derivatives segment so they will take the NSE's side on the issue; brokerage revenue is driven by getting the public to trade, and this the derivatives segment does very well with its high leverage, huge volumes, and weekly/monthly contract tenures. Finally, and true to its historical role, the speculating public will clamour for a leveraged product after it has been withdrawn, but they are usually happy with whatever is substituted – like (say) a straightforward margining system in the cash market. (During the

[72] For an argument that the high leverage offered by India's thick SSFs markets helps participants overcome funding constraints and influences spot price discovery, see Nidhi Aggarwal and Susan Thomas, 'When Stock Futures Dominate Price Discovery,' *Journal of Futures Markets*, 39 (3), 2019, 263–78. Short constraints in the cash market imply that the effect is more pronounced for price reactions to negative news flow; market participants find it simply easier to initiate short positions in the SSF markets because of their high leverage and liquidity. In turn, this implies that SSF markets sometimes lead price discovery, particularly when there is negative news flow.

Century of Marking Time, a margin system could not have worked as a badla substitute because it required an active public in a country with a threshold of capita income;[73] it also needed a strong institutional interface, through big brokers who could bring the public to the market. Both were missing in the badla era, but are present in today's market.)

Still, winding up the derivatives segment might produce one cosmic advantage. After all, lopsided development of the derivatives market also draws away much needed trading capital from the cash market. Assuming there's a limited pool of trading capital to move stocks up to fair value, any drawing away of trading capital – especially on this scale – has deleterious effects on price discovery and market efficiency, and this is an underappreciated side effect of derivatives dominance. So, in theory, winding up the derivatives segment might free up a lot of trading capital to move into the cash market and improve valuations there. It is admitted that winding up the derivatives segment would reduce the liquidity benefit to the cash market that arbitrage between the cash and derivatives segment brings about. Nevertheless, the freed-up trading capital that would enter the cash market if the derivatives segment was wound up might compensate for that.

But winding up the derivatives market – or even reducing its overwhelming dominance in the market's microstructure – is a pipe dream, given the vast constituencies and interest groups that the phenomenon has spawned, and besides its genesis and rise are seen as crowning achievements of India's financial sector reform. Even if the derivatives segment was wound up, the market's historical need for a speculative leveraged product is so strong that someone out there would simply construct substitutes and trade in them. So, the final reason for the presence of derivatives is the substitutes that would anyway be created by their absence.

[73] Bombay Stock Exchange, *Profile of Stock Exchange Activity in India*, Bombay: BSE, 1970, x.

21

THE HOWLING

The Media and the Market

Imagine a television channel that covered the steel industry for 24 hours a day. *Oh dear*, the ore inventory's building up. *My my*, now they're adding lime and coke to the ore. *Hai la*, they just fired up the electric furnace. *Geez*, they've moved the flats and longs off the floor, to the storage area. *Uff oh*, the night shift on fabrication just started.

Strange results.

But daylong coverage of the securities industry produces analogous results and no one says anything about it. Perhaps that's because coverage of the steel industry would only have to deal with events relating to that industry but coverage of the securities business pertains to events relating to the scores of industries whose securities it has issued and traded; this is besides a host of other factors that are causative, such as world events or liquidity or interest rates. Consequently, media coverage of the stock market is obsessive and, whether you like it or not, that rascal Mr Market will hammer away at you on CNBC and various other channels for most of the day. Saurabh the Student and Hema the Housewife and all the others love it.

Robert Shiller brings out the historical coincidence between the earliest speculative bubbles and the advent of newspapers as a mass medium.[1] The rise of the media industry in India in the early nineteenth century, too, coincided with the stock market's founding, with both seeing their early days in Calcutta and Bombay. Before physical gatherings of traders created a market, it was convenient to publish quotes for stocks in newspapers, and early newspapers published in both cities functioned almost like over-the-counter (OTC) pink sheets for stocks. As seen, from about the 1820s, stock quotations for the Bank of Bengal and the Union Bank appeared with some regularity in Calcutta newspapers such as the *Bengal Hurkaru and Chronicle* (1795).

Bombay newspapers had also started carrying quotations for stocks and one of the earliest quotes – for the Agra Bank at ₹250 – appears in an 1835 issue of the *Bombay Courier*.[2] In fact, in Bombay, the media and the market were physically adjacent to one another, with Bazaar Gate, where the early newspapers were located, next to the Horniman Circle area where the first traders gathered. Asia's oldest extant newspaper the *Bombay Samachar* (1822) is located only a few buildings away from the BSE, and one of the exchange's two entrances is on Mumbai Samachar Marg. Yet eyewitness accounts of the time that detail the initial gatherings at Horniman Circle and the Cotton and Share Mania of the 1860s, are surprisingly devoid of media references. An editor of the *Times of India's* predecessor, *The Bombay Times and Journal of Commerce* (1838), was present at the meeting when the news of Robert E. Lee's surrender at Appomattox – the event that ended the Cotton and Share Mania in 1865 – was first received by the market, but other than this incident, there is not much recorded on the media as a participant in the market's founding episode.

Subsequently, by the mid-nineteenth century, the tendency of traders to gather physically in one place became apparent, and this did

[1] 'The history of speculative bubbles begins roughly with the advent of newspapers.' Robert Shiller, *Irrational Exuberance*, 2nd ed., Princeton: Princeton University Press, 2005, 85.

[2] *The Bombay Courier*, Saturday, 18 April 1835.

away with the need to publish quotes (or requests for quotes) in the newspapers. During the Century of Marking Time, the equity market at Dalal Street was a physical market with its own trading hall. The key market participants – the 500 odd brokers – also had offices located on or around Dalal Street itself, usually within walking distance of each other. So, even when there was occasion for the media to transmit information, newspapers were unreliable and slow compared to the actual crowd transmission that occurred in a physically proximate environment with its own trading floor.

Through most of this period it was print media through newspapers that was the only source of market coverage. Most newspapers from the early years, such as the *Bombay Courier* or the *Bombay Times*, did not carry a regular stock market column, but some had a small business section which covered general business news with an occasional article on the market. The sleepiness of that epoch was apparent even in the media coverage. Flare-ups in the media's interaction with the market occurred after the First and Second World War, and the tops of 1920 and 1946 saw newspaper coverage of the new issue mania that reported on kerb rates and grey market premia. Newspapers also carried much advertising for these issues that was noteworthy for tall claims that tried to bring the public into the primary market's stagging operations.

The *Federal Observer*'s special editions on the stock market – which came out in 1940 and 1941 probably after someone realized that the market's centennial had passed by unnoticed some years previously – are an important source on the exchange's early years. Written in the hagiographic style common at that time, they nevertheless contain much biographical information on the movers and shakers of that era.[3] After Independence, occasional market incidents – especially those dealing with the settlement compromises of the badla era – also featured in the *Economic and Political Weekly* (1949).[4]

[3] *Federal Observer*, Stock Exchange Special Number, Vol. 1, Nos. 36 and 37, 10 November 1940; *Federal Observer*, Stock Exchange Special Number, Vol. 1, Nos. 42 and 43, 30 March 1941.

[4] 'Deliberate Default,' *Economic and Political Weekly, Around the Markets*, 29 March 1952.

Given the profit motive, one would expect that demand for market news was considerable even in the early years, but that was not the case. This is because trading based on inside information was widely prevalent. The 1956 SCRA never found insider trading important enough to even mention, and with no official proscription, insider trading on an event cycle was extensive. Journalist Aditi Roy Ghatak records how a secretary at a Calcutta managing agency would finish typing out a dividend announcement and then pick up the phone to place an order with her broker.[5] In fact, it was an era when statutory disclosures were negligible, so it is conceivable that without insider trading the incorporation of information into price simply would not have happened. Because of the insider trading, public news flow through the media was at the end of an event cycle – it was always 'buy the rumour, sell the news' and never 'ignore the rumour, buy the news'. This left the media, as generator of that news, at a disadvantage, and it did not offer much incentive to invest in a news gathering infrastructure for financial markets.

From about the 1960s there was a marked acceleration in the media's engagement with the market, mainly through the launch of the first business newspapers. The *Economic Times* (1961), *Financial Express* (1961), and *Business Standard* (1975) were pioneers among the pink papers, and they continue to be market leaders today. To these must be added *BusinessLine* (1994), *Mint* (2007), and *Business Guardian* (2022). This roster of six broadsheets comprises print media's present newspaper coverage of the stock market and business. Even the US, the world's largest media market, does not have six national-level broadsheets to cover business or the market, which simply indicates the saturation level in today's media.

In the 1970s, print's engagement with the market expanded with the start of business magazines. *Business India* (1978) and *Business World* (1981), together with other magazines were founded around this time, but most were focused on policy and industry and carried negligible market coverage. In fact, there was much sniffing and condescension

[5] Aditi Roy Ghatak, *Down Lyons Range*, Kolkata: P.K. Ray for the Calcutta Stock Exchange Association, 2008, 63.

towards the raffish stock exchange crowd in that era, and as a result, the early magazine coverage lacked the savvy frontline view from the trenches of newspapers such as the *Economic Times*.

The business magazines were followed by a rash of personal finance magazines, and stock market coverage created the personal finance segment in the magazine space. *Capital Market* (1986) and *Dalal Street Investment Journal* (1986), with their exclusive focus on stock investing and trading, were the pioneers in what later evolved into the segment of personal finance magazines. The tipster format and the profit motive sent these magazines on their merry way as they offered stock picking advice to the public, and both are extant and thriving to this day. Later, other magazines such as *Outlook Money* (1998), *Money Today* (2006), and *Money Life* (2006) also engaged with the market and offered stock picking advice within the broader personal finance segment but without the exclusive equity focus of *Capital Market* or *Dalal Street.* Among regional language publications, a range of Gujarati magazines, including *Chanakya Ni Pothi* and *Smart Investment*, also offer stock advice.

The press takes the credit for the only episode where the media figures both as observer and participant in the market's drama. In 1992, Sucheta Dalal's coverage in the *Times of India* of G-Sec clearing and settlement problems unearthed the Harshad Mehta scam and ended the first major bull market of the modern era.[6] The *Times*'s coverage was factual and sober but much of the other coverage – focusing as it did on Mehta's foreign cars and flashy lifestyle – would set a trend for breathless and sensational schadenfreude that was seen as the kiss of death by later day participants and operators. This would also mark the last occasion when a single media segment scooped a story. After that, the presence of a house across multiple segments, together with the simultaneous breaking of stories across newsprint, broadcast, and digital would ensure that no single segment of the media could take the credit for a market scoop. CNBC TV 18, a television channel, did

[6] Debashis Basu and Sucheta Dalal, *The Scam: Who Won, Who Lost, Who Got Away*, New Delhi: UBS Publishers' Distributors Ltd., 1993.

scoop the Satyam scam based on a confessional its promoter wrote to the channel's newsroom, but that remains a company event rather than a market-wide systemic event.

Among media segments, print was always private but broadcast – starting with radio in 1930 and later television in 1959 – was under state control till private entry was allowed in the early 1990s.[7] State control of radio and television ensured that there was negligible coverage of the stock market. It was only from the early 1990s that private broadcasting (which meant television/cable, as radio had negligible market coverage) started coming into its own and ended the indifference of the state-controlled Doordarshan towards the market.

Despite significant coverage by the print segment, it was only with the advent of private television that media started playing an important role in the market's drama. That influence also worked in the other direction and the market's hold over television (particularly business channels) was greater than over other segments like print or digital, an influence that has carried forward. Perhaps this is because market hours and daytime programming coincide. As a result of that alignment, the stock market provides the framework around which television organizes its coverage of the business day. At one time, four business channels covered economic and financial news and all had the stock market as their focus: *CNBC TV 18* was the leader, while *ET Now*, *Bloomberg UTV*, and *NDTV Profit* all offered competition. Today, the field is effectively left to *CNBC TV 18* and *ET Now*. Two business channels, *CNBC Awaaz* and *Zee Business*, cover the markets in Hindi, and besides these, the stock market also figures in scores of regional language news channels. India now has over 400 news channels, and on many of them, the stock ticker has become ubiquitous across the bottom of the screen.

The defining event in the media's coverage of the markets was the IPO wave of the early 1990s. For the first time, the stock market became a revenue stream for the media, as the mania briefly led to a

[7] The first private radio broadcasts were made in the 1920s through the Presidency Radio Clubs, followed (for a brief period) by the Indian Broadcasting Company.

new practice – financial services – in the advertising and public relations industries. Promoters discovered that spends on IPO publicity and advertising could be financed from the issue proceeds itself, which was convenient, and this fuelled a huge boom in financial services advertising. Specialized agencies sprang up to offer Dalal Street access to the media and sophisticated outreach techniques were created to connect the Street with various investing publics. This was the heyday for such activity, a brief period of freedom before SEBI started throwing regulations at it and formalized the haphazard techniques of the IPO grey market. By now, disclosure issues were not about untrue facts as much as vague claims like 'latest and proven technology', 'assured markets', 'low breakeven point', and 'guaranteed dividend'.[8] This IPO wave also marked the start of SEBI's influence on the media-market relationship; statutory requirements that companies publish quarterly results in media date from this period, and thousands of companies that listed in this wave continue to provide a steady revenue stream to the pink papers because of this regulatory requirement.

From the late 1990s, the internet and digital media start coming into their own, and a new seamlessness emerged between segments as they went about their nonstop market coverage. From its early years, the internet was found suitable for that bedrock practice of Indian financial markets – rumour mongering. *Moneycontrol*, part of the same group that owns *CNBC TV18*, is a good example of a site that provides financial information and a platform for market rumours through its chat boards. The internet and social media would change coverage of the markets by making that coverage granular, customizable, and subject to instant feedback. The flipside was a lack of quality control and the absence of a certain gravitas that print brought. Internet and social media have also brought immediacy to market action, but it is an immediacy that the average retail investor can do without and only contributes to the speculative nature of the market. To get an idea of the intensely personal

[8] M.R. Mayya, 'Regulatory Framework for Stock Markets: The Indian Experience,' *Symposium on Capital Market Development and Privatisation*, Mumbai: Commonwealth Secretariat, 1990, 185.

relationship a trader can have with a stock, check out its message board on *moneycontrol*.

With the ELOB going online by the turn of the millennium, there was no physical market and consequently no physical crowd. If the market is a crowd nowadays, it must be a virtual one, and if that virtual crowd has to develop a mental unity and get mobilized behind a single idea, it needs a vector of contagion. That vector of contagion is the media, and this gives the media a certain importance that was missing in the old days when transmission took place in a physically proximate market. The pros have their own channels of information, so the demand for media coverage of the market comes mainly from the crowd – the public.

The public's main objective is to make a killing without being killed and the public wants to be told how to do it.[9] The great desire of the public to be told – this demand if you will – generates its own supply, and a vast media industry now caters to that desire. As a result, media coverage of the markets is nonstop when the market is open, and after it closes, there's the usual port-mortem. All major tops of the post-Independence era occurred only after 1991 which corresponds to the opening up of broadcast media from that date. Per Shiller's observation, this is no coincidence, and in other countries too, the occurrence of speculative bubbles is concurrent with the rise and profusion of mass media.

With the rise of broadcast media in recent years, much of this plays out on television.[10] India, today, is a chronically saturated media market, that by some measures is the second largest in the world; by 2020, the country had almost 1,40,000 registered publications and over 900 TV channels, of which close to half were news

[9] This combines insights from Gerald Loeb and Edwin Lefèvre.

[10] For an account of television broadcasting, see Nalin Mehta, *Behind a Billion Screens: What Television Tells us about Modern India*, New Delhi: HarperCollins India, 2015.

channels.[11] The obsession of business channels with the market is understandable, but in recent years, it is not through them, but through the regular news channels that the stock ticker has become ubiquitous. Despite the market's marginal influence in the wider scheme of things, all this coverage gives the market a prominence it does not deserve. That big, always-on display of a business channel next to the portrait of Lakshmi in the BSE's lobby is simply an indication of that prominence.

On balance, it is television and the talk shows that contribute to media's influence on the stock market. The talk show is an echo chamber within which the media influences and gets influenced by the stock market. Here, participants appearing as guests vie with one another to provide insight on the market's movements; nobody gets paid for all this effort, so for participants it is the chance to raise their company's profiles that persuades them to appear. Participants vary their appearances in the echo chamber: the technical traders appear habitually, the fundies and brokerages regularly, the FIIs occasionally, the dervishes on Diwali (typically), and LIC never. The public emerges when given the chance at talk shows with a call-in format. But despite the attempts at providing insight, most commentary is irrelevant because of the well-known tendency of participants to 'talk their book', i.e., to rationalize and tout their market approach and positions to a wider audience in the hope of influencing them to buy (typically) or sell (occasionally).

Consider the usual suspects among the guests on your typical channel.

The fast-talking *technical analysts* babble away, reading out levels of support and resistance at various times during the trading day. They have thousands of stocks to tout, so finding things to say is easy; at any point, many stocks are in various stages of breakout or breakdown, and these tend to be the phases that attract the trend-following technical crowd. The techies are wont to talk both ways. A typical comment is: 'If the stock crosses 45, then it can touch 50, but if it breaks support to

[11] According to the Registrar of Newspapers for India (RNI), by early 2020, the total number of registered publications stood at over 1,40,000. The full list is available at http://rni.nic. in/pdf_file/ whatsnew/list_of_registered_newspaper.pdf. Naturally, all this generates much competition among channels for advertising budgets, and the struggle for share of ad spend is continuous and relentless.

the downside at 40, then 35 is a strong possibility.' This is a wonderful statement to make. A stock usually does two things – go up or down – so this announcement covers both of its states and almost 20 per cent in either direction at that. Accuracy is therefore guaranteed. Technical analysts are the mainstay of most channels, both because of their availability and the public's fondness for the magical thinking of technical analysis. Critically, for the channels, there is the chance to economically fill broadcast time covering the squiggles and wiggles of thousands of stocks.

The *economists* intone their growth predictions after a fair amount of diddle-daddle and fiddle-faddle, gravely announcing that they 'expect it to come in at 7.3 per cent next year'. This proclamation is treated with great respect by the channels, more so if it comes from what the pink papers – in their 'Heard on the Street' gossip columns – call the Golden Socks brokerage or the Murugan Srini brokerage. There will be an obligatory news flash in the middle of the trading day, announcing the grand prediction. The anchors then fret and worry about the difference between Murugan Srini's 7.6 and Golden Socks's 7.1 forecast, so after a while the panjandrum who arrived at the figure is hauled on to the channel to talk in measured tones about the estimate. Never mind that the figure is not from a general equilibrium model of the economy with accurate inputs. Never mind that the prediction is guesswork based on a careful survey of other economists' guesswork about the growth rate. Finally, never mind that the learned economists are all huddled together for warmth and safety in the herd's centre, as a result of which all their estimates anchor neatly around a figure. Actually, most participants couldn't care less about growth predictions, as there is little connection between such predictions and market levels. Then why does so much effort go into the whole shebang? The answer is that the brokerages get a fair amount of market exposure with the exercise, an act of free indirect subliminal advertising. So, the main role of the learned economists has less to do with analysis or prediction and more with building their organization's profile on market media.

The *fund managers* drone on about the importance of being fully invested because their job is to be fully invested most of the time. This is apparent on the way to a high, but at the highs the message changes and the polite euphemism is that the market is 'fairly valued'. With the fundies, the market is never overvalued but always 'fairly valued', and the longer they use that term, the higher the chance of an approaching top. Fundies are very fond of quoting forward multiples for the market and irrespective of a market level, a typical media comment is: 'The market is fairly valued at 18 times forward earnings.' At market highs, such a comment is guaranteed. After all, fiddling with earnings per share projections in the denominator will always lead to a reasonable multiple irrespective of the actual market level; project earnings two years forward and market valuations turn more reasonable. Fund manager appearances are geared towards getting the public into the market and also towards getting them to stay there when redemption pressures rise. Consequently, their voices get a little shrill while trying to get the public to stay invested during a down move, but at the bottom itself, they disappear altogether from the media as the public is sullen and in no mood to listen to their prognostications.

The *industrialists* make their pleas for lower interest rates, though they'd only be happy when rates are at their lower bound of zero. At the first hint of an upturn in the rate cycle, industry lobbyists start yelping about how high interest rates are bad for the economy and employment. Attempts are made to influence RBI policy by mobilizing public opinion in favour of lower rates and television is the most effective channel for this. Industry's tendency to talk its book on rates was most apparent in 2010, just when the RBI had to clear the decks to ensure interest rates went higher; industrialists and their association heads were then seen smoothly intoning how high interest rates would affect growth, and there was considerable twisting and turning as they came up with ingenious arguments against rate hikes. On this occasion at least, the RBI listened too closely to this talk and went wrong; it commenced tightening later than it should have and inflation became a significant problem. The absence of think tanks, university economists, or people with less self-serving bias is quite apparent in India, and as a result, the hijacking of the media by special interests often takes place.

For *brokerages*, the favourite media theme during a bull move is growth and during a down turn is reform. During a bull move, the up move is rationalized as discounting the growth that lies ahead. During a down move, something has to be done to stop the down turn and so the government – the *maa baap ka sarkar* – has to rescue the market with Stakhanovian bouts of reform, and the brokerages can be seen egging on the government to do just that. It's almost uncanny how there is virtually zero talk of reform during a market up move and how such talk mounts during a down turn. During the first big break, the brokerages are busy just getting their clients to breathe, so there is no such talk, and it is only during the listless drift to the bottom in the bear's final stages that such talk reaches a crescendo. Along these lines, the chatter on reform surged in 2009, 2013, and briefly in 2020.

This brings us to the *government*. The government usually restricts its media presence to periods of market turmoil. Naturally, the move to the upside is a pleasant affirmation of India Shining or government policies, but successive Indian governments, while quick to take credit for many things, have been strangely reluctant to take credit for market upside. So, it is only turmoil to the downside that elicits government comment. Markets grind higher slowly but fall faster, so when the downside break presents itself and the government is suddenly called on to talk its book, it does not have much time for sensible comment. Besides, it is only occasionally that the breaks have proximate causes – either domestic or international. So, irrespective of the presence of a proximate cause, the government talks its book by saying '*Aaaaall is well*' followed by '*Main hoon na*', and soothing bromides from a mandarin or a minister are the default course of action. In the usual format, an anxious media corners a worthy outside the finance ministry and bombards the person with questions. The response is a series of calming comments on how the 'India growth story' is intact; statistics, most of which are only distantly connected with the proximate cause of the crash are sometimes reeled off, following which the media moves on to the next story.

All this can sound quite confusing to participants because of the even balance in Indian markets between the technical crowd and the fundamental gang. When a stock – or the entire market – has made a considerable down move, the technical crowd and the trend followers are screaming 'sell' as it's in a downtrend, but the fundamental gang who buy value are shouting 'buy' because it's cheap in their eyes, and the media are happy to play along and air both views with equal aplomb.

Still, it's all quite civilized and respectful compared to the political coverage and this is understandable. Political coverage runs into the inherent vulgarity and coarseness of public discourse and in fact contributes to that coarseness; besides, there's the lip service that has to be paid to the general equality of conditions. But in the stock market conditions are more unequal and guests are 'they' – those with the competence and capital to take stocks higher – the 'they' of *eh lokho upar lehse* or 'they'll take it up'. As a result, the deference flows naturally. So, the beast has to be stroked by staying with the polite bromides and the anchors do precisely that. Go too far and lean on your guest and they'll just hop over to the next channel. There seems to be an unwritten rule about how far one can go, and anchors going through with their anodyne questions is about as far as it does go.

The basic problem is having something sensible to say, day in and day out, about an insensible process – the market. The ideal solution would be a daily 10-minute program on the market, which would leave the channels free to do what they liked with the remaining programming time. But this suggestion would be shot down as dangerously naïve, or worse still, irredeemably facetious. Besides, that freedom would be impossible to handle and most channels would be incapable of filling programming time on a daily basis. The cost would also be prohibitively high.

The media effect is resplendent if the market tops out around Diwali after a long up move, as it did in 2007, 2010, and 2019. In keeping with the festive season, the studios are decked in colourful lighting and twinkling *diyas* and the dervishes and fundies come out in style, looking immaculate in their shimmering silk kurtas. The anchors eagerly ask them questions and try to get their secrets. Sometimes the anchors try to inject a dose of skepticism into the discussion, but get swept away by the forceful enthusiasm of the bulls and India Shining.

The anchors' questions – in accents that are usually clipped Bong or sing song Tam Bram – get deflected and rolled over by the fundies and dervishes, always bullish. And there are the dervishes, talking with sweet reasonableness about the market's majestic upward move, inexorable in its march; they make eminently sensible arguments on why the public should drop its perennial distrust of the stock market. One of the fundies might have words of caution but this is to be expected from the 'prudent man' investing the life savings of thousands; the doubts are raised and then self-dismissed with vigour a few moments later. An occasional voice of dissent does speak up and The Mustachioed One from among the dervishes simply might not fall in line. *How dare he?* How can you be bearish on Diwali, the festival of lights? So, the highlight of the evening might be a petulant exchange between this character and one of the bullish dervishes. But the overarching theme of this little scene playing out in the media is to get that elusive Yeti – the Indian public – back into the market, and if it is already there, to keep it there.

At least the dervishes speak their minds and the market – that bloodless and anonymous arena in which they made their wealth – allows them that luxury. Other guests are not so fortunate and the weight and power of the government has a chilling effect on public opinion in the market, as it does elsewhere. This is most apparent in programs involving the banking fraternity and the central bank. On these programs, the combination of majority government ownership and convoluted regulation that no one seems to really understand produces a 'Daddy Knows Best' attitude towards the RBI, or worse, a paralysing fear that leads to wretched and slavish adherence. If the RBI does X, the entire banking industry can be seen solemnly agreeing and intoning 'X X X' on the channels, and if the RBI does Y, equally ingenious choruses of 'Y Y Y' will arise. A typical comment by a public sector bank head might go like this: 'Yaar Bee Yiii, by keeping rates unchanged, has acted in a mature and steady fashion.' If instead of keeping rates unchanged the rate action was a hike, we'd have: 'Yaar Bee Yiii, by raising rates, has acted in a mature and steady fashion.'

In any case, monetary policy coverage has pretensions to being a communication channel between the central bank and bond markets, but stock market coverage has no such airs about it. Nowadays, debt market participants and the learned economists even have a 'citizen's monetary policy committee' where they vote on rate actions and such like, but the stock markets have no such device to influence policy through the media.

Despite that, in large part it is the media that accounts for the disproportionate influence the stock market has on economic policy making. The real economy may be doing well or badly but it's usually only when the stock market – as played out in the media – says the economy is doing well or badly that everybody sits up and pays attention. Bureaucrats keep an eye on the Sensex or Nifty all the time, perhaps because of the sheer availability of that pesky number and the way it wiggles around; the market's inherent moodiness and drama as depicted in the media forces a sense of crisis on a situation, often even when the situation is far from a predicament and undeserving of a government response. Even the language contributes to this and stocks don't just rise, they 'soar' or 'spurt', and they don't just fall, they 'slump' or 'slide'.

All this was apparent in 2008 when one of the biggest bear market drops took the Sensex from 21,000 to almost 8,000 in a little over a year, but this over 50 per cent fall presaged a drop in output growth of just 2.5 percent. This is just another example of substantial market variations that cannot be explained by release of news on the real side.[12] In this case, the sell-off preceded the output drop and played out massively

[12] For early evidence that a substantial amount of return variation is simply not supported by release of macroeconomic news (or release of non-economic news events), see David M. Cutler, James M. Poterba, and Lawrence H. Summers, 'What Moves Stock Prices?' *Journal of Portfolio Management*, 15, No. 3 (Spring 1989), 4–12.

in the media, which pressured policy makers into the most significant monetary easing in a generation, a response that in turn was to have significant inflationary repercussions some years later.

It is the strong retail presence that guarantees the media coverage which gives stock markets this prominence. Unlike debt or currency markets – which are wholesale, institution-driven, interbank, and usually over-the-counter – stock markets in India have wide ranging retail participation, and so, lots of people watch their coverage, which leads to that large audience. Reaching this audience results in the total rating points (TRPs) which are a sine qua non for broadcast media, and this incentivizes channels to organize daily coverage around the market framework. As a result, stock markets dominate media coverage which gives them a high profile in public discourse and policy making. The market's classical role is that of the barometer, soaring when it senses better times ahead, or swooning when it anticipates a downturn in economic activity. But in India, the market or rather the 'market in the media' is not a barometer but an electroencephalogram (EEG) that reflects the patient's current moods rather than future health.

The entire spectacle should be a side show, but that does not register. The stock market is open from morning till late afternoon (9 a.m. to 3.30 p.m.), and this provides a solid framework around which the business media organizes its coverage for the day. That framework has stayed essentially the same since the early 1990s when private broadcast media came into existence and ended Doordarshan's state monopoly. This period also coincided with the market's liberalization, and since then the stock market and television have symbiotically fed off one another in a chain of mutual dependence.

Business media has used the market framework for its coverage for some time now, and even when the coverage moves to another event it always swings back to the market lodestar; in this sense, the market firmly anchors the coverage framework for the business day. Similarly, the stock market uses media extensively and much of the market's influence over economic policy comes from its hold over broadcast media. The market's framework dominates the Hindi and regional language business channels even more than it does the English channels; compared to the English channels, Hindi and regional ones have less access to analytical economic or business content and consequently tend to fill more programming time with stock tips and the like. In fact, when the market is closed on a weekday, the media coverage on all business channels seems a little lost and forlorn as it moves from one filler program to the next.

The problem is not with the media. It's only trying to do its job by reporting the news within a certain framework, and within that framework, the media does an excellent job. The tendency of the market's operating hours to create the framework within which the media must produce the business news is what creates the problem. That framework leads to an environment of nonstop noise, and it is noise that remains the defining feature of the media-market relationship. The framework itself ensures the very definition of noise – the idea that a large number of small events matter more than a small number of large events.[13] Because of that noise, sometimes it becomes difficult to discern the important stuff – that small number of large events – and so what is important tends to simply slip through. In turn, this puts a premium on the participant's skill and ability to hear through all that din. Most people would be thankful to have a competent and objective observer guide them like a skilful host gently leads a guest by the elbow through the crowd towards the right person the host would like that guest to meet. But there are few who can distil and provide such guidance, and for the most part, the chatter is all that there is.[14]

As noted earlier, the media anyway has an impossible job – trying to explain the present and discern the future by talking sensibly about an insensible topic. On most occasions, the media will look for the reason behind a move after the move has taken place. Given manifold

[13] Fischer Black, 'Noise,' *Market Efficiency: Stock Market Behaviour in Theory and Practice Vol I*, ed. Andrew W Lo, Lyme, NH: Edward Elgar Publishing, Inc., 1997, 3–15.

[14] Consider that even in sophisticated markets, much of the news does not release fresh information to be incorporated in fundamentals or prices. Paul Tetlock, 'Giving Content to Investor Sentiment: The Role of Media in the Stock Market,' *Journal of Finance*, 62, No. 3, June 2007, 1139–68.

causality and the infinite variety of news events, this is not a difficult task; positive news and negative news are used as explicatory for price rises and falls respectively. The BSE's *Stock Exchange Reviews* of the 1990s and thereafter had 'all round buying' followed by 'short covering' as standard explanations for any rise in the markets, but these days – with the vast increase in channels and the media's rise to prominence – such anodyne explanations will not do.[15] The search for causation has now become continuous and relentless. That there was just a little more buying than selling when the market moved up 300 points will not do as the reason behind a move. The move has to be explained. Even when that explanation is patently absurd – nowadays, short covering cannot be the reason for a rally in the near complete absence of short selling – it still must be made.

And so, the media basically acts as an echo chamber for the long side. India has no short side, though it is admitted that in speculative markets the biggest bear can be a bull who has just sold out and is waiting to get back in at lower prices; a bear case can also be made for the brave souls shorting in the derivatives market, but in fact, all they do is trade noise over the monthly periods the contract tenors allow them. Except for these two cases there are no real bears, and so, the one-sidedness of bull opinion in the media's echo chamber can be mind-numbing in its intensity. The absence of the short side, together with the long corner and the lack of global diversification results in a homogeneity of opinion on the long side that is so pervasive that it isn't even noticed.

With the fundies, this one-sidedness is particularly pervasive. Give a person ₹50,000 crores to put on a line and tell him his life, his well-being, his family's well-being, his name and reputation, and everything else he holds dear in this world depends on that line going up, and he will keep saying that the line will go up. Add to that the thousands of people who have contributed to that ₹50,000 crores and their lives and well-being that the fundie holds in his hands, and the pressure to say that the line

[15] See for example, Bombay Stock Exchange, *The Stock Exchange Review: July 1989*, Bombay: BSE, 1989, 15.

will go up mounts even further. Now you can call that line a clothes line or you can call it a Sensex and it will not matter, for that line has to keep going up and if it does not go up, it has to be talked up. This the entire buy side does with energy and alacrity.

Media coverage at turning points can be important and especially to contrarians; that sameness of opinion as it plays out in the media becomes the contrarian's food for thought and allows a contrarian trade to be put on. Successful fundies reportedly have the ability to mingle with those holding a contrary opinion on a stock, which allows them to carefully extract negative views which are then balanced out against their own bullishness. So, contrarians looking to cross the market will listen carefully to the coverage at what they believe are turning points, and analysing that sameness of opinion as it plays out in the media becomes critically important at market highs and lows. What applies to a stock should apply to a country – and yet it does not – so there is no one to mingle with who holds a contrary opinion on India itself. As noted earlier, domestic bias and the complete lack of international diversification imply that close to 100 per cent of all folios are invested in India and this allows for a sameness and uniformity of opinion on the country that does not brook any opposition.

The media also amplifies the information cascades and feedback loops often associated with rising or falling prices. The influence is such that while tape reading it is possible to see a stock jump a couple of points when CNBC has a news announcement on a company, or better still, moves to cover the company itself. The channel shines a spotlight on the stock, singles it out from the over 2,000 stocks trading on that day, and brings it to the attention of the trading public.[16] This attention is especially useful for the small- or mid-caps that have negligible media coverage, and often the stock will spike higher even if there are only

[16] Brad Barber and Terence Odean, 'All That Glitters: The Effect of Attention and News on the Buying Behavior of Individual and Institutional Investors,' *Review of Financial Studies*, 21, No. 2, January 2008, 785–818. They find that attention-driven (rather than preference-driven) choice as a solution to the search problem affects individual investors (the public) more than it does professionals.

banalities in the news item.[17] So profitable and regular is the effect that sometimes anchors have been caught front running their own programs.[18]

More technically, the media is amplifying an information cascade that has feedback loops.[19] Investors practise herding behaviour, which leads to momentum, much of which is broadcast through an information cascade with positive feedback. Most of us have participated in an information cascade at one time or another. Walking down a road of empty restaurants, people naturally gravitate towards the one that is half-full – that half-full status itself arose because an initial agent went in, followed by others. Absent other information, the crowd assumes the food is a little better at the half-full restaurant as compared to the empty ones. In this sense, information cascades can help as they may reduce search and transaction costs. But in a stock market cascade, agents (in this case, retail investors) make sequential decisions rationally based on the information they have – which is purely price action as seen on television – and without access to the information of others. Problems arise when such cascades are based on improper beliefs or valuation models. Further, even if agents are rational and valuation models are sound, people might practice greater fool investing; traders buy assuming that someone is out there whom they can offload to, while the media broadcasts the price action and acts as a vector for all this. Then the result is a positive feedback loop. An initial action leads to a

[17] Lily Fang and Joel Peress find this effect globally, and typically for stocks with 'high individual ownership, low analyst following, and high idiosyncratic volatility' which are typical characteristics of small- and mid-cap stocks that make up the bulk of Indian listings. See Lily Fang and Joel Peress, 'Media Coverage and the Cross Section of Stock Returns,' *Journal of Finance,* 64, No. 5 September 2009, 2023–52. For evidence that this effect is subject to mean reversion, see J. Felix Meschke, 'CEO Interviews on CNBC,' Working paper, Arizona State University, Phoenix, AZ, 2004.

[18] Samie Modak, 'SEBI Bars TV Anchor Hemant Ghai, Wife and Mother for "Fraud in Trading",' *Business Standard,* 13 January 2021.

[19] For early work on feedback loops, see Sushil Bikhchandani, David Hirshleifer, and Ivo Welch, 'A Theory of Fads, Fashion, Custom, and Cultural Change as Informational Cascades,' *Journal of Political Economy,* October 1992, 992–1026; Abhijit Banerjee, 'A Simple Model of Herd Behavior,' *Quarterly Journal of Economics,* 107, 3, August 1992, 797–818.

continuation of the same action, high prices result in higher prices, with these new higher prices resulting in even higher prices, and so on.

The internet and social media have democratized access to information and this trend has been amplified by the spread of smart phones with low priced data packs. Presently, the issue is not access to information – in fact there is a chaotic surfeit of it – but the processing and analysis of that information. The recent rise of social media contributes further to the information overload and intensifies media's effect on the market. According to Heckyl Technologies, a social media data analytics firm, X (formerly Twitter) messages with the terms 'Nifty' or 'Sensex' have recorded considerable increases in recent years.[20] In X's case, the concision of the medium (at 280 characters) makes it useful for touting tips; the brevity is also a good excuse for the absence of any further explanation. Building up a list of followers also becomes that much easier with technology. Rumour mongering through *khabar* – that bedrock practice in India's stock markets – and customizing the spread of those rumours are now possible at the touch of a button. Equally remarkable on social media is the rising ant heap of digital apps that focus on financial education – sites such as YouTube are rife with short videos that offer trading advice from 'finfluencers' or finance influencers. Like the drafters and solicitors of Roychand's time, these intermediaries have also made good in the SIP Bull run of recent years. But here too, content gravitates towards the lowest common denominator. The inane simplicity of content was usually a deliberate choice and one 'finfluencer' was publicly quoted as saying he wanted to develop content that would make his toddler proud.

[20] Shailesh Menon, 'D Street Plugs into the Social Network,' *Economic Times*, 19 November 2015.

22

WE'RE ONLY GOING HIGHER

Highs and Lows

Nobody wants to buy at a high or sell at a low, and yet enough people do to make it happen. Highs and lows have become the subject of lore and studying them can offer pointers on what to look for at a turning point, albeit with the caveat that historical analogy in the stock market is always clear in retrospect and rarely so in prophecy.

Three noted tops – those of 1920, 1929, and 1946 – took place in the pre-Independence era.[1] Following these, there is a hiatus of almost half a century till the Harshad Mehta top of 1992, and over these two generations, the market loses its historical memory of what a top looks like. The Mehta high is then followed by the more recent highs of 2000, 2008, and 2020. As a rule, lows followed between one and three years after these highs, though the duration of Indian bear markets seems to be compressing over time.

The 1920 top came at the end of a sustained bull run that coincided with the First World War and its aftermath. The Cotton and Share Mania of the 1860s had produced no aggregate market data, while only sectoral moves were recorded after that – jute in the 1870s, tea in

[1] K.R.P. Shroff's indexes from the BSE's archives have been used to discern these movements.

the 1890s, and coal in the 1900s[2] – and so, the Great War move was the first bull run in the Indian market that was actually measured and recorded as a bull market. The outbreak of hostilities in Europe had led to exchange closure and all-round pessimism, but the mood changed when businesses realized that the war would cut-off imports from Europe and lead to a spurt in local manufacturing activity.[3] War-related demand for cotton and jute – which dominated listings in Bombay and Calcutta – also soared, and this led to a boom in the Calcutta and Bombay exchanges. Calcutta led Bombay in the fireworks, and Dunbar Cotton in Calcutta went up 76 times over a six-year period that ended in 1920, making it India's first multi-bagger.[4] Critically, price controls on commodities reduced trading activities in those markets and a flood of trading capital left bullion and agri-commodities, only to find its way into the stock market.[5] An extended period of prosperity followed, peaking in 1920. Many of the big Marwari trading houses of Calcutta would use this period to accumulate capital that would be ploughed back into industry, and more generally, this episode marks the beginning of local business ascendency over British agency houses.[6] Since stock indexes were missing at that time, market movements were judged in hindsight, using indexes with base years selected to coincide with the cycle's start. One such index constructed by K.R.P. Shroff shows a rise from 100 to 296 between 1914 and 1920.[7]

This activity also led to a new issue boom, where promoters allotted watered stock to themselves and then sold that stock to the public

[2] Sectoral moves in jute, tea, and coal were recorded in Calcutta and the coal boom-bust sequence led to the 1908 formation of the Calcutta exchange. Aditi Roy Ghatak, *Down Lyons Range*, Kolkata: P.K. Ray for the Calcutta Stock Exchange Association, 2008, 9–10.

[3] Bhulabhai J. Desai, 'Minority Report of Mr. Bhulabhai J Desai,' Sir Wilfrid Atlay, *Report of the Bombay Stock Exchange Enquiry Committee*, Bombay: Government Central Press, 1924, 21–22.

[4] K.R.P Shroff, *History and Present Position of the Stock Market in India*, Bombay: The Stock Exchange, Bombay, 1962, 12.

[5] Appendix 5, Official Representation of The Native Share and Stockbrokers' Association, Sir Wilfrid Atlay, *Report of the Bombay Stock Exchange Enquiry Committee*, 41.

[6] Aditi Roy Ghatak, *Down Lyons Range*, 49–50.

[7] K.R.P Shroff, *History and Present Position of the Stock Market*, 11–12.

at high premia.[8] After the Cotton and Share Mania, this is the first occasion when a buoyant market's final stages led to new issue activity and the pattern would repeat itself in later years. Here too, we see for the first time the promoter tendency to keep free floats as low as possible, which prompted the Bombay exchange to insist that at least 33 per cent of equity be sold before a company qualified for an official quotation and listing; the exchange would subsequently raise the requirement to 50 per cent, which later became irrelevant with the enactment of the 1956 SCRA regulations that prescribed 49 per cent.[9] When the boom ended, K.R.P. Shroff's makeshift index registered a drop from 296 to 169 between 1920 and 1923, a fall of over 40 per cent.[10] This was the first recorded bear market, and it would set a pattern for bear market drawdowns of between one-third and half.

The 1929 top coincided with the end of the worldwide expansion of the Roaring Twenties and with Wall Street's own bull high. But the expansion was a subdued affair in India, and the only observation from the archives is that the makeshift index rose from 93 in April 1927 to 101 by September 1929.[11] The up move was more apparent at the sector level; commodities like cotton and jute staged a comeback and shared leadership with collieries and steel. This time, Bombay eclipsed Calcutta, and Tata Steel would establish itself as a trading favourite for the first time, rising from an all-time low of 8, recorded just after the 1923 Kanto earthquake in Japan to a high of 88 by June 1929.[12] Near ruinous strikes among Bombay's cotton mills brought the bull move to an end a little before the worldwide move topped out in September 1929, which also explains the restrained performance of the indexes.

In the depression that followed, political considerations and a nascent Independence movement would impinge on market conditions for the

[8] Ibid., 13.

[9] Ibid., 34.

[10] Ibid., 14.

[11] Ibid., 18.

[12] Ibid.

first time, and the index drawdown from the September 1929 high to the June 1932 low of 58 was a little over 40 per cent. The low was marked by the 1933 bankruptcy of Currimbhoy Ebrahim, a well-known managing agency house. Some brokers ran into settlement difficulties and could not meet their commitments, but bona fide investors who had traded through them were rescued by a fund of ₹3 lakhs put together by the brokers themselves.[13] This marks the first creation and use of an investor protection fund in India.

The 1946 top was the last of the colonial era highs and followed a period of unprecedented volatility in the market, occasioned by the Second World War and its conclusion. When Germany broke its borders in 1939, the commencement of European conflict actually triggered a huge surge in prices – perhaps on recollections of the earlier war boom – and the market almost doubled, but the advance was tempered by Allied losses in the early years. War time price controls and the unexpected imposition of an Excess Profits Tax in January 1940 then precipitated a decline in values, which accelerated into panic with the fall of France in 1940 and Germany's Barbarossa victories on the Eastern Front in 1941.[14] For a brief period, the Calcutta exchange shut down and badla trading was suspended in Bombay, but later Calcutta was reopened and forward trading resumed. A mini surge in late 1941 was followed by a collapse in 1942, as Japanese land advances across the China–Burma–India (CBI) theatre of operations looked like they would reach Calcutta. The situation was exacerbated by Congress's launch of the Quit India movement, and as the Independence movement gathered momentum, political conditions continued to impact market operations and briefly brought them to an end.

Crucially, the 1943 Defence of India Rule 94-C banned the forward badla market which effectively moved the trading floor to the street outside. As a result, kerb markets, share bazaars, bucket shops, and

[13] Ibid., 19.

[14] P.J. Thomas, *Report on the Regulation of the Stock Market in India*, New Delhi: Ministry of Finance, 1948, 5–6.

independent firms saw activity soar.[15] These share bazaars and bucket shops displaced legitimate exchanges, and by one estimate, Calcutta's *katni* market on the street outside was many times the size of the regular market in Lyons Range.[16] Entire new exchanges also came up (6 in Ahmedabad and 5 in Lahore alone), and briefly the number of exchanges grew from 7 at the war's outbreak, to 21 by 1947.[17] Rule 94-C – in one of the earliest cases of regulatory arbitrage – had caused an upsurge in informal kerb market and bucket shop activity. Following Allied victories, the market situation stabilized from 1943 onwards and then violently reversed itself to the upside, helped along by deficit spending and inflationary financing. The war's end and the abolition of wartime controls – both the Excess Profits Tax and Rule 94-C were repealed – then brought about a runaway boom that peaked in September 1946. Rolling back state dirigisme proves a big trigger for up moves in India and this was an early example. Through all this, K.R.P. Shroff's index lurched from 100 to 382 between 1939 and September 1946 – at both the 1920 and 1946 tops, the market had risen between 3 and 4 times over its trough value, as computed by Shroff.[18]

Like the previous bull run, this move also provoked a primary market boom, with kerb manipulation of new issues. Here too are witnessed early instances of stag operations in the IPO market, though such manoeuvres had taken place in the 1920 boom.[19] The chaos of Partition and the transfer of power brought about a free-for-all in commercial operations and open warfare flared up among various managing agency groups for control of assets.[20] Much of this played out in the stock

[15] Ibid., 8–12, 75–80. Independent firms were distinct from the kerb, and there is no parallel to them in today's operations. Some were managing agencies, NBFCs, brokers, arbitrageurs, and OTC market makers all rolled into one.

[16] Ibid., 6, 42. Indian Iron and Steel Company (IISCO) dominated Calcutta's *katni* market as much as it did trading on the regular bourse. The regular market was usually open from noon to 2 p.m., but the *katni* market stayed open till late into the night.

[17] Ibid., 10–12.

[18] K.R.P Shroff, *History and Present Position of the Stock Market*, 24–25.

[19] Ibid., 26–27.

[20] Ibid.

market and this marks the only time in Indian corporate history when, for a brief while, a market for corporate control through the stock market became more than a theoretical possibility.

The 1946 high then ran headlong into the events of Partition and the resulting political uncertainty and communal violence put paid to the bull movement. But the real end came when Liaquat Ali Khan presented the interim government's budget in February 1947. For the first time, the market got a preview of Nehruvian India's attitude towards it, and a string of taxes, including a business profits tax, capital gains tax, corporation tax, and a super-tax, were imposed. Collectively, the proposals were confiscatory in nature but it was not the proposals as much as the tenor of public debate, with its discussions on nationalization and dividend limitation, that signalled a change. The slump that resulted saw K.R.P. Shroff's index fall from its 1946 peak of 382 to a July 1949 low of 131, a drawdown of almost two-thirds.[21] To date, this remains the most severe of bear markets.

The auction value of BSE card prices confirms the accuracy of Shroff's informal indexes and provides another way of gauging tops in the pre-Independence era. The BSE card rose from ₹1,800 in 1910 to ₹48,000 at the 1920 top, before dropping to ₹6,700 at the end of the Great Depression in 1932.[22] Card prices rose again to ₹64,000 during the 1946 high and slumped to ₹14,000 by 1954, indicating remarkable correspondence with the market cycle.[23]

The three highs of the pre-Independence colonial era offer some parallels with modern episodes. The tops were preceded by a displacement – usually from an international source, in keeping with the open markets of that era; there was government intervention bordering on dirigisme and much of its consequences were dealt with through regulatory arbitrage; and there was significant stoking of primary market activity in the later stages of the bull move. There was also a rough trebling of market levels followed by a drawdown of about half from the higher values. But too

[21] K.R.P Shroff, *History and Present Position of the Stock Market,* 24.

[22] Ibid., 6.

[23] Ibid.

much must not be read into these similarities – the analogies are dulled both by the makeshift nature of the indexes that measured the moves and the wide-ranging differences between the market then and now. Since this was the Municipal Era, there was no real national market and most of the action remained confined to the metropolises of Bombay, Calcutta, and Ahmedabad, with some orders dialled in from cities like Delhi and Madras. Critically, the organized buy side was non-existent, and action was usually confined to individuals and other private players.

After 1946, the Indian stock market went through its longest period between bull runs. From that date till the early 90s, there are no up moves of sufficient magnitude to find mention in the record, and it is striking that no name or label attaches to any market move. The interregnum is remarkable for its longevity, and the Century of Marking Time closed in on the market as it grappled with that era's inherently hostile attitude towards equities. The period also coincided with three wars (with China in 1962 and with Pakistan in 1965 and 1971) and a currency devaluation in 1966, and is generally known as a time of high inflation and stagnant growth. It is the worst period ever in the history of Indian markets, though this is difficult to see as the Sensex was created only in 1982.

And yet – as seen in accounts from Atlay, Shroff, and Thomas – the period before 1946 had been one of intense market activity, when the market responded vibrantly to domestic and international events. But so long is the break between 1946 and 1992 and such is the disregard for time, that the market loses its historical memory of the era before Independence. Besides the BSE archives, nothing written down of any note is available, and it is common to find most accounts of the stock market start from the period of the 90s, when the Harshad Mehta bull commences its fireworks.

In the modern era, four noted peaks took place in 1992, 2000, 2008, and 2020; on the way to the highs, the market itself goes up between three and seven times from its previous trough levels. Market analysts usually decompose these moves into multiple expansion and earnings expansion. Multiple expansion takes place through an increasing PE ratio, as the market gets more comfortable paying higher ratios for earnings; the PE ratio typically increases from 10 to 30 on the move from trough to peak.[24] Earnings expansion by companies then accounts for the rest of the market's up move. Towards the top, the market keeps assigning progressively higher multiples to higher earnings, which is the sweet spot of a bull market. The period between peaks is about eight years, and this is the duration of a market cycle (that is, if one thinks in terms of cycles), though in the latest move the interval between the tops of 2008 and 2020 is 12 years.

Market lows were reached and formed in 1993, 2003, and 2009. Lows are reached between one and three years after the peaks are formed, but note that the duration of down moves has been reducing over the years. So far – and we are a generation into the new millennium – there has not been a down move to rival the IT bear's duration between 2000 and 2003.

The April 1992 Harshad Mehta top is the closing bang of the Municipal Era and the first bull move of modern times. It is also the first and only high to be forever associated with a personality. Unlike the earlier highs that were discerned through Shroff's indexes, the Mehta market was the first bull documented through a regularly calculated index – the Sensex. The 10-year upswing from 225 to 4,467 between 1982 and April 1992 gives us a record that will, in all probability, never be surpassed.[25] Over this period, the market became a 20-bagger, and on a logarithmic scale, this is the largest decadal move – about 1,900 per cent – in the market's history.[26] The 1991 reform measures

[24] Exchange websites.

[25] Bombay Stock Exchange, *The Stock Market Today: 1987*, Bombay: The Stock Exchange Foundation, 1987, 12.

[26] To see why such a move might never happen again, consider that a corresponding decadal move even from the 2009 low of almost 9,000 would imply a level of 1,80,000 by 2019, instead of the 41,000 that actually resulted.

and Mehta's exertions in the G-Sec market had removed a century of severe undervaluation, but the market went to the other extreme and multiples of 50 and above were recorded at the top. In the near half century between the 1946 and Mehta highs, the market lost its memory of what a top looked or felt like and made the move from extreme undervaluation to extreme overvaluation in a short time span of less than two years. The Mehta Bull's multiples of over 50 that were set in April 1992 have also never been exceeded.

When FIIs were allowed entry for the first time, the market retested its previous 1992 high during a second surge in 1994, in effect making the only double top in a bull move. The Mehta Bull took place before the modern microstructure was put in place, so the high was reached despite the unlimited naked shorting capacity of the badla system, and this gives us an idea of the power behind the bull surge. The Shamiana Coffee Shop at Mumbai's Taj Mahal Palace Hotel was packed with traders flush with easy money and sober industrialists referred to the man at the centre of it all as the Napoleon of Finance. Lore also has it that the market would surge whenever the Napoleon of Finance's Lexus entered Dalal Street and this recollection is common among participants of that era.[27]

The February 2000 IT top followed years of range-bound movement during which the modern microstructure with its electronic limit order book (ELOB) was developed and put in place. The trading floor was done away with, and from now on, all the action was on screen; some old timers took to the new environment with difficulty, but for most it was a seamless transition. The IT high was the last to take place under the old badla system of lightly margined forwards and the system's abolition and replacement with a derivatives market took place a year later. So, this is the last occasion when the market did not have to compete with a vast derivatives segment and all trading capital sloshed into the cash market. But the Sensex high of over 6,000 (by now there

[27] Mehta also used the Lexus on his periodic visits to State Bank of India to explain discrepancies in G-Sec clearing and settlement, which alerted the media to his shenanigans.

was an alternate index, the NSE's Nifty) was recorded on the narrowest of market moves and most action remained confined to a few sectors such as software, media, and telecom. Even within that narrow space, much of the action was confined to the K-10 scrips of Ketan Parekh, the bull operator most associated with the top. A subsequent parliamentary investigation found that in some sessions, almost two-third of market volumes came just from this group.[28]

The IT high was also the first of the modern era to form in exact correspondence with international trends. This had happened with the tops of the pre-Independence era, but the half century of autarky since then had dulled participants' instincts and most did not see this simple connection with international markets; due to that correspondence, this was also the first top to end because of an international event, and the March 2000 Nasdaq crash was the trigger that provoked the fall. To date, it remains the last bull move to end in response to a scam; changes to the microstructure have now resolved the clearing and settlement issues that usually led to such scams.

The January 2008 Rate Bull top is canonical in our list of market highs. It is the first one to occur after the market's new microstructure was put in place, and many of its features seem destined to repeat in the highs that follow. The most distinguishing feature was momentum, and the gap between the 200 day moving average (DMA) and the market line was the widest it had been in years. The Sensex high of about 21,000 (Nifty 6,400) was defined by price increases on the back of colossal volumes. In turn, those price increases were just the end point of a bull surge that lasted almost five years and sent some stocks up over 2,000 times. Price increases of this magnitude had never happened before and were driven in large part by the long corner and the short selling constraint – this is the first bull that did not have to deal with the unlimited shorting capacity of the old badla system, and it showed in the price moves to the upside. But valuations stayed sweet

[28] Joint Parliamentary Committee, *Joint Committee on Stock Market Scam and Matters Relating Thereto*, Thirteenth Lok Sabha, Volume I - Report, New Delhi: Lok Sabha Secretariat, 2002, 188.

and reasonable till the very end, primarily because of massive earnings expansion brought about by the interest rate displacement and general improvement in economic conditions.

So, the Sensex trough to peak move of about seven times (from 3,000 to 21,000) remains the largest in the modern era, and yet such was the corporate earnings surge caused by the rate displacement and economic improvement, that compared to the other tops, it is the Rate peak that is the easiest to justify in valuation terms. Unlike the narrow IT Bull that preceded it, the Rate Bull's breadth was broad and deep with advance-decline ratios overwhelmingly in favour of advances, and this market breadth is in keeping with the nature of the interest rate displacement that impacted most companies. Finally, and unlike other highs that all ended because of proximate causes, the 2008 Rate top had no proximate cause that led to the subsequent sell-off; as seen earlier, the last buyer simply came in, following which various technical factors such as excess leverage in the derivatives market and the stop-loss honeycomb led to a crash.

The January 2020 SIP Bull high is the only top that formed over a substantial length of time, and this remains its distinguishing feature. From mid-2019 till the early 2020 Sensex level of 42,000, the market traded range bound with an upward bias, and so, the 200 DMA indicator crept up to the market line; by contrast, the other tops had had large momentum induced gaps between the DMA and the market line. Nevertheless, and unlike earlier highs, the SIP top had the least amount of earnings support, resulting in the market trading at close to 30 times earnings at the high.[29] Also unlike other tops, the IPO market did not appear frothy and the new issue pipeline was dormant. In contrast to previous highs where the market went off a cliff with tops followed immediately by crashes, the first 2020 top took its own time ending and the three-week gap between the 20 January high and the real sell-off that started on 12 February is noteworthy.[30]

[29] Exchange websites.

[30] The market fell from its all-time high of 42,200 on 20 January 2020 to 41,100 on 20 February following which there was a crash to 25,800.

Striking also is the fact that the public's presence – which was considerable – did not lead to any sort of euphoria. One explanation comes from the displacement itself; the SIP inflows that displaced the bull movement were from a public whose presence was (in the main) mediated through mutual funds with their rupee cost averaging plans. Finally, after the coronavirus pandemic outbreak, the liquidity-induced pull back was so massive that it took the market comfortably to another high; the market doubled off the low of about 25,000 and would go on to cross 60,000 (Nifty 18,500) in 2021. The real economy collapsed in the wake of the pandemic but the market sailed through it all, disconnecting the market from the economy in a way that could only be described as bubble-like. Yet it all seemed sweet and reasonable, and the brokerages and fundies rationalized it all through the device of forward earnings. In keeping with lore, by 2021 the public was also heavily in the market, but much of the trading action was online, geographically widespread, and mainly transacted through discount brokers.

Tops have contours that are clearer in retrospect rather than when they actually form. At market highs – most have happened in January or February, except for the Mehta bull that topped out in April – lore has it there is mania with the public foaming at the mouth and quacking for stock. When the ducks go 'quack quack' it's time to feed them, so the pros sell into the mania and feed the public with their stock. The brokerage fraternity is divided, with the usual mix of people touting the differing opinions that make up horse races and stock markets – some suggest caution and others urge buying, but the market see-saw is clearly loaded in favour of buyers.

Price surges on huge volumes are the central feature of a top and usually the culmination of a steady price increase that's gone on for years. In the moves that culminated in 2000 and 2008, many stocks were up 50 to 100 times and this was seen as normal. Momentum was the distinguishing feature of the bull surges that culminated in the tops of 1992, 2000, and

2008, though it did not distinguish itself in the 2020 high; the earlier tops give the impression of a rampaging bull that went over a cliff, but the 2020 high feels like a softly leaping jaguar that finally tired out.

The market has been making lifetime highs for months before the top, and during that period, its shenanigans are often on the front page of the *Times of India*. But by the time an actual top is reached, the newspapers have stopped writing about a passé detail like a lifetime high. The fact loses its novelty, and the fact that the fact loses its novelty is itself of some significance. Like many important things in India, what does not happen is more significant than what happens; sometimes in public affairs, this is even done deliberately and so the significance of what is left out gets drowned out in all the noise and chaos generated by what is let in.

Delivery volumes as a percentage of total volumes fall during market tops, and the trading public scrutinizes this figure closely as it is easily available in the ELOB window for individual stocks. The figure is low simply because many blue chips are also trading favourites, and the large day trading volumes that momentum generates, reduce the delivery percentages. At the peak, FIIs are usually buying heavily. Though they were not present at the 1992 high, this tendency to come in at the top has emerged repeatedly across the remaining highs of the modern era. As asset allocators, rather than pickers or timers, they don't obsess over a market where their allocations are usually less than 5 per cent. By contrast, almost all DII capital gets socked away in the local market, and they regard it as home turf that they need to protect. This they do by crossing the FIIs, and so, most DIIs sell into the mania at a high, in keeping with market lore that has the pros *thoko-ing* (hitting) it to the public at a top.

Corporate results at the top tend to be outstanding. This was not so apparent in 1992 but became clear during the 2000 IT Bull high – consider that Infosys's quarterly results just before that high showed earnings growth of almost 100 per cent.[31] January 2008, however, is

[31] Infosys, 'Reports and Filings Quarterly & Annual Reports,' *Infosys*, Accessed 20 January 2017, 2–3, 7, https://www. infosys.com/investors/Documents/QR6k/Q3-1999-00.pdf.

the best example of good fundamental news coming in at a top; results for the preceding December quarter were excellent – economic growth was at over 9 per cent, profits had compounded at over 20 per cent for years, and the interest rate environment was moderate, despite the RBI being well into its rate tightening cycle. Here too, 2020 was an anomaly and corporate results were terrible for some years before that high. By January 2020, the SIP Bull had become the Reluctant Bull; it was a high that almost did not want to happen but happened nevertheless because of those gushes of international liquidity.

Because of excellent corporate results, valuations at tops are usually stretched but reasonable, with the market trading at the top of its valuation band – between 25 to 30 times earnings. In 1992, the market traded at over 50-times earnings but there are questions about the index's methodology in that period;[32] in 2000 and 2008, the market traded at 24- and 26-times earnings respectively; at the 2020 high, it traded at almost 30-times earnings, so the valuation band's upper end in the modern era is somewhere between these figures.[33]

Still, it remains unclear how such numbers can be used for market timing or trading because these situations can continue for years, typically because earnings can catch up as bull markets progress. It is possible for a market to trade at 25-times earnings and still keep going higher, as earnings expansion get priced at the same 25 multiple, which takes the market higher. As a bull progresses, the key point is that for years earnings have been growing faster than prices, and as a result, price-earnings multiples look nice and reasonable despite the market's continued advance. Crucially, on the way to the top the market gets more comfortable placing progressively higher multiples on those nicely growing earnings.

Besides, the analysts who've got egg on their faces predicting the up move's end are now on for the ride. They're projecting earnings a year or two ahead at high growth rates, thus making the market sweet and

[32] Bombay Stock Exchange, *BSE Books–Financial Ratios of BSE Indices*, (Bombay: BSE, 1992) 22.

[33] Exchange websites.

reasonable from the perspective of these forward earnings; at market tops, brokerage fantasies about forward earnings can rationalize most market levels. So, it's all 'fairly valued' using forward earnings, and it stays 'fairly valued' all the way to the top.[34] This is especially true of the fundies, for among them saying the market is overvalued is a mortal sin punishable by death. At the top, some of the pros fret privately and worry about cash earnings per share and other more sophisticated yardsticks dealing with the quality of earnings; public fretting gets shouted down by the multitude. Most of the skeptical pros then simply give up, join their colleagues in the chorus, and insist that the market is pricing in two years of forward earnings and is 'fairly valued' on that yardstick.

There is a full pipeline of new issues as the investment bankers get busy with IPO season and selling paper such as Reliance Power or Paytm becomes easier in this atmosphere. That crucial Street function of raising risk capital for companies gets lost in the usual din of secondary market operations, and it is only during a short window on the way to a high that this most basic of functions gets exercised. Since the primary market is dormant most of the time, a real pickup in IPO tempo is potentially one sign that a top is not far away.

John Kenneth Galbraith, in his classic work *The Great Crash 1929*, adds an important piece of lore to the study of tops and sell-offs.[35] The great tops happen after the market actually becomes a part of society. Paresh the Pro listens to cousin Raju rave about that killing he just made, while Hema the Housewife hears Mrs K's chatter at the cocktail party and both – together with countless others – then join that giant surge as it reaches its pathological stage. Galbraith's is a tall standard to meet and yet part of that norm was met during the tops of 1992, 2000, and 2008. More generally, at the top the sun is shining and the beer is nice and cold. It's just perfect for the bulls but the bears are too finished to talk. India has no real bears, so this applies mainly to those brave souls in the huge derivatives market who are shorting with leverage while

[34] Googling – Sensex 'fairly valued' – pulls up thousands of entries.

[35] John Kenneth Galbraith, *The Great Crash 1929*, Boston and New York: Houghton Mifflin, 1997.

trying to find a top and getting hammered as a result; the derivatives market is retail dominated so there are a fair number of such folk.

So, of all participants, it is the public whose presence is sought after and mulled over at tops, and it remains lore that the public is heavily present at highs. In recent years, this tradition has been called into question, and it is a general observation that directly attributable public presence has been declining at market highs. Dalal Street is no longer a geographic focus for the market and the action has migrated online, so direct observation of the public's presence is difficult. Though there is little indication nowadays of excessive public presence, this does not mean the public is absent at the top; it only means that the form of its presence has changed.

In recent years, the public has chosen the SIP (and similar rupee cost averaging products) as a preferred mode of entry, and 2019 was a record year for such plans.[36] So, the public came in at the top in 2020 but mostly through the indirect route, with its presence moderated by the mutual funds. The presence of 3-in-1 online trading accounts also means that much action is now online, and surges in demat account openings are another sign of a direct public presence at tops. By late 2020, the pandemic's work-from-home ethos also led to an increase in the public; 2020 was a record year for demat account openings with over 10 million opened, which led to the demat base crossing 50 million. By August 2022, demat accounts would cross 100 million.

During market highs, excellent news also brings with it that belief in a *naya daur* or a new era, and this talk rises to a crescendo as the realness and immediateness of surging prices confirms the observations, however far-fetched. The siren song can be something as basic as Harshad Mehta's intriguing 'replacement cost' theories of 1992; India's IT service companies were the local equivalent of the brave new world of dot-coms and the internet, and they brought new era thinking with them in 2000. In 2008, it was Chindia – the interest rate displacement

[36] Association of Mutual Funds of India (AMFI) and Crisil, *SIP-shape: Retail Investors Catalyzing Growth of Mutual Funds in India*, August 2019, accessed 10 April 2019, 5, 14.

misled many observers into believing something fundamental had happened to the economy along the likes of China, and the resulting Chindia phenomenon was trumpeted by Western media and eagerly lapped up by India's political and business elite.

Faced with the prospect of assigning explanations for the bull move, the wire houses trot out old warhorses including the demographic dividend, the Great Indian Middle Class, and something called the consumption story. There's even talk of a 'liquidity super-cycle', a marvellous concatenation of events that occurs as a younger population in an economy with a high savings rate and low dependency ratios benefits from investor education, takes on more risk, and buys equities.[37] There is an uncanny and time-honoured correlation between brokerage reports that carry such themes and the big market tops.

In 2020, again, we have a break in the pattern and the January 2020 top was the most sober and businesslike of them all; there was nothing captivating or *naya daur* about the market chatter from this episode. Perhaps by now the market was maturing and sensed that the pieces of paper it traded represented residual ownership claims in companies operating in a dysfunctional real economy that was not going anywhere in a hurry. Besides, in 2020 there was clarity about Western quantitative easing being the source of a liquidity-driven global rally, and so it was difficult to summon up that carefree and wanton exuberance so characteristic of a market top.

Auguries like the Wall Street shoeshine boy who's in the market don't exist on Dalal Street. But activities at the BSE's eastern entrance could figure in the list of events that signify tops, especially among those who go looking for such portents. The bronze statue of the BSE bull at the Bombay Samachar Marg eastern entrance was installed in January 2008, exactly at the Rate Bull's top.[38] This coincidence should have added 'Installation of Iconic Sculptures on Exchange Premises' to the

[37] PTI, 'India in Midst of Domestic Liquidity Supercycle: Morgan Stanley,' *Economic Times*, 8 September 2017.

[38] Virendra Verma, 'How the Bull Came of Age,' *Business Today*, 27 December 2009.

list of omens, but to date not many have recognized this quirk. The crash that followed shook up traders – usually among the most superstitious of people – and many insisted that the *vaastu* was all wrong, as the bull's backside faced into the exchange.[39] Despite the grumbling, the bull was left untouched, but the eastern entrance's sporadic openings have had unfortunate coincidences with other market tops. Coinciding with the Mehta high, the entrance was opened in 1992 but shut shortly thereafter; it was reopened in 2001 just after the IT top, closed after that and reopened once again in 2008 at the Rate Bull's top for the sculpture's installation.[40]

All tops formed in the modern era were immediately followed by terrible crashes, and this is a remarkable coincidence. After the top is formed – the years are 1992, 2000, 2008, and 2020 – the market simply thunders off a cliff, and there is no hint of an alternate scenario like (say) a gradual sell-off over a few months. Compressed drawdowns between 25 and almost 40 per cent happened in all four cases. In the first three cases, crashes followed within days of a high being reached, but in 2020, over a month lapsed between the January top and the crash. Yet no work has been done on this important phenomenon that is responsible for large amounts of wealth destruction. Perhaps that's because most of the damage happens to the speculative, leveraged side of the market, while the politically influential 'buy and hold' crowd comes through relatively unscathed as the market resumes its inexorable upward march.

Crashes are never apparent *ex ante*, or before the event, but always *ex post*, or after the event. This is a fancy way of saying that most participants and economists are clueless about when or why they happen and get seized of the matter only after the event has taken place. So much for

[39] Girish Kuber, 'BSE Brokers Blame Bull Vaastu for Bear Maul,' *Economic Times*, 29 January 2008. The sculpture was created by Bhagwan Rampure of Solapur.

[40] Ibid.

prediction. It is a commonplace that the market looks for the reason behind an event after the event has taken place, and market crashes are the single best example of that.

During crashes, the pink papers will usually put out that stock photo of a trader, head in hands, staring in dazed and pitiable fashion at his screen. There goes the Honda! After big crashes, the search for a fundamental cause takes place, usually through learned analysts writing in the newspapers but more diligently through the brokerage strategists in their reports. Much ink is spent searching earnestly and futilely for a fundamental cause. Perhaps there is none, and it is simply that the last buyer came in and after that there was no one left to buy and so the deluge.

Rather than fundamental causes, it is better to think in terms of proximate causes, and but for 2008, all crashes have had proximate causes attached to them. The 1992 crash started with Sucheta Dalal's exposé of Harshad Mehta's G-Sec manipulations; 2000 was triggered by the great Nasdaq sell-off; and 2020 by the coronavirus pandemic breakout. History suggests that the proximate cause interacts with the technical internal composition of the market, and this interaction causes the crash. Microstructure and the market's technical internal composition play a big role in all this, and as noted in the Rate Bull discussion – the 'stop loss' honeycomb, naked intraday shorting without an uptick rule, the absence of the inter temporal short covering trade, and leverage unwinding in India's colossal derivatives markets – are the main technical causes behind these episodes. So, the proximate cause – the Sucheta Dalal expose, a Nasdaq sell-off, or a virus pandemic – results in initial long unwinding, and this later interacts with the market's technical composition to produce these spectacular collapses.

Ever since badla's 2001 abolition, it is long unwinding rather than short selling that causes these crashes. Long unwinding from the proximate cause triggers a sequence of events starting with the stop-loss honeycomb that was most apparent in the Rate and SIP Bull tops of 2008 and 2020. In both cases, trend-following traders had got their calls right on a nicely trending bull market for many years – almost five years for the Rate Bull and 11 years for the SIP Bull – and were trailing market prices with their 'stop loss' sell orders. As a result, swathes of sell orders were placed below the market price of all front-line stocks, and both the magnitude and duration of the up moves contributed to the bunched up sell orders. Long unwinding from the proximate cause then led the market to crash through this honeycomb of sell orders. On those days when the crash seemed most terrifying, day traders – in the absence of an uptick rule such as SEC's Rule 10a-1(a)(1) – were pressing the naked intraday short and contributing to the downside momentum. In fact, the astute and adventurous among them were pressing naked intraday shorts in an active search for the honeycomb, which triggered more stops of the numerous trend-following traders and led to the selling climax. Through all this, a short covering trade should have provided an inbuilt pillar of support to the market, but that did not exist because of constraints to the short side.

A related set of events then took place in both 2008 and 2020 in the colossal derivatives market where daily trading volumes of over ₹14,00,000 crores ($196 billion) were now considered normal. Leverage unwinding is a big cause of crashes worldwide, but the cash market in India offers negligible leverage, as both margin trading and the loans against shares product have low volumes. So, leverage unwinding took place in an indirect fashion through the derivatives market which acted like a house of cards that tottered and fell. India's derivatives segment is dominated by the public and many among them – who were overtrading and abusing the leverage inherent in such markets – were long at the top. In fact, many had taken abusing leverage to another level and were 'pyramiding' into the move; they were using the unbooked profits on their open derivatives contracts as capital to buy more contracts.

Most traders had been lulled into complacency by the Rate and SIP Bulls' steady up moves, and so, the honeycomb's initial break caught them unawares. Many were novices, part of that steady stream the demographic dividend is luring into the markets, and many were also cross-margining between their cash and derivatives holdings, i.e., using their actual share portfolios as security for derivatives margin, which was then used to pyramid into the up move. The honeycomb break exposed all this hidden leverage and triggered a rash of margin calls from the brokerages, which in turn forced cross-margining traders to sell some of their portfolio holdings in the cash market to meet the calls, further exacerbating the cash market's collapse. Even traders who were not cross-margining because they were adequately capitalized might have had to sell some of their portfolio holdings to meet margin calls. When all this happened, interactions between the cash and derivatives markets became critical. Consequently, the proximate cause and microstructure issues caused a sell-off in the cash market, which caused the excess leverage to get wrung out of the derivatives market through the cross-margining mechanism, which in turn caused further sell-offs in the cash market. Contagion moved from the cash to the derivatives market and then back to the cash market.

In extreme cases and only for a few terrifying moments, reverse arbitrage also takes place between the cash and derivatives markets, which aggravates the down move. As shown earlier, the normal position in arbitrage's first leg is to *buy* in the cash and *sell* in the derivatives (futures) segment, as futures prices are always higher than cash prices due to the spot-futures parity theorems (or the 'cost of carry' relationship). But in severe market crashes, prices fall so far and so fast that futures prices are below corresponding cash prices.[41] Then the first leg of the arbitrage transaction is inverted to *sell* in the cash segment and *buy* in the futures segment to capture the basis; this cash market selling further increases the downside momentum.[42] Because India's cash markets don't have an uptick rule like the SEC's Rule 10a-1(a)(1), this trade is relatively easy to execute on the few occasions it presents itself.

Note also that in India, reverse arbitrage can take place on a wide range of blue-chip stocks, including those that make up the index,

[41] More technically, fleeting market imbalances rather than fundamentals or warehousing effects are responsible for this backwardation.

[42] For an analysis of this phenomenon during the Wall Street crash of October 1987, see Larry Harris, *Trading and Exchanges: Market Microstructure for Practitioners*, New York: Oxford University Press, 2003, 562–63.

and this has systemic effects; in countries without single stock futures (SSFs), this reverse arbitrage is possible only between the index futures contract and baskets of stocks that make up that index, which can be cumbersome. But India's huge SSFs market – there are close to 150 blue chips where the above trade is possible – means that the arbitrage could easily take place on individual counters rather than through a cumbersome index basket, and this magnifies the impact of reverse arbitrage on the market.[43] The 30 (or 50) stocks that make up the market indexes are also in that group of 150 that make up the SSF segment, which also increases reverse arbitrage effects on the widely watched market index. All the above factors come into play during a crash – as they did in January 2008 and March 2020 – leading in turn to a selling climax and meltdown.

In the modern era, lows were recorded in 1993, 2003, and 2009. Lows are tricky to call but most fall in place between one and three years after a high. Markets tend to form lows slower in India than other countries and short constraints in the cash market may account for this tendency; because short selling in the cash market is so restricted, stocks take their own time drifting to lower levels as long traders lose hope and sell out only gradually. And yet, it is at market lows that short constraints seem merciful.

The singular feature of a market bottom is a giant flushing sound as stocks get thrown out of the window. The low is usually the last stage of a sell-off that's happened in three stages – the three-stage lurch downwards in an Indian bear market. This was apparent in the period from 2000 to 2003 as the IT bubble burst and more obvious between 2008 and 2009; on the later occasion, the compressed and telegraphic

[43] Because of the dominance of single stock futures, most participants also see the securities lending and borrowing mechanism (SLBM) as necessary for reverse arbitrage rather than anything more; viewing it as a source of stock for short selling – its real purpose – is uncommon.

nature of the down move was remarkable. Another striking observation is that the longevity of Indian bear markets seems to be compressing over time and since the 2000–03 bear, there has been no long-lasting time correction. Price corrections that qualify as bear markets happen but for microstructure-driven reasons, and they qualify more as crashes than as time-bound bear markets.

At market bottoms, the fundamental news is terrible and much debate takes place on whether it has been incorporated in the price. Many participants think prices will go lower. Stocks appear cheap but the brokerages have been saying that for some time – perhaps since stocks were two or three times higher than their present lows. Analysts have got crushed into submission after seeing prices repeatedly decline below their targets and are busy reworking their spreadsheets with an anxious eye on current levels. The confidence is gone, so the models are tweaked and massaged to come out with one-year price targets just a little higher than the extant low prices. This is not difficult given the assumptions that go into discounted cash flow models, but the anchoring also means that the research reports and their predictions are basically worthless; coming off the great bottoms of 2003 and 2009, those modest one-year price targets were reached in a few days.

The brokerage reports are mercifully devoid of talk on Chindia, the Great Indian Middle Class, or that 'liquidity super-cycle', and this is as it should be. At market bottoms, there's less need for this nonsense. Stocks have simply got cheap and valuation considerations will prevail. The fat man cometh and just as we don't need to guess his exact weight to know he's fat, so too will experienced observers not have to guess at the market's valuation to know it's cheap.

The bulls have already been tempted – both by the research reports and their own proclivities – to purchase stock at higher levels, so by the time these throwaway prices arrive, they're simply too smashed up to buy. They've exhausted their gunpowder getting in at higher levels, and so, many stocks are down 70 and 80 per cent on moderately high volumes, with no real buyers. Some hardy souls have been trying to find the bottom using derivatives and some have been destroyed by the leverage inherent in those contracts; India's vast derivatives markets are retail dominated so there are a fair number of such folk. A lucky few may actually buy the lows and pyramid into the up move by using unbooked profits from earlier contracts as capital for later positions, resulting in vast fortunes being made overnight.

Often, at market lows, there is bad fundamental news like an international bankruptcy. Till recently at least, companies in India got 'sick' rather than bankrupt, so the bankruptcy news usually came from abroad. The Second Gulf War in 2003 and the General Motors bankruptcy filing in 2009 are examples of bad news coming out at the bottom. Experienced observers will carefully watch the market's reaction to such news. The absence of further downside after such bad news is usually seen as signalling a low, and in fact, the market simply shrugged off the newsbreaks on the Gulf War and the GM bankruptcy.

India's markets now correlate strongly with international indexes and this is truer of lows than of highs. The Mehta low of 1993 was driven by local factors, but in 2003 and 2009 there was a close correspondence with world indexes; in 2009, this correspondence was taken to an extreme, as both the S&P 500 and Sensex bottomed out within days of one another. So, correlations with world markets have been rising steadily; for FIIs at least, the diversification benefits to investing in Indian markets have been falling steadily, but are nevertheless present.[44]

At the bottom, the market is on the front pages of the *Times of India* and the headlines are frightening. The market chorus is going on about how the 'India Growth Story' has been derailed. FII outflows may be considerable and have contributed to the down move. The fundies are too embarrassed – given their earlier predictions – to come on television; besides, the public is subdued and sullen and in no mood to listen to their prognostications. The public is buying heavily on the way down and this was apparent at the 2003 bear low; the public's shareholding of stocks rumoured to be Ketan Parekh favourites (the so called K10)

[44] For evidence on negligible correlations from the early years, see Roger Ignatius, 'The Bombay Stock Exchange: Seasonality and Investment Opportunities,' Discussion Paper 29, Bond University School of Business, *Discussion Papers*, 1992, 21.

showed striking increases even as the fundies reduced their holdings.[45] The ₹2,000 stock seems throwaway cheap when down 90 per cent at ₹200, but that it should be 0 is not internalized.

Fund redemptions used to be high at bottoms but this tendency is reducing, which is not surprising; the public – egged on by a large financial advisory industry – is getting contrarian in its mindset and so there is little redemption at lows. The public has wised up, but only by so much. The redemptions will start as the next bull comes off the bottom and will reach their peak usually just when the up move gets going, which ensures that the public will miss out on a section of the next bull run.[46]

In the past, these events have prompted a regulatory response but that tendency has been reducing with each cycle. The last big regulatory response at a market low came in 2003, but since then the bureaucracy has shown little inclination to wring its hands and do something in response to the howling mob of public opinion. Perhaps this is because the microstructure has been in place for some time now and its coming has lessened the bureaucratic need to fiddle. But the lambs have been taken to the shearing shed, and so, there is some bleating on the talk shows. The talk shows allow people to call in, discuss their losses, and seek anxious advice – the anonymity of the talk show format protects the ego, and so, there is a long queue to get on such programs. The usual advice is to hold on, which is good and sound; at these low prices no one is inclined to sell, and besides disposition effects that lead to loss aversion are very strong in Indian markets. So 'wait for a pull back to sell' is standard gyan (advice) and this counsel is responsible for those mutual fund redemptions that peak early into the next surge.

As the RBI leans against the wind, interest rates have been headed lower for some time before the bottom and that next up move is usually not far away. Value starts manifesting again, Liquidity chases

[45] Nithya Subramanian and Ambarish Mukherjee, 'FIs Crawl out of K10 Stocks: Retail Investors, Who Bought Them, Burn Their Fingers,' *The Hindu*, 16 February 2001.

[46] Udit Prasanna Mukherji, 'Record 53k Demat Accounts Closed in Feb,' *Times of India*, 14 April 2014.

Value which sends the market on its next upswing and that improves Sentiment. The seeds of the next bull move are being sown. And so it goes.

Yet much of all this is not even noticeable on a long-term chart. On a 40-year Sensex graph, most highs and lows are not apparent, and even when they are, seem more like bumps set against the market's majestic long-term upswing. What looked like a massive sell-off in 1993 or 2000 is now just a small trough on the long-term chart – the graphs are linear rather than logarithmic and this accounts for the tendency.[47] Critically, the market moves higher by offering higher multiples on corporate profits, which are measured in nominal non-inflation adjusted figures that anyway rise with inflation. Even if multiples stayed the same and corporates have some pricing power, just the inflation effect of higher nominal profits would send markets higher over time (note also that India is an inflation-prone country where this effect is exacerbated). So, the market always rises, just as a graph of a fixed deposit (FD) that compounded at 8 per cent would always rise over time. Except that the FD would plot as a neat series of rising and progressively larger half rectangles over time, but the market's progress is more jagged and uncertain, and it is this uncertainty that allows the value investor or contrarian to make an occasional move.

Since autarky's end in 1991, there is three decades' worth of stock market data available, but this is trivial in long historical terms. The cyclical movement of the market is not so apparent when surveying this period on the Sensex and Nifty charts. It is only that glorious one way up move over time that is visible on the charts, and there are only hints of cyclical activity. The cycle's rise and fall is better charted through the

[47] Logarithmic charts mark off equal differences between price points according to the percentage change rather than the actual price change. As a result, long term moves from low initial values plot better on logarithmic as compared to linear charts.

expansion and contraction of the market's PE ratio – more technically, the trailing 12-month PE ratio expressed on a free-float adjusted basis. This is the Sensex (or Nifty) level divided by the earnings of its components over the past twelve months, with those earnings suitably weighted by the proportion of each stock in the index and further adjusted for that stock's free float. Charting this shows ratios ranging from between 9 and 11 at a bear low, to between 35 and 40 at a high; the median range is usually between 15 and 18, though the distortions of unconventional monetary policy have shifted that range a little higher in recent years.

Is there a stylized market cycle between these tops and bottoms? It is indisputable that there were highs in 1992, 2000, 2008, and 2020 and each got taken out as the market continued its inexorable march up. It is also clear that there were lows in 1993, 2003, and 2009 and that none of these lows were violated as the market kept going higher. So, why should it matter if there are highs and lows, as long as the market keeps going up? It should not, and this answer provides the raison d'être for the fundies as they invest to capture that long upward swing. And yet to a lot of people it does matter because the monetary rewards of getting it right – of getting in near a low and selling out near a high – are large, in fact large enough to tempt many into guessing at those highs and lows and acting on that guesswork. Even getting it right occasionally over a lifetime of trading or investing would yield considerable rewards.

It also matters to stock pickers, who are the bulk of India's investing public; for most of their picks, they need an upward-trending market (or at least a range-bound market) for the approach to work, and many discover this the hard way when a bear takes away most of their gains. It matters most of all to traders and speculators, as they use the turning points to judge market trend and direction. Finally, it also matters to the small savers, who are constantly comparing the opportunity cost of equity investing to the myriad small savings schemes that offer guaranteed returns. Prolonged periods between highs and lows, together with an extended down cycle, can bring out the high opportunity cost of Indian equity investing and cause money to drift away from the market as the opportunity from guaranteed returns of small schemes gets attractive. In fact, the opportunity cost of equity investing brought about by India's segmented and distorted debt markets is high enough to make even short periods of downturn really matter, though this effect has lessened over the years with the compression in bear durations.

Many would say that a cyclic world view is typically Indian but it is not uncommon across cultures as the works of Vico and Spengler, or those dealing with Chinese dynastic cycles, would indicate. From Ecclesiastes we get: 'To everything there is a season, and a time to every purpose under the heaven / A time to be born, and a time to die'.[48] From Hindu cosmology, we get those cycles encompassed within vaster cycles, from *yugas* and *mahayugas* to *manvantaras* and *kalpas*, and so on. With this encompassing world view it would not be uncommon to think about the market in cyclical terms, and in India one is struck by the frequency with which participants implicitly assume this cyclical approach to the markets. The instinct has been dulled by the one-way bull markets of recent years, but is nevertheless present.

So perhaps in the market, too, there is a time to live and a time to die, more so in some periods than others; the compressed and telegraphic nature of the cycles between 1992 and 2000, and later between 2000 and 2008 simply brings this out. As seen earlier, interest rates and corporate profits are the prime determinants of a cycle, though liquidity also plays an important role. They interact in that trinity of Value, Liquidity, and Sentiment, and it is at market highs and lows that interactions become most apparent. At market lows for example, Value becomes apparent; Liquidity, attracted by the cheap valuations, pours in from foreign and domestic sources and the buying pulls the market up; Sentiment is improved and attracts the trend following technical crowd. This starts the market on its upswing and the cycle takes off.

An offbeat way of looking at the market is through participants' reactions to each stage of this cycle. There is always a chorus in the market's background, almost like the chorus in a Greek tragedy who

[48] Ecclesiastes, 3:1-8 (KJV).

comment with a collective voice on the dramatic action.[49] In the market, that chorus consists of a motley bunch of fund managers, equity strategists, brokerages, technical traders, research analysts, media commentators, and the public; occasionally even the listed industrialists, economists, and lobbyists will have a go at it, but their views are restrained and they are less carried away by the action. As the market moves through its cycle from low to low, the chorus – in stylized form – might go something like this:

The bottom:	'The end of the world is near'
Getting off the bottom:	'Just a bear market rally'
Climbing the wall of worry:	'Be cautious'
The pullback sell-off:	'Short'
Climbing the wall again:	'Buy'
The top:	'India Shining'
The first big break:	'Just a correction'
The slide starts:	'Buy on dips'
The violent pullback:	'The bull market resumes'
The collapse continues:	'We're in a bear market'
The bottom:	'The end of the world is near'

What does one make of all this? Sometimes – usually in the middle of a move rather than at turning points – it appears that the chorus is in sync with what actually happens in the market, while sometimes it appears that the refrain is actually the opposite of what is required to be done. For example, notice the point at which caterwauling about how it's time to be cautious because it's 'just a bear market rally' begins, and yet that seems to be the right time to load up. And what about the point when participants are banging on about 'India Shining' and how

[49] John Train has his version of a market chorus in *The Money Masters*. See John Train, *The Money Masters*, New York: Harper Business, 1994.

it's all just perfect? Isn't it time to lighten up a little because of the big break that's just ahead? Is it that most of the time – in the middle of the move when the market is climbing the wall – most people are right, but something happens at turning points, at the highs and lows? And yet at the turning points, the belief behind these responses is that most participants are wrong most of the time, but is that even possible, or is it arrogance to even think that this can actually happen?

Actually, this stylized market cycle (and the chorus's response to that cycle) is the basis for that famous and dangerous approach to the market – contrarianism – and these are the same questions buzzing around in a contrarian's head. It is this gap between the market chorus and the contrarian's own thoughts (and the questions which result) that will shape the contrarian's view, and so, market highs and lows matter more to the contrarian than (say) the fundie. Without highs and lows and without a chorus along the above lines at those turning points, contrarianism would, in fact, be impossible. Over the years, the correspondence between market moves and this stylized cycle has been remarkable. Equally notable has been the refusal of the market to behave in this pattern since about 2009; as seen earlier, those vast tides of liquidity coursing through world markets in response to unconventional Western monetary policy are mainly responsible for the present disjointedness. Whether in future years the Indian market reverts to the stylized pattern or exhibits other behaviours is something only a brave observer will guess at.

23

EVALUATING PERFORMANCE AND THE FINANCIAL ADVISOR

Performance evaluation of the buy side is a recent idea in India. Informal indexes go back many decades but formal indexes date only from 1986, so any notion of performance that beat an index was also non-existent before that date. Evaluation applies mainly to actively managed portfolios, as passively indexed folios simply replicate market performance and so have little need for evaluation (though evaluative work like tracking error studies can also be applied to passive folios). In India, practically the entire buy side actively manages portfolios, which makes performance doubly relevant; despite that, evaluation is not a focus area. Among participants, performance evaluation applies to mutual funds more than anyone else: LIC's performance is not disclosed, the dervishes' performance is a private matter, FII's performance matters only to them, portfolio management schemes are only beginning to deal with statutory provisions on evaluation, and the public does not care to evaluate itself.

Evaluating performance can be a tricky task and is not as straightforward as it seems. Even when done well, performance evaluation runs into the contradictions of mandated disclaimers like, 'Past performance is no guarantee of future returns.' For practical purposes, there are absolute or relative measures of return. With absolute returns, you'd like to know if your folio returned, say, 12 per cent or some other absolute figure. That 12 per cent – the holding period return – consists of three components: the folio's price appreciation over the relevant period, dividends received on the folio, and any cash yield for the time the manager chose to be in cash rather than fully invested in stocks.[1] With relative returns, you'd like to know if that 12 per cent beat the market's return of (say) 10 per cent over the relevant period. This excess return of 2 per cent over the index is called 'alpha', and most professionals worry about whether they can generate this market-beating return. Alpha is something that most fund managers in the West live or die by, but in India, beating a market benchmark (or bogey) is considered less important; like their peers worldwide, most Indian fund managers can't do it consistently anyway.

The bogey, in turn, is sometimes calculated after both price appreciation and dividend reinvestment, i.e., assuming dividends on index stocks are reinvested in the index. This leads to a total return index that over long periods will be higher than the actual Sensex or Nifty level because of the compounding effects of dividends; dividend yields on the Indian market are usually 1 to 1.5 per cent, so including and compounding this in the bogey over long periods makes it that much harder to beat. Regulations put in place since 2018 have mandated performance evaluation relative to this total return index.[2]

The public, however, typically cares only about the absolute return figure and India tends to be an absolute return equity shop with most investors unconcerned about measuring their portfolio against a bogey like the Sensex or Nifty. Instead, most investors implicitly and mentally benchmark equity returns to small savings products such as post office schemes or public provident funds. Many of these products also enjoy favourable tax treatment which adds to their appeal.

So far quite straightforward, but performance measurement also gets complicated by risk. What matters then – more to professionals than

[1] The last component is usually negligible, but can be important in India, as managers tend to give themselves the flexibility of timing the market by going to cash with large amounts.

[2] Securities and Exchange Board of India, Circular No. SEBI/HO/IMD/DF3/CIR/P/2018/04, 4 January 2018.

to the public – is risk-adjusted performance. If your manager's been a naughty boy and is juicing performance by buying just 7 stocks, it's not the same as having that same performance come from a well-diversified portfolio of 50 stocks. In the latter case, the risk is less and *ceteris paribus* that's a much better situation to be in; in fact, given the volatility and risk in India's equity markets, it's the only situation to be in. This example applies especially to the portfolio management scheme (PMS) side of the fund business. By running concentrated folios, the entire portfolio management industry thrives on this inability of the customer to understand risk-adjusted performance. One would expect the fundies to be more circumspect than the portfolio management side, but Indian regulations allow up to 10 per cent of a fund to be invested in a single company, and this is twice as much as usually allowed in developed markets. So, even among the fundies there is a pronounced bias towards running concentrated folios and, by and large, fund performance in India comes from concentration married to turnover.[3]

As seen earlier, there is little attempt at forming mean variance efficient portfolios, and so, the concentration allows for higher returns with higher risk. The key point is that even after sexing up the portfolio by concentrating it, there is little rise in risk perception among the public or the advisors, and this is because the entire market is an absolute return equity shop. So, the evaluation needed to judge whether the enhanced return was due to stock picking skill – or just juicing up the folio by concentrating it in a few stocks – does not happen, and here too the buy side gets away with it all. One measure which adjusts for that risk is the Sharpe ratio which measures the portfolio's excess return per unit of risk taken.[4] In India, such measures are disclosed but never fully appreciated, and they rarely enter an investor's consideration set. So, the adjustment for risk that takes place in the West does not happen here and intuitions about risk are only beginning to take hold.

[3] Portfolio churn is the euphemism applied to this phenomenon.

[4] Here the portfolio's excess return over a risk-free rate (say a G-Sec) is divided by the portfolio's standard deviation (roughly the extent by which it varies around its average return). A trio of measures includes those named after Sharpe, Treynor, and Jensen.

Fees are another complication and, ideally, you want a product that beats the market even after fees (such as mutual fund loads), or better still, beats the market after fees and transaction costs. But adjusting for fees and/or transaction costs is rarely done and even studies that systematically find market-beating performance are usually not adjusted for the vigorish – the total of all those brokerages, fees, and commissions that are needed to lubricate any process of financial intermediation. A final complication is survivorship bias, and this is an important issue in India. With survivorship bias, poor performers exit or are merged into other funds but the time series data does not correct for that; over time, the data only reflects the high-performing survivors, and this tends to introduce positive biases on aggregate.

Luck and skill interplay in complex ways when judging performance. Some studies indicate that it takes about 22 years of time series data (and the use of analytics like 't statistics') to judge if a manager's performance is due to luck or skill.[5] But most fundies become managers in the early to mid-forties and retire by their late fifties. Consequently, most fundies have career spans less than the 22 years needed to judge whether performance was due to luck or skill, which implies that a fundie can have an excellent career run with most of it due to luck. As always, in financial markets it's good to be lucky and skilful, but given a choice, it's better to be lucky than to be skilful.

This brings us to the business of financial advisors. For many years – perhaps because of the dominance of equities as an asset class – financial advice simply meant stock picking advice and tips. Nowadays, financial advice encompasses a broader area than just equities, and in recent years, the field has had to deal with the problem of shifting boundaries. Presently, financial advice and planning is a broad field that includes estate planning, insurance policies, and tax advisory, together

[5] This is with a low confidence interval of 75 per cent. See Larry Harris, *Trading and Exchanges: Market Microstructure for Practitioners*, New York: Oxford University Press, 2003, 457.

with investment advice and planning; so, giving advice on equities gets subsumed under the broader rubric of investment advice and planning. This discussion will be confined to pure play equity counsel, through advisors and distributors (of manufactured products like mutual funds). Principally, the focus here is on the interface between financial advisors/ distributors and equity markets, together with regulatory attempts at changing that interface.

For most of the Century of Marking Time, the advisory business was informal with little sign of the range of services people associate with financial advice. Brokers typically doubled up as financial advisors and assorted professionals like chartered accountants also gave advice of varying quality. From the mid-1980s, magazines such as *Dalal Street Investment Journal* dispensed advice on equities, but besides these, there were few other channels for equity counsel. On the distribution side, till the early 1990s, there were no mutual fund distributors other than the UTI sales force. From about the turn of the millennium, this informal way of life ended and the advisory and distribution businesses became the focus of regulatory attention. Brokers had been the focus of regulatory attention in the early 1990s, followed by the fundies a short while later, and now it was the turn of the advisors. As is usually the case in India, all this regulatory attention produced mixed results.

Sales of financial products gained momentum during the Rate Bull between 2003 and 2007, which led to the occasional episodes of mis-selling that brought about the regulatory focus. Among these episodes was a fiasco involving unit-linked insurance plans (ULIPs), which were insurance plans with investment features that went south during the financial crisis that followed the Great Recession. Besides the ULIP affair, the 2009 abolition of entry loads for mutual funds also called for clarification on the roles of advisors versus distributors.

Subsequently, two bouts of regulatory attention in the years leading up to 2013 and 2020 essentially created the investment advisory business and then rendered it comatose.

The first period of regulatory attention led up to the SEBI (Investment Advisers) Regulations of 2013. Starting from about 2007, the tortuous process of creating regulation via committee was apparent in the following sequence of events and milestones: consultative paper; public comments; a memorandum before the SEBI board; referral to a high-level consultative committee; the high-level committee's referral to another committee headed by D. Swarup; the D. Swarup committee's referral back to the high-level committee; further discussions with a Financial Stability and Development Council sub-committee; a concept paper by SEBI based on the above inputs; a draft; and finally a copy of the 2013 Investment Adviser Regulations.[6]

Much of this six-year process of 'death by committee' took place against the backdrop of the Great Recession's boom–bust cycle and the ULIP incident in particular, influenced the committees and convinced them that mis-selling was rampant. Committees that got into the act would make repeated references to the ULIP affair as they went about drafting a regulatory framework for advisors.[7] In effect, the ULIP fiasco aggravated the dirigisme that underlay much state activity in India, and this pattern of dubious activity by one party resulting in heavy-handed regulation for the remaining 99 was to remain a pervasive feature of Indian regulation. Like generals fighting the last war, regulators dealing with the last bad apple put in place rules that made life more difficult for the majority into the future and this tendency towards the fallacy of composition became pervasive.

All this introduced the advisory and distribution space to the same regulatory risk other parts of the financial services industry were now facing. At least, manufacturers (like mutual funds) and brokers were large organizations that could deploy resources and influence the process, but

[6] The 2011 concept paper on investment advisor regulations contains an overview on regulation formation in its Background Section. Securities and Exchange Board of India, *Concept Paper on Regulation of Investment Advisors*, Mumbai: SEBI, 2011.

[7] The ULIP episode's influence on investment advisor regulations can be seen in the D. Swarup committee report. The phrase 'ULIP' (or its expansion) was used 28 times in the report and Annexure 1 of the report contained three pages of interviews with customers who claimed they were victims of ULIP mis-selling. See Ministry of Finance, *Financial Well-Being: Report of the Committee on Investor Awareness and Protection*, New Delhi: Ministry of Finance, 2009.

most advisors and distributors were individuals or small businesses who had fewer resources to deal with all this regulatory risk.

The regulations were notified in January 2013, with an October deadline for advisors to register themselves, but only 11 advisors had signed up a month before the deadline.[8] On deadline expiry, barely 70 had entered the fold as Registered Investment Advisors and this number remained essentially unchanged for a full year after the regulations were notified.[9] Embarrassed, SEBI then exempted certified financial planners (CFPs) – many of whom had already been grandfathered into the profession by the Financial Planning Standards Board – from taking a certification exam required to register as investment advisors.[10] As a result, over 2,000 of such planners found themselves automatically eligible to register as advisors. Despite these exertions, by mid-2016, only 512 advisors (across individuals and firms) had signed up, and by now, more than three years had passed since the 2013 regulations were notified.

A second bout of regulatory attention then followed between 2016 and 2020. When the trade's tepid response became apparent, SEBI reacted with a further flurry of regulation, and three consultation papers were released in 2016, 2017, and 2018, seeking public comments on further changes.[11] Following the third paper's release in 2018, a working group was constituted, and it performed the crucial tasks of agenda setting, issue framing, and actual proposal generation; the members of the working group were never disclosed and its composition is not publicly available. Following this working group's recommendations, a fourth consultation paper that subsumed the suggestions of the earlier

[8] Lisa Pallavi Barbora, '11 Investment Advisers Registered under SEBI's New Regulations,' *Mint*, 3 September 2013.

[9] BS Reporter, 'SEBI Gets 70 Applications under Investment Advisors Regulation,' *Business Standard*, 19 October 2013.

[10] Securities and Exchange Board of India, Notification No. LAD-NRO/GN/201-14/42/118, 27 January 2014.

[11] Securities and Exchange Board of India, *Board Memorandum on SEBI (Investment Advisers) Regulations 2013*, Mumbai: SEBI, 2020, 2.

papers was issued for public comments in early 2020.[12] Over 2,800 comments were received and the public consultation gave the impression of a democratic process, except that the public were offering comments on what was already framed by the mysterious working group.[13]

In turn, all this led to the June 2020 amendments to the 2013 regulations that further tightened rules, and which will, in all probability, make the trade less attractive. Consider that by 2018, over a 1,000 had signed up, but by some estimates, most were in the business of stock tips or research and only 400 were advisors; of these 400, less than 100 were 'fee only' advisors – whose increase was the sole object of all this regulation – and the remaining were both fee and commission agents.[14] By January 2020, a date deliberately chosen because it avoids any attrition caused by the coronavirus pandemic, the regulations had resulted in a total of 1,277 registered advisors.[15] All this in a country with over 250 million households. To put things in perspective, the US had over 300,000 personal financial advisors, of which over 100,000 were certified financial planners.[16]

And yet, as seen from the above account, the response was not for want of trying on SEBI's part.

What had happened? Some of the 2013 regulation was unexceptionable, but other parts were more problematic and much of it was reiterated in the 2020 changes. Net worth, qualification, and certification requirements were introduced and then tightened even further; additional infrastructure and personnel (like compliance officers) were included in the long list of 'must haves'; another long list of day-

[12] Securities and Exchange Board of India, *Consultation Paper on Review of Regulatory Framework for Investment Advisers (IA)*, Mumbai: SEBI, January 2020.

[13] SEBI, *Board Memorandum on SEBI (Investment Advisers) Regulations 2013*, 3–4.

[14] Dhaval Kapadia, 'Why the RIA Model Has Not Picked up in India,' *Morningstar*, 5 December 2018.

[15] Of these, about three quarter are individuals or partnerships. SEBI, *Board Memorandum on SEBI (Investment Advisers) Regulations 2013*, 1–2.

[16] US Bureau of Labor Statistics at https://www.bls.gov/oes/2023/may/oes132052.htm. CFB Board, CFP® Professional Demographics, at https://www.cfp.net/knowledge/reports-and-statistics/professional-demographics.

to-day operational requirements was tacked on and included client risk profiling, confidentiality, more disclosure, recordkeeping, yearly audits, and so on; and finally, the regulator gave itself powers of inspection to ensure the above.[17] Capping fees in percentage and absolute terms was also attempted in the concept papers, but at least that was not included in the final 2020 changes. Much of this rose from the usual heavy-handed attempt to drive out small players, but other changes were more substantial and changed the basic character of the industry. Critically, advisors were made fiduciaries, the advisory and distribution businesses were segregated at the client level, advisors were banned from offering distribution services even in their family members' names, and so on.

All this took place in a confused tangle of regulation whose general tone reeked of suspicion and circumspection. Like many concept papers in regulation, the concept papers on advisors also started off with ritual demonization of the group that was the object of regulation. It was clear that the end result had further marginalized the industry. Improbably enough – in a country with those 250 million households – moving the needle from about 1,000 advisors to something more would continue to remain an elusive undertaking. Occupational closure that shut amateurs and 'non experts' out of the advisory profession should have happened after the profession was created, but excessive credentialism ensured it happened before that. Using credentialism to create that new *jaati* of advisors has proved difficult, perhaps because the brahminical rank ordering of hierarchy that credentialism depends on clashes with the 'in your face' egalitarianism of the market. Media coverage should have clarified the issues, but the reporting is typically through tick-tocks that contribute to the noise.

By now, it was apparent that it was not just the public who needed protection from the advisors, but the advisors who needed protection from the regulator. Some of SEBI's regulatory action was unexceptionable and noteworthy in itself and yet the general tenor was

[17] The proposals – and their rationale – are outlined in the 2020 Consultation Paper and Board Memorandum.

driven by the *aam aadmi* (ordinary man) bias that typified much of the regulator's actions. Like the fundies, the advisors now had to deal with a regulator inherently biased in favour of the *aam aadmi*, and as a result, advisory income streams also faced regulatory risk. As seen earlier, regulatory action brought about by the *aam aadmi* bias appropriated industry profits that accrued from economies of scale and distributed it back to the *aam aadmi* in their avatar as customers. It had happened after the mutual fund industry reached economies of scale, but now the pattern repeated with the advisory business even before it could reach economies of scale, and this sent the advisory trade into a coma.

Nevertheless, and despite the attention showered on the advisors, the real action took place among the distributors. By 2022, there were over 1,00,000 mutual fund distributors in India as compared to a little over 1,000 registered advisors, so distributors outnumbered advisors by almost 100 to 1.[18] Some of the leading national distributors, such as NJ Invest and Bajaj Capital were large organizations that pulled in considerable sums in commission; four of the five largest fund distributors were banks that took advantage of their huge branch networks to distribute mutual funds. Gross mutual fund distribution fees for the top 1,000 (or so) distributors peaked at about ₹8,000 crores ($1.1 billion) in 2018–19 before dropping by about a fifth in the next year.[19] The amount seems large, but this was marketing and distribution spend that supported the entire Indian buy side and its base of about ₹24,00,000 crores at that time. In fact, the distribution commissions are much less than what the FMCG industry would spend on marketing and distribution in a given year to support business activity of a lower order of magnitude; it is also less than the brokerage commission pool, which in recent years has moved between ₹15,000 and ₹20,000 crores. But SEBI's *aam aadmi* bias viewed the fund commissions as too much, and so the regulator kept hammering away at the commissions, often to the detriment of the industry's basic economics.

[18] Some studies put the number of active distributors at between 10,000 and 40,000.

[19] Ravi Samalad, 'Top Distributors See a Drop in MF Commission Earnings,' *Morningstar*, 7 July 2020.

From about 2013, the distributors were also in a state of unrest brought about by another SEBI swipe at the vigorish.[20] This time, it was SEBI's introduction of direct plans that allowed customers to buy mutual funds directly on an exchange, bypassing distributors and reducing their trail commissions.[21] This added to the turmoil on the distribution side. More generally, the distributors were getting exposed as only relationship people, who were not as credentialed as the advisors. Despite that, distributors were important market participants. In fact, distributors accounted for the bulk of SIPs, and AMFI data usually showed that as much as 85 to 90 per cent of SIP flows came from regular plans handled by distributors.[22] So, the market's future was as much in their hands as it was with the FIIs, and organizing among themselves might have improved their bargaining power. Mysteriously, the distributors themselves chose not to exercise their influence, perhaps because there were so many of them in a fragmented industry.

Distributor earnings were tied to the assets invested through the distributors in regular or direct plans. With regular plans and trail commissions, mutual funds paid distributors an annual percentage (say 0.5 per cent) of the amount the distributor had garnered for the fund; in turn, this amount was paid out of the total expenses charged to the fund. With direct plans, the customer bought the fund directly through a stock exchange, or by approaching a fund directly, and so, there were no annual trail commissions. Trail commissions had profound (if underappreciated) effects on switching costs. Trail commissions applied to the original distributor who got the capital into the market, and so, a new distributor whom a customer switched to got no trail commissions; only fresh investments qualified.[23] This reduced the new distributor's

[20] Narendra Nathan, 'MF Distributors Behaving Like Angry Birds. Here's Why,' *Economic Times*, 14 January 2016.

[21] Ibid.

[22] For example, AMFI data for the month of September 2019 showed that direct plans mobilized through distributors accounted for ₹7,147 crores of the ₹8,263 crores collected through SIPs – or about 86 per cent of flows. Ravi Samalad, '86% of SIP Inflows Came via Distributors in September 2019,' *Morningstar*, 18 October 2019.

[23] Neil Borate, 'Unhappy with Your Mutual Fund Distributor? Switching Is Not Easy,' *Mint*, 10 December 2019.

incentive to take up the customer's business, and also made it difficult for the customer to switch distributors. Later, the total expense ratio of funds was also reduced, which caused them to cut back on commissions to distributors, which in turn reduced entry into the distribution business.[24]

The overall impression was of an industry where the vigorish was being squeezed out of the system by the regulator's *aam aadmi* bias, with attendant complications for industry structure and incentives to key players. Structural surges in assets under management (AUM) should have caused huge increases in industry bottom lines, but this did not happen.

SEBI, faced with the advisors' reluctance to respond to its fiddling, then attempted another solution – it tried to convince distributors to become advisors. It proposed that distributors had till March 2019 to decide if they wanted to be advisors or distributors, and then went ahead and implemented that proposal. Initially, the trade arbitraged through the family, and distributors tried to set up separate entities controlled by relatives where they lodged the advisory business. But the advisory side paid so little and now came with such bizarre and onerous regulations that most simply opted out of the advisory business and chose to stay as distributors. Many certified financial planners who had been grandfathered into the advisory fold and were both advisors and distributors, also now chose to remain only as distributors.[25] One aim of the original 2013 regulation had been to get many distributors to give up that activity and become advisors, but so convoluted had the compliance environment become, that the reverse took place. The determined effort to grow the advisory community had the opposite effect.

---

[24] Himadri Buch, 'Ban on Upfront Commission Hits New Individual Distributor Registrations in FY20; Plummets 51% YoY,' *Moneycontrol*, 23 April 2020.

[25] Fund distributors are registered with AMFI and required to abide by AMFI's guidelines and code of ethics. Prospects who clear exams conducted by the National Institute of Securities Markets are issued an AMFI Registration Number which permits them to distribute and sell mutual funds. This license is valid for a period of three years. Cafemutual.com is a website for mutual fund professionals.

You have a financial advisor not to manage your investments but to manage yourself. This is especially true if you fancy yourself as a *khiladi* (player), and the trading temptations of India's stock market means that there are many such fanciers. In such cases, good advisors act as a first line of defence against an investor's stupidity. They protect people from the consequences of their own idiocy but are rarely thanked for the money they save people this way. Visualizing the counterfactual is difficult for most clients – except those who've taken on advisors after getting whacked on their backsides through direct trading in the markets; in fact, such clients tend to be the most loyal.

Financial advisors benefit from the relationship-oriented nature of Indian society and commercial life. Everything is the relationship, and 'Do we have a relationship with them?' is the usual anxious question at Monday morning meetings on business development. In India, the 'trust, but verify' dictum is not as important as simply 'trust', and this is because verifying has always been difficult in such a chaotic environment. As a result, much gets subsumed under the rubric of 'trust', and yet not much data is available on this global issue. One study by the CFA Institute found that 87 per cent of Indian retail investors were likely to 'completely trust' or 'trust' the financial services industry as compared to 46 per cent for retail investors surveyed globally.[26] This result is at odds with the actual state of India's financial services industry and attributable in large part to the backstop provided by government's ownership of most of the banking system, together with the relative youth of the trading population.

Most advisors run into the Indian tendency to avoid paying for advice. Financial advisors add another layer of fees to the investor's costs and are judged on whether those fees were worth it. In an environment that does not value advice, they are constantly assessed on the added value they bring to the advisory product, and this introduces a certain

[26] The results are from a 2020 CFA Institute and Greenwich Associates global survey of over 3,500 retail investors and over 900 institutional investors that included India. CFA Institute, 'Earning Investors' Trust,' *Fourth Investor Trust Survey*, https://trust.cfainstitute.org/wp-content/uploads/2020/05/CFAI_TrustReport2020_FINAL.pdf.

tension to their work. Because of this, in the early years there was a general reluctance to charge fees and even today most get by in a sort of shadow world between fees and commissions. The key point is that most advisors will go on and on about risk but none take any risk themselves, and for most, the equity component of their advice is confined to recommending high performing mutual funds. Advice on direct stock picking would be anathema to most of them. So, for most advisors – after the asset allocation process – a selection of mutual funds delivers the advisory product and gives clients the relevant equity exposure.

The business model of most advisors and distributors is geared not toward fiduciary standards, as much as towards suitability standards. Under fiduciary standards, a financial advisor works for a fixed fee (or some such lump sum amount), computed either on an annual basis or as a percentage of assets under advice placed with the advisor. Fiduciary standards then run into the traditional Indian problem of wanting free advice. But free advice is usually worth what you pay for it, and yet most don't get this basic fact (the exception to this rule is advice between parties with some prior relationship). Nevertheless, the public's attitude is now shifting and many from the younger generation seem willing to pay for advice; besides, the industry is being nudged by the regulator towards this fiduciary standard.

Still much of the industry presently runs under suitability standards, where an advisor recommends products based on their suitability to the client, and then receives commissions; these are paid to the advisor by the relevant manufacturer (like a mutual fund) whose product was recommended. Here there may be agency issues, and products that offer large commissions (or better still, large upfront commissions) might be recommended despite being less than suitable for a client, leading to a conflict of interest. The most recognizable manifestation is churning, as when an advisor repeatedly churns a client's folio by getting the client in and out of various mutual funds just to earn the commission; this practice has reduced with the 2009 decision to do away with entry loads for mutual funds.[27]

[27] PTI, 'SEBI Removes Entry Load on MF Schemes,' *Economic Times*, 18 June 2009.

Because of agency issues, the suitability standard has been getting a bad rap in recent years and one would expect that the fiduciary standard is the gainer. But nothing in India is as straightforward as it should be, and the negligible number of fee-only financial advisors – despite vigorous regulatory encouragement – suggests that the fiduciary standard also has acceptance issues.[28]

Generally, formal advice on equities flowed to the public from five sources: mutual fund distributors, bank/brokerage relationship managers (RMs), independent financial advisors (IFAs), registered investment advisors (RIAs), and portfolio management schemes (PMSs). Of these, the PMSs ran discretionary and non-discretionary schemes, and the discretionary PMS product was the most direct form of equity advice offered, running equity-only portfolios with fixed and performance based variable fees similar to what hedge funds charged. But the PMSs had entry requirements on folio size which only well-heeled clients could meet, which left the majority with the first four types. Distributors, RMs, and IFAs work on a suitability model where the recommended product's manufacturer pays them commissions, while the RIAs are an attempt to introduce a fiduciary model based on lump sum payments to advisors. Finally, all this is the formal market, but in a relationship-oriented society, much financial advice is also generated from informal sources.

By not paying for advice, clients drive the advisory business towards the suitability model, while SEBI uses regulatory action to drive it towards the fiduciary model. This unstable dynamic leads to a conflicted business where regulatory action is the biggest variable acting on industry top and bottom lines. The situation is familiar to other participants such as the fundies, except that fundies are big corporates who can 'manage the environment' better than advisors, who are usually individuals with fewer resources. So, now one end of the industry spectrum is 'fee only' or fiduciary driven, while the other end is 'commission only', which is suitability driven.

[28] Neither 'suitability' nor 'fiduciary' are commonly used as terms when describing advisory business models.

In the spectrum's middle are 'fee-based' activities, which are a combination fee and commission model; in a form of virtue signalling, advisors charge low fixed fees to signal they are respectable fiduciaries, while informally receiving commissions from manufacturers on recommended products, commissions that clients know nothing about. This hybrid fee and commission model lost 'regulatory forbearance' in 2020 and complicated guidelines came out that tried to do away with it; the same advisor was barred from offering commission-based distribution and advice to the same client, and further twists tried to minimize the trade's attempt to carry out regulatory arbitrage through other family members.[29] This sort of manoeuvring over the vigorish has now become common in India, but despite all the moves India remains an agent-driven market running on a suitability model.

The vigorish is like oxygen that keeps the undergrowth of the financial jungle alive, and the denizens of that undergrowth – advisors and distributors among them – do all they can to keep the flow of that life-giving commodity coming, driven in large part by a digitized back office where the country was anyway a world leader. The vigorish has always been in play in India.[30] This is easier to see on the trading side, where the daily value of trading in cash and derivatives markets exceeded $200 billion by 2021; that sum was spread over 100 million demat accounts and considerable amounts could be made by shaving off miniscule amounts from these huge flows as they sloshed between the market and the public's demat accounts. Something similar happens with mutual funds and other manufactured products the advisors deal with, but here the chattering classes are aware of the vigorish's effects on long term returns, and so, a vig that is privately decided in the brokerage/trading space is controlled through regulatory fiat in the advisory space. In turn, that regulation is usually a well-meaning but heavy-handed affair, with

[29] Neil Borate, 'SEBI Tightens Norms for Advisers, Restricts Use of Terms Like IFAs,' *Mint*, 8 July 2020.

[30] Vigorish components such as impact costs and bid-ask spreads are less relevant to the advisory business.

that silent bias in favour of the *aam aadmi* rather than the industry's bottom line, a bias so pronounced that it would be denounced as almost communist, if it did not apply to the most capitalist of industries.

All this results in that peculiar cat and mouse game between manufacturers, advisors, distributors, and the regulator. SEBI takes regular swipes at the vig, so the more disguised its flow the better for the industry, and this leads to dizzy manoeuvring between the regulator and participants.

Dirigisme – directive state control of economic activity – was pervasive in India's financial sector, and it was often unclear where that dirigisme ended and regulation began. The advisory business lived in the same quiet dread of SEBI's regulatory activity as the fundies. One example of this dirigisme involved fiddling with net-worth norms and constantly raising them to drive participants out of the industry; the purpose behind such fiddling was unclear, as advisory firms were services that anyway had negligible capital requirements. It was a common pattern for net-worth norms to be set low to encourage entry into an industry segment, following which they would be progressively raised. Raising net-worth norms was invidious because those who could not meet the raised norms would be forced to admit their own capital constraints, which proved embarrassing to many and consequently brought about silent compliance or exit. Many participants left the industry, but this also restricted entry and protected bigger incumbents from competition.

Strange also was the fiddling over credentials; increasingly, postgraduate qualifications in finance or accounting were needed, which hit the scores of advisors without these pieces of paper who had built up competence in the school of hard knocks. Under these requirements, someone with a background in the social sciences or humanities who had succeeded on a titanic scale in investments (like a Soros or a Templeton) would have been deemed unworthy. The obsession with credentials also resulted in pages filled with qualification requirements for market participants.[31]

[31] Clause 7 of the 2013 and 2020 regulations contains two pages of certification requirements.

Dirigisme was not the only cause behind all this and another reason was regulatory capture. The members of SEBI's assorted working groups, more often than not were the larger and more aggressive names from among the regulated entities themselves. For example, a 2019 working group on portfolio managers had six out of seven members from among the larger portfolio managers, and sure enough these worthies raised net worth and qualification norms to widen the moat around their industry segment and drive out smaller firms, whom they openly branded as 'fringe players' in their report.[32] So, the initial impression was of faceless SEBI dirigistes perennially trapped in 'reform' mode, who tinkered with regulations that wore down smaller participants and drove them – through a process of regulatory arbitrage – into the informal economy. But to that must be added, participants who sat on the working groups and set the compliance and reform agenda behind the scenes to their advantage. 'Death by compliance' was now also 'death by committee'. The unrecognized hypocrisy of having working groups that often dealt with conflicts of interest, themselves being so brazenly conflicted, was considerable even by Indian standards.

It was also common to find regulatory logic where a certain set of rules applied if a business was limited to X in turnover or assets or some such, but once that limit X was exceeded, a further set of rules and regulations applied, that materially affected the business and changed its basic character. For example, the 2020 changes to the advisor regulations forced advisors whose client list had crossed 150 clients to give up their individual registrations and 'corporatize'.[33] All this led participants into severe but underappreciated regulatory risk. Many small enterprises that met all compliance norms on entry into an industry segment later found themselves entangled in regulatory changes put in place after

[32] Securities and Exchange Board of India, *Report of the Working Group on SEBI (Portfolio Managers) Regulations, 1993*, Mumbai: SEBI, 2019, 6. In this example, the six members included: UTI Asset Management Company Pvt Ltd; ASK Group; Marcellus Investment Managers Private Limited; NJ Advisory Services Private Limited; Aequitas Investment Consultancy Private Limited; and Kotak Wealth Management, Distribution arm of Kotak Mahindra Bank. The 7th member was a former Executive Director (Legal), SEBI.

[33] Section 13 (e) of the SEBI (Investment Advisers) (Amendment) Regulations, 2020.

their entry. Many simply gave up and exited, without realizing they were victims of a game being played out behind the scenes.

Disturbing also was the absence of outrage at all this regulatory overreach and most lived in apprehension of a SEBI that had the power to enforce ever-shifting guidelines. The necessity of going to the regulator every three years (or so) to renew a license, gave a faceless bureaucrat power over a profitable business if there was any dissent. As a result, bizarre regulation only elicited silence or resigned pushback, but never red-blooded reaction. And so, in this deafening silence, the costs of complying with absurd regulations kept increasing. Watching the market was SEBI's job but watching the watchers was nobody's job. *Quis custodiet ipsos custodies?*[34]

Successful trading and investing usually calls for knowledge of a wide range of fields including finance and accounting methodology, investment policy, competitive strategy, valuation, psychology, sociology, financial history, market microstructure, and open economy macroeconomics. Many successful participants have got by without a formal introduction to these fields, while many succeeded by picking up knowledge along the way through the school of hard knocks; rather than command of the above subjects, it was that broad gauged experience and a certain savvy on how the world worked, which distinguished them. Nowadays though, it is becoming harder to come across participants who have succeeded without a working knowledge of some of the above fields.

In turn, finding this level of knowledge among financial advisors is not easy, and to be fair, it is not even expected of them. Paradoxically, in an efficient market where prices reflect available information most of the time, there should be little need for a high level of investing knowledge. In such a market, most stocks are efficiently priced most of the time, so rather than the expertise necessary to pick stocks, what matters is well

[34] 'Who will watch the watchers?'

diversified exposure to systematic market risk – and the higher returns that should follow after taking such risk – and in this limited sense, efficient markets actually protect those without high skill levels. Then what really matters is getting people exposed to equities, and this is what most financial advisors do for their clients anyway. Consequently, the advisor's job is directing clients to other participants such as fundies, whose track records demonstrate competence in that long list of fields. In turn, India is an inefficient market where some managers can be better (or luckier) than others at generating returns by buying mispriced stocks; financial advisors can then add commensurate value by pointing clients toward such managers.

Advisors can be independent or associated with an entity. Strangely enough, the catastrophic cases of mis-selling have more often than not taken place among advisors associated with large organizations – there are just a lot more relationship managers from large organizations to spread the wrong party line among the public. Chartered accountants sometimes double up as informal advisors, but given their training in audit and taxes (more than anything else), often produce mixed results. For the independents, Bengaluru is a key centre as its IT ecosystem produces large numbers of upwardly mobile high-salaried professionals – and these are a coveted client base. Independent advisors need to have a strong entrepreneurial streak and many have an evangelical bent as well. In fact, some of them seem almost spiritual in what is otherwise the most worldly of processes, and the way the best among them deal with a client's urge to time the market (or worse still, to trade) is reminiscent of an Alcoholics Anonymous councillor wrestling an addict off the bottle. The desire to change lives by spreading the word on equities figures strongly among their reasons for being, or so they say, and this also accounts for the evangelical bent.

Perhaps because they lack the assurance that comes from belonging to more credentialed professions such as chartered accountancy or law, many advisors are autodidacts, with a keenness to learn and desire for continuous self-improvement. The bigger advisors graduate and become wealth managers. Both do essentially the same thing, but saying you're a wealth manager rather than an advisor signals that you have bigger clients. Many work as one-stop interfaces between clients and a complex digital world and help clients navigate that world just as other intermediaries have sprung up to help small businesses navigate the shoals of the GST.

All this overlaps with a financial planning profession that is also going through its own process of credentialism. Because of the poor response to its proposals on registered investment advisors, SEBI had attempted to grandfather a nascent financial planning vocation into the investment advisory business, and this led to some confusion among the public on nomenclature. But an unofficial financial planning profession has existed for some time, and it is going through its own process of formalization. Some say that Gaurav Mashruwala is the founder of India's financial planning industry. Many years later, someone looking back on the profession might also count Lovaii Navlakhi, Dilshad Billimoria, Suresh Sadagopan, and Brijesh Dalmia among the first generation of pioneers. An overseas institute has entered and is attempting to create a *jaati* of certified financial planners (CFPs), with its own certification and entry requirements. Some experienced participants have been grandfathered into existence as financial planners by giving them a CFP certification without examination, but others that follow will have to go the hard way of examination and certification.

The advisory process usually starts with a one-on-one consultation and a detailed questionnaire, both of which attempt to probe risk profile. Advisors are typically asset gatherers who gather and then farm out assets to other participants like fundies, usually after deciding on a basic allocation between debt and equity based on the client's risk profile. The usual aim of all this is helping investors as householders reach goals on savings and retirement, after all other householder obligations are met.

Onboarding clients, risk profiling, asset allocation, and fund selection, followed by ongoing customer relationship management and hand holding, is the basic sequence on the equity advisory product. Actual stock picking as part of the advisory process is uncommon nowadays, and the emphasis is on asset gathering and farming out to mutual funds. The basic heuristic on asset allocation has been internalized and is used as the foundation for much advice – younger clients with greater risk-bearing capacity get socked with a little more equity, and so on. Clientele effects – the idea that different tax or regulatory changes will have different effects on clients as investors – are particularly important in India's bizarrely complex and frequently changing environment, and keeping on top of them is important for sophisticated advisors.

For an upper-middle class salaried household, a reasonable heuristic for every 100 in household income is to spend 20, save and invest 20, get taxed with 20, and drawdown debt (or pay EMIs) with 20. That leaves 20 unaccounted for and this is the 'disappearing 20' – that part of a household's budget that mysteriously disappears on items like costumes for the children's school play, the upgraded annual vacation that should never have happened, and so on. This 'disappearing 20' gets added to the 'spend 20' for a total of 40 which should have been the original 'spend' allocation anyway, but it's more tolerant of human frailty to think in terms of such mental buckets. If the housing loan is large (a common situation in cities nowadays), the 'save and invest 20' gets clubbed with the 'drawdown debt (or pay EMIs) 20' for a total of 40 towards the housing loan EMI; in this case, the household is only building real assets, with not much left over for building financial assets.

Most personal financial advice should operate along these simple heuristics but rarely does so, and this is because of the well-known Indian tendency to complicate things that don't need to be complicated.

Acquisition costs can be significant. Client acquisition runs into the key issues of trust and relationships, so getting a client is an exercise in psychology as much as business development; this is not surprising, given the role behavioural issues play in handling money. Being a good listener, getting the client to open up, and demarketing are also key to client acquisition; the demarketing sounds odd, but it builds credibility by tempering return expectations and introduces a dose of realism into the advisory process right from the beginning. Most acquisition and new business occurs through referrals, but getting those referrals depends on providing a few years of returns, which allows for the development of 'comfort levels' that lead to an established relationship.[35] For newcomers, getting over this hump can be an issue; the hump acts as a moat around the more established advisors who have been around for a while. SEBI's 2009 decision to do away with entry loads, further raises the advisor's capital requirement for the first few years and deepens the moat.

Once that moat is crossed though, clients can be sticky. Clients tend to stay on, and in turn, the best advisors grow with their clients; if the advisor is doing a good job and growing client assets, the same percentage fee on a larger asset base increases the advisor's top line, and this continuity is key to the business model. Because of that stickiness, it is also common to see clients move around with their advisors and relationships tend to be trust based. Wealth management firms and brokerages try to exploit this stickiness, and it is common to see firms trying to build an asset base by hiring relationship managers. The hope is that the relationship manager moves with clients' assets, which also justifies the cost of hiring the manager. The result is a merry-go-round for relationship managers who move with their clients' money and recruitment advertising for such managers is widespread.

The archetypal client of a financial advisor or distributor is the salaried, upper middle class, and Double-Income-One-Kid unit. Persistent tropes in client acquisition include that of the hard-charging executive who has no time for his investments, or the profligate who – horror of horrors – violates unspoken Indian middle-class norms on spending and extravagance. For such types, the trope has the 'advisor as saviour' and the papers are filled with stories that usually have picture-perfect upper middle class DIOKs in ideal settings who strayed from the path, but were rescued by the financial advisors.[36] For the self-reliant, the best

[35] For profiles of some leading financial planners/advisors and the issues involved in building an advisory practice in India, see Manish Chauhan and Nandish Desai, 'Secrets of 10 Successful Financial Advisors in India,' *cafemutual,* EBook, https://cafemutual.com/ UploadPdf/ 634957564005172500_Secrets-of-10-Successful-Financial-Advisors-In-India-cafemutual.pdf. Websites for advisors include Networkfp and IFA Galaxy.

[36] Nilanjana Chakraborty, Disha Sanghvi, Deepti Bhaskaran, Sunita Abraham, and Lisa Pallavi Barbora, 'Your Money in 2019: Financial Planning for a New Beginning,' *Mint,* 2 January 2019.

advice was to be your own financial advisor but that meant financial literacy and learning, which was painful.[37]

Once an advisory relationship is initiated, the client's responsibility for his own stupidity shifts to the advisor, and this is one of the main services for which the advisor gets paid. For the client, having an investment adviser is almost like buying psychological protection for his (the client's) ego. If things turn out well, the client congratulates himself for choosing the advisor. If things turn out badly, the client blames the advisor. A client handling his own portfolio would see his ego sink with the folio, but with an advisor the client's ego gets protected. In this sense, hiring an advisor amounts to a client buying a protective put option on his own ego with the advisor's fees as the put premium.

Advisors and distributors play an important role in keeping the public fully invested. They handhold the public through downturns, and this is a vital function that has gone unrecognized to date. Handholding is more important for uneducated than educated clients, as the latter anyway take more risk; educated clients tend to vent more than they need to, though what they are really looking for is the comfortable caterwauling of shared misery. In their handholding function, the advisory *jaati* is helped along by the media, and during downturns, a lot of column space is filled by advisors writing articles that urge the public to stay invested. In recent years, regional media have also got into the act and much personal finance content is also published by them. Herding among advisors and distributors has never been studied in India, and this is despite their key role in keeping the flock together and in line.

The buzzword in all this is the self-regulating organization (SRO) and compared to the SEBI-led alternative, it is not a bad thing.[38] Turning

[37] Dhirendra Kumar, 'Be Your Own Financial Advisor,' *valueresearchonline*, 17 January 2020, https://www.valueresearchonline.com/stories/47221/be-your-own- financial-advisor/.

[38] US-based Financial Planning Standards Board Ltd. (FPSB), owner of a certified financial planner certification program works with the National Institute of Securities Markets, a SEBI sponsored certification body. Their Certified Financial Planner certification has now been accredited in India. The latest attempt at a self-regulating organization (SRO) model involved delegating regulatory responsibilities to stock exchange subsidiaries. See Neil Borate and Jayshree P Upadhyay, 'SEBI Issues Norms for Stock Exchange Subsidiary to Regulate Investment Advisors,' *Mint*, 7 August 2020.

themselves into a self-regulating organization, or at least an industry lobbying group, might help the advisors and distributors. Often, they sounded like foot soldiers in the foxholes of a combat zone – capable of seeing their small portion of a fire-swept battlefield, but incapable of seeing themselves as part of something larger – and without the leadership that could make them think in terms of a larger battle plan. Their public comments reflected this and contributed to the deafening noise levels the media generated on the issue. But turning themselves into a self-regulating organization would still run into the usual issues such frameworks face in India. Most want the freedom and absence from heavy handed regulation that the self-regulating organization framework provides, but lack the discipline and wisdom to make the trade-offs the self-regulating organization framework demands.

With its digital ecosystem in an otherwise underdeveloped economy, India is uniquely positioned for what some see as the future of the advisory business – robo-advising.[39] Like someone with a hammer who went looking for nail-like problems, India's digital evangelists went around with their apps looking for programmable solutions. The rationale is clear on the surface. Despite SEBI's best efforts – or perhaps because of them – there are fewer than 1,500 registered investment advisors in a country with over 250 million households; this 250 million includes a vast number of poor and marginal entities with little investible surplus, but even a figure one-twentieth of that number indicates a substantial gap between demand for advisory services and available advisory resources. Conceivably, this gap can be filled through automation or robo-advising, and here the relevant phrases are fintech, artificial intelligence, machine learning, and some such.

Prima facie, treating the basic questionnaire used by the advisory firm as input to an algorithm allows for a computer to spew out standardized and programmatic financial advice without any human interface. Robo-advising is useful for low net-worth clients with common sense

[39] Himadri Buch, 'AI disruption: Is Robo-advisory a Threat to Financial Planners?,' *moneycontrol*, 3 August 2018.

advisory needs and these comprise the majority of salaried middle-class clientele in India. As most financial advisory work in India simply ends up recommending the best performing mutual funds as part of a basic asset allocation exercise, this sort of advice is very digitizable. Besides, direct plans where clients bypass distribution agents and buy mutual funds directly on a stock exchange are now a reality, and it is possible to conceive of a no-frills service where robo-advising leads to a client buying direct plans, thus reducing costs. Individual stock picking would be impossible with robo-advising but most advisors lean away from it anyway.

Nevertheless, robo-advising runs contrary to the traditional Indian regard for the personal touch, trust, handholding, or such like, and many of the country's contradictions are bound to surface when dealing with the issue; the CFA study mentioned earlier found that as many as 92 per cent said they preferred the 'latest technology platforms and tools' to a human when it came to advising and executing on their own investment strategies, and yet the same study found that 82 per cent of respondents said they preferred human to robo-advice.[40] Perhaps older cultural values relating to trust are clashing with a younger generation's tech savvy, and a 'high tech, high touch' synthesis is still elusive.

For the self-reliant investor, it may be possible to go one up on robo-advising. A 'do it yourself' program is a 50:50 allocation to equity and debt with the equity component made up of one or two diversified all equity mutual funds. The growth (rather than the dividend) option is selected to allow for the maximum effect of long-term compounding, and the mutual fund units are bought on an exchange through a direct plan, which minimizes costs. When the equity component rises substantially during a bull run, occasional rebalancing is done by selling some units and buying debt with the proceeds, which brings the folio down to its original allocation. The rebalancing can be done in stages, as and when the market multiple crosses (say) 27 times earnings, or some such figure the investor is comfortable with. Multiples below (say) 15,

[40] CFA Institute, *Fourth Investor Trust Survey*.

lead to rebalancing by sale of debt components and purchase of more equity units.

This sort of program allows the investor to capture the upward swing of the market over many years, while keeping costs to a minimum; the periodic rebalancing takes money off the table, and if done with some common sense, should perform as well as much of the fancy (and costly) advice out there. The catch is that nowadays most equity funds give themselves the flexibility of going to cash (or debt) in large proportions, often of up to 30 per cent. This runs the risk of the fundie and the investor both rebalancing in different ways at different times, which messes with the self-reliant investor's asset allocation. The solution is to look for a fund that does not give itself this flexibility, and therefore a fund that is fully invested all the time. Alternately, with the flexible funds there should be no need for the investor to rebalance at all, as that task (with its associated risks) is left to the fundie.

A client's laundry list of advisor qualities would include – passion, knowledge, experience, style practised, lock ins, track record, presence in other asset classes, and critically, the advisor's third-party compensation from other participants that sets up conflicts of interest. In practice, in a relationship-oriented country, all this gets subsumed into that typically Indian phrase, i.e., 'comfort levels'. The advisor's laundry list of client qualities would include – return expectations, risk profile, emotional stability, capital needs, income levels, tax clientelism, lock ins, and critically, the client's need for 'action', that itch which can only be relieved through poorly understood speculation. In practice, most advisors are grateful to have a savvy client who invests in equities.

When listening to the sales pitch, it is common sense for a client to watch out for the following terms: no downside, huge upside, technicals, no brainer, commodities, 'our proprietary computer model', *khabar*, 'you'll be sorry if you don't', options strategies, derivatives, sure thing, or 'this will move'.[41] In the digital age, 'our proprietary computer model'

[41] A larger list of such terms is in Benjamin Graham, *The Intelligent Investor,* New York: HarperCollins, Revised Edition, 2006, 275. Chapter 10 offers Graham's take on the investor and his advisors.

sounds a little old fashioned. So, consider the latest version of the above jargon, as directed at a new generation of traders called 'Millennials' and taken word for word from an *Economic Times* article, circa July 2020:

> … customised semi-automated trading strategies, robot-based advisory and stock picks, customised basket portfolios managed by professionals at a much lower cost than portfolio management services (PMS), spread-based option strategies to trade on any platform and automated rule-based trading engines for high-frequency players.[42]

Really.

[42] Rajesh Mascarenhas, 'Regulatory Reality May Shatter Millennials' Stock Dreams,' *Economic Times*, 27 July 2020.

24

WHY WE'RE ALL MESSED UP IN OUR HEADS

Behavioural Finance

You can feel it in the first stage of a bull move, and you felt it especially well coming off the bottom in that great V-shaped pull back of 2009. It came at you in those little rooms in the rabbit warren of the Bombay Stock Exchange, and its smell was almost palpable. The shouts of '*Maal lao, Maal lao*' (bring on the goods) as stocks soared. The rising apprehension and disbelief as stocks doubled in a few weeks, followed by that perfectly rational feeling that it was all happening too fast for it to end well. One part of the mind screaming, 'Buy, Buy, Buy', and the other part – because of that rational feeling – saying, 'Wait for a pullback to enter.' You saw the trapped look in the eyes of shorts in the derivatives segment, who thought the move was a bear market rally. You heard the bulls frantically calling bank 'loans against shares' departments for more leverage and capital. You saw and felt it like a rush, and behind it all, the feelings. At first, it was not greed like the books said, just the overwhelming feeling – the regret – that you would be left out of the move. If stocks fell, you knew they often came back, but if they rose you never knew how far they would rise from those low prices. That combined with the psychological impossibility – the fear – of buying stocks that had doubled in weeks, just after they had halved in the weeks before they started doubling. Fear was supposed to happen when stocks fell, but this was fear when stocks rose, the fear of being the last buyer in a rally that most people thought was only punctuating a catastrophic and ongoing bear. It was a terrible, insane kind of fear, far worse than the fear of falling prices. It was the fear that the courage to buy was not there. And against that, as prices roared higher – the greed – that mad feeling, that irresistible, visceral, feral, desire to buy with everyone else and buy at any price.

Welcome to the start of your first bull market.

Notice there is no talk here of market efficiency or asset pricing models; no math or big equations or fancy talk on interest rates. There's not even talk of valuations or PE ratios. The stock market is also about people – sweating, heaving, feeling human beings – and with all the talk about valuations and interest rates, participants sometimes forget that. Behavioural finance reminds us that we should not forget. It reminds us that there's a human being behind the 'Buy' button.

As a field of study, behavioural finance began as a reaction to the efficient market hypothesis (EMH) and the asset pricing models that were subsequently developed.[1] By the 80s and to some people at least, the EMH and asset pricing models such as the CAPM had become theology bordering on dogma, and the people who articulated it had become a priesthood. Some of the field's early developments also came in reaction to the Wall Street crash of 1987. The textbooks said that 40 to 50 per cent sell-offs in stocks over a day or two could not happen. Yet happen they did – and crucially, without significant information releases that could have acted as a trigger.

At issue here is the efficiency school's view on human rationality, above all its belief that individuals are perfectly rational utility maximizers. Alternately – and the issues can get technical – is rationality less than perfect, i.e., is it bounded, either by the complexity of the decision or

[1] Robert J. Shiller, 'From Efficient Markets Theory to Behavioral Finance,' *Journal of Economic Perspectives*, Vol. 17, No. 1, Winter 2003, 83–104.

by cognitive limitation? If that's a stretch, do people at least subjectively maximize their expected utilities and accurately update their belief structures consistent with newly arriving information?

Behavioural finance owes its origins to the pioneering ideas of Israeli psychologists Daniel Kahneman and Amos Tversky who, together with Richard Thaler and Robert Shiller, are generally acknowledged as the field's founders. Kahneman and Tversky were the forces behind the development of prospect theory and its extensions into behavioural economics.[2] The marriage of psychology and finance, behavioural finance claims to be a richer way of describing stock market reality. Behind the 'Buy' button is a human being, and humans make mistakes. Behavioural finance deals with those mistakes – called bias – in a formal fashion. In its present state, it is yet to develop into a general equilibrium model of asset pricing such as the CAPM, though theoretical advances are moving the field in that direction; rather, it is presently a series of powerful observations about human behaviour in financial markets. As behavioural finance's default mode is examining market efficiency in the breach, it should be a prolific line of inquiry in an emerging market like India, where deviations from efficiency can be pronounced.

Much of finance is suspended in reaction between the efficiency school and the behavioural school, and whether the field moves in one direction or the other is yet to be decided. The Royal Swedish Academy of Sciences also couldn't make up its mind, and in an unusual move, decided to recognize the leading lights from both schools – Eugene Fama and Robert Shiller – for the 2013 Nobel Memorial Prize in Economic Sciences, one of the few occasions in Nobel history when pro and contra on the same idea were honoured in the same year.

Judgement heuristics are mental shortcuts and informal rules of thumb that people use to process information quickly and make choices under

[2] Much of the psychology of behavioural economics is detailed in Daniel Kahneman's classic treatment, *Thinking, Fast and Slow*, London: Penguin, Allen Lane, 2011. System 1 and System 2 are the metaphors used in this dual-process framework on the interplay between intuition and reason. System 1 thinking relies on heuristics and is fast and intuitive, but prone to bias and error even in day-to-day decision making; System 2 thinking is more deliberate, logical, and used for thinking through problems in an orderly series of steps.

conditions of uncertainty. These informal rules are fast and intuitive, but though they often work, they can sometimes produce errors in reasoning called bias. One example of a rule of thumb that produces peculiar results in Indian investment advisory work is '*100 minus your age is the percentage of your folio that should be allocated to equities.*' One is never surprised by the frequency with which this chestnut pops up in advisory work.[3] Financial advisors who work for banks seem especially partial to the rule. Yet, this heuristic, based as it is on a lifecycle model of investing, would reduce the asset allocation to equities as one got older. At the same time, it makes no allowance for risk profile, income levels, tax clienteles, or wealth effects. For example, it discounts the fact that many Indians live with their children in old age, which means that intergenerational transfers of wealth and risk preference have different repercussions in India; because of the inherent safety net in such social arrangements, risk profiles and income levels have to be judged differently here.

And yet, the alternate to this heuristic would be a judgment on a complex attribute: how much should equities contribute to an individual's financial goals. Far better, therefore, to substitute a simpler attribute that relates equity allocation to a readily available measure like a person's age. This sort of attribute substitution is a major factor behind the reliance on heuristics.[4]

Two themes (or building blocks) run through the extensive literature of behavioural finance that has built up over the past few years – the *limits to arbitrage* and *psychology*.[5] *Limits to arbitrage* arguments, building

[3] For a recent article outlining various heuristics and thumb rules that are used by Indian financial planners, see Sunil Dhawan, 'Financial Planning Thumb Rules,' *Economic Times*, 12 October 2018.

[4] Daniel Kahneman and Shane Frederick, 'A Model of Heuristic Judgment,' *The Cambridge Handbook of Thinking and Reasoning*, eds. Keith J Holyoak and Robert G Morrison, New York: Cambridge University Press, 2005, 267–94.

[5] The classification is from Nicholas Barberis and Richard Thaler, 'A Survey of Behavioral Finance,' *Handbook of the Economics of Finance*, eds. George Constantinides, Milton Harris, and René Stulz, Vol.1, Part 2, Oxford and Amsterdam: Elsevier, North-Holland, 2003, 1053–1128.

on the insights of economists Andrei Shleifer and Robert Vishny, tend to emphasize the difficulties and limitations that rational traders face in their attempts to undo the dislocations caused by irrational traders. *Psychology*, building directly on the work of psychologists Kahneman and Tversky, catalogues the mistakes made in equity markets that may result in deviations from rational asset pricing.

Arbitrage

Arbitrage – together with its result 'The Law of One Price' – is a fundamental law of finance and almost a self-evident truth. Arbitrage works with the idea that the same piece of paper, representing the same contractual claim on a firm's cash flows cannot trade very differently in price from one market to another. If it did, rational traders acting in costless and risk-free fashion, would just buy the paper in the underpriced market and simultaneously sell – or short sell it – in the overpriced market. This mispricing would briefly result in abnormal risk-free profits, but buying the paper in the underpriced market would drive up prices, and selling it in the overpriced market would drive down prices, resulting in the same price – The Law of One Price – across markets. The mispricing – in the classical Friedman view of an efficient market – has been arbitraged away by rational traders, often at the cost of irrational (or noise) traders.[6]

For many years, entire rooms in the BSE were filled with nimble-fingered traders who bought, say, Reliance stock on the NSE if it was a little cheaper there, and simultaneously sold it on the BSE, where the quote was a little higher.[7] Standing outside the rooms, one could heard the continuous clatter of 20 or more keyboards manually carrying out this simple arbitrage; the practice continued till recently, and now

[6] Milton Friedman, 'The Case for Flexible Exchange Rates,' *Essays in Positive Economics*, Chicago: University of Chicago Press, 1953, 157–203.

[7] For an early treatment of arbitrage based on different settlement cycles between the NSE and BSE, see Ashok Jogani and Kshama Fernandes, 'Arbitrage in India: Past, Present and Future,' *Derivatives Markets in India*, ed. Susan Thomas, New Delhi: Tata McGraw-Hill, 2003.

computers do the same thing at a fraction of the cost.[8] In an earlier generation, price differentials as high as 10 per cent between Bombay and the regional exchanges were among the notable inefficiencies of the Municipal Era, which allowed similar arbitrages to take place.[9]

The above are examples of inter-exchange arbitrage, i.e., across exchanges within the same time span, but arbitrage can also be (and usually is) inter-temporal, i.e., across time but within the same market or exchange. In the most obvious example, value buyers may buy stocks they believe are too cheap and short sell overpriced stocks, thereby returning the market to some sort of equilibrium. More complex forms of arbitrage involve betting on merger risk or convertibles.

Much finance theory and practice devotes itself to constructing arbitrage portfolios that – going by technical definitions at least – are risk free, costless, zero investment, and profitable. But profitable arbitrage is an oxymoron, as it is a perpetual and perfect money machine that can endlessly generate risk free profits. This is not possible over prolonged periods, so the above mechanisms come into play, end (or arbitrage away) the opportunity, and drive markets into equilibrium. Left with arbitrageurs are normal profits consistent with their cost of capital, which also implies that being competitive on the cost of capital is necessary for successful arbitrageurs to stay in business. Because of its pervasiveness, the 'law of one price' is a useful property to build on, and much asset pricing literature also uses arbitrage-based arguments to model financial markets in equilibrium.[10]

In a seminal paper, Andrei Shleifer of Harvard and Robert Vishny of Chicago showed the limits to this classical view of a financial market.[11] In an inefficient market driven by rational and irrational traders,

[8] Inter-exchange arbitrage is now largely driven by simple algorithms. See Deepak Shenoy, 'Algos Are Changing India's Stock Markets,' *Mint*, 13 January 2020.

[9] M. Narasimhan, *Financial Sector Reform and the Capital Markets*, Fourth Phiroze Jeejeebhoy Memorial Lecture, Bombay: The Stock Exchange, Bombay, 1992, 23.

[10] Besides asset pricing models, an array of other financial propositions – including put call parity relationships, the spot-futures parity theorems, and binomial option pricing models – use arbitrage-based arguments.

[11] Andrei Shleifer and Robert W. Vishny, 'The Limits of Arbitrage,' *Journal of Finance,* 52, No. 1, March 1997, 35–54.

irrationality can have a substantial and long-lived impact on prices. Rational traders, despite the classical model's predictions, can find it difficult to arbitrage away mispricing and, as a result, deviations of current price from fundamental value can persist for long periods. Further, prices below fundamentals may lead to further deviation to the downside and prices above fundamentals may lead to further deviation to the upside.

Consider by way of example, a hedge fund manager who was convinced that Unitech's epic 2,30,000 per cent run to the upside by early 2008 had led to the stock being massively overvalued. If he could short sell the stock, he would have been right in subsequent years – and spectacularly so – as the stock went to nothing. Further, the short selling would itself have driven down Unitech's price and aided the adjustment to its fair value. Yet the manager would be constrained and unable to do anything about it. As seen earlier, Indian markets impose so many limits on short selling in the cash market that any attempt to arbitrage away Unitech's mispricing would not have been feasible. Short constraints since the badla system was abolished and the absence of a credible automated lending and borrowing (ALBM) mechanism, make short selling in the cash market next to impossible in India, leading to considerable deviations from fundamental value to the upside. Crucially, because of the short constraints, Unitech's example generalizes to the aggregate stock market resulting in deviations from fair value.

Further, in India, the fund management business does not have many professional arbitrageurs or 'arbs' as the jargon goes. But even if present, arbitrageurs face agency risk, and in this they are no different from other intermediaries; they handle money for others, who may not be willing to wait for the long periods required for price to go back to fair value, i.e., for the arbitrage to work out. Besides, even if the short side was allowed, the arbitrageur doing it might be concerned that noise traders in the stock would keep taking it higher, forcing liquidation at higher prices, and this fear makes the arbitrageur reject the trade in the first place. To the downside, when prices get driven too low, buying is often done with collateral or borrowing; people lending collateral might ask for more collateral just before the trade starts getting profitable, which also limits the capacity of arbitrageurs to arbitrage away irrational pricing. So, time horizons can be forced and limited, which places temporal restrictions on the capacity to arbitrage away mispricing. All this places limits on the arb's capacity to arbitrage away irrationality, and so, in the real world, arbitrage is neither risk-free nor costless, which restricts its use as an activity that can bring markets into efficient equilibrium. Hence, if arbitrage is limited and noise traders have biases, prices can deviate from fundamental value for substantial lengths of time.

Psychological Errors

Psychological errors – heuristics and bias – in financial decision-making are a focus area of behavioural finance and cataloguing them is something of a growth industry in academia.[12] Recently, a Wikipedia page titled 'List of Cognitive Biases' catalogued over 190 items.[13] Some of the noted biases investigated by Kahneman, Tversky, and others include representativeness, adjustment/anchoring, overconfidence, and loss aversion.

Representativeness

Consider the following statement, itself a version of the famous Linda Problem from Kahneman and Tversky:[14] 'Asha in Mumbai, is quiet, studious, bookish and very concerned about environmental and social issues.' Based on this, rank the probability that:

☐ One: Asha is a librarian.
☐ Two: Asha is a librarian, and a member of the Bombay Environmental Action Group (BEAG).
☐ Three: Asha works in the banking industry.

[12] The early papers on heuristics and prospect theory are Daniel Kahneman and Amos Tversky, 'Judgment under Uncertainty: Heuristics and Biases,' *Science*, New Series, Vol. 185, No. 4157, September 1974, 1124–31 and 'Choices, Values, and Frames,' *American Psychologist*, 39(4), 1984, 341–50.

[13] 'List of Cognitive Biases,' *Wikipedia*, https://en.wikipedia.org/wiki/List_of_cognitive_biases.

[14] Daniel Kahneman and Amos Tversky, 'Extensional versus Intuitive Reasoning: The Conjunction Fallacy in Probability Judgment,' *Psychological Review*, 90(4), 1983, 293–315.

Most people would choose **Two** because it just seems right. After all, librarians do work in surroundings that are 'quiet' and 'studious', and they deal in books, so it all sounds very right and very *representative* of 'bookish' Asha. And member of the BEAG? That's a dead giveaway and also very representative of Asha's interest in environmental and social issues. Actually, Two is simply a subset of **One**, so by definition, One has a higher probability ranking than Two and is the better choice. But notice also that there are just a lot more bankers than librarians in any city; there's just a higher base rate, incidentally more so in Mumbai which is the centre of the financial services industry. The base rate priors or prior probabilities are simply larger, though neglected. Therefore, the correct answer is **Three**: despite being quiet, studious, bookish, and very concerned about environmental and social issues, the odds – and the base rate – favour Asha as a banker.

This example also illustrates the conjunction effect: the conjunctive statement, 'Asha is a librarian *and* a member of the BEAG' receives a higher probability than it deserves. But what is really going on here is judgment based on stereotypes, or similarity. Decision makers use similarity – or representativeness – as a substitute for probabilistic thinking. In fact, India's complexity and social biases further encourage the construction of little mental boxes to put people into, and doing so simply makes the messiness of daily reality a little easier to deal with. So, the Tam Bram is clever but narrow minded, the Bong is cultured but emotional, and the Parsi is straightforward but eccentric and so on; that you can have straightforward Tam Brams, clever Bongs, and cultured Parsis takes a little longer to sink in. Similarity (or stereotyping, often based on gut familiarity) cannot be a substitute for probability, and results in bias when used to judge how representative membership of Element A is in Class B.[15]

Stereotypes may not even be necessary to encounter this bias, as evident from the following statement: 'Microsoft is a good company, so

[15] The insight that stereotypes about PSUs may bias values to the downside (and allow a stock picker to find value) is found in Parag Parikh, *Value Investing and Behavioral Finance*, New Delhi: Tata McGraw-Hill, 2009, 142–43.

Microsoft belongs to the class of good stocks.' Actually, a good company does not have to be a good stock at all; it also depends on the price. Microsoft was a good company in 1999, but its price was discounting the happily ever after. After the stock sold off, Microsoft, one of the world's great franchises, took till 2015 – or the better part of a generation – to come back to its 1999 level.

Adjustment and Anchoring

Adjustment bias happens when people insufficiently adjust from starting values to predicted values, and this happens mainly because the starting point acts as an anchor to the estimate.

In answering the question: 'Is the Ganga more or less than 1,500 km long?', answers that subsequently estimate its length will cluster around the 1,500 km anchor laid down in the question, though the correct answer is a little over 2,500 km. In answers to this experimental question from a 2013 study: 'How many states in India have a population greater than 25 million?' the correct answer at that time was 14, but respondents anchored heavily around the starting points offered; with 3 states offered as an anchor, respondents' mean estimate was 5 states, but with 25 states offered as an anchor the mean estimate of respondents rose to 18 states.[16] Likewise, in response to the question: 'How many years was the Indian soap opera *Kyunki Saas Bhi Kabhi Bahu Thi* on television?' the correct answer at survey time was 9 years, but mean responses with anchors of 2 and 16 came in at 7.5 years and 12.2 years respectively.[17]

So, subjects make predictions without adjusting sufficiently from starting values, and those predictions tend to cluster around the value anchors laid down in the question. The starting point thus acts as a

[16] Andrew R. Smith, Paul D. Windschitl, and Kathryn Bruchmann, 'Knowledge Matters: Anchoring Effects Are Moderated by Knowledge Level,' *European Journal of Social Psychology*, 43, 2013, 97–108. The study was conducted among US and Indian subjects who answered anchored target questions on both US and Indian topics. The results documented that increased knowledge lowered anchoring effects, with Indian subjects exhibiting larger anchoring bias for US domain knowledge questions than Indian domain knowledge questions.

[17] Ibid.

heavy anchor, even when it is bizarrely generated – in Kahneman and Tversky's famous example, subjects asked to estimate the number of African countries who were United Nations members anchored around numbers generated by spinning a rigged wheel of fortune. The bias is heightened when people have to make snap decisions, or if they don't have much time to think about the problem – and this is a common situation among equity analysts updating their valuation models following breaking news.

The above examples revolve around insufficient adjustment from a starting value but another explanation involves suggestion and priming; subjects take the information in the question as a hint or suggestion towards the answer, and that hint activates associative memories and compatible thoughts that primes subjects into believing.[18] As a result, asking someone the average price of, say, German cars will evoke a higher answer when subjects are primed with names like BMW or Mercedes and a lower answer when primed with mass-market brands such as Volkswagen.[19]

Anchoring has been a crucial bias in India. Analysts usually anchor their targets to the current price and their reports are elaborate, fact-filled justifications for that extant market price. Timidity in forecasting has been pervasive, usually through short-term forecasts of earnings and prices over horizons of three months to a year, which effectively reinforces 'speculative investment' as the dominant approach to the market. Few stick their necks out and make the long-range forecasts essential for long-term investing.

Since the end purpose of all equity research is a target value V, equity research during bull markets simply involves repeated upward reassessments of V over short time periods. So, it has been possible for a stock that went up 25 times over a few years, to have reports about it brought out every 3 months during the up move that, in effect, rationalized the prevailing price P by setting a target value V that was 5

[18] Daniel Kahneman, *Thinking, Fast and Slow*, 122–23.

[19] Ibid.

to 10 per cent above that prevailing price. Noise alone – and the Indian market is overwhelmed with noise – guarantees that the target value V is repeatedly met, and this allows the analyst to tom-tom the accuracy of the forecast. But for the customer at least, acting on such research might involve selling the stock early on one of the many occasions when the price target was repeatedly met. In later years, studies have described this phenomenon of selling winners early as the disposition effect, but it is also naïve clients acting on equity research that is heavily influenced by anchoring.

Related to this is the tendency of analysts to react conservatively to new information and not adjust estimates enough. Unanticipated positive news flow is factored into estimates and results in an upward revision of targets but only by so much, and the current price serves as a terrible and heavy mental anchor to a timid analyst. Consequently, in a bull market, upward revisions tend to be excessively conservative, and as a result, positive news surprises are likely to be followed by further positive news surprises. The reverse happens to the downside in a bear market. As a result, prices repeatedly overshoot on both sides of analyst estimates. Rare is the report that makes a long-term prediction over a cycle, and rarer still is the report that predicts one of those steep and precipitous declines that routinely wipe out most of a mid-cap's equity. Analysts, such as Isaiah Berlin's hedgehogs, usually have excellent company and industry knowledge, but judging whether all of that is 'in the price' and arriving at a price prediction happens with the usual variability in results.

Similar concerns arise when adjusting asset allocation beyond the 1/N heuristic. As seen earlier, the absence of formal portfolio optimization implies that Talmudic (or naïve) diversification using variations of the 1/N heuristic is pervasive in India. Given a menu of N choices, allocations will anchor around the 1/N level and adjusting beyond that is an issue. So, setting a menu of, say, large-cap stocks, small-cap stocks, tech stocks, and banking stocks can lead, more often than not, to a 25 per cent allocation to each and adjusting beyond that is due to guesswork rather than formal optimization.

Overconfidence

In a survey of drivers asked to rate their own ability, 80 to 90 per cent rated themselves above the median.[20] This is a mathematical impossibility in a normally distributed population and an unbiased sample should yield answers closer to 50 per cent. Investors suffer from the same problem of overconfidence, and it is widespread when trading and investing in stocks. Overconfidence in personally gathered information is especially common, as is overconfidence after periods of good past performance. Overconfidence is worse for men than for women,[21] and so, the problem assumes added significance in India, a country where most household financial decisions are still made by men. People simply do not ask themselves: 'What informational advantage do I have over other traders?' One consequence of overconfidence is bad bets and wrong trading decisions, but at least this can be handled by the stop-loss discipline. A second and more pernicious consequence is a tendency to trade more often than necessary. This leads to a rise in transaction costs, of which the direct components like brokerage and taxes are not as important as the invisible components such as impact costs and the bid-ask spread.

As a final example of overconfidence, consider the following problem posed by economists Roger Clarke and Meir Statman to survey participants: The Dow Jones Industrial Average (DJIA) index was created in May 1896 with a starting value of 40. In 1998, its value was 9,000. What would this value be with dividend reinvestment, i.e., assuming all dividends received on the Dow's 30 stocks were reinvested in the index itself?[22] (More technically, the answer required subjects to convert the Dow from a price index to a total return index, and then make a prediction.) Answers from subjects in experimental situations yielded figures far lower than the correct value, but this is not surprising.

[20] The original study (subsequently replicated) is Ola Svenson, 'Are We All Less Risky and More Skillful Than Our Fellow Drivers?,' *Acta Psychologica*, 47 (1981), 143–48.

[21] Brad M. Barber and Terrance Odean, 'Boys will be boys: Gender, overconfidence, and common stock investment,' *The Quarterly Journal of Economics*, 2001, 116(1), 261-292.

[22] Roger G. Clarke and Meir Statman, 'The DJIA Crossed 652,230,' *Journal of Portfolio Management*, Winter 2000, 26 (2), 89–92.

The correct answer for a 1998 Dow value with dividend reinvestment was a staggering 6,50,000 – a consequence of dividend reinvestment and the magic of compounding over a very long period, in this case over 100 years. The experiment is often cited as another example of predictive overconfidence, but note that even experienced subjects would have issues adjusting their answers away from the anchor of 9,000 offered in the question.

Loss Aversion

Consider the following mind problem. Anil does 2 trades, and the first results in a ₹1 lakh profit, while the second results in a ₹1 lakh loss. The ₹1 lakh profit obviously results in pleasure, while the ₹1 lakh loss results in pain. Because the change in Anil's wealth – in either direction – is exactly the same at ₹1 lakh, it follows that the magnitude of pleasure Anil gets from a ₹1 lakh profit should equal the magnitude of pain Anil gets from a ₹1 lakh loss but in the opposite direction. After all, the change in his financial position – his net worth – in either direction is exactly the same, and only the sign is different. Actually, it doesn't work out that way. It turns out that the pain Anil feels from a ₹1 lakh loss is greater than the pleasure he feels from a ₹1 lakh gain.

More technically, the value function is concave for gains, convex for losses, and is generally steeper for losses than for gains.[23] This central insight of Kahneman and Tversky's prospect theory can lead to pernicious consequences, foremost among which is loss aversion.[24] People – feeling losses more than gains, usually by as much as 2 to 1 – simply do not book their losses, and this can lead to dangerous situations in financial markets. Combine this loss aversion with the speculative nature of Indian equity markets and one comes across a common character – the involuntary investor. This is the trader who buys for a price turn, simply

[23] Daniel Kahneman and Amos Tversky, 'Prospect Theory: An Analysis of Decision under Risk,' *Econometrica*, 47, 2, March 1979, 263.

[24] Nicholas Barberis and Ming Huang, 'Mental Accounting, Loss Aversion and Individual Stock Returns,' *Journal of Finance* 56, 2001, 1247–92.

doesn't take his losses because of loss aversion, and stays 'invested' till he gets his money back. Sometimes that never happens.

The situation exacerbates because many retail investors in India deal with loss aversion by averaging on the way down, i.e., they buy more as the stock heads lower and reduce their average cost. Even a small pullback in the stock's price then brings the position to breakeven, which is followed by a profitable exit. This strategy – a catastrophic violation of the laws of speculation outlined earlier – is indicative of market-wide belief in short-term mean reversion (as opposed to international work that points to long-term mean reversion). It might work 8 times out of 10, but on the two occasions it does not, the stock heads to single digits, the commitment becomes exceptionally large, and the losses are often fatal. Finally, the short constraint and the absence of a bankruptcy regime (till recently at least), imply that stocks can linger for years as penny stocks before heading to zero, which tempts retail investors to average down for extended periods of time.

Some research is recognizing the behavioural issues traders and investors face in India's market, and that acknowledgement is long overdue. Due to the absence of formal optimization techniques, heuristics or thumb rules are used extensively in financial advisory work – in fact, that is just how work gets done – and studying the biases that result from extensive use of these heuristics should result in a fertile line of academic inquiry. Critically, it could improve the advisory product itself. The country also offers a laboratory for academic research in emerging markets. Unlike the US, India's microstructure is neatly symmetric: two exchanges, two depositories, two clearing houses, and so on; also, digital data is now available from the early 1990s, allowing for empirical research over a slightly larger time frame. So, applying behavioural finance's insights to the issues traders and investors commonly face should be a productive field of inquiry.

Consider an application of behavioural finance to the *diversification* levels of retail investors. Investors in India diversify less than they should, and much less than the prescriptive behaviour suggestive of rational investors in portfolio optimization models. As seen earlier, this tendency has been apparent from L.C. Gupta's first surveys of the 1990s and continues into the present day.[25] Inadequate attention to diversification has also been found in various international surveys, but the extent of the problem in India is still surprising. One survey found 70 per cent of Indian respondents agreeing with the statement: 'Buying a single company stock usually provides a safer return than a stock mutual fund.'[26] This is a higher response rate than the 50 per cent that could be expected from random guessing by a large group and many times larger than the close to 0 response rate that should have occurred if respondents had even the slightest idea about the benefits of diversification. As mentioned before, the problem of diversification gets exacerbated by severe domestic bias. The rupee, for many years convertible on the capital account only for foreigners and NRIs, now offers liberal investing options to domestic residents that make it – for all practical purposes – convertible for them too. Yet considerable home country bias exists, and even seeing it as bias appears eccentric; domestic bias gets replicated in studies of other markets, but here too, the extent of the problem in India is surprising.

One study found that inadequate diversification is also responsible for heterogeneous returns that increase the inequality of account size; the lack of diversification means that some concentrated folios do randomly well or randomly poorly, and this increases idiosyncratic

[25] The problem was first noticed by L.C. Gupta and his collaborators in their early surveys. See L.C. Gupta, *Indian Shareowners: A Survey*, New Delhi: Society for Capital Market Research and Development, 1991 and L.C. Gupta, Naveen Jain, and Yash Kulshreshtha, *Shareholders' Geographic Distribution, City-wise, Urban-rural, and State-wise*, New Delhi: Society for Capital Market Research and Development, 1994.

[26] Josh Beshears, James J. Choi, David Laibson, and Brigitte C. Madrian, 'Behavioral Household Finance,' *The Handbook of Behavioral Economics: Foundations and Applications Volume 1*, eds. B. Douglas Bernheim, Stefano Dellavigna, and David Laibson, Oxford and Amsterdam: Elsevier, North-Holland, 2018, 198.

wealth inequality among participants[27] (in turn, this allows participants who use the tactic to trumpet their randomly generated higher returns and much financial advertising flows from this random performance). Finally, another study found that larger accounts tend to be better diversified than smaller ones, lowering their idiosyncratic risk and allowing them to earn higher log returns, which in turn increased their account size (and wealth inequality over the smaller accounts) during the study period.[28]

In India, the diversification problem is compounded by *local hero* bias. Shareholder registers reveal that the majority of retail shareholders in a company tend to be located in the same state – or often the same city – where the company is headquartered.[29] This can be an issue if the company is a Satyam, for example. Chances are a big portion of Satyam's shareholder register would have been made up of Hyderabad shareholders rather than (say) Delhi shareholders. There is similar bias for excessive holdings in the company one works for, a bias that does not take into account the economics of the industry the company is embedded in. This phenomenon is also international; many Lehman and Enron employees were sophisticated enough to realize the importance of this bias, but they would still have had significant weightings of these companies in their folios, and both stocks went to 0.

More generally, in a relationship-oriented society like India, people feel a great affinity for familiar situations, as opposed to ambiguous situations where the gamble's probability distribution is difficult to evaluate. Much of this affinity is captured by cunning marketers under the rubric of 'trust', and it is a common theme of bewitching marketing campaigns to loudly proclaim how trustworthy the campaign's locally

[27] Large accounts tend to have higher average log returns not by earning higher average simple returns, but by lowering uncompensated idiosyncratic risk that lowers average log return for any given level of average simple return. The rich get richer, but it also depends on how the measuring is done. John Y. Campbell, Tarun Ramadorai, and Benjamin Ranish, 'Do the Rich Get Richer in the Stock Market? Evidence from India,' Working paper no. 24898, National Bureau of Economic Research, Cambridge, MA, August 2018.

[28] Ibid.

[29] L.C. Gupta, Naveen Jain, and Yash Kulshreshtha,, *Shareholders' Geographic Distribution*, 8.

connected products are. As a result, familiar 'our town' assets get over invested in, compared to ambiguous 'other town' assets, and this also results in insufficient diversification.

So don't buy certain Kolkata companies – whose accounting practices may differ from yours – just because you're from Kolkata. If you're a medical representative buying the pharma company where you're working, you should be okay because of the inherently sound economics of that industry, but what happens if you buy real estate companies just because you're a real estate agent? Similarly, if you are from a community that might have a communal disposition towards a certain stock market style – remember the old saw about the Gujjus being always long and the Maddus being always short – recognize the inherent bias that the style produces in you as a trader.

Paradoxically, at the other end of the spectrum you have the nervous Nellies, whose portfolios hold 10 to 12 funds across sizes, sectors, and styles. Because most mutual funds hold between 50 to 100 stocks, this leads to excessive diversification even after the common holdings are cancelled out. The trend has surfaced in recent years, driven in large part by agency issues within the advisory community; the default mode of many advisors is to recommend multiple funds to clients and then churn those recommendations for commissions.[30]

In line with international evidence, another documented bias is '*gambling with the house's money*'. Since the market (the house) has provided profits through a winning streak, getting aggressive and overconfident with those profits when on a roll is gambling with the house's money. Recent research indicates Indian traders increase both frequency and volume of trading when on a roll.[31] So strong is this

[30] Sunita Abraham and Mitra Joshi, '5 Common Investment Mistakes to Avoid,' *Mint*, 1 June 2015.

[31] Sankar De, Naveen R. Gondhi, and Bhimasankaram Pochiraju, 'Does Sign Matter More Than Size? An Investigation into the Source of Investor Overconfidence,' Working paper, Indian School of Business, Hyderabad, 2010, http://papers.ssrn.com/sol3/papers.cfm?abstract_id=1657926. The study covered 111 million transactions made by about 1.32 million investors in the NSEs Nifty index stocks between January and June 2006. Similar results are documented in John Y. Campbell, Tarun Ramadorai, and Benjamin Ranish, 'Getting Better or Feeling Better? How Equity Investors Respond to Investment Experience,' Working paper no. 20000, National Bureau of Economic Research, Cambridge, MA, March 2014.

tendency that it persists irrespective of the size of past profit outcomes – traders increase both trading frequency and trade size in the future irrespective of whether (say) ₹10,000 or ₹1,00,000 was made in past trades.[32] This aggression usually means that the proceeds of the winning streak are surrendered back to the house. Las Vegas casinos are known to gently steer winning gamblers back to the tables, but in the stock market, even that isn't necessary, as traders stay of their own volition and often give it all back. The above applies to past profits or past trades with positive signs. Negative signs or losses in past trades often lead to '*geteventitis*' which is the understandable desire to get even with the market and recover account equity; the increased risk taking often has the opposite effect. The money management rule of periodically skimming away profits, but without additions to account equity that make it whole again after losses, is designed to deal with these tendencies. If the profits are large enough, the rule reduces to taking out the original commitment, which leaves only the profits (the house's money) as capital for future trading.

Excessive trading due to predictive overconfidence is another common feature, both in world markets and India.[33] In a rational world, there would be negligible trading, because of the vigorish and the odds against a trader, and yet the observed volume of trading is massive. The vigorish – that combination of brokerage, taxes, impact costs, and bid ask spreads – eats away the returns of excessive trading, and as seen earlier, its real effects are often hidden. Also, dividend yields that practically never accrue to frequent traders are an opportunity cost of trading that nobody considers. Overconfidence in one's predictions is the main reason for excessive trading, and this is encouraged by a brokerage industry that persuades participants to use the magical thinking of technical analysis to make predictions. As a result, most participants feel they have the information to justify a trade when in fact they do not, and as a result,

[32] Ibid.; Sankar De, Naveen R. Gondhi, and Bhimasankaram Pochiraju, 'Does Sign Matter.'

[33] Terence Odean, 'Do Investors Trade too Much?,' *American Economic Review* 89, 1999, 1279–98; Brad Barber and Terence Odean, 'Trading Is Hazardous to Your Wealth: The Common Stock Performance of Individual Investors,' *Journal of Finance*, 55, 2000, 773–806.

uninformed traders lose out to informed ones. In India, business communities tend to be prone to overconfidence and excessive trading, but then again, these communities also lay claim to trading traditions and greater skill. Also, as seen, high past performance leads to bouts of overconfidence and excessive trading, which take away a big part of past gains.[34]

A related application is *herding behaviour*. Herding occurs when market participants ignore their own information or signals and rely on the observed behaviour of other participants, often even when they consider that behaviour to be wrong.[35] Certain fund managers might even see such behaviour as natural and protective of reputational capital; herding among fundies is also easy to implement as regular disclosures of fund portfolios are a compliance requirement. Herding can also be rational as with information cascades, or when investors herd by copying the decisions of better-informed investors; in India, entire websites carefully track the dervishes' holdings, and this allows retail investors to herd by mimicking the dervishes' decisions.

Some work indicates herding behaviour in Indian markets, but the research differs on its extent and offers few causal explanations for the phenomenon.[36] In particular, the empirical work on herding has not

[34] Overconfidence is more of a problem among individuals and less so for institutions. See Sankar De, Naveen R. Gondhi, and Subrata Sarkar, 'Behavioral Biases, Investor Performance, and Wealth Transfers between Investor Groups,' Working paper, Indian School of Business, Hyderabad, 2012. The study also found that for the average trader, overconfidence results in more wealth loss than disposition effects.

[35] An extensive literature examines herding in financial markets. Some studies focus on market wide herding behaviour while others study herding effects of particular groups, usually on the institutional side.

[36] Poshakwale and Mandal find herding across the market cycle and Lakshman et al. find mutual funds more prone to herding. See Sunil Poshakwale and Anandadeep Mandal, 'Investor Behaviour and Herding: Evidence from the National Stock Exchange in India,' *Journal of Emerging Market Finance*, 13, no. 2, August 2014, 197–216; Lakshman M.V., Sankarshan Basu, and R. Vaidyanathan, 'Market-wide Herding and the Impact of Institutional Investors in the Indian Capital Market,' Working paper 327, Indian Institute of Management, Bangalore, 2011. For evidence of some herding among FIIs, see Amita Batra, 'The Dynamics of Foreign Portfolio Inflows and Equity Returns in India,' Working paper no. 109, Indian Council for Research on International Economic Relations, New Delhi, September 2003. One study found herding more prevalent in China than India, with the Indian market exhibiting the phenomenon more during upswings than down moves. See Paulo Lao and Harminder Singh, 'Herding Behavior in the Chinese and Indian Stock Markets,' *Journal of Asian Economics*, 22 (6), 2010, 495–506.

(to date at least) identified technical and momentum traders as sources of herding in the market. Herding behaviour should be apparent in a market dominated by technical or momentum traders, and both types are prominent in India's markets; together, they produce positive feedback trades that emphasize buying recent winners and selling recent losers. Technical analysis is especially conducive to herding behaviour; besides the obvious tendency to pile onto a trend, the belief that 'it's all there on that line' is prominent among Indian chartists, which induces the trader to ignore other extant information and makes it easy to herd into a counter. Similarly, momentum is a fundamental-technical hybrid approach that lends itself to herding; selecting mid-caps based on some sort of fundamental analysis but waiting for them to show momentum on the chart before herding into the counter is a common strategy among fund managers. In fact, the speculative investment approach used by large sections of the market also encourages herding, as it involves keeping an eye on the crowd and guessing where the market herd will be next.

Studies of herding among institutions (only domestic or domestic/foreign as a group) are confounded by the offsetting positions they take against one another. Studying just the domestic buy side – mutual funds and LIC – for instance, is complicated by the inherently contrarian positions LIC takes in its investment policy. Examining the entire buy side – domestic and foreign together – also runs into the uncanny tendency of the domestic side to protect turf by buying when FIIs are selling and vice versa. Since these effects cancel out, studies of herding among institutional participants should produce confounding results. Consequently, results of studies on institutional herding are confounded, while studies of the broader market show herding because of the technical and momentum traders.

Another well documented bias is the *disposition effect* – the tendency to sell winners early and hold on to losers.[37] India provides fertile ground for studying disposition effects because high noise levels in the

[37] The effect was first proposed by Hersh Shefrin and Meir Statman in 'The Disposition to Sell Winners Too Early and Ride Losers Too Long: Theory and Evidence,' *Journal of Finance* 40, no. 3 (1985), 777–90.

trading environment go together with the uncertain quality of financial disclosure; both should increase trader tendency to sell early and take money off the table. The speculative character of Indian markets and the standard broker advice to 'book the profit' also leads retail investors to sell winners early. Further, as seen previously, the tendency of much research to anchor and make short-term predictions that are repeatedly met over a stock's long move also contributes to the disposition effect; the short-term price targets get repeatedly met, and on one of many such occasions, the retail investor gets drawn into selling out early. Loss aversion also contributes to the tendency to hold on to losers. In a volatile and trading-oriented market, loss aversion can quickly lead to erosion of previous gains; a 50 per cent down move is all it takes to give up a previous 100 per cent gain but many retail traders have difficulty grasping this basic insight behind price movements.

Because of the above, research finds that disposition effects are higher in India than in markets such as US, Japan, China, and Finland.[38] Some research also finds lower disposition effects from informed trading around earnings announcements – the higher the level of informed trading, the lower the disposition to sell at a small gain in the post-announcement period.[39] Finally, besides the common effects in secondary markets, disposition effects also occur in primary markets; research finds disposition effects in gains made from randomly allocated shares during the IPO process.[40]

[38] Shailesh Menon, 'Disposition Effect and Over-confidence Trigger Investor Losses in Stock Markets: Sankar De, ISB Professor,' *Economic Times*, 29 November 2012; Sankar De, Naveen R. Gondhi, and Subrata Sarkar, 'Behavioral Biases, Investor Performance.' The study period – between January 2005 and June 2006 – was in the middle of the Rate Bull that ended in early 2008. Strongly trending markets with large numbers of speculators will intensify the disposition effect of selling winners early; trading range markets should lower that effect, but this hypothesis is yet to be tested.

[39] De and Mukherjee find lower levels of the disposition effect with higher levels of informed trading in post announcement periods. Saptarshi Mukherjee and Sankar De, 'Are Investors Ever Rational?,' Working paper, Indian School of Business, Hyderabad, 2012, http://papers. ssrn.com/sol3/papers.cfm?abstract id =2156047.

[40] Santosh Anagol, Vimal Balasubramaniam, and Tarun Ramadorai, 'Endowment Effects in the Field: Evidence from India's IPO Lotteries,' *Review of Economic Studies* 85, no. 4 October 2018, 1971–2004. Related effects include portfolio tilts in favour of the winning IPO's sector and higher trading frequency.

Intriguing also is recent work which finds that *traders learn* from past experience. Because of the demographic dividend and the continuous churn of traders entering and leaving, Indian markets are fertile ground for studies on how traders learn in financial markets. Recent research finds that some biases such as the disposition effect and excessive trading due to overconfidence are capable of being reduced through learning and experience;[41] positive feedback effects also lead to reinforcement learning. The market tends to reward experience, so longer running accounts tend to have better returns than novice accounts.[42] But diversification continues to remain an issue and under diversification is not remedied through learning and hard experience.[43] Similarly, despite learning well, many traders run into other behavioural phenomena like gambling with the house's money to their own detriment. Moreover, both value and momentum continue to be favoured strategies among novice and experienced investors,[44] indicating the dominance of speculative investment as an approach to the market. So, the road to trading proficiency is long and slippery. Learning curve effects work in tandem with account draw downs, and hopefully the former happens faster than the latter.

The dervishes of Dalal Street have an intuitive knowledge of the implications of behavioural finance, but it usually stops at that, except in the more intellectually inclined among them. Massive success has deadened the desire for any further knowledge, and some even believed there was a royal road to learning; it was not uncommon for the dervishes to ask a person more learned to summarize a book and regurgitate its contents to them. Besides, the stop-loss discipline in their trading positions takes care of most of the biases that concern behavioural finance, so why go through the trouble of learning about them. The dervishes have their hand on the market's pulse just like a doctor would take a patient's pulse. They try to banish emotions from their

[41] John Y. Campbell, Tarun Ramadorai, and Benjamin Ranish, 'Getting Better or Feeling Better?'

[42] Ibid.

[43] Ibid.

[44] Ibid.

decision making and prefer to operate without anxiety. The dervishes are especially good at handling regret, always a more powerful emotion in India than fear or greed. In India, fear is moderated by fatalism and greed is moderated by Gandhiism but regret has no natural moderator. If the stock goes up, the average retail investor lives in regret because he wishes he had bought more. If the stock goes down, there is the obvious regret of loss, together with the more subtle regret of having stupidity proven – but at least the latter can be overcome by the conviction to stay invested all the way down to single digit prices.

To see the average retail investor's emotional involvement with a stock, one only has to peruse message boards like *moneycontrol*, where the market crowd gathers. Scrutinizing these boards would show that for most of the crowd, any semblance of rationality disappears once a position is opened. It is this cauldron of emotions that the dervishes avoid. To most of the dervishes, in the markets there can be no emotion – no greed or regret or fear or hope. The dervishes are also good at handling hope, especially as it applies to their trading positions. Some types of hope are good: a cancer patient must hope for a cure and a young executive must hope to become chairman. But for many of the dervishes, while trading there must be no hope. You can start a day in hope but ending it in hope leaves you hungry.

More generally, all this is especially important in trading but less so in investment, where time and the dividend cushion come to the rescue. Behavioural insights are also important to participants in India's vast derivatives segment, where the leverage – and the exaggerated pay-offs – magnify the emotional strain in a way that trading in the cash market does not. Nevertheless, making an investment approach from all this is not attempted in India, though in the West some hedge funds use it as an input while formulating strategy. Behavioural finance's precepts and their use to an individual are of a negative kind: don't anchor, don't trade excessively, don't ride losses, and so on (also, don't buy the market the day after India loses a cricket match; one study found that daily returns after India loses a match played on home pitches are eight times lower than returns that accrue when the country wins).[45] There is little on the nitty gritty of company appraisal and valuation, activities that dominate day-to-day work in a market of stock pickers. Behavioural finance's focus is more on telling us what not to do, rather than what to do; even when applied, its tenets only complement the traditional approach. By contrast, Graham and Dodd tell us what to do and this is a big difference.

[45] See Vinod Mishra and Russell Smyth, 'An Examination of the Impact of India's Performance in One-day Cricket Internationals on the Indian Stock Market,' *Pacific-Basin Finance Journal*, 18, 2010, 319–34. This study is part of a sub-field that finds causality between the performance of national teams (in widely followed sports) and the stock market.

CONCLUSION

Catching Lakshmi

Bringing a historical account to its end in the present implies not an end as much as reaching a present moment. And yet, concluding in the 2020s is satisfying in itself, as this period represents the bicentennial decade of the Indian stock market. But to date, no account outlines those two centuries of market activity and the change of the 1990s is responsible for this. That sudden disjointed break from the past has hidden many things and the recentness combines with the culture's ahistoricity to obscure market activity before our time. But behind today's computers and razzmatazz, ancient attitudes remain in the world's oldest emerging market. The past appears as a blur – unexamined and unthought of by the majority – and yet in spite of that, or perhaps because of that, many of the past's attitudes carry forward into the present. In India, it is not the past that intrudes on the present but the present that creeps up on a hazily understood past, just as the suburbs of an expanding city of Hyderabad now lap away at Golconda's ramparts.

But in the market, it was not the present creeping up on the past as much as the present peeping into the future through a price forecast that really counted. And yet here too, the past mattered. Successful investing was a kind of futurology where only after a successful judgement on the past's incorporation in present price was a peep into the future possible. Notice in the previous sentence the degree of mental effort required to go back and forth in linear time, and contrast that with a mythological view where time itself is seen as irrelevant to the point of easy timelessness.

Habits of the heart and mind that allowed the 1990 reforms to take hold so quickly were built up by over a century of market activity, but to the whiz kids of that era, that past was of little consequence, and in fact, most of their work simply assumes it did not exist. The whiz kids may be forgiven their insouciance because of their closeness to those events, but this attitude was pervasive in India and symptomatic of a people affected – more than anything else – by their inability to distinguish myth from history. That a god king was helped in his wife's rescue by an army of talking monkeys led by a head monkey who flew is very clearly myth and not history, as monkeys don't talk or fly. Yet to many, the Ramayana's events were possible as history rather than as myth. On record are ministers stating that a causeway of natural rock formations between India and Lanka was actually a bridge built by those talking monkeys, followed by the claim that the bridge stood as evidence of ancient India's prowess at civil engineering. Much of this emerged from the dense tangle between myth and history in the Indian mind, where both existed all intertwined like the undergrowth of a garden. An extensive right wing school network often taught myth as history, which intensified the tangle and spread it among a wider population.[1]

This made history – an analytical recounting of events whose central theme was to combine fact and idea while telling it like it was, while finding out 'what really happened' – a difficult undertaking in the country. The Sanskrit word *itihasa* clearly meant the Mahabharata and Ramayana epics – with their interwoven myths of flying machines and talking monkeys – but it also meant history as moral precept. Then again it also signified history as stories recorded by witnesses, and in

[1] For a summary of early attempts at rewriting history, see William Dalrymple, 'India: The War over History,' *New York Review of Books*, 7 April 2005, 52, 6.

fact, Panini's exact meaning of *iti ha āsa* renders from the Sanskrit as 'so indeed it was'. But notice this is not very different from Leopold von Ranke's famous admonition to professional historians in the Western tradition, to tell it – *wie es eigentlich gewesen* or 'how it essentially was'. Finding out what really happened. But did that include those talking monkeys?

Equally was this attitude prevalent among the talking heads who dominated public discourse in India and here Richard Hofstadter's comment is appropriate:

> The activist historian who thinks he is deriving his policy from his history may in fact be deriving his history from his policy, and may be driven to commit the cardinal sin of the historical writer: he may lose his respect for the integrity, the independence, the pastness, of the past.[2]

This lack of respect 'for the integrity, the independence, the pastness, of the past' was pervasive in India, not just among those who derived their history from their policy, but among the public who derived their history from their myth. As a result, heated and voluble public debates revolved around conflicting 'narratives' which had to be 'controlled', and where 'optics' had to be handled. Much of this sinister Orwellian doublespeak substituted for the plain task of telling it like it was, and India, unable to agree on a common idea of its past, continued to thrash around in its own peculiar historical schizophrenia. Why did this country have such a different sense of continuity over linear time, alternating violently between indifference to that continuity and obsession over it? It was these alternations, more than anything else, that made the country fertile ground for bizarre ideologies.

Just as history mattered for good citizenship, presumably some knowledge of the market's past mattered for good 'participant-ship' in it, but this attitude would also be seen as strange by most participants.

[2] Richard Hofstadter, *The Progressive Historians: Turner, Beard, Parrington*, New York: Knopf, 1968, 464–65.

Because of this lack of historical sense and memory, documentation of India's market also remains negligible, and so, every generation entering the market discovered its rigors the hard way – only through their own experience, rather than also through the vicarious experiences of those who came before. Yet the archives existed, mute and mouldering and patient, waiting for decades till someone came along to unshackle them from their obscurity.

Those archives reveal a market, little changed over a century, that was subjected to a sudden break in the early 1990s. That earlier market – a collection of municipal monopolies – had borne the brunt of Nehruvian India's official mistrust and, in fact, its survival was a wonder. It had been a quote-driven physical market mostly in unmargined naked forwards, self-regulated with contract enforcement through compromises and bargaining over 'relief'.

The system worked till the late 1980s, following which it was strained by significant volume surges, exacerbated by the Harshad Mehta bull run. In the early 1990s, a burst of reform to the microstructure – led largely by the NSE – resulted in an order-driven screen-based market, together with the creation of an organized buy side with domestic and foreign components. This founding generation of the new market, lasting as it did till about 2009, stands out as a period of scandals and cycles. The scandals (and early cycles) take their names from operators such as Harshad Mehta and Ketan Parekh, but with the later cycles the market becomes too big for one person, and nomenclature for later movements comes from fundamental causes such as interest rates and systematic investing plans.

The upshot of all this is a one-time rise in valuation parameters from the 4 to 6 multiples of an earlier era to the 15 to 30 range of modern times. In doing so, the market moves from its base level of 100 in 1978–79 to over 60,000 by 2023. From about 2008, unconventional monetary policy starts distorting markets worldwide, and India is no exception to this trend. But the domestic buy side's access to local savings and a 'defend your turf' mindset that eschews global diversification compels the domestics to cross foreign investors and smoothen out foreign flows as they enter and exit. Markets rise irrespective of the real economy or corporate performance, aided by the long corner, the absence of a short selling product, and an index drawn from a handful of high-performing sectors. The rise is more apparent in rupees, as dollar returns get eaten away by a rupee in secular decline. Nevertheless, growth and corporate performance continue to drift as religious majoritarianism destabilizes the body politic, while rising social and political tensions further disconnect an always expensive market from the real economy. By the new millennium, the Indian market was a first-rate microstructure that traded mainly second-rate companies operating in a difficult environment.

The study on catching Lakshmi in India's stock market brings out various themes, among which are: The Search for Value amidst Volatility, The Balance of Speculation and Investment, The Primacy of Return over Risk, The Disconnect from the Real Economy, The Permanence of Reform, The Absurdity of Regulation, The Rise of Domestic Investors, and The Dominance of Derivatives.

The Search for Value amidst Volatility is the essence of the Indian stock market. By itself, this statement is a commonplace, as on balance all stock markets share that feature. Nevertheless, special to the Indian market is the extremes to which volatility and value both go. Consider a partial list of factors influencing the market over a randomly selected six month period during the recent bull run: unanticipated changes in inflation and rates, signals from the central bank, corporate profits and their quality, economic news and leading economic indicators, news on Greece and the Eurozone, foreign investment flows, policy action by an aggressive newcomer in the central bank, government avowals on tax rates, oil prices and the geopolitics behind them, future quantitative easing (QE) by Western central banks, regime change, effects of the fits and starts of reform on listed sectors, external balances and their funding, El Nino and its effect on agriculture, emotion, and mood.

As if this were not enough to unnerve the average trader, go down to the company level where the volatility of the environment becomes more apparent. At the company level, consider: quarterly results, management changes, production issues, CBI criminal inquiries, predatory tax notices, FDA rulings, product launches, figuring out winners and losers of a perennial and fitful reform process, concerns over promoters and their squabbles, erratic government and regulatory policy affecting the company, incoherent court rulings on those regulatory pronouncements, law suits, fraud or corruption (the polite euphemism is 'corporate governance concerns'), valuations, regime change effects on companies, and so on. This is a volatile environment, so complex that it is even possible for insiders acting on inside information to lose money, as unanticipated flare ups of these factors impinge on their trades.

As blue chips halve and then treble when the above factors act on their prices, it is the ensuing volatility which generates the occasions to find value. Here, political, social, and economic change all unfolding at the same time, impinge relentlessly on those pieces of paper that trade on the exchange. It is the extremes to which value and volatility go that give meaning to this assertion on the market's essence.

The sample factors listed are extrinsic and collectively amount to noise – the idea that a large number of small events matter more than a small number of large events. Amidst all this noise, discerning the few factors that really move the market is vital, and astute observers devote much time to sifting through the noise for signals on the two or three factors that are actually driving the market at any given moment. But besides extrinsic factors and noise, volatility arises from factors intrinsic to the Indian market's microstructure and these include technical trading, short selling constraints, the 'stop loss' honeycomb, the colossal derivatives segment, and the uptick rule's absence. Intrinsic forces are influential during downturns rather than advances, and as seen from the analysis of crashes, they sometimes precipitate widespread collapses in the general list. The intrinsic forces acting together lead to the observation that stocks rise at different times, for different reasons, and over different periods, but fall together and all at once. As a result, waiting for the break or the bear, and timing the bottom right – that Holy Grail of active investing that is always just out of reach – carries disproportionate rewards in India. When the fat man cometh, he really cometh.

Noise trading is widely practiced worldwide, but in India's markets, the extrinsic and intrinsic factors allow for noise investing as an approach to the market. This is usually the 6 to 18 month long pull trade of 'speculative investment', and it is widely practiced even among the professional buy side.

The Balance of Speculation and Investment is a second enduring theme, though it is only recently that investment even enters the picture as a market approach. For most of the Century of Marking Time, speculative approaches were more prevalent, mainly because trading communities honed techniques in inherently speculative commodity markets before transplanting them to the exchange. Badla's trading in mark to market differences on unmargined naked forwards was tailor made for speculation, and most market volumes came from that activity. Without a buy side and proscriptions on bank lending for market activities, badla was what it took to run a stock market and it worked – but only too well. The speculative mindset would continue into the modern era through widespread practices such as day trading and technicals, but it is with derivatives that the speculative mindset gets taken to extremes. Because they lack a hedging clientele, India's outsized derivatives markets – the world's largest by number of contracts traded – are also the most speculative of enterprises, but a vast conspiracy of silence hides that simple fact. The NSE has gone and created one of the world's largest gambling casinos and convinced everyone about the greatness of that achievement.

Equities are a business of future possibilities, but catching Lakshmi has to contend with a basic characteristic of Indian civilization – that focus on human limitations rather than human possibilities. This leads to an excessive concern for the short term and a difficulty in taking the long view. From this, flows the speculative approach's dominance – those blue chips halving and trebling need a reason – but from this also come opportunities for those who can take the long view necessary for investment.

It is only from the 1990s and the buy side's birth that investing comes into its own. But investing is not investment policy, as much as stock picking. As noted earlier, formal investment policy that uses Modern Portfolio Theory's insights on mean variance optimization and efficient diversification does not happen, mainly because of problems with computing the input list for Indian stocks. Instead, the asset allocation heuristic (or thumb rule) is informally used, which only allows for Talmudic or naïve diversification, which is inefficient. But that does not matter, because the risk of inefficient diversification that Markowitz warns about is less important than the risk of overpaying which is Graham's concern. So, it is Graham rather than Markowitz who is the patron saint of the Indian buyside, and that is mainly because of the rampant inefficiency that makes Graham's stock picking – despite its hit or miss nature – more relevant and, in fact, synonymous with investment.

It is the even balance between investment and speculation that is a singular feature of the modern era. The buy side's growth, FII entry, and the SIP have all contributed to investment's spread as an approach; the millennium's trending (rather than trading) markets have further ensured its popularity. Against this must be balanced the speculative aspect arising from: vast numbers of traders and chartists who believe in technical analysis's magical thinking, the demographic dividend that leads to jobless graduates who drift into markets and attempt to trade their way to fortunes, the colossal derivatives segment with its monthly tenor instruments, and finally, habits of the heart and mind developed by trading communities over centuries. Crucially, the clearing and settlement revolution made it easier for back offices to manage small values spread over many players, which also increased the speculative element. Investment deals with large values spread over a few (usually professional) players, but speculation deals with small values spread over a large group of players, and that large group of small players is readily available in India. So, digitization contributed to speculation rather than investment.

It is tempting to criticize speculation, but in fact its role is so critical that the Indian market cannot be considered without it. The reasons for this are not difficult to see. Firstly, the present microstructure's electronic limit order book (ELOB) simply collects and stacks orders, without any specialists or market makers; sans them, it is speculation that provides thickness to the order book. Secondly, it is speculation's excesses that create the volatility which takes valuations to extremes, and this produces the opportunity – the search for value amidst volatility – that investors can exploit. Finally, the great cash-futures arbitrage engine that links the speculative derivatives market with the cash market, allows for the cash segment volumes which further build the thick order books that make all other market activities possible.

Ending the speculative orientation of India's old market was a focus area of the reform effort, so the present market with its speculative orientation is another unrecognized irony. Those trading habits of the heart and mind developed over centuries of market activity have proved difficult to change. But there is little need to tilt at windmills by fretfully running around and trying to curb the market's speculative activity. The activities of traders and speculators allow for the large order books the investing buy side uses to pick up stakes, and the balanced coexistence between both elements is a distinctive feature of the modern market. Without that even balance between speculation and investment, there would be no market.

The Primacy of Return over Risk comes up repeatedly over many decades of the market's history. By and large, India remains an absolute return equity shop with little concern for risk and even the idea that there is a risk-return trade-off is internalized but rarely acted on. That such an attitude should prevail among the public is understandable, but its pervasiveness among professionals is surprising. Perhaps the revolution in buy side finance that changed the West's attitudes towards risk bypassed India's equity markets, and the catch-up period after 1991 was not used to formalize ideas on risk.

Badla's extreme risk led to the near universal view that the market was a dangerous sort of place, but with the asset allocation heuristic came the idea that it is not the market as much as the portfolio's exposure to that market which brought risk. The idea is not entirely correct – as the portfolio itself has to be efficiently constructed – but it is still an improvement over badla days. Public markets were the first to be affected by this attitudinal change, but now private illiquid markets such as alternate investments are seeing these changing attitudes to risk.

Nevertheless, in public markets at least, the primacy of return over risk is still pervasive. Markowitzian mean variance optimization, that optimizes return per unit of risk taken, does not happen as a matter of investment policy, and for practical purposes, a diversified equity fund is taken as an efficient portfolio. As a result, diversification is Talmudic or naïve, and based on the experience and belief systems of managers. In turn, this naïve diversification is inefficient and risky, but that does not carry reputational costs to the manager, as the market has internalized intuitions on return rather than risk, and rewards participants accordingly.

Once naïve diversification allocates to asset classes or sectors, the all-important search for the next Tiddlywinks can commence. This in turn is based on Graham's criteria of value investing through stock picking. As finding value through stock picking is the basis of all investment policy, overpaying for value must be the basis for all risk. This attitude is second nature in India's market, dominated as it is by frugal trading communities who are obsessed with bargaining. Consequently, it is Graham's risk of overpaying for value rather than Markowitz's risk of inefficient diversification that gets internalized in India. In turn, overpaying (or underpaying) for value puts the focus squarely on expected returns. The primacy of return over risk then follows.

Fund marketing also emphasizes return rather than the diversification benefits of lower risk, as does the nascent global investing movement. The fundies cannot be blamed for this though, mainly because of the rampant inefficiency that makes Graham more relevant than Markowitz. In turn, the cavalier attitude to risk allows the buy side to get away with concentrated portfolios and the regulations also encourage this. In fact, Indian mutual funds – small to begin with – can put as much as 10 per cent of their folios in a single stock, a high concentration level that brings its own risk. Because of return primacy, the higher returns from concentration often get attributed to stock picking skill rather than greater risk taking, which makes it difficult to judge whether picking skill or risk assumption are responsible for outperformance; small and mid-cap managers benefit the most from such return primacy, despite operating in the riskiest of spaces.

The Disconnect from the Real Economy seems to be increasing with time, and this is paradoxical. That disconnect was understandable during the Century of Marking Time when the market was a small enterprise centred around Bombay or Calcutta, and when the information flow to price the real economy was absent, or at best sporadic.

But the disconnect continues into the modern era, made clear by the causality – the displacements – behind the big moves. Both the Mehta and IT Bulls were tenuously connected with the real economy's performance. The Mehta Bull was displaced by the promise of reform – after a half century of autarky – rather than any real economy surge; other causal factors such as Mehta's G-Sec exertions and FII entry were liquidity based and also had little connection with the real economy. With the IT Bull, a small and nascent sector responded to the displacement of a worldwide mania, which together with the bull's compressed time frame and its one-on-one moves with Nasdaq also indicates a tenuous real connection.

But unlike Mehta and IT, the great Rate Bull from 2003 to 2008 was canonical in its real economy connections, and the period was marked by both market and real side booms. The near 900 basis point fall in rates between 1996 and 2003 marked a historic break from high interest rates of the past, and the displacement was conducive to a real economy surge. This led to an across-the-board rise in corporate bottom lines and consequently of stock prices, and the resulting breath was another key feature of the Rate Bull, showing the gravity-like effects of interest rates on asset prices more clearly than ever before. Earnings grew faster than prices across market breadth for a significant time period, which was another distinguishing feature of the move. That this was the first bull since badla's 2001 abolition removed the short trade, that the domestic buy side was now coming into its own, and that global conditions were very conducive, are important, but secondary to the primary factor of the interest rate displacement.

If the Rate Bull was definitive in its real connections, the ongoing SIP Bull from 2009 to about 2020 and onwards, is definitive in its disregard, and herein hangs a tale. The market goes back to echoing the Mehta and IT disconnects. The disconnect is more apparent in the bull's later stages and assumes surreal proportions when the coronavirus pandemic hits. With much of the economy locked down, calendar year 2020 is the worst year in independent India's economic history, and yet the market rises 12 per cent. Clearly something has happened.

Confounding factors responsible for the SIP Bull's disconnect include: distortions caused by Western monetary policy and QE, the long corner that reduces free float so much that QE type liquidity surges cause disproportionate effects on prices, a buy side with a cavalier disregard for global investing that uses the SIP to defend its own turf from foreign flows, a market index whose narrowness lends itself to index management, and the short constraint.

Working together, these factors led to a fantastic disconnect from the real economy during the pandemic downturn. Despite a GDP collapse of 24 per cent for the quarter that ended June 2020 and a near 8 per cent contraction for 2020–21, the market doubled off the bottom formed by the March 2020 sell-off and continued to chug higher through a lockdown and second wave of the pandemic that was catastrophic for the economy. The extreme dislocations caused time series data based on year-on-year comparisons to jump around, but through these dislocations the market consistently traded at over 30 times earnings (at one point it even touched 40 times) with dividend yields that consistently went below 1 per cent. The wire houses rationalized it all by trotting out the familiar forward earnings fudge, as a result of which the market was usually 'fairly valued' at about 20 times forward earnings.

There are multiple levels of disconnect in this Twilight Zone: between a real economy and its controversial measurement; between that real economy (as contentiously measured) and those 30 or 50 stocks that are selected for index inclusion based on financial performance rather than how they mirror the real economy; between the bottom lines of those index stocks and the bottom lines of over 2,000 stocks that make up the traded broader market; and critically, between liquidity flows and valuations.

As a result, cycles are becoming tenuous to the point where the market is in danger of losing its traditional role as a barometer for the economy. In the old days before QE, the SIP, and other factors, talk of a cycle seemed possible, but history as it comes into the present loses some of its rhythm and a certain immediacy sets in, which together with these confounding forces, makes a cycle difficult to discern. Since about 2010, the cyclical violence that characterized the market in the early modern era seems to have abated, but the immediacy of current events and the confounding factors make it difficult to say if the cycle has abated for good. In turn, the long bias of the confounding factors allows for stock picking to work in a steadily rising market that rises despite fundamentals – the market is 'micro efficient' but 'macro inefficient' – and this happens till the market violently reasserts itself, usually via a sell-off triggered by intrinsic factors unique to the microstructure. But these are few and far between. In the generation between the 2002 IT bear sell-off and 2020, the only period of falling prices was 2008.

The Permanence of Reform arises from the myth of Sisyphus. In this dominant myth of our time, the central character is eternally condemned to push a rock up a hill only to have it roll down as he nears the top, following which he wearily starts all over again. Like that, reform in India is an unending Sisyphean task that never ceases. Consider that in the stock market there was a time when the task began and was ended, and yet it continues. Even by its widest conception, the reform era of the early 1990s should have been done over the next three decades, but the bureaucrats never saw it as such. Lacking the historical imagination to conceive of a reform era in the first place, they found it difficult to believe it could have ended.

As a result, the equity markets have been continuously in reform mode. Every few years a different area becomes the subject of reform efforts, often with mixed results – first the brokers, then the microstructure, the mutual funds, the advisors, then the distributors, and so on. Observers returning after a few years are usually dazed by all this and remark that the country is always changing. Eternal India has now become Eternally Changing India. To SEBI, change usually meant tinkering with regulations, and the tinkering – the media's favourite phrase was 'tweaking' – raised compliance burdens for all and mirrored the wider reform anxiety in the country. Invidious to smaller players was the risk of being caught on the wrong side of these reform efforts, but more sinister was the risk of being driven out for the terrible crime of being small.

Market participants unwittingly contribute to this, howling for 'reform' with a market fall and ceasing such talk on a market surge. SEBI's proximity to the market doubly obliges it to do something and the next lurch of the reform movement then gets going. There was a pervasive tendency to believe that every isolated incident had system-wide implications, and such incidents often acted as a trigger to the next bout of reform. Recently, a broker's isolated abuse of margin trading led to an overhaul of the market-wide system that left most people scratching their heads, followed in turn by media reporting that was unintelligible even to astute participants. Founded in the early 1990s to reform markets, SEBI found it difficult to move away from the reform embedded in its DNA. Lacking a historical account that could bring the reform era to an end, the bureaucrats who regulated the market appeared perennially trapped in reform mode. Convinced that reform had led to great things, it was only logical to summon up 'reform' as a prelude to more great things.

M.R. Mayya, India's first regulator, himself saw reform of the stock markets as a perennial process – whatever that meant – and his successors at SEBI continued with that view. A people with no institutional memory or understanding of the past could draw little comfort from it, and were incapable of understanding how far they had progressed from that past into the present. Having little idea about how far they had come, they complained loudly about how far they needed to go. As a result, they were reduced to contemplating a present that always seemed less perfect than what could be summoned up through 'reform'.

The market's eternal reform mode contrasted with the wider body politic, where the belief had caught hold that India reformed only in a crisis. Actually, a crisis was the worst time to reform. Governments were usually firefighting in a crisis, which rarely allowed for the calm reflection on trade-offs necessary for reform; critically, assembling the human bandwidth necessary to pull it all off was rarely possible in a crisis. Yet among the chattering classes 'never waste a good crisis' became another glib term to be bandied around, perhaps because of the brief constellation of pro-reform forces that the political economy allowed for during 1991. With SEBI though, the problem was the reverse, and it was continually trapped in a sort of reform anxiety similar to a constant low-grade fever.

The Tangle of Regulation is a recent phenomenon, as the market was a self-regulating organization (SRO) for most of its existence. Ruinously expensive contract enforcement made self-regulation a necessity, but the SRO framework had issues scaling up from the colonial period's small market into the reform era. Agency issues were responsible for this, as brokers chose to be both principals for themselves and agents for their clients, and these principal-agent problems – usually referred to as 'conflict of interest' issues – rose in proportion as the market scaled up. Most wanted the flexibility of SROs but lacked the discipline or judgment to make the statesman-like trade-offs necessary to get the SRO framework to work, and as a result, many SROs degenerated into a quagmire of self-interested self-assertions. This undid the SRO model and became most apparent as volumes surged through the Mehta and IT Bulls.

Besides, it was only with the 1956 passage of the Securities Contracts (Regulation) Act that the government gave itself rule making authority over the market's microstructure. But with resource mobilization mainly through plan rather than market, there was little occasion for the government to use that authority, till recognition of the market's resource raising potential and SEBI's creation allowed for more formal regulation.

In an age without a buy side, SEBI's founding mission of investor protection marked a clear declaration in favour of the little guy – the trading and investing public. This emphasis, together with the pervasive democratic ethos, later translated into the *aam aadmi* bias – a regulatory predisposition backing the masses against the classes, which also meant backing the public against any participant who mediated between that public and corporates. This combines with a certain dirigisme – the belief that there is a considerable state role in organizing economic activity – and the combination produces the tangle of regulation. This unchecked and unbridled regulatory activity was often the decisive element in participants' fortunes, and its manipulation or channelling would be crucial to participants like brokers, funds, or advisors. As the section on advisors showed, dealing with all this regulatory friction could be fatal for smaller participants who did not have the same resources as larger ones.

The tangle became apparent in the new millennium. Typically, dubious action by one party triggered the dirigisme that led to heavy-handed regulation for the remaining 99, as the regulator went about protecting the *aam aadmi* from the next dubious instance. This was to remain a defining pattern of Indian regulation. This also arose from the inability to distinguish between corporate events, such as the Satyam and Yes Bank frauds, and market-wide systemic events that had been largely extinguished by changes to the microstructure. It is unlikely corporate events would ever end, but a regulator perennially trapped in reform mode did not recognize this, and kept raising requirements in response to such events, which raised compliance burdens to staggering levels.

Incremental regulation's default mode dealt with further filings rather than doing away with existing filings. Once in place, regulation and levies are rarely removed as indicated by the temporary IPO restrictions of the 1940s that stayed in place for a half century as the Capital Issues

(Control) Act. The SEBI tax of the 1990s is also still in place. America's SEC commissioners would presumably be strung up from the nearest lamp post for even suggesting that every US market trade be taxed privately by the SEC. But the SEBI tax on trillions of such market trades, like most government levies, continues with a life of its own.

Some regulatory action was unexceptionable, and some was noteworthy – as in derivatives risk management. Some action could even be serendipitous – the cavalier FERA dilutions of the 1970s stand as one of the earliest recorded cases of the *aam aadmi* bias, and yet they jumpstarted the equity culture. The cultural change from *sākh* to systems is also a significant achievement of Indian regulation. Nevertheless, in later years the tenor of all this could change industry dynamics. More generally, regulatory action arising from the *aam aadmi* bias appropriated industry profits that accrued from economies of scale and distributed it back to the *aam aadmi* in their avatar as customers. That a financial market needed some regulation was clear, but that the government's heavy handedness could ruin a segment's prospects was equally clear, and the vehemence with which both views were held pointed to a strange situation. Keeping up with product innovation was usually why regulatory balance proved difficult worldwide – but note that innovation was never a concern in India because there was so little of it anyway, and yet the balance proved difficult.

The tangle of regulation raised compliance costs, but these were concealed somewhat by the huge bull surges of recent years. More invidious was the effect on industry structure, profitability, and incentives. The result was 'death by compliance'. It was easier to handle for the big boys who had both the resources and the larger volumes to spread the costs over, but smaller players had less of both and were more vulnerable to regulatory change. As a result, regulatory action tended to change industry structure by driving out smaller players – often deliberately – as the PMS and advisory segments demonstrated. Micromanagement of industry structure and incentives was also apparent in the mutual fund space, and their changing fee regimes show the disincentivization of scale economies. Business was about building a better mousetrap, following which the world beat a path to the entrepreneur's door. But in India much time and effort went into intermediating between the mousetrap and the environment, and it was those intermediaries (like the chartered accountants, company secretaries, tax filers, and lawyers) who benefited most from the system.

Another obvious consequence was regulatory arbitrage. *Dabba* trading and Calcuttta's *katni* market were early examples, but lately, as further examples of regulatory arbitrage in a globalized world, consider that currency hedging and short selling have also left India and moved abroad. The alternative to regulatory arbitrage was to hope for leniency, and market participants could survive for years on the wretchedly appropriate 'regulatory forbearance' as shown by the regional exchanges. But that example also brings out the severe regulatory and reform risk that participants face, as in a few years the regionals went from being essential to the microstructure to being a regulatory burden, and were therefore abolished. Yet heavy-handed regulation brought forth timid responses, as short duration licenses led to the coercive necessity of repeatedly approaching the regulator for their renewal.

The usual industry response to all this was a cat and mouse game with the regulator over the vigorish that only expert accountants seemed to understand. Much of this also played out in an area where the country anyway had significant experience – the back office – and fiddling with back-office settings to siphon out tiny amounts from a colossal account base had topline benefits. As noted earlier, skimming ₹8 (9 cents) a month from those 100 million demat accounts could lead to jam of almost ₹1,000 crores ($125 million) a year, with none the wiser. Nevertheless, as a result of all this, business in India increasingly resembled a chaotic football match, where besides the play, the rules, goalposts, umpires, and shape of the ground all changed with the play itself. The budget's annual ritual – where the crowd eagerly watched for change while the government obliged by fiddling with change – even institutionalized this metaphor of a football match where everything was in play, and all at the same time.

The Rise of Domestic Institutions is epochal and marks an age. The ascendency's 1963–93 first phase was noticeable for its exclusively public sector focus and marginal access to resources, while the 1993–2010 second phase was marked by private sector entry, the learning curve of the Mehta, IT, and Rate cycles, and favourable tax treatment for fund products. The third phase from about 2010 is marked by the rise of averaging products such as the SIP, but the date's recentness makes it suspect, and it remains to be seen if this third phase is temporary or something more structural. Nevertheless, the growing deployment of SIP money leads to a waning of FII influence over the market, and in this sense, 2010 marks an inflexion point.

So much of the DII rise is a recent phenomenon. Despite India's high savings rate and the household search for yield, DII performance in the early years belied the hopes of liberalization. High interest rates provided better opportunities from debt, while chronic distrust of equities challenged the mutual fund industry till it discovered the wonders of averaging products. Nevertheless, despite the recent surge, industry AUM is much lower than the 40 to 60 per cent of GDP featured in emerging market peers such as South Africa and Brazil.

Behind the DII rise are two significant transitions: household moves from real to financial assets, followed by a move from other financial assets into equities. The first reduced somewhat the obsession with land and gold, while the second has been led by SIP-type averaging products. Sticky and inclined towards inertia by philosophy and design, SIPs are spectacularly successful in the steadily upward trending markets of recent years.

Traditionally, customer acquisition and asset gathering were expensive because of mistrust and the absence of pension allocations at source; third-party distributors dominate asset gathering channels, which raises costs further. Besides high gathering costs, mutual funds have had to deal with the regulator's *aam aadmi* bias, which tinkers away at the industry's fee structure and top line. Despite that, annual AUM growth rates of about 15 per cent are higher than the market's compounded 13 per cent advance, which in the absence of new fund offerings indicates rising net inflows. SEBI's incentive schemes to nudge distribution into smaller towns and digitization have helped as much as the structural shifts in savings. During the coronavirus pandemic, action did shift to smaller towns – though digitization also ensured that activities such as derivatives trading on smart phones benefited more than asset gathering.

The buy side cracks its distribution and redemption problems through the SIP and digitization. The distribution problem resolves as the small monthly sizes of averaging plans – the smallest are less than ₹1,000 ($14) – allow for wide distribution and acceptance, while digitization lowers the costs of product handling. The redemption problem resolves as the averaging philosophy behind monthly inflows leads to stickiness, which allows for lower redemption. Together, the SIP and the buy side's ascendency also reduced the concern with liquidity exhibited by previous generations of market participants.

The ascendency also changed the relative position of foreign investors and reduced the market's obsession with them. Since their entry in 1993 to about 2010, FIIs had an influential presence in the market as the domestic buy side rarely had enough capital to counter their flows. DIIs now use SIP flows to act as a countervailing force to FII entry and exit. Foreign flows are tied to global liquidity and asset allocation fashions, but the domestic buy side is only invested locally and has an incentive to smooth out the volatile foreign flows that influence their performance. So, from about 2010, DIIs use SIP inflows to prop up the market, and in so doing, give FIIs a free option to sell and exit. This is the SIP put, and FIIs are happy to benefit from it.

DIIs do not diversify internationally despite being allowed to do so for some time, and instead prefer to defend a domestic market by crossing FIIs. A cultural bias towards the home market and the India Growth Story, lack of experience in other markets, and the tendency to think in terms of local stock picking rather than global asset allocation are all responsible for this situation. Rather than compete with everyone else in an international asset market for returns, DIIs see themselves as defenders of a domestic market that has to be propped up at all cost when everyone else leaves. The resulting capital market segmentation that cuts India off from the rest of the world is now de facto rather than de jure, and yet from the market's standpoint, today's domestic institutions have stepped into the breach at the right time in its history. Even recent slowdowns in growth rates and the coronavirus pandemic were not enough to convince domestic institutions about the benefits of global diversification, though that situation might change going forward.

The Dominance of Derivatives continues into the modern era. Such was the dominance that this account revealed not much else by way of other practice during most of the market's existence. In the early years, India's trading communities adapted commodity trading techniques to the stock market, and among these were Premchand Roychand's time bargains. During the Century of Marking Time, most of the stock market consisted of unmargined or lightly margined naked forwards with embedded option features and monthly (later fortnightly and weekly) tenors that kept getting rolled over on the Friday of tenor expiry. Cash markets were negligible for most of the market's history, as the banking system was reluctant to finance market activity and also because no cash margining system could match badla's leverage and volumes.

So, right from its founding, the market's superstructure was dominated by some form of derivatives trading but the inability to go back far enough in time hides this simple fact. The influence of derivatives continues into the present because of path dependency dating from the 1990s. The reform objective of separating the cash from the forward market effectively put paid to the BSEs badla product, but the market's need for a leveraged trading product was always strong. In the complex manoeuvring over microstructure that followed, a brand-new derivatives segment won out over both continuation of the badla product or alternate arrangements such as a margining system. International best practice at that time also pointed to a derivatives market, as did the improvement in risk management that could result, and these were the main reasons behind the creation of a derivatives segment.

The NSE then proceeded to monopolize the derivatives market with its Futures and Options segment. Nowadays, the NSE's volumes in the derivatives segment are so large that they need an explanation. By July 2020, the NSE was reporting daily derivatives volumes of over ₹19,00,000 crores ($255 billion), but much of that number came from deep 'out of the money' options reckoned at notional face value.

Despite that, derivatives volumes are staggering. As a result, the dominance of derivatives has increased in the post reform era, and in this sense, nothing has changed. India, today, has the world's largest derivatives market by measures such as number of contracts traded and the market's superstructure continues to be dominated by that segment. This is ironical as reducing the system's reliance on badla's derivative-like features had been an important reform objective. A related objective – improving risk management by allowing for a hedging product – also did not materialize. The short monthly tenor of most derivatives contracts makes is difficult for the buy side to use them for hedging purposes; even if tenors were increased, it is unlikely that India's retail dominated derivatives market would take to longer tenors, and here the absence of sophisticated players such as hedge funds is especially felt.

Without any hedging activity, practically all derivatives volume is speculative, and the NSE runs what is, in effect, one of the world's biggest casinos.

Of the two basic instruments – futures and options – futures are more important from a systemic standpoint. This is because the cash leg of the arbitrage between cash and futures markets brings in substantial volumes to the market's cash segment, all of which accrue to the NSE. By contrast, options with weekly or monthly tenors are less useful for risk management or hedging, and are used mainly as speculating instruments.

Doing away with derivatives allows for the vast margin money paid into the derivatives market to be used as trading capital in the cash market but would also end the cash market's volumes (and therefore liquidity) from the cash futures arbitrage trade. Whether this trade-off is net beneficial from a public policy perspective is anybody's guess, and the issue may never reach a stage where such trade-offs are even contemplated. For discontinuing the derivatives segment is a pipe dream and the colossal derivatives market – despite providing no real utility in price discovery, raising resources, or risk management – seems destined to be around for a long time. India's vast demographic dividend pours into the markets through new traders trying their hand and that public's need for a leveraged product is simply too strong. Besides, a big part of the NSE's valuation of almost $10 billion (in 2021) depends both on its monopoly of the derivatives segment and the cross-margining advantages that come with that. The marquee investors who enter and leave the NSE's valuation game in that discreet game of musical chairs may not brook any interference with that valuation.

The NSE's derivatives dominance was also responsible for the BSEs future plans as an exchange. Denied the equity market by the NSE's dominance, the BSE would move into other areas and now saw itself as a fintech company and platform, rather than as an exchange. The BSE would morph into a fund distribution platform cum exchange, and then go on to seed a wide variety of ventures including almond trading and power trading that had little in common with equities. Rather than functional businesses, these were more in the nature of bets on the future and the exchange was beginning to look like the fintech segment of a private equity fund. Steeped in a past it knew little about, the exchange obsessed about its options in a digital future that was always just around the corner, and in this sense, the BSE was a metaphor for India itself.

The democratization of investing is a final trend and a satisfying one to contemplate in the world's largest democracy. It is a recent development, as for much of its history the market remained confined to wealthy individuals located in the big metros. Even the post-Independence period does little to change this, and it is only from the millennium's turn that things begin to change. Much of this is led by SEBI, and its founding mission is clearly loaded in favour of the little guy, but that is only a reflection of wider forces. The dominant force of Indian political life – the political economy of competitive populism – cannot leave the financial system alone and the market wide ecosystem, as part of a larger social milieu, is not immune to it. Politicians compete through the ballot box, but SEBI does not even need to do that and ensures populism through regulatory fiat as it goes about realizing its founding mission.

But as much as regulatory fiat and SEBI, it is technology that makes many things possible, and it is the digitization of investing and trading that also makes possible its democratization. Digitization contributes to that most pervasive of Indian phenomena – the tendency of small values to get spread over large volumes – and it isn't only in the markets; the banking system has *jandhan* or bank accounts for all, while the stock market has the SIP, or investing for all, and so on. By now it was possible to invest as little as ₹500 ($6) at regular monthly intervals in the markets; in most other countries, the vigorish alone would make this impossible, yet here it happens routinely.

So, this plebeianization via fiat and technology is pervasive, and the tendency towards a commonality of conditions is getting pronounced. But in the stock market, it is moderated by that winner take all culture which pervades all markets, and the market still disproportionately rewards those who delve into and master its secrets, with a little luck thrown in for good measure.

Over sufficient lengths of time, stock markets only go higher, and there are three reasons for this. First, all market returns are nominal before taking inflation into account. Company sales and earnings are priced nominally before inflation, and if companies have some pricing power, which is a reasonable assumption in India, sales and bottom-line earnings rise with inflation; in an inflation prone country such as India, this effect is even more pronounced. The stock market simply prices this nominal growth through the ratio of price to earnings, and even if that ratio was a constant and never changed, markets would still head higher over time because of nominal increases in bottom-line earnings. Second, companies reinvest a substantial portion of their profits through retained earnings. If dividend payout ratios are not large, also a reasonable assumption in India, this automatic compounding through reinvestment of retained earnings, also in nominal terms before inflation, will take stocks and markets higher. The third reason is not even a financial reason, and yet it is the most powerful – it lies in the nature of humankind to advance. As Gibbon pointed out, whatever is human must retrograde if it does not advance, and it is this tendency to advance that manifests in corporate life and the stock market. Because the equity contract is a perpetuity that lasts forever, some of that tendency of humankind to advance must get captured in nominal terms through holding a diversified number of good stocks, and this remains the one enduring lesson from the stock market's history.

GLOSSARY

aam aadmi. An ordinary person.

aam aadmi bias. Mental construct in the Indian regulatory mind which ensures that disputes between intermediaries and the aam aadmi will usually be resolved in favour of the latter.

absolute valuation approach. Determination of a stock's intrinsic value by projecting its income streams as a perpetuity to find its present value. Usually done through discounted cash flow (DCF) analysis. *Contrast* **relative valuation approach**.

active management. Predominant form of portfolio management in India, typically involving asset allocation, security selection, and market timing to exploit undervaluation. *See also* **passive management**.

agency issues. Issues arising out of conflicts of interest between shareholders, bondholders, and management. Shareholders as principals/owners usually bear most of the costs of dealing with agents such as management. For example, incentivizing management to maximize shareholder value rather than management's own well-being (and then monitoring the process) involves agency costs. *See also* **principal–agent problem**.

ALBM. Automated Lending and Borrowing Mechanism (ALBM) launched by the NSE in February 1999 as a mechanism to borrow and lend stocks under a forward system. The BSE equivalent was BLESS (Borrowing and Lending Securities Scheme). With the introduction of derivatives, both were done away with in 2001 but reintroduced in later years.

alpha. Excess return over a defined benchmark (bogey) or over a return predicted by an asset pricing model such as the Capital Asset Pricing Model (CAPM).

announcement date. The date on which market-moving information on a stock is released.

anomaly. A regularity in stock prices that can be exploited in a manner anomalous to the Efficient Market Hypothesis. *See also* **Efficient Market Hypothesis**.

arbitrage. Construction of a costless, riskless, zero-investment portfolio that yields a sure profit. Practically, any attempt made across financial markets to exploit differences in the price of the same security as it trades in different markets. *More under* **Law of One Price**.

ask. The rate a seller demands in a financial market.

asset allocation. Choosing among various asset classes and the allocation of capital among them.

asset pricing model. General equilibrium models that determine the theoretically appropriate pricing of financial assets in equilibrium, usually after positing relationships between expected returns and risk. Single-factor models such as the Capital Asset Pricing Model (CAPM) posit return relationships with a single factor (e.g., a stock's variability with the market), while multifactor models such as Arbitrage Pricing Theory seek to find other factors (besides the market) that can act as proxies for systematic risk.

autarky. Economic self-sufficiency that isolates an economy from the world. The absence of international trade and capital flows.

backwardation. In futures markets, when futures prices are lower than the expected future spot price. *Contrast* **contango**.

badla. Trading in marked to market price differentials of unmargined (or lightly margined) naked forward contracts which was the predominant form of Indian stock trading till 2001.

badni trading. Commodity trading, usually in grains.

balance of payments. Summary of flows between a country and the rest of the world on current and capital accounts. More technically, the official settlements balance, the net supply of foreign currency (or the net demand for domestic currency) after the private sector has made all its desired transactions on the current and capital accounts, and after adjusting for errors and omissions.

balance sheet. Financial statement of a firm's financial position at a point in time, detailing assets, liabilities, and owners' equity.

bania. A member of trading/business communities, traditionally drawn from the Vaishya grouping in the four groups of the *chaturvarna* caste system.

basis. The difference between a stock's cash price and its futures price in the derivatives segment. *See also* **convergence**.

bear. A trader who sells for the fall in a financial market.

behavioural finance. The application of psychology and its principles to the study of investor behaviour in financial markets.

benchmark. *See* **bogey**.

beta. The standardized covariance of a stock with a market. A measure of systematic risk in single-factor asset pricing models that measures a stock's response to market movement.

bias. Systematic errors, typically emotional or cognitive, that individuals make in financial decision-making.

bid. The rate a buyer demands in a financial market.

bid-ask spread. The difference between the best (or highest) buyer and best (or lowest) seller rates in a market.

Black–Scholes–Merton option pricing model. Formula for the pricing of a call option that uses five inputs: the risk-free interest rate, the price of the underlying stock, the variance of the underlying stock, the option's exercise price, and the option's time to expiration.

blank transfers. Transfer deeds signed by parties as sellers but left blank for particulars on the buyer's name. Market custom of the badla era that facilitated its high trading velocity.

blue sky laws. In the US, state-level laws that protect investors from parties trying to sell them little more than 'blue sky'.

bond. Fixed-income instrument paying out a specific cash flow over a specified period.

bogey. Benchmark index that fund managers are compared with for performance evaluation.

bonus share. *See* **stock dividend**.

book value. For a firm, an accounting measure that is the total of its paid-in capital and retained earnings. Alternately, the excess of total assets over total liabilities.

broker. Intermediary offering search or execution capabilities to buyers and sellers in a market.

bull. A trader who buys for the rise in a financial market.

business cycle. Repetitive expansion and contraction of an economy around its long-term growth path.

buy side. Collective term for institutions such as mutual funds or pension funds, who buy and hold stocks for an investing public.

call option. The right, but not the obligation, to buy a stock or other financial instrument.

Capital Asset Pricing Model (CAPM). Single-factor asset pricing model which shows that equilibrium returns on risky assets are a function of their covariance with a market portfolio; model that posits a linear relationship between a stock's expected return and its beta (a measure of market risk).

capital gains. The excess of proceeds over cost from the sale of a capital asset.

capital market segmentation. Absence of integration between a country and global capital markets, because of convertibility controls, exchange regimes, taxes, or belief systems.

capital markets. Markets that provide long-term debt and equity capital to a firm.

card. The right of nomination that entitled BSE members to transfer their membership with the approval of the Governing Board. Similar to a seat on the London and New York exchanges. The card value was the value of that right.

clearing and settlement. Back-office function where securities and payment change hands. When clearing, all parties determine their obligations and agree on them, following which they match their records with those of the exchange and its clearing house. At settlement, buyers pay in cash and sellers pay in shares; following reconciliation and pay-out, buyers receive shares and sellers receive cash.

clearing house. Microstructure institution that facilitates securities clearing and settlement.

clientele effect. The idea that different tax or regulatory changes will have different effects on demands and goals of shareholders as clients, with corresponding effects on a firm's stock price. Company policies on issues such as dividends can also create clientele effects on a firm's stock price.

collateral. Asset pledges made by a borrower to secure a loan against default risk.

common stock (share). A share in the share capital of a company.

comparative advantage. The idea that trade can take place even if one nation is less efficient than another in the production of all goods. The less-efficient nation specializes in and exports the good in which its absolute disadvantage is smaller (where it has some comparative advantage) and imports the other commodity.

compounding. The process of reinvesting each interest payment to earn more interest. The reverse of discounting.

concentration. Common buy side practice of inadequately diversifying portfolios by focusing them on a few stocks. *Contrast* **diversification**.

contango. Situation in futures markets where futures prices are higher than the expected future spot price. *Contrast* **backwardation**.

contrarianism. In stylized form, buying from the crowd what it hates and selling to the crowd what it loves.

convergence. The convergence of a futures contract to the price of its underlying stock on maturity of the contract.

convertible bond. Fixed-income instruments with options that allow the holder to exchange the instrument for a specified number of shares.

corner. Artificial scarcity created on a counter that lowers its free float to the point where the counter's price is affected. Typically refers to short corners, but in India, the long corner is also a possibility. *See also* **squeeze**.

correlation. A statistical measure of the dependence between two random variables, defined as the covariance of two variables divided by their standard deviations. *See also* **covariance**.

cost of capital. Actual costs incurred by an entity to finance its investing and operating activities. For listed entities, often seen by the market as a hurdle to be crossed before the entity can generate value.

cost of carry. *See* **spot-futures parity theorem**.

counter. Alternate name for the activity in a stock. Now archaic.

counterparty risk. The risk that a counterparty to a contract will not perform their part of the contract, such as repay a deposit of cash, settle an invoice, or supply goods when due.

coupon. The interest rate per rupee of par value payable by a fixed income instrument.

covariance. A measure of how much two securities vary in relation to each other in a portfolio. A statistic that scales covariances between –1 and +1 is called the correlation coefficient. *See also* **correlation**.

cross-margining. Using share portfolios as collateral to fund derivatives trading positions.

dabba. A dud.

dabba trading. Informal bucket shop trading, usually only in marked-to-market price differentials.

Day Moving Average (DMA). A technical analysis tool that smooths out price data by averaging the closing prices of an asset over a specific number of past days.

day trading. A pastime in which trades are closed out on the same trading day.

demat account. Short form for a dematerialized account in which an investor's shares are held in electronic form.

dematerialization. The process of converting physical share certificates to electronic (dematerialized) form.

demutualization. Among stock exchange members, the separation of ownership interests from trading interests; done to reduce principal–agent issues.

depository. A centralized entity that holds financial securities in electronic dematerialized form.

derivative. Securities whose pay-offs are contingent and derived from the value of another asset (the underlying); underlying assets can include stocks, bonds, commodities, currencies, and even intangibles such as interest rates and indexes. Common types of derivatives include options and futures.

dervish. A big professional trader on Dalal Street.

DIOK. Double Income One Kid. Salaried couples with one child and capacity to invest, seen as a persistent trope in the advisory business's client acquisition.

dirigisme. Directive state control of economic activity in a market economy. Someone with this orientation is a dirigiste.

discounted cash flow (DCF) analysis. Absolute valuation approach that uses earnings and their growth rates, risk levels, and market interest rates as inputs to value a stock by projecting and then discounting its free cash flows. *Contrast* **relative valuation** and **price-earnings ratio**.

discounting. Calculating the present (current) value of amounts received in the future. The reverse of compounding.

displacement. *See* **trigger**.

diversifiable risk. Risk that affects a single asset like, say, a single company's stock; usually eliminated by holding an efficient portfolio. Also called unsystematic risk or non-market risk. *See also* **non-diversifiable risk**.

diversification. Investing a portfolio in various assets or asset classes to minimize exposure to a single source of risk.

dividend. Cash reward paid out by a company to its shareholders, either from present profit or earmarked reserves. In some jurisdictions, dividends can be paid in property, stocks, or scrips (notes payable).

dividend discount model (DDM). Estimating the value of a firm by calculating the present value of its expected future dividends.

Domestic Institutional Investors (DIIs). Categorization of the domestic buy side that includes (among others) mutual funds, insurance companies, pension funds, and portfolio management schemes.

Dow Theory. Technical theory aimed at identifying minor, intermediate, and primary trends in the stock market; signals then generate buy and sell calls.

earnings yield. The reciprocal of a price-earnings ratio.

economic rents. What a resource holder would get over and above the market price of a resource, that market price itself being what the resource could command when used in an alternate opportunity. An excess return over and above the opportunity cost of resources.

efficiency. The extent to which, and the speed at which, information release is captured in a stock's price.

efficient frontier. Upward portion of a hyperbolic curve representing the optimized set of efficient portfolios that maximizes expected return for every given level of portfolio risk; alternately, the optimized set that minimizes risk for every given level of portfolio return. The hyperbolic curve is also known as the Markowitz bullet.

Efficient Market Hypothesis (EMH). The idea that prices of securities usually reflect all available information on them. In turn, this implies that investors receive an equilibrium rate of return commensurate with the risk they take.

Electronic Limit Order Book (ELOB). Screen depiction of an order-driven market's order listing that aggregates buyers' and sellers' orders with a price/time priority rule. In India, all participants view the market for a stock through its ELOB.

empiricism. Knowledge based on, concerned with, or verifiable by observation or sensory experience, rather than theory or pure logic; the belief that knowledge or justification comes only from (or primarily from) sensory experience.

event study. A controlled experiment in a financial market that isolates the effect of firm-specific information release on a stock's price during an event window; the event window is typically a defined period of a few weeks preceding an event, such as an earnings announcement.

evergreening. Further loan disbursement to distressed borrowers that keeps the distressed borrower's account current and performing.

ex ante. Looking forward.

ex poste. After the event.

exchange rate. The price of one currency in terms of another currency.

exercise price. Price at which a call option holder can buy an underlying stock; alternately, the price at which a put option holder can sell an underlying stock. Also called the strike price.

expected returns. Average of all possible return scenarios weighted by their probability of occurrence.

family office. Private offices set up by promoter families to manage their wealth.

fatkas. Indigenous commodity futures.

fiduciary. Agent who manages money or property for someone else with the legal obligation to act in trust for that other person's benefit.

fiduciary standard. Advisory standard under which a financial advisor works for a fixed fee (or some such lump sum), computed either on an annual basis or as a percentage of assets under advice placed with the advisor. *Contrast* **suitability standard**.

First In First Out (FIFO). Inventory valuation technique in which ending inventory is computed from most recent purchases, while the cost of goods sold is computed from oldest purchases, including beginning inventory. *Contrast* **Last In First Out (LIFO)**.

flipping. In the primary market, sale of IPO allotments on listing day.

floating stock. *See* **free float**.

folk devils. Groups seen as threatening to established society norms or community interests.

Foreign Institutional Investors (FIIs). Categorization of the foreign buy side in India's stock market.

forward contract. Any agreement calling for future delivery (or settlement) of an asset at an agreed-on price. *See also* **futures contract**.

free float. The outstanding shares actually available to the public in a market, after taking off promoter group holdings, government holdings, and shares locked-in for other purposes.

front running. The practice of an intermediary buying (or selling) ahead of a client's order, thereby raising the client's impact cost.

fundamental analysis. The use of relative or absolute valuation approaches to arrive at a stock's value; based (typically) on its earning power.

futures contract. Standardized traded contracts that oblige traders to buy or sell an asset at an agreed-on price on a specified future date. *More under* **marking to market**.

G-Secs. Government securities issued by the central bank on behalf of the Union of India to cover its fiscal deficit. The typical tenor is 10 years.

general equilibrium. A situation in which all markets and agents in an economy are simultaneously in equilibrium.

greenshoe options. Provisions that give an underwriter the option to purchase additional shares at the IPO price to cover over-allotment; effectively a short cover of a deliberately oversold IPO.

grey market. IPO kerb markets where unseasoned issues trade before listing. Always informal and subject to manipulation.

Growth at a Reasonable Price (GARP). Hybrid of the growth and value approaches that involves buying stocks with moderately high retrospective earnings and valuation parameters only slightly less than an industry average.

guarantee broker. In comprador capitalism, a local broker or intermediary who found creditworthy small firms and guaranteed to reimburse a larger firm or capital provider for losses it made on its advances to these small firms.

hedging. Taking positions in negatively correlated instruments to reduce the overall risk of a portfolio.

heuristics. Thumb rules and shortcuts used to simplify financial decision-making under uncertainty.

holding period return. A portfolio's return over a period, consisting of the folio's price appreciation, dividends received on the folio, and any cash yield for the time the manager chose to be in cash rather than fully invested in stocks.

honeycomb. The build-up of 'stop loss' sell orders below a stock's present price or below a market level, usually after a long duration up move in severely short constrained markets with a trading orientation.

income statement. Statement of revenue, expenses, gains, and losses for a period that ends in reckoning profits/losses for that period.

index fund. Funds whose corpus exactly replicates the proportions of a market index.

Initial Public Offering (IPO). First issue of shares by a company to the public. *See also* **primary market** and **grey market**.

investment banker. Typically, an underwriter who specializes in primary market operations and selling new issues. Also, an intermediary who performs a range of functions, including broking (both individual and institutional), providing corporate financial advice, and proprietary trading. *See under* **sell side**.

jaati. Occupational sub-caste.

jobber. In the Bombay market, brokers who doubled up as market makers and quoted bid and ask.

katni market. Kerb market, typically located on the streets outside an exchange.

Keynesian beauty contest. Beauty contest, where rather than contestants, it is the judges who compete for a prize, with a prize going to the judge whose opinion most closely matches the winning opinion of the panel as a whole. Used as an analogy for stock picking.

khabar. Market news about a stock; usually difficult to distinguish from rumour mongering or hearsay.

khangi bhao. Kerb trading quotations. Also known as *band ke bhao*.

khiladi. A player, usually of a speculative orientation.

Last In First Out (LIFO). Inventory valuation technique in which ending inventory is computed from oldest purchases, while cost of goods sold is computed from most recently acquired purchases. *Contrast* **First In First Out (FIFO)**.

Law of One Price (LOOP). For financial assets, the idea that the same security must trade at the same price in various markets, provided arbitrage is costless and risk-free. *See also* **arbitrage**.

leading indicator. An indicator whose peaks and troughs tend to occur earlier than corresponding peaks and troughs of the business cycle.

leverage. Buying in excess of the capital on hand. Done either by using the capital at hand as margin to fund a much larger position or by borrowing to buy stock.

limited liability. The idea that stockholders have no liability to the creditors of a firm in the event of an insolvency.

liquidation values. Value that arises when a company is liquidated and has its assets (excluding intangibles) sold and used to pay off debt; realization happens when the residual liquidation value is distributed to shareholders via liquidation dividends.

liquidity. The speed and ease at which an asset can be converted into cash.

loans against shares. Common form of leverage involving pledging fully owned shares and obtaining credit against them, which is then typically used to buy more shares. Similar in effect to a cash margining system.

managing agent. Agent, usually self-appointed, who would manage affairs of a joint-stock company under a management contract. Company operations and financing were arranged by the agent in exchange for a fee, and the arrangement allowed for control with negligible shareholdings. The managing agency system was abolished in the late 1960s.

managing the environment. Euphemism for a broad swath of activity – usually involving some type of rent-seeking – that takes place when the Indian state interacts with business. *See also* **strong-arm promoter**.

mandi. Indigenous put options. Also jargon for a market in a bear phase. Another word for a market, usually large and rural. *Contrast* **teji**.

margin call. Call from a broker to a trader to replenish account equity with cash or securities when a trader's margin falls to (or below) a maintenance margin. *See also* **margin trading**.

margin trading. Purchase by investor after borrowing part of the stock's purchase price from a broker. The percentage margin is typically the value of the account's net worth (or equity) to the value of the securities in it. *See also* **margin call**.

market breadth. The percentage of a listed stock universe that takes part in a market up (or down) move.

market capitalization. The market price times a company's outstanding shares.

market cycle. Periodic market highs and lows, usually seen through expansion and contraction of the market's multiple of price to earnings. *Contrast* **business cycle**.

marking to market. Daily estimation and settlement of obligations in a futures position.

mean reversion. The tendency of a time series value to revert or move back towards its average (or mean) value.

mean-variance optimization. Portfolio optimization technique that seeks to minimize risk (variance) subject to a return constraint or vice versa.

micro-prudential norms. Firm-level rules, typically on capital adequacy, margining, leverage, and liquidity, that are put in place to ensure firm solvency and customer protection.

microstructure. The study of processes and outcomes involved in exchanging financial assets under a specific set of rules. Microstructure deals with how specific trading rules affect the price formation process.

moat. Something a company benefits from, or does very well at, which throws a protective barrier (or moat) around the company and allows it to earn economic rents above the opportunity cost of resources.

Modern Portfolio Theory (MPT). Theoretical core of modern buy side finance that combines interrelated intuitions on efficient markets, diversification, and the risk–return trade-off, while developing models for the pricing of financial assets in equilibrium.

moral panic. Defined by Stanley Cohen as the process of arousing social concern over an issue – usually the work of moral entrepreneurs and mass media.

moving average (200 day). Indicates the average closing price over the previous 200 trading sessions. Regarded as an important technical indicator in the market.

multi-bagger. A stock that goes up many times.

Municipal Era. Period that lasted till the mid-90s, during which every major municipality had its own exchange with a monopoly on transactions within that area. Sections 13 and 19 of the 1956 Securities Contracts (Regulation) Act (SCRA) further established the municipal monopolies that provided much of the *raison d'être* for regional exchanges.

mushroom companies. Companies that approached the primary market, realized the subscription, and then disappeared. Also known as vanishing companies.

mutual fund. Investment vehicle that pools the public's savings and invests it through professional fund management.

naïve diversification. Inefficient diversification, i.e., done without looking for risk-return trade-offs or the highest expected return for any defined level of portfolio risk.

naya daur. New era.

nazrana. Option premia on teji and mandi contracts.

net current asset (NCA) rule. Benjamin Graham's rule of buying a stock at two-thirds or less of its net current assets value, i.e., taking current assets, deducting all liabilities (short and long term) in full, while ignoring all fixed assets and claims ahead of the common (like preferred stock).

noise. Fisher Black's idea that a large number of small events matter more than a small number of large events.

noise investing. The long pull trade of speculative investment. *See also* **speculative investment**.

non-diversifiable risk. Risk common to an economy or a market that cannot be diversified away. Also called systematic risk. *Contrast* **diversifiable risk**.

novation. Clearing house assumption of counterparty risk on itself by becoming the legal counterparty to all trades, in effect interposing itself between all parties; feature of derivatives clearing houses that was adapted by the NSE to the stock market.

open interest. The aggregate number of derivatives contracts outstanding for a stock (or for a market) during a settlement period.

open offer. Offer made by an acquiring company to the shareholders of a target company, inviting them to sell their shares at a particular price to the acquirer. Done to provide an exit option to the target company's shareholders when there is a change in control or substantial acquisition of shares.

operator. Participant who actively uses their ability to move price while buying and selling stocks.

order-driven market. Market, usually screen-based, where orders are collected in a single electronic limit order book and then matched using a price/time priority rule. *See also* **quote-driven market**.

over-the-counter (OTC) market. Network (often phone-based) of dealers and traders who negotiate securities purchase and sale with one another. Also called a dealer-driven market. Usually quote-driven and distinct from an auction market.

passive management. The construction of a portfolio that replicates a market index and its performance. Typically done by holding the same stocks that make up a market index and in the same proportions. *See also* **active management**.

path dependency. The idea that the present state of a system or process depends on the historical sequence of prior processes (together with the actions of involved actors) that led to the present state.

peak. That point in a business cycle where economic activity stops rising and starts falling. *Contrast* **trough**.

penny stock. Conventionally, any stock that trades in single digits. A very low-priced stock.

perpetuity. An instrument that yields a perpetual stream of cash flows, such as British government consols.

political business cycle. Ruling party's use of expansionary aggregate demand policy to stimulate the economy in election season.

portfolio management scheme (PMS). Discretionary or non-discretionary investment scheme with fewer compliance restrictions that invests larger amounts on behalf of a wealthy clientele.

preferred stock. Stock (usually without voting privileges) whose holders are offered fixed dividends that are prioritized over common stockholders.

price-earnings ratio. The ratio of a stock's current market price to its earnings (or profits) per share; a heuristic that values stocks based on a relative valuation approach. *See also* **relative valuation approach**.

price-earnings to growth ratio (PEG). The ratio of a ratio (a stock's price-earnings ratio) to a rate (its earnings growth rate expressed as an absolute number).

primary market. The market for initial public offerings where new and unseasoned issues are offered to the public for the first time.

principal–agent problem. How a principal (say a customer) can get an agent (say a broker) to act in the principal/customer's interest rather than only in the agent/broker's interest. In India, the term 'conflict of interest' is often used to refer to the problem. *More under* **agency issues**.

priors. Bayesian prior probabilities that express belief systems before further empirical evidence is taken into account.

promoter. Entrepreneur or family who is predominantly associated with a business venture, usually as its largest shareholder.

prudent man rule. Rule directing fiduciaries 'to observe how men of prudence, discretion and intelligence manage their own affairs, not in regard to speculation, but in regard to the permanent disposition of their funds, considering the probable income, as well as the probable safety of the capital to be invested.'

pump and dump. Stock manipulation that involves accumulating a stock, making exaggerated claims about the company behind it, and then distributing the stock at a higher price.

put–call parity theorem. A theorem positing the correct relationship between puts and calls.

pyramiding. Futures trading technique that uses accumulated profits on existing positions as capital to fund new positions.

quadruple witching. The simultaneous expiry of all four classes of derivative instruments – futures and options on indexes, together with futures and options on stocks. Occurs during the final trading hour on the last Thursday of every month.

quantitative easing. Unconventional monetary policy involving central bank asset purchases when interest rates are at lower bounds.

quote-driven market. Market in which prices are determined from bid and ask quotations made by market makers, dealers, or specialists. Market makers or dealers fill orders either from their own inventory or by matching them with other orders. *See also* **order-driven market**.

random walk. The idea that stock prices are unpredictable and random. *See also* **efficiency**.

regulatory arbitrage. Tendency of participants to exit or enter security jurisdictions based on regulatory and compliance requirements. Typically, high-compliance jurisdictions that are viewed as high cost are exited, and lower-compliance jurisdictions are entered.

related party transactions. Material transactions typically between a promoter group, its listed (reporting) entity, and a promoter group's various unlisted entities.

relative valuation approach. Deciding on a stock's price relative to another variable such as its underlying earnings, the earnings of comparables, or the earnings of the market. *Contrast* **absolute valuation approach**.

replacement cost. The present market price that will purchase another similar asset that offers the same future benefit or service potential to a firm.

repo. Ready forward deal or repurchase agreement. Sale of government securities (G-Secs) by a borrowing bank with an agreement to repurchase at a slightly higher price on a future date. A reverse repo is a purchase with an agreement to resell at a specified price on a future date. Tenors are typically short term and sometimes even overnight.

resistance. In technical analysis, the level at which a price advance stalls because it faces resistance from supply coming into the market. *Contrast* **support**.

return on capital employed (ROCE). The ratio of a firm's earnings before interest and taxes divided by its total assets net of current liabilities.

return on equity (ROE). The ratio of a firm's profits to its equity book value (share capital plus reserves).

reverse arbitrage. Rare inversion of the usual first leg in arbitrage between the cash and futures markets, executed through simultaneously buying in the futures segment and selling in the cash segment, followed by its reversal a short while later. Results from market conditions and not from special equity transactions or dividend announcements. Unlike commodity backwardation, it usually occurs only during extreme stock market events.

risk. The lack of certainty in an asset's return. In modern portfolio theory, the standard deviation of a stock price over time; also, the extent to which it contributes to a portfolio's risk. *More under* **diversifiable risk, non-diversifiable risk, Modern Portfolio Theory,** and **variance**.

risk-free asset. An asset that has a certain future rate of return and no possibility that it will lose its value. Government securities and treasury instruments are examples of risk-free assets.

robo advising. Standardized advice generated by a computer through an algorithmic process with little human interface.

ryot. Farmer.

sākh. A participant's standing in a market. Now archaic.

satta. Speculation.

scalability. A company's ability to ramp up into a sunrise sector with a clearly addressable market opportunity, which then translates into scalable growth over many years.

scalper. Trader who trades for small amounts.

scuttlebutt. The informal, yet structured, exchange of information about stocks that takes place among professionals.

seasoned stocks. Stocks that presently trade on an exchange. *Contrast* **primary market.**

security selection. Activity that seeks to buy stocks at prices less than what they are believed to be worth. Stock picking.

self-regulatory organization (SRO). Industry or trade body that exercises some degree of regulation over the same industry or trade.

sell side. Institutions such as brokerages who (in the main) sell stocks through primary offerings or who intermediate for other institutions and the trading public. *See under* **investment banker**.

separation theorem. In portfolio theory, the idea that the investment process or investment policy can be separated into two distinct steps: First, the construction of an efficient portfolio, which technically is a mathematical outcome of mean variance optimization that is irrelevant to risk preference; and second, the decision to combine that efficient portfolio with a risk-free asset, such as a bank deposit. *More under* **Modern Portfolio Theory**.

short constraint. Microstructure and legal constraints that make the short side more difficult to take than the long side.

short sale. Borrowing and sale of shares not owned by an investor in expectation of a fall in price. Since the shares are not owned by the investor, they are borrowed through a market lending/borrowing mechanism and sold short, following which they are bought back at a profit if the stock falls in price (short covering) and returned to the lending/borrowing mechanism. This reverses the normal order of purchase followed by sale. A short sale without borrowing is the naked short and was normal practice in the badla system. *See also* **corner** and **squeeze**.

single stock futures (SSFs). Futures on individual stocks; uncommon in most countries but extensively traded in India.

skin in the game. The extent and value of an agent's personal stake in an enterprise. Typically done to get around the principal–agent problem. *More under* **agency issues**.

specialist. Floor intermediary who has both rights and obligations while making a fair and orderly market in pivotal counters.

specified list. The list of stocks on which badla was allowed. Also called the 'A' List or 'contracts for the clearing' or 'cleared securities'. *More under* **badla**.

speculation. Decision-making exclusively on the basis of price action, not dividend receipts or valuation, and using what is known to predict and act on a single future state of nature – the behaviour of price.

speculative investment. Long pull trade, usually between 6 and 18 months in duration. Typically done to exploit fundamental displacement of a sector that takes it to a higher valuation. *See also* **noise investing**.

spot-futures parity theorem. Relationship between a stock's cash price and its futures price. Under the parity relations, futures usually – but not always – will trade at a slight premium to their underlying cash (or spot) price. That premium (basis) is the cost of financing the position that must be borne by its holder; the cash price financed or 'carried' at a risk-free interest rate over the time to expiry (net of dividends) should equal the futures price. Also called the cost of carry relationship.

squeeze. Inability of short sellers to meet their short covering obligations, usually because the stock was cornered and had little floating stock available. This often resulted in the price being bid higher to irrational levels and was a common feature of the badla era. *See also* **short sale** and **corner**.

stag. Participant (usually non-institutional) who buys into IPOs hoping to flip for a profit at listing.

Statutory Liquidity Ratio (SLR). Percentage of a bank's net demand and time liabilities that banks are compelled to invest in government securities to fund the Indian government's fiscal deficits. The ratio has ranged from almost 40 per cent to its present level of just under 20 per cent.

sterilization. Simultaneous central bank intervention in the foreign exchange and bond markets to offset the effects of foreign exchange intervention on the monetary base.

stock dividend. Nonreciprocal issuance by a company of its own stock to shareholders on a pro rata basis, and usually done by reclassifying amounts from earned capital (retained earnings) to contributed capital (common stock). *See also* **bonus share** and **dividend**.

stock exchange. Market where seasoned issues are bought and sold.

stock split. Cosmetic increase in the number of outstanding shares through reductions in face value, without making any material changes in shareholder equity.

'stop loss' order. Popular type of order whereby a sell order is executed if the stock's price falls below a certain level. Other types of orders include limit buy, limit sell, and stop buy orders.

strong-arm promoter. Promoter, usually politically connected and from the infrastructure space, who demonstrates aggressive risk-taking and the capacity to get things done, together with the ability to manage the environment. *See also* **managing the environment**.

suitability standard. Advisory standard under which a financial advisor recommends products based on their suitability to a client and receives commissions from the relevant manufacturer (say a mutual fund) accordingly. *Contrast* **fiduciary standard**.

support. In technical analysis, a level at which a price decline stalls because it faces support from buying coming into the market. *Contrast* **resistance.**

survivorship bias. The tendency of databases or performance studies to skew to the upside as they document only winners (who are survivors), while excluding the losers who are left out of the data collection.

Systematic Investment Plan (SIP). Rupee cost averaging product that involves investing predefined amounts at regular intervals into listed equity.

Talmudic diversification. *See* **naïve diversification**.

technical analysis. The study of past price and volume action – as depicted on a chart – in search of recurrent or predictable patterns that can be clues to future price action; the study of other phenomena that impact a stock's demand supply situation in a market.

teji. Indigenous call options. Also jargon for a market in a bull phase. *Contrast* **mandi**.

tenor. The maturity of a financial instrument.

term structure of interest rates. The structure of interest rates appropriate for discounting cash flows of different maturities.

Tiddlywinks. A perfect stock pick. A company with a strong moat around the business, scalable growth over many years, a small to middling market capitalization, presence in an area playing either to India's international comparative advantage or with exposure to the consumption side of its large domestic market, negligible unorganized sector competition, sound management with integrity, a low to moderate price-earnings ratio, a high return on equity (ROE) or high return on capital employed (ROCE), a low ratio of price/earnings to growth, earnings visibility that reflected in cash flows together with the deployment of those cash flows in successful reinvestment or dividend payout, moderate leverage, no accounting red flags, a high promoter shareholding, a low free float, and little government or regulatory interaction.

time bargain. Unmargined naked forward contract traded through giving and receiving marked-to-market price differences. Early version of the badla trade. *See also* **badla**.

timing. The idea that a market (or a security) goes through bull/bear phases that a portfolio manager can exploit by timing asset allocation or security selection. *More under* **active management**.

Tobin's *q*. The ratio of the market value of a firm's debt and equity to the replacement cost of its assets less liabilities. *More under* **replacement cost**.

total return index. Index that includes price performance and dividends when calculating total returns.

Treasury bills, notes, bonds. Fixed-income instruments of varying tenors issued by a sovereign and therefore seen as free from default risk.

trigger. Market terminology for a displacement that makes a stock or a sector go higher.

trough. That point in a business cycle where economic activity stops falling and starts rising. *Contrast* **peak**.

uptick rule. A price test for short sales that allows traders to short a security only at a price higher than the security's last trade. The idea is to prevent the buildup of catastrophic downside momentum during a single trading session. The SEC's Rule 10a-1(a)(1).

vaastu shastra. Rules of architectural layout and spatial geometry based on ancient Indian knowledge systems.

value at risk (VAR). Statistical measure that quantifies the risk associated with a portfolio. Usually defined as the maximum amount of loss that can be borne over defined time periods and confidence intervals.

variance. Statistical measure of risk that summarizes the dispersion (or variability) of possible stock returns around an average; the expected value of the squared deviations from an average or expected return. Taking its square root arrives at a standard deviation. *More under* **risk** and **Modern Portfolio Theory**.

vehicle currency. Focal currency (and currency of invoicing) around which foreign exchange trading volumes will cluster in a market. In India, the dollar is the vehicle currency and rupee–dollar is the dominant currency pair from which other cross rates are typically computed.

Very Small Aperture Terminal (VSAT). Small-sized earth station used to transmit/receive data over a satellite communication network. Pioneered by the NSE for stock trading.

vigorish. That combination of brokerage, taxes, impact costs, and bid-ask spreads that the market (the house) takes away from a trader on a round-trip transaction. Brokerage and taxes are visible parts of the vigorish, while impact costs and bid-ask spreads are its invisible parts. In the gaming industry, the vigorish (known variously as the juice/take/house edge/vig) is what a bookmaker charges to accept a wager.

Weighted Average Cost of Capital (WACC). What a company is expected to pay on average to the debt and equity capital providers who finance the company's assets; costs of debt and equity are weighted by their proportions in a firm's capital structure.

wire house. Brokerage.

BIBLIOGRAPHY

A

Afsharipour, Afra. 'The Indian Private Equity Model,' NSE Working Paper, WP/8/2013, July 2013.

Agarwal, Gaurav. 'Monetary Policy Announcements and Stock Price Behavior: Empirical Evidence from CNX Nifty.' *Decision*, Vol. 34, No. 2, 2007.

Agarwal, Manish, and Harminder Singh. 'Merger Announcements and Insider Trading Activity in India: An Empirical Investigation.' *Investment Management and Financial Innovations*, Vol. 3, No. 3, 2006.

Aggarwal, Nidhi, and Susan Thomas. 'When Stock Futures Dominate Price Discovery.' *Journal of Futures Markets*, Vol. 39, No. 3, 2019.

Aiyar, Swaminathan S. Anklesaria. 'Despite Modi, India Has Not Yet Become a Hindu Authoritarian State.' *Cato Institute*. 24 November 2020.

Aleem, Abdul. 'Transmission Mechanism of Monetary Policy in India.' *Journal of Asian Economics*, Vol. 21, 2010.

Allen, Franklin, Rajesh Chakrabarti, Sankar De, Jun Qian, and Meijun Qian. 'Law, Institutions and Finance in China and India.' In *Emerging Giants: China and India in the World Economy*. Oxford: Oxford University Press, 2010.

AMFI and Crisil Intelligence, The *Sahi* Journey, AMFI-Crisil Factbook, 2024

Ammer, John, Clara Vega, and Jon Wongswan. 'International Transmission of U.S. Monetary Policy Shocks: Evidence from Stock Prices.' *Journal of Money, Credit and Banking*, Vol. 42, No. 1, September 2010.

Anagol, Santosh, Vijaya Marisetty, Renuka Sane, and Buvaneshwaran Venugopal. 'On the Impact of Regulating Commissions: Evidence from the Indian Mutual Funds Market.' *World Bank Economic Review*, Vol. 31, No. 1, 2017.

Anagol, Santosh, Vimal Balasubramaniam, and Tarun Ramadorai. 'Endowment Effects in the Field: Evidence from India's IPO Lotteries.' *Review of Economic Studies*, Vol. 85, No. 4, October 2018.

Anstey, Vera. *The Economic Development of India*. London: Longmans, Green and Co., 1931.

Aristotle, *Politics*.

Arthur Andersen & Associates. *Blueprint of a National Stock Market System*. Bombay: Arthur Andersen, August 1992.

Arthur Andersen & Associates. *Review of International Experience of National Stock Market Systems*. Bombay: Arthur Andersen, 1992.

Association of Merchant Bankers of India (AMBI). *Infrastructure for the Capital Markets* (Dave Committee). Mumbai: AMBI, 1997.

Association of Mutual Funds of India (AMFI). Website.

Atlay, Sir Wilfrid. *Report of the Bombay Stock Exchange Enquiry Committee*. Bombay: Government Central Press, 1924.

B

Bagehot, Walter. *Lombard Street: A Description of the Money Market*. Wiley Investment Classics. Hoboken, NJ: John Wiley and Sons, Inc., 1999; first published 1873.

Baker, Kent H., and Sujata Kapoor. 'Why Indian Firms Issue Stock Distributions.' *Managerial Finance*, Vol. 41, No. 7, 2015.

Balfour, Ian. *Famous Diamonds*. London: Antique Collectors Club, 2008.

Banaji, Jairus. 'Investor Capitalism and the Reshaping of Business in India.' Working paper series, no. 54, Queen Elizabeth House, Oxford Department of International Development, University of Oxford, September 2000.

Banerjee, Abhijit. 'A Simple Model of Herd Behavior.' *Quarterly Journal of Economics*, Vol. 107, No. 3, August 1992.

Barber, Brad, and Terence Odean. 'Trading Is Hazardous to Your Wealth: The Common Stock Performance of Individual Investors.' *Journal of Finance*, Vol. 55, 2000.

———. 'Boys will be boys: Gender, overconfidence, and common stock investment,' *The Quarterly Journal of Economics*, 2001, 116(1), 261-292.

———. 'All That Glitters: The Effect of Attention and News on the Buying Behavior of Individual and Institutional Investors.' *Review of Financial Studies*, Vol. 21, No. 2, January 2008.

Barberis, Nicholas, and Ming Huang. 'Mental Accounting, Loss Aversion and Individual Stock Returns.' *Journal of Finance*, Vol. 56, No. 4, 2001.

Barberis, Nicholas, and Richard Thaler. 'A Survey of Behavioral Finance.' In *The Handbook of the Economics of Finance*, Vol. 1, Part 2. Edited by George Constantinides, Milton Harris, and René Stulz. Oxford and Amsterdam: Elsevier, North-Holland, 2003.

Barua, Samir, K.V. Raghunathan, and J.R. Varma. 'Research on the Indian Capital Market: A Review.' *Vikalpa*, Vol. 19, No. 1, 1994.

Barua, Samir, and Jayanth R. Varma. 'Securities Scam: Genesis, Mechanics, and Impact.' *Vikalpa*, Vol. 18, No. 1, January–March 1993.

Baruch, Bernard M. *Baruch: My Own Story*. New York: Henry Holt and Company, 1957.

Barzun, Jacques, and Henri F. Graf. *The Modern Researcher*. 4th ed. New York: Harcourt Brace Jovanovich, 1985.

Basham, A.L. *The Wonder That Was India*. New York: The Macmillan Co., 1954.

Basu, Debashis, and Sucheta Dalal. *The Scam: Who Won, Who Lost, Who Got Away*. New Delhi: UBS Publishers' Distributors Ltd., 1993.

———. *The Scam: From Harshad Mehta to Ketan Parekh*. Mumbai: KenSource Information Services, 2007.

Batra, Amita. 'The Dynamics of Foreign Portfolio Inflows and Equity Returns in India.' Working paper no. 109, Indian Council for Research on International Economic Relations, New Delhi, September 2003.

Bayly, C.A. *Rulers, Townsmen and Bazaars: North Indian Society in the Age of British Expansion: 1770–1870*. Cambridge: Cambridge University Press, 1988.

BBC News.

Beckert, Sven. 'Emancipation and Empire: Reconstructing the Worldwide Web of Cotton Production in the Age of the American Civil War.' *American Historical Review*, Vol. 109, No. 5, December 2004.

Bengal Hurkaru (and Chronicle). 1 January 1805. 28 October 1829. 19 November 1834.

Berkshire Hathaway. *Annual Report*. 2008.

Berle, Adolf, and Gardiner Means. *The Modern Corporation and Private Property*. New Brunswick and London: Transaction Publishers, 1991; first published 1932.

Beshears, Josh, James J. Choi, David Laibson, and Brigette C. Madrian. 'Behavioral Household Finance.' In *The Handbook of Behavioral Economics: Foundations and Applications Volume 1*. Edited by B. Douglas Bernheim, Stefano Dellavigna, and David Laibson. Oxford and Amsterdam: Elsevier, North-Holland, 2018.

Bhabha, Cooverji Hormusji (C.H.). *Report of the Company Law Committee, 1952*. New Delhi: Government of India Press, 1952.

Bhatt, R.S. 'Revival of the Capital Market.' In *35th Meeting of the Standing Committee of the Presidents of the Stock Exchanges in India*. Bombay: BSE, 1988.

Bhattacharya, Rudrani, Ila Patnaik, and Ajay Shah. 'Monetary Policy Transmission in an Emerging Market Setting.' *IMF Working Paper* No. 11/5, 2011.

Bhole, L.M. 'The Indian Capital Market at a Crossroads.' *Vikalpa*, Vol. 20, No. 2, April–June 1995.

Bikhchandani, Sushil, David Hirshleifer, and Ivo Welch. 'A Theory of Fads, Fashion, Custom, and Cultural Change as Informational Cascades.' *Journal of Political Economy*, October 1992.

Birdwood, Sir George C.M. 'Sett Premchund Roychund.' In *Sva*. London: Oxford University Press, 1915.

Birla, Ritu. 'Speculation Illicit and Complicit: Contract, Uncertainty, and Governmentality.' *Comparative Studies of South Asia, Africa and the Middle East*, Vol. 35, No. 3, December 2015.

———. *Stages of Capital: Law, Culture, and Market Governance in Late Colonial India*. Durham, NC: Duke University Press, 2009.

Black, Fischer. 'Noise.' In *Market Efficiency: Stock Market Behaviour in Theory and Practice Volume I*. Edited by Andrew W. Lo. Lyme, NH: Edward Elgar Publishing, Inc., 1997.

Bloomberg.

BloombergQuint.

Bodie, Zvi, Alex Kane, and Alan J. Marcus. *Investments*. 3rd ed. Chicago: Richard D. Irwin, 1996.

Bogle, John C. 'The Economic Role of the Investment Company.' Thesis, Princeton University, 1950.

Bombay Congress Bulletin, 24 June 1930.

Bombay Courier. 18 April 1835.

Bombay Stock Exchange (BSE). *Draft Rules of the Native Share and Stock Brokers' Association*. Bombay: BSE, 1937.

———. 'K.R.P. Shroff: Patriarch of the Stock Exchange and the Father of the Stock Market in India.' Bombay: BSE, 1966.

———. *Profile of Stock Exchange Activity in India*. Bombay: BSE, 1970.

———. Governing Board. *Minutes*. 28 June 1971. Available at https://www.sebi.gov.in/History/BSE_1971-80.pdf.

———. 'How the Stock Market Functions.' (n.p., n.d.). Bombay: BSE, Undated.

———. *The Stock Market Today*. 1987 to 1993. Bombay: The Stock Exchange Foundation, 1987–1993.

———. *The Stock Exchange Review*. 1989 to 2001. Bombay: BSE, 1989–2001.

———. *Settlement, Share Depository, and Trading Systems*. Bombay: BSE, 1991.

———. *National Stock Market System*. Bombay: BSE, 1992.

———. *One Day Training Programme on the Carry Forward System (Badla)*. Mumbai: BSE, 1999.

———. *Inspection Manual: Revised Edition*. Mumbai: BSE, 2000.

———. Website.

Le Bon, Gustave. *The Crowd: A Study of the Popular Mind*. Mumbai: Sterling Book House, 2002.

Boorstin, Daniel J. *The Discoverers: A History of Man's Search to Know His World and Himself*. New York: Random House, 1983.

Bose, Suchismita. 'Securities Market Regulations: Lessons from US and Indian Experience.' *ICRA Bulletin: Money & Finance*, Vol. 2, Nos. 20–21, 2005.

Brinson, Gary P., L. Randolph Hood, and Gilbert L. Beebower. 'Determinants of Portfolio Performance.' *Financial Analysts Journal*. July–August 1986.

Bubna, Amit, and Nagpurnanand R. Prabhala. 'IPOs with and without Allocation Discretion: Empirical Evidence.' *Journal of Financial Intermediation*, Vol. 20, No. 4, Elsevier, October 2011.

Buchanan, James M., Robert D. Tollison, and Gordon Tullock. (eds.) *Toward a Theory of the Rent-seeking Society*. College Station, TX: Texas A&M University Press, 1980.

Buffett, Warren. 'The Superinvestors of Graham-and-Doddsville.' In Benjamin Graham. *The Intelligent Investor*. New York: HarperCollins, Revised Edition 2006; first published 1973.

Buiter, Willem H. 'James Tobin: An Appreciation of His Contribution to Economics.' Working paper no. 9753. National Bureau of Economic Research, Cambridge, MA, June 2003.

Business Standard.

Business Today.

C

Cafemutual.com. Website.

Cakici, Nusret, Frank J. Fabozzi, and Sinan Tan. 'Size, Value, and Momentum in Emerging Market Stock Returns.' *Emerging Markets Review*, Vol. 16, 2013.

The Calcutta Monthly Journal. Asiatic News. Vol. XXVI, January 1837.

Calhoun, Ricky-Dale. 'Seeds of Destruction: The Globalization of Cotton as a Result of the American Civil War.' Ph.D. diss., Kansas State University, Manhattan, Kansas, 2012.

Campbell, John Y., Tarun Ramadorai, and Benjamin Ranish. 'Getting Better or Feeling Better? How Equity Investors Respond to Investment Experience.' Working paper no. 20000, National Bureau of Economic Research, Cambridge, MA, March 2014.

———. 'Do the Rich Get Richer in the Stock Market? Evidence from India.' Working paper no. 24898, National Bureau of Economic Research, Cambridge, MA, August 2018.

Capitalideasonline.com. Website.

Capital Market.

Carhart, M.M., J.N. Carpenter, A.W. Lynch and D.K. Musto. 'Mutual Fund Survivorship.' *Review of Financial Studies*, Vol. 15, No. 5, 2002.

Carret, Philip. *The Art of Speculation.* Wiley Investment Classics. Hoboken, NJ: John Wiley and Sons, Inc., 1997; first published 1930.

CFA Institute. 'Earning Investors' Trust.' *Fourth Investor Trust Survey 2020.* Charlottesville, VA: CFA Institute, 2020.

Chakrabarti, Rajesh. 'IPOs in a Major Emerging Market Economy: India.' In *The Oxford Handbook of IPOs.* Edited by Douglas Cumming and Sofia Johan. New York: Oxford University Press, 2019.

Chakrabarti, Rajesh, and Sankar De. 'Introduction.' In *Capital Markets in India.* Edited by Rajesh Chakrabarti and Sankar De. New Delhi: Sage Publications, 2010.

Chancellor, Edward. *Devil Take the Hindmost: A History of Financial Speculation.* New York, NY: Plume, 2000.

Chang, Eui Jung, Eduardo José Araújo Lima, and Benjamin Miranda Tabak. 'Testing for Predictability in Emerging Equity Markets.' *Emerging Markets Review*, Vol. 5, No. 3, 2004.

Chang, James J., Tarun Khanna, and Krishna Palepu. 'Analyst Activity around the World.' Working paper no. 01–61, Strategy Working Paper Series, Harvard Business School, Cambridge, MA, January 2000.

Chatterji, Angana P., Thomas Blom Hansen, and Christophe Jaffrelot (eds.), *Majoritarian State: How Hindu Nationalism is Changing India.* New York, NY: Oxford University Press, 2019.

Chidambaram, P. Remarks at the 20th Anniversary Celebrations of the National Stock Exchange of India. Mumbai. 14 December 2013.

Chitale, Rajendra P. 'Use of Derivatives by India's Institutional Investors: Issues and Impediments.' In *Derivatives Markets in India.* Edited by Susan Thomas. New Delhi: Tata McGraw-Hill, 2003.

Choksey, K.R. Interview by author. Mumbai, 2018.

Chong, Terence Tai-Leung, Sam Ho-Sum Cheng, Elfreda Nga-Yee Wong. 'A Comparison of Stock Market Efficiency of the BRIC Countries.' *Technology and Investment*, Vol. 1, 2010.

Christiano, Lawrence J., Martin Eichenbaum, and Charles Evans. 'The Effects of Monetary Policy Shocks: Evidence from the Flow of Funds.' *Review of Economics and Statistics*, Vol. 78, 1996.

Civil Supplies, Ministry of. *Report of the Committee on Forward Markets*. New Delhi: Ministry of Civil Supplies, 1994.

Clarke, Jonathan, Arif Khurshed, Alok Pande, and Ajai K Singh. 'Sentiment Traders & IPO Initial Returns: The Indian Evidence.' *Journal of Corporate Finance*, 37(C), 2016.

Clarke, Roger G., and Meir Statman. 'The DJIA Crossed 652, 230.' *Journal of Portfolio Management*, Vol. 26, No. 2, Winter 2000.

Cohen, Stanley. *Folk Devils and Moral Panics: The Creation of the Mods and Rockers*. 3rd ed. London: Routledge, Taylor and Francis, 2002; first published 1972.

Computer Maintenance Corporation (CMC). *Technical Project Report, Online Trading and Trade Support System: Executive Summary*. Bombay: CMC, 1991.

Copeland, Thomas E., and David Mayers. 'The Value Line Enigma (1965–1978): A Case Study of Performance Evaluation Issues.' *Journal of Financial Economics*, Vol. 10, No. 3, November 1982.

Crawford, Arthur Travers. 'Silver Times in Bombay.' *Federal Observer*. Stock Exchange Special Number 1, Nos 42 and 43, 30 March 1941.

Crisil.

Crowell, Maddy. 'The Messengers: One Small Magazine's Fight for the Indian Mind.' *Virginia Quarterly Review*, Vol. 96, No. 4, Winter 2020.

Cutler, David M., James M. Poterba, and Lawrence H. Summers. 'What Moves Stock Prices?' *Journal of Portfolio Management*, Vol. 15, No. 3, Spring 1989.

D

Dalal Street.

Dalal Times.

Dalal, Sucheta, and Debashis Basu. *Absolute Power*. Mumbai: KenSource Books, 2021.

Dalrymple, William. 'India: The War over History.' *New York Review of Books*, Vol. 52, No. 6, 7 April 2005.

Damani, M.G. 'Revival of Capital Market.' In Bombay Stock Exchange (BSE). *The Stock Exchange Review: July 1998*. Bombay: BSE, 1989.

———. 'Comments on the Report of the Committee on Derivatives.' 2 December 1997. In *Report of the Committee on Derivatives* (L.C. Gupta Report of 1998). Mumbai: SEBI, March 1998.

Damodaran, Ashwath. *Investment Fables*. New York: FT Prentice Hall, 2004.

Das, Gurcharan. 'Introduction.' In Thomas A. Timberg. *The Marwaris: From Jagat Seth to the Birlas*. New Delhi: Penguin Books, 2014.

Dasgupta, Swapan. 'Preface.' In *Awakening Bharat Mata: The Political Beliefs of the Indian Right*. Edited by Swapan Dasgupta. New Delhi: Penguin Random House, 2019.

De, Sankar, Naveen R. Gondhi, and Bhimasankaram Pochiraju. 'Does Sign Matter More Than Size? An Investigation into the Source of Investor Overconfidence.' Working paper, Indian School of Business, Hyderabad, 2010.

De, Sankar, Naveen R. Gondhi, and Subrata Sarkar. 'Behavioral Biases, Investor Performance, and Wealth Transfers between Investor Groups.' Working paper, Indian School of Business, Hyderabad, 2012.

Deb, Soumya Guha, Ashok Banerjee, and B.B. Chakrabarti. 'Persistence in Performance of Indian Equity Mutual Funds: An Empirical Investigation.' *IIMB Management Review*, Vol. 20, No. 2, 2008.

De Bondt, W.F.M., and Richard Thaler. 'Does the Stock Market Overreact?' *Journal of Finance*, Vol. 40, No. 3, 1985.

DeMiguel, Victor, Lorenzo Garlappi, and Raman Uppal. 'Optimal versus Naive Diversification: How Inefficient Is the 1/N Portfolio Strategy?' *Review of Financial Studies*, Vol. 22, No. 5, 2007.

Desai, Bhulabhai J. 'Minority Report.' In Sir Wilfrid Atlay. *Report of the Bombay Stock Exchange Enquiry Committee*. Bombay: Government Central Press, 1924.

Dhar, Joyjit and Kumarjit Mandal. 'Market Timing Abilities of Indian Mutual Fund Managers: An Empirical Analysis.' *Decision*, Vol. 41, No. 3, 2014.

A Dictionary of Sociology. 4th ed. Edited by John Scott. New York: Oxford University Press, 2014.

Dimson, Elroy, and Massoud Mussavian. 'A Brief History of Market Efficiency.' In *European Financial Management*, Vol. 4, No. 1, March 1998.

DNA India.

Douglas J.P., James. *Glimpses of Old Bombay and Western India-With Other Papers*. London: Sampson Low, Marston and Company, 1900.

Dremen, David. *Contrarian Investment Strategies: The Next Generation*. New York: Simon and Schuster, 1998.

Dwivedi, Sharada. *Premchand Roychand: His Life and Times*. Mumbai: Eminence Designs Pvt. Ltd, 2006.

E

Echeverri-Gent, John. 'Political Economy of India's Fiscal and Financial Reform.' Working paper no. 105. Stanford University, Center for International Development, Palo Alto, CA, August 2001.

———. 'Why Do Some Financial Markets Develop and Others Do Not? Politics of India's Capital Market Reform.' Paper presented at The Workshop on States, Development, and Global Governance. University of Wisconsin Law School. Madison, WI, March 2010.

———. 'Politics of Market Micro-Structure: Towards a New Political Economy of India's Equity Market Reform.' In *India's Economic Transition: The Politics of Reforms*. Edited by Rahul Mukherji. New Delhi: Oxford University Press, 2011.

Economic and Political Weekly.

The Economic Times.

Ehrmann, Michael, and Marcel Fratzscher. 'Taking Stock: Monetary Policy Transmission to Equity Markets.' *Journal of Money, Credit and Banking*, Vol. 36, No. 4, August 2004.

Elliott, Jennifer E. 'Demutualization of Securities Exchanges: A Regulatory Perspective.' *IMF Working Paper*, WP/02/119, July 2002.

Equityfriend.com. Website.

Equitymaster.com. Website.

F

Fama, Eugene F. 'The Behavior of Stock-Market Prices.' *Journal of Business*, Vol. 38, No. 1, January 1965.

———. 'Efficient Capital Markets: A Review of Theory and Empirical Work.' *Journal of Finance*, May 1970.

———. 'Efficient Capital Markets II.' *Journal of Finance*, December 1991.

———. 'Market Efficiency, Long-term Returns, and Behavioral Finance.' *Journal of Financial Economics*, Vol. 49, 1998.

Fama, Eugene F., and Kenneth R. French. 'The Cross Section of Expected Stock Returns.' *Journal of Finance*, Vol. 47, 1992.

Fama, Eugene F., and Michael C. Jensen. 'Separation of Ownership and Control.' *Journal of Law and Economics*, Vol. 26, 1983.

Fang, Lily, and Joel Peress. 'Media Coverage and the Cross Section of Stock Returns.' *Journal of Finance*, Vol. 64, No. 5, September 2009.

Federal Observer. Stock Exchange Special Number 1, Nos. 36 and 37, 10 November 1940; Special Number 1, Nos. 42 and 43, 30 March 1941.

Finance, Ministry of. Department of Economic Affairs. *Report of the High Powered Committee on Stock Exchange Reforms* (G.S. Patel Committee). New Delhi: Controller of Publications, 1985.

———. Stock Exchange Division. Circular F14 (2)/SE/85, 23 September 1985.

———. Stock Exchange Division. Press Note 14/3/SE/86 Apt, 1986.

———. *Report of the High Powered Study Group on Establishment of New Stock Exchanges* (Pherwani Committee). New Delhi: Ministry of Finance, June 1991.

———. *Report of the Study Group to Examine the Issue and Problems Relating to Unregulated Share Trading Counters and Other Dealers in Securities* (Convenor: Ajit Day). New Delhi: Ministry of Finance, 1991.

———. *Economic Survey 2005–2006, 2009–2010, 2010–2011*. New Delhi: Ministry of Finance, 2006, 2010, 2011.

———. *Financial Well-Being: Report of the Committee on Investor Awareness and Protection* (D. Swarup Committee). New Delhi: Ministry of Finance, 2009.

Financial Times.

Finapolis.

Fisher, Irving. *The Rate of Interest*. New York: The Macmillan Company, 1907.

Fisher, Philip A. *Common Stocks and Uncommon Profits.* New Jersey: John Wiley and Sons, 1996.

Forbes.

Ford Foundation. *Annual Report 1966*. From The Ford Foundation website.

Friedman, Milton. 'The Case for Flexible Exchange Rates.' In *Essays in Positive Economics*. Chicago: University of Chicago Press, 1953.

———. 'The Role of Monetary Policy.' *American Economic Review*, Vol. 58, No. 1, 1968.

G

Gadgil, D.R. *The Industrial Evolution of India in Recent Times*. 3rd ed. London: Oxford University Press, 1933; first published 1924.

Galbraith, John Kenneth. *The Great Crash 1929*. Boston and New York: Houghton Mifflin, 1997; first published 1954.

Garg, Ashish Kumar, and Pankaj Varshney. 'Momentum Effect in Indian Stock Market: A Sectoral Study.' *Global Business Review*, Vol. 16, No. 3, 2015.

Gertler, Mark, and Simon Gilchrist. 'Monetary Policy, Business Cycles, and the Behavior of Small Manufacturing Firms.' *Quarterly Journal of Economics*, Vol. 109, 1994.

Ghatak, Aditi Roy. *Down Lyons Range*. Kolkata: P.K. Ray for the Calcutta Stock Exchange Association, 2008.

Ghosh, Pulak, Jayant R. Kale, and Venkatesh Panchapagesan. 'Do Indian Business Group Owned Mutual Funds Maximize Value for Their Investors?' National Stock Exchange. NSE–NYU Stern School of Business. Initiative for the Study of Indian Capital Markets. January 2014.

Goetzmann, William N. *Money Changes Everything: How Finance Made Civilization Possible*. Princeton, NJ: Princeton University Press, 2016.

Gorwala, Astad Dinshaw (A.D.). *Report of the Committee on Proposed Legislation for the Regulation of Stock Exchanges and Contracts in Securities*. New Delhi: Government of India Press, 1951.

Goswami, Chandana. 'How Does Internet Stock Trading in India Work?' *Vikalpa*, Vol. 28, No. 1, January–March 2003.

Goswami, Omkar. *Goras and Desis: Managing Agencies and the Making of Corporate India*. New Delhi: Penguin Random House, 2016.

Graham, Benjamin. *The Intelligent Investor*. New York: HarperCollins, Revised Edition 2006; first published 1973.

Graham, Benjamin, and David Dodd. *Security Analysis*. 6th ed. New Delhi: Tata McGraw Hill; first published 1934.

Grant, Alfred. *The American Civil War and the British Press*. Jefferson, NC: McFarland and Co. Inc., 2000.

Griffin, John M., Patrick J. Kelly, and Federico Nardari. 'Do Market Efficiency Measures Yield Correct Inferences? A Comparison of Developed and Emerging Markets.' *Review of Financial Studies*, Vol. 23, No. 8, 2010.

Grossman, Sanford J., and Joseph E. Stiglitz. 'On the Impossibility of Informationally Efficient Markets.' *American Economic Review*, Vol. 70, No. 3, 1980.

Grubb, W. Dennis. 'Foreword.' In *The Future of India's Stock Markets*. Edited by Tushar Waghmare. New Delhi: Tata McGraw-Hill, 1998.

Gunasekarage, Abeyratna, and David Power. 'The Profitability of Moving Average Trading Rules in South Asian Stock Markets.' *Emerging Markets Review*, Vol. 2, No. 1, March 2001.

Gupta, Ashish, Kush Shah, and Prashant Kumar. 'House of Debt.' Credit Suisse. Asia Pacific/India Equity Research. 21 October 2015.

Gupta, Ila Bharat. Interview by author. Mumbai, August 2021.

Gupta, L.C. *Expert Study of Trading in Shares in Stock Exchanges*. Volumes 1 and 2. New Delhi: The Society for Capital Market Research and Development, 1991.

———. *Indian Shareowners: A Survey*. New Delhi: Society for Capital Market Research and Development, 1991.

———. *Stock Exchange Trading in India: Agenda for Reform*. New Delhi: Society for Capital Market Research and Development, 1992.

———, (ed.). *India's Financial Markets and Institutions*. New Delhi: Society for Capital Market Research and Development, 1999.

Gupta, L.C., Naveen Jain, and Yash Kulshreshtha. *Shareholders' Geographic Distribution, City-wise, Urban-rural, and State-wise*. New Delhi: Society for Capital Market Research and Development, 1994.

Gupta L.C., P.K. Jain, and C.P. Gupta. *Indian Stock Market PE Ratios*. New Delhi: Society for Capital Market Research and Development, 1998.

Gupta, Ramesh. 'Derivatives Committee Report: Four Queries.' In *The Stock Exchange Review: June 1998*. Mumbai: BSE, 1998.

H

Hagstrom, Robert G. *Investing: The Last Liberal Art*. 2nd ed. New York: Columbia University Press, 2013; first published 2000.

Hardgrove, Anne. 'Marwaris and Moral Economies: From Rain to Ghee.' In *Community and Public Culture: The Marwaris in Calcutta, c. 1897–1997*. New York: Columbia University Press, 2004.

'Harjivandas Nemidas Securities Private Limited.' In *Yugvandna*. Stock Exchange Edition: 125 Years of the BSE, February 2003.

Harris, F.R. *Jamsetji Nusserwanji Tata: A Chronicle of his Life*. London: Oxford University Press, 1925.

Harris, Larry. *Trading and Exchanges: Market Microstructure for Practitioners*. New York: Oxford University Press, 2003.

HDFC Asset Management Company Ltd. Draft Red Herring Prospectus.

Herdeck, Margaret, and Gita Piramal. *India's Industrialists*. Boulder: Lynne Reiner Publishers, 1985.

Hession, Charles Henry. *John Maynard Keynes: A Personal Biography of the Man Who Revolutionized Capitalism and the Way We Live*. New York: Macmillan, 1984.

Himal Southasian.

The Hindu.

The Hindu BusinessLine.

Hiremath, Gourishankar S., and B. Kamaiah. 'Variance Ratios, Structural Breaks and Non-Random Walk Behaviour in the Indian Stock Returns.' *Journal of Business & Economic Studies*, Vol. 18, No. 2, Fall 2012.

Hofstadter, Richard. *The Progressive Historians: Turner, Beard, Parrington*. New York: Knopf, 1968.

I

ICFAI Centre for Management Research. 'The US 64 Controversy' and 'Derivatives Trading in India.' In *Case Studies in Finance, Volume II*. Hyderabad: ICFAI Centre for Management Research, 2004.

ICICI Securities Ltd. Draft Red Herring Prospectus. Filed December 15, 2017.

ICICI Securities. Website.

ICRA Research Services. 'Indian Brokerage Industry.' Mumbai: ICRA, September 2017.

ICRA Press Releases.

Ignatius, Roger. 'The Bombay Stock Exchange: Seasonality and Investment Opportunities.' Discussion Paper 29. Bond University School of Business *Discussion Papers*, 1992.

India Today.

Indian Express.

Indian Law Reports. Bombay Series.

Infosys. *Annual Reports*.

Investing.com. Website.

Investment Company Institute (ICI). *2018 Investment Company Fact Book: A Review of Trends and Activities in the Investment Company Industry*. Washington DC: ICI, 2018.

Investor's India.

J

Jaffrelot, Christophe. *Modi's India: Hindu Nationalism and the Rise of Ethnic Democracy*. Princeton, NJ: Princeton University Press, 2021.

Jain, Pawan, and Mark A. Sunderman. 'Stock Price Movement Around Merger Announcements: Insider Trading or Market Anticipation?' *Managerial Finance*, Vol. 40, No. 8, 2014.

Jain, Prashant. Interview. 'Prashant Jain on His Stock Picking Strategy [Video]'. *NDTV*. 2016.

Janis, Irving. 'Groupthink.' *Psychology Today*, Vol. 5, No. 3, November 1971.

Jameson, Melvin, Andrew Prevost, and John Puthenpurackal. 'Controlling Shareholders, Board Structure, and Firm Performance: Evidence from India.' *Journal of Corporate Finance*, Vol. 27, 2014.

Jeejeebhoy, Phiroze J. *A Blueprint of Economic Democracy: A People's Stock Market and People's Joint Stock Enterprise.* Bombay: Bombay Stock Exchange, 1979.

Jegadeesh, Narasimhan, and Sheridan Titman. 'Returns to Buying Winners and Selling Losers: Implications for Stock Market Efficiency.' *Journal of Finance*, Vol. 48, 1993.

Jensen, Michael C. 'The Performance of Mutual Funds in the Period 1945–1964.' *Journal of Finance*, Vol. 23, 1968.

Jensen, Michael C., and William H. Meckling. 'Theory of the Firm: Managerial Behavior, Agency Costs, and Ownership Structure.' *Journal of Financial Economics*, Vol. 3, 1976.

Jobst, Andreas A. 'The Development of Equity Derivative Markets.' *International Journal of Emerging Markets*, Vol. 3, No. 2, 2008.

Jogani, Ashok and Kshama Fernandes. 'Arbitrage in India: Past, Present and Future.' In *Derivatives Markets in India.* Edited by Susan Thomas. New Delhi: Tata McGraw-Hill, 2003.

K

Kahneman, Daniel. *Thinking, Fast and Slow.* London: Penguin, Allen Lane, 2011.

Kahneman, Daniel, and Amos Tversky. 'Judgment under Uncertainty: Heuristics and Biases.' *Science*, New Series, Vol. 185, No. 4157, September 1974.

———. 'Prospect Theory: An Analysis of Decision under Risk.' *Econometrica*, Vol. 47, No. 2, March 1979.

———. 'Extensional Versus Intuitive Reasoning: The Conjunction Fallacy in Probability Judgment.' *Psychological Review*, Vol. 90, No. 4, 1983.

———. 'Choices, Values, and Frames.' *American Psychologist*, Vol. 39, No. 4, 1984.

Kahneman, Daniel, and Shane Frederick. 'A Model of Heuristic Judgment.' In *The Cambridge Handbook of Thinking and Reasoning.* Edited by Keith J. Holyoak and Robert G. Morrison. New York: Cambridge University Press, 2005.

Kale, Jayant R., and Venkatesh Panchapagesan. 'The Indian Mutual Fund Industry: Opportunities and Challenges.' *IIMB Management Review*, Vol. 24, No. 4, 2012.

Kamiyama, Tetsuya. 'India's Mutual Fund Industry.' *Nomura Capital Market Review*, Vol. 10, No. 4, Winter 2007.

Kampani, Mahendra. 'Share Transfer Simplification Through Stock Holding Corporation.' In *35th Meeting of the Standing Committee of the Presidents of the Stock Exchanges in India.* Bombay: BSE, 1988.

Kampani, Nimesh N. 'Marketing of Corporate Capital Issues: Role of Merchant Bankers as Intermediaries between Companies and Brokers.' In *Primary*

Capital Market: Seminar July 9, 1988. The Calcutta Stock Exchange Association (CSEA) Ltd. Calcutta: CSEA Ltd, 1988.

Keay, John. *The Spice Route: A History*. Berkeley: University of California Press, 2006.

———. *India: A History–From the Earliest Civilisations to the Boom of the Twenty-First Century*. London: Harper Press, 2010.

Keegan, John. *The Mask of Command.* New York: Penguin Books, 1987.

Kenia, Vikram. Discussions with the author. Mumbai, 2005–2014.

Keynes, John Maynard. *The General Theory of Employment, Interest and Money*. London: Macmillan, 1936.

Khanna, Tarun. *Billions of Entrepreneurs: How China and India are Reshaping Their Futures*. Boston, MA: Harvard Business School Press, 2011.

Khanna, Tarun, and Krishna Palepu. 'Is Group Affiliation Profitable in Emerging Markets? An Analysis of Diversified Indian Business Groups.' *Journal of Finance*, Vol. 55, No. 2, April 2000.

Khosla, Tanuj. 'Challenging Times Ahead for Indian Foreign Currency Convertible Bonds.' *Institutional Investor*, 3 June 2011.

Khundrakpam, Jeevan Kumar. 'Credit Channel of Monetary Transmission in India: How Effective and Long Is the Lag?' Working Paper Series WPS (DEPR): 20/2011, Reserve Bank of India, Department of Economic and Policy Research, Mumbai, 2011.

Khundrakpam, Jeevan Kumar, and Rajeev Jain. 'Monetary Policy Transmission in India: A Peep Inside the Black Box.' Working Paper Series WPS (DEPR): 11/2012, Reserve Bank of India, Department of Economic and Policy Research, Mumbai, 2012.

Kindleberger, Charles. *Manias, Panics, and Crashes*. New York: Basic Books, 1978.

Kling, Blair B. *Partner in Empire: Dwarkanath Tagore and the Age of Enterprise in Eastern India*. Berkeley: University of California Press, 1976.

Knightley, Phillip. *The First Casualty: The War Correspondent as Hero and Myth-maker from the Crimea to Kosovo*. Baltimore: Johns Hopkins University Press, 2000; first published 1975.

Kochhar, Sameer. *BSE: Journey of an Aspiring Nation*. New Delhi: Skoch Media, 2015.

Kohli, Rasmeet. 'Venture Capital and Private Equity Financing in India.' National Stock Exchange, Mumbai, 2009. Unpublished paper.

Kolman, Joe. 'The World According to Nassim Taleb.' *Derivatives Strategy*, December/January 1997.

Kothari, Hemendra M. 'Expansion of the Primary Capital Market.' In *Primary Capital Market: Seminar 9 July 1988*. The Calcutta Stock Exchange Association Ltd. Calcutta: CSEA Ltd, 1988.

KPMG India. 'Indian Mutual Fund Industry: Distribution Continuum Key to Success.' Mumbai: KPMG India, 2014.

Kudaisya, Medha. *The Life and Times of G.D. Birla*. New Delhi: Oxford University Press, 2003.

Kumar, Manish. 'Returns and Volatility Spillover between Stock Prices and Exchange Rates: Empirical Evidence from IBSA Countries.' *International Journal of Emerging Markets*, Vol. 8, No. 2, 2013.

L

Lakonishok, Josef, and Baruch Lev. 'Stock Splits and Stock Dividends: Why, Who, and When.' *Journal of Finance*, Vol. 42, No. 4, 1987.

Lakshman, M.V., Sankarshan Basu, and R. Vaidyanathan. 'Market-wide Herding and the Impact of Institutional Investors in the Indian Capital Market.' Working paper 327, Indian Institute of Management, Bangalore, 2011.

Lala, R.M. *The Creation of Wealth: The Tatas from the 19th to the 21st Century*. New Delhi: Penguin Books India, 2006.

———. *Beyond the Last Blue Mountain: A Life of J.R.D. Tata*. New and updated edition. New Delhi: Viking, 1993.

Lao, Paulo, and Harminder Singh. 'Herding Behavior in the Chinese and Indian Stock Markets.' *Journal of Asian Economics*, Vol. 22, No. 6, 2010.

Lebergott, Stanley. 'Through the Blockade: The Profitability and Extent of Cotton Smuggling, 1861–1865.' *Journal of Economic History*, Vol. 41, No. 4, December 1981.

Lefèvre, Edwin. *Reminiscences of a Stock Operator*. New York: John Wiley and Sons, 1994.

Lento, Camillo. 'Tests of Technical Trading Rules in the Asian-Pacific Equity Markets: A Bootstrap Approach.' *Academy of Financial and Accounting Studies Journal*, Vol. 11, No. 2, 2006.

Life Insurance Corporation of India. *Annual Reports*.

Lintner, John. 'The Valuation of Risk Assets and the Selection of Risky Investments in Stock Portfolios and Capital Budgets.' *Review of Economics and Statistics*, Vol. 47, No. 1, 1965.

Ljungqvist, Alexander. 'IPO Underpricing.' In *Handbook of Corporate Finance: Empirical Corporate Finance Volume 1*. Edited by B. Espen Eckbo. Amsterdam and Oxford: North-Holland, 2007.

Lo, Andrew W. 'Introduction.' In *Market Efficiency: Stock Market Behaviour in Theory and Practice, Vol. I.* Edited by Andrew W. Lo. Lyme, NH: Edward Elgar Publishing, Inc., 1997.

Loeb, Gerald M. *The Battle for Investment Survival.* Wiley Investment Classics. Hoboken, NJ: John Wiley and Sons, Inc., 2007; first published 1935.

Lucassen, Jan. Email message to the author. 13 January 2020.

Lukose P.J., Jijo and S. Narayan Rao. 'Market Reaction to Stock Splits: An Empirical Study.' *ICFAI Journal of Applied Finance*, Vol. 8, No. 2, 2002.

M

Mackay, Charles, *Extraordinary Popular Delusions and the Madness of Crowds*; Joseph de la Vega, *Confusión de Confusiones.* Wiley Investment Classics. Hoboken, NJ: John Wiley and Sons, Inc., 1995.

Madras Stock Exchange Association Ltd. Proceedings of the Council of Management.

Maher, Daniela, and Anokhi Parikh. 'The Turn of the Month Effect in India: A Case of Large Institutional Trading Pattern as a Source of Higher Liquidity.' *International Review of Financial Analysis*, Vol. 28, 2013.

Maheshwari, Basant. Interview. 'Basant Maheshwari's Investment Mantra [Video].' *NDTV*, 2015.

Malkiel, Burton. *A Random Walk down Wall Street.* 11th ed. New York: W.W. Norton, 2015; first published 1973.

———. 'The Efficient Market Hypothesis and Its Critics.' *Journal of Economic Perspectives*, Vol. 17, No. 1, Winter 2003.

———. 'Reflections on the Efficient Market Hypothesis: 30 Years Later.' *Financial Review*, Vol. 40, No. 1, February 2005.

Malle, Louis, director. *Phantom India.* Nouvelles Éditions de Films, 1969. (51:50).

Markowitz, Harry M. 'Portfolio Selection.' *Journal of Finance*, Vol. 7, No. 1, March 1952.

Martineau, John. *Life and Correspondence of Sir Bartle Frere, Volume 2.* New York: Cambridge University Press, 2012; first published 1895.

Massey, Joseph. 'The Inter-connected Stock Exchange of India.' In *The Future of India's Stock Markets.* Edited by Tushar Waghmare. New Delhi: Tata McGraw-Hill, 1998.

Mayya, M.R. 'Recent Developments in Stock Exchanges.' In *Seminar on Capital Markets: Problems and Prospects*, 4 February 1988. The Stock Exchange, Bombay. Bombay: BSE, 1988.

———. 'Regulatory Framework for Stock Markets: The Indian Experience.' In *Symposium on Capital Market Development and Privatisation*. Mumbai: Commonwealth Secretariat, 1990.

———. 'Reflections on the Changing Scenario of the Indian Stock Markets.' A.D. Shroff Memorial Lecture 1994. In *Glimpses of Indian Stock Markets*. Mumbai: Indian Institute of Capital Markets, 2010.

———. *Glimpses of Indian Stock Markets*. Mumbai: Indian Institute of Capital Markets, 2010.

Mehta, Chhavi, Surendra S. Yadav, and P.K. Jain. 'Managerial Motives for Stock Splits: Survey Based Evidence from India.' *Journal of Applied Finance*, Vol. 21, No. 1, 2011.

Mehta, Nalin. *Behind a Billion Screens: What Television Tells Us about Modern India*. New Delhi: HarperCollins India, 2015.

Mehta, Nipun. *OTC Exchange of India: The Stock Exchange for You and Me*. Bombay: Jaico, 1992.

Melamed, Leo. 'The Rise of Financial Futures: The CME and Beyond.' In *The Stock Exchange Review: May 1998*. Mumbai: BSE, 1998.

Meschke, J. Felix. 'CEO Interviews on CNBC.' Working paper, Arizona State University, Phoenix, AZ, 2004.

Michie, Ranald C. *The London Stock Exchange: A History*. New York, NY: Oxford University Press, 2001, first published 1999.

Minsky, Hyman P. *Stabilizing an Unstable Economy*. New Haven: Yale University Press, 1986.

Mint.

Mishra, Ankita, Vinod Mishra, and Russell Smyth. 'The Random-walk Hypothesis on the Indian Stock Market.' *Emerging Markets Finance and Trade*, Vol. 51, No. 5, 2015.

Mishra, Prachi, Peter J. Montiel, and Antonio Spilimbergo. 'Monetary Transmission in Low-Income Countries: Effectiveness and Policy Implications.' *IMF Economic Review*, Vol. 60, No. 2, 2012.

Mishra, Prachi, Peter Montiel, and Rajeswari Sengupta. 'Monetary Transmission in Developing Countries: Evidence from India.' *IMF Working Paper* WP/16/167, August 2016.

Mishra, Vinod, and Russell Smyth. 'An Examination of the Impact of India's Performance in One-day Cricket Internationals on the Indian Stock Market.' *Pacific-Basin Finance Journal*, Vol. 18, 2010.

———. 'The Random Walk Hypotheses on the Small and Medium Capitalized Segment of the Indian Stock Exchange.' In *Information Efficiency and*

Anomalies in Asian Equity Markets: Theories and Evidence. Edited by Qaiser Munir and Sook Ching Kok. Routledge Studies in the Modern World Economy, Vol. 162. Abingdon and New York: Routledge, 2017.

Mitra, Subrata Kumar. 'How Rewarding Is Technical Analysis in the Indian Stock Market?' *Quantitative Finance*, Vol. 11, No. 2, 2011.

Mody, Zia. 'Securities Regulation.' In *Capital Markets in India*. Edited by Rajesh Chakrabarti and Sankar De. New Delhi: Sage Publications, 2010.

Mohan, Rakesh. 'Monetary Policy Transmission in India.' In *Transmission Mechanisms for Monetary Policy in Emerging Market Economies*. BIS Papers No. 35. Basel: Bank for International Settlements, January 2008.

Mohanty, Deepak. 'Evidence on the Interest Rate Channel of Monetary Policy Transmission in India.' Working Paper Series WPS (DEPR): 6/2012, Reserve Bank of India, Department of Economic and Policy Research, Mumbai, 2012.

Moneycontrol. Website.

Moneylife. Website.

Morarjee J.P., Seth Jamnadas. 'The Native Share and Stock Brokers' Association: Origin and Growth of the Bombay Stock Exchange.' In *Federal Observer*. Stock Exchange Special Number 1, Nos. 36 and 37, 10 November 1940.

Morison, Walter B. *Report of the Stock Exchange Enquiry Committee*. Bombay: Government Central Press, 1937.

Morningstar.

Morris, Morris D. 'The Growth of Large-scale Industry to 1947.' In *The Cambridge Economic History of India: Volume 2, c. 1751–c. 1970*. Edited by Dharma Kumar and Meghnad Desai. Cambridge: Cambridge University Press, 1983.

Mossin, Jan. 'Equilibrium in a Capital Asset Market.' *Econometrica*, Vol. 34, No. 4, 1966.

Motilal Oswal Financial Services Ltd. (MOFSL). *Annual Reports*.

Mudraa.com. Website.

Mukherjea, Saurabh. *Gurus of Chaos: Modern India's Money Masters*. New Delhi: Bloomsbury India, 2014.

———. *The Unusual Billionaires*. Gurgaon: Penguin Random House India, 2016.

Mukherjee, Saptarshi, and Sankar De. 'Are Investors Ever Rational?' Working paper, Indian School of Business, Hyderabad, 2012.

N

Nair, R.R. 'A Computerized System for Improving the Liquidity of Thinly Traded Securities in the Bombay Stock Exchange.' In *35th Meeting of the Standing Committee of the Presidents of the Stock Exchanges in India*. Bombay: BSE, 1988.

Nair, Santosh. *Bulls, Bears and Other Beasts*. New Delhi: Pan Macmillan, 2016.

Narasimhan, M. *Financial Sector Reform and the Capital Markets*. Fourth Phiroze Jeejeebhoy Memorial Lecture 1992. Bombay: The Stock Exchange, Bombay, 1992.

Narayan, Badri. *Republic of Hindutva: How the Sangh Is Reshaping Indian Democracy*. New Delhi: Penguin Random House India, 2021.

Narayan, Paresh Kumar, and Deepa Bannigidadmath. 'Are Indian Stock Returns Predictable?' *Journal of Banking & Finance*, Vol. 58, 2015.

Narisetty, Vijaya B., and Marti Subrahmanyam. 'Group Affiliation and the Performance of Initial Public Offerings in the Indian Stock Market.' *Journal of Financial Markets*, Vol. 13, 2010.

National Council for Applied Economic Research (NCAER). *How Households Save and Invest: Evidence from NCAER Household Survey 2011*. New Delhi: NCAER, 2011.

National Securities Depository Limited. Website.

National Stock Exchange. *Annual Reports*.

National Stock Exchange. Website.

NDTV Business.

Newslaundry.

The New York Times.

Niebuhr, Reinhold. *The Irony of American History*. Chicago: The University of Chicago Press, 2008; first published 1952.

O

Odean, Terence. 'Do Investors Trade too Much?' *American Economic Review*. Vol. 89, 1999.

O'Hara, Maureen. *Market Microstructure Theory*. Cambridge, MA: Blackwell, 1995.

Oonk, Gijsbert. 'The Emergence of Indigenous Industrialists in Calcutta, Bombay, and Ahmedabad, 1850–1947.' *Business History Review*, Vol. 88, No. 1, March 2014.

Outlook Magazine.

Outlook Money and Outlook Profit.

P

Pandit, B.L., Ajit Mittal, Mohua Roy, and Saibal Ghosh. 'Transmission of Monetary Policy and the Bank Lending Channel: Analysis and Evidence for India.' Reserve Bank of India, Department of Economic Analysis and Policy, Study No. 25, January 2006.

Pandit B.L., and Pankaj Vashisht. 'Monetary Policy and Credit Demand in India and Some EMEs.' Working paper No. 256, Indian Council for Research on International Economic Relations, New Delhi, May 2011.

Parekh, H.T. *The Bombay Money Market.* Bombay: Oxford University Press, 1953.

———. 'Indian Capital Market: Past, Present and Future.' A.D. Shroff Memorial Lecture 1975. Bombay: A.D. Shroff Memorial Trust, 1975.

———. 'The Changing Pattern of the Indian Capital Market.' In *Seminar on Capital Markets: Problems and Prospects.* 4 February 1988. Bombay: BSE, 1988.

———. 'The Capital Market.' Phiroze Jeejeebhoy Memorial Lecture 1989. Bombay: The Stock Exchange, Bombay, 1989.

Parikh, Anokhi. 'The December Phenomenon: Month-of-the-year Effect in the Indian Stock Market.' January 2009. Retrieved from nseindia.com/content/press/NS_jan2009_1.pdf.

Parikh, Chetan, Navin Agarwal, and Utpal Seth. *India's Money Monarchs: Conversations with Leading Investors.* Mumbai: Cerebrum Online Pvt. Ltd, 2005.

Parikh, Parag. *Value Investing and Behavioral Finance.* New Delhi: Tata McGraw-Hill, 2009.

Parliament. Joint Parliamentary Committee. *Joint Committee on Stock Market Scam and Matters Relating Thereto* (Thirteenth Lok Sabha). Report: Volume I. New Delhi: Lok Sabha Secretariat, 2002.

Parson, Rahul Bjørn. 'The Bazaar and the Bari: Calcutta, Marwaris, and the World of Hindi Letters.' Ph.D. dissertation, University of California, Berkeley, CA, 2012.

Patra, Michael Debabrata, Sitikantha Pattanaik, Joice John, and Harendra Kumar Behera. 'Global Spillovers and Monetary Policy Transmission in India.' Working Paper Series (DEPR): 03/2016, Reserve Bank of India, Department of Economic and Policy Research, Mumbai, 2016.

Pattanaik, Devdutt. *Lakshmi: The Goddess of Wealth and Fortune – An Introduction.* New Delhi: Vakils Feffer & Simons Ltd, 2009.

Paz, Octavio. *In Light of India.* New York: Harcourt Inc., 1997; first published 1995.

Pendharkar, V.G. *Unit Trust of India: Retrospect and Prospect.* New Delhi: UBS Publishers and Distributors, 2002.

Petram, Lodewijk. *The World's First Stock Exchange.* New York: Columbia University Press, 2014.

Piramal, Gita. *Business Maharajas.* New Delhi: Penguin Books India, 1996.

Planes, Alex. 'Why Did the Greatest Bull Market in History Last So Long?' *The Motley Fool*. At https://www.fool.com/investing/general/2013/09/03/why-did-the-greatest-bull-market-in-history-last-s.aspx.

Planning Commission. *Report of the Working Group on the Development of the Capital Market* (Abid Hussain Committee). New Delhi: Planning Commission, 1989.

Poitras, Geoffrey. 'The Early History of Option Contracts.' In *Vinzenz Bronzin's Option Pricing Models: Exposition and Appraisal*. Edited by Wolfgang Hafner and Heinz Zimmermann. Berlin and Heidelberg: Springer-Verlag, 2009.

———. *Valuation of Equity Securities: History, Theory and Application*. Singapore: World Scientific Publishing, 2011.

Poshakwale, Sunil. 'Evidence on Weak Form Efficiency and Day of the Week Effect in the Indian Stock Market.' *Finance India*, Vol. 10, No. 3, 1996.

Poshakwale, Sunil, and Anandadeep Mandal. 'Investor Behaviour and Herding: Evidence from the National Stock Exchange in India.' *Journal of Emerging Market Finance*, Vol. 13, No. 2, August 2014.

Prabhala, N.R. Interview by author. Mumbai, 2017.

Prabu, Edwin A., Indranil Bhattacharyya, and Partha Ray. 'Is the Stock Market Impervious to Monetary Policy Announcements: Evidence from Emerging India.' *International Review of Economics and Finance*, Vol. 46, 2016.

Prasad, Bandi Ram. 'The Securities Industry.' In *Capital Markets in India*. Edited by Rajesh Chakrabarti and Sankar De. New Delhi: Sage Publications, 2010.

Press Trust of India (PTI).

Prichard, Iltudus Thomas. *The Administration of India from 1859–1868: The First Ten Years of Administration under the Crown*. London: Macmillan and Co., 1869.

The Prime Database. New Delhi: Praxis Consulting and Information Services Pvt. Ltd., 2017; first published 1994.

The Print.

R

Raj, Mahendra, and Damini Kumari. 'Day-of-the-week and Other Market Anomalies in the Indian Stock Market.' *International Journal of Emerging Markets*, Vol. 1, No. 3, 2006.

Rajeshwer, C.H. 'FIIs: A New Force of Support and Discipline.' In *Equity Markets: A New Paradigm*. Edited by G. Kumara Swamy Naidu. Hyderabad: ICFAI Press, 2002.

Raju, Anjana, and Kanak Sapra. 'Convenience to Curse: Pledging of Promoter

Shareholding in India under Scanner.' *Journal of Wealth Management*, Vol. 12, No. 4, 2010.

Ramkrishna, Chitra, and Madhu Sudan Sahoo. 'Equity Markets.' In *Capital Markets in India*, Edited by Rajesh Chakrabarti and Sankar De. New Delhi: Sage Publications, 2010.

Ramakrishna, G.V. *Two Score and Ten: My Experiences in Government.* Delhi: Academic Foundation, 2004.

Ramesh, Jairam. *Making Sense of Chindia: Reflections on China and India*. New Delhi: India Research Press, 2005.

Ranade, Rekha. *Sir Bartle Frere and His Times: A Study of His Bombay Years, 1862–1867*. New Delhi: Mittal Publications, 1990.

Rand, Ayn. *Atlas Shrugged.* New York: New American Library, reprint, 1999.

Ray, Partha, and Edwin Prabu. 'Financial Development and Monetary Policy Transmission across Financial Markets: What Do Daily Data Tell for India?' Working Paper Series (DEPR): 04/2013, Reserve Bank of India, Department of Economic and Policy Research, Mumbai, 2013.

Rediff on the Net.

Reserve Bank of India. *History of the Reserve Bank of India: Volume 1, 1935–1951.* Mumbai: RBI Central Office, 2005; first published 1970; *Volume 3 1967–1981*, Mumbai: RBI Central Office, 2005.

———. Website.

Reuters. Website.

Rigobon, Roberto, and Brian Sack. 'Measuring the Reaction of Monetary Policy to the Stock Market.' *Quarterly Journal of Economics*, Vol. 118, No. 2, May 2003.

The Rig Veda. Translated by Ralph T.H. Griffith.

Ritter, Jay, and Ivo Welch. 'A Review of IPO Activity, Pricing, and Allocations.' *Journal of Finance*, Vol. 57, 2002.

Roberts, J.M., and Odd Arne Westad. *The Penguin History of the World.* 6th ed. London: Penguin Books, 2013; first published 1976.

Rosen, George. *Some Aspects of Industrial Finance in India*. Glencoe, IL: Free Press, 1962.

Ross, Stephen A. 'The Economic Theory of Agency: The Principal's Problem.' *American Economic Review*, Vol. 63, No. 2, May 1973.

Rouwenhourst, K. Geert. 'The Origins of Mutual Funds.' Working paper No. 04–48, Yale International Center for Finance, New Haven, CT, December 2004.

Roy, Tirthankar, and Anand V. Swamy. *Law and the Economy in Colonial India.* Chicago and London: The University of Chicago Press, 2016.

Rungta, Radhe Shyam. *The Rise of Business Corporations in India 1851–1900.* London: Cambridge University Press, 1970.

Russell, Richard. *The Dow Theory Today*. Vermont: Fraser Publishing Company, 1997.

Rustomjee, Adil. 'The Dilemma of Being an FII in India: Only Entry, No Exits.' *Firstpost.* February 2014.

———. 'Dr Rajan, Your Next Crisis is Coming up in Banking.' *Firstpost.* November 2013.

S

Sabarinathan, G. 'SEBI's Regulation of the Indian Securities Market: A Critical Review of the Major Developments.' *Vikalpa*, Vol. 35, No. 4, October–December 2010.

Sahoo, M.S. *Historical Perspective on Securities Laws.* N.p., n.d. Available at http://citeseerx.ist.psu.edu/viewdoc/download?doi=10.1.1.603.5591&rep=rep1&type=pdf.

Samuelson, Paul A. 'Proof That Properly Anticipated Prices Fluctuate Randomly.' *Industrial Management Review*, Vol. 6, Spring 1965.

Samuelson, Paul A., and William D. Nordhaus. *Economics*. 13th ed. Singapore: McGraw Hill, 1989; first published 1948.

Sarkar, Jayati, and Subrata Sarkar. 'Large Shareholder Activism in Corporate Governance in Developing Countries: Evidence from India.' *International Review of Finance*, Vol. 1, No. 3, 2000.

Sarkar, Subrata. 'Mutual Funds in India: Structure and Regulatory Framework.' In *Institutions Governing Financial Markets*. Edited by Shubhashish Gangopadhyay. Mumbai: Allied Publishers, 1997.

Sasidharan, Anand. 'Stock Markets Reaction to Monetary Policy Announcements in India.' Munich Personal RePEc Archive, 2009.

Saunders, A.J. 'The Indian Central Banking Inquiry Committee, 1931.' *Economic Journal*, Vol. 42, No. 165, 1 March 1932.

Schwert, G. William. 'Anomalies and Market Efficiency.' In *Handbook of the Economics of Finance, Vol. 1, Part B.* Edited by G.M. Constantinides, M. Harris, and R. Stulz. Amsterdam: Elsevier B.V., 2003.

Screwvala, J.R. 'Mr. K.R.P. Shroff, President of the Bombay Stock Exchange.' In *Federal Observer*. Stock Exchange Special Number 1, Nos. 36 and 37, 10 November 1940.

———. 'Share Bazaar in 1864–65.' In *Federal Observer*. Stock Exchange Special Number 1, Nos. 42 and 43, 30 March 1941.

———. 'Rain Gambling.' In *Federal Observer*. Stock Exchange Special Number 1, Nos. 42 and 43, 30 March 1941.

Securities and Exchange Board of India (SEBI). *Report on the Working Group on Recognition and Regulation of Sub Brokers*. Mumbai: SEBI, 1989.

———. *Report of the Committee on the Review of the Present System of Carry Forward Transactions*. (G.S. Patel Committee, 1995). Mumbai: SEBI, February 1995.

———. *Report of the Group to Review the Revised Carry Forward System*. (J.R. Varma Committee, 1997). Mumbai: SEBI, July 1997.

———. *Report of the Committee on Derivatives*. (L.C. Gupta Committee, 1998). Mumbai: SEBI, March 1998.

———. *Report of the Group on Risk Containment Measures in the Indian Stock Index Futures Market*. (J.R. Varma Committee, 1998). Mumbai: SEBI, October 1998.

———. *Report of the Committee on Carry Forward under Rolling Settlements*. (J.R. Varma Committee, 2000). Mumbai: SEBI, January 2000.

———. *Report of the Group on Deferral Products in Rolling Settlement*. (J.R. Varma Committee, 2001). Mumbai: SEBI, April 2001.

———. Advisory Committee on Derivatives. *Report on Development and Regulation of Derivative Markets in India*. Mumbai: SEBI, 2002.

———. 'Concept Paper on Regulation of Investment Advisors.' Mumbai: SEBI, 2011.

———. 'Board Memorandum on SEBI (Investment Advisers) Regulations 2013.' Mumbai: SEBI, 2013.

———. *SEBI Investor Survey 2015*. Mumbai: SEBI, 2016.

———. 'Discussion Paper on Growth and Development of Equity Derivative Market in India.' Mumbai: SEBI, July 2017.

———. 'Issue of Capital and Disclosure Requirements, Regulations.' (ICDR Regulations). 2018.

———. *Report of the Working Group on SEBI (Portfolio Managers) Regulations, 1993*. Mumbai: SEBI, 2019.

———. 'Consultation Paper on Review of Regulatory Framework for Investment Advisers (IA).' Mumbai: SEBI, January 2020.

———. *Orders* Mumbai: SEBI.

———. *Annual Reports*. Mumbai: SEBI.

———. *Handbooks of Statistics*. Mumbai: SEBI.

Selarka, Ekta, and Susan Thomas. 'The Mutual Fund Industry in India: Growing with Regulatory Reform.' *Finance Research Group Technical Note*. Indira Gandhi Institute of Development Research. Mumbai, November 2010.

Shah, Ajay. 'The Indian IPO Market: Empirical Facts.' Centre for Monitoring Indian Economy, Mumbai, June 1995. Mimeographed.

———. 'Market Efficiency on the Indian Equity Derivatives Market.' In *Derivatives Markets in India.* Edited by Susan Thomas. New Delhi: Tata McGraw-Hill, 2003.

Shah, Ajay, and Susan Thomas. 'Developing the Indian Capital Market.' In *India: A Financial Sector for the Twenty-first Century*. Edited by James A. Hanson and Sanjay Kathuria. New Delhi: Oxford University Press, 1999.

———. 'David and Goliath: Displacing a Primary Market.' *Journal of Global Financial Markets*, Vol. 1, No. 1, Spring 2000.

———. 'Policy Issues in Indian Securities Markets.' In *Reforming India's External, Financial and Fiscal Policies.* Edited by Anne Krueger and Sajjid Chinoy. Stanford Studies in International Economics and Development. Redwood City: Stanford University Press, 2003.

Shah, Ajay, Susan Thomas, and Michael Gorham. *India's Financial Markets: An Insider's Guide to How the Markets Work.* Noida: Elsevier, 2008.

Shankar, V. 'Automation Plans of the Bombay Stock Exchange.' In *Handbook of Articles from The Stock Exchange Review 1989–1991*. Bombay: BSE, 1992.

———. 'IT Architecture at the Bombay Stock Exchange for the Nineties.' In *Handbook of Articles from The Stock Exchange Review 1989–1991*. Bombay: BSE, 1992.

Sharma, J.L., and R.E. Kennedy. 'A Comparative Analysis of Stock Price Behaviour on the Bombay, London and New York Stock Exchanges.' *Journal of Financial and Quantitative Analysis*, Vol. 12, 1977.

Sharma, Prateek, and Samit Paul. 'Testing the Skill of Mutual Fund Managers: Evidence from India.' *Managerial Finance*, Vol. 41, No. 8, 2015.

Sharpe, William F. 'Capital Asset Prices: A Theory of Market Equilibrium under Conditions of Risk.' *Journal of Finance*, Vol. 19, No. 3, 1964.

———. 'Mutual Fund Performance.' *Journal of Business*, Vol. 39, No. 1, January 1966.

Shefrin, Hersh, and Meir Statman. 'The Disposition to Sell Winners Too Early and Ride Losers Too Long: Theory and Evidence.' *Journal of Finance*, Vol. 40, No. 3, 1985.

Shepley, George F. 'Copy of Grant Telegraph on Lee Surrender.' Papers of George F. Shepley. Maine Historical Society. Available at http://www.mainememory.net/artifact/76625.

Shiller, Robert J. 'Do Stock Prices Move Too Much to Be Justified by Subsequent Changes in Dividends?' *American Economic Review*, Vol. 71, No. 3, 1981.

———. 'From Efficient Markets Theory to Behavioral Finance.' *Journal of Economic Perspectives*, Vol. 17, No. 1, Winter 2003.

———. *Irrational Exuberance.* 2nd ed. New York: Crown Business, 2006.

Shleifer, Andrei, and Robert W. Vishny. 'A Survey of Corporate Governance.' *Journal of Finance*, Vol. 52, No. 2, 1997.

———. 'The Limits of Arbitrage.' *Journal of Finance*, Vol. 52, No. 1, March 1997.

'Shree MR Mayya.' In *Yugvandna*. Stock Exchange Edition: 125 Years of the BSE, February 2003.

Shriram College of Commerce, *Business Analyst.*

Shroff, Ardeshir Darabshaw (A.D.). *Report of the Committee on Finance for the Private Sector, 1954.* New Delhi: Government of India Press, 1954.

Shroff, Kaikhushru Ruttonji Pestonji (K.R.P.). 'The History of the Bombay Stock Exchange.' In *The Bombay Investors' Year Book 1940.* Bombay: Devkara Nanjee Printing and Publishing Co., 1940.

———. *History and Present Position of the Stock Market in India.* Bombay: The Stock Exchange, Bombay, 1962.

Silver, Arthur W. *Manchester Men and Indian Cotton 1847–1872.* Manchester: Manchester University Press, 1966.

Singh, Ajit. *Corporate Financial Patterns in Industrializing Economies: A Comparative International Study.* International Finance Corporation. Technical Paper No. 2. Washington DC: World Bank Group, 1995.

Singh, Bhupal. 'How Important Is the Stock Market Wealth Effect on Consumption in India?' *Empirical Economics*, Vol. 42, No. 3, 2012.

Singh, Kanhaiya, and Kaliappa Kalirajan. 'Monetary Transmission in Postreform India: An Evaluation.' *Journal of the Asia Pacific Economy*, Vol. 12, 2007.

Singh, Kavaljit. *Tax Financial Speculation: The Case for a Securities Transaction Tax in India.* New Delhi: Public Interest Research Centre, 2001.

Skidelsky, Robert. *Keynes: The Return of the Master.* New York: Public Affairs, 2010.

Smith, Adam. *The Money Game.* London: Michael Joseph, 1968.

Smith, Andrew R., Paul D. Windschitl, and Kathryn Bruchmann. 'Knowledge Matters: Anchoring Effects Are Moderated by Knowledge Level.' *European Journal of Social Psychology*, Vol. 43, 2013.

Society for Capital Market Research and Development. *Indian Householders' Investment Survey: 2004.* New Delhi: SCMRD, 2005.

Somanathan, T.V. *Derivatives.* New Delhi: Tata McGraw-Hill, 1998.

Somnarayan, Rajendra. 'Welcome Address at the Diamond Jubilee Celebrations of the Bombay Stock Exchange, April 24, 1936.' Bombay: Bombay Stock Exchange, 1936.

Streeter, Edwin. *The Great Diamonds of the World: Their History and Romance.* London: George Bell and Sons, 1882.

Stringham, Edward Peter. *Private Governance: Creating Order in Economic and Social Life.* New York: Oxford University Press, 2015.

Subramanian, Arvind. 'India's GDP Mis-estimation: Likelihood, Magnitudes, Mechanisms, and Implications.' CID Faculty Working Paper, 354. Center for International Development, Harvard University, June 2019.

Subramanian, Arvind, and Josh Felman. 'India's Great Slowdown: What Happened? What's the Way Out?' CID Faculty Working Paper, 370. Center for International Development, Harvard University, December 2019.

Subramanian, Lakshmi. *Three Merchants of Bombay.* New Delhi: Allen Lane/ Penguin, 2012.

Sur, A.K. 'History of the Stock Exchange.' In *The Stock Exchange: A Symposium.* Edited by AK Sur. Calcutta: Calcutta Stock Exchange Association, 1958.

Svenson, Ola. 'Are We All Less Risky and More Skillful Than Our Fellow Drivers?' *Acta Psychologica*, Vol. 47, 1981.

Swensen, David F. *Pioneering Portfolio Management: An Unconventional Approach to Institutional Investment,* Fully Revised and Updated. Florence, MA: Free Press, 2009.

T

Taleb, Nassim. *The Black Swan: The Impact of the Highly Improbable.* New York: Random House, 2007.

The Telegraph.

Tetlock, Paul. 'Giving Content to Investor Sentiment: The Role of Media in the Stock Market.' *Journal of Finance*, Vol. 62, No. 3, June 2007.

Teweles, Richard J., and Frank J. Jones. *The Futures Game: Who Wins, Who Loses, and Why.* New York: McGraw Hill Professional, 1998.

Thomas, P.J. *Report on the Regulation of the Stock Market in India.* New Delhi: Ministry of Finance, 1948.

Thomas, Susan. 'How the Financial Sector in India was Reformed.' In *Documenting Reforms: Case Studies from India.* Edited by S. Narayan. New Delhi: Macmillan India, 2006.

Thomas, Susan, and Jayanth Rama Varma. 'Derivatives Markets.' In *Capital Markets in India.* Edited by Rajesh Chakrabarti and Sankar De. New Delhi: Sage Publications, 2010.

Timberg, Thomas A. *The Marwaris: From Jagat Seth to the Birlas.* New Delhi: Penguin Books, 2014.

The Times of India.

Tindall, Gillian. *City of Gold: The Biography of Bombay*. New Delhi: Penguin Books, 1992.

Tobin, James. 'Liquidity Preference as Behavior Towards Risk.' *Review of Economic Studies*, Vol. 25, No. 2, February 1958.

———. 'A General Equilibrium Approach to Monetary Theory.' *Journal of Money, Credit and Banking*, Vol. 1, No. 1, 1969.

———. Interview with David Fettig. In *The Region*. Federal Reserve Bank of Minneapolis. 1 December 1996.

Tomlinson, B.R. 'Colonial Firms and the Decline of Colonialism in Eastern India 1914–1947.' In *Power, Profit and Politics: Essays on Imperialism, Nationalism and Change in Twentieth-century India.* Edited by Christopher Baker, Gordon Johnson, and Anil Seal. Cambridge: Cambridge University Press, 1981.

Tradingeconomics.com.

Train, John. *The Money Masters*. New York: Harper Business, 1994.

Treynor, Jack L. 'Toward a Theory of Market Value of Risky Assets.' Unpublished Manuscript. Fall 1962.

———. 'How to Rate Management of Investment Funds.' *Harvard Business Review*, Vol. 43, No. 1, January–February 1965.

The Tribune.

Tripathi, Dwijendra. *The Oxford History of Indian Business*. New Delhi: Oxford University Press, 2004.

Twain, Mark. *Following the Equator: A Journey around the World*. Hartford, CT: American Publishing Company, 1897.

U

Unitech Limited. *Annual Reports*.

United Kingdom. Parliament. *Report of the Commissioners Appointed to Look into the Failure of the Bank of Bombay,* Volume 4, No. 4162, 1869 and Minutes of Evidence.

United Nations. Department of Economic and Social Affairs. *World Urbanization Prospects: The 2014 Revision, Highlights*. New York: United Nations, 2014.

United States. Board of Governors of the Federal Reserve System. *102nd Annual Report, 2015*. Washington, D.C.: Government Printing Office, 2016.

United States. Congress. Joint Economic Committee. *The Economic Outlook*. 109th Congress, 1st session, 3 November, 2005.

United States. Department of State. 'The Blockade of Confederate Ports, 1861–1865.' At http://history.state.gov/milestones/1861-1865/blockade.

United States. Department of the Treasury. *Macroeconomic and Foreign Exchange Policies of Major Trading Partners of the United States*, April 2018 and May 2019.

United States. Federal Reserve Bank of New York. 'Emerging Equity Markets in the Global Economy.' By John Mullin. *Quarterly Review*, Summer 1993.

United States. Securities and Exchange Commission (SEC). *Regulation of the Indian Securities Markets: A Preliminary Survey,* by Norman S. Poser and David Silver. Washington, D.C.: January 1965.

United States. Securities and Exchange Commission. Website.

University of Delhi (South Campus). Department of Commerce. *Proceedings of a National Seminar on Indian Securities Market: Thrust and Challenges*. New Delhi: Department of Commerce, University of Delhi (South Campus), 1988.

V

Valueresearchonline. Website.

Varottil, Umakanth. 'Corporate Law in Colonial India: Rise and Demise of the Managing Agency System.' Working paper no. 2015/016. National University of Singapore, Singapore, 2015.

W

Wacha, Sir Dinshaw Eduljee. *A Financial Chapter in the History of Bombay City*. Bombay: A.J. Combridge and Co., 1910.

———. *Premchund Roychund: His Early Life and Career*. Bombay: The Times Press, 1913.

———. *Shells from the Sands of Bombay*. Bombay: Indian Newspaper Co., 1920.

Waghmare, Tushar (ed.). *The Future of India's Stock Markets*. New Delhi: Tata McGraw-Hill, 1998.

Watts, Dickson G. *Speculation as a Fine Art and Thoughts on Life*. Vermont: Fraser Publishing Company Edition, 1979.

Wealth Insight.

White, Bouck. *The Book of Daniel Drew*. New York: Doubleday, Page and Company, 1910.

The Wire.

Williams, John Burr. *The Theory of Investment Value*. Cambridge, MA: Harvard University Press, 1938.

Worthington, A.C., and H. Higgs. 'Weak-form Market Efficiency in Asian Emerging and Developed Equity Markets: Comparative Tests of Random Walk Behaviour.' Working paper series no. 05/03, University of Wollongong, School of Accounting and Finance, NSW, Australia, 2005.

Y

Young, John Russell. *Around the World with General Grant*. New York: The American News Company, 1879.

Z

Zweig, Jason. 'Investing Experts Urge "Do as I Say, Not as I Do".' *The Wall Street Journal*, 2 January 2009.

ACKNOWLEDGEMENTS

Many people have helped in the writing of this book.

To the late Amit Dave, one of the old-style brokers, is owed a karmic debt for introducing me to this world.

Among authors and academicians, I would like to thank Liaquat Ahamed, Nandini Bhattacharya, Ritu Birla, Eliot A. Cohen, Farrukh Dhondy, Martin Fridson, Sunil Khilnani, Jan Larrsen, Zareer Masani, Dinyar Patel, N. Prabhala, Tirthankar Roy, and Ashwin Sanghi.

I would also like to thank Anuj Bahri, Ashishkumar Chauhan, Ila Gupta, R. Jagannathan, Nawshir Khurody, Rashna Nicholson, Giovanni Papotto, Jehangir Patel, and Farrokh Suntook.

Jeffrey Lilley was the first person to see parts of the book in finished form and to perform that most unselfish of tasks – commenting on another writer's work.

Thanks also to Thomas Abraham, Riti Jagoorie, Kanishka Gupta, Sonali Jindal, Dipanjali Chadha, Ananya Bhatia, and Sai Prasanna for ably shepherding this book through publication.

K.R. Choksey – who with 60 years of stock trading and investing under his belt qualifies as a Grand Old Man of the Market – recollected his early years in the stock market. Nikunj Modi brought a day-to-day perspective on derivatives markets, gained from over two decades of running a trading desk.

At the BSE Archives and the Seth Chunilal Motilal Library, Pradip Name provided much assistance. Thanks also to A.K. Sahu, General Manager and Chief Librarian, and Mrs S.G. Telang at the RBI Central Library in Mumbai for access to the RBI's resources. At the Maharashtra State Archives, Mrs Bhale Rao helped me access and plough through records on the stock market's founding.

Among the lawyers, thanks to Harsh Desai, Amit Desai, Abhay Mahimkar, Chetan Damre, and Rahul Theckedath. Their contribution to this book is of an indirect kind which only they can comprehend.

Finally, that 10th floor gang at the Bombay Stock Exchange. Thanks to Yogesh Kothari, Nihar Dave, Vikram Kenia, Sanjiv Bhambri, and Mahesh Talreja, both for the countless cups of tea and the many years of conversation on '*kevo lagech market*'.

INDEX

Symbols

2G spectrum scam 365
2008 financial crisis 254, 255, 261–63

A

Act XXVIII of 1865 47, 49, 85
Active fund management 345–346, 598
A.D. Gorwala Committee, 1951 92
Ahluwalia, Montek S. 152
Ahmedabad 52, 207
  regional exchanges of 297, 692
  trading market of 147, 485, 493, 499, 601, 694
AkzoNobel 213
Alpha, stock market ratio 590, 719
American Civil War 19–20, 38, 53. *See also* Cotton and share mania
  Lee, Robert E., General 20, 44
  Indian cotton market, effect on 21–24
  Indian stock market, effect on 42–47
American Stock Exchange 148, 150
Andersen, Arthur 149
Andersen report 153
  arguments against the NSE 149–150
Anomalies, stock market 334, 335–38, 341
April effects 337
Arbitrage 660, 750–51
Asiatic Banking Corporation 26
Assam Company 67
Asset plays 460
Asset price channels 313–314
Assets under management (AUM), Indian mutual funds 576, 577, 580–81, 586, 588–89, 729
Associated Cement Companies (ACC) 121
Association of Mutual Funds of India (AMFI) 585
Atlay Committee 82, 84, 90, 112, 136, 139, 182, 485, 694
Automated lending and borrowing mechanism (ALBM) 214, 645, 646, 752

Average daily turnover (ADTO) 375, 604

B

Bachelier, Louis 327, 651
Backbay Reclamation Company 25, 26, 28, 49
 auction of 27
Badhwar Park 56
Badla 70
 bans 108, 214, 646, 691
 Bombay vs Calcutta 77
 broker coalitions in exchange elections 138
 BSE board, relationship with 138, 399
 call market 79, 137
 cash and derivatives market, combination of 639
 cash market 108
 cash market, distinction from 88, 89
 clearing and settlement systems 78
 derivatives-like nature 79
 financiers 73
 infinite stock supply 107
 J.R. Varma committee 645, 646
 Madras 77, 78
 mainstay 78
 old market principle, led to 107
 repeated crises 647
 Roychand time bargain 638
 Rule 94-C 91
 SSFs 644
 unmargined naked forwards 79
 vital attributes 107
Bajaj Capital 727
Banajee, Rustomjee Cawasjee 65
Bank of Bombay 28
 1840 founding act, modifications to 28, 29
 end 48
 management speculation 33
 Saraiya, connection with 81
 share capital expansion 29, 125
Banyan tree 17, 18, 46, 56
Baruch, Bernard 387
Basu, Basistha 112
Behavioural finance 746
 absence of formal optimization techniques 760
 adjustment bias 755, 756
 anchoring bias 756, 757
 disposition effect 766
 diversification levels of retail investors 761, 762
 excessive trading 764
 gambling with house's money 763
 herding behaviour 765
 how traders learn 768
 limits to arbitrage and psychology 749
 loss-aversion bias 759, 760
 overconfidence 758, 759
 rationality 747
 representativeness bias 753, 754, 755
Behramjee Hormusjee Cama 46
Bengal Hurkaru and Chronicle 64, 668
 East India Company trade in debt securities, record of 17
Berle and Means, conception of modern corporations 445
Berlin, Isaiah 596, 757
Bernanke, Ben 261

Beta, stock market ratio 402
Bhabha, Cooverji H. 182
Big Bull. *See* Mehta, Harshad
Birdwood, George C.M., Sir 36
Birla, G.D. 384
Birla, Ritu 380
BJP-led government, effect on market 259, 264, 269, 270, 271
  Aadhaar 264
  corporate profits between FY 2008 and FY 2020 271
  demonetization 265
  GDP controversy 268
  introduction of GST 265
  Jan Dhan financial inclusion scheme 264
  Rate Bull 269
BLESS 645–46
Bombay, 1800 24, 25
  currency shortage 30
  Diwali of 1864 34, 35
  first market activity peak 33
  Gandhi arrest, market effect of 55
  traders, impact of British newspapers on 43
Bombay Baroda and Central India (BB&CI) Railway 25, 52
Bombay Green. *See* Elphinstone Circle
Bombay Paperie 20
Bombay Securities Contracts Control Act, 1925 59, 85, 86, 92
Bombay Stock Exchange (BSE) 55, 191, 193, 746
  advantages of 177
  appeals for relief 84
  Articles of Association 83, 111
  BSE Online Trading System (BOLT) 163, 175
  BLESS 645–46
  broker control 118, 140–42, 145, 215
  bull sculpture 20
  differences from other markets 165, 166
  G.S. Patel Committee 118
  jobbers' role 166, 167
  leadership 114–121
  Manu Manek's influence 110–111
  margining system 171, 172
  poor liquidity 177
  Reliance complaint 111
  reputation effects and brokers 85
Brokers 167, 170, 185, 189
  bankers as 630, 631
  commission pool 603, 630
  conflict of interest issues 609
  control of exchanges 118, 140–42, 145, 215
  coronavirus pandemic, effect on 611
  digitization of 606, 632
  discount brokers 631
  foreign brokers, entry of 601
  industry setup 599–632
  KYC norms 606
  RBI and 325
  regulatory authority 605
Bucket trading. *See* Dabba trading
Buffett, Warren 353, 395
  Berkshire Hathaway 569, 570
Bull market
  corporate profits, first pillar of 310
Bull run and rate cycle
  domestic liquidity conditions 226
  interest rate, displacement 223
  violently reversed 222
Burr, John 308
Business Guardian 670

BusinessLine 670
Buttonwood Agreement 346

C

Calcutta
  India's IPO market, progenitor of 64
  pre-exchange trading in 64
  sole regional exchange 300
  tea shares, boom in 66
Calcutta exchange 96, 210, 217, 218, 691
Calcutta Stock Exchange Association (CSEA) 66
Capital Asset Pricing Model (CAPM) 401, 402, 519–21, 747, 748
Capital Issues (Control) Act of 1947 183, 616
Capital Market (1986) 671
Capital market segmentation 409, 554, 559, 561, 564
Cards. *See* Membership, stock exchange
Cash reserve ratio (CRR) 306, 311
Center for Research in Security Prices (CRSP) 328
Central Depository Services Ltd (CDSL) 189
Certified financial planners (CFPs) 738
Chakravarty, Sukhamoy 306
Chanakya Ni Pothi 671
Chartered accountants 737
Chauhan, Ashishkumar 197
Chidambaram, P. 254
Clientele effects 739
Cobden, Richard 32, 33
Companies Act of 1956 92
Compounding 308
Computer Maintenance Corporation (CMC) 145
Constitution of India, stock exchange in 86, 92, 599
Contracts for difference (CFDs) 496
Contrarianism 465–71
  BSE 171
  LIC 395, 468, 572, 766
  Media influence on 685
Controller of Capital Issues (CCI) 91, 183, 613, 616
Cooverji H. Bhabha Committee 93
Corner, market strategy 80–82, 111
Cotton and Share Mania 20–36, 125
  American South, cotton plantations 21
  Asiatic Banking Corporation 26
  Backbay Reclamation Company 26
  Bank of Bombay, involvement in 28–29, 33, 48, 125
  cotton market frenzy 24
  financial associations, founding of 26
  Indian cotton exports, increase in 22, 23, 217
  infrastructure development, spur in 52–53
  Overend Gurney panic 47
  real estate boom 24
  Roychand, involvement in 20, 25, 26, 28, 36–42
Coronavirus pandemic
  brokerage industry boost 611
  Indian stock market crash 282
  public participation, effect on 496
  second wave 286
Crashes, stock market 705, 706, 707

causes and microstructure issues 708
leverage, unwinding of 707
'stop loss' honeycomb structure, break in 706
Credit channels 312–13, 316
Credit market segmentation 318
Criterion, liquidation value approach 436
Crowd psychology
contagion 504
suggestibility 503
Cyberspace Infosys 203
Cyclical plays 460
Cyclical stocks 425, 440

D

Dabba (bucket shop) trading 71
Dalal Street 57, 105, 202, 235, 398, 399, 671
Dalal Street Investment Journal 671, 722
Dalal, Sucheta 129
Dalmia, Ramkrishna 384, 638
Damani, M.G. 549
Dave Committee 298, 299
Dave, S.A. 183
Day moving averages (DMAs) 413, 697
December effects 331
Defence of India Rules of 1943 91
Demat statements 189
Demonetization 265
Demutualization 159
Depositories 189
Depositories Act, 1996 189
Derivatives
commodity derivatives 377
forward trading, gambling in differences 71–72
futures 649–51
futures, American 637
options 74, 76, 284, 295, 604, 636, 649
turnovers 377
Desai, Ashok 150–51
Desai, Bhulabhai 484
Development finance institutions (DFIs) 91
Digitization
brokerage industry, impact on 632
Dinshaw, F.E. 515
Dirigisme 734–35
Discounted cash flow (DCF) model 423, 430–32
Discounting 308
Discount brokers 631
Displacement approaches 439–41
Diversification, stock portfolio 395
lessons in 410, 411
Divided discount models 431
Dodd, David 382, 435, 436
Domestic Institutional Investors (DIIs) 226
big players 568
insurance companies 570
LIC 227
Dot-com boom 200
Dow, Charles 414
Dow Theory 414

E

Early stock trading 17–20, 63–68
Echeverri-Gent, John 135–36
Edwards, Robert 414
Efficient Market Hypothesis (EMH)

327–29, 341, 747
basic assumptions 343
core beliefs 343–44
forms 329
noise 333
philosophical ideals 340
proofs and refutations 344
theoretical core 332
variance tests 334
Electronic limit order book (ELOB) 173–78, 378, 631, 674, 696
Elphinstone Circle 19, 52, 56, 57, 307, 599, 668
Employees' Provident Fund Organisation (EPFO) 279
Equity research 628–30
Event studies 330
Excess Profits Tax 692
Exchange rate 552–55

F

Fama, Eugene 328, 748
Federal Observer 669
FERA dilution rules 545
FIFO (first in, first out) 454
Financial associations 26
Financial scandals, India. *See* Scams and scandals
Financial Stability and Development Council sub-committee 723
First World War 61, 82, 86, 688
Fiscal Responsibility and Budget Management (FRBM) Act 254
Fisher, Irving 308
Fisher, Philip 471
Fixed deposits 400
Foreign Currency Convertible Bonds (FCCBs) 249
Foreign Exchange Regulation Act (FERA) 98, 616
Foreign institutional investors (FIIs) 130, 226, 228, 470, 548
Atmanirbhar Bharat, impact of 561
colonial era 548
dominance in equities 549, 551
factors determining performance 555
Ford and General Motors case 557, 558
incessant accumulation of Indian equity 550
index stocks 564, 565
'India Growth Story', belief in 556–58
investment strategies and patterns 559
post-2010 phase 551, 562–63
presence in market 566
quantitative easing 261–62, 565
underperformance 553
Forward Contracts (Regulation) Act 637
Franchises and moats 441–44
Free floats 456–59, 451
Frere, Bartle, Sir 25, 26, 33, 34, 41
Fundamental analysis 342, 412–38
Fundies 594, 596
fundamental analysis 597
macroeconomics 598
Fund management business 389, 501, 752–53

G

Galbraith, John Kenneth 702
Gambling 379–80, 411
Barsaat ka Satta 373

Lakdi Satta 373
Global Trust Bank (GTB) 209
Gold (Control) Act,1962 95
Golden Cross, technical indicator 419
Golden Socks brokerages 676
Goods and Services Tax (GST) 265
Graham and Dodd 435, 436
Graham, Benjamin 271, 382, 395, 435, 436, 535
Grant and Ward 51
Grant, Ulysses S. 20, 50, 51
Great Depression 261
Great Recession. *See* 2008 financial crisis
Grey markets. *See* Kerb markets
Growth at a reasonable price (GARP) 451, 452, 473
G-Secs 122
G.S. Patel Committee 118
Guarantee brokers 37
Gulf Crisis 125
Gupta, L.C. 102, 491–92, 761

H

HDFC 586
Heckyl Technologies 687
Hedging 375
Henry, Frederick 84
Highs, stock market 688
1946 high 693
2008 Rate top 698
2020 SIP Bull high 698
central features 699–702
IT high 696, 697
Mehta high 688
modern era, four noted peaks 694, 695
Rate peak 697–98
SIP top 698
Hindu rate of growth 89
Höganäs, Sandvik 213
Horniman Circle/Circle Garden. *See* Elphinstone Circle
Hot hand fallacy 205, 207
House Price Index (HPI), RBI 360
Hume, David 387
problem of induction 388
Hussain, Abid 102

I

Independent financial advisors (IFAs) 584, 732
Indexing
issues 347–48
legitimacy 347
Indian capitalism
company ownership structure 238, 240
emergence of corporations 239
Indian Central Banking Enquiry Committee 574
Indian Clearing Corporation Limited (ICCL) 186
Indian Iron and Steel Company (IISCO) 96, 97, 383
India Shining 233
Individual retirement accounts (IRAs) 583
Industrial Development Bank of India (IDBI) 152
Infotech 206
Initial public offerings (IPOs) market, India 611–28
aggressive pricing 624

Calcutta, progenitor of Indian IPO market 64
CCI abolition 618
concerns 627
first significant IPO 66
post-2010 620
pre-Independence 613
regulations 627
second wave and mushroom company phenomenon 616
Union Bank issuance, 1829 65
Inter-connected Stock Exchange of India (ISE) 299
Interest rates 223–25, 307
Interest rate channels 312
Intermarket Trading System 149
International Securities Consultancy 154
Intraday short selling 243
Investment policy 393
asset allocation 393
efficient portfolio construction 397
market timing 394
risk and diversification 393
securities selection 394
IT services companies, India 206

J

Jain, Anand 111
January effects 336
Jeejeebhoy, Phiroze 116, 117, 189
Jeevandas, Seth Purbhoodas 59
Jegadeesh, Narasimhan 340
Jehangir, Cowasjee 28
Joint Parliamentary Committee (JPC) 209
J.R. Varma Committee 180
Jutha, Seth Morarjee 58

K

Kahneman, Daniel 748
Kampani, Mahendra 142
Katni markets. *See* Kerb markets
Keene, James 42, 458
Kenia, Vikram Chandrakant 109
Kerb markets 18, 67, 78, 170, 210, 212, 216, 487, 614–15, 691–92
Keynes, John Maynard 391
Khan, Liaquat Ali 693
Know Your Customer (KYC) norms 606
Krishnamachari, T.T. 574
Kumar, K. 197

L

Large Scale Asset Purchases (LSAPs) 319
L.C. Gupta Committee 180, 642, 643
Leading economic indicators (LEIs) 249, 406
Le Bon, Gustave 503
Lefèvre, Edwin 238
Lehman Crisis. *See* 2008 financial crisis
LIC
accumulation phase 572
contrarian approach 395, 468, 572, 766
handmaiden and rescuer 571, 572
India's largest player 570
opacity 571
oversized influence 573
LIFO (last in, first out) 454
Liquidation values 434

Lo, Andrew 334
Loans against shares product 251
London Stock Exchange (LSE) 165
Long corner 242, 246, 274, 456, 457
Lows, stock market
  bad fundamental news, response to 711
  crashes 705
  FII outflows 711
  fund redemptions 712
  high inflation and stagnant growth 694
  Indian bear markets, longevity of 709–10
  market bottoms 710
  regulatory response, 2003 712
  reverse arbitrage 708
Lyons Range 217, 218

M

Mackay, Charles 503
Madhavpura Mercantile Cooperative Bank (MMCB) 209, 211–13, 216
Madras Stock Exchange 78
Magee, John 414, 415
Maharaj, Nisargadatta 382
Maharashtra Mushrooms 512
Malkiel, Burton 347
Malle, Louis 168
Manek, Manu 108–10, 640
Margin of safety concept 437
Market efficiency 327, 352, 666. *See also* Efficient Market Hypothesis
Market inefficiency 439, 470, 748. *See also* Efficient Market Hypothesis
Market makers 165. *See also* Jobbers
Market microstructure rents 136
Markowitz, Harry 395, 396, 401
Mashruwala, Gaurav 738
Mayya, M.R. 118–21, 156, 176, 299, 617
Mean variance optimization (MVO) 396, 403
Media
  Influence on market 667–87
Mehta Bull 122
  end 129
  high 688
  replacement cost theory 128
  valuation 127
Mehta, Deena 168
Mehta, D.R. 648
Mehta, Harshad 121–26, 128, 151, 204, 292, 392
  scam 151, 640, 646, 671
Membership, stock exchange 54, 69
Merrill Lynch 59
Mid-cap mutual funds 359
Mill, John Stuart 388
Mint 670
Modern Portfolio Theory (MPT) 394, 402, 404, 407, 408
Momentum 477–80
Monetary transmission 311
  asset price channel and exchange rate channel 313, 314
  banking system 317
  credit channel 312, 313
  interest rate channel 312
  issues 315, 316, 317
  micro-prudential measures 315
  priority-sector lending 317
  statutory liquidity ratio (SLR) 317
  wealth effect 314

Moneycontrol.com 353, 673, 769
Monopolies and Restrictive Trade Practices (MRTP) Act of 1969 95
Morarjee, Jamnadas 58, 67, 169, 612
Morgan Stanley Growth Fund 550
Morison Committee, 1937 77, 182
Morison Report, 1937 374
Morningstar® EnCorr® 402
Motilal, Chunilal 81
Mukherjea, Saurabh 442
Multi-baggers 243, 247
Municipal era 93–94, 101–102, 146–49, 296–301
Mundhra–LIC scam 87
Murugan Srini brokerage 676
Mutual funds 272, 407–08, 574–94. *See also* Systematic Investment Plan (SIP)
- 1970 BSE study of 591
- assets under management (AUM) 580
- efficient portfolios construction 398
- household savings pool 582
- issues faced 581, 586–94
- leverage/short sell 593
- mutual fund theorem 398
- private-sector dominance 581
- three phases of industry 575–80

N

Naked short 467, 469, 646, 696, 707
Narain, Ravi 196
Nasdaq 203, 211, 697
National Council of Applied Economic Research (NCAER) 488
National Democratic Alliance (NDA). *See* BJP–led government, effect on market
National Exchange for Automated Trading (NEAT) 173
National Investment Commission 182
National Securities Clearing Corporation Limited (NSCCL) 185, 186
National Securities Depository Ltd (NSDL) 189
National Stock Exchange (NSE) 133, 157–76
- ALBM 645
- beginnings 151–55
- controversies 195
- demutualization 159
- derivatives market operations 641, 645, 648, 649, 658, 665
- ELOB 173–75
- financial market reform 192
- major founders 158, 159
- management salaries 160
- microstructure 164–69
- monopoly 295–96
- NEAT 173, 298
- Nifty 50 192
- NSE building 293–94
- pan-national market for securities 192
- R.H. Patil 159
- strategy and business model 161
- trading hours 169, 170
- transaction-based revenue model 163

National Stock Market System (NSMS) 146, 147, 298
Native Share and Stock Brokers' Association 54, 599
Nehruvian era 63
- advisory business 722

and margin system 666
BSE's leaders, longevity of tenure during 114
end with entrance of party 130
equity market at Dalal Street 669
long-term investing, during 541, 542
market condition 291, 292
Northern Pacific Corner 81
short corner 238
technological view 289
time series, 1970 BSE study 290
Net asset values (NAVs) 358, 577
Newspapers, stock quotations in 18, 64, 69, 167, 668,
New York Cotton Exchange 373
New York Stock Exchange (NYSE) 79, 137–38, 166, 177, 346
Niebuhr, Reinhold 157
Nifty 50 192, 276, 277
NJ Invest 727
Noise trading and investing 333, 390, 440, 460, 684, 750, 757
Non-banking financial companies (NBFCs) 267, 610
Non-member Short Sales Ratio 500
Northern Pacific Corner 81

O

Operation Twist 319
Options 74, 76, 284, 295, 604, 636, 649
Order-driven non-specialist markets 177
Outlook Money 671
Overreaction and underreaction, trading 338–39
Overseas investing 409, 410
Over-the-Counter Exchange of India (OTCEI) 150, 152

P

Parekh, Deepak 392
Paras Defence & Space Technologies 623
Parekh, H.T. 156
Parekh, Ketan 200, 203, 205
arrest 212
circular trading 213
counter associations 207
financial stress 210
hot hands association 205
K-10 counters 208
Kolkata payment crisis 211
promoters, financed by 209
scam 200, 204–13, 219, 645
Passive fund management 346–48
Patel, G.S. 102
Patil, R.H. 159, 197
Pay-in and pay-out 187
Penny stocks 505
Pension funds 568
Pentafour Bull. *See* Mehta, Harshad
Performance evaluation 718–21
Petit, Dinshaw Maneckjee 57
Pherwani Committee 146, 147
Pherwani Report 146, 148, 152, 154, 155
Pherwani, M.J. 102
Physical assets 583
Pink papers 544, 618, 668, 670, 673, 676
P.J. Thomas Report 486, 613
Portfolio management services (PMS) 390, 568–89, 720, 732, 745
Price discovery 664
Price-earnings (PE) ratio 412, 423–30
Price-Earnings-to-Growth (PEG) ratio 451, 452

Price to book ratio 432, 433
Primary market, India. *See* Initial Public Offering (IPO) market, India
Private equity 237, 351
Private markets 400
Promoters 444–48
Public participation
  2015 survey on 495
  definition 509
  demat accounts 497, 498
  Gujarati and Marwari communities 500
  Gupta, L.C., surveys on 491, 492
  preference for low-denomination shares 490
  professional traders, eye on 502, 544
  SEBI annual reports on 493
  susceptibilities 503–06
Putran, Raghavan 197
Pyne, Ganesh 112

Q

Quadruple witching 660
Quit India movement 691
Quotation announcements/displays 18, 64, 119, 668
Quote-driven market systems 145, 147, 149, 164, 173, 177, 258

R

Radio Corporation of America (RCA) 350
Rajabai Tower 52
Ramkrishna, Chitra 196
Ramakrishna, G.V. 152, 176
Rate Bull 409, 592, 223
  benefits to brokerages 236
  Dalal Street and public 235
  economic expansion 233
  final glittering peak 249
  interest rates 223
  IT Bull, contrast with 234
  'Naya daur' thinking 233
  policy rates reductions 223, 228
  strong-arm promoters 229, 240
RBI Act of 1934 305
Real estate, asset class 360–70
Real Time Gross Settlement (RTGS) 187, 325
Regional exchanges, India 101, 299–300, 602
Registered investment advisors (RIAs) 732
Relative Strength Indexes (RSIs) 480
Reliance 285
Replacement cost theory 128
Report of the High Powered Committee on Stock Exchange Reforms 102
Reserve Bank of India (RBI) 213, 225, 255, 305–26
  attitude towards stock market 307, 322–24
  debt markets regulation 325
  interest rate channel 307, 309
  RBI Act of 1934 305
  RTGS 325
Return on capital employed (ROCE) 449, 450
Return on equity (ROE) 278, 449, 450
Revised Carry Forward System 640
Risk, definition and treatment of
  management 665
  Markowitz on 404
  valuation risk 405

Risk-free assets 397, 400
Ritchie Steuart 37
Roaring Twenties 690
Robo-advising 742, 743
Rothschild 38
Rothschild, Nathan 39
Roussac's Daily Money Market Report 66
Royal Swedish Academy of Sciences 748
Roychand, Premchand 20, 25, 26, 29, 36, 38, 47, 165, 392
  as guarantee broker 37, 42
  as Pied Piper 41
  as promoter 28
  Bank of Bombay, directorship 28
  insolvency 48
  recovery and return to market 49
  Sir Bartle Frere's views on 41
  Wacha's description of 39, 40
Rule 94-C 91, 692
Rungta, Radhe Shyam 67

S

Samuelson, Paul A. 275, 327–38
Saraiya, Chunidas Dharamdas 81
Satyam scandal 257
SBI Magnum scheme 104
Scandals and scams
  2G spectrum 365
  Harshad Mehta 151, 640, 646, 671
  Ketan Parekh 200, 204–13, 219, 645
  Mundhra–LIC 87
  MS Shoes scam 618
  Satyam 257, 672
  UTI 577–78
SCRA 86, 92–94, 296–97
  Section 13 93, 101, 191, 296–97
Scuttlebutt 542, 543
SEC's Rule 10a-1(a)(1) 243
Securities and Exchange Board of India (SEBI) 133, 182–90
  annual reports 493
  clearing and settlement 184–87
  criticism of 216
  dematerialization 187–90
  founding objectives 182
  legislative activity 183
  SEBI Act and Depositories Act 183
  SIP incentive schemes 507
Securities and Exchange Commission (SEC), USA 182
Securities Contracts (Regulation) Act of 1956 84, 638
Securities Transaction Tax (STT) 215, 420
Securitisation and Reconstruction of Financial Assets and Enforcement of Securities Interest Act, 2002 (SARFAESI) 232
Segmented credit markets 318
Self-regulating organizations 741, 742
Sensex 119, 231, 262–63, 276, 277
Share and Stock Brokers' Association 54
Sharpe, stock market ratio 720
Shiller Home Price Indices 360
Shiller, Robert 334, 335, 668, 674, 748
Shirras, G. Findlay 90
Shleifer, Andrei 751
Short sales/short selling 79–85, 107
  Nehruvian era 238
Shroff, K.R.P. 114–16, 155, 488, 600, 690
  annual salary 116

BSE tenure 114–115
father of the stock market 116
Singh, Manmohan 152
Single stock futures (SSF) market 79, 244, 252, 293, 467, 522, 644
SIP Bull 271–74
Small and medium enterprise (SME) credit 318
Smart Investment 671
Smith, Adam 596
South Sea Bubble, England 19
Speculation 383–88
Speculative investment 388–90
Spreads 166, 167, 420, 764
Standard industrial classification (SIC) 277
Standard deviation 395
Statutory liquidity ratio (SLR) 306, 317
Stock Brokers' Association 599
Stock Exchange Division, Finance Ministry 134
Stock Exchange New Building 58
Stock Exchange Old Building 57
Stock picking 391, 403–05, 407, 412, 424, 439–64
Stock splits 489
Suez Canal 53
Sun Mills 81
Surats 23
Survivorship bias 539
Swensen, David F. 400
Systematic investment plans (SIPs) 227, 260, 271
counterweight to foreign flows 274, 552, 564–65, 579, 580
democratization of finance 272
domestic buy side access 227, 260, 271
liquidity source 271
public participation, rise in 506–08
rise in 563

T

Tagore, Dwarkanath 65
Taleb, Nassim 388
Talmudic diversification 403
Tata Iron and Steel Company (TISCO) 60–62, 489
Tata, J.N. 46, 384
Technical analysis (TA) 342, 386, 412–22, 597, 676, 764
Telegraph, establishment of in India 45
Tennessee Valley Authority (TVA) 294
Tenors, contracts 30–31, 383, 593, 653, 655, 658, 660, 661
The Companies (Temporary Restrictions on Dividends) Act 97
The Real Estate (Regulation and Development) Act, 2016 (RERA) 370
Thomas, P.J. 486, 615
Tiddlywinks, perfect stock pick 460–62
Times of London 43
Time bargains 30
Tobin, James 215, 396–99, 401
Tobin's *q* 128, 433
Tokyo Stock Exchange 17
Trailing and forward earnings 427–30
Transaction costs 419
Transitory multi-bagger 359
Treacher and Company 56
Tulip Mania, Holland 19
Tversky, Amos 748

Twain, Mark 51, 52, 363
  Roychand, writing on 51, 52

U

Union Bank 65, 66
Union Budget, 2001 211
Unitech 349–71. *See also* 2G spectrum scam
United Progressive Alliance (UPA)-led government 231–33, 254, 262–64
United Technical Consultants Pvt. Ltd. 356
Unit Trust of India (UTI) 96, 106, 158, 208, 218, 722
  early years 574–48
  financial scandal 577–78
  Unit Scheme (US)-64 96, 218, 575, 576
Uptick rule 243–44
UTI India Fund 549
Unmargined naked forwards 37, 70, 71, 75, 374, 381, 399, 636

V

Valuation approaches 423–38, 448–64
Value at Risk (VAR) methodology 644
Value Line Enigma 336
Value Line Investment Survey 336
Variance bounds tests 334
Varma, J.R. 102
Vigorish 419, 733
Vlamingh, Willem de 387
Volatilities 401

W

Wacha, Dinshaw Eduljee, Sir 34, 36, 39, 40, 56
Walmart 458
Wall Street 690
Watts, Dickson 386
Weighted average cost of capital (WACC) 450, 451
Western monetary policy 228, 242, 261, 322, 470, 717
Working capital 229, 308
World Trade Organization (WTO) 224

Z

Zerodha 663